FROM SERRA TO SANCHO

Currents in Latin American & Iberian Music

WALTER CLARK, SERIES EDITOR

Nor-tec Rifa!
Electronic Dance Music from Tijuana to the World
Alejandro L. Madrid

From Serra to Sancho:
Music and Pageantry in the California Missions
Craig H. Russell

FROM SERRA TO SANCHO

Music and Pageantry in the California Missions

Craig H. Russell

OXFORD
UNIVERSITY PRESS
2009

OXFORD
UNIVERSITY PRESS

Oxford University Press, Inc., publishes works that further
Oxford University's objective of excellence
in research, scholarship, and education.

Oxford New York
Auckland Cape Town Dar es Salaam Hong Kong Karachi
Kuala Lumpur Madrid Melbourne Mexico City Nairobi
New Delhi Shanghai Taipei Toronto

With offices in
Argentina Austria Brazil Chile Czech Republic France Greece
Guatemala Hungary Italy Japan Poland Portugal Singapore
South Korea Switzerland Thailand Turkey Ukraine Vietnam

Copyright © 2009 by Oxford University Press, Inc.

Published by Oxford University Press, Inc.
198 Madison Avenue, New York, New York 10016
www.oup.com

Oxford is a registered trademark of Oxford University Press

Library of Congress Cataloging-in-Publication Data

Russell, Craig H.
From Serra to Sancho : music and pageantry
in the California missions / Craig H. Russell.
p. cm. – (Currents in Latin American and Iberian music)
Includes bibliographical references and index.
ISBN 978-0-19-534327-4
1. Church music—California. 2. Church music—Catholic church.
3. Franciscans—Missions—California. I. Title.
ML3011.7.C15R87 2009
781.71'2009794–dc22   2008018417

Visit the companion Web site at http://www.oup.com/us/fromserratosancho
Access with username Music2 and password Book4416

9 8 7 6 5 4 3 2 1

Printed in the United States of America
on acid-free paper

For Astrid, Peter, and Loren
who encouraged me and inspired me at every step

Acknowledgments

THROUGH THE PAST years, many individuals and institutions have been exceedingly generous, unselfish, patient, and trusting in helping me accomplish my research. Museums, missions, archives, and libraries have allowed me to consult their most precious treasures; without this privilege and patience I never would have been able to accomplish almost anything.

For those people and institutions that reside in California, I would like to extend my most heartfelt and profound thanks. I am indebted to Lynn Bremer, the Director of the Santa Barbara Mission Archive-Library; Brother Tim, Berta, and Pat at the Santa Barbara Mission Archive-Library; Susan Snyder, Anthony S. Bliss, Jack von Euw, and the entire professional staff at the Bancroft Library; Matthew L. Weber, Manuel Erviti, and Cheryl Griffith-Peel at the Music Library of the University of California at Berkeley; Monsignor Francis J. Weber, Director and Curator of the Archival Center for the Archdiocese of Los Angeles at the San Fernando Mission; Anne McMahon, Head Archivist at the Orradre Library of Santa Clara University, and her assistant Sheila Conway; Jean MacDougall, Collections Manager at the de Saisset Museum at Santa Clara University; Ramona López Nadel, Administrative Assistant to the Rector, and Brittany Hill of the de Saisset Museum at Santa Clara University; Sheila Benedict, Parish Administrator and Archivist at Old Mission Santa Inés; Dorothy Macchio at the Old Mission Santa Inés; James Perry, Archivist at Mission San Juan Bautista; Father Edward Fitz-Henry and Dr. Rubén Mendoza at Mission San Juan Bautista; Mary L. Morganti, the Director of Library and Archives at the California Historical Society; Debra Kaufman and Allison Moore at the California Historical Society; Tim Noakes (the Department of Special Collections), Nancy Lorimer (Head of Music Technical Services), and Claire Perry (Curator of Cantor Arts Center) at Stanford University; the Green Library at Stanford University; Louis Sanna, Business Manager and Facility Administrator at the Carmel Mission; Father Carl Faría at the Archive of the Archdiocese of Monterey; Teresa Carey, Parish and Retreat Coordinator at Mission San Antonio;

the Doe Library at the University of California at Berkeley; Eunice Schroeder, Cathy Jones, and Temmo Korisheli at the Fine Arts Library at the University of California at Santa Barbara; the Davidson Library at the University of California at Santa Barbara; and the Sutro Library in San Francisco. In addition, I owe a debt of gratitude to Katrina Rozelle Topp, Ken Pierce, Eric Topp, Carolynn Patten, and Karen Topp for graciously allowing me to stay as a personal house guest for weeks or months at a time while I did archival research in the San Francisco Bay area.

In Spain and Mexico, many offered generous access to archival materials or indispensable knowledge. In Mexico, I owe a debt of gratitude to the following: Licenciado Salvador Valdés and the Catedral Metropolitana de México; the Archivo General de la Nación; Mónica Salazar López at the Colegio de San Ignacio de Loyola, Vizcaínas, in Mexico City; Liborio Villa Gómez and Candelaria Orduña at the Biblioteca Nacional de México; Luis Jaime Cortes and the Conservatorio de las Rosas in Morelia; Cristina Peñaloza Torres, Silvia Ruís, and Adriana Macías Levin at the Subdirección de Documentación of the Museo Nacional de Antropología e Historia; Aurelio Tello of the Centro Nacional de Investigación, Documentación e Información Musical «Carlos Chávez» (CENIDIM); Ricardo Miranda of CENIDIM and the Universidad Veracruzana; Eduardo Contreras Soto (CENIDIM); Leonora Saavedra (previously of CENIDIM, now at the University of California, Riverside); Thomas E. Stanford and the Universidad Anahuac del Sur; Álvaro Días Rodríguez at the Universidad de Baja California; and Luisa Vilar Payá of the Universidad de las Américas, Puebla.

In Spain, several scholars and institutions offered invaluable help, including the Biblioteca Nacional de España; the Arxiu del Regne de Mallorca in Palma de Mallorca; the Arxiu de la Esglèsia Parroquial de Artà in Mallorca; Joan Vives of the Universitat de les Illes Balears; Llorenç Vich Sancho; Joan Parets i Serra; Francesc Bonastre at the Universitat Autònoma de Barcelona; plus María Gembero Ustárroz, Emilio Ros-Fábregas, and Antonio Martín Moreno at the Universidad de Granada.

To the previous generations of scholars who pioneered research in music of the missions or of the American Southwest I am grateful, especially to fathers Maynard Geiger and Owen da Silva. Several distinguished scholars (and dear friends) offered repeated advice and unselfishly shared their most recent research and discoveries, and to them I owe a special debt. Bill Summers and John Koegel, in particular, have been sounding boards for my ideas through the entire process, and many of the most notable features of this book would be absent were it not for their wisdom, perceptive eye, and generosity. In Palma, Mosen Gili i Ferrer invited me to be a private house guest (even though I was complete stranger!) and was my guide through the various archives in Mallorca.

I also would be remiss not to honor other colleagues who provided me with invaluable information at critical stages of my work, much of which has helped shape this book into its present form. My thanks to Robert M. Stevenson, Antoni Pizà, Dan Krieger, Bob Hoover, Drew Edward Davies, Keith Paulson-Thorp, Alfred E. Lemmon, Paul Laird, Bernardo Illari, Piotr Nawrot, Leonardo Waisman, Miriam Escudero, Thomas E. Stanford, Robert Snow, Gerard Béhague, Dieter Lehnhoff,

Neal Zaslaw, John Spitzer, Rose Marie Beebe, Bob Senkewicz, Margaret Cayward, Grayson Wagstaff, Theodor Göllner, Mark Brill, and Louise Stein. In addition, several young scholars have helped to shape my perspective through writings and conference presentations, and—most important—through personal conversations in which they taught me countless things that I needed to know. Without them, several points in this book would have gone astray. I especially want to thank Stewart Uyeda, Irerí Chávez Bárcenas, Dianne Lehmann, Jesús Herrera, Fernando de Jesus Serrano Arias, Alejandro Barceló Rodríguez, Nelson Hurtado, Bárbara Pérez Ruiz, Sherrill Blodget, Jessica Getman, and Jeremy "Spud" Schroeder.

Several music performing groups have collaborated with me in realizing California mission music in performance. Our experiences have also left their mark in the present publication. I extend my deep appreciation to Joseph Jennings and Chanticleer; Paul Gibson and Zephyr; Laura Spino and Musica Angélica of Los Angeles; Grant Gershon and the Los Angeles Master Chorale; Thomas Davies and the Early Music Ensemble of Cal Poly; John Warren and Eric Greening of the New World Baroque Orchestra of San Luis Obispo; Juan Pedro Gaffney and the Coro Hispano de San Francisco; Jordan Sramek and the Rose Ensemble; Philip Brunelle and Vocalessence; my own performance ensemble, Ramo de Flores; and María Jette, whose voice has served as an exquisite interpreter of Colonial Latin American music.

For the past years I have received considerable help from the California Polytechnic State University; none of this book would have come to fruition without its unfailing support and encouragement. I wish to thank President Warren Baker; Provost Bill Durgin (and the previous provost, Bob Detweiler); Dr. Linda Halisky, the Dean of College of Liberal Arts (and our previous dean, Harry Hellenbrand); Music Department Head Terry Spiller (and my previous department heads, Clifton Swanson and John Russell); and Susan Opava, the Dean of Research and Graduate Programs. Obviously, the Kennedy Library at Cal Poly was a bastion of support through the whole process. Hats off to the following: Dean Michael Miller; Ken Kenyon, and Nancy Loe in Special Collections; plus Janice Stone, Linda Hauck, and the other hardworking staff in Interlibrary Loan. The College of Liberal Arts allowed me to take a year of absence in 2004–5 to lay the groundwork for this book—and I thank all concerned, especially my fellow faculty members who had to row that much harder in my absence. Several members made unselfish sacrifices to keep things afloat, especially professors Alyson McLamore and Clif Swanson. Several other colleagues on our music faculty contributed to this book in some demonstrable way: professors Antonio "Greg" Barata, Terry Spiller, Tom Davies, David Arrivée, Ken Habib, Paul Rinzler, Meredith Brammeier, Bill Johnson, and Chris Woodruff.

My editor at Oxford University Press, Suzanne Ryan, has been stellar in every respect, and Walter Clark, the supervising editor of the series Currents in Latin American and Iberian Music, has been a sounding board for my ideas. They have encouraged me at every turn and have allowed me to shape this book into something quite elegant and worthy—instead of pressuring me to do things cheaply and in a rushed fashion. Also, thanks to Lora Dunne, Katharine Boone, Norm Hirschy, Susan Ecklund, and Paul Hobson for their help through this journey.

Last, and most important, my family has assisted me throughout the process. Our younger son, Loren, has inspired me to write with more grace and humor. Our older son, Peter, has reminded me of the value of meticulous attention to detail and the value of beauty, even for things that otherwise would seem inconsequential. My mother, Catherine "Kitty" Q. Russell, kept my spirits up whenever I became fatigued. And most, I thank my amazing wife and best friend—Astrid. She has helped immeasurably in almost every aspect of this book and my life. Her consummate mastery of Castilian has been a constant help in untangling some of the more obtuse texts. Her artistic flair has helped in the physical design of the music editions. Her impressive command over software programs helped her "rescue" some of my photos that would have been hard to read were it not for her "restoration" of these digital images. Her artistic sensibility has been a blessing repeatedly, and her energy and support have been critical components during this colossal project. In short, my whole family has inspired me and stood with me in every adventure and every challenge, even when it meant real sacrifice on their part—so to my family members, I give each one of you my most exuberant and heartfelt "thank you!"

Contents

About the Web Site

IN CONJUNCTION WITH this book, the reader will find five appendices online at the Oxford University Press Web site at the following address:

http://www.oup.com/us/fromserratosancho

To access this protected site, one can find the necessary "username" and "password" on the copyright page of this printed volume.

The five appendices include:

Appendix A: Catalogue of California Mission Sources. This appendix provides a systematic catalogue of contents, clarifying such things as a source's location, physical size and number of pages, appearance or makeup, repertoire, instrumentation, and so on. For each piece, in addition to indicating the page number where a work is found, I provide comments regarding notational aspects, performance style, context, and links to facsimiles or music editions that I provide elsewhere in this book.

Appendix B: Photos of Missions and Mission Music Sources. Since music editions and transcriptions from fragmentary primary sources are highly subjective—through necessity—I have tried to supply in this appendix a large number of facsimiles for the reader's perusal.

Appendix C: Translations of Primary Texts. This appendix provides complete texts of important documents in side-by-side translations, with the original Spanish at the left and my English translation at the right.

Appendix D: Music Editions. This section provides eleven extended musical works from the California repertoire in modern, performing editions.

Appendix E: Bibliography.

Editorial Procedures

PRESENTLY, THERE IS no universally accepted standard with regard to naming the California missions. Some of the institutions prefer to have the word "Mission" before their town name, and others prefer to place it after the town name. For consistency and for clarity in alphabetizing the book's index, I have placed the word "Mission" *after* the town of origin in each instance: "San Juan Bautista Mission," as opposed to "Mission San Juan Bautista."

When quoting primary documents and in making my Catalogue of California Mission Sources, I have not "modernized" spellings but have tried to preserve the author's decisions. The thousands of "wrong" spellings that the reader will encounter are actually "right" (excluding my typos made by human error). Much information can be gleaned by an author's choice in lettering. For instance, Sancho abbreviates words on a regular basis in writing out song texts, whereas Durán prefers to spell out words most of the time. Some of Durán's words slip into Catalan spellings momentarily. And the pile of music Sancho presumably carried with him from Mallorca to Mexico and then California occasionally has a mishmash of spellings that swirl together Latin, Castilian, and Mallorquín all in the same title. In the music manuscripts that Sancho wrote out while still in Palma de Mallorca, he occasionally indicates the soprano part by writing "tible" or "tipble" above the first staff. I could have standardized the spelling into "tiple" but in so doing would have expunged useful information. Pedro Cabot writes out "Kyrie eleison" and "Alleluia" whereas Durán inevitably prints out "Kirie eleison" and "Alleluÿa." The list could go on for pages, but my point is this: spelling is like fingerprints—the choice of lettering tells us something about who was at the writing desk when the ink was flowing from the pen. A spelling choice can help us determine the provenance of a source or maybe even who wrote out an "anonymous" sheet. Therefore, I have chosen not to alter spellings if possible, simply to make them conform to "standard usage"—because in so doing, I would have been scrubbing away the evidence that the next scholar might need.

The one exception to this policy concerns my addition of accents to title pages of old sources when I cite them in the end notes or bibliography—for the following reason. Very often, old Spanish sources capitalized all the letters of the main words on their title pages, and in so doing accents generally were omitted. Since I am not preserving the all-caps spelling from the original source whenever I cite them, I see no reason to avoid the accent marks that would have appeared if the word had been spelled using lowercase lettering. Therefore, I have added these "implied" accents that had been omitted from the all-caps orthography of a title page.

My policies were slightly different with respect to my music examples and editions, for I have "translated" the note shapes into modern half notes, quarter notes, eighth notes, and so on. Additionally, I have used only modern treble and bass clefs instead of the multiple clefs used in the mission era. These decisions seemed courteous, even necessary, because I cannot really expect everyone to be conversant in eighteenth-century *canto figurado* notation and plainchant notation, as well as the single-staff colored polyphony of the musicians—these are too many scribal "languages" for the nonspecialist to handle. As I explain in my purpose statement, I hope my book is used by performers. I have transcribed, translated, and updated the friars' notation systems into something that can be played, "right off the shelf," so to speak, so that we can hear this music in the concert hall or sanctuary in the near future.

In order to make user-friendly performance editions, several other alterations or additions were necessary. Sometimes I have added or moved bar lines, but the action is not as radical as it first might seem (see my discussion of bar lines in chapter 4). The mission notation system does not always function under the same rules that we do with respect to meter and the placement of bar lines. Initially, I tried to footnote or indicate every occasion that I had to add, remove, or shift a measure line, but I ended up with such a forest of vertical lines and indigestible mountains of footnotes that all the meaningful information on the page became obscured. To resolve the issue I have not formally annotated each and every bar line change but instead have tried to provide facsimile pages of those works where that is an issue: in that way, the reader can make his or her decisions and not be confined by the decisions that I used. If a particular work required bar line alterations when I made my transcription, then I make a statement to that effect at the beginning; if my edition has no comment on this issue, then the bar lines are unaltered from the manuscript source.

Another large problem confronted me if I were to reach my goal of making editions that could actually help revive this music as performed literature—that of instrumental accompaniment. During the mission period, instrumental accompaniment was obligatory for most styles, even though extant performance parts for these ensembles are almost nonexistent. For most of my music editions, therefore, I have supplied instrumental accompaniments of my own invention rather than print out an unedited and horribly sparse urtext edition with nothing added. If I were dealing with the cantatas of J. S. Bach or piano concertos of W. A. Mozart, then an urtext edition would be practical and highly desirable, since there are few gaps; almost all the primary source material is still extant. But that is not the case with mission music. Even though notated instrumental parts are rare, we know that instrumental performance was essential, so it seemed bizarre for me to print up only the extant material that gives a visual sense that the music was a cappella. That result is unsatisfactory—almost a fib—since what we see on the page is *not* what the early California residents would have heard in the mission or plaza. I therefore felt it useful to supply a plausible accompaniment to the best of my ability, trying to be aware of the style and era of the transcribed work.

The editorial decisions described thus far clearly accommodate the performer, but what of the scholar? My purpose statement includes scholars as well, and I hope that my music editions will be of use in their research. Except for the types of changes explained here, I have tried not to add or remove anything without explanation or indication. In research, though, transcriptions can only go so far in revealing a work's hidden secrets. There is nothing better than consulting an original document, but the next best thing is a good photograph. For the scholar who wants to see the notational nuances of the original, I therefore have tried to include facsimiles whenever possible (see appendix B). This seemed to be the most logical two-pronged approach to solving editorial dilemmas. My performing editions resolve most obstacles encountered by the performer, and the facsimiles resolve most issues confronting the researcher.

FROM SERRA TO SANCHO

Introduction

IN FEBRUARY 1982, after leaving North Carolina in one of its horrid freezing rainstorms, I wondered what I would find in this funny-sounding place, San Luis Obispo, where I was scheduled for a job interview at Cal Poly. After several hours and a couple of connecting flights, I found myself in a cramped, airborne toothpaste tube about to land in this green, lush Eden on the central coast of California—no slush or icy crud anywhere. There stood the welcoming party to greet me, and once I had collected my bags, we jumped into Ron Ratcliff's station wagon to make the journey into town. We were headed to campus for my guest lecture on Classicism before an unsuspecting music appreciation class, and after driving down Broad Street and making a few zigzags through an old Victorian-era district, we soon arrived in the heart of downtown. And there it stood—the San Luis Obispo Mission—a gorgeous and quizzically inviting building mounted on a small hill, a structure that marked the center of that village geographically, culturally, historically, and even spiritually. One could approach it on foot by passing a gently gushing fountain with a fabulous sculpture of a bear and a young Chumash girl, some superabundant gardens, and a pedestrian plaza that was buzzing with college students, couples with baby strollers, retirees on shopping errands, and lawyers from the county courthouse on lunch break. The structure's facade was whitewashed, with the wooden numerals "1772" above the entrance reminding passersby of its founding date, long ago. The slightly lopsided bell tower, asymmetric L-shaped floor plan, colonnade of wooden supports that ran alongside the parish hall, and stunning rose garden all intrigued me, and I found myself asking, "What did the music sound like in this building two centuries ago?"

Twenty-seven years later, that question still intrigues me. And that one question has a thousand related ones that have piqued my curiosity. Who actually performed the music? Was it the neophyte converts who performed at functions, or was it primarily the European-trained padres? Was there primarily a single style, or were there several coexisting simultaneously? Were there instruments, and did they combine with the voices? Was the music complicated or rustic? Or was it even competent in a technical sense? Was there any trace of a "California" character, or was the whole thing imported from other traditions? Did women get to participate, or was it another case of "guys only"? Were there any composers on the West Coast? At a mission, was there any "nonreligious" activity that was accompanied by music? How was music woven into the fabric of daily life?

This book, hopefully, will provide possible answers to some of these questions. But as with any scholarly endeavor, I inevitably will end up raising more questions and problematic issues than I answer with any purported certainty. That is half the fun—bringing the reader along on a journey where ambiguity and blurred interpretations are part of the landscape, and where a good puzzle or mystery can leave us scratching our heads in amazement and wonder. If I leave the reader with a good puzzle or two, hungering for more information and evidence, then I will consider my book successful.

Obviously, I am not starting from scratch. My research is more like a relay race in which previous scholars (such as William John Summers, John Koegel, Owen da Silva, Antoni Gili i Ferrer, Hubert Howe Bancroft, Zephyrin Engelhardt, and Maynard Geiger) have run many miles and then graciously handed me the musicological baton as I try to move our understanding a few feet further toward an understanding of music in the mission period. Before embarking on this trek, I would like to assess just "where we are" with respect to previous authors, their contributions, viewpoints, and biases. We can triangulate our position by assessing other scholarly contributions and the directions they have pointed, using three criteria: (1) consideration of what constitutes "American music" and where California fits in that discussion; (2) an examination of scholarship in California history, including its music, especially in the context of authors' outlooks, perspectives, or biases; and (3) a summary of the methodologies and obligations of a historical musicologist so that the course we set has the greatest chance of success and lasting value.

If one reads any of the recent books on "American music" or some of the standard histories of nineteenth-century California, one gets the impression that its music was—at best—peripheral or an inconsequential nonentity, unworthy of any real research or discussion.[1] The most common reaction to California's musical traditions in modern musicological studies is that of omission. A general lack of intellectual curiosity perpetuates a sort of self-fulfilling prophecy, where ignorance of the repertoire or of its existence produces no sense of awe or wonder, so there is little incentive to dig in and examine the music in any depth. And the uncurious mind then simply assumes, "Because *I* know nothing of interest about California music during the mission period, there wasn't anything of value." And the cycle repeats itself in blissful laxity and inattention. This same problem crops up in historical writings, as well as musicological ones; as David J. Weber has observed, there is the unfortunate tendency for "American histories" to be explanations of the English colonies and their expansion westward, into lands that are peculiarly considered "vacant."[2] This perception precludes the possibility of elegant or worthy music existing in the West before the Yankees brought their tunes to California with the Gold Rush.

My harsh assessment of present scholarship has its exceptions, most notably the rigorous and inspired work of William John Summers, John Koegel, Robert Stevenson, Sister Mary Ray Dominic, Norman Benson, Theodor Göllner, Owen da Silva, James A. Sandos, Kristin Dutcher Mann, Margaret Cayward, and Antoni Gili i Ferrer.[3] But for the average reader, their work is largely inaccessible, since much of it is buried in rare journals that are found in but a few research institutions in the country. One may have Summers's articles from the *Ars Musica Denver* from Denver University or *Miscellanea Musicologica* from Australia but not yet obtained a copy of his work in the *Revista Musical Chilena* issued in South America (all good publications but difficult to acquire).[4] Gili's research is published on the island of Mallorca, written in Catalan.[5] Benson's best work is published in the journal *Student Musicologists at Minnesota*, not exactly on everyone's library shelf.[6] Some of Koegel's historic and ingenious discoveries are tucked into the handouts that he distributed when he spoke at meetings of the International Musicological Society or the American Musicological Society—but those "handouts" do not surface on any of the traditional search engines or published bibliographies, in spite of their inestimable value.[7] And even if someone obtains one or two of these items, the insight loses its full import and the attention it deserves because the information is dispersed without the reinforcing material to give it structure and context. With a single article, we see a snapshot of a single issue, but that perspective usually does little to clarify a wider vision of how the various music traditions interrelated and how cultures either collided or intertwined.

Of course, any discussion of California mission music is indebted to the first pioneer in the field, Father Owen da Silva, who, in 1941, published his puissant *Mission Music of California*, the most consequential publication on the topic.[8] It remains the only single-volume work dedicated to *music* during the mission period and still is a bedrock of valuable information. Any author could be proud if his or her work remained as useful as da Silva's tome, sixty years after its initial printing. Nevertheless, the errors that are contained within the covers of da Silva's book—and there are glitches that pop up here and there—have taken on a life of their own in subsequent retellings. These mistakes, like arrows loosed from a bow, have taken on trajectories that fly farther from their point of origin with each passing year and each repetition. When da Silva described the sounds of early California, minute errors in the angle of his aim have resulted in an ever-larger distance from the desired target (the *actual* sounds of California mission music) and the final destination of da Silva's arrows (his mistaken *impressions* of those sounds). For instance, his lack of experience in music theory of the eighteenth and nineteenth centuries has left many observations in a muddle or—worse—has conveyed the opposite of what writers actually intended to express. Da Silva is off the mark when he says that the Indian musicians were not particularly accomplished and could not sight-read music and that Narciso Durán far surpassed the other mission fathers in musical importance. Each of those conclusions is flawed, as will be discussed in future chapters. Nevertheless, those views have become enshrined as essential elements of the California style by subsequent authors, his errors having been told again so many times that they have grown in veracity and magnitude with each retelling. The lack of performable music editions, other than the invaluable ones found in da Silva, has also caused the handful of works there to become rather timeworn "chestnuts" while the rest of the engaging repertoire remains completely unknown to the public and most scholars. It is rather like being in Los Angeles or San Francisco and eating the same dinner entrée at the same restaurant for sixty years; there are more flavors and cuisines to discover and enjoy.

Any historical view inadvertently gives as much information about the author's perspective as it does of the object that is being examined. With regard to California mission music, a variety of positions or biases have inflected the debate. Several authors have little use for Catholicism and couch the story of California in pejorative descriptions of the Franciscans, questioning their motives, their capabilities, and their moral character. As Francis J. Weber has observed, the writings of Alexander Forbes and Captain Frederick William Beechey in the mid-nineteenth century are overtly anti-Catholic missives authored by "men imbued with the intolerance of Protestantism,...[men who are] inclined to ridicule and cast insinuations on the activities of the Fathers."[9] Hubert Howe Bancroft, California's first preeminent historian, authored dozens of indispensable, yet colored, historical writings in the 1880s in which he displayed little affection for Spain, Mexico, or the Catholic Church.[10] One gets the sense from Bancroft that California was a natural paradise and that until the coming of the Yankees, it was populated by a collection of flawed inhabitants—such as selfish, manipulative friars, lazy Mexican immigrants, or slow-witted Native Americans incapable of deep intellectual or artistic sophistication. In his chapter "General Characteristics," he presents a variety of stories and ultimately arrives at the conclusion: "They were not a strong community in any sense, either morally, physically, or politically; hence it was that as the savages faded before the superior Mexicans, so faded the Mexicans before the superior Americans."[11]

Bancroft's California was a leisurely and pastoral Eden, corrupted by Catholic friars and populated by quaint dullards. Bancroft's organized and indefatigable efforts to preserve California's history are as astounding as they are colossal, yet in collecting and recounting the firsthand accounts of the *californios* who remembered the mission years, Bancroft tends to select the negative condemnations of the friars made by disgruntled or abused neophytes, at the expense of the high number of laudatory reminiscences that portray these same Franciscans in a positive light.[12] It is not that Bancroft is disingenuous or false—but he is highly selective in his emphasis on negative portrayals. His views on Mexico and its culture reflect the attitudes of his era, complete with its stereotypes and prejudices.

Of course, each of us is the product of the era in which we live, replete with its passions, perspectives, stereotypes, and prejudices; in that respect, Bancroft is no different than anyone else. He repeats with frequency the mistaken stereotypes of his age, including the demeaning generalization that Mexicans are lazy. He paints a picture of "Mexican settlers" in California as all possessed with "inherent indolence."[13] He develops the theme of slothfulness for pages: "Day after day, at morning and at night, lazily they told their rosary, lazily attended mass, and lazily ate and slept."[14] Three "lazies" in one sentence: if we were to expunge that single adjective, the sentence would portray a more accurate view of California mission life. Reading Bancroft's prose, one could ask just who it was that tended the livestock, slaughtered and prepared the beef, planted the wheat, irrigated the crops, built the storage bins, and cooked the feast so that these lethargic settlers could "lazily eat" their meals in the California paradise. And one might ask why American historians have proclaimed the religious devotion and faithful church attendance by the Puritans as incontrovertible proof of a "Protestant work ethic," yet Catholic fealty and regularity in worship among Mexican settlers seem proof enough for Bancroft that they were lackadaisical loafers. The daily regimen of the faithful was similar in both sets of colonies on the two North American coasts, but the assessments of the two religious traditions by scholars are often diametrically opposed, one being laudatory and the other circumspect. Bancroft's assessments are not peripheral to an examination of mission music, for the intrinsic value that we assign the *californios* has a direct bearing on how we perceive their music—as the ragtag product of quaint yet incompetent country bumpkins, on the one hand, or the product of rugged yet astute artisans who were skilled in the mastery of pageantry, complexity, and sophistication, on the other. Extant evidence suggests the latter.

Friar Zephyrin Engelhardt takes the opposite view of Bancroft in his exuberant praise of the Franciscan fathers and of mission life.[15] He admires the padres and takes to task the *gente de razón* (non-Indian Californians who lived in a Mexican or European lifestyle), stating that they "certainly lacked the necessary religious instruction, [for] otherwise the ignorance of the later Californians in official circles, and their little regard for Religion and morals are incomprehensible."[16] He saw them as "unsympathetic seculars." He is discomforted by Bancroft's anticlerical stance. Whereas Bancroft only begrudgingly acknowledges virtues here and there, Engelhardt is remiss in accepting severe criticism of the religious fathers. For example, in recounting the poisoning of several friars, Engelhardt opens the discussion with a sweeping generalization that sets two groups on fundamentally different moral planes: "While the Fathers sacrificed themselves for the Indians, they received little gratitude from their wards."[17] Fray Andrés Quintana's poisoning at Santa Cruz in 1812 was the result of "Indian treachery," according to Engelhardt.[18] After detailing the testimony of the accused and the severe penalties meted out to the guilty parties, he then expands: "Malevolent writers, as well as malevolent Indians, have frequently endeavored to fasten the reproach of cruelty upon the missionaries. Documentary evidence has demonstrated that there was little or no truth in such charges."[19] To support his case, he then produces a long quotation from Governor Solá in 1816 that sets out Solá's findings as to whether or not the Indians were treated cruelly by Father Quintana, as was charged by the neophytes in their trial defense.[20] Engelhardt's conviction that the friars were untainted is only partially corroborated, for Solá confirms that lashings were a regular occurrence—he simply argues that the beatings were not as cruel as the neophytes had described. Solá's report explains:

> I find that they [the Missionary Fathers]...look upon them [the Indians] with perhaps more love than natural parents look upon their children. In

some missions they do not use the whip; in others the lash is made of two ropes with which they punish the public sins of fornication and theft... [and] when reprimands have failed to be effective, they apply the punishment of the lash; twelve or fifteen strokes are then administered to each one. This whipping is more adapted to children of six years than to men, most of whom receive it without an exclamation of pain.[21]

Solá's apology actually reinforces the unsettling reality that whipping was considered "no big deal." The lashing for the convicted parties in Fray Quintana's case was hardly lenient: five were flogged with 200 lashes and sentenced to two to ten years of hard labor in chains; only one culprit survived the punishment. That floggings and lashings were customarily meted out to the Indian converts, often for the most trivial of offenses, is a historical fact that is recounted by many observers of the time, be they apologists or disputants. Whereas Bancroft almost takes glee in the retelling, Engelhardt goes to great lengths to dismiss the beatings as "normal" and of little consequence.

Native American potential to achieve excellence is underrated repeatedly in modern studies of the era. Jessie Davies Francis provides considerable information on the virtues of Mexican administration in California after it passed from Spanish control following the successful fight for Mexican independence, but Native Americans in his study are pushed to the side as incapable or irrelevant, a degrading view that is nowhere substantiated and is clearly contradicted by evidence in the field of music performance.[22] Da Silva's study placed Indians on the lowest rung intellectually, for no apparent reason except that of preconceptions on the part of the author.[23] William Summers has brought the issue of racism to the table, revealing its ugly presence and fighting for its extrication from the discussion.[24] Samuel Edgerton develops this theme in the visual arts, wondering why historians have automatically assumed that Indians were incapable of any technique or quality: he is disgusted by the knee-jerk reaction by some that an artwork had to have been the work of European rather than indigenous artisans if the creation is in any way elegant, technically proficient, or refined.[25]

Of course, there is plenty of racist ammunition available from nineteenth-century accounts, but historian Jack D. Forbes takes us to task for simply reprinting those views without seeking out the other side of that cultural interaction and accepting at face value the Anglo-American perspective as the only valid one. He eloquently argues his case:

Practically every such work [dealing with the history of America] exhibits an unconscious or conscious Anglo-European point of view: the hero is always the English-speaking pioneer while the native is the alien, an enemy, a non-American. Now, it cannot be denied that the Anglo-European newcomer regarded the Indian as an alien, and indeed the native was alien to the developing colonial culture of the Atlantic seaboard; nevertheless, the historian would seem to make a serious mistake when he takes the point of view of the pioneer as his own. To be properly a history of America, a work must be more than just a repetition of the prejudices and attitudes of one portion of the population.[26]

Once again, context is crucial—how Native Americans are perceived is central to an understanding of California mission music. There were but a handful of Mexican immigrants at each mission, and even fewer European-born friars. To examine the mission music separate from an examination of Native American culture is, quite frankly, bizarre—as if the Indians who danced traditional ceremonies on feast days were different than those people who sang mass earlier on the same day. These artists are one and the same.

Several polarities of view refract the vision of California mission music, depending on one's focal point of California life in the nineteenth century. There has long been a polarized viewpoint, with one lens seeing California as a Romantic, pastoral paradise (as with Bancroft's picturesque portrayal of "Lotus-Land")[27] as opposed to the opposite view, where the missions are seen as agents of suffering, intentional conquest, or genocide.[28] Several scholars have represented the latter stance, such as Robert H. Jackson, Edward Castillo, Beth Aracena, Kroeber, Cook, and Randall Milliken.[29] Kroeber and Cook see the missions as providing only one thing—death.[30] Milliken's study is less condemnatory, and his rigorous scholarship is well documented and persuasive. He asks the question:

"Why did people leave their homelands and move to the mission communities?" If I had to propose a single explanation, it would focus on people's loss of faith in the feasibility of continuing their traditional ways within the context of a new reality. Each new migration involved emotionally ambivalent people who had reached the conclusion that they had no other choice but to join a mission; they felt both dread and hope as they made that journey.[31]

Milliken does not see the missions as diabolical, but neither does one sense that they can be regarded as "contributions." I find no fault with his scholarship and in fact admire his knowledge and approach, but I would suggest that one gets a different view (and a completely different "feeling") if one considers architecture, painting, music, and so on, as well as demographic evidence of birth and death rates, migrations, legal proceedings, punishments, and the like.

Unfortunately, the view that the missions brought primarily suffering to Indian converts and little else is the view perpetuated in some California textbooks. The approved text *California* published by Harcourt Brace Social Studies pounds away at mission life, painting a picture primarily of loss, abuse, disease, malnutrition, poor living conditions, indignity, and revolt.[32] The denial of customs is presented as a major cause of resistance. Indians at San Antonio are referred to as "servants"—as if the friars there were spoiled plantation owners living in posh luxury while the underlings did all the work.[33] The documents clearly contradict that: the friars at San Antonio, Pedro Cabot and Juan Sancho, toiled in the fields and in the construction projects, working side by side with the other residents at the mission. The most distorted excursion is the one that associates the friars and mission life with slavery:

> A French explorer [Le Pérouse] who visited the missions in the late 1700s wrote that the missions had made the Indians "too much a child, too much a slave." A *slave* is a person who is owned by another person and made to work.[34]

Out of the hundreds of documents and accounts describing mission life, there is plenty of praise and plenty of condemnation, but the reference to Indians as "slaves" by Le Pérouse is almost unique—and it is misleading to select this one account as the snapshot of the mission system. The textbook impression is clear, however; the missions were oppressive institutions by their nature, condoning a sort of slavery and thus generating rebellion and revolt. These themes are taken up again in the teacher's edition with the insert "Meet Individual Needs: English Learners," in which the authors suggest this mission section would be an opportune moment to discuss word roots using words such as "revolution" and "slavery."

> Point out to students how identifying the root of a word can help them decode unfamiliar words. For example, write the word *resistant* on the board. Underline the word *resist*, and explain that it means *to fight* or *to go against*. Review the definition of *resistant* as a person or thing that resists. Then check students' understanding by asking them to identify the roots in *revolution, resistance, slavery*, and *customary*.[35]

Although this insert purports to be a discussion of word roots, the choice of terms in this context leaves an unmistakable taste in one's mouth regarding the friars, all sour. I am not trying to deny the authors' observations, which have more than a kernel of truth to them. I only point out that if the authors included other parameters—such as music—the image of mission life would be expanded substantially and portray an equally important and valid vision of life in the mission era. The music sources show some friars had a certain permissiveness to Native American musical customs, and at times even active collaboration. Suffering and punishment are only a part of mission history (or of any history, for that matter); there also is the story of magnificent accomplishment, emotional reverence, inspired spectacle, prolonged and negotiated cooperation, a respect and admiration for the abilities of the neophytes, and, I would argue, even kindness and affection. To paint the Catholic friars as malicious slave drivers is but a continuation of the anti-Catholic and anti-Spanish attitudes that I addressed earlier.

A more moderated position surfaces in writings of Robert Kirsch and William S. Murphy, who debunk the pastoral myth as a bunch of "saccharine prose."[36] They do not see the destruction of native culture as *willful* on the part of unfeeling friars but nevertheless bemoan a system that left the Indians unprepared for the historic changes that were to sweep away the remnants of the old traditions. As they aptly state:

A myth emerged under the benevolent eyes of the padres, the Indians labored happily in the fields, while the dons lounged on their verandas, or cavorted nightly at a round of gay fandangos. While the Franciscan system of converting the Indians was a sound one, and was undoubtedly one of the most successful methods of colonization devised, it also had serious limitations. For one, it reduced the Indian to a state of servitude, and while he learned many useful arts and crafts under the tutelage of the mission fathers, he was entirely dependent upon them for their subsistence. Whatever initiative may have carried over from his ancestors, who were forced to hunt, dig, and look to the sea for means to clothe and feed themselves, was now lost. The mission provided the necessities, and thereby weakened the whole social structure of the Indian tribes. When the Mexican government ordered that they be secularized, that is, freed from their bondage to the missions, the final disaster occurred. They were not prepared to take their place in society, and so became outcasts, neglected and persecuted by the white man. It was only a question of time until the native races would become virtually extinct.[37]

The two summaries that make the most sense to me—for they meld the cataclysmic misfortunes suffered by Native Americans with the contrasting evidence that suggests certain aspects of mission life were beneficial to New World life—are those by Robert Hoover and Samuel Edgerton. Whereas many of the aforementioned authors present a well-documented view that, from one perspective, has veracity and a certain unassailable "truth," that vision is rather like a painting that captures one side of the issue. That is, the utility and perspective is useful when viewed staunchly where the historian stood to paint it, but if one takes other parameters into account that force one from to side to side, the perspective on the canvas can become skewed and no longer depict a precise representation of a reality one perceives from this new viewpoint. Hoover and Edgerton, on the other hand, present their history more as sculpture than painting, where they shift their focus and position to accommodate conflicting and contradictory evidence, and in so doing provide us a vision that is more three-dimensional. Robert Hoover beautifully describes the two extremes of California-as-paradise versus California-as-prison:

The public image of the Franciscan missions of California has been misrepresented constantly over the last 150 years, beginning in every fourthgrade class. Early fiction writers portrayed the missions as idyllic earthly paradises: rose gardens, fountains and soft romantic guitar music feature prominently in this image. Later writers, with their own special agendas, countered this picture with a view of the missions as prison camps holding thousands of unwilling neophytes in bondage, even implying some vague connection with the genocidal horrors of Nazi Germany.

In truth, both images are incorrect. The Franciscan missions were the best and most humane approach to contact with native cultures in the 18th century. Instead of killing or driving the natives off the land, as was done by Anglo-Americans, the Spanish saw the Indians as human beings with souls and the potential to become full Spanish citizens. "Missionization" in the 18th century involved not just a change in spiritual beliefs, but visible signs of being "Christian," such as living in permanent planned settlements, wearing European-style clothes, speaking Spanish and forming or learning a trade. Baptisms were voluntary but, once baptized, Indian neophytes were expected to follow the rules of the mission community for the common good.[38]

Edgerton's *Theaters of Conversion: Religious Architecture and Indian Artisans of Colonial Mexico* provides the most inspired and thoughtful explanation of the American experience yet. Through the course of this masterful book, he convincingly proves that life and religious practice were *negotiated* in the field between the Franciscans and the Indians and were not a simple dictatorial mandate from Spain to its colonies. In his chapter on New Mexico missions, he reminds the reader that a friar had a Herculean task. He had to leave his home and journey to the farthest corner of the earth, alone, and upon arrival somehow convince the Native Americans (1) that he meant no harm and was peaceful, (2) that they should abandon native religious practice and become good Catholics, and (3) that they should supply their own toil and sweat—at no charge or clear sense of remuneration—to build a church and other buildings that the friar might propose. And, to Edgerton's astonishment, they succeeded! He goes on to question the model of friar-as-oppressor (and he backs up his claim with scores of examples in support of his thesis). He concludes:

> Once again, the question arises as to how much the Indians were "forced" against their will to work on these massive structures. I reject the explanation by some authors that the Indians only begrudgingly participated in servile submission out of fear of physical punishment.[39]

Hoover's and Edgerton's assessments play out well when examining music in early California. If the *intent* of the missions was one primarily of subjugation or annihilation, it would make little sense to spend enormous effort building up choirs and orchestras at the various missions. Death camps rarely supply their victims with violins and cellos. A meticulous scrutinizing of the manuscripts also indicates that the Native Americans and missionaries negotiated several aspects of religious ceremonies and celebrations. The fact that these collaborations occur in events of deep religious significance for both cultures would indicate they had more than tolerance for each other; they had genuine respect (at least in these documentable instances). That is not to say that Jackson, Castillo, Kroeber, Cook, and Milliken are incorrect or off base when they reveal the abhorrent miseries and frequent injustices that the neophytes suffered. But societies and their interactions are complex and multifarious organisms; to see only misery or only the triumph is to miss the greater "sculpture" to which I referred earlier. A valid historical model should be multifaceted and accept seemingly contradictory conclusions, depending on the parameters or momentary viewpoint of the author.

To Hoover and Edgerton should be added the most recent contribution to understanding life in California during the mission era—Rose Marie Beebe and Robert M. Senkewicz's *Lands of Promise and Despair: Chronicles of Early California, 1535–1846.*[40] Tucked into its covers are a wealth of primary documents in English translation that provide an invaluable glimpse into government, life, and the arts in the words of those who lived in early California. As the title implies, the authors take the good and the bad, the sacred with the secular. They have no "axes to grind" except those of rigorous analysis, artful expression, and clear thinking. The introductory prefaces to each source reading provide a context and structure for what is to follow, and they are so stunningly well done that the reader is drawn into the experience with vibrant clarity. For anyone hoping to understand better the music of colonial California, this book would provide the exquisite foundation to make the experience worthwhile and believable.

In researching any musical topic, one must decide how broad a perspective is required. The opening line of Jim Pruett and Thomas Slavens's *Research Guide to Musicology* crystallizes the issue:

> Musicologists, like most humanists and social scientists, give order to their work through conceptual frameworks that reflect relationships among the various activities they engage in and the research that results from them. These schemata offer more than simply a justification for types of research and methodologies; they offer conceptualizations of a field of research that aim to show a gestalt for the discipline, to suggest a general meaning for the entire endeavor, and to demonstrate the interrelatedness of the parts of the field.[41]

Joseph Kerman has argued that the only thing of real interest is the artwork itself, and the scholar's task is aesthetic criticism. He takes aim at the stodgy "positivists" who merely stick around archives and labor over a litany of "facts"; he instead advocates evaluation, discrimination, and the making of value judgments.[42] So far, so good, but he ends up implying that if a work is "flawed" and not up to snuff, then why bother? William Prizer has articulated, however, that there are difficulties with an object-centric approach to music research where one considers only the artwork itself devoid of the other aspects surrounding its creation. The discussion can degenerate into "a kind of narrow Kermanism that admits only 'criticism' of the art work as a valid field of study."[43] Robert Stevenson has stated that a careful study of any musical tradition requires an approach that is both *biographical* and *musical*; he calls these two the Tigris and Euphrates of musicological fieldwork.[44]

Scope of the Book

The present volume intends to row up both those two rivers that Stevenson sets before us—the *biographical* and the *musical*. With respect to the *biographical* journey, I will emphasize the life of Juan Bautista Sancho and, to a lesser extent, that of Junípero Serra as prime examples of California's padre-musicians. Summers may well be correct in his belief that Sancho represents the pinnacle of artistry in the California experience.[45] I stress, however, that this book just as easily could have selected as a centerpiece almost any of the other musical friars, such as Narciso Durán, Florencio Ibáñez, Estevan Tapís, Pedro Cabot, or Felipe Arroyo de la Cuesta. Each has a vital place in the music of the California missions, and they all make many appearances in my book—but not with equal emphasis. That is intentional; if I had tried to cover all the friars and their accomplishments equally, space restrictions would have forced me to slash and trim their stories down to uninspired stubs. In the end I would have ended up with a rather bland, homogenized list of names, a few paragraphs on each, and no real "story" that could have explained what it *meant* to be a padre or a *californian* in those early years. By delving into Sancho's life in some depth, I hoped to capture—at least for a moment—a sense of the human experience. This book is not "complete." On purpose, I have chosen to write a human narrative at the expense of encyclopedic equality.

Although I mention secular music in the villages and military *presidios* during the mission period, I do so only to amplify various points regarding the missions and their music. Again, were I to treat all aspects of life in California, I would end up with yet another story, yet another volume. With respect to dates, my text's emphasis is centered on the eight decades beginning with Serra's founding of the San Diego Mission (1769) and running up to the Treaty of Guadalupe Hidalgo (1848), which ended the Mexican-American War and pushed California definitively from the orbit of the Mexican government into that of the westward-expanding United States of America.

For the *musical* journey (the Euphrates that flows parallel to the "biographical" currents of the Tigris), I will discuss general trends and currents and then select a few pieces that represent the larger whole. It is not my goal to be comprehensive and treat every piece in the repertoire and every mission equally. Many archives and missions generously opened their doors to my project, giving me unfettered access to their treasures (and for their generosity I will be forever grateful); some missions had difficulty making primary source materials available, since they were on display in their museums (and removing them for extended study presented a real hardship). Also, geographic proximity to my home made some missions more accessible to me than others. In the end, I had to write a story about the missions using the materials available. I ask for the reader's indulgence and understanding when I leave certain stories untold. I have not tried to write a *complete* history, but only a *representative* one.

One problem that has plagued scholars and musicians for years has been a paucity of available music editions. Da Silva's book has been a blessing, but there is a desperate need to explore new repertoire, resolve the "historical" and musical problems, and then produce meaningful commentary and performable scores. That is harder to do than it might seem, for the following reasons.

The dilemma of discerning just what the music actually "is" becomes particularly problematic when looking at California sources. An examination of the musical "notes" on the page is not very revealing. For one thing, many manuscripts that actually should be conjoined look shockingly different in their notational style, so they have been regarded as separate entities. Many pieces look quite modern, keenly displaying the latest musical fads in Mexico and Europe, and others look like plainchant from a thousand years ago. But in California missions and Mexican cathedrals of the late eighteenth and early nineteenth centuries, the medieval and the Mozartean are thrown together in stark juxtaposition, to remarkable effect. Even today, a stroll along the streets surrounding the Alameda Park in Mexico City will present the individual with a vibrant alternation architecturally between the ancient and ultramodern. This compatibility of the enduring "old" with the adventuresome "new" is a central feature of that culture. In a similar way, California mission music entailed the simultaneous practice of multiple traditions from many different epochs: if one were to examine the "old" chant without considering the "new" Haydnesque material that borders it, the entire structure is misrepresented—both in sound and in dramatic effect.

At first glance, the musical sources themselves look like a hodgepodge of unrelated material, and that impression is heightened by the many different notational styles and disparities in physical size, ranging from gargantuan chant books to tiny scraps with a few musical jottings. When these resources were still in daily use at the missions, they produced radiantly different sounds that were often combined in a single musical experience. The various musical sources can be likened to the ingredients found in a kitchen. The milk is in the refrigerator and looks nothing like the flour in the pantry. The sugar sits in a canister on a kitchen shelf, and the dark chocolate is still in its foil jacket, ready to be unwrapped; but if one knows the proper recipe, these disparate elements can be combined to create a scrumptious cake. Similarly, the enormous choirbook is on the lectern and looks nothing like the folder containing a vocal quartet. A stack of photostatic copies of now-lost instrumental accompaniments sits on a neglected archival shelf. A booklet of scratch paper (with little ditties that are squeezed into any available spaces) is tied up in an acid-free folder, waiting for the scholar to untie the knot and unwrap this musical "desert." Like the chef in the kitchen, the musicologist can take these ingredients that look so strikingly different and have them baked into a magisterial *himno* or *sequencia*, in the California cuisine.[46] Without context, however, one simply has no cake. The "recipe" is critical. And that is why I have chosen to pursue a model that is broad and inclusive of many, many kinds of historical and musical materials, rather than limit myself exclusively to a diet of aesthetic criticism.

In this book, then, I plan to examine some of the "recipes" that will enable us to reconstruct the sonorities of mission music by regarding these choirbook pages or short "compositions" more as ingredients than as finished, self-standing works. The evidence needed is multifarious and widely dispersed over many sources and dozens of locations. To execute my plan I intend to examine the following: the musical notes; the notational system to indicate those notes; the genre of the piece to determine what sounds would be expected; the kind of paper or velum on which the pieces are written; the handwriting to determine who is writing all this down (and when); the instructions to the musicians in the margins; travelers' accounts by those who heard the music; government questionnaires and invoices; calendars and the order of the liturgy for the services as they progressed through the year; maps, geography, and the resources available at certain institutions but not found at others; architectural or physical spaces where performances took place; musical instrument inventories; instrument construction; shipping records that provide clues as to musical needs; and letters, diaries, passenger lists, baptismal and burial records, and other biographical information that turns up along the way. In short, this book on California mission music is not just about the musical pitches on pieces of paper—for that would be as flavorful as unsifted flour. My goal is to assemble ingredients from seemingly disjointed and far-flung resources, to decipher the appropriate recipes, and then to bake the audible "pastries" that were once heard in the missions of California.

Available Resources in This Book

Hopefully, the reader will be able to enjoy and utilize the text and accompanying materials that I have prepared over the past years in writing this book. In the main printed text there is, of course, considerable commentary on the musical pieces, their origins, and so forth. My notes accompany the text, but for more complete citations I refer the reader to the bibliography (appendix E) that is available online. I also supply other resources electronically, including the following appendices.

Appendix A: Catalogue of California Mission Sources

To help researchers navigate the confusing and often fragmentary sources of California mission music, I describe and catalogue the contents of many (but not all) available primary sources. Truthfully, this has been a colossal and time-consuming task. Whenever possible, I have consulted the original manuscripts or original publications. In the contents listed in this appendix, I generally go through each resource page by page or photo by photo, so that future researchers will not have to waste needless time searching uncharted waters. I have tried to clarify such things as location, physical size and number of pages, description of a source's appearance or makeup, format, watermarks, paper type, handwriting, repertoire, instrumentation, and so on. With respect to melodies or musical settings, I detail the musical style that an example represents and its notational details. In that way the reader will know not only the title of a work and its location but whether it is plainchant, strummed homophony, polyphony, and so on. The context for the repertoire is examined with respect to its appearance in the Christian year. For chants from the Divine Office, I cross-reference the piece with its identification number in Renato-Joanne Hesbert's *Corpus Antiphona-*

lium Officii. Also, I generally compare the chant melodies to the same text as found in the *Liber Usualis*. I realize this is an anachronism, since the *Liber Usualis* is a modern invention and could not have influenced the mission repertoire in any way. However, it is my hope that my book will be useful to *performers* as well as to *musicologists*. If a modern choral director were to program a concert of music known in the New World (and California specifically), it would be helpful to have a comparison between the Roman rite as found in the *Liber Usualis* (because it is readily available anywhere) and the almost inaccessible mission manuscripts. In that way a choral director could be aware of those chants encountered in the *Liber* that would have sounded familiar to the neophytes and friars at the California missions. In a practical performance context, that is useful information—and it is in that spirit that I have gone to the trouble to provide it.

Appendix B: Photos of Missions and Mission Music Sources

The visual image is helpful, and at times necessary, in the search to understand the missions and their mission. Therefore, I offer in appendix B a large number of engravings or paintings from the era that depict the missions, as well as old mission photos dating from the opening of the twentieth century. Furthermore, my musical discussions in my printed text are almost unintelligible if one cannot see the music notation in question. In addition, the music manuscripts are a delight just for their visual beauty, completely divorced from a consideration of their utility in a musical setting. For that reason, as well, I have tried to assemble a large assortment of beautiful and varied images. In addition, many of the facsimile photos in this appendix have direct relevance to the music manuscripts covered in my printed prose.

Appendix C: Translations of Primary Texts

While reading my chapters, one will frequently come across short quotations that I have excerpted from larger documents. Some of these are of such interest that I felt it would be useful for the reader to have access to the documents in their entirety. Therefore, online in appendix C, I provide the complete texts both in the original Spanish and in English translation of several important documents such as Narciso Duran's extensive "Prologue" to choirbook C-C-59 at the Bancroft Library or the musical discussions in the *Interrogatorio (Questionnaire)* that some of the friars filled out between 1812 and 1814. Another document of potential interest is the list of musical goods that the missions requested be sent to them from the motherhouse of the Apostolic College of San Fernando in Mexico City for the upcoming years of 1807 and 1808. These requisition orders include musical instruments, strings, music books, music stands, and so on. These requests for music supplies also appear in appendix C.

Appendix D: Music Editions

I have already laid out the problems one encounters if he or she wants to study or perform California mission music, not the least of them being the relative inaccessibility of performable scores. Therefore, I offer in the online appendix D many reconstructions of mission music repertoire.

Appendix E: Bibliography

Purpose Statement

In short, I had several goals in writing my book and will have several ways to measure its success. First, I want this book to further scholarship and be a helpful guide to scholars and enthused amateur sleuths who find themselves immersed in research of the California missions. Second, I hope this book will leap beyond its musicological shelf and be a companion to performers and conductors trying to bring these treasures to life before an attentive public. Third, I hope this book will help correct the bizarre misimpressions with regard to mission life that are spewed out in our public schools' textbooks. Fourth, I hope this book will resound as a reminder to North Americans that part of *our own American culture* came to us not only from the eastern seaboard but from Mexico and Spain as well. This fact is too often shoved aside in modern-day discourse whenever tempers become superheated and disrespectful. If we do not understand our own past, how can we responsibly resolve our present-day problems? Finally, nothing would please me more than seeing and hearing this music sound again within the walls of the missions as part of worship of our Creator. The Franciscans bravely sailed halfway across the earth with a passionate desire to build a better world, devoid of materialistic greed, dedicated to a higher purpose. The native Californians—who learned and sang this amazing music—also had a history of passion, bravery, and purpose, devoid of materialistic self-indulgence, ever cognizant of Mother Earth and their Creator. I see them both as part of the same story—now our story. And I hope this book will sufficiently honor them both.

Notes

1. For a thorough discussion of books on "American music" and its treatment of California mission music (or lack thereof), consult William John Summers, "Recently Recovered Manuscript Sources of Sacred Polyphonic Music from Spanish California," *Revista de Musicología*, vol. 16, no. 5 (1993), esp. 2842–43. Previously, two articles by Robert Stevenson sounded a rousing call to action for historians to broaden their perspectives to encompass not only the European traditions but those of Latin America as well. See [Robert M. Stevenson], "The Latin American Music Educator's Best Ally: The Latin American Musicologist," *Inter-American Music Review*, vol. 2, no. 2 (1980), 117–19; and Stevenson, "The Last Musicological Frontier: Cathedral Music in the Colonial Americas," *Inter-American Music Review*, vol. 3, no. 1 (1980), 50.

2. David J. Weber, *The Spanish Frontier in North America* (New Haven, Conn.: Yale University Press, 1992), 5.

3. Some of the impressive contributions of these scholars can be found in the bibliography for this book located online as part of the Oxford University Press Web site. In addition to previous musicologists, a new generation of energetic scholars is helping dig into the music of New Spain to unlock its secrets and help focus our perspective (and their research will be applicable in some way to California). In the foreseeable future, we can anticipate more published findings by scholars such as Drew E. Davies, Margaret Cayward, Alicia Doyle, Dianne Lehmann, Írerí Chávez, Stewart Uyeda, and Jeremy "Spud" Schroeder.

4. William John Summers, "Recently Recovered Manuscript Sources of Sacred Polyphonic Music from Spanish California," *Ars Musica Denver*, vol. 7, no. 1 (1994), 13–30; Summers, "The Spanish Origins of California Mission Music," in *Transplanted European Music Cultures: Miscellanea Musicologica*, Adelaide, Australia: Studies in Musicology, vol. 12, papers from the Third International Symposium of the International Musicological Society, Adelaide, 23–30 September 1979, pp. 109–26; and Summers, "Orígenes hispanos de la música misional de California," *Revista Musical Chilena*, nos. 149–150 (1980), 34–48.

5. Antoni Gili i Ferrer, "Evangelitzadors Artanencs al Nou Món," in *Congrés Internacional d'Estudis Històrics Les Illes Balears i Amèrica* (Palma, Mallorca: Gener, 1992); and Gili, "Contribució a la història musical de Mallorca (segles XIV–XVIII)," *Boletín de la Sociedad Arqueológica Luriana*, vol. 49 (1994), 97–104.

6. Norman Benson, "Music in California Missions, 1602–1848," *Student Musicologists at Minnesota*, vol. 3 (1968–69), 128–67; 4 (1970–71), 104–53.

7. John Koegel, "Sources of Hispanic Music of the Southwest (United States)," paper presented at the fifty-ninth annual meeting of the American Musicological Society, Montreal, 4–7 November 1993; Koegel, "The Lummis Collection of Cylinder Recordings as a Source for Nineteenth-Century Hispanic Music in Southern California," handout from the paper presented at the Fifteenth Congress of the International Musicological Society, Madrid, 7 April 1992"; Koegel, "*Órganos, Violines, Cornetos, y Tambores*: Musical Instruments in *Mission, Presidio, Pueblo* and *Rancho* in Spanish and Mexican California, Arizona, New Mexico, and Texas," paper presented at the annual meeting of the Sonneck Society for American Music, Pacific Grove, California, February 1993.

8. Owen da Silva, O.F.M., *Mission Music of California: A Collection of Old California Mission Hymns and Masses* (Los Angeles: Warren F. Lewis, 1941).

9. Francis J. Weber, *Catholic Footprints in California* (Newhall, Calif.: Hogarth Press, 1970) 17. Alexander Forbes traveled in California in 1835. For an account of his views and travels, see Alexander Forbes, *California: A History of Upper and Lower California from the First Discovery to the Present Time...(1839)*, introduction by Herbert Ingram Priestley, reprint of San Francisco: John Henry Nash, 1937 (New York: Kraus Reprint, 1972). Captain Beechey was on the English ship *Blossom* that visited San Francisco and Monterey in 1826–27. Many of his accounts are found in Irving Berdine Richman, *California under Spain and Mexico, 1535–1847* (New York: Cooper Square, 1965).

10. For this study, the contributions of most importance are Bancroft's *The Works of Hubert Howe Bancroft*. vol. 19, *California, vol. 2, 1801–1824* (San Francisco: A. L. Bancroft, 1885), and vol. 34, *California Pastoral, 1769–1848* (San Francisco: San Francisco History Company, 1888).

11. Bancroft, *California Pastoral, 1769–1848*.

12. For instance, Bancroft selects an extremely unflattering story about Juan Bautista Sancho arbitrarily beating one of his servants over a stomachache on page 203 yet retells no story that is favorable to Sancho, in spite of the many extant accounts that extol his virtues. Similarly, Narciso Durán is portrayed as taking delight in whipping his converts on Sundays (*California Pastoral*, 214, 238), yet the adulations heaped on him by Robinson and the de la Guerra family are left unsung.

13. Bancroft, *California Pastoral*, 260.

14. Ibid., 263.

15. See, for example, Fr. Zephyrin Engelhardt, O.F.M., *The Missions and Missionaries of California*, 4 vols. (San Francisco: James H. Barry, 1916); and Engelhardt, *Mission San Antonio*

de Padua: The Mission in the Sierras, Missions and Missionaries in California, New Series: Local History (Ramon, Calif.: Ballena Press, 1972).

16. Fr. Zephyrin Engelhardt, O.F.M., *The Missions and Missionaries of California. Volume III: Upper California*, pt. 2, *General History* (San Francisco: James H. Barry, 1913), 8.

17. Engelhardt, *Upper California*, 11.

18. Ibid., 12.

19. Ibid.

20. Ibid.

21. Ibid., 14.

22. Jessie Davies Francis, *An Economic and Social History of Mexican California, 1822–1846, vol.* 1, *Chiefly Economic*, The Chicano Heritage, Carlos E. Cortés, adviser and editor (New York: Arno Press, 1976).

23. See, for example, da Silva, *Mission Music of California*, for his description of "Primitive Music" on pp. 4–6, his entirely conjectural and unflattering description of vocal timbre on p. 13, and the prologue by John Steven McCroarty that sets the tone for the volume on p. ix. Silva's views serve as the springboard for Regina M. Gormley's assessment of the Indian neophytes' capabilities (or lack thereof) in her dissertation, "The Liturgical Music of the California Missions 1769–1833," Ph.D. diss., Catholic University of America, 1992, esp. 46, 69–71, 94.

24. Summers, "Recently Recovered Manuscript Sources," *Revista de Musicología*, 2843.

25. Samuel Y. Edgerton, *Theaters of Conversion: Religious Architecture and Indian Artisans in Colonial Mexico*, photographs by Jorge Pérez Lara (Albuquerque: University of New Mexico Press, 2001), esp. 107–10, 151–53, 198.

26. Jack D. Forbes, "The Historian and the Indian: Racial Bias in American History," *The Americas*, vol. 19, no. 4 (April 1963), 351.

27. One of the most sympathetic recollections of an idyllic California in the mission and rancho periods is that of Mariano Guadalupe Vallejo. He published an extremely engaging description of his early childhood—before the coming of the Yankees—and the details of daily life during that era are richly informative as well as heartwarming. See Mariano Guadalupe Vallejo, "Ranch and Mission Days in Alta California," *Century Magazine*, vol. 41, no. 2, series 19 (December 1890), 183–92.

28. Robert L. Hoover explains the opposing viewpoints of the pastoral versus the prison, concisely and clearly, in his review of Robert H. Jackson and Edward Castillo, *Indians, Franciscans, and Spanish Colonization: The Impact of the Mission System on California Indians*, in *Ethnohistory*, vol. 14, no. 2 (Spring 1996), 352–54. Another concise and lucid summary is found in James A. Sandos's introduction to *Converting California: Indians and Franciscans in the Missions* (New Haven, Conn.: Yale University Press, 2004), esp. xiii. Sandos explains the two opposing schools of the "Christophilic Triumphalists," who are adamantly pro-mission, and the differing "Christophilic Nihilist" camp that regarded the missions in an unfavorable light.

29. In addition to Hoover's review of Jackson and Castillo, consult C. Alan Hutchinson, "The Mexican Government and the Mission Indians of Upper California, 1821–1835," *The Americas*, vol. 21, no. 4 (April 1965), 337–38. Beth Aracena argues that missionary work, with its compulsion to install new musical traditions for its Christian worship, is, in and of itself, aggressive repression. She observes, "The musical strife associated with evangelization was no less repressive. That Western musics changed and replaced traditional indigenous practices may be viewed as political aggression. The fact that indigenous musics also influenced Jesuit practices lessens the sting only slightly." Although her work explores the Jesuit missions in Chile rather than Franciscan missions in California, some will argue that her main point concerning mission evangelization is applicable in both geographic contexts. See Aracena, "Viewing the Ethnomusicological Past: Jesuit Influences on Araucanian Music in Colonial Chile, *Latin American Music Review*, vol. 18 (1997), 22.

30. Hutchison, "Mexican Government," 337–38.

31. Randall Milliken, *A Time of Little Choice: The Disintegration of Tribal Culture in the San Francisco Bay Area 1769–1810*, Ballena Press Anthropological Papers No. 43 (Menlo Park, Calif.: Ballena Press, 1995), 220–21.

32. Richard G. Boehm et al., *California*, teacher's edition, Harcourt Brace Social Studies (Orlando, Fla.: Harcourt Brace, 2000). The text published by McGraw Hill covers many of the same themes, such as the kind of work, the needs of the missions, and Indian revolts, but there is little or no vilification of the Franciscans or their motives. Its presentation of the good with the bad is a more balanced one. See James Banks et al, *California: Adventures in Time and Place*, teacher's multimedia edition (New York: McGraw Hill School Division, 2000).

33. Boehm et al., *California*, 158.

34. Ibid., 156.

35. An insert labeled "Meet Individual Needs: English Language Learners," in Boehm et al., *California*, 155.

36. Robert Kirsch and William S. Murphy, *West of the West: Witnesses to the California Experience, 1542–1906. The Story of California from the Conquistadores to the Great Earthquake, as Described by the Men and Women Who Were There* (New York: Dutton, 1967), 102.

37. Ibid., 102–3.

38. Robert L. Hoover, "A Window on the Past: Mission San Antonio de Padua," *The Way of St. Francis* 7, no. 3 (May–June 2001), 18.

39. Edgerton, *Theaters of Conversion*, 261.

40. Rose Marie Beebe and Robert M. Senkewicz, *Lands of Promise and Despair: Chronicles of Early California, 1535–1846* (Santa Clara, Calif.: Santa Clara University; Berkeley: Heydey Books, 2001).

41. James W. Pruett and Thomas P. Slavens, *Research Guide to Musicology*, Sources of Information in the Humanities, No. 4 (Chicago: American Library Association, 1985), 3.

42. See Joseph Kerman, *Contemplating Music: Challenges to Musicology* (Cambridge, Mass.: Harvard University Press, 1985), esp. chap. 4, "Musicology and Criticism." See also Kerman's "A Profile for American Musicology" and "How We Got into Analysis, and How to Get Out" in his collection *Write All These Down: Essays on Music* (Berkeley and Los Angeles: University of California Press, 1994), 3–11 and 12–32, respectively. One of the most important essays to examine the role of criticism in musicology (an approach that Kerman zealously advocates) is William S. Newman's "New Musicology—What, Wherefore, Whither?" in which he defines the pro-criticism approach as "New Musicology" and compares its values and limitations with those of "Old Musicology." In his words, "New Musicology" is "research in any music recognized as such, *plus* a critical consideration of the findings"; he explains that "Old Musicology" is devoted to "discovering or recovering facts founded on demonstrably objective evidence." William S. Newman, "New Musicology—What, Wherefore, Whither?" in *Res musicae: Essays in Honor of James Pruett*, edited by Paul R. Laird and Craig H. Russell (New York: Harmonie Park Press, 2001), 1–6.

43. William F. Prizer, "The Study of Patronage at the Italian Courts," *Revista de Musicología*, vol. 16, no. 1 (1993), 611.

44. Robert M. Stevenson, "Tendencias en la investigación de la música colonial," *Heterofonía*, vol. 9:4, no. 49 (1976), 3.

45. William J. Summers emphasizes this theme in the following articles: "Sancho: The Preeminent Musician of Alta California," in Antoni Pizà, William J. Summers, Craig H. Russell, and Antoni Gili Ferrer, *J. B. Sancho: Compositor pioner de Califòrnia*, edited and coordinated by Antoni Pizà (Palma de Mallorca, Spain: Universitat de les Illes Balears, Servei de Publicacions i Intercanvi Cientific, 2007), 23–90; "Fray Juan Bautista Sancho, Alta California's Preeminent Musician," handout for a paper presented at the tenth annual conference of the California Mission Studies Association, Mission San Antonio de Padua, California, 12–14 February 1993; "Orígenes hispanos de la música misional de California," *Revista Musical Chilena*, nos. 149–50 (1980), 34–48; "Recently Recovered Manuscript Sources," *Revista de Musicología*; and "Recently Recovered Manuscript Sources," *Ars Musica Denver*.

46. A similar approach was advocated at the Study Session on New Musicology in Latin America held during the meeting of the International Musicological Society, Madrid 1992. See "Study Session XIII: Relación entre la investigación-musical y la etnomusicología en Latinoamérica," chaired by Luis Merino, *Revista de Musicología*, vol. 16, no. 3 (1993), 1741–75. There were several recurring themes, such as the advocacy of a Latin American perspective and incorporation of cultural context into musical analysis, achieved largely through combining ethnomusicology with historical musicology.

CHAPTER 1

Musical Style and Performance in Mission Life

AS THE STORM clouds of revolutionary war were building on the East Coast of North America in the 1770s, another revolution was brewing in the West (albeit a more peaceful one)—for at the very moment when Jefferson, Madison, Washington, and Adams were mapping out a plan for a newly conceived "United States of America," the Franciscan friars Serra, Lasuén, and Tapís on the Pacific were simultaneously mapping out a plan to establish a series of missions in Alta California that eventually would stretch from the San Diego Mission in the south to the San Francisco Solano Mission in the north. (See photo 1-1, "El Camino Real: Outline map of California.")

California was forever transformed—and there are few aspects where that radical transformation is more evident than in music. The Franciscan friars who established and governed the missions were well informed in the musical arts, many of them having undergone extensive training in music theory and performance. The Indian neophytes who constituted the choirs and orchestras of this era performed music on a daily basis, and much of it was resplendent, impressive, varied, complex, erudite, and even virtuosic. Well into the mid–nineteenth century, Native American sacred pageants and religious rites—which included music and dance as inextricable elements—continued to be practiced alongside the newly introduced customs of sacred liturgy from Mexican and European religious traditions. And life in the military presidios or civilian pueblos or towns also produced a vibrant musical culture where the strains of the guitar and harp were the "sound track" to daily life, and where serenading, festive dancing, and regal processions marked special occasions.

The primary documents in California provide a wealth of information through their eyewitness accounts of the era's soundscape. But before tackling the music sources and the writings themselves, it would be helpful to establish a glossary of terms, for without some understanding of music theory and terminology from the late eighteenth century, a translation may get the "words" correct (and that is the case

Photo 1-1 El Camino Real: Outline map of California drawn by Mabel Emerton Prentiss, ca. 1903, the Bancroft Library, Map G 04361 A1 1834 P7 case C Bancroft. (Photo courtesy of the Bancroft Library, University of California, Berkeley.)

with Geiger's and da Silva's translations) but entirely muddle the musical *concepts* and even generate a sort of gobbledygook. The first task at hand will be the clarification of musical styles as conceived and described by the musicians of the era.

Compositional Styles

Spanish treatises from the Renaissance onward put forward two or three styles of sacred music performance, contrasting *canto llano* (literally "plainsong" or "plainchant"), with *canto de órgano* (literally "organ singing," but implying rhythmic music conforming to a steady underlying meter). To these two is added another intermediary style, *canto figurado* (or "figured music") by many authors who consider it a sort of middle ground between plainchant and independent counterpoint. *Cantar a voces* reflects the ability of a composer and performers to combine several contrapuntal lines simultaneously. Yet another aesthetic, *estilo moderno* or *música moderna*, describes the more avant-garde style that made it to the California missions that remind one more of Vivaldi than of the Middle Ages or Renaissance. Each of the aforementioned terms has underlying it a history worthy of exploration if we are to understand the musical heritage of North America's West Coast.

For us to understand the unfamiliar assortment of terms, it is essential that we examine two specific repositories of information in order to decipher the mysteries of musical styles in the missions. First, all the friars received their musical

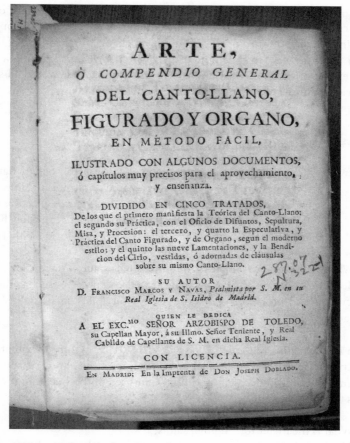

Photo 1-2 Title page for Marcos y Navas's *Arte, o compendio general del canto-llano, figurado y órgano*, Santa Barbara Mission Archive-Library, Copy MT860 M37 1776. (Permission to include this image courtesy of the SBMAL; photo by the author.)

training in Spain while studying in their Franciscan convents, well before leaving for the New World. Therefore, Spanish treatises of the time provide a window into the musical culture that helped formulate the friars' musical views as young men. Second, the specific treatises and music publications that the padres brought with them to Alta California are of particular importance, for these would have served as the daily reference points for the friars as they poured the cultural foundations of musical practice in their respective missions. Three key sources in this second category include Marcos y Navas's *Arte, ó compendio general del canto-llano, figurado y órgano, en método fácil* (See photo 1-2), Vicente Pérez Martínez's *Prontuario del cantollano gregoriano*, and Daniel Traveria's *Ensayo gregoriano, o estudio práctico del canto-llano y figurado en método fácil*.[1]

Canto llano

Canto llano, or "plainchant," was a free-flowing style where the length of notes was determined by the flow and rhythm of the text—as opposed to proportionally lengthened or shortened notes depending on changes in the shape of the note heads. It admitted no accompaniment or harmonizing, thus creating a monophonic texture. Even if an entire choir were performing, they would all sing the same melodic thread together and in the same way.[2] Francisco Marcos y Navas elucidates:

> Q[uestion]: What is...plainchant [*canto llano*]?
> ...
> A[nswer]: Plainchant is the simple and equal measuring out of figures
> and notes, which cannot be augmented or diminished in value.
> *Musica plana est notarum simplex, & uniformis prolatio, qua
> nec augeri, nec minui possunt.* It is also called Gregorian Chant,
> since it was Gregory the Great who gave it form so that the
> Church would be able to sing.
> Q: Why is one not able to augment or diminish the value of these said notes?
> A: Because plainchant has no hierarchical metric structure—such as mode,
> tempus, and prolation—nor does it have variability in its note-shape
> values.[3]

Later in his treatise, Marcos y Navas allows for some rhythmic flexibility where the rhythm of the words actually shapes the rhythm of the phrase, particularly in the singing of Psalms (and by implication, Canticles, and other sung verses). He provides the following advice:

> Q: What is the meter for singing Psalms?
> A: That which does not aim to make all the notes the same, but instead
> measures out long and short syllables according to the rules of
> Grammar.[4]

Traveria's *Ensayo gregoriano* iterates principles similar to those of Marcos y Navas: "Plainchant is a simple and uniform unfolding of note shapes, that can be neither lengthened nor shortened, in contrast to *canto de órgano* that has diverse note-values as well as measure-groupings."[5] Pablo Nassarre, in 1700, defines *canto llano* as "a fluid connecting of shapes or notes, without allowing any lengthening or shortening."[6] In 1724 he defines *canto llano* as "a species of music where the notes are of equal value" but then goes on to distinguish the different subdivisions of chant, "Gregorian" style being but one of several, including Ambrosian (from Milan) and Roman.[7] Ignacio Ramoneda similarly defines *canto llano* as being "a simple and regular delivery of the notes, of which one can neither lengthen nor shorten them. That is to say, that the notes or notation symbols in this type of singing are of equal value and timing, without prolonging some shapes more than others, even though they appear different in their notated shapes."[8]

Some modern authors have translated *canto llano* as "Gregorian chant," but this approximation can lead us down the wrong road if we travel very far.[9] There actually are several sources for the plainchant melodies used in the California missions, and a sizable portion of them are not based on "Gregorian" models.

Pope Gregory the Great, who served between 590 and 604, has assumed legendary status as the composer, codifier, and arranger of the chant melodies into the body of music we now call "Gregorian chant." Throughout the Middle Ages, authors credited Gregory with having arranged these melodies into an organized cycle, in which specific tunes became associated with specific days of the church year.[10] More recent scholarship has shown these romanticized accomplishments to be more legendary than factual. Although Gregory's importance is indisputable, it is highly unlikely that the tunes as performed in the seventh century had much in common with the repertoire as written down centuries later.[11] The "Gregorian" repertoire was, in fact, the outcome of a dynamic process of creation, reform, and standardization that took place over the course of several centuries. There arose an immense effort to standardize chant usage, beginning with Charlemagne, that extended at least until the Council of Trent, when Pope Pius V sent forth the official Roman Breviary in 1568.[12] With few exceptions, the papal authorities discouraged and expunged regional branches and unorthodox tributaries of chant singing: it is this widely disseminated corpus of melodies that now receives the label "Gregorian chant."[13]

But other currents of chant tradition continued to flow.[14] For our purposes, the most influential tributary that runs through the California mission repertoire is the one that issued forth from Toledo, Spain, under the auspices of the cardinal of Toledo, Francisco Jiménez de Cisneros.[15] He attempted to have the "Old Spanish" or "Mozarabic" chant copied out in clearly decipherable notation and then published these adaptations in a Missal (1502) and a Breviary (1504).[16] How the enigmatically written chants from the Middle Ages relate to the later sixteenth-century versions in the precisely decipherable notation of Cisneros's repertoire is not entirely clear. David Hiley observes that these later versions do not really match up with the early sources.[17] Casiano Rojo and Germán Prado see no relationship between them at all, explaining that it was a modern invention in the sixteenth century.[18] At any rate, Toledo received special papal dispensation to continue practicing its regional tradition during the reign of Ferdinand and Isabella—a privilege afforded few other traditions in all of Europe.[19] For purposes of clarity, I will use the terms "Gregorian chant" or "Roman rite" to refer to the relatively standardized body of chant associated with the Church in Rome and use the terms "Toledo chant" or "Toledo rite" to refer to the repertoire emanating from the Primate Church of Toledo and distributed throughout the Hispanic world, beginning with the efforts of Cardinal Cisneros in the early sixteenth century.

This corpus of chant emanating from Toledo under the Cisneros revision cast its shadow across the Atlantic to the California missions. Works specifically associated with Toledo and its heritage surface in several loose sheets and choirbooks from the missions, such as the "MissaToledana, Quarto tono, punto alto" (Mass of Toledo in Mode 4, a step higher) in the enormous "Serra choirbook M.0612 now housed at Stanford; a "Gloria Todedana [*sic*]" (Gloria of Toledo) in the handwriting of Padre Juan Bautista Sancho; and the "Missa Toletana, St. Joan Baptista

Photo 1-3 *Missa Toledana, Quarto Tono*. Kyrie, from Serra choirbook M.0612, fol.15. (Photograph courtesy of Stanford University.)

(Mass of Toledo for Saint John the Baptist)" copied by Felipe Arroyo de la Cuesta on 3 May 1834.[20] (See Photo 1-3, *Missa Toledana. Quarto Tono.* Kyrie, from Serra choirbook M.0612 at Stanford University.)

This latter mass for John the Baptist probably occupied an important place in Arroyo de la Cuesta's California experience, given that he served most of his years at the San Juan Bautista Mission, an institution that certainly would have celebrated the feast day of its namesake, John the Baptist. The manuscript bears an annotation on the top margin of page 2, stating that "this mass is exactly the one that is sung in my homeland of Cuba on feast days of greatest importance"—a curious observation given that Arroyo de la Cuesta was born in Burgos, Spain, and that there is no demonstrated link between him and Cuba.[21] The friars sought out chant books with the Toledo repertoire, as seen in the requisitions for the upcoming year of 1807, in which Fray Marcelino Cipres and Fray Luis Antonio Martínez include "1 chant book of the Roman rite with the Appendix of the Toledo tradition" on their wish list.[22] At the San José Mission, the Toledo rite was also in demand: Fray Narciso Durán asks that "1 book of the rite of Toledo" be sent with the supplies for 1809.[23]

One of the strongest verifiable links to a Toledo tradition is found in Vicente Pérez Martínez's *Prontuario del cantollano gregoriano.* (See photo 1-4.) Although published in Madrid, the *Prontuario* includes a clarifying link to Toledo as part of its title: "Handbook of Gregorian plainchant...according to chant as practiced in the Most Holy Primate Church of Toledo, Royal Chapel of Your Majesty and of various Church-Cathedrals."[24]

Bill Summers observes, "One of the chant manuscripts prepared by Estevan Tapís at Mission San Juan Bautista was based directly upon this plainsong source."[25] Apparently, Florencio Ibáñez had this two-volume publication in his possession, since one exemplar of the *Prontuario* now housed at the Santa Barbara Mission Archive-Library includes a "Benedictus qui venit" carefully inscribed by him on page 1034 and yet another one tacked on to the last page (p. 1074).[26] Ibáñez is the scribe for at least two other California sources: Santa Clara Ms. 3 at the Orradre Library at Santa Clara University, and choirbook C-C-68:2 at the Bancroft Library in Berkeley. We can ascertain Ibáñez's authorship through his annotation on folio 81v of Santa Clara Ms. 3, in which he signs his work and dates the completion of these latter pages on 8 June 1812: "8 de Junio de 1812 se acabáron estos 15 pliegos en Lunes, y Luna 29 visperas de Conjuncion. Ybañez." (See photo 1-5.)

A comparison, then, of Santa Clara Ms. 3 and choirbook C-C-68:2 with the printed *Prontuario* reveals Ibáñez's chant books to have been largely planted in the Toledo tradition. For instance, the Mass for the Dead that is tucked into the pages of the *Prontuario* match splendidly with the same service as found in Santa Clara Ms. 3.[27] For example, the Introit (*Requiem æternam*) and Tract (*Absolve Domine*) are nearly identical in Ibáñez's Santa Clara Ms. 3 and Vicente Pérez's *Prontuario*; the version that we find in standard Roman chant departs from these two in small but observable ways. More significant, the *Dies irae* in the *Prontuario* is a rhythmic setting in an impulsive triple meter—a twin to the version found in Santa Clara Ms. 3.[28] This attraction to metric settings of hymn and sequence texts is a feature

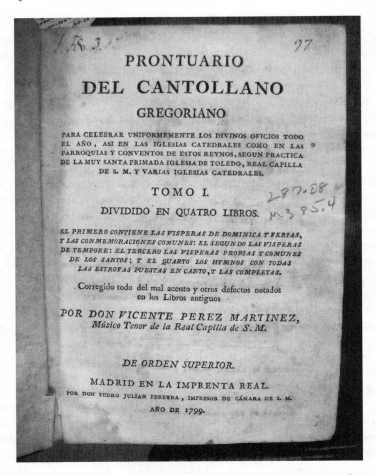

Photo 1-4 Title page for Vicente Pérez Martínez's *Prontuario del cantollano gregoriano,* Santa Barbara Mission Archive-Library, M2907 L99 P47, vol. 1. (Permission to include this image courtesy of the SBMAL; photo by the author.)

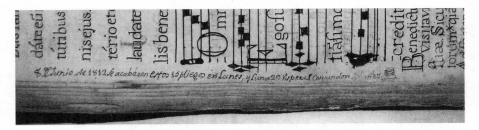

Photo 1-5 Ibáñez signature on side of p. 81v from Santa Clara Ms. 3. (Permission to include this image courtesy of the Santa Clara University Archive; photo by the author.)

strongly associated with the Toledo rite that was widely disseminated throughout California. A meticulous comparison of the *Prontuario* and Ibáñez's choir manuscripts falls beyond the scope of this present study, but a few samples would indicate the shadow of Toledo on this friar's work.[29]

The Toledo chant tradition was widespread in California, if we are to judge by other examples, such as the chant *In medio Ecclesiæ*.[30] Pedro Cabot and Juan Bautista Sancho both wrote out copies of this chant in nearly identical orthographic detail, indicating that they probably had a common model or that one was copying from the other. The *Prontuario* supplies most of the same pitches as these two friars, but not always; the visual aspect of the *Prontuario* (the choice of note shapes) differs from the twin versions sketched out by Cabot and Sancho. I strongly suspect that the two friars had a common model (not yet identified but from the same repertoire tradition as found in the *Prontuario*) and that it probably was generated from or distributed through the motherhouse of the Franciscans in Mexico City.[31] It is not surprising that these two friars wrote out *In medio Ecclesiæ*, for this chant serves not only as the Introit for the Common of the Church Doctors (Augustine, Dominic, Jerome, and Ambrose), but, more important, it also functions as the Introit for the Feast Day of Saint Anthony—the patron saint of their home mission, San Antonio de Padua. In Santa Barbara Mission Document 7, Father Tapís (or possibly Father Viader) wrote out the same basic tune that Sancho and Cabot had used as well; this "match" of a shared melodic contour is particularly intriguing, given that Santa Barbara Doc. 7 generally used a core repertoire of melodies and simply recycled them over and over, adapting them as necessary to accommodate the changing texts during the liturgical year. It uses a one-size-fits-all approach to liturgical chant. Therefore, for *In medio Ecclesiæ* to have a *nonformulaic* tune shows it was important enough to merit special treatment; as already observed, the melody that is jotted down is quite close to the one used by Sancho and Cabot. Another manuscript, Santa Barbara Doc. 12, has a nearly identical version of *In medio Ecclesiæ* to that of the Tapís (?) manuscript, Santa Barbara Doc. 7.[32] These two latter sources have an extra pitch F at the very beginning that is not found in the other sources mentioned thus far. In addition, these two have an ascent and descent encompassing a third (f-g-a'-g-f) at the word *ejus* that sets this version apart from the others. In short, Santa Barbara Documents 7 and 12 are stenciled from the same common model. Given the similarities in all the previously mentioned California manuscripts, it seems reasonable to believe that all of them are siblings, reflective in some way of the Toledo chant repertoire as conveyed to the *casa matriz*, or motherhouse, of the Apostolic College of San Fernando in Mexico City, which then migrated with (or was shipped to) the Franciscan friars in Alta California.[33] With respect to these chant melodies originating from Toledo, their inclusion in California's liturgy would have reflected a certain "nationalistic" pride in the Spanish church—simultaneously praising the Creator and the Spanish Crown in a single musical tradition.

Florencio Ibáñez was one of the many talented Franciscan musicians and holds a place of honor as the scribe of several of California's most intriguing plainchant volumes.[34] In his two books mentioned earlier (Santa Clara Ms. 3 and the Bancroft Library fragment choirbook C-C-68:2), he provides the applicable Proper chants for the various feast days, including the Introit, Alleluia, Offertory, and Communion. Ibáñez habitually includes the Offertory settings, unlike Narciso Durán's choirbooks that omit that genre almost entirely. As a young man he was the *maestro de capilla* at the Convento de Nuestra Señora de Jesús in Zaragoza, one of the important musical centers in Baroque Spain, and later held the same post at the Franciscan convent at Catalayud.[35] Upon his arrival in California in 1801, he spent two years at the San Antonio Mission and then, in 1803, moved north to the neighboring mission of Nuestra Señora de la Soledad, where he spent his remaining years, eventually dying there in 1818. His extensive training on the Iberian Peninsula in sacred music bore fruit in the New World with his profound knowledge of plainchant and liturgy, as evidenced in the four illuminated Antiphonaries at the Santa Barbara Mission.[36]

The Ibáñez choirbook at Santa Clara provides an intriguing clue to chant performance that conjoined aspects of Native American sacred tradition with those of Spain, at least with respect to the Alleluia and sequence *Veni Sancte Spiritus* for Pentecost. Ibáñez inserted along the margin of page 33 the following annotation: "Estarán arrodillados todos todo el tpō qᵉ la Tambora haga un ruido como el cañon gᵈᵉ del organo" (Everyone will kneel here for the whole time that the drum makes a ruckus like the big metal organ stop of the organ). (See photo 1-6.) Historically, this Alleluia required that the choir kneel at the Psalm verse—but the inclusion of a drum is obviously a California innovation![37] The fact that this aspect of indigenous religious practice was folded into Catholic liturgy reveals Ibáñez's respect and even reverence for his fellow *californios*.

Chant performance at the San José Mission and later Santa Barbara, under the guidance of Padre Narciso Durán, was at odds with the repertoire and performance tradition of Ibáñez at the Soledad Mission. The discrepancy might be due—at least partially—to the different musical experiences of these two friars. Whereas Ibáñez was highly trained (as is evidenced by his triumphant winning of the position of chapelmaster at Nuestra Señora de Jesús in Zaragoza), Durán himself admits that his training was only rudimentary. From the outset, he offers a disclaimer regarding his rather shaky musical expertise:

> In the first place, I confess that I am no music professional; I have never been a studious pupil. And although several times I have overheard music students engaged in conversation, speaking about the theoretical rules of Chant, I assure you that never have I been able to catch on or to understand them. I will only tell you that, thanks be to God, nature has favored me with a good ear, delicate enough in order to discern something about the material.[38]

Later in the same preface to his opulent choirbook, he emphasizes that learning to read music and understanding the rudiments are necessary for any choir, but that he felt underqualified as a teacher of this art. As he explains:

Photo 1-6 "Alleluia and *Veni Sancte Spiritus*" from Santa Clara Ms. 3, p. 34. (Permission to include this image courtesy of the Santa Clara University Archive; photo by the author.)

And not being able to persuade myself that the native choirboys might be capable of digging into music and chant according to the rules that the masters of this art have set down—and neither could I teach them the rules due to not knowing them—I made up my mind to do it with arbitrary rules that form a system or method that I am going to explain to you now.[39]

Durán's musical inexperience and reluctance to delve into the subtleties of the eight modes explain his shocking departure from the chant repertoire that had been transmitted in an almost immutable form for generations. This colossal repertoire of the Proper of the Mass (that is, the repertoire that was destined for specific days during the church year as opposed to those text that were reutilized generically day after day) was pruned, trimmed, and amputated down to a few core melodies that were then adapted for the many texts that circulated through the liturgical year. In a highly unorthodox practice, Durán hammers *all* the Introits

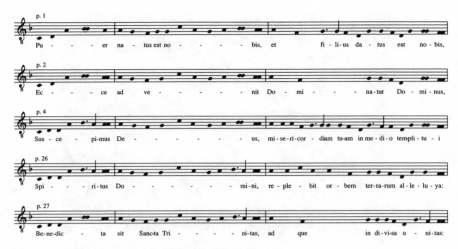

Figure 1-1 Introits in Durán's choirbook C-C-59

into the same melodic mold of the *Gaudeamus omnes*, shapes *all* the Alleluias into the same formula, and pushes all the Communions into the same melodic contour.[40] (See figures 1-1, 1-2, and 1-3 and photo 1-7—with a color version of this same photo appearing as B-100 in appendix B online. Also consult photos B-101 and B-102.)

The Alleluias are somewhat modern sounding, emphasizing triads that banter between tonic and dominant tonal areas: not only do these Alleluias conform to the same general outline time and time again, but even their Psalm verses adhere to the same tune. So far, no Gregorian chant model has been found as the jumping-off point for either Durán's Alleluias or his Communions (although each

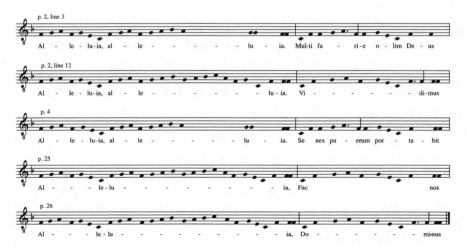

Figure 1-2 Alleluias in Durán's choirbook C-C-59

Figure 1-3 Communions in Durán's choirbook C-C-59

of these genres has a standard tune that is utilized for each feast day).[41] The Introit *Gaudeamus omnes* serves as the model for all the other Introits, a propitious choice by Friar Durán given its association with the Feast of Saint Francis.[42] He elucidates the procedure in his preface:

> Likewise, I need to point out that the Introits, Alleluias, and Communions are all in the same mode or key, a feature that possibly will annoy someone. But it is necessary to realize just how little promise the Indians show presently, in order for them to enter into that variety of modes that are used by other choirs, in which there is usually no lack of teachers. But these poor folks are out there having to perform all of the functions by themselves, and it is necessary to facilitate things for them so that they will sing well, and for this reason it occurred to me that putting everything in only one mode is easier for them. So the Introits are in Mode 1, conforming to or in imitation of the *Gaudeamus* (which is the one that I have heard celebrated): except the Introits for Ash Wednesday and Holy Week, for which I thought it more in keeping with the Spirit of the Church in the mysteries of these days to set them in Mode 4. The Alleluias and Communions of the year are in Mode 6 for the same reason—it seemed to me that they create an appropriate mood that is fitting for their place or presentation of the Mass. And just to make sure all of this does not annoy you, keep in mind the fact that until now nobody has gotten upset with the Orations, Epistles, Gospels, Prefaces, Lord's Prayer, etc., in spite of them always being sung in just one key.[43]

Durán may not have been schooled in the deepest intricacies of music theory, but one cannot help but admire his ingenuity and knack for crafting workable

Photo 1-7 Octave of Christmas and Mass for Epiphany from Santa Clara Ms. 4, p. 1. (Permission to include this image courtesy of the Santa Clara University Archive; photo by the author.)

solutions to the problems he encountered. He maps out a system and rationale for combining instrumental and vocal performance of the sacred liturgy and explains his goals and procedures for notating all chants with a tonal center F and exclusively using the F clef. This radical departure from tradition is not really very constricting given that Durán uses but a handful of core tunes for his settings of the Proper. He also advocates instrumental support for chant singing, not so much for the enriched texture but for the security it provides in keeping the choir at pitch, and for the invaluable assistance it provides in physically and graphically teaching the difference between half steps and whole steps—an issue that confounds beginning music theory students to this day. Durán puts forth his case:

> As the first fundamental principle, I mandated that there would never be a distinction between instrumentalists and singers, but that hands and

mouth should do the task that was assigned to them; that is to say, that singers and players should be one and the same. In the beginning they hit many roadblocks, but now they accomplish it without any problem whatsoever. It also seemed desirable to me to always have the instruments accompany the singing, even having two cellos for the Requiem. There are two reasons for this. First, in order to maintain the voices of the choirboys at a steady level, neither going flat nor sharp in pitch, as regularly happens without this precaution. The second, so that seeing the distances from one another that the notes have on the instruments in the positioning of the fingers, they might acquire some idea of the same distance that the notes in singing have from one another in the various modulations of the voice. Then I made them learn the scale, that I called the "natural notes," having them sing and play at the same time. After that, the scale of "half-steps" indicated by the flats and sharps as written below [later on folios B^v and C of this choirbook]. But there still remained the most difficult and tangled aspect of music and chant, which—it seems—is the variety of clefs with which the musical notes—such as C, D, E, et cetera—change their place of residence and location on the staff. And this struck me as inaccessible to the Indians, especially since chant is always to be accompanied by instruments—which have fixed, invariable pitch locations. I say, for example, it seemed to me unhelpful to say "ut" or "C" for a note on the bottom space of the staff when using the F clef, and then with a different clef to have to say "re" (D) or "mi" (E) for a note in the same place. For this reason I resolved to put this problem to one side, and to make use only of the F clef.[44]

In spite of Durán's advice in his preface that instruments invariably double the vocal line during the singing of chant, he nevertheless inserts annotations elsewhere in the volume that mark out a few exceptions. For example, the setting of the Canticle of Zechariah, *Benedictus Dominus Deus Israel* (*Blessed Be the Lord, God of Israel*), was performed by a gradual ascent, artfully expressing the passion of this text.[45] Periodically the whole tonal level is jacked up progressively, step by step, much like those old Barry Manilow songs that abruptly modulated up a level or two near the end of the number in order to give it more emotional bounce. Durán observes that instrumental doubling is too risky due to the barrage of sharps and flats that suddenly come flying at the performer as the melody marches upward, veering from key to key, so he therefore counsels against the use of instruments altogether in this context. As Durán states in his instructions:

Note: This Psalm or Canticle should be sung by rising upward, ascending a step every two verses; one should do the same for the verse *Illuminare* and the *Ad dirigendos* as well. But it is strongly advised not to accompany on any instrument, no matter what, because this is way too full of flat and sharp notes, and to succeed demands a lot of work and a masterful teacher.[46]

Ironically, then, Durán's admonition *not* to employ instruments in this case reveals that they must have been used as the rule of thumb under normal circumstances.

The next addendum scribbled on this page also makes reference to instrumental performance, this time with respect to the Lamentation settings for Matins of Maundy Thursday.[47] This service consumes almost twenty pages, constituting one of the most extensive settings in the choirbook. The Lamentations have long expanses of repeated notes (the voices frozen on the Great Plains of the staff) that are then separated by rolling hills of highly motivic and memorable recurring gestures (on a kind of melodic Piedmont). The phrases are not so much melodies as they are intoning formulas in free-flowing polyphony, reminiscent of some medieval organum. Unlike medieval polyphony, though, Durán explains that the melodies are to be distributed to two people: one choirboy and one *violón* (that is, a cellist).[48] He states:

> Another Note: The Lamentations were arranged as a duet so that one boy sings them and one cello plays. And be it advised that wherever you see parentheses like this, { }, I'd say that you can omit the pitches that are contained inside, in the event that the boys are unable to reach up to the high notes. One text and two lessons that are missing have been omitted so that the performers can choose what to do and so they can sing them however they like.[49]

A third and final word of advice is subsequently written at the bottom of this same sheet, where Durán tells us that he and his choir at San José mounted a performance of the complete Matins service in 1814 and that it was excessively long—so in the future he has decided to do only the first third of the piece (the first Nocturn), and then follow it up and draw the sacred service to a close with Lauds. He explains:

> Another Note: In this year, 1814, the complete Matins service was sung, and the service is way too long—for which reason it is felt that [in future years] no more than the first Nocturne and Lauds should be sung.[50]

Besides the manuscript at the Bancroft Library, choirbook C-C-59, we can add another major treasure related to Narciso Durán—the grandiose and dazzling choirbook Santa Clara Ms. 4 at the Santa Clara Mission.[51] The lettering appears to be modeled on his script, and the tome's notational and organizational features are so similar and idiosyncratic that they bear his stamp as well. Perhaps it is the fruit of a scriptorium or copy center at the San José Mission during Durán's residency there. The same handful of core melodies that Durán adapts for the Introits, Alleluias, and Communions in the Bancroft Library's choirbook reappears as the fundamental basis for the Propers in Santa Clara Ms. 4. We could hardly find a more definitive fingerprint or retinal scan to establish Durán as the supervising presence in this volume. On page 76, Durán provides more clues that clarify his practice of having instruments play along with the vocalists—not only in polyphonic or concerted works but in plainchant as well. He writes out the elaborately complex chant *Subvenite Sancti Dei* at the conclusion of the *Vigilia de Difuntos (Matins for the Dead)*, and he provides the following advice before writing down the *canto llano* melody:

> Continue on with the Subvenite, transposed to F with A flats and D flats, so that the cellos accompany in a good key for the choirboys.[52]

These fascinating and repeated references by Durán to instrumental doubling of the voices in plainchant do not surface in other mission sources and probably do not reflect standardized mission practice. However, instruments were an indispensable element of three other representative styles that permeated California mission life—those known as *canto de órgano, canto figurado*, and *música moderna*.

Canto de órgano

The second main style prevalent in Spain, Mexico, and California was that of *canto de órgano*, a term that easily befuddles modern scholars who translate it word for word as "song of the organ" or "singing and organ music." In actuality, the term refers to metric or mensural music; that is, the pulses are arranged repeatedly into groups of two, three, or four pulses, and the shapes in music notation convey mathematical and proportional relationships between the note lengths, so one can determine precisely how long or short each note should sound. *Canto de órgano* first surfaces in treatises in the early Renaissance when musicians had solved the thorny rhythmic problems of music notation: because it produced a recurrent meter, it was sometimes called *canto mensural* or *canto métrico*. The list of theorists with nearly identical definitions is a long one.[53] Antonio Ventura Roel del Río explains that *canto de órgano* "is a progression of harmonic sounds that is perceived by means of notes that are notated and measured out differently."[54] In 1761, Jerónimo Romero de Ávila defines *canto de órgano* as "an aggregate of note figures or note shapes which are lengthened or shortened depending on the meter."[55] Similarly, in his *Fragmentos músicos*, theorist Pablo Nassarre mentions the metric quality of *canto de órgano* and then elaborates:

> Q: Well, we have arrived at a commitment to treat metric or mensural music; what is understood by these kinds of music?
> A: By metric music, one means *canto de órgano*.
> Q: Well, why is *canto de órgano* called mensural or metric music?
> A: Because all the music of *canto de órgano* is sung in a measured way.
> Q: And why is it called "song of the organ" or *canto de órgano*?
> A: Because for this kind of music one always uses the instrument of the organ [to accompany].
> Q: Well, then, just what sort of thing is *canto de órgano*?

A: *Canto de órgano* is a collection of note shapes which one makes longer or shorter depending on the [three hierarchies of rhythmic organization,] mode, tempus, and prolation.[56]

During the Renaissance, *canto de órgano* designated polyphonic writing (as well as hierarchical rhythm). When sixteenth-century Iberian writers discuss the Renaissance counterpoint of masters such as Josquin, Gombert, Palestrina, Lasso, Morales, and Victoria, they refer to *canto de órgano*, which they contrast with the older monophonic and meterless singing of *canto llano*.[57] But by the early nineteenth century, *canto de órgano* could include (or even emphasize) homophonic settings within its definition.

Spanish theorists in the seventeenth and eighteenth centuries divide their treatises into major sections, beginning with plainchant (*canto llano*), continuing on to metric music (*canto de órgano*), and then moving on to explain polyphony and the process used to write it, which they label *composición* and *contrapunto* (composition and counterpoint).[58] The discussion unfolds naturally, progressing from the simplest textures to the more complex; that is, from monophony (a single unaccompanied vocal line) to homophony (a main melody with a subordinate chordal accompaniment that supports the tune), and concluding with polyphony (the simultaneous combination of two or more independent melodic lines). Although *canto de órgano* does not inherently limit itself solely to homophony, the very origin of the term refers to a singer providing a melodic thread that is accompanied and supported by subordinate harmonies on the organ, and it is relevant that any homophonic examples occur primarily in the section of *canto de órgano*. On the other hand, polyphony, with its web of independent melodic lines that one associates with the late Baroque (the music of Corelli, Bach, Handel, etc.), falls under the designations *composición* or *contrapunto* more often than under *canto de órgano*. Another term, *cantar a voces*, indicates polyphonic performance. In theoretical discussions, *voz* denotes any independent line of melody, be it vocal or instrumental. Therefore, *cantar a voces* roughly translates as "to sing or perform with several different melodic lines."

Visually on the page, *canto de órgano* looks very much like plainchant with its square and diamond note shapes, but whereas all the symbols have equal weight in *canto llano*, in *canto de órgano* the square notes (called *breves*) are either twice as long or three times as long as diamond notes (called *semibreves*), depending on the metric understructure. One also finds regularly placed bar lines to keep track of the measures as they pass by. Additionally, *canto de órgano* employed primarily the traditional-looking C clef and F clef found in chant; if one comes across a "modern" bass clef or treble clef, then the musical style has entered the up-to-date realm of *música moderna* (which will be discussed shortly).

In addition to the foot-tapping rhythmic qualities of *canto de órgano*, this style also requires the use of instruments to accompany the voice(s). Although the instrument of choice initially was the organ, by the late 1600s *canto de órgano* admitted large ensembles with a wide spectrum of sonorities: bowed strings, reed instruments and flutes, brass instruments, harps and archlutes, and so on. The inclusion of instruments is one of *canto de órgano*'s defining aspects, according to Nassarre, who distinguishes between three performance genres: *canto llano* is for voices alone; *canto de órgano* is for voices with instruments; and the third style, *instrumentos artificiales*, is instrumental music by itself with no vocals.[59]

Canto de órgano must have supplied a sense of pageantry and magnificence to religious services, if we are to believe Nassarre's description of the style as practiced in Spanish churches of the eighteenth century. He gives three reasons that *canto de órgano* was a valued practice, stating that it provides (1) spiritual benefit; (2) solemnity; and (3) confirmation of the authority and prowess of the church or cathedral.[60] In supporting his first thesis of spiritual benefit, he explains that song itself provides spiritual nourishment; it causes one to raise his or her heart toward God. Furthermore, the benefit is garnered not only by the performers but also by all who are in attendance; many attend the divine services primarily because they are attracted by the exquisite delight and enrichment that the music causes. He provides an anecdote of the powerful effect made by an organist on a soldier who was in the congregation. The keyboardist produced such a realistic imitation of military effects and battle scenes that the soldier—forgetting where he was—hit the pavement out of reflexive conditioning. When asked by neighbors what was going on, he responded that he had become agitated by the sounds of war and had simply forgotten where he was. Nassarre continues:

> Goodness, if the music of only one instrument by itself (the organ) can cause similar effects to those just described, one simply has to admire how many more [emotional] effects would be caused by the expanded sonorities that are created by church musicians employed in today's Cathedrals, composed of a variety of voices and instruments—winds as well as strings and organs—and with the variety of sweet consonances that they create.[61]

Resuming his presentation, Nassarre then elaborates on his second point: that *canto de órgano* provides solemnity for important feast days. He presents a summary of the hierarchy of church days, some being regular affairs, some significant, and others extremely important. Those days of preeminent stature deserve greater musical attention. Nassarre explains that in cathedrals "they use *canto de órgano* in the major church celebrations at those feast days of the first and second class. That is when music is most often employed that expresses the greatest solemnity and joy with which the festivity should be consecrated; because, just as Durando states, song signifies the joy of Heaven."[62]

Nassarre concludes this discussion with his third point—that *canto de órgano* confirms the authority and prowess of the church or cathedral. He argues that for prestigious cathedrals it is obligatory to have a music chapel with many musicians to realize the divine ritual; the more prestigious the institution, the more musicians it should employ.[63] A few pages earlier, Nassarre observes that any institution that could afford to do so mounted performances of *canto de órgano*, but that the expense could prove to be formidable. It required many musicians to take the various lines of the sopranos, altos, tenors, basses, wind players, string players, harpists, archlutenists, and so on.[64]

That the organ was one of the primary instruments available for this "accompanied style" is self-evident not only by the etymology of the term itself, *canto de órgano*, but by the instructions for conceptualizing and playing a chordal backup in Nassarre's section on organ and harp accompaniment.[65] But the inclusion of organ in *canto de órgano* was merely an option, not an obligation. For instance, the *villancicos* of Lucas Fernández corroborate most of Nassarre's main views but stamp it with a folkloric flavor rather than that of Nassarre's semiorchestral instrumentation.[66] As with all *villancicos*, his are "sacred" works poured from a "secular" mold: they are written in regular language and dialects that one would hear in the country or on cosmopolitan street corners (as opposed to Latin); they are sung by character types drawn from everyday life such as shepherds, Gypsies, sailors, and so on; and musically they are meant to capture the rhythms and flavor of the street, the sea, the pasture, or the farm.[67] The fusing together of *canto de órgano* and this pop-oriented *villancico* style is explicit, for Fernández concludes these works with phrases such as "this is written in *canto de órgano*" or, in his Christmas skits, "finally, all go to adore him [baby Jesus] singing a *villancico* that ultimately is notated as *canto de órgano*."[68] Since *villancicos* are meant to capture the thrill and flavor of secular pop music, so the chordal accompaniments were usually realized by harps and baroque guitars, not keyboards.[69] It is a rare shepherd who wanders from hill to dale with a harpsichord or organ strapped to his back.

Canto figurado

References to *canto figurado* surface in musical discourse by the music theorists and mission padres, derived from the term *figura*, or "note shape." It is regarded as synonymous with *canto de órgano* by many writers, such as Ignacio Ramoneda, who states, "Metric song, mensural song, figured song [*canto figurado*] and *canto de órgano* are all one and the same thing: and they are defined as 'a collection of notated figures unequal in value'—and upon encountering them, they are lengthened or shortened, depending on what is required by the metric hierarchies of mode, tempus, and prolation."[70] Similarly, Comes y Puig tells us that we can expect "a mensural rendition of many Credos, Glorias, and *prosas* where the pulses are grouped in twos or threes, depending on its composition, and these Credos will be known and referred to as being *canto figurado* or *canto de órgano*, but they are not to be found in *canto llano*."[71] For him, the two terms are used interchangeably.

But some authors treat *canto figurado*, or "figured" song, as a special subcategory under *canto de órgano* or even as its own separate genre—a substyle that John Koegel has succinctly and accurately defined as "rhythmicized elaborations of chant or harmonized devotional songs."[72]

For these theorists, *canto figurado* is a simpler, less adorned style that falls in the middle territory between the sparse simplicity of *canto llano* and the spectral possibilities offered by *canto de órgano*.[73] It should be noted that these authors present examples of *canto de órgano* whose erudite complexity and modern-sounding phrases hardly resemble the antiquated sounds presented by some of their fellow musicians writing at the same time. In truth, the apparent stodginess or trendiness of *canto de órgano* depends immensely on who is speaking; but all the musicians of the era were in agreement on the central defining features—*canto de órgano* was a rhythmic and metric style, and its notation used different note shapes to refer to different lengths of sound. A rift divides them on other points. For those authors who explore the distinctions between *canto figurado* and *canto de órgano* (rather than equating them), *canto figurado* most often lilts along with strings of "longs" and "shorts," written out in an antiquated system using the square and diamond note heads of the *breve* and *semibreve*. Once in a blue moon there might be a handful of the faster *minims* for a fleeting moment, but rapid-fire virtuosic passages are almost nonexistent. Only a handful of meters arise, as seen in Tomás Gómez in his *Arte de canto llano, órgano y cifra* (1649), where he allows only binary and triple meters with the possibility of dividing pulses into duplets or triplets—a total of four possibilities.[74] *Canto de órgano*, on the other hand, could use the modern notational system with which we are familiar today, using "rounded" shapes rather than the "squared" ones; it is jotted down using whole notes, half notes (*blancas*), quarter notes (*negras*), eighth notes (*corcheas*), and so forth, and the instrumental parts often subdivide the pulse even further into minuscule sixteenth notes or thirty-second notes that can race by in spectacular runs or arpeggios. Such is the case in Pérez Martínez's *Prontuario* hymn and sequence settings and in Marcos y Navas's *Arte, ó compendio general del canto-llano, figurado y órgano*, where his last section on *canto de órgano* is chock-full of Baroque-sounding snippets, complete with florid motion and ornamentation. Additionally, the number and variety of meters in *canto de órgano* cover a wide spectrum in comparison to *canto figurado*'s Spartan options. Similarly, *canto figurado* and *canto de órgano* can be distinguished from each other in texture; the former style is homophonic, with a single melodic thread or a duet in parallel thirds tripping along, supported by unwritten but implied chords. *Canto de órgano*, on the other hand, admits more independent vocal and instrumental parts and can interweave them in true contrapuntal polyphony, a texture rarely seen in any discussion of *canto figurado*.

All these refined distinctions surface in Marcos y Navas's *Arte, o compendio general del canto llano, figurado y órgano*; he provides dozens of mensural hymns and sequences with breves and semibreves as musical examples in his section on *canto figurado*. They are direct and simple, unmuddied by any distracting flourishes or racing figuration. The antiquated note shapes mark out a single tune on the staff (although it would have been accompanied by improvised instrumental chording), and once in a while the texture expands to a duet in parallel thirds.[75] Nothing fancy at all. His choice of examples reflects the strong connection of *canto figurado* with metric hymns, sequences, and *prosas* (i.e., Spanish-texted sacred pieces).

Marcos y Navas's explanations match his musical examples—he draws a crisp line between *canto figurado* (a straightforward homophonic style with a few available meters and note values) and *canto de órgano* (a more complex contrapuntal style with a rich variety of time signatures and great diversity in note values and articulations). In chapter 3, he instructs the beginner on the note shapes and meters of *canto figurado*:

Treatise Three: The Theory and Practice of *Canto Figurado*

Q: How many note types does one find in *canto figurado?*
A: Four.
Q: And what are they?
A: Long, breve, semibreve, and minim.
....
Q: How may time signatures or meters are there that are employed in *canto figurado?*
A: Just two: binary and ternary.[76]

Turning the pages through this tutorial, we arrive later at Marcos y Navas's explanation of *canto de órgano*, which has many more note shapes and meters at its disposal. He explains:

Treatise Four: The Theory and Practice of *Canto de Órgano*

Q: What is *canto de órgano?*
A: It is the combining of various and diverse figures that are lengthened or shortened in value, depending on the time signature.
Q: What is understood to be a figure in *canto de órgano?*
A: A representative note shape of the melodic line.
Q: How many of these "figures" or note shapes are there?
A: Seven, and they are: double whole-note, whole note, half note, quarter note, eighth note, sixteenth note, and thirty-second note.
...and some modern musicians use even one more—the sixty-fourth note.
....
Q: How many meters are in use presently with respect to *canto de órgano?*
A: Six
Q: What are they?
A: Cut time, common time, 2/4 time, 6/8 time, 3/8 time, and 3/4 time.[77]

Marcos y Navas then details the other symbols commonly found in *canto de órgano*, that include the multitude of different clefs one would find in Bach or Corelli (whereas *canto figurado* used only the C clef and F clef drawn in the same way as in plainchant). He then explains the accidentals and articulation marks available in *canto de órgano*—but that are avoided in *canto figurado*. His handy notational symbols include all the sharps, flats, and naturals that provide a full chromatic gamut; he explores the dots needed for making dotted rhythms (yet another effect prohibited in *canto figurado*), slurs, fermatas, measure lines, repeat marks, appoggiaturas, trills, and "guides" to indicate the pitch that is coming up on the next staff or next page turn.[78] In short, both *canto figurado* and *canto de órgano* have note values and meter, but the former is straightforward and uncluttered, whereas the latter presents a full spectrum of possibilities with respect to rhythm, meter, structure, tonality, and articulation.

Jerónimo Romero de Ávila reflects a similar outlook in his treatise *El arte de canto llano y órgano*, evidenced in the tome's grouping into four books. The first deals with theoretical aspects of *canto llano*, the second approaches it from a practical performance standpoint, and then—in book 3—he sets forth the theory and approach for singing metric hymns, sequences, and *prosas*, before concluding with the fourth and last book on *canto de órgano* "in the modern style." This repertoire of hymns, sequences, and *prosas* gets its own chapter, and just as we saw with Marcos y Navas, this material is sandwiched between the ancient and the modern, between plainchant and the modern Baroque, between monophony and polyphony. That the singing of hymns in a steady meter was regarded somewhat as a hybrid, a middle ground stylistically between plainchant and the Baroque, is further hinted at by Roel del Río, who explains that "although the metric singing of hymns is sometimes called plainchant, it really isn't—but instead it is a sort of 'plain' organ chant."[79] (For a typical example of *canto figurado* notation, see photo 1-8.)

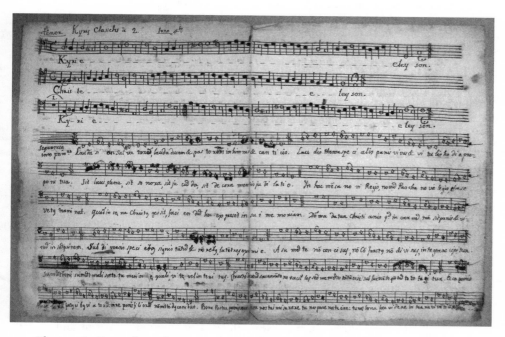

Photo 1-8 *Canto figurado* as seen in *Lauda Sion Salvatorem*, San Fernando Mission, Archival Center of the Archdiocese of Los Angeles, manuscript S-2. (Permission to include this image courtesy of the ACALA; photo by the author.)

Canto figurado implied "concerted performance," that is, the combining of voices and instruments, as opposed to a purely vocal or purely instrumental performance. In his prohibition against theatrical and profane features from entering into the Lima Cathedral, Archbishop Pedro Antonio de Barroeto y Ángel describes in 1754 why plainchant and *canto figurado* are more respectful of the grave and serious ambience needed for devotional worship. He begins by railing against the inappropriate nature of minuets, operatic arias, and Spanish-texted songs for instilling reverence.[80] He then summarizes the ancient and beneficial use of Gregorian chant and the later inclusion of instrumental music largely to keep good Catholics from entering the "Temples of the Heretics" who might be drawn in, due to the sensual attraction of their music to the ear. He then says that Flaviano of Antioch, Saint Christósomo of Constantinople, Saint Augustine, and Saint Ambrose all "permitted the combining of instruments with voices and of figured music [*música figurada*] that finally became standard usage in the Churches."[81] He then returns to the inappropriate nature of sonatas, arias, minuets, and vernacular songs in the temple. From Barroeto y Ángel's edict we can conclude several things: "figured" music mixes together voices with instruments; just as important, it is subdued and reverent—unlike the "the operatic," showy, or virtuosic sounds seen in "modern" music.

Instrumentation in *Canto figurado* and *Canto de órgano* Accompaniments

I will return to the controversy concerning "modern" music in the next section, but at this point, a few words considering instrumentation are in order. Both *canto figurado* and *canto de órgano* were "concerted" styles in which voices and instruments mixed together into one swirling blend of sound. The fundamental choices in "orchestration" are defining elements of their respective styles. For *canto figurado*, what were the accompanying instruments that supplied the harmonic rivers of chords upon which the melody floats? For *canto de órgano* settings with a figured bass line, what were the chordal instruments in the continuo grouping? With respect to realization of *acompañamiento* or basso continuo lines in Spain, the most common chordal instruments were the organ, harp, and guitar.[82] Louise Stein aptly summarizes continuo writing in the Spanish Baroque:

> The characteristic Spanish continuo ensemble included harps and guitars, the preferred accompaniment instruments in Spain since at least the middle of the sixteenth century. In a sense, then, Spanish continuo practice was a compromise of new techniques and older traditions....
>
> Because the guitar and harp were the principal accompaniment and continuo instruments in Spain, Spanish continuo practice also retained the native style until the eighteenth century, and the repertory for guitar and harp was closely aligned with that of secular and theatrical songs.[83]

The guitar and harp combination was such a defining element of Spanish style that it was used in foreign works where a non-Spaniard composer wanted to portray a "Spanish" feeling for his audience. Such is the case with Jean-Baptiste Lully's *Mascarade* of 1664, in which he includes a "Dance Number of Spaniards with Spanish-sounding Music with Harps and Guitars," further specifying that the actual performers in this spectacle should be Spaniards, and that they were to play those two specific instruments.[84]

Harps and guitars were seen in sacred performance as well as in secular settings. In addition to being a preferred choice in theatrical song and dance, the harp was a near-mandatory member of the continuo ensemble in Spanish and Mexican cathedrals as well. Any decent-sized church had at least two chordal instruments in the continuo grouping—an organ and a harp. For polychoral works, the harp was assigned to the smaller Choir I (with one singer on a part), and the heftier Choir II that doubled vocalists on each line was accompanied by the organ.[85] That guitars were part of a mission orchestra is demonstrated by their ubiquitous presence in the mission inventories of South America.[86]

The "Spanish feeling" became the basis for the California and Texas sonorities as well. If we examine the purchase orders sent by the mission fathers in 1807 to their motherhouse, the Apostolic College in San Fernando, Mexico, we see their insatiable appetite and need for guitars, guitar strings, guitar tutors, guitar chord charts, *bandolas, bandolones* (tenor *bandolas*), and bass *bandolas*.[87] The Franciscans are not asking for these instruments so they can put on fandangos (although we do find the secular authorities at the presidios asking for guitars or guitar strings, probably for that purpose);[88] no, the friars clearly needed these instruments for religious music making and were buying them out of their church budget.

Thomas Oliver Larkin observed that "almost every *Californio* can play on harp and guitar."[89] The harp was a favorite among Los Angeles's most distinguished citizens at midcentury, and Soledad Coronel, daughter of military officer Ignacio Coronel, established a glowing reputation as a skilled harpist and helped her father open a reputable school in Los Angeles in 1844.[90] In Texas, as well, during the 1700s, the most common instruments were the irrepressible guitar, harp, and violin.[91]

That the harp and guitar were pervasive in the entire Spanish Empire—including California—is not that surprising. In the remote frontiers of the empire, the highly portable guitar, harp, and *bandola* were natural choices for chordal accompaniments. When it comes to documenting keyboard instruments in California, however, things are more elusive and befuddling. Some scholars have leapt to the erroneous conclusion that the friars had access to pipe organs, since they talk about *canto de órgano*, a term that refers to polyphony and part-writing as opposed to a musical instrument. To add to the confusion, some friars actually do mention organs in the context of musical instruments—but they usually are referring to *barrel* organs. These mechanical instruments have no keyboards to select individual pitches but instead utilize prefabricated wooden sleeves with holes that can be dropped into a big barrel that has bellows and a crank. The "performer" would turn the crank and pump the bellows; once set in motion, the sleeve with the holes allowed certain reeds to sound, making a credible performance in much the same way that a player piano uses punched holes in a paper roll (or a music box uses raised pegs on a prefabricated disk). The measured distances between the holes or the pegs generate the correct pitches at the appropriate time.[92] Keyboards with movable keys, on the other hand, were exceedingly rare in California life before the mid-nineteenth century. A few notable exceptions arise, however. Father Narciso Durán repeatedly requested that the motherhouse of San Fernando in Mexico City send him an organ with three contrasting ranks of pipes.[93] At some point before 1842, Santa Barbara achieved Durán's dream of obtaining an organ; Sir George Simpson was in attendance at mass there when a self-taught neophyte played several hymns on the organ, one of them being *Ein feste Burg ist unser Gott.*[94]

Durán was not the only Californian to put keyboard instruments on his wish list. The petitions for supplies annually sent to the *casa matriz* in Mexico City often include keyboard instruments, such as pianos, spinets, or organs. In 1809, the San Fernando Mission pleads for "1 fortepiano, if one can be found at a fair price, and if not, then a spinet or a monochord," along with "Keyboard lessons for beginners with their corresponding sonatas."[95] The San José Mission similarly asks for "1 Spinet" along with "4 volumes of explanatory lessons on harmony."[96] San Miguel asks for "an organ with one stop, as our Quartermaster [?] Don Mariano [Payeras?] has been informed, that it should be coming along with the two that the Most Reverend Fathers of Mission San Luis Obispo are ordering."[97] Father Durán—before asking for the organ—was hopeful that Mexico would send him a piano. On 3 February 1806, he writes: "That which is requested for the new is the following: a forte-piano for the Church liturgy, not to exceed 200 pesos in price; the work by [Francesc] Valls titled *Keyboard Lessons.*"[98] Sadly, there is no evidence that any of these aforementioned instruments were ever delivered.

For a short period, the San Diego Mission had a spinet that was brought there by Friar Ángel Fernández Somera in 1771. It had already fallen into disrepair by the time Pedro Font used it to accompany mass on 14 January 1776. Sometime thereafter the spinet found its way to the San Gabriel Mission.[99] In 1824, the officiating padre at San Francisco Solano used a small clavichord (a rare treasure that had been left by the Russians) both as the accompaniment for voices during mass and as the altar. Dimtry Zavalishin remembers the events and multitasking, stating:

> There were not enough musicians or musical instruments (they used organs [?]), and for me it was very strange to see that in the new mission of San Francisco Solano some old, jingly clavichord (virtually abandoned [in 1806] by Rezanov, our emissary to Japan), set inside a shed that substituted for a church, served as an altar and an organ, and that Padre José Altamira celebrated the rites and played piano simultaneously, performing the duties of a priest, organist, reciter, and chorister.[100]

A precious handful of other keyboard instruments made their way to California by midcentury. A shipment of pianos by Captain Stephen Smith brought three pianos from Baltimore to the West Coast. He sold the treasures to José Abrego in Monterey, Eulogio Celio in San Pedro, and Mariano Guadalupe Vallejo in San Francisco.[101] After the Gold Rush, keyboards began to trickle into California along with the flood of new Yankee settlers. None of these instruments, however, would have been available to the friars during the height of the mission period.

To summarize, then, we can conclude that *canto figurado* with its chordal accompaniments—and the harmonies needed for *acompañamiento* or basso continuo lines—were realized in the California missions by ensembles of multiple plucked strings, including guitars, harps, and families of *bandolas* in different registers. With few exceptions, keyboard accompaniments were not viable options for mission performance.

Música moderna or *Estilo moderno*

So far we have seen three main style classifications of mission music: *canto llano, canto figurado*, and *canto de órgano*. Yet another style, *música moderna*, makes its appearance in the California missions in a few isolated but noteworthy examples, particularly in some of the manuscripts brought by Juan Bautista Sancho and used by his choir and orchestra at the San Antonio de Padua Mission. In many respects, it reflects the cutting-edge developments in Europe and New Spain, such as thrilling violin figuration with rapid repeated notes, exuberant arpeggios or lightning fast runs that rocket across the fingerboard, and gigantic leaps that plunge or jump from one register to another. The theatricality of this showy aesthetic caused furious debate throughout the eighteenth century that was not totally resolved even by century's end.

The Italianate aspects of the vocal and instrumental writing became flash points for raging polemics in Spain, as theorists discussed whether or not this "invading" style was appropriate for preserving a reverent attitude at worship. The shift in timbral preference from wind and brass instruments to the increasing prominence of paired violins takes place more or less concurrently with the appearance and rising importance of this newer *música moderna*. The role of the instruments also shifts; in *canto de órgano* (also labeled *música antigua* by the theorists who discuss the "modern music"), wind parts often double the vocal lines to reinforce them and make them more secure, whereas in *música moderna* the violins are often entirely liberated, leaping about, running over and under, from high to low, energizing the texture—without being tethered to the singers. In addition, melodic lines become increasingly embellished with ornaments such as trills, mordents, slurs, suspensions, appoggiaturas, turns, passing tones, and the like.

Newer trends shape the vocal lines of the *música moderna* or *estilo moderno* as well; the recitatives and da capo arias are unmistakably modeled on the latest trends in Italian operas, oratorios, and cantatas, complete with recitatives and da capo arias. The more subdued rhythmic features of *canto de órgano* pale in emotive effect to the variety of rhythms in *música moderna* and its flamboyant displays of technical skill. In general, accidentals are few and modulations are rarer in *canto de órgano*, but they are sprinkled more liberally throughout the compositions of *estilo moderno*. Furthermore, the bass lines of the modern style are much more daring, exhibiting a wide harmonic vocabulary, seventh chords, diminished and augmented triads, secondary dominants, and so forth. Finally, the modern style admits much greater variety in clef selection. The treble clef and bass clef predominate, with the C clef becoming less and less frequent, and even then, its use is confined to vocal parts.

The newer trends met with controversy when first introduced in the eighteenth century. Padre Feijoo and Pablo Nassarre threw themselves into the thick of the debate and rapidly assembled a plethora of supporters and detractors.[102] Feijoo authored several collections of essays that set in motion the discourse regarding musical aesthetics in sacred music of eighteenth-century Spain. His first collection, the *Teatro Crítico Universal*, came out over a period of years, with volume 1 appearing in 1726 and volume 6 arriving in 1734. The fascinating and oft-quoted *Música de los templos* is tucked into volume 1 of the *Teatro Crítico Universal*. His next series, the *Cartas eruditas y curiosas*, began in 1742 with volume 1 and concluded with volume 5, which closed things off in 1760. In general, Feijoo was against the Italianate arias and "theatrical" elements that were creeping into liturgical music; his true love was the intricate polyphony and more choral-dominated sound of the previous century, where the instruments clearly played a subservient role to the fabric of choral counterpoint. He was perturbed by the treble-dominated sonorities of the violin. He observes:

> Violins are inappropriate in the sacred arena. Their squeals—although harmonious—are shrieks and they excite in our spirits a liveliness akin to immature childishness, very distant from that proper respect that is owed the majesty of the Mysteries, especially in this era when those who compose for violins take care to make the compositions go so high that the performer has to make a bridge with his fingers.[103]

Lining up alongside Feijoo's conservative positions were Juan Francisco de Sayas and Gaspar Molina de Saldívar; they were offended by the inclusion of violins in the sanctuary and felt that operatic-style singing was unseemly.[104] However, it is notable that Feijoo, although conservative, was nevertheless flexible, capable of changing his mind on occasion. By his last publication, his views on Italian influence have softened (preferring the Italians over the French), and his disgust with the violin has been tempered. His adulation for Corelli is seen in his claim that if one were to take all the musicians in France and put them together, they would not equal one Corelli.[105]

On the other side of the aisle during the eighteenth century were several irate musicians who were offended by Feijoo's "stodgy" reluctance to accept the new concerted style where violins and chamber orchestras supported the choral sonorities.[106] A musician in the Royal Chapel published the *Diálogo harmónico sobre el Teatro Crítico Universal en defensa de la Música de los templos* (1726) under the pseudonym Eustaquio Cerbellón de la Vera. He lumps together the older styles of *canto llano* and *canto de órgano*, labels them "ancient music (*música antigua*)," and contrasts them to the trendy *música moderna*. He praises the craftsmanship and structure of the old ways but says that when one takes into account good taste and style, modern music (*música moderna*) greatly sur-passes *música antigua*.[107] Juan Francisco de Corominas, the first violinist at the University of Salamanca, takes a similar tack, contending that musicians should not be governed by the sounds of their grandparents and praising the pantheon of great contemporary composers who employ violins in concert with voices—artists such as Antonio Vivaldi, Arcangelo Corelli, Joseph de Torres, Tomaso Albinoni, José de Nebra, and Antonio Literes.[108] The artistry of several of these composers would have been familiar to the Franciscan friars, since their music constituted a significant core of the Mexico City Cathedral repertoire.[109] In addi-tion, Fray Juan Bautista Sancho, active at the San Antonio Mission in California, surely would have known the music of Literes, since they both were extremely esteemed musicians from the small island community of Mallorca (although from very different generations). In short, the *música moderna* that Corominas espouses would have been at the heart of Sancho's musical experience (and per-haps of other Franciscans as well).

The Mission Performance Styles in the Americas

John Koegel's research has demonstrated both *canto llano* and *canto de órgano* were standard occurrences in San Agustín, Florida, shortly after the Spanish arrived, and they were the bread and butter of music performance in early New Mexico, beginning with the first wave of settlers after Oñate's venture into the territory. By the early 1600s, there were already approximately thirty Franciscan missions where polyphonic performance in *canto de órgano* was normally expected.[110] Bernardo Illari and Piotr Nawrot, through their pioneering research and gorgeous music editions, have shed light on the richly variegated music performed with regularity by the indigenous Guarení at the Jesuit missions in South America.[111]

The Jesuits' Chiquitos missions in Bolivia resonated with music similar to that of California, as described by Leonardo Waisman, who classifies their extant reper-toire in four different categories.[112] The first one he labels *estilo misional*: it is typi-fied by syllabic declamation, a narrow melodic range, emphasis on the harmonies I, IV, and V, short phrases in parallel thirds, simple sequences, and the alternating of passages that juxtapose three or four singers against a smaller group of one or two—all of which describe the preponderance of the California manuscripts written in *canto de órgano* or *canto figurado*. Waisman's second category includes more ambitious and adventuresome works of larger dimensions, and more daring harmonies and modulations—an apt description of the *música moderna* found in Mexican cathedrals and a few of the California missions. His remaining cat-egories deal with a repertoire from the middle and late nineteenth century and therefore are not relevant to the present study. All descriptions of mission life in Baja California under the Jesuits, until their expulsion by Carlos III in 1767, are consonant with the same daily features of mission life as described in Sonora, New Mexico, Florida, and South America, including the singing of chant and music accompanied by harp and guitar—whose appearance as chordal backup to sung vocal lines constitute an implied reference to *canto de órgano*.[113]

Alta California falls in the same orbit, as is evidenced by the fathers' letters, government documents, accounts by travelers who were visiting the missions, and the music manuscripts themselves. Mission routines for daily life and worship were quite similar, from one tip of the Americas to the other, and the mission repertoire promulgated by the mendicant orders invariably included *canto llano* and *canto de órgano*. Friars Pedro Cabot and Juan Bautista Sancho confirm this and provide a fascinating snapshot of music making at San Antonio de Padua in their response to the *Interrogatorio (Questionnaire)* that they were asked to fill out by the bishop of Sonora and the father-president of the California missions, José Señan. Cabot and Sancho list the instruments that the neophytes have mastered, then meticulously describe Native American instruments and songs—including some theoretical analysis of Indian scale systems—after which they go over the sorts of European styles that the converts have learned, and finally sign their names and date, "26 February 1814."[114]

Unfortunately, much of Cabot's and Sancho's description of mission life has been mistranslated; it would make sense at this point to excerpt and scrutinize their treatment of European-style music and correct the misconstrued terminology that has marred the translations of Geiger, Engelhardt, and da Silva, especially since their garbled misconceptions of this document have been the passages most often quoted in subsequent research.

That they had an orchestra at San Antonio is illuminated by their opening sentence that spotlights the instruments they are using:

> *Tienen mucha inclinacion á la Musica, y tocan violines, violon, flautas, trompa, tambora, y otros instrumentos que la Mision les ha dado.*

The aforementioned scholars have translated this passage by listing a series of instruments: Geiger states, "They are much inclined to music. They play the violin, cello, flute, trumpet, drum, and other instruments supplied by the mission"; Owen da Silva's version is similar when he observes, "They like music very much. They play the violin, the bass-viol, the flute, the trumpet, the drum, and any other instrument given them"; Engelhardt omits this passage and begins his translation with the material on Native American music.

Several patches are needed right off the bat to rectify some misconceptions in terminology. A *violón* is not usually a bass viol, as da Silva mistakenly concludes, but a violoncello. As Evguenia Roubina explains in her engaging study of string instruments in New Spain, the term had been ambivalent for a good part of the seventeenth century. At the outset of the 1600s, it could apply to *any* member of the violin family, including the high-pitched violin and extending down to the cello. Little by little, its usage was winnowed down to designate a cello—especially in instances where both *violín* and *violón* appear in the same document.[115] The term for contrabass or bass viol was *bajo, contrabajo,* or *violón contrabajo;* this dis-intinction is borne out in the employment rosters of the music chapels of Spain and Mexico, as well as the request for instrument shipments to the California missions.[116] Da Silva and Geiger both erroneously translate *trompa* as "trumpet," when in fact it means "horn." In eighteenth-century scores, a trumpet is identi-fied either as *clarín*—denoting a valveless clarion trumpet, a bit like a bugle—or as *trompeta,* a designation that starts appearing in the nineteenth century. Signifi-cantly, some of the names that Cabot and Sancho jot down are plural and others are singular, a detail that da Silva and Geiger miss; the preponderance of treble instruments that are in the plural (violins and flutes) suggests that they were dou-bling with more than one instrument on a part. The lower register, on the other hand, apparently was slugging it out with a single cello (or perhaps a bassoon or string bass added to the soup as one of the "otros instrumentos" to which Cabot refers). The top-dominated instrumentation with multiple violins is one of the main characteristics of a Classical-period orchestra as opposed to a mere ragtag collection of instruments that happen to be present at a particular institution or venue.[117] That instrumentation looks remarkably similar to the Spanish "orches-tras" from the era, such as the theater orchestra in eighteenth-century Valladolid that consisted of 4 violins, 2 horns, 2 flutes, a cello, and a bass; the opera orchestra in Granada that in 1770 consisted of 4 violins, cello, bassoon, oboe, 2 horns, and guitar; the orchestra in the Chapel of the Royal Palace in Valencia in 1776 that consisted of 4 violins, viola, cello, bass, a pair of flutes (that doubled on oboe), a pair of horns (that doubled on trumpet), and bassoon; or the orchestra in the Salamanca Cathedral that by 1740 had a top-dominated ensemble of 4 violins, oboe, flute, recorder, *flauta de pico* (a smaller flute in the register of a piccolo), cello, bass, organ, harp, and perhaps some of the older wind instruments from the older "antique" style.[118] Similarly, nearly the same instrumentation was employed in the late eighteenth century at the Coliseo, the main theater in Mexico City. In 1786 its payment roster included "2 first violins, 2 second violins, another vio-lin who also is a singing master, a violoncello who is a singing master, a viola, a contrabass, 2 oboes, and 2 horns."[119] The same tendencies surface during the mid-eighteenth century in many of the *reducciones* or Jesuit missions of South America, where they performed exquisite pieces by Domenico Zipoli and other *galant* or "Classical" composers; their orchestras, too, were top-dominated, with multiple violins in the high register and a few low-sounding instruments such as the *bajón* or *violón.*[120]

I will to return to the theme of California's "orchestras" later, in chapter 7, but for now I wish to emphasize a central point: Cabot and Sancho are not just giving a haphazard grocery list of instruments in the marketplace; they are telling us that they have a full Classical-period orchestra that could handle representative works written in the *estilo moderno.* If the above-mentioned glitches are rectified, a more accurate translation would read:

> The neophytes have a lot of musical talent, and they play violins, cello, flutes, horn, drum, and other instruments that the Mission has given them

[implying that there were even more kinds of instruments available and that they collectively constituted a full orchestra].

In the middle section concerning Native American traditions, Geiger, da Silva, and Engelhardt interject several statements that misconstrue the original text. For instance, at one point Geiger translates "*y nunca cantan a voces, si solamente quando cantan muchos juntos, algunos van octava alta*" as "the only time they sing anything like part music is when many sing together." Here, Geiger's translation implies that polyphony (or "part music") was integral to the Indian tradition— but actually Cabot and Sancho are stating the opposite! Da Silva's interpretation of the passage is considerably closer: "The only time that they sing anything like part music is when many sing together; then some sing an octave higher than the others." Stymied by this same passage and some other equally demanding phrases, Engelhardt gathers up these amputated limbs, cut from various sentences that are found in completely different contexts, and then stitches them together into a sort of Frankenstein translation that is highly interpretive: "In their pagan state they have songs which they employ at their dances and elsewhere. They sing together, never any solos, though some sing high and others low." The idea that "they sing together" is not such a stretch, since the *Interrogatorio* does indeed state, "*cantan muchos juntos*," but nowhere is any mention made that they never sang solos. The closest reference to "high and low" arises in Cabot's and Sancho's discussion of Indian scale systems and the manner that they "go up and down"; but scales and the way they work have little or no bearing on whether singers are in high or low registers. Granted, the friars do mention that some vocalists "*van octava alta*" (sing an octave higher), but that is much more specific than Engelhardt's over-generalized "some sing high and others low." Goodness, "singing high and low" could describe almost any music after 1200, from medieval organum, to the Verdi *Requiem*, to the Temptations: but singing "an octave higher" reflects something else altogether. In order to set the derailed translations back on track, I propose the following:

[In their traditional music, the Native American converts] *never* sing independent polyphonic lines; but in the unique cases when many sing together, some of them sing an octave higher.

Skipping to the document's closing sentences, we encounter Cabot and Sancho returning to the field of European-style music. They state:

Las letrillas en castilla las cantan por perfeccion, y aprenden con facilidad todo canto, que se les enseña, asi llano, como figurado; y desempeñan un coro, una Misa â voces, mas que sean papeles obligados; á todo esto les ayuda las [sic] voz clara, y el buen ohido que tienen todos, asi Hombres como Mugeres.

Again, this passage has stumped scholars in this effort to divine the secrets of California's mission style. Geiger's translation is quite good but runs off on the shoulder or gets bumped off the road a time or two. Both he and da Silva translate "*las letrillas en castilla*" as "Spanish airs." Technically, *letrillas* is not a kind of song but the lyrics to them. Even today, when one wants to refer to the song's words, the term that pops up is *letra*. Cabot and Sancho are thus praising how perfectly the neophytes sing the *text*, at least as much as they are complimenting the singing. Geiger, da Silva, and Engelhardt all approximate the friars' reference to *canto llano* (plainchant) as "plain music": as we have just seen, *canto llano* is a specific musical genre that has many attendant aspects beyond its simplicity or "plainness." The same holds true for "figured music."

The next conundrum arises in trying to figure out the padres' statement "y *desempeñan un coro, una Misa â voces, mas que sean papeles obligados*." Da Silva's and Geiger's translations greatly resemble each other. Geiger translates, "They are members of a choir and sing a mass as a group, but they cannot sing by sight," and da Silva's rendition similarly reads, "They form a choir, and can do a part mass, but cannot sing by sight." These two interpretations fall short in explaining the passage, beginning with the term *coro*. The California manuscripts that juxtapose alternating sections of monophonic chant with sections of polyphony place the word *coro* over the plainchant sections.[121] When Cabot and Sancho state, therefore, that their local musicians join together as a *coro*, they probably mean that the group is successfully negotiating passages of plainchant.[122] The next few words in the *Interrogatorio* refer to contrapuntal performance, showing that the neophytes could handle both contrasting styles (monophony and polyphony) with ease. As we just established in the previous section, the phrase *a voces* means the work has separate, independent, and interweaving melodic lines. The performance of a repertoire written *a voces* requires several well-trained performers who can read music at an advanced level and can stay on pitch even when others nearby are going in a myriad of directions. It also presupposes a societal structure where music education is organized and accessible, and where rehearsals are the expected norm for the preparation of almost any music performance. Geiger's assessment that the neophytes could "sing mass as a group" sorely understates the accomplishment of the San Antonio choir. As Geiger and da Silva struggle with the text "*mas que sean papeles obligados*," they leap to the unfounded conclusion that the native choir "cannot sing by sight." Nowhere is that implied or vaguely suggested. A more rigorous translation yields "unless there are the obligatory sheets or papers," a clause that makes no sense unless joined to the previous words that it modifies. Once we glue the two segments together, however, we get a perfectly lucid explanation:

> They can perform a polyphonic mass with separate, independent melodic lines—as long as there are the necessary performance parts.

The friars are clear: their choir *can* perform polyphonic music, but instead of relying on an oral tradition and singing by memory, this style demands that they must have in front of them the written performance parts so that they can read their individual lines. In short, the native musicians could read music—and they did it well (as will be evidenced by travelers' accounts and by aspects of the music manu-scripts themselves). How ironic and unfortunate that Geiger's and da Silva's trans-lations take a position that is diametrically opposed to the original statements made by Cabot and Sancho. Engelhardt fares no better, with his cursory reduction: "They sing in choir at Holy Mass and at other occasions." These "other occasions" are not spelled out in the answer to the *Interrogatorio* although this editorial inser-tion does happen to be true.

Two intriguing issues arise when inspecting the final sentence and its transla-tions: the first concerns subtleties in punctuation and their impact on meaning, and the second concerns a flaw of omission in the various translations and the resulting repercussions. The report's last sentence reads, "*á todo esto les ayuda las* [sic] *voz clara, y el buen ohido que tienen todos, asi Hombres como Mugeres.*" Geiger and Engelhardt sound like siblings in their conclusions, with the former translat-ing the passage in question as "In all these they are aided by clear and sonorous voices and a good ear, which all have, both men and women," and the latter offer-ing a similar rendition, "In this they are aided by their clear and sonorous voices and sharp ear with which men and women are blessed." The sound in the mission must have been bounteous and resonant, as Cabot and Sancho describe it, and we can gather that the native choir sang in tune, since the friars praise the vocalists for their "good ear." This is not a portrait of shoddy performance, as has often been stated by Bancroft, Arnaz, Beatfield, and others.[123]

We can glean another rather startling aspect of performance practice regarding female performers if we focus on the details of Cabot's and Sancho's answer to the *Interrogatorio*. Notably, in their original manuscript, this last phrase is preceded by a semicolon, not a period. That seemingly minuscule detail has huge impli-cations, for it joins together in one extended sentence the previous description of plainchant, choral singing, and the performance of polyphonic masses with this final description of men's and women's voices. The wording, "in this they are aided," is connective as well, for it explicitly directs back to the previous musical remarks, supplying even more syntactical glue to bond all these ideas together into one gestalt. The shocking aspect at this juncture is the implied inclusion of women musicians in sacred settings; although this paragraph can be read several ways, each pointing to different conclusions, one could make a persuasive case that Cabot and Sancho are placing women in the heart of their discussion of poly-phonic vocal performance.[124] Another solution might imply that women sang in church but as members of the congregation, not as members of the chapel choir, who would be singing the Latin text of the mass. In either case, Cabot and Sancho unmistakably include women's voices as a part of mission worship.

Whereas Geiger and Engelhardt both tackle the ultimate words of Cabot's and Sancho's report (*á todo esto les ayuda las* [sic] *voz clara, y el buen ohido que tienen todos, asi Hombres como Mugeres*), da Silva simply lops off the quotation and stops translating before arriving at these key words.[125] His abrupt truncation deprives the modern reader of critical information—that Native Americans per-formed plainchant and European polyphony with an ample, sonorous fullness, and furthermore, that women may have sung in the missions. The omission is made worse by da Silva's unsubstantiated statement that "no women were allowed in these choirs."[126]

In fairness to da Silva, he actually *does* translate this passage elsewhere in his volume, but he distorts its meaning by removing it from the original context and instead inserts it into his section "Primitive Music" (primarily meaning the indigenous music in North America before European contact). The pseudo-compliments are dismissive and have a derogatory aftertaste: "Although the California Indians stood on a lower physical and intellectual plane [!] than a great many other tribes of North America, they were not devoid of music talent. In fact, both men and women, according to the padres of Mission San Antonio, possessed 'clear and sonorous voices and a sharp ear.'"[127] Da Silva then spends the next paragraphs describing the flutes, fifes, drums, and percussion sticks of Native American music. Da Silva's relocation of material ends up distorting Cabot's and Sancho's intent. What initially had been praise for the neophyte converts' performance of European "art music" has been thrown into a grab bag of disparaging assumptions concerning the inherent inferiority of California's first peoples.

Pulling the various revisions and conclusions into one paragraph, I suggest the following as a plausible translation for Cabot and Sancho's section on European music in the San Antonio Mission:

> The neophytes have a lot of musical talent, and they play violins, cello, flutes, horn, drum, and other instruments that the Mission has given them [implying that there were even more kinds of instruments available and that they collectively constituted a full orchestra].
>
> ....
>
> The Indian converts sing Spanish lyrics perfectly, and they easily learn every kind of singing that is taught to them, *canto llano* or plainchant as well as the metric singing of *canto figurado* [and accompanied by instruments]. Also, they can successfully perform as a choir, or even manage the singing of a polyphonic mass with separate, independent melodic lines—as long as there are the necessary performance parts. In all this they are aided by a clear voice and good ear that they all have, both men and women alike.

By the early 1800s, across Europe and Mexico the fervor surrounding the combining of voices with rather showy instrumental lines, the top-dominated florid structures of burgeoning Classicism, and the "scandalous" use of violins had subsided. These features were now commonplace and inoffensive aspects of much church music throughout Europe and the main cities of Mexico. The *Interrogatorio* filled out by Cabot and Sancho here indicates that California was experiencing a parallel transformation. In actuality, all four styles mapped out so far were essential ingredients in the "recipe" of California mission life. *Canto llano, canto figurado, canto de órgano*, and *música moderna* all enjoyed deep roots in the mission environment—and the context of their usage will occupy the coming chapters.

Notes

1. Francisco Marcos y Navas, *Arte, ó compendio general del canto-llano, figurado y órgano, en método fácil* (Madrid: Joseph Doblado, 1716). Five copies at the Santa Barbara Mission Archive-Library (SBMAL): MT860 .M37 1776, formerly catalogued as 287.07 N322-1 (with an ex libris of Juan Bautista Sancho on the title page, "Del simple uso de Fr. Juan Bau^ta Sancho"); MT860 .M37 1816, formerly catalogued as 287.07 N322 c.2 (with an ex libris to the San Rafael Mission on the title page, "pertenece a la Mision de S. Rafael"); 287.07 N322 c.3; 287.07 N322 c.4 (with an ex libris for the San Francisco Solano Mission on the paper facing the title page, "Pertenece a la M^n de S Fr° Solano"). Also copy MT860 .A2M25 1816 Case X at the UC Berkeley Music Library.

Vicente Pérez Martínez, *Prontuario del cantollano gregoriano para celebrar uniformemente los divinos oficios todo el año... según practica de la muy Santa Primada Iglesia de Toledo*, 2 vols. (Madrid: Julian Pereyra, 1799, 1800). Copy M2907 .L99 P47, vols. 1 and 2, formerly catalogued as 287.08 M385.4 in the SBMAL, with annotations on pp. 1034 and 1074 in the hand of Friar Florencio Ibáñez (active primarily at the San Antonio Mission and then the Soledad Mission). The binding for the second volume is a bit confusing, since its spine reads volume "3," even though the title page on the inside clearly reads "TOMO II."

Daniel Traveria, *Ensayo gregoriano, o estudio práctico del canto-llano y figurado en método fácil* (Madrid: Widow of Joachín Ibarra, 1794), Copy 287.09 T779 in the SBMAL with an ex libris to Fr. Malabehar ("F. A. Malabehar, / de la Purisima Concepcion").

2. Nearly every Spanish theorist from the late Middle Ages forward includes a discussion of *canto llano*. For a superb summary of these theorists, with copious footnotes that facilitate further research, consult Francisco José León Tello, *Estudios de Historia de la Teoría Musical* (Madrid: Consejo Superior de Investigaciones Científicas and Instituto Español de Musicología, 1962), esp. 403ff. that contain the chapter "Teoría del canto llano." Of equal importance is his subsequent volume that emphasizes later theorists, the one that would be most applicable to the present study. See León Tello, *La teoría española de la música en los siglos XVII y XVIII* (Madrid: Consejo Superior de Investigaciones Científicas, 1974). In English, several useful sources of plainchant include David Hiley, *Western Plainchant: A Handbook* (Oxford: Clarendon Press, 1993); Willi Apel, *Gregorian Chant* (Bloomington: Indiana University Press, 1958) reprinted in paperback (Bloomington: Midland Books, 1990); and Richard Hoppin, *Medieval Music*, Norton Introduction to Music History Series (New York: Norton, 1978).

3. P[regunta]. Qué es... Canto-Llano?
....
R[espuesta]. Canto-Llano es una simple é igual prolacion de figuras ó notas, las quales no se pueden aumentar ni disminuir. *Musica plana est notarum simplex, & uniformis prolatio, qua nec augeri, nec minui possunt.* Llámase tambien Canto Gregoriano, por haber sido San Gregorio el Magno quien le puso en forma, para que se pudiese cantar en la Iglesia.
P. Por qué no se pueden aumentar, ni disminuir las dichas notas?
R. Porque el Canto-Llano no tiene modos, tiempos, prolaciones, ni variedad de figuras.
Marcos y Navas, *Arte, ó compendio general*, 1.

4. P. Quál es el compas de los Psalmos?
R. El que no mira á hacer los puntos iguales, sino que vá midiendo las sílabas longas, y breves, segun las reglas de Gramática.
Marcos y Navas, *Arte, ó compendio general*, 55.

5. "El Canto-Llano es una simple, y uniforme prolacion de figuras, que ni se pueden aumentar, ni disminuar (a), a diferencia del canto de Organo, que las tiene diversas, como tambien sus compases." Traveria, *Ensayo gregoriano*, 1.

6. "Canto Llano es una firme prolacion de figuras, ò notas, las quales no se pueden aumentar, ni disminuir." Pablo Nassarre, *Fragmentos músicos, repartidos en quatro tratados en que se hallan reglas generales, y muy necessarias para canto llano, canto de órgano, contrapunto, y composición* (Madrid: Joseph de Torres, 1700), vol. 1, facsimile ed., intro. by Álvaro Zaldívar Gracia (Zaragoza: Institución «Fernando el Católico» and Consejo Superior de Investigaciones Científicas [C.S.I.C.], 1988), 3.

7. Canto llano: "que en esta especie de música fuesen las notas de igual valor." Quotation in vol. 1, p. 91 of Pablo Nassarre, *Escuela Música según la práctica moderna, dividida en primera y segunda parte*, 2 vols. (Zaragosa: Herederos de Diego de Larumbe, 1724); facsimile edition (Zaragosa: Institución «Fernando el Católico» and C.S.I.C., 1980).

8. "Una simple, è regular prolacion de notas, la qual no puede aumentarse, ni disminuarse. Quiere decir, que las Notas, ò Figuras cantables en este Canto, son de igual valor, y tiempo, sin detenerse mas en unas, que en otras, aunque sean diferentes en la figura." See Ignacio Ramoneda, *Arte de canto-llano en compendio breve, y méthodo muy fácil* (Madrid: Pedro Marín, 1778), 3; copy at the UC Berkeley Music Library, MT860.A2 R3 Case X.

9. For instance, Joseph Halpin utilizes the term "Gregorian masses" to refer to the repertoire in Santa Clara Ms. 3, when in fact the repertoire is drawn from a different tradition, that of Old Hispanic chant. See Halpin, "A Study of Mission Music Located at Mission Santa Clara de Asís," M.A. thesis, San Jose State College, 1968, 31ff. Similarly, James A. Sandos uses the term "Gregorian chant" exclusively to refer to mission plainchant. See Sandos, *Converting California: Indians and Franciscans in the Missions* (New Haven, Conn.: Yale University Press, 2004), esp. 131–33. Although not incorrect, this usage presents certain limitations.

10. For one of the most thorough discussions of the hierarchy of feast days and their order in the liturgical year, consult Luis Hernández, *Música y culto divino en el Real Monasterio de El Escorial (1563–1837)*, 2 vols., Documentos para la Historia del Monasterio de San Lorenzo El Real de El Escorial, vol. 10 (El Escorial, Spain: Ediciones Escurialenses, 1993). Of particular value are the large number of primary sources that Hernández quotes in full. Brief summaries also appear in Apel, *Gregorian Chant*, 4; John Harper, *The Forms and Orders of Western Liturgy from the Tenth to the Eighteenth Century: A Historical Introduction and Guide for Students and Musicians* (Oxford: Clarendon Press of Oxford University Press, 1991), esp. chap. 3, "The Liturgical Year and Calendar," 43–57; and *Liber Usualis, with an Introduction and Rubrics in English*, ed. by the Benedictines of Solesmes (Tournai, Belgium: Society of St. John the Evangelist and Desclée, 1947), xl–xlix.

11. Perhaps the best summary of "Gregorian chant," its origins, its notational development, and its relationship to other chant traditions is Helmut Hucke's "Toward a New Historical View of Gregorian Chant," *Journal of the American Society*, vol. 33, no. 3 (1980), 437–67. His summary on pp. 464–67 is outstanding. David Hiley provides an excellent study of chant, its origins, and its developments through the centuries in *Western Plainchant*. Of particular note with regard to "Gregorian" chant is his chapter 6, "Plainchant up to the Eighth Century." He states, "The first codification in a form of musical notation of the chant we know as 'Gregorian' is the result of the Frankish endeavors to establish Roman liturgy and its chant as normative in their land" (479). Hiley devotes an entire section to Gregory (503–13). In the introductory words to this section, he explains: "The 'Gregorian' chant repertory bears the name of St. Gregory the Great, pope from 590 to 604. Gregory's actual share in its composition, or the regulation of its liturgical use, has been much debated. Since there is no gap of nearly three centuries between Gregory's life and the appearance of the first completely notated chant-books, it is unlikely that what finally entered the written musical record is what Gregory knew, even if we subtract the chants for those days whose liturgies were added to the calendar after Gregory's time. It is nevertheless impossible to argue that an ancient core of the repertory, in something very much like the state in which we find it in the late ninth century, might date back to Gregory" (503).

12. Robert Stevenson discusses the Roman Breviary of 1568 and its impact on Spanish music in his volume *Spanish Cathedral Music in the Golden Age* (Berkeley: University of California Press, 1961), esp. 91ff.

13. Some authors prefer to refer to this body of music as "Roman rite" or "Roman chant." As Willi Apel observes, "the term *Roman chant*...has the advantage of implying nothing

but the incontestable fact of the chant's intimate connection with the Church of Rome, thus distinguishing it from other bodies of Christian chant." Apel, *Gregorian Chant*, 4.

14. Kenneth Levy, in "The Iberian Peninsula and the Formation of Early Western Chant," *Revista de Musicología*, vol. 16, no. 1 (1993), 435–37, discusses four traditions: Gregorian; Urban Roman; Milanese (also called Ambrosian); and Old Hispanic (sometimes called Old Spanish, Mozarabic, or Visigothic). In addition to Levy, Don M. Randel, Michel Huglo, and Ismael Fernández de la Cuesta have delved into the tradition of Old Hispanic chant in considerable detail. Consult Don M. Randel, *An Index to the Chant of the Mozarabic Rite* (Princeton, N.J.: Princeton University Press, 1973); Randel, "El antiguo rito hispánico y la salmodía primitiva en Occidente," *Revista de Musicología*, vol. 8 (1985), 229–38; Michel Huglo, "Recherches sur les tons psalmodiques de l'ancienne liturgie hispanique," *Revista de Musicología*, vol. 16, no. 1 (1993), 477–90; Ismael Fernández de la Cuesta, "El canto viejo-hispánico y el canto viejo-galicano," *Revista de Musicología*, vol. 16, no. 1 (1993), 438–56; and Fernández de la Cuesta, *Desde los orígenes hasta el "ars nova,"* vol. 1 of *Historia de la música española*, esp. chap. 5 "Fuentes de la música hispano-visigótica," series under the direction of Pablo López de Osaba (Madrid: Alianza, 1983).

15. Toledo long occupied a place of importance in Spanish plainchant. During the push to standardize liturgical practice first by Pope Alexander II (1061–73) and then by his successor, Pope Gregory VII (1073–85), Toledo—which had only been recaptured from the Moors in 1085—nevertheless was permitted by Rome to continue with its old sacred tunes, a repertoire sometimes called "Mozarabic," "Old Hispanic," "Old Spanish," or "Visigoth."

16. Fernández de la Cuesta, "El canto viejo-hispánico," 438. Fernández de la Cuesta gives slightly different information in his book *Historia de la música española: Desde los origenes* in the section titled "Los cantorales de Cisneros," p. 114. He states that Cisneros's *Missale mixtum secundum regulam beati Isidori, dictum Mozarabes* was released in 1500, and his *Breviarum Gothicum* was published in 1502. For an enlightening discussion of the music for Holy Week as it was shaped by Cardinal Cisneros and its repercussions in the New World, consult Robert J. Snow, *A New-World Collection of Polyphony for Holy Week and the Salve Service "Guatemala City, Cathedral Archive, Music MS 4,"* edited and with an introduction by Robert J. Snow (Chicago: University of Chicago Press, 1996).

17. Hiley, *Western Plainchant*, 558.

18. Casiano Rojo and Germán Prado provide a superb historical analysis of the Mozarabic tradition in their *El Canto Mozárabe: Estudio histórico-crítico de su antigüedad y estado actual*, Publicaciones del Departamento de Música, vol. 5 (Barcelona: Diputación de Barcelona, 1929). They deal directly with its origins: "Al canto de la antigua liturgia hispana se le suele llamar eugeniano. Pero semejante atribución, lejos de arraigar en una tradición antigua, parece pura invención moderna" (13); "El gran cardenal Jiménez de Cisneros, al proponerse rehabilitar los antiguos ritos españoles, no restauró la liturgia mozárabe tal como se había practicado en tiempos antiguos y como se conservaba en los libros que en las iglesias de Toledo venían usándose, y en los vetustos códices de nuestros templos y catedrales se encontraba, sino que hizo un nuevo arreglo, es decir, una nuevo [*sic*] misal y un nuevo breviario. En ellos se conservan los textos y la forma substancial de la liturgia mozárabe, pero no sin notables transformaciones y traslados, entrando también numerosos elementos de la liturgia romanotoledana, que por entonces se practicaba en nuestra Península" (96).

19. Luis Robledo, "Questions of Performance Practice in Philip III's Chapel," *Early Music*, vol. 22, no. 2 (May 1994), 200.

For purposes of clarity, from here on I will use the terms "Gregorian chant" or "Roman rite" to refer to the relatively standardized body of chant associated with the Church in Rome and use the terms "Toledo tradition," "Toledo chant" or "Toledo rite" to refer to the repertoire emanating from the Primate Church of Toledo and distributed throughout the Hispanic world, beginning with the efforts of Cardinal Cisneros in the early sixteenth century.

20. The Serra choirbook is catalogued as manuscript M.0162 at the Green Research Library at Stanford, with the "Missa Toletana" being found on fols. 15–16v. The Department of Music at the University of California at Berkeley owns an invaluable collection of photos catalogued as "WPA Folk Music Project. Items 45–87, Box 2 of 12. California Folk Music Project Records, ARCHIVES WPA CAL 1." The photographs were made in 1937 as part of the Work Projects

Administration (WPA) that later changed its name to the Works Progress Administration. For a detailed account of this collection's history, including its rediscovery by John Koegel, consult the file "WPA Folders" in appendix A online. From here onward, I refer to this collection with the abbreviation "WPA." This collection contains several works from the Toledo tradition, written in the hands of Juan Bautista Sancho and Felipe Arroyo de la Cuesta. The "Gloria Todedana [*sic*]" is on page I-3 of folder 63; and the "Missa Toletana, St. Joan Baptista" is located on sheet 1 of folder 79. Although the Arroyo de la Cuesta selection appears to be chant without a discernible meter, the rhythmic features of the Serra and Sancho selections place it squarely in the rhythmic or "metric" tradition of *canto de órgano*.

21. "Esta misa es justamente la que se cantaba en mi Patria de Cuba [!] los días de primera clase," WPA folder 79, sheet 2.

22. "Mision de San Luis Obispo. Memoria q. ᴾ. la expresada Mision pide pᵃ el año de 1807. / ... 1 Ritual Romano con el Apendice toledano." Expediente 10, dated 1 July 1806, from the larger document Archivo General de la Nación: Número de Registro 53860, Grupo Documental 8, Archivo de Hacienda, Número de Soporte, 283 (hereafter AGN, Hacienda, N° 53860).

23. "Memoria de la Mision del Sr. Sn. Josef para el año de 1809. / ... 1 Ritual toledano." Expediente 41, dated 31 January 1808, located in AGN, Hacienda, N° 53860.

24. "PRONTUARIO / DEL CANTOLLANO / GREGORIANO ... SEGUN PRACTICA / DE LA MUY SANTA PRIMADA IGLESIA DE TOLEDO, REAL CAPILLA / DE S. M. Y VARIAS IGLESIAS CATEDRALES." Pérez Martínez, *Prontuario*, title page.

25. William Summers, personal correspondence with the author, 23 August 2006. I wish to express my thanks to Professor Summers for sharing with me his important discovery.

26. The "Benedictus qui venit" on p. 1034 of vol. 2 is a new text underlay for a Sanctus movement appearing on that page. It is set to the music originally destined for the third appearance of the word "Sanctus." The "Benedictus qui venit" on the last page (p. 1074) is appended after the last printed music, and its mensural rhythms place it in the *canto figurado* tradition as opposed to plainchant.

27. The Mass for the Dead is found in Santa Clara Ms. 3 on pp. 1–10. The same service appears in Vicente Pérez, *Prontuario*, vol. 2, pp. 687ff.

28. Vicente Pérez, *Prontuario*, vol. 2, pp. 690–92; and Santa Clara Ms. 3, pp. 3–6. In truth, this setting is no longer even *canto llano* but is instead *canto figurado*—a style defined by its steady meter and homophonic textures. I will address *canto figurado* in more detail shortly. For facsimiles of the *Dies irae* as found in these two sources, consult photos B-88 and B-92 in appendix B, available online in conjunction with this book.

29. The following concordant chants, for example, reveal strong links between the *Prontuario* and Ibáñez's books: *Pange lingua* in choirbook C-C-68:2 at the Bancroft Library (p. 70) and the *Prontuario* (vol. 1, p. 655); *Vultum tuum* in Santa Clara Ms. 3 (p. 17) and the *Prontuario* (vol. 2, p. 645); *Spiritus Domini* in Santa Clara Ms. 3 (p. 100), plus choirbook C-C-68:2 (p. 56) and the *Prontuario* (vol. 2, p. 669); *Cibavit eos* in Santa Clara Ms. 3 (fol. 46v), plus choirbook C-C-68:2 (p. 66) and the *Prontuario* (vol. 2, p. 687).

Notably, the chant *Cibavit eos* in Santa Clara Ms. 3 appears under the heading "Corpus Xʳi. Del Libro de Madrid" (Mass for Corpus Christi, *from the Madrid Book*) [italics added]. Significantly, Vicente Pérez's *Prontuario del canto llano ... de la muy Santa Primara Iglesia de Toledo* was published in *Madrid* by Julian Pereyra, 1799 and 1800. Equally important, the last pages in the SBMAL copy of the *Prontuario* has Ibáñez's handwriting—he owned this very book. We can assume, then, that the heading for *Cibavit eos*, "from the Madrid book," is Ibáñez's specific reference to this book that he owned—Vicente Pérez's *Prontuario*. That being established, we can further establish that this setting of *Cibavit eos* is drawn from the Toledo chant tradition, since it appears in the *Prontuario* that is explicity devoted to that repertoire.

Although a link between Ibáñez and the Toledo chant tradition is verifiable, it is not the sole source of his chant melodies. It should be noted that the *Prontuario* version of some chants and those texts as set in Santa Clara Ms. 3 or choirbook C-C-68:2 sometimes are completely different. Some examples of discrepancies include the following: *In nomine Jesu* (*Prontuario*, vol. 2, p. 697) different than Santa Clara Ms. 3 (p. 26); *Clamaverunt justi* (*Prontuario*, vol. 2, p. 743) different than choirbook C-C-68:2 (p. D at the back); *Stabant juxta crucem Jesu* (*Prontuario*, vol. 2, p. 748) different than Santa Clara Ms. 3 (p. 18); *Clamaverunt justi* (*Prontuario*, vol. 2, p. 774) different than choirbook C-C-68:2 (p. D at the back); *Charitas Dei diffusa est* (*Prontuario*, vol. 2, p. 812) different than choirbook C-C-68:2 (p. 74), but very close to Roman rite, as found in the *Liber Usualis*, 1472.

30. See photo B-90, *In medio ecclesiæ* in Santa Clara Ms. 1; and photo B-97, *In medio Ecclesiæ* in Santa Clara Ms. 3.

31. Pedro Cabot wrote out *In medio Ecclesiæ* on fol. 1 of Santa Clara Ms. 1. Juan Bautista Sancho wrote out the same piece on fol. 7v of San Fernando Mission's *Artaserse Ms.* (sometimes referred to as manuscript As-3). Their tune is close to the one found in Pérez Martínez's *Prontuario* (vol. 2, p. 610), but as has been observed, the orthographic features differ.

32. Santa Barbara Doc. 7 is in the same hand as several other mission manuscripts, including Santa Inés Ms. 1 and San Fernando Ms. A320.

33. Several scholars have already put forward the theory that many of the anomalies in California mission music (and not limited to plainchant) are probably explained by a strong link to a standardization of its repertoire as projected from the Casa Matriz in the Colegio Apostólico de San Fernando or, at the very least, a separate Franciscan tradition that was not identical to the broader general trends in Spain. See Theodor Göllner, "Two Polyphonic Passions from California's Mission Period," *Yearbook for Inter-American Music Research*, vol. 6 (1970), 67–76; Grayson Wagstaff, "Franciscan Mission Music in California, c. 1770–1830: Chant, Liturgical and Polyphonic Traditions," *Journal of the Royal Music Association*, vol. 126 (2001), 54–82; and William J. Summers, "The *Misa Viscaina*: An Eighteenth-Century Musical Odyssey to Alta California," in *Encomium Musicae: Essays in Memory of Robert J. Snow*, ed. by David Crawford and G. Grayson Wagstaff, Festschrift Series, No. 17 (Hillsdale, N.Y.: Pendragon Press, 2002), 127–41.

The Apostolic College of Santa Cruz was the *casa matriz*, or "motherhouse" in charge of its offspring, the Apostolic College of San Fernando, which in turn became the governing body or *casa matriz* for the twenty-one missions in Alta California. The Colegio Apostólico de San Fernando was established on 15 October 1733, an extension of the Colegio Apostólico de Santa Cruz that was established in 1683 in Santiago de Querétaro by Fr. Antonio Llinás with the purpose of Christianizing the Native Americans of the Sierra Gorda. Bartolomé Font Obrador delves into the founding and history of both the Colegio Apostólico de Santa Cruz and the Colegio Apostólico de San Fernando in his "La Sierra Gorda de Fray Junípero," in *América y Mallorca del Predescubrimiento hasta el siglo XX. Miscelánea Humanística. Tomo 1*, introduction by Prof. Dr. Bartolomé Escandell (Palma de Mallorca: Ajuntament de Palma, Edicions Miramar, 1991), esp. 166. The work of Llinás has been detailed by Bartolomé Escandell Bonet in *Baleares y America* (Madrid: Editorial Mapfre, 1992), 240–46, basing his research on that of Antoni Gili i Ferrer's *Antoni Llinás: Misionero de misioneros* (Monacor, Mallorca: Informacions Llevant, 1990); another important work on Llinás is the article by Antoni Picazo and Bartolomeu Tous, "Fray Antonio Llinás y el primer Colegio de Propaganda Fide de América," in *América y Mallorca del Predescubrimiento*. For a thorough treatment of the Colegio Apostólico de San Fernando, consult the excellent article by Maynard Geiger, O.F.M., "The Internal Organization and Activities of San Fernando College, Mexico (1734–1858)," *The Americas*, vol. 6, no. 1 (July 1949), 3–31. Kristin Dutcher Mann describes the daily routine at the Colegio de Santa Cruz in Querétaro in "The Power of Song in the Missions of Northern New Spain," Ph.D. diss., Northern Arizona University, 2002, 80–82.

34. In addition to Santa Clara Ms. 3 and choirbook C-C-68:2 at the Bancroft Library, another impressive source in Ibáñez's hand is found at the SBMAL: "Antiphonarium Romanum cum Himnis de Tempore et Sanctis...scribi â P.P. Præd F.F. Paolo Font & Florentio Ibáñez. Die VII Aprilis Anni Domini MDCCLXXIV, 1774." The title credits the scribal work of this enormous 364-page volume to Paolo Font and Florencio Ibáñez. Paulo Font was a friar at the Apostolic College of San Fernando in Mexico City, where this manuscript was prepared. His brother, Pedro Font, was the famous chronicler of the de Anza expedition that made it to California by a treacherous overland route in 1776. For information on both Paolo and Pedro Font, consult Maynard Geiger's *Franciscan Missionaries in Hispanic California 1769–1848: A Biographical Dictionary* (San Marino, Calif.: Huntington Library, 1969), 276–78. Obviously, the 1774 date predates Serra's founding of the first mission at San Diego in 1776. Geiger informs us that this

impressive manuscript did not actually arrive in Santa Barbara, California, until 1882—well after the mission period had come to a close. See Geiger, *Franciscan Missionaries*, 124.

35. For a discussion of Florencio Ibáñez and musical aspects of his life, consult Geiger, *Franciscan Missionaries in Hispanic California*, 124–25, 233–25, and the following articles by Summers: "Sancho: The Preeminent Musician of Alta California," in Antoni Pizà, William J. Summers, Craig H. Russell, and Antoni Gili Ferrer, *J. B. Sancho: Compositor pioner de Califòrnia*, edited and coordinated by Antoni Pizà (Palma de Mallorca, Spain: Universitat de les Illes Balears, Servei de Publicacions i Intercanvi Cientific, 2007), 26, 46, and 69; "New and Little Known Sources of California Mission Music," *Inter-American Music Review*, vol. 11, no. 2 (Spring–Summer 1991), 21; Orígenes hispanos de la música misional de California," *Revista Musical Chilena*, nos. 149–150 (1980), 46–47, esp. note 27; and "The Spanish Origins of California Mission Music," in *Transplanted European Music Cultures: Miscellanea Musicologica*, Adelaide, Australia: Sudies in Musicology, vol. 12, Papers from the Third International Symposium of the International Musicological Society, Adelaide, 23–30 September 1979, 125n27. Also see Hoskin, *A History of the Santa Clara Mission Library*, 46.

36. Owen da Silva, O.F.M., *Mission Music of California: A Collection of Old California Mission Hymns and Masses* (Los Angeles: Warren F. Lewis, 1941), 22. Also see Summers, "New and Little Known Sources," 21.

37. For instructions concerning kneeling during the performance of the Alleluia for Pentecost, consult the *Liber Usualis*, 880. Although the inclusion of the drum here is a peculiarlity of California performance practice—at least when compared to European convention—it nevertheless was probably imported from indigenous practice from some other American location. The drum was not really used as a common instrument by the native Californians. Elsewhere, throughout the Americas, indigenous cultures employed the drum with regularity to sanctify the physical space during religious ceremonies. For a discussion of the commingling of indigenous American and European customs in musical worship in the Americas, consult Guillermo Wilde, "El ritual como vehículo de experiencias sonoras indígenas en las doctrinas jesuíticas del Paraguay (1609–1768)," in *Música Colonial Iberoamericana: Interpretaciones en torno a la práctica de ejecución y ejecución de la práctica. Actas del V Encuentro Simposio Internacional de Musicología* (Santa Cruz, Bolivia: Asociación Pro Arte y Cultura, 2004), 43–57. To hear a recording of the "Alleluia and *Veni Sancte Spiritus*"—the facsimile of which appears as photo 1-6 in this chapter—consult the CD *Mission Road*, Chanticleer and Chanticleer Chamber Ensemble, directed by Joseph Jennings and with artistic consultant Craig H. Russell (Claremont, Calif.: Warner Classics and Jazz and the Rhino Entertainment Company, 2008).

38. "En primer lugar te confieso que yo no soy maestro, pues nunca he sido discipulo. Y aunque varias veces he oido en conversacion / a discipulos hablar de las reglas teoricas del Canto, te aseguro que jamas las he podido apear ni comprehender. Solo te dire *in honorem / Domini* que la naturaleza me ha favorecido con el oido bastante delicado para dicernir [*sic*] algo sobre la materia; y ve aqui la regla / principal me ha guiado para los fines y motivos que te voy a decir." Bancroft choirbook C-C-59, fol. 1. I include a complete translation of Durán's entire preface as item C-1 in appendix C that is available online at the Oxford University Press Web site in conjunction with this book. Also, on that same Web site one can consult a facsimile of this preface as part of appendix B, photos B-1, B-2, and B-3.

39. "Yo no pudiendome persuadir / de que sean capaces de entrar en la musica y canto baxo las reglas que ponen los maestros del arte, ni pudiendo yo enseñarselas por ignorarlas,/ me determine a hacerlo con unas reglas arbitrarias que forman el sistema ó metodo que te voy a explicar." Bancroft choirbook C-C-59, fol. 1v.

40. It should be noted that on occasion Durán does remain faithful to the traditional chant melody instead of taking the one-size-fits-all approach that we see in his treatment of the Mass Proper. For instance, the Mass for the Dead that he records on pp. 62–64 is nearly identical to the same service as it appears in the Roman rite (see *Liber Usualis*, 1806–15). For Holy Week, he replicates the entire Matins service for Good Friday on pp. 75–92; this corresponds closely to the material in the Roman rite (see *Liber Usualis*, 665–88). The subsequent Lauds service for Good Friday in Durán's choirbook C-C-59 (pp. 92–96) is also faithful to the version in the *Liber Usualis*, 689–94. Note, however, that Durán associates both of these services with Maundy

Thursday (providing the title "Jueves S. a la tarde") instead of Good Friday, as this material appears in other chant books, including the *Liber Usualis*. These same principles hold true for the other two choirbooks in Durán's hand (Santa Clara Ms. 4 and Santa Barbara Doc. 1). In addition, the small Santa Barbara Mission fragment Ms. VI-B-6 (which consists of one large sheet, folded in half to make four folios) utilizes the same "standardized" melodic cores as found in the Durán choirbooks. This small sheet begins with the Introit *Adjutor et protector* for San José. Given the fact that Narciso Durán served at the San José Mission for many years, it is not surprising that this sheet that maps out the service for the Feast Day of San José would exhibit the melodic idiosyncrasies associated with its most famous mission padre. A manuscript that takes this standardization even further is Santa Barbara Doc.7, in which the Introit melody *Statuit ei Dominus* serves as the model for all the remaining members of the Proper (not just the Introits); in other words, its melodic contours are used to sing the Introit, the versicle to the Alleluia, the Offertory, and the Communion for each of the feast days in this manuscript. Although the versicle of the Alleluia is based on the Introit's tune, the Alleluia's antiphon is a different tune, but it recurs as well in a "standardized" form on every occasion. In short, the Alleluia's tune was the same for each day. During Paschal time the Introit model shifted from *Statuit ei Dominus* to *Protexisti me Deus*; as in the previous case, this Introit melody then served as the basis for the ensuing movements of the Proper.

41. A careful perusal of the various chant repertoire as indexed by Bryden and Hughes turns up no matches that even approach these two melodies (for the Alleluias and Communions) that constitute so much of Durán's manuscript. Consult John R. Bryden and David G. Hughes, *An Index of Gregorian Chant*, 2 vols. (Cambridge, Mass.: Harvard University Press, 1969).

42. The Introit chant *Gaudeamus omnes* occupied a place of prime importance in Franciscan liturgical practice. Not only was it used as the Introit for the Feast of the Assumption of the Virgin, celebrated every year on 15 August, but for the members of the Franciscan Order the Introit bore special significance as the Introit for the Feast Day of Saint Francis, celebrated on 4 October. It resurfaces again as the Introit for All Saints' Day (1 November) and for the Feast of Our Lady of Guadalupe (12 December). See Bancroft choirbook C-C-59, pp. 35, 38, and 40. *Gaudeamus omnes* also was a staple of "regular" Gregorian liturgy. Many feasts for female saints and the Virgin—in addition to the Assumption of the Blessed Virgin Mary—also utilize this tune and text for its Introit. See, for example, the Feasts of Agatha (L.U.1368); Anne, the mother of Mary (L.U.1571); Josophat (L.U.1751); Our Blessed Lady of Carmel (L.U.1556); and the Immaculate Conception (L.U.1316). It also makes its appearance on All Saints' Day (L.U.1724) and the Feast of Saint Thomas (L.U.427).

43. "Igualmente advierto que todos los Introitos, Alleluyas, y Comunios son de un mismo tono lo que tal vez para fastidiar a alguno / pero es menester hacerse cargo de lo poco que por aora prometen los Indios, para hacerlos entrar en aquella variedad de tono que se usa / en otros coros, en que por el regular nunca faltaran maestros; mas estos pobres estan expuestos á haber de hacer ellos solo las funciones, / y es menester facilitarles a que se impongan a cantar bien, y para esto me ha parecido que poniendoselas en un mismo tono les es mas facil. / Los Introitos pues van primer tono, conformes ò á imitacion del *Gaudeamus*, que es el que he oido celebrar: a excepcion de los de Ceniza y Sema-/ na Santa, que me parecio mas conforme al Espiritu de la Iglesia en los misterios destos dias; echarlos de 4° tono. Los Alleluyas y Comu-/ nios del año son 6^tos por las mismas razones de haberme parecido que hacen sensacion conforme a estado o representacion de la / Misa. Y paraque esto no fastidie, acordarse que hasta aora nadie se habra fastidiada de las Oraciones, Epistolas, Evangelios, Prefacios / Pater Noster &c. sin embargo de cantarse siempre de un mismo tono." Bancroft choirbook C-C-59, fol. 2.

44. "Por base primera ordené que jamas hubiese distincion entre musicos y cantores, sino que las manos y la boca hiciesen / el oficio que les toca, esto es que unos mismos canten y toquen. Al principio se embarazaban, mas aora lo hacen sin trabajo algu-/ no. Tambien me parecio conveniente que los instrumentos acompañasen siempre todo lo cantado, aun lo de Requiem los dos / violines; y esto por dos razones. La primera para mantener las voces de los muchachos en un estado de firmeza sin ba-/ xar ni subir de tono, como sucede regularmente sin esta precaucion. La segunda paraque con las distancias que guardan / entre si los puntos en los instrumentos en las varias posiciones de los dedos, adquieran alguna idea de la misma

distan-/ cia que tienen entre si los puntos del canto en las varias modulaciones de la voz. Desp[s] les impuse en la escala que yo llamó / de puntos naturales haciendosela cantar y tocar a un mismo tiempo. Luego la de medios puntos señalada con los be-/ moles y sostenidos del modo que estan abaxo. Pero faltaba imponerlos en lo mas dificultoso y enredado de la musica y can-/ to, que segun parece, es la diversidad de Claves, con las quales las notas musicales *Vt, Re Mi &c.* varian de domicilio ô collocacion / en la pauta. Y esto me parecia inapeable para indios, especialmente habiendo de ir el canto siempre acompañado de instrumentos, / las quales tienen dicho domicilio invariable. Me parecia, digo, inapeable, decir V.G. *Vt* en el primer blanco abaxo con la clave / de *Ffaut*: y luego con otra clave haber de decir *Re* ô *Mi* en el mismo lugar. Por lo que resolvi arrimar esto a un lado, / y echar mano de la sola Clave de *Ffaut*." Bancroft choirbook C-C-59, fol. 1v. The final statements concerning clefs make sense if one fills in the necessary implied details. Durán places his F clef invariably on the third line up from the bottom on the staff, unlike the modern tendency to place it on the fourth line. This practice does indeed produce the pitch ut or C for a note in the bottom space, just as Durán articulates. If the C clef is placed on the fourth line up of the staff, then the bottom space would elicit the note mi or E. If the C clef is placed on the bottom line of the staff (a common occurrence for soprano parts, as will be seen later in this study), then the bottom space produces the note re or D.

45. "Benedictus Dominus Deus Israel" is drawn from Luke 1:68–79, in which Zechariah offers God this heartfelt prayer at the birth of John the Baptist. See Michael Martin, "Benedictus, Canticle of Zechariah," http://home.earthlink.net/~thesaurus/thesaurus/Cantici/Benedictus. html. This canticle appears in Bancroft choirbook C-C-59, in the context of Lauds for Maundy Thursday; this is probably an error, for normally this appears on Good Friday.

46. "Nota: Este Salmo ô Cantico se cantara levantando un punto en cada dos versos, como tambien / al Verso *Illuminare*, y al *Ad dirigendos*; pero se advierte que de ningun modo acompañe instru/mento porque está demasiado lleno de puntos bemolados y sostenidos; y para este era necesario mucho / trabajo y maestro." Bancroft choirbook C-C-59, p. 96. It is worth observing here that the two specific lines to which he refers (the *Illuminare* and *Ad dirigendos*) occur in the last verse of the Canticle, with the net effect that the elevation in pitch level becomes fast and furious at the end of the piece, creating even more ecstatic excitement. The last line reads: "*Illuminare* his qui in tenebris et in umbra mortis sedent: *ad dirigendos* pedes nostros in viam pacis," or "[the dawn from on high will break upon us], *to shine* on those who sit in darkness and the shadow of death, *to guide* our feet in the way of peace."

47. Durán identifies this setting as pertaining to "Jueves S. a la tarde (Maundy Thursday in the Afternoon)," but this may be an inadvertent slip. Historically (and in the other sources of the time), the texts that Durán sets down here apply to Good Friday, not Maundy Thursday.

48. One of the most elusive and misunderstood Spanish terms of the era is *violón*. In the sixteenth, seventeenth, and early eighteenth centuries, it referred to a member of the viol family that was tuned in fourths and was constructed with frets and a shorter neck. Luis Robledo correctly observes, however, that by the late seventeenth century the term *violón* could be used to designate members of the violin family as well. By the early Classical era and the influx of the *style galant*—with its modern Mozartean string writing—the violin family had supplanted its viol cousins. By the time of the mission period in California, *violón* referred most often to the cello (but in some instances it still might have indicated the bass viol, whose full designation most accurately would read *violón contrabajo*). For more detailed discussion of the *violón* and its elusive ambiguities, consult Francis Baines, "What Exactly Is a *Violone?* A Note towards a Solution," *Early Music*, vol. 5, no. 2 (April 1977), 173–76; Xosé Crisanto Gándara, "El violón ibérico," *Revista de Musicología*, vol. 22, no. 2 (1999), 123–63; Gándara, "La Escuela de contrabajo en España," *Revista de Musicología*, vol. 23, no. 1 (2000), 147–86; and Luis Robledo, "Los cánones enigmáticos de Juan del Vado (Madrid? ca. 1625–Madrid, 1691), Noticias sobre su vida," *Revista de Musicología*, vol. 3, nos. 1–2 (1980), 129–96, esp. 147–48.

49. "Itt. Las lamentaciones eran puestos á duo para q[e] las cante un muchacho y 1 violon. Los tratados pueden can/tarlos 5[?] ô 6 muchachos juntos con un Violon. Y se advierte que donde esta; este parentesis { } / [tu]viese decir: que se pueden omitir las solfas que se contienen dentro, en caso que los muchachos / no puedan llegar á los puntos altos: Vn tratado y dos lecciones que faltan se han omitido para q[e] / *puedan elegir [?]* que hacer à los aficionados, y los canten del modo que gusten." Bancroft choirbook C-C-59, p. 96.

50. "Itt: Este año de 1814 se han cantado todos los Maytines, y es demasiado larga la función; / por lo que se piensa no cantar mas que el Primer Nocturno y Laudes." Bancroft choirbook C-C-59, p. 96.

51. As already stated, there is a hodgepodge of contradictory numbering systems to identify the Santa Clara Mission music books. I call the source in question "Santa Clara Ms. 4" drawing upon the numbering system put forward in the microfilm of these sources that is available in the Archives Section of the Orradre Library of the Santa Clara University Library. This same choirbook is labeled Manuscript No. *1* (as opposed to No. *4*) in the Hoskin and Spearman books. Yet another manuscript with the "Durán repertoire" and apparently in his hand is Santa Barbara Doc. 1.

52. "Siguese el Subvenite trasporta por fa con el la ÿ re bemoles, para acompañar / los violones en un punto bueno para los muchachos." Santa Clara Ms. 4, p. 76. The *Vigilia de Difuntos (Matins for the Dead)*, to which this chant belongs, is found on pages 69–77 of this same choirbook.

53. For a thorough discussion of dozens of Spanish theorists who treat this theme, consult León Tello, *La teoría española de la música en los siglos XVII y XVIII.* Also of great use is Ana Serrano Velasco, María Pilar Sauco Escudero, Juan D. Martín Sanz, and Celso Abad Amor, *Estudio sobre los teóricos españoles de canto gregoriano de los siglos XV al XVIII* (Madrid: Sociedad Española de Musicología, 1980).

54. "[Canto de órgano] es una progresión de sonidos armónicos que se percibe por medio de notas distintamente figuradas y medidas." Antonio Ventura Roel del Río, *Institución harmónica, o doctrina musical, theórica, y práctica, que trata del canto llano, y de órgano; exactamente, y según el moderno estilo*... (Madrid: Herederos de la Viuda de Juan García Infazón, 1748), 211. M.1877 in the Biblioteca Nacional in Madrid.

55. "Es canto de órgano un agregado de figuras o notas las cuales se aumentan o disminuyen según el tiempo." Jerónimo Romero de Ávila, *El arte de canto llano y órgano*... (Madrid: Joaquín Ibarra, 1761), 167; cited in León Tello, *La teoría española de la música en los siglos XVII y XVIII,* 587.

56. "P[regunta]: Pues avemos llegado à empeño de tratar de Musica Metrica, ò Mensural, què se entiende por dicha Musica? / R[espuesta]: Por Musica Metrica, se entiende el Canto de Organo./ P. Pues porquè el Canto de Organo se llama Musica Metrica, ò Mensural?/ R. Porque toda Musica de Canto de Organo, se canta debajo de medida. / P. Y Canto de Organo porqué se llama?/ R. Porque en el Instrumento de Organo, siempre se usa de dicha Musica./ P. Què cosa es Canto de Organo?/ R. Canto de Organo, es una quantidad de figuras, las quales se aumentan, ò disminuyen, segun el modo, tiempo, y prolacion." Nassarre, *Fragmentos músicos,* 31. Several years after his *Fragmentos músicos*, Nassarre provides in his *Escuela música* a similar explanation where he defines *canto de órgano* as "an aggregate of figures or note shapes of unequal value, of which one either lengthens or shortens, according to [three hierarchies of rhythmic organization], mode, tempus, and prolation" (*Canto de órgano*: es un agregado de figuras, o notas de desigual valor, las quales se aumentan, y disminuyen, según el modo, tiempo, y prolación). Nassarre, *Escuela Música,* bk. 1, p. 210. Andrés Lorente covers similar territory, stating that *canto de órgano* is "a diverse number of notated figures that are not the same, which are lengthened or shortened depending on the mode, tempus, and prolation" ([Canto de órgano:] diversa cantidad de figuras no iguales, las cuales se aumentan o disminuyen según el modo, tiempo, o prolación demuestra). Andrés Lorente, *El porqué de la música, en que se contiene los quatro artes de ella, canto llano, canto de órgano, contrapunto, y composición*... (Alcalá de Henares, 1672), 146. R.9271, in the Biblioteca Nacional in Madrid. Also consult the discussion in León Tello, *La teoría española de la música en los siglos XVII y XVIII,* esp. 29. For a thorough explanation in English of these hierarchies to which Nassarre refers of mode, tempus, and prolation, consult Willi Apel, *The Notation of Polyphonic Music, 900–1600,* 5th rev. ed. (Cambridge, Mass.: Mediaeval Academy of America, 1953); Alejandro Planchart, "Tempo and Proportion," in *Performance Practice: Music before 1600,* ed. by Howard Mayer Brown and Stanley Sadie, Norton/Grove Handbooks in Music, vol. 1 (New York: Norton, 1989), 126–44; and Thomas Morley, *A Plain and Easy Introduction to Practical Music* (London: Peter Short, 1597), modern edition, 2nd paperback reprint, ed. by Alec Harman, foreword by Thurston Dart (New York: Norton, 1973), esp. 23ff.

57. The controversy caused by Felipe II's ban on polyphony in the monastery he built at San Lorenzo de El Escorial near Madrid has been the topic of much scholarly debate and research. The discussion in the sixteenth century used the term *canto de órgano* to refer to this polyphony.

58. Some important Spanish theorists who use this basic organizational structure include Lorente, *El porqué de la música*; Romero de Ávila, *El arte de canto llano y órgano*; and Antonio de la Cruz Brocarte, *Médula de la música theórica cuya inspección manifiesta claramente la execución de la Práctica, en división de quatro discursos; en los quales se da exacta noticia de las cosas más principales, que pertenecen al Canto llano, Canto de Órgano, Contrapunto, y Composición*... (Salamanca: Eugenio Antonio García, 1707), M.875, in the Biblioteca Nacional in Madrid. Other treatises as well are confirmed in León Tello, *La teoría española de la música en los siglos XVII y XVIII*.

59. Nassarre, *Escuela Música*, bk. 1, p. 209.

60. Ibid., 212–13.

61. "Pues si la Musica de un solo instrumento causa semejantes efectuos, que avrà que admirar, causen otros muchos aquellas crecidas armonias, compuestas de variedad de vozes, de instrumentos, assi flatulentos,como de cuerda, y Organos, con variedad de dulces consonancias, que forman, y de que estàn pobladas las capillas en las Iglesias Cathedrales?" Ibid., 212.

62. "En las Iglesias Cathedrales, y otras muchas, en que se usa la Musica de Cāto de Organo en las mayores celebridades, como son las de primera, ò segunda classe, es, quando mas se exercita, expressando la Musica la mayor solemnidad, y la alegria, con que se debe solemnizar la fiesta; porque como dize Durando, el canto significa la alegria del Cielo." Ibid., 212–13.

63. Ibid., 213.

64. Ibid., 210.

65. Nassarre, *Escuela Música*, bk. 2, esp. chap. 20. Note that *canto de órgano* is derived from the word *organum*, a medieval term for polyphony. Therefore, its etymology is linked as much to the idea of counterpoint as it is to the *organ* as a musical instrument. The two ideas (texture and instrument) are intertwined here and not easily separated.

66. Maximiano Trapero, "La música en el antiguo teatro de Navidad," *Revista de Musicología*, vol. 10, no. 2 (1987), 445.

67. The definitive scholar on *villancico* literature, Paul R. Laird, has authored several important writings, such as *Towards a History of the Spanish Villancico* (Warren, Mich.: Harmonie Park Press, 1997); "The Coming of the Sacred Villancico: A Musical Consideration," *Revista de Musicología*, vol. 15, no. 1 (1992), 139–60; "Fray Diego de Torrijos and the Villancicos at San Lorenzo del Escorial, 1669–1691," *Revista de Musicología*, vol. 12, no. 2 (1989), 451–68; and "*Dulcísimo Dueño* by Sebastián Durón: A 'Poster Child' for the Baroque Villancico," in *Encomium Musicae: Essays in Memory of Robert J. Snow*, 493–507. See also Paul R. Laird and José Luis Palacios Garoz, "The Dissemination of the Spanish Baroque Villancico," *Revista de Musicología*, vol. 16, no. 5 (1993), 2857–64.

68. "Está puesto [en] canto de órgano" & "Y finalmente se van todos a le adorar cantando el villancico que en fin es escrito en canto de órgano." Cited in Trapero, "La música en el antiguo teatro de Navidad," 445.

69. The importance of the harp in Spanish Baroque *villancicos* is addressed by Thomas F. Taylor in "The Spanish High Baroque Motet and Villancico. Style and Performance," *Early Music*, vol. 12, no. 1 (February 1984), 64–73. Cristina Bordas [Ibáñez] details the use of two harps to accompany the processional *villancicos* at the Royal Chapel, especially during the festivities of Corpus Christi. See Bordas, "The Double Harp in Spain from the Sixteenth to the Eighteenth Centuries," *Early Music*, vol. 15, no. 2 (May 1987), 156.

70. "El canto métrico y mensurable, figurado o de órgano, que toda es una misma cosa, se define así: una cantidad de figuras no iguales, las cuales se encuentran, aumentan o disminuyen según pide el modo, tiempo y prolación." Ramoneda, *Arte de canto llano*, 3, cited in León Tello, *La teoría española de la música en los siglos XVII y XVIII*, 517. The hymns and sequences that Ramoneda places under the rubric *canto figurado* (such as *Veni Sancte Spiritus*, on pp. 129–31, *Lauda Sion Salvatorem*, on pp. 136–38, and *Pange lingua*, on pp. 143–44) are the same kind of settings that one finds elsewhere in other theorists such as Marcos y Navas under the term *canto figurado*. This general lumping together of these metric styles continues in chapter 7, where he

melds *canto métrico* and *canto figurado* together, selecting as the main criterion the appearance of a predictable meter. He then provides numerous metric hymns to illustrate this section. See Ramoneda, *Arte de canto-llano*, 85–95.

71.   "Muchos credos, glorias y prosas hay que se cantaron con la medida o compás binario o ternario, según su composición y estos credos serán llamados y conocidos por canto figurado o de órgano y no se tendrán por canto llano." Bernardo Comes y Puig, *Fragmentos músicos, caudalosa fuente gregoriana en el arte de canto llano*...(Barcelona: Herederos de Juan Pablo and María Martí, 1739), 134, cited in León Tello, *La teoría española de la música en los siglos XVII y XVIII*, 488. *Prosa* is an extended text added to the "normal" liturgical order of the mass after the Tract and just before the Sermon and Credo. Its placement in the liturgy is graphed out by Louis Jambou in "La función del órgano en los oficios litúrgicos del Monasterio de El Escorial a finales del siglo XVI," in *La Música en el Monasterio del Escorial. Actas del Simposium (1/4-IX-1992)*, (San Lorenzo de El Escorial: Estudios Superiores del Escorial and Ediciones Escurialenses, 1992), 402. Also, an eighteenth-century document in the Archivo del Palacio Real, Sección San Lorenzo, Legajo no. 49, clarifies that the *prosa* is placed in this location: "Item 276. En la Missa siempre se canta el: *Introito*, los *Kiries, Gloria in excelsis*, Gradual, Tracto, y la Prosa quando lo hubiere, *Credo*, ofertorio, *Sanctus, Benedictus qui venit, Agnus*, la Comunicada." Quoted in Jambou, "Las funciones del órgano," 422. That these *prosa* were sung, allowing for the practice of alternating choral phrases with instrumental ones, is clarified by a document in the Biblioteca Nacional in Madrid: M 1 183, *Ceremonial de los officios divinos*...(Toledo: Pedro Rodríguez, 1591), fol. 143v, where it states, "Las prosas muy largas se podrán tañer a versos de tal manera que las comiencen los cantores, y las prosiga el organo alternativamente con el choro." Quoted in Jambou, "La función del órgano," 423.

72.   John Koegel, "Spanish and French Mission Music in Colonial North America," *Journal of the Royal Music Association*, vol. 126 (2001), 41.

73.   Léon Tello explicitly draws this conclusion after hundreds of pages of examination. He states, "In the treatises of the 18th century, *canto figurado* is clearly delineated as an intermediary step between ancient mensural notation and the modern" (En los tratados del siglo XVIII el canto figurado queda claramente delineado ante la antigua notación mensural y la moderna). León Tello, *La teoría española de la música en los siglos XVII y XVIII*, 608. Several theorists make the distinction between *canto figurado* and *canto de órgano*, including Tomás de Iriarte in his extended poem *La Música*, where he divides "sacred art" into three genres: *canto llano, canto figurado*, and *canto de órgano*. See León Tello, *La teoría española de la música en los siglos XVII y XVIII*, 391.

74.   Tomás Gómez, *Arte de canto llano, órgano y cifra junto con el de cantar sin mutanzas, altamente fundado en principios de Aritmética y Música* (Madrid: Imprenta Real, 1649). See León Tello, *La teoría española de la música en los siglos XVII y XVIII*, 459.

75.   As William Summers has pointed out, the parallel thirds that define much of the California repertoire fit hand in glove with the musical examples in parallel thirds and the notation methods of Jaime Vila y Pasquas in his *Método fácil y breve* (1848). Vila y Pasquas lived and worked at the Monasterio de San Gerónimo near Barcelona. Once again we see a Catalan source (Vila y Pascuas) with the same musical features as the California manuscripts, a relationship that should not be surprising given the large percentage of Franciscans in California who were born and raised on Catalan soil. See Summers, "Orígenes hispanos,"40; and Summers, "The Spanish Origins of California Mission Music," 111–13.

76.   "Tratado Tercero. Teórica, y Práctica del Canto Figurado / P. Quántas son las figuras, ó notas que se hallan en el Canto Figurado? / R. Quatro. / P. Quáles son? / R. Longa, breve, semibreve, y mínima. / ... / P. Quántos son los tiempos, ó compases que se usan en este Canto? / R. Dos: binario, y ternario." Marcos y Navas, *Arte, ó compendio general*, "Tratado Tercero. Teórica, y Práctica del Canto Figurado," p. 266.

77.   "Tratado Quarto. Teórica y Práctica del Canto de Organo. / Capitulo General / P. Qué es Canto de Organo? / R. Es un conjunto de varias y diversas figuras, que se aumentan, y disminuyen segun el tiempo. / P. Qué se entiende por figura en el Canto de Organo? / R. Una señal respresentativa del canto. / P. Quántas son estas figuras? / R. Siete: que son breve, semibreve, mínima, semínima, corchea, semicorchea, y fusa.... [Pictures of note shapes] ... / Algunos modernos usan de otra mas, á quien llaman semifusa, la qual se figura así: [= and a

picture of 64th notes]. / . . . / [p. 356] P. Quántos son los tiempos que segun hoy se usan en el Canto de Organo? / R. Seis./ P. Quáles son? / R. Compasillo, compas mayor, dos por quatro, seis por ocho, tres por ocho, y tres por quatro." Marcos y Navas, *Arte, ó compendio general*, "Tratado Quarto," pp. 355–56.

78. "P. Quantas son las señales que comunmente se hallan en el Canto de Organo? / R. Doce: que son claves, sustenidos, bemoles, bequadros, ligaduras, puntillos, divisiones, calderones, repeticiones, poyaturas, trinos, y guiones. / P. Como se señalan? / R. Segun abaxo se demuestra." / (Chart of clefs, sharps, flats, naturals, slurs, points, measure lines, fermatas, repetition marks, grace notes, trills, guides.) Marcos y Navas, *Arte, ó compendio general*, "Tratado Quarto," p. 359.

79. "[De los himnos] aunque se llamen canto llano no lo es tal sino llano de órgano." Roel del Río, *Institución harmónica*, 70. See León Tello, *La teoría española de la música en los siglos XVII y XVIII*, 201.

80. "Edicto de 27 de septiembre de 1754. En que se mandad, no se toque, ni canten en las Iglesias minuetes, arias, ni demás canciones profanas, ni theatrales, sobre que el Maestro de Capilla [Roque Ceruti] de esta Santa Iglesia tendrá cuidado, de que la Música de los templos sea grava, seria, y correspondiente á la Santidad del lugar. . . ." Quoted and discussed in Andrés Sas Orchassal, *La música en la Catedral de Lima durante el Virreinato*, vol. 1, *Primera Parte: Historia General*, Colección de Documentos para la Historia de la Música en el Perú (Lima: Universidad Nacional Mayor de San Marcos and Casa de Cultura del Perú, 1971), 41–42.

81. "El Canto, que desde la primitiva Iglesia, siendo común á todo Fiel, fué vn solemne modo de celebrar los Divinos Oficios, passó de su primera simplicidad a vna más armoniosa composición, y después de haverse limitado en el quarto siglo a solo los Ecclesiásticos, por disposición del Concilio Leodicense, el gran Gregorio compuse el firme, que tomó su nombre, con la gravedad, y decoro de su Autor, haviéndose permitido antes el uso de la Música instrumental, solo á fin de evitar, que los Cathólicos entrassen en los Templos de los Hereges, que con este alhago del oydo incitaban las gentes diabólicos congressos; por esso S. Flaviano en Antioquía, S. Chrisóstomo en Constantinopola, S. Agustín en Hipponna, y S. Ambrosio en Milán permitieron en sus Iglesias este concento, y música figurada, que finalmente tuvo su uso en las Iglesias. . . ." Sas, *La música en la Catedral de Lima*, vol. 1, p. 42.

82. The importance of harp and guitar in continuo realization is emphasized by many primary and secondary sources.

Harp: With respect to harp, one of the most outstanding articles on chordal accompaniments in Spanish music of the Iberian Peninsula and the Americas is Cristina Bordas [Ibáñez's], "The Double Harp in Spain." She sees the "tradition revered among Spanish musicians [to consist primarily] of the 'trio' of polyphonic continuo instruments—organ, harps, and vihuela (or guitar)." Bordas, "The Double Harp in Spain," 148–63, esp. 154. Louis Jambou also emphasizes the harp as an indispensable part of the cathedral chapel, but correctly observes that the musician is often employed under the title of "organist." In the context of a juried contest to select qualified instrument makers in Madrid in the late 1600s, Jambou remarks: "La réalisation de la harpe, instrument très répandu en Espagne tant dans la société civile que religieuse (rare est la cathédrale au XVIIᵉ siècle et jusqu'au milieu du XVIIIᵉ qui n'ait son harpiste titulaire, lequel prétend souvent au titre d'organiste) est éxigée des sept candidats. Il s'agit dans tous les cas de la *arpa doppia* adoptée en Espagne à la fin du XVIᵉ siècle." See Louis Jambou, "La lutherie à Madrid à la fin du XVIIe siècle," *Revista de Musicología*, vol. 9, no. 2 (1986), 437. Jambou delves further into aspects of instrumental accompaniment for *canto figurado* in his recent contribution, "Dos categorías de canto litúrgico y su acompañamiento en los siglos modernos: Canto llano y canto figurado," in *Concordis Modulationis Ordo, Ismael Fernández de la Cuesta in Honorem: Festschrift in Honor of Royal Academician Don Ismael Fernández de la Cuesta*, published in two volumes as volume 17, numbers 1–2 (2007) of the *Inter-American Music Review*, edited by Robert M. Stevenson, vol. 1, pp. 39–47. Luis Robledo describes Spanish festivities in the early 1600s whose sonorities were typified by harps and guitars. See Luis Robledo, "Música de cámera y música teatral en el primer tercio del siglo XVIII: A propósito de Juan Blas de Castro," *Revista de Musicología*, vol. 10, no. 2 (1987), 492. Other noteworthy articles dealing with the importance of the harp as a continuo instrument in Spain include Colleen R. Baade, "La 'música sutil' del Monasterio de la Madre de Dios de

Constantinopla: Aportaciones para la historia de la música en los monasterios femeninos de Madrid a finales del siglo XVI–siglo XVII," *Revista de Musicología*, vol. 20, no. 1 (1997), 221–30; Louis Jambou, "Arpistas en la Catedral de Toledo durante la segunda mitad del siglo XVII. Del testamento de Diego Fernández de Huete a su música: 'Zien láminas de bronze poco más o menos,'" *Revista de Musicología*, vol. 23, no. 2 (2000), 565–77, esp. 566–68; Louis Jambou, "José Solana (1643–1712), Trayectoria de un organista compositor," *Revista de Musicología*, vol. 4, no. 1 (1981), 61–101, esp. 104; Leopoldo Fernández Gasalla and Javier Garbayo, "Gregorio y Juan Galindo. Aportaciones documentales a sus biografías en el contexto de la Galicia de el siglo XVII," *Revista de Musicología*, vol. 17, nos. 1–2 (1994), 41–60, esp. 46; Rafael Pérez Arroyo, "El arpa de dos órdenes en España," *Revista de Musicología*, vol. 2, no. 1 (1979), 89–107; Mariano Pérez Prieto, "La capilla de música de la Catedral de Salamanca durante el período 1700–1750: Historia y estructura," *Revista de Musicología*, vol. 18, nos. 1–2 (1995), 145–73, esp. 158, 171–72; Lothar Siemens Hernández, "José Palomino y su plan de reforma para el mejoramiento de la capilla de música de la Catedral de Canarias (1809)," *Revista de Musicología*, vol. 3, nos. 1–2 (1980), 293–305, esp. 296.

Baroque guitar: Some of the theorists who delve into aspects of continuo performance on guitar include Juan Carlos Amat, Gaspar Sanz, Santiago de Murcia, Joseph de Torres, Antonio Vargas y Guzmán, and Lucas Ruiz de Ribayaz. Modern authors who examine continuo performance as explained in these treatises (and many with English translations of the original) include Gerardo Arriaga, "El método de guitarra de Juan Antonio de Vargas y Guzmán," *Revista de Musicología*, vol. 8, no. 1 (January–June 1985), 97–102; Cristina Azuma Rodrigues, "Les musiques de danse pour la guitare baroque en Espagne et en France (1660–1700), Essais d'étude comparative," 2 vols., Ph.D. diss., Université Paris-Sorbonne, 2000; Eloy Cruz, *La casa de los once muertos: historia y repertorio de la guitarra* (Mexico City: Universidad Nacional Autónoma de México and Escuela Nacional de Música, 1993); Rodrigo de Zayas, introduction and study of Gaspar Sanz's *Instrvccion de mvsica sobre la gvitarra española*, Series "Los Guitarristas," Colección Opera Omnia, (Madrid: Editorial Alpuerto, [1985]); Juan José Escorza and José Antonio Robles-Cahero, "Dos tratados de música instrumental del siglo XVIII," *Heterofonía*, vol. 7, no. 84 (January–March, 1984), 63–64; Escorza and Robles-Cahero, *Juan Antonio de Vargas y Guzmán's "Explicación para tocar la guitarra de punteado por música o cifra, y reglas útiles para acompañar con ella la parte del bajo (Veracruz, 1776),"* 3 vols. (Mexico City: Archivo General de la Nación, 1986); Luis García Abrines, introduction and study of Gaspar Sanz's *Instrvccion de mvsica sobre la gvitarra española* (Zaragoza: Herederos de Diego Dormer, 1674, 1697), (Zaragoza: Institución «Fernando el Católico» de la Excma. Diputación Provincial and the Consejo Superior de Investigaciones Científicas, 1979); Monica Hall, "The Guitar Anthologies of Santiago de Murcia," 2 vols., Ph.D. diss., Open University [England], 1983; Paul Murphy, study and translation of *Jose De Torres's Treatise of 1736: General Rules for Accompanying on the Organ, Harpsichord, and Harp, by Knowing Only How to Sing the Part, or a Bass in Canto Figurado* (Bloomington: Indiana University Press, 2000); Craig H. Russell, "Radical Innovations, Social Revolution, and the Baroque Guitar," in *The Cambridge Companion to the Guitar*, ed. by Victor Anand Coelho (Cambridge: Cambridge University Press, 2003), 153–81; Russell, *Santiago de Murcia's "Códice Saldívar No. 4": A Treasury of Guitar Music From Baroque Mexico*, 2 vols. (Urbana: University of Illinois Press, 1995); Russell, "Santiago de Murcia: Spanish Theorist and Guitarist of the Early Eighteenth Century." 2 vols., Ph.D. diss., University of North Carolina at Chapel Hill, 1981; [Robert Stevenson], "A Neglected Mexican Guitar Manual of 1776," *Inter-American Music Review*, vol. 1, no. 2 (Spring–Summer 1979), 205–10; Stevenson, "Un olvidado manual mexicano de guitarra de 1776," *Heterofonía*, vol. 8, no. 44 (September–October 1975), 5–9, and vol. 8, no. 45 (November–December 1975), 5–9; Robert Strizich, *The Complete Guitar Works of Gaspar Sanz*, transcription and translation by R. Strizich (Saint-Nicolas, Quebec: Les Éditions Doberman-Yppan, 2000); and James Tyler, *The Early Guitar: A History and Handbook*, Early Music Series, no. 4 (London: Oxford University Press, 1980).

83. Louise K. Stein, "Spain," in *The Early Baroque Era from the late 16th Century to the 1660s*," ed. by Curtis Price, Music and Society (Englewood Cliffs, N.J.: Prentice Hall, 1994), 330, 338.

84. "Entrée des Espagnols a concert espagnol avec des harpes et guitarres." Lully names eight "espagnols" to perform this piece: "Espagnols qui jouent de la harpe et les guitares." See Albert

Cohen, "Spanish National Character in the Court Ballets of J.-B. Lully," *Revista de Musicología*, vol. 16, no. 5 (1993), 2984.

85. For an example of the separation of the vocal resources into two divisions—Choir I with harp accompaniment and Choir II with organ accompaniment—see Paul Laird, "Fray Diego de Torrijos and the Villancicos at San Lorenzo del Escorial, 1669–1691," *Revista de Musicología*, vol. 12, no. 2 (1989), 457.

86. Francisco Curt Lange provides the inventory for the Convento de San Lorenzo de Nuestra Señora de la Merced in Córdoba, Argentina: its list for 1780 contains "una guitarra grande para la Capilla." See Francisco Curt Lange, "Convento de San Lorenzo de Nuestra Señora de la Merced, Córdoba, Argentina," *Latin American Music Review*, vol. 7, no. 2 (Autumn 1986), 227, 236. The guitar also appears in the list of available instruments at the Jesuit mission of Yapeyú in Río de la Plata, 1799, as inventoried by Francisco C. Brabo. For complete information concerning Brabo's list, see Lange, "El extrañamiento de la Compañía de Jesús del Río de la Plata (1767). Los bienes musicales de los inventarios practicados," *Revista Musical Chilena*, pt. 1 in vol. 165 (January–June 1986), 4–58, esp. 28 for citation of the guitar. Additionally, four guitars (and many harps) are in the instrumental resources of Pueblo de San Luis Gonzaga in Mesopatamia de Argentina in 1772. See Lange, "El extrañamiento de la Compañía de Jesús del Río de la Plata (1767)," *Revista Musical Chilena*, pt. 2 in vol. 176 (July–December 1991), 57–96, esp. 71.

87. The Archivo General de la Nación in Mexico City has a huge volume that documents requisitions from the California missions for the upcoming year of 1807. Archivo General de la Nación: Número de Registro 53860, Grupo Documental 8, Archivo de Hacienda, Número de Soporte, 283, "TEMPORALIDADES Misiones en California," AGN, Hacienda, N° 53860. These purchase orders list items needed for agricultural cultivation, light manufacturing, visual art for the mission chapels, cloth, and so on. The musical instrument requests are particularly interesting, and I include them as item C-4 in appendix C. Missions that were asking for guitars, guitar strings, guitar tutors, *bandolas, bandolones,* or bass *bandolones* included the missions at San Francisco (expediente 3), San Antonio (expediente 9), San Miguel (expediente 11), San Buenaventura (expediente 15), San Luis Rey (expediente 19), San Fernando (expediente 28), Santa Barbara (expediente 30), Santa Clara (expediente 37), and San José (expedientes 42 and 64).

88. Giorgio Perissinotto provides the purchase order documentation for the Santa Barbara Presidio; in the lists of requested items, strings are recurring necessities, especially for the violin, cello, guitar, and *vihuela.* See Giorgio Perissinotto, ed., *Documenting Everyday Life in Early Spanish California: The Santa Barbara Presidio "Memorias y Facturas, 1779–1810* (Santa Barbara, Calif.: Santa Barbara Trust for Historic Preservation, 1998), esp. 186–87, 286–87, 356.

With respect to these documents, a few words concerning terminology are in order. *Entorchados* are "wound" strings where a thread of some material is wrapped tightly around another "core" thread, creating a thicker string but of a precisely controlled diameter. The *violón* is a cello, not a violin as Perissinotto translates. A *bandola* is not a mandolin, as Perissinotto translates, but instead a slightly larger instrument (see note 87). Perissinotto uses the English word "guitar" to translate the Spanish words *guitarra* and *vihuela.* Both have similar body shapes, tied frets, and gut strings. Although there is some overlap and ambiguity in those two words, they are not automatically synonymous. The guitar during this era sometimes used double strings for each course and could be strung in a "re-entrant tuning" with only treble strings and no *bordones* or bass strings. That is not the case with *vihuelas*; the pitches extend from the high register down into the lower register, thus using some bass strings. Obviously, this distinction is important when it comes to placing string orders, since the wound or *entorchado* strings are thicker in diameter and would be needed only for the bass notes. Conversely, *entorchados* are not applicable for guitars if they were using treble, "re-entrant" tunings. For more information concerning guitar tuning systems, consult my book *Santiago de Murcia's "Códice Saldívar No. 4,"* esp. vol. 2, pp. xv–xviii; or my article "Radical Innovations, Social Revolution, and the Baroque Guitar," esp. 156–57. Given the enormous ambiguity and potential confusion surrounding these two terms, I recommend preserving the original terms in making an English translation, rather than assume that "guitar" and *vihuela* are indistinguishable.

Below I provide the citations of the Santa Barbara Presidio inventory as they appear in Perissinotto's book but have supplied my own English translations, in order to incorporate the points that I have just presented.

Invoice: Mexico City, 9 December 1791, signed by Pedro Ignacio de Aríztegui:
"2 Dozˢ de Entorchados de Seda pᵃ Violin, a 12 rˢ."
2 dozen wound violin strings of silk for 12 reales.
"3. Dozenas de Entorchados de Seda para Viguela a 10 rˢ."
3 dozen wound vihuela strings of silk for 10 reales.

Requisition: Santa Barbara, 28 February 1797, signed by Felipe de Goycoechea:
"1. Begiga˙ de Cuerdas de bihuela y Violin."
1 bag of strings for vihuela and violin
[˙Technically, a *vejiga* is a bladder.]
"4 Docenas de entorchados pᵃ bihuela."
4 dozen wound strings for vihuela

Requisition: Santa Barbara, 14 January 1808, signed by José Joaquín Maitorena Arrillaga:
"2. Mazos de cuerdas y 4 docenas de Entorchados gordos pᵃ Guitarra
2 bundles of [treble] strings and 4 dozen thick, wound strings for guitar.
"2. Dozenas de Cuerdas de Violin 12 Entorchados de id[e]m
2 dozen [treble] violin strings & 12 wound ones for the same [i.e., the violin])
"1. [Encorda?] dura doble˙ de vandola y otra id[e]m pᵃ Violon
1 durable set of strings for bandola and another for cello.
[˙Note: there is something puzzling about the Spanish provided. *Encorda* is not a standard word, although *encordar* is a verb, meaning "to string." *Dura doble* is not standard Spanish; perhaps the scribe actually wrote *duradero*. Without seeing the original script, it will be hard to come up with an alternate reading of this citation.]

89. Thomas Oliver Larkin quotation, cited in John Koegel, "*Órganos, Violines, Cornetos, y Tambores*: Musical Instruments in *Mission, Presidio, Pueblo* and *Rancho* in Spanish and Mexican California, Arizona, New Mexico, and Texas," handout accompanying paper presented at the annual meeting of the Sonneck Society for American Music, Pacific Grove, California, February 1993.

90. Robert M. Stevenson, "Music in Southern California: A Tale of Two Cities," *Inter-American Music Review*, vol. 10, no. 1 (Fall–Winter 1988), 57.

91. Friar Juan Agustín Martí, a Franciscan missionary to Texas, writes in 1777 that the local neophytes played harp, violin, and guitar very well. The trio of instruments (violin, harp, guitar) were also chronicled as being important at San Juan Capistrano in Texas (1731) and Misión La Purísima Concepción near San Antonio (1778). See Koegel, "Spanish and French Mission Music in Colonial North America," 31, 33–34.

92. Captain George Vancouver gave Padre Fermín de Lasuén a barrel organ with three sleeves and a total of thirty-four playable tunes. It was played on 27 December 1793, at San Juan Capistrano, and it left the California neophytes in awe. For discussions of barrel organs in California, including the one gifted by Vancouver to Lasuén, consult Norman Benson, "Music in California Missions, 1602–1848," *Student Musicologists at Minnesota*, vol. 4 (1970–71), 104–13; da Silva, *Mission Music of California*, 22; Geiger, *Franciscan Missionaries in Hispanic California*, 19; Beryl Hoskin, *A History of the Santa Clara Mission Library* (Oakland, Calif.: Biobooks, 1961), 44; Robert Kirsch and William S. Murphy, *West of the West: Witnesses to the California Experience, 1542–1906: The Story of California from the Conquistadores to the Great Earthquake, as Described by the Men and Women Who Were There* (New York: Dutton, 1967), 114–26; Koegel, "*Órganos, Violines, Cornetos, y Tambores*; and Abel du Petit-Thours, *Voyage of the "Venus": Sojourn in California*; excerpt from *Voyage au tour du monde sur la frégate* Venus *pendant les années 1836–1839*, trans. by Charles N. Rudkin (Los Angeles: Glen Dawson, 1956), 57.

For excellent discussions of barrel organs and other mechanical music-making devices from the Enlightenment, consult David Fuller, "An Introduction to Automatic Instruments," *Early Music*, vol. 11, no. 2 (April 1983), 164–66; Arthur W. J. G. Ord-Hume, "Cogs and Crotchets:

A View of Mechanical Music," *Early Music*, vol. 11, no. 2 (April 1983), 167–71; Ord-Hume, "Ornamentation in Mechanical Music," *Early Music*, vol. 11, no. 2 (April 1983), 185–93; and William Malloch, "The Earl of Bute's Machine Organ: A Touchstone of Taste," *Early Music*, vol. 11, no. 2 (April 1983), 172–83.

93. For a discussion of Durán's repeated petitions soliciting an organ, consult Francis Price, "Letters of Narciso Durán from the Manuscript Collections in the California Historical Society Library," *California Historical Society Quarterly*, vol. 37, no. 2 (June 1958), 97–128; vol. 37, no. 3 (September 1958), 241–65; and also Maynard Geiger, "Harmonious Notes in Spanish California," *Southern California Quarterly*, vol. 57, no. 3 (1975), 243–50. Both Price and Geiger provide translations into English of the relevant letters that Durán authored to the *casa matriz* in Mexico City. The original letters are housed at the California Historical Society, catalogued as "Durán, Narciso. Transcriptions and Translations. Vault Ms. 17." Of greatest utility is letter no. 30, written by Durán on 7 January 1821, while at the San José Mission.

94. See the section titled "The Orchestra in California" in chapter 7 and note 69 in chapter 7 for a full quotation of the passage. For further comments regarding the organ in California, consult Summers, "The Spanish Origins of California Mission Music," 123n9; and Larry Warkentin, "The Rise and Fall of Indian Music in the California Missions," *Latin American Music Review*, vol. 2, no. 1 (1981), 50.

95. "1 fortepiano, si se halla â precio comodo, y en su defecto una espineta ô monucordio [*sic*] / ... Lecciones de Clave pᵃ principiantes con sus sonatas correspondientes." Petition for the year 1809, Expediente 28 in AGN, Hacienda, N° 53860.

96. "1. Espineta / 4. Tomos de serm̃s [sermones?] de armonia." Petition for the year 1808, request dated 31 January 1807, Expediente 63 in AGN, Hacienda, N° 53860.

97. "1 Registro de Organo, como esta inteligenciado nuestro Oterm° [?] Dn Mariano el qᵉ deve venir con los dos que piden para esta Mision los RR. PP. de la Mision de S. Luis Obpo." Petition for the year 1807, Expediente 11 in AGN, Hacienda, N° 53860.

98. "Lo que se pide por los nuevos Ministros es lo siguiente: Un Fuerte-piano para el culto de la Iglesia que no pase de dos cientos pesos: La obra de Bails intitulada *lecciones de Clave*." Petition for the year 1807, Expediente 6 in AGN, Hacienda, N° 53860.

99. Stevenson, "Music in Southern California," 40–41.

100. Dimtry Zavalishin, "California in 1824," translated and annotated by James R. Gibson, *California Quarterly*, vol. 55, no. 4 (Winter 1973), 386.

101. Hubert Howe Bancroft, vol. 34 of *The Works of Hubert Howe Bancroft*, vol 34, *California Pastoral, 1769–1848*, (San Francisco: San Francisco History Company, 1888), 428.

102. For a discussion of Feijoo's theories regarding the "modern style" and the debate it stirred, consult Antonio Martín Moreno, *El Padre Feijoo y las ideologías musicales del XVIII en España* (Orense: Instituto de Estudios Orensanos «Padre Feijoo», 1976); and Martín Moreno's *Siglo XVIII*, vol. 4 of *Historia de la música española*, series directed by Pablo López de Osaba (Madrid: Alianza Editorial, 1985). Both Feijoo and Nassarre are dealt with thoroughly in Paul R. Laird's *Towards a History of the Spanish Villancico* (Warren, Mich.: Harmonie Park Press, 1997), esp. 147–48; and in León Tello's *La teoría española de la música en los siglos XVII y XVIII*, esp. 89–190. Some recent scholars have called into question as erroneous the idea that these traits were merely a sort of "Italian invasion" or "decadence" (as many have argued for years) but instead convincingly present a case that these newer trends are manifestations of "modernization and Europization" of musical currents in Spain. Consult four articles in *Music in Spain during the Eighteenth Century*, ed. by Malcolm Boyd and Juan José Carreras (Cambridge: Cambridge University Press, 1998), including Juan José Carreras, "From Literes to Nebra: Spanish Dramatic Music between Tradition and Modernity," esp. 7–8; Xoán M. Carreira, "Opera and Ballet in Public Theatres of the Iberian Peninsula," esp. 17; Álvaro Torrente, "Italianate Sections in the Villancicos of the Royal Chapel, 1700–40," esp. 73–74; José González Valle, "Liturgical Music with Orchestra, 1750–1800," esp. 67; plus the article by Juan José Carreras, "Entre la zarzuela y la ópera de corte: Representaciones cortesanas en el Buen Retiro entre 1720 y 1724," in *Teatro y música en España (siglo XVIII): Actas del Simposio Internacional, Salamanca, 1994*, ed. by Rainer Kleinertz (Kassel and Berlin: Edition Reichenberger, 1996), 51–52; and finally, Rui Vieira Nery, review of Alfred E. Lemmon, ed., *La música de Guatemala en el siglo XVIII* (Antigua, Guatemala: Centro de Investigaciones Regionales de Mesoamérica; South

Woodstock, Vt.: Plumsock Mesoamerican Studies, 1986) in *Latin American Music Review*, vol. 9, no. 1 (1988), 109.

103. "Los violines son impropios en aquel Sagrado Teatro. Sus chillidos, aunque harmoniosos, son chillidos y excitan una viveza como pueril en nuestros espíritus, muy distante de aquella decorosa atención que se debe a la majestad de los Misterios, especialmente en este tiempo que los que componen para violines ponen estudio en hacer las composiciones tan subidas que el ejecutor vaya a dar en el puente con los dedos." Feijoo, *Música de los templos*, 309, cited in Martín Moreno, *El Padre Feijoo*, 135.

104. Juan Francisco de Sayas, *Música canónica, motética y sagrada...* (Pamplona, 1761); and Gaspar Molina de Saldívar, Marqués de Ureña, *Reflexiones sobre la arquitectura, ornato y música del templo* (Madrid, 1785). See Martín Moreno, *Siglo XVIII*, 430–31.

105. Vol. 5 of the *Cartas eruditas*, 1760, quoted in Martín Moreno, *Siglo XVIII*, 424.

106. Three of the more persuasive advocates of *música moderna* or the *estilo moderno* include Joaquín Martínez de la Roca, *Elucidación de la verdad...* (Valladolid, n.d. [ca. 1715?]); Roel del Río, *Institución harmónica* (1748) and another version in manuscript (1766); and Antonio Rodríguez de Hita, *Diapasón instructivo, consonancias físicas y morales, documentos a los profesores de música* (1757). They are discussed in Martín Moreno, *El Padre Feijoo*, 210–14, 218–23; and Martín Moreno, *Siglo XVIII*, 417–19, 422–28.

107. "No hay duda, señores, que la Música antigua, en cuanto al primor del Arte (así por el enlace de las voces como por la solidez e ingeniosa progresión de sus intentos) por lo general hace grandes ventajas a la Música Moderna: pero si atendemos al gusto, su principal objeto, bien saben Vs. mds. que, por lo común, excede en mucho esta música moderna a la antigua." Eustaquio Cerbellón de la Vera, *Diálogo harmónico sobre El Theatro Crítico Universal, en defensa de la Música de los Templos* (Madrid: Francisco López, 1726), 53, cited in Martín Moreno, *El Padre Feijoo*, 210.

108. Juan Francisco de Corominas, *Aposento Anti-Crítico desde donde se ve representar la gran Comedia que en su Teatro Crítico regaló al pueblo el RR. P. M. Feijoo contra la Música Moderna y uso de los violines en los Templos* (1726). See Martín Moreno, *Siglo XVIII*, 423; and Martín Moreno, *El Padre Feijoo*, 218. A study and facsimile of the relevant passages is found in Mariano Lambea, "Edición facsímil del *Aposento Anti-Crítico de Juan Francisco de Corominas*," *Revista de Musicología*, vol. 24, nos. 1–2 (2001), esp. 21.

109. For a listing of works by Torres, Nebra, and Corelli in Mexican and Latin American archives, consult E. Thomas Stanford, *Catálogo de los Acervos musicales de las Catedrales Metropolitanas de México y Puebla de la Biblioteca Nacional de Antropología e Historia y otras colecciones menores* (Mexico City: Instituto Nacional de Antropología e Historia, Gobierno del Estado de Puebla, Universidad Anahuac del Sur, Fideicomiso para la Cultura México/USA, 2002); and Robert Stevenson, *Renaissance and Baroque Musical Sources in the Americas* (Washington, D.C.: General Secretariat, Organization of American States, 1970). For a discussion of Corelli's music in the Hispanic and Hispano-American world, see Craig H. Russell, "An Investigation into Arcangelo Corelli's Influence on Eighteenth-Century Spain," *Current Musicology*, vol. 34 (1982), 42–52.

110. Koegel, "Spanish and French Mission Music," 7–17.

111. One of the most thorough and insightful treatments of mission music in the New World is the huge (but carefully crafted) dissertation by Bernardo Illari: "Polychoral Culture: Cathedral Music in La Plata (Bolivia), 1680–1730," 4 vols., Ph.D. diss., University of Chicago, 2001 (UMI No. 3029501). Piotr Nawrot's work also explores the music and culture at the *reducciones* (missions) of Mojos and Chiquitos. His music editions are exquisite and reveal a repertoire worthy of attention from both scholars and performing musicians. See Piotr Nawrot, s.v.d. (Sociedad del Verbo Divino): *Canto chiquitanos: Arias, cantos eucarísticos y de acción de gracias, cantos devocionales, letanías, música instrumental. Anónimos & Domenico Zipoli*, ed. by Piotr Nawrot, Indígenas y Cultura Musical de las Reducciones Jesuísticas, vol. 2, Colección: Monumenta Música, 2. Festival de Música Renacentista y Barroca Americana (Cochabamba, Bolivia: Verbo Divino, 2000); *Cantos guaraníes y moxeños: cantos sacros de los guaraníes, música autóctona de los moxos, música post-reduccional de los moxos, plan de gobierno de Lázaro de Ribera*, ed. by Piotr Nawrot, Indígenas y Cultura Musical de las Reducciones Jesuísticas, vol. 5, Colección: Monumenta Música, 5. Festival de Música Renacentista y Barroca Americana

(Cochabamba, Bolivia: Verbo Divino, 2000); *Domenico Zipoli (1688–1726): Salmos, himnos, canto sacro, motete, letanía laurentana. Vol. II: Partituras,* ed. by Piotr Nawrot, Colección: Monumenta Música, 7. Archivo Musical de Chiquitos y Archivo Musical de Moxos, Bolivia (Cochabamba, Bolivia: Verbo Divino, 2002); *Indígenas y cultura musical de las reducciones jesuíticas. Guaraníes, Chiquitos, Moxos,* vol. 1, ed. by Piotr Nawrot, Colección: Monumenta Música, 1. Festival de Música Renacentista y Barroca Americana (Cochabamba, Bolivia: Verbo Divino, 2000); *Música de vísperas en las reducciones de Chiquitos-Bolivia (1691–1767): Obras de Domenico Zipoli y maestros jesuitas e indígenas anónimos,* ed. by Piotr Nawrot (Concepción, Bolivia: Archivo Musical Chiquitos, 1994); and *Requiem chiquitano: Missa mo unama coñoca,* ed. by Piotr Nawrot, Indígenas y Cultura Musical de las Reducciones Jesuísticas, vol. 4. Colección: Monumenta Música, 2. Festival de Música Renacentista y Barroca Americana (Cochabamba, Bolivia: Verbo Divino, 2000).

Other scholars who provide valuable insight regarding Jesuit mission work in South America include Francisco Curt Lange, Leonardo Waisman, and Alfred Lemmon. Lange provides plentiful primary documents for the missions of Chiquitos, Gran Chaco, Mojos, and Mesopotamia de Argentina. See Francisco Curt Lange, "El extrañamiento de la Compañía de Jesús del Río de la Plata (1767), Los bienes musicales de los inventarios practicados," *Revista Musical Chilena,* pt. 1 in vol. 165 (January–June 1986), 4–58; and pt. 2 in vol. 176 (July–December 1991), 57–96. Also see Leonardo Waisman: "Música misional y estructura ideológica en Chiquitos (Bolivia)," *Revista Musical Chilena,* vol. 176 (July–December 1991), 43–56; and "¡Viva María! La música para la Virgen en las misiones de Chiquitos," *Latin American Music Review,* vol. 13, no. 2 (1992), 213–25. Alfred Lemmon is the world authority on music in the Jesuit missions of Mexico (see the bibliography in appendix E for a long list of publications). He summarizes several important points in "Musicología jesuítica en la Provincia de Nueva España: El rol de la música," *Revista Musical de Venezuela,* 2° Festival de la Música del Pasado de América, vol. 21, nos. 30–31 (January–December, 1992), 211–23.

112. Waisman, "¡Viva María!" esp. 216–18.

113. Several excellent books and articles have appeared that treat this topic. Robert M. Stevenson deals with the role of the various mendicant orders in his *Music in Aztec and Inca Territory* (Berkeley: University of California Press, 1968); and his *Music in Mexico: A Historical Survey* (New York: Crowell, 1952). Koegel discusses the use of *canto de órgano* and mission life in Sonora, New Mexico, and Florida in "Spanish and French Mission Music in Colonial North America," esp. 7–17, 22–30. The role of music in the Jesuit missions of California has been addressed by: Harry Crosby, *Mission and Colony on the Peninsular Frontier, 1697–1768,* published in cooperation with the University of Arizona Southwest Center and the Southwest Mission Research Center (Albuquerque: University of New Mexico Press, 1994), esp. 237–40; Francis J. Weber, "Jesuit Missions in Baja California," *The Americas,* vol. 23, no. 4 (April 1967), 408–22; Alfred E. Lemmon, "Los Jesuitas y la música de la Baja California," *Heterofonía,* vol. 10:4, no. 55 (July-August 1977), 13–17; and its continuation in vol. 10:5, no. 56 (September-October 1977), 14–17; and although the following article by Lemmon deals with the sixteenth century in Mexico, it nevertheless has bearing on the present study—consult Lemmon, "Los jesuitas y la música colonial de México," *Heterofonía,* vol. 10:2, no. 52 (December 1976 and January 1977), 7–10; and its continuation in vol. 10:3, no. 54 (May–June 1977), 31–32.

114. *Interrogatorio (Questionnaire)* or "Preguntas y Respuestas," 26 February 1814, Mission San Antonio. "Al R.P. Presid^te Fr. José Señan," Santa Barbara Mission Archive-Library. The entire text of this document is reprinted along with an accompanying translation in the article by Maynard Geiger, O.F.M., "Documents: Reply of Mission San Antonio to the Questionnaire of the Spanish Government in 1812 Concerning the Native Culture of the Indians," *The Americas,* vol. 10, no. 2 (October 1953), 211–27. Owen da Silva also translates most (but not all) of this document and without supplying the original Spanish text in his book, *Mission Music of California,* 5. A translation of selected portions also appears in Fr. Zephyrim Engelhardt's *Mission San Antonio de Padua: The Mission in the Sierras,* Missions and Missionaries in California, New Series: Local History (Ramona, Calif.: Ballena Press, 1972), 38–39. Engelhardt's translation serves as the basis for the quotations included in Beatrice [Tid] Casey, *Padres and People of Old Mission San Antonio,* reprint King City: Casey Newspapers in conjunction with Franciscans of San Antonio, 1976 of (King City: The Rustler-Herald, 1957), 24–25.

115. "En esto lo que repercutió también en el uso del vocablo *violón*, que inicialmente, como ya se había dicho, fungió como apelativo común para toda la familia de violines o cualquiera de sus miembros (aunado o no a la especificación del registro), pero al cabo del siglo XVII empezó a mostrar su ambivalencia de manera distinta, pudiendo aplicarse tanto al violín (tiple), como al bajo de la familia.

La doble identidad del violón, que plantea la disyuntiva de decidir entre el registro tiple y bajo de la familia de violín, se infiere forzosamente de las líneas de la hoja de servicios de un tal Nicolás Grinón, quien durante la década de 1642 a 1652 desempeño el cargo de música de arpa y violón en las capillas de las catedrales de Puebla y de México. Pero es obvio que la diversidad de las posibles acepciones del término violón se reducen sólo a una, la del violín bajo, o sea el violonchelo, cuando las fuentes documentales mencionan al cordófono así denominado al lado de los violines de registro agudo." Evguenia Roubina, *Los instrumentos de arco de la Nueva España* (Mexico City: CONACULTA and FONCA, 1999), 100–101.

116. Antonio Martín Moreno lists the *planta* or musician rosters of Spain's most important music institutions in *Siglo XVIII*, vol. 4 of *Historia de la música española*, series directed by Pablo López de Osaba (Madrid: Alianza Editorial, 1985). Evguenia Roubina explores the distinction between the *violón* and *bajo* in *Los instrumentos de arco de la Nueva España*, esp. chapter 6 on pp. 95–103. The instrument requests for the California missions between 1806 and 1808 are found in the Archivo General de la Nación in Mexico City as Número de Registro 53860, Grupo Documental 8, Archivo de Hacienda, Número de Soporte, 283, Expediente 3. These California mission documents—as with those for the Royal Chapel of Madrid and cathedrals of Spain and Mexico—are careful to make a distinction between the *violón* (cello) and *bajo* (contrabass). It should be noted that the *bajo* or contrabass was undergoing considerable changes in its construction during the eighteenth century, and those alterations certainly affected the sonorities of the missions orchestras. For the definitive study on the *bajo* of this era, consult Xosé Cristano Gándara, "De arcu contrabassi," *Revista de Musicología*, vol. 25, no. 1 (June 2002), 157–73.

117. For the most perceptive and persuasive discussion of "what constitutes an orchestra," consult John Spitzer and Neal Zaslaw, *The Birth of the Orchestra: History of an Institution, 1650–1815* (Oxford: Oxford University Press, 2004). Zaslaw published an excellent article previously, "When Is an Orchestra Not an Orchestra?" *Early Music*, vol. 16, no. 4 (November 1988), 483–95; and John Spitzer similarly authored "The Birth of the Orchestra in Rome—An Iconographic Study," *Early Music*, vol. 19, no. 1 (February 1991), 9–27. Also of value is Robert Weaver's "The Consolidation of the Main Elements of the Orchestra: 1470–1768," in *The Orchestra: Origins and Transformation*, ed. by Joan Peyser (New York: Scribner's, 1986), 1–35, esp. 23. A primary source from the Classical period that provides helpful advice as to the size of an orchestra and appropriate strength of the instruments that double up is found in Joseph Joachim Quantz, *On Playing the Flute*, trans. and with an introduction by Edward R. Reilly (New York: Free Press, 1966), esp. chap. 18, items 13–18, on pp. 211–15.

118. See María Antonia Virgil i Blanquet, "La música teatral en Valladolid en el siglo XVIII," *Revista de Musicología*, vol. 8, no. 1 (1985), 119–23; Xoan M. Carreira, "Recepción de la ópera italiana en Granada," *Revista de Musicología*, vol. 13, no. 1 (1990), 231–51; Andrea Bombi, "La música en las festividades del Palacio Real de Valencia en el siglo XVIII," *Revista de Musicología*, vol. 18, nos. 1–2 (1995), 175–228; and Mariano Pérez Prieto, "La capilla de música de la Catedral de Salamanca durante el período 1700–1750: Historia y estructura," *Revista de Musicología*, vol. 18, nos. 1–2 (1995), 145–73. The general trend toward top-dominated sonorities in the orchestras of the eighteenth century is borne out in the musician rosters as reproduced by Antonio Martín Moreno in his excellent book *Siglo XVIII*. He provides the musicians' names and instruments for the Real Capilla in Madrid, the convent Descalzas Reales, and the cathedrals of Ávila and Aránzazu. Similar tendencies in the orchestras occur in the palace life of Fernando VI in midcentury. Again, violins dominate the Real Sitio de Aranjuez (10 violins, 2 violas, 2 cellos, 2 basses, plus winds and brass), and the Real Coliseo del Buen Retiro is quite similar. See Martín Moreno, *Siglo XVIII*, 28–33, 55–56, 66–69, 358–61.

119. Luis González Obregón, *Época Colonial, México Viejo: Noticias históricas tradiciones, leyendas y costumbres por Luis González Obregón. Nueva edición aumentada y corregida, con profusión de ilustraciones: dibujos originales, retratos, vistas, planos, sacados de antiguos cuadros*

al óleo, láminas y litografías; y fotografías, tomadas directamente de monumentos, monedas y medallas (Mexico City: Editorial Patria, 1945), 352–53.

120. For examples of top-dominated orchestras in Chiquitos, consult the music inventories as replicated in Francisco Curt Lange, "El extrañamiento de la Compañía de Jesús del Río de la Plata (1767). Los bienes musicales de los inventarios practicados," *Revista Musical Chilena*, pt. 2 in vol. 176 (July–December 1991), esp. 85–90. The 1767 inventory of Brabo in Río de la Plata replicates this trend toward top-dominated instrumentation in the Jesuit missions of South America. See Lange, "El extrañamiento de la Compañía de Jesús," pt. 2, p. 28. Lange also details the 1776 inventory of instruments at the Convento de San Lorenzo de Nuestra Señora de la Merced in Córdoba, Argentina, that was dominated by "English violins." See Lange, "Convento de Predicadores de Nuestro Padre Santo de Córdoba (Argentina)," *Latin American Music Review*, vol. 7, no. 2 (1986), esp. 225–27. The Guaraní Indians in Mojos and Chiquitos also performed *galant*-style music with top-dominated orchestras. Jesuit friar José Cardiel, writing in the mid–eighteenth century in his "Breve relación de las misiones de Paraguay," states: "En cada Pueblo hay una música de 30 o 40, entre tiples y tenores, altos, contraltos, violinistas y los de los otros instrumentos. Los instrumentos comunes a todos los Pueblos son violines de que hay 4 o 6; bajones, chirimías 6 o 8; violines [violones?] 2 o 3; uno o dos órganos; y 2 o 3 clarines, en casi todos los Pueblos. En algunos Pueblos hay otros instrumentos más. Les buscamos papeles de las mejores músicas de España y aún de Roma para cantar y tocar." Passage quoted in Nawrot, *Indígenas y cultura musical de las reducciones jesuíticas*, 12–13. See also Bernardo Illari, "El sonido de la misión: práctica de ejecución e identidad en las reducciones de la provincia de Paraguay," in *Música Colonial Iberoamericana: Interpretaciones en torno a la práctica de ejecución y ejecución de la práctica. Actas del V Encuentro Simposio Internacional de Musicología* (Santa Cruz, Bolivia: Asociación Pro Arte y Cultura, 2004), 5–25.

121. The Bancroft Library choirbook C-C-59 has several works marking *coro* above the chant sections that are interpolated in between polyphony: "Kyrie," "Gloria," and "Credo" from the "Misa de Quarto Tono a 4 Voces," pp. 122–27; "Credo de la Rosa 6° T[on]o," 129–31; "[Gloria]" from the "Misa a 4 Voces, 6° T[on]o," 137–38. The aforementioned "Gloria" from pp. 122–23 in the Bancroft choirbook C-C-59 has concordant versions (although these other sources do not necessarily include the *coro* indications found in choirbook C-C-59). These concordant versions include the following: "Gloria simple, 4. Tono," WPA folder 55; "Gloria" in loose sheets at the San Fernando Mission, catalogued as S-1v, S-2v, and S-3 by Summers in his article "*Opera seria* in Spanish California: An Introduction to a Newly-Identified Manuscript Source," in *Music in Performance and Society: Essays in Honor of Roland Jackson*, ed. by Malcolm Cole and John Koegel (Warren, Mich.: Harmonie Park Press, 1997), 276–77; and "[Gloria]" in Santa Clara Ms. 4, pp. 123–24. The aforementioned "Credo" on pages 124–26 of choirbook C-C-59 is concordant with the "Credo" on pp. 125–27 of Santa Clara Ms. 4. This same Credo also appears in Sancho's *Misa en sol*, M.0573, Box 1-1-1 at the Green Library, Stanford University. This same mass appears as folder 65 in the WPA collection at UC Berkeley.

122. Several Mexico City manuscript sources from the time (such as the large-scale Choirbooks 1-4, 5-1-1, and 5-2-6) similarly shape the density of textures in their *canto figurado* mass settings, frequently using instructions such as "solo," "duo," or "coro" over individual phrases.

123. Benson summarizes many of these condemnations in "Music in California Missions, 1602–1848," pt. 1, *Student Musicologists at Minnesota*, vol. 3 (1968–69), esp. 142–44.

124. Although this is nowhere stated, I wonder if the context is that of sacred processional music outside the church walls (with songs such as *¡O qué suave!* and *¡O Rey decorazones!*) or common devotional hymns such as "Ya viene el alba" (the *canción del alba*). This would maintain the sanctity of Latin and male performance *within* the sanctuary but simultaneously acknowledge the vital aspect of female performance that Cabot and Sancho articulate. Until further evidence is found, however, my proposal remains an unproved hypothosis.

125. Da Silva, *Mission Music of California*, 5.

126. Ibid., 8.

127. Ibid., 4.

CHAPTER 2

Notation and Music Theory

HANDWRITTEN PROSE HAS more than one surface meaning—it conveys more than mere "words." A careful eye might see if a page was written with care or in a hurry, whether it was for personal use or government work, whether it was read repeatedly through the years or—on the other hand—read once and then summarily filed. Similarly, music notation has more than one surface meaning—it conveys more than just the pitches and rhythms. An attentive inspection might reveal the subtleties of style and interpretation, who is singing, how many people are performing, whether or not instruments are playing, if the pitch is lower than written, and so on. Much information remains concealed in the mission manuscripts. This chapter, then, is a guide to unlocking their secrets through an examination of the clues found in their musical notation.

Note Shapes

In California mission manuscripts, the desired performance style is often implied by the type of note shapes that are drawn onto the velum or paper. *Canto llano* uses the standard chant notation from the Middle Ages, with its squarish note heads and neumes (compound shapes that lump together several tones into a single, larger notational symbol).[1] An exception to this general rule occurs in the chant manuscripts of Felipe Arroyo de la Cuesta, who carefully blocks off the borders of each note with a vertical line on either side and then connects the two with a slanted, oblique line. The result is a visual zigzag effect. Also, the chant passages in Sancho's loose sheets are sometimes drawn with hollow notes instead of blackened ones, but this idiosyncratic practice seems to apply when he is writing a sheet for a single performer as opposed to a group.[2] Few other mission padres utilized hollow notes for notating plainchant.

Canto figurado greatly resembles *canto llano* in its square and diamond note shapes (the breve and semibreve, respectively), but several significant differences are readily apparent: (1) *canto figurado* never employs the composite-shaped neumes found in chant that map out a cluster of notes; (2) for fast-moving notes, *canto figurado* employs minims (diamond-shaped notes with a stem), a shape completely foreign to *canto llano*; (3) *canto figurado* usually employs regular bar lines to mark off each measure, unlike chant, where vertical lines mark the end of large phrases or sections; and (4) *canto figurado* can stack notes on top of each other to indicate duet singing, usually in parallel thirds—where black ink indicates the main, lower voice and the newly added upper voice is marked in red.[3] Once again, Juan Sancho is a peculiar case among the padres in that he is the only one who writes entire pieces of *canto figurado* using hollow note heads as opposed to solid ones.[4]

In California, there were two different but compatible traditions to notate *canto de órgano*, one of them old-looking and the other modern. The antique system resembles *canto figurado* in nearly every respect: note shapes are squarish, notes can be hollow or filled in, notes can be either black or red, and bar lines are frequent and regular. The other notational system is our modern one, using the "rounded" shapes of whole notes, half notes, quarter notes, and so on, as opposed to the antique breves, semibreves, and minims. To the eye, the two systems look radically different, yet to the ear they are indistinguishable. In fact, several pieces are notated in the antique system in one manuscript and notated in "modern" notation in another.[5]

As we saw with *canto figurado*, a duet could be indicated by stacking notes in a two-color system of reds and blacks. This ingenious colored notation is expanded in *canto de órgano* to a four-voice capability on a six-line staff where the low-sounding bass voice is solid black, the tenor above it is solid red, the alto uses "hollow" outlines in black ink, and the top soprano part is demarcated in "hollow" red outlines.[6] Even though all four melodic lines are crammed onto one staff, each singer keeps track of his own part by following the appropriate color. By far the most common texture is a four-voice one, but Narciso Durán takes the system one step further, sometimes indicating yet another fifth voice in much smaller hollow note heads, etched out in a grayish ink that is lighter than the raven black alto and bass lines. Of course, the traffic jam of note heads presents a real notational dilemma when two or more melodic lines end up on the same pitch at the same moment. In such cases, some California manuscripts have the note heads bump up next to each other, elbow to elbow, thus depicting a shared unison through notational neighborliness. The other solution has note heads split in half at the note's midriff or beltline, and then plops the head of one melodic line (with its designated color) on top of the feet of the other part (along with its designated color).[7] When an alto melody ends up sharing a pitch momentarily with the tenor, the hollow black outline of the alto can frame the solid red tenor; obviously, black-and-white photos make this difficult to detect, and microfilms are nearly worthless. Another color system occurs in various sources where the four voice types are written as yellow (soprano), red (alto), "white" or hollow black (tenor), and solid black (bass).[8] This old-looking "square" notation using colors appears in the enormous choirbooks or large-scale folios intended for group use; that is, several people could simultaneously read from the same king-size sheets. For obvious reasons, the small pages intended for individual performers utilized notational systems with only one (or two) parts on a staff.

Da Silva attributes the origin of colored notation to Estevan Tapís: "Perhaps the most engaging feature of Old Mission music is the colored notation. Due to the crowding of two, three, or four parts onto a single staff of five or six lines, it was often difficult to follow an individual voice, especially when the voices crossed. Some inventive padre, and local tradition says Fray Estevan Tapís of Mission San Juan Bautista, overcame this problem by the use of colors."[9] Certainly, Tapís utilized this system effectively, but Theodor Göllner and Bill Summers have demonstrated that the use of colored notation was actually a long-lived Italian and Spanish practice, not a newfangled invention in the nineteenth century.[10] Göllner cites Italian precedents for using different colors on a single staff to indicate separate voices, tracing this practice back to at least the thirteenth century.[11] Furthering their case, Göllner and Summers reproduce a painting of Elías Salavería standing in front of a choral book in Cataluña that has red notes written above black ones, closely resembling the same notational practice as found in the choirbooks of California. Therefore, we must conclude that even tough Tapís may have been a proponent of colored notation, he could not have been its actual inventor.

All told, a variety of notational options are open to the scribe in "squared" *canto de órgano*—contrasting filled-in notes with hollow ones, red versus black ones. The scribe, then, can signal the desired voice type not only in polyphonic passages where all voices are sharing the staff, but in monophonic passages as well, merely by choosing the appropriate note shapes. For instance, Narciso Durán indicates that the *coro* (or full choir) should perform a monophonic thread as a unified group when he writes solid-black breves and semibreves. He reinforces this instruction often by writing "*coro*" above the staff to avoid any ambiguity. But in the same composition, Durán might jot down brief passages of a single melody in hollow notes, indicating that the soprano is desired (if the ink is red) or an alto (if the ink is black). He is, in effect, "orchestrating" the passage, selecting different vocal timbres for different phrases and carefully coloring the sound by coloring the notes (literally!) on the page.

This "orchestrating" through choices in solid or hollow note shapes is not a universal policy, however. In Sancho's collection of loose sheets, both at the University of California at Berkeley and at the San Fernando Mission, he often notates several complete works of *canto figurado* (with a single melodic line or occasional polyphony plus an implied chordal backup) in either blackened note heads or hollow ones, but he seems to do so indiscriminately: in both cases the voice falls in the low register, not in the alto or soprano range.[12] What is most significant in these manuscripts is not the type of note head as much as the physical dimensions of the pages; their small scale would make them appropriate for a single performer but rather impractical for a group to be reading from a single sheet.[13]

In addition to the antiquated or exotic notational styles discussed, a considerable number of works in modern notation use the customary clefs, key signatures, meters, and note heads that one would expect. Not surprisingly, the more adventuresome and up-to-date works of *música moderna* are written in this modern system, as well as a few of the more complicated *canto de órgano* works. The early compositions of Ignacio de Jerusalem, Francisco Javier García-Fajer, and Sancho (particularly with respect to his *Misa en sol*) that are found in California missions have much in common with Haydn and the Classical style. These artists habitually write out their compositions with half notes, quarter notes, eighth notes, and all of the other symbols familiar to modern performers.

Misa "de Jesús" and the *Misa Italiana*

In the California missions, the note shapes can tell us much about text expression and word painting. Sometimes the note heads provide clues with regard to performance resources (whether a line is sung by a soloist or the *coro* or choir). Often a work is not written down from start to finish in one place but instead is made up of components of pieces that are separated from one another. The following paragraphs take a few examples and explore how the "hidden" information in manuscripts can be divined: the *Misa "de Jesús"* and the *Misa Italiana* are excellent case studies of notational puzzles and their resolutions.

Sancho manuscripts in the WPA collection at the University of California that use "hollow" square notation of *canto figurado* include a "Credo de Angeles" that is written out on the lower half of a sheet in folder 61. The upper staves contain a Lamentations setting for either bass or tenor, written in modern notation on a bass clef.[14] This particular combination, where a *canto figurado* or *canto llano* selection "shares" a manuscript with a modern-looking bass or tenor performance part, is a common occurrence in California sources, especially those ones brought to the New World by Juan Sancho from his native Mallorca.[15] Of course, in this instance the aspect that binds the two differing selections together is their low register—for as a general rule, the bass and tenor voices performed plainchant and most *canto figurado* in the missions, not the sopranos or altos.

Within the same folder there is a "Kiries tono 4to un punto alto" (Kyrie in mode 4, one tone higher) written in "hollow" notation; it is overwritten with corrections or additions to such an extent that it is difficult to tell whether the selection is mensural *canto figurado* or meterless *canto llano*.[16] The bleed-through from the opposite side of the sheet and the general mediocre quality of the photograph further exacerbate the difficulty in ascertaining the intended pitches. Immediately succeeding this short setting is the "Kyries de Jesus. T^{o} 5to" (Kyrie of Jesus in mode 5) which is set as single-staff polyphony of *canto de órgano* with the middle voice in white mensural notation and the upper part and lower parts both notated in blackened mensural notation.[17]

Other folders have portions of a "Jesús" mass as well, such as the "Credo de Jesus, tono 5to" (Credo of Jesus in mode 5) in folder 63, notated in white mensural notation.[18] Most likely, it is part of the same "Jesús" liturgy as the "Kyrie of Jesus in mode 5" that was just discussed. At first glance this Credo appears to be monophonic or homophonic *canto figurado*, for the dominant note shapes on the page are those of white mensural notation—a single melodic line being placed on the staff in white breves and semibreves with an unwritten but implied harmonic backup. But if one looks closely, one discovers microscopic notes sprinkled over the "main notes" in some of the phrases, creating a duet texture at these points. A performance of the work, then, consists of alternating sonorities; the "single" line is interrupted with an occasional duet. The most obvious visual occurrence of paired voices occurs on line 5, where a newly added voice in blackened breves and semibreves is suddenly written above the "hollow" notes of the main tune. The text of this phrase centers on God's *humanness*, the nature of Jesus as an actual person as well as divine spirit: "Et incarnatus est de Spiritu Sancto, ex Maria Virgine, et homo factus est" (And was incarnate of the Holy Spirit, born of the Virgin Mary, and was made man). Significantly, this phrase is nearly always set in duet texture in the numerous *canto figurado* settings found in California. One might imagine a sort of word painting taking place, for humans adore the sensual and are drawn to things that are enticing and richer; in this way, the "human" aspect of the Credo's text at this point is set in a style that deliberately appeals to the human ear. The Credo's text then changes course in its tone and content, somberly depicting Jesus' suffering and Crucifixion, which is then followed by the jubilant news of the Resurrection and ascent into heaven. The musical setting makes the same journey as the text. It leaves the "worldly" sound of man's music and returns to the more divine simplicity of a single melodic thread—reminding the congregation of the centuries of plainchant as practiced in God's holy church.[19]

In addition to the duet phrase "Et incarnatus est . . ." concerning the human aspect of Jesus, one finds many other sections where a duet texture results through the placement of tiny dots above the "hollow" notes. The dots are so small they could be mistaken for staccato marks, but close examination reveals another purpose—their precise location unmistakably maps out a second, added voice. It sweetens the texture with parallel thirds and sixths. Octaves crop up here and there, especially at cadences. Significantly, these added notes occur in every other phrase, so that an alternation between single-voice and duet textures results—and in both cases, the vocals are probably accompanied by an improvised chordal support on strummed guitars or harp.

Yet another Credo in mensural white notation is found in folder 63 of the WPA collection in Berkeley. Bearing the title "Credo Ytaliano t° 4°" (Italian Credo in mode 4), it bumps along in steady duple meter with only a single melodic line at any given time (except the fourth measure, where the singer is given a choice of which octave to sing C on the text "factorem"). Once again, though, small cues suggest an alternation between single-line and duet texture; the instructions *duo* or *coro* are scribbled above the beginning of each phrase, the two switching back and forth. One might reasonably ask why there is only one notated melody at any given time, even for those phrases marked "duo." Is there a "missing" vocal line that would complete the duet texture?

The answer is divulged in a concordant version of this piece, located in folder 66. Its title page reads, "Credo Italiáno [*sic*] â Duo & con acõpaña[to] to. 4to" (Italian Credo for two parts with accompaniment in mode 4).[20] The photos can be broken out into four performance parts, judging from the bleed-through of pages where one can see the faint image of the "back" of any sheet, and from the order of numbers that Sidney Robertson assigned to each photo.[21] Clearly, she systematically photographed the front and then the back of each sheet, so the recto and verso sides of a folio invariably have adjacent numberings in her cataloguing system. Using Robertson's numbering of the photos and visual evidence of bleed-through as clues, we can establish that the manuscripts in folder 63 originally consisted of four booklets, each of which was destined for different performers: (1) a *coro*, or choir, performing *canto figurado* in unison; (2) an alto vocalist; (3) a bass vocalist; and (4) a basso continuo line that would have been realized by a melodic bass instrument, such as a *violón* or cello, plus an improvising chordal instrument, such as a harp or guitar.[22]

A comparison of the bass vocalist's tune in folder 66 with the melody found in folder 63 unearths a close match between them—in spite of the fact that their notations look radically different. Although no voice types are specifically indicated in the "duos" in folder 63, we can deduce from folder 66 that the lowest vocal timbre of these duets should be a bass. The other vocal line is undoubtedly the alto—the only other voice to sing in these "duo" passages.

With respect to the bass vocal line, in folder 63 its tune is sketched out in mensural white notation: the same basic core is translated to modern notation in folder 66, but with a few rhythmic discrepancies. These rhythmic differences, although relatively small, would nevertheless be enough to generate some messy moments in performance with fumbled text declamation and harmonies of colliding seconds, if these two manuscripts were sung together, since one voice would sometimes get slightly ahead of the other. These fleeting (yet painful) moments might explain why the whole setting in folder 63 has been crossed out with sweeping *X*'s by Sancho, or some other exasperated musician. If these minor collisions between versions had become too grating, it might have made sense to simply scrap the sheet and start over with a cleaned-up version.

A variety of notational systems are used in these four booklets from folder 66, and each system has its stylistic implications regarding performance practice. The performance parts for the basso continuo and alto each consisted of a large sheet that was folded so that the "outside" made a sort of title page and cover, and the "content" with the staves and musical notes was on the "inside"—exactly like a Hallmark greeting card made of a single sheet of folded cardboard. The basso continuo part had on its cover the title "Credo Italiáno â Duo & con acõpaña[to] to. 4 [to]" (Italian Credo for two parts with accompaniment in mode 4), and there was yet another heading on the inside above the first musical staff: "Para Acomp[to] del Credo Italiano â Duo. con el coro" (For the basso continuo part of the Italian

Credo, written as a duet and with a choir). The alto similarly had a heading on the inside above the music, "Alto del Credo Ytalia^{no} a Duo. con el coro alternando" (Alto part to the Italian Credo, written as a duet alternating with a choir). The alto's title page provides invaluable information, for it reveals the scribe to have been Juan Sancho: it reads "Credo Ytaliá. Â duo: con el coro. Del uso de Fr. Juan Sancho. Año 1796" (Italian Credo, written as a duet and with a choir, for the use of Friar Juan Sancho, in the year 1796). The penmanship is unquestionably Sancho's. He took the trouble to date his effort—the year 1796—a time when he was still in Palma de Mallorca at the Convent de San Francesc. The provenance here is of critical importance, for it reveals that this piece at one time constituted part of the repertoire at the Franciscan monastery in Mallorca, and it further reveals that the alternating style where accompanied duets flip-flop with choral renditions in rhythmic *canto figurado* was a staple in Spain as well as California. The sheet for the bass vocalist in folder 66 included much more music than the alto, since it recorded both the duet phrases and the choir's *canto figurado* lines (the latter choral phrases being absent in the alto's manuscript). The extra music necessitated using both sides of the music sheet, using up the available space that otherwise would have been the "title" page. Neatly inscribed over the top staff, however, is a functional heading that identifies the work: "Baxo del Credo Ytaliáno â Duo. con el coro" (Bass voice for the Italian Credo, written as a duet and with a choir). The *coro* sheet ("Coro para el Credo Italiano") also is chock-full of music, so every square centimeter is utilized on both sides, sacrificing no space for a title page. Not only does it contain the choral melody for the Credo, but on the opposite side of the folio we encounter the music for the Kyrie, Gloria, Sanctus, and Agnus Dei as well. For *all* these movements, the text is cut short or snipped apart into fragments; *only* the group choral lines in *canto figurado* appear on these pages, and the rest of the work (presumably performed by soloists in accompanied duets or the like) must be obtained on their separate performance sheets.

This bears out a theme that will recur with incessant regularity regarding California mission manuscripts: rarely is a "piece" written down in only one place; instead, these notated "pieces" (either separate or even bound into a choirbook) are most likely ingredients to a larger recipe. They are components that must be combined with the other elements—very often found on completely different sheets, different folders, or even different choirbooks—in order to complete a finished "composition."

The key to divining this Credo's "recipe," that is, what elements are needed and how they fit together, is most evident in the vocal bass part of this folder. Textually, this sheet is the most complete. Granted, it is missing the opening words "Credo in unum Deum," but that is the norm rather than the exception. The *Missale Romanum*, the instruction book on how to sing the mass, explains that the incipit for both the Gloria and the Credo were to be intoned in chant by the cantor, giving the musicians the correct pitch so that the body of the choir and the orchestra (if accompanied) could plunge in at the ensuing words—"in excelsis Deo" for the Gloria, and "et in terra pax" for the Credo. The intoned incipit was the "kickoff," so to speak, a way of getting the piece in play before all the other singers or partici-pants joined in together.[23] So, once the beginning had been intoned, the bass voice for the "Credo Italiano" has all the remaining text. That the bass replicates the full text is a direct result of his role in the two contrasting styles apparent in the work; he sings as one of the two soloists in the accompanied duets, and he sings in the choral sections as well—unlike the higher alto voice, who would have sounded out of place in the cellar with the lower tenors and basses. Visually, the bass part clari-fies the obvious changes in style through its changes in notation: the duets with basso continuo are *canto de órgano* notated in "modern" notation with quarter notes, half notes, and so forth, whereas the shift to *canto figurado* in measured homophony or pseudo-monophony (that is, the whole choir singing a single line but perhaps with a guitarist improvising some unobtrusive chords) is notated in "blackened" breves and semibreves, denoting an older and simpler style.

The *acompañamiento* or basso continuo line is also helpful in patching this Credo together. Notated in the bass clef in modern notation, its melody is nearly identical to the bass vocalist's line, but there is no text underlay. However, several cues—including textual ones—are provided in order to assure that everyone is in the same place, all playing the same phrase. One such aid is the inclusion of the first words and a few "squared" notes of each *canto figurado* section; clearly, the continuo player is not expected to play, since the phrase is abruptly cut short. But the thumbnail-sized excerpts that map out phrase beginnings *do* help assure that the continuo players do not get lost whenever the choir embarks on another line of *canto figurado*. Also, two or three words of the appropriate text are scribbled below the staff at the beginning of each *canto de órgano* phrase, where the con-tinuo grouping actually does play along. Again, this courtesy helps prevent the calamity of having the continuo ensemble lose its place with respect to the vocal-ists. With so many starts and stops and interpolated phrases of one style interrupt-ing another, it is quite easy to leave someone back at the ranch. By jotting down the text incipits, the scribe provides signposts to keep everyone going down the same road at the same time.

Yet another quizzical aspect of this Credo deserves comment. The back page of the alto part (the section that would be the outside left of our Hallmark greeting card) has sixteen measures in blackened *canto figurado* notation. Above the staff is a heading, "1ra voz, â Duo" (First voice, for a duet). At first glance, these few measures seem dramatically out of place, perhaps even pertaining to a different work, since they are the only measures in this style on the alto's performance sheet. Or maybe these breves and semibreves are merely a sketch on improvised scratch paper, where Sancho is working out some musical detail. That last possibility seems plausible, since the San Fernando Mission Archive does have in its possession a sketchbook where Sancho doodled and scribbled various incomplete, musical ruminations. The text, however, provides a critical clue for the mystery's resolution: "Et incarnatus est de Spiritu Sancto, ex Maria Virgine, et homo factus est" (And was incarnate of the Holy Spirit, born of the Virgin Mary, and was made man). As we saw earlier in the discussion of "Credo de Jesús," this is the specific line from the Credo that customarily is fleshed out in richer polyphony in California settings, reflecting humanity's desire for sensuality and the pleasure of the senses. This alto melody, then, is a melodic line that can be added to launch us into polyphony at this juncture; it provides a touch of counterpoint to the bass's melody at the expected moment, thickening the otherwise sparse texture of this *canto figurado* setting.

Clefs

One of the great contributions to Western music notation was the ingenious idea of graphing out the precise location of pitches on a "staff," composed of four or five lines; notes that fell on the same line or space were identical in pitch, and the elevated position of a note on the staff corresponded to the sensation to the human ear that the pitch was higher as well. As Alfred W. Crosby has noted in his superb and insightful book, *The Measure of Reality*, music was part of a new visualization of nature and the universe that began to take place in the late Middle Ages and early Renaissance; he enthusiastically observes, "The musical staff was Europe's first graph."[24] He ruminates that the West's ability at this time to subdivide natural phenomena into equal components, or "quanta," and then to *visualize* them, was the main impulsive force behind its "ascent" in the following centuries.[25]

The staff, by itself, does not indicate to the musician which notes fall on which lines or spaces any more than empty graph paper tells us the "value" of any given line or point. That is done by assigning a specific value to a spot on the axis. In music notation, that function falls to the clef that assigns a specific pitch to specific line. A C clef actually resembles the letter *C*, its two "arms" embracing the line that will be assigned to the pitch middle C; an F clef most often appears like a trio of diamonds with two of them placed on either side of the line that will represent F below middle C; and the G clef has a scroll that spirals smaller and smaller around the line that fixes the note G above middle C (see figure 2-1).[26]

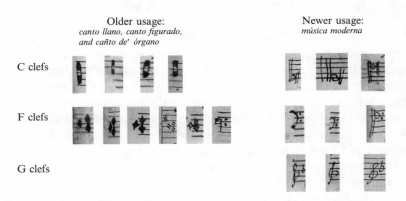

Older usage:
*canto llano, canto figurado,
and canto de' órgano*

Newer usage:
música moderna

C clefs

F clefs

G clefs

Figure 2-1 Clefs in California manuscripts

All three clefs occur with frequency in California mission music, but their locations and their notational idiosyncrasies convey more meaning than simply pitch
location. The choice of clef or the manner in which it is drawn can help indicate
such things as the following:

1. whether a piece is performed as *canto llano, canto de órgano, canto
   figurado*, or *música moderna*;
2. whether a specific timbre or voice type is requested to sing a particular
   line;
3. whether the composition is "concerted," that is, whether it combines
   voices with instruments, as opposed to being a cappella;
4. whether a piece is performed in a direct or an antiphonal manner;
5. whether the notes should be played at pitch as written or, on the other
   hand, whether they should be transposed down a fifth;
6. whether the piece is in a particular scale system (a *tono*) that implies a
   specific power or mood associated with the *tono*; and
7. whether a manuscript can be attributed to a particular location or
   associated with a specific scribe or scriptorium.

For California sources, *canto llano* and *canto de órgano* utilize almost exclusively the first two clefs of C and F and only rarely G. Pablo Nassarre explains why
in his *Fragmentos músicos*: "The G clef is not used in *canto llano*, but only the F and
C clefs that are appropriate for grave or low voices—which are those that always
sing *canto llano*. Because the G clef is for sopranos, it is used only in canto *de
órgano*."[27] His last statement, allowing the G clef in *canto de órgano*, appears to contradict my previous observation that disallows it from that style, but that is merely
because Nassarre makes no distinction in his work between *canto de órgano* and
canto figurado. If one does make a more refined subdivision of the possibilities,
as does Marcos y Navas in his treatise where he distinguishes between the older
homophonic-style *canto figurado* (of a vocal line accompanied by chords) and the
newer *canto de órgano* or *música moderna* (which, as we have already seen, is more
modern and even Italianate in style), then the observation holds true. One can
safely assume, then, that the G clef in California mission music implies not only a
higher treble or "soprano" register but also a more modern stylistic rendition.

The C clef is not always in the shape of the letter *C*; in many cases, such as the
many loose sheets copied out by Juan Bautista Sancho, it is drawn as a double bar
followed by a circle that marks the line for middle C, followed by another, smaller
double bar. Other friars use a similar design, but the circle becomes more boxlike
in shape—still enclosing the critical line for middle C. Significantly, this circle-
shaped clef is never found in the chant books (whose central repertoire is that
of *canto llano, canto figurado*, and some *canto de órgano*) but instead is the norm
for the more complicated *canto de órgano* and *música moderna*, with its modern-
sounding pieces scribbled onto loose sheets intended for performance, one on a
part. Each singer or player has his own sheet—rather small, but big enough for
one performer—unlike the group singing of *canto llano* that is facilitated by the

enormous physical scale of the choirbooks; their colossal size made it possible for many singers simultaneously to see their notes clearly, even if standing several feet from the lectern. This particular "circle" or "boxed" C clef, then, informs us that the piece should be realized as chamber music with only a few singers, as opposed to the massing of choral resources on that particular line.

Additionally, I would argue that this clef (along with the use of modern note shapes such as whole notes, half notes, quarter notes, and so forth, as opposed to squared-off breves and semibreves) implies that instrumental lines supported the melody when the work was performed in the missions—even if those instrumental parts are not readily found today. This is difficult to prove categorically, since most of the loose-sheet instrumental parts from the missions are no longer extant or have been misplaced. But a thorough examination of the repertoire at other musical institutions active at the same time would support my thesis. For example, there are hundreds of delightful pieces from the eighteenth century at the exquisite Conservatorio de las Rosas in Morelia, Mexico, a charitable institution founded in 1743 for destitute young girls, dedicated to advanced music instruction.[28] The repertoire for these girls is of the first rank; it is written in a modern, informed style by Mexican masters such as José Gavino Leal, Manuel de Zendejas, and Francisco Javier Ortiz de Alcalá that in many respects resembles that of the premier European artisans of the time: José de Nebra, Francisco Corselli, Alessandro Scarlatti, Leonardo Leo, or Johann Adolf Hasse. In these manuscripts, vocal lines are habitually sketched out with the boxlike C clef and with the modern "rounded" note shapes of whole notes, half notes, quarter notes, and so forth—and without exception, these works in *música moderna* style have a basso continuo accompaniment. The lion's share of them also incorporate a pair of busy violins (and sometimes flutes) to enhance the luxuriant texture. The vocal lines of Sancho's "Pues sois sancto sin igual" or his "Altera autem die" look very much like the writing of "A ti mi Jesús amado," "Jesús, mi dulce amor," or "Celebren los astros" from the Conservatorio, but alas, the Sancho folders are clearly incomplete, lacking the attendant instrumental support.[29] Since the notation styles and musical effects of Sancho's "Pues sois sancto sin igual" are cut from the same cloth as "A ti mi Jesús amado" or "Jesús, mi dulce amor," it seems reasonable to me to finish both of these garments with matching instrumental accompaniments.

In addition to pitch location, instrument usage, and performance style, the clef also can imply the desired vocal timbre. Nassarre explains that although there are four standard voice types, one only needs three different clefs. He elucidates:

> Although there are four voices types, they are split up as two extremes and a middle; the highest one, which is the Soprano part, corresponds to the G clef; the lowest sounding voice [the Bass] corresponds to the bass clef; and although two voice parts remain, they are in the middle region between the extremes, for which one clef [the C clef] is sufficient. For the Altos and Tenors, one can go up and down as far as might be necessary, all within the span of the staff's five lines, depending on the line that the clef might be situated.[30]

Nassarre then develops clef associations even further, showing that the C clef's position on the staff can indicate any of the four voice types, merely by selecting the proper line for middle C. He explains:

> The C clef is for Sopranos, and it is ordinarily drawn on the first or lowest line of the staff. For the Altos, the C clef falls on the second line sometimes and on others it's on the third. For Tenors, the clef is on the third line, and at other times on the fourth. The Bass part ordinarily is notated with a C clef on the fourth line, but never on the first [meaning the very top line]— because in the situations where it is necessary to descend down low, one notates it using the F clef or bass-clef on the third line. It turns out that the note names match up on the same lines and spaces [for both the C clef on the top line and the F clef on the third line], and that is even better reason to use the F clef, for it is more appropriate for low-sounding pitches since it is located on one of them. And most often, one puts this clef on the fourth line, but it is not ever necessary to place it on the fifth, because if once in a while one needs to go lower, a small ledger line can be added, or even two ledger lines when needed.[31]

Marcos y Navas (whose treatise was in the hands of many of the California friars) maps out a similar pattern for clef usage. For four-voice polyphony, he explains that the soprano uses a C clef on the bottom line; the alto places the C clef on the middle line; the tenor's C clef falls on the fourth line up; and the bass uses an F clef on the fourth line. For Marcos y Navas, the G clef on the second line (our modern "treble clef") is the domain of high-pitched instruments such as the violin, oboe, and so on.[32]

Nassarre's and Marcos y Navas's advice proves beneficial in determining the voice types for the Lamentations in folder 61 of the WPA collection at Berkeley. Sancho has three different settings of texts taken from the Lamentations of Jeremiah, each serving as a Lesson during a Matins service during Holy Week.[33] The duet with the text "Iod, Manum suam misit hostis" has the voice types "tenor" clearly marked at the top of both vocal parts, and it also has the C clef on the second line down as described by Nassarre. The same clef is used for the duet "Aleph. Quo modo obscuratum," so one could safely assume that it also is intended for a pair of tenors (or perhaps basses), since Nassarre admits those two possibilities for this clef. The other duet, "De Lamentatione Jeremie...Heth. Cogitavit Dominus," is clearly for sopranos, given the range and Sancho's choice of clef, a C clef on the bottom line.

Changes in clef can imply a shift to antiphonal exchanges between two separate choirs, as in the *canto figurado* setting of *Lauda Sion Salvatorem* in an incomplete mission choirbook C-C-68:2 in the Bancroft Library.[34] This hymn is related textually to the ancient sequence—that legend has associated with Saint Thomas Aquinas in the Middle Ages—but its style, texture, melody, and musical structure are completely different. The *canto figurado* setting wafts along in graceful triple meter (although no bar lines are drawn in). It is built entirely of two phrases that alternate throughout the piece, creating a pattern that could be graphed as *a-b-a'-b'-a''-b''-a'''-b'''*, and so on. Although it could easily be written out from start to finish using only one clef, it nevertheless changes clefs with each new phrase. All of the *a* phrases employ an F clef on the middle line, (perhaps requesting an alto sound); all of the *b* phrases use a C clef on the second line from the top (thus possibly requesting a tenor or bass timbre, according to Nassarre's explanation of clef usage).

A smidgen of caution regarding coloristic implications is justified here, since this version of *Lauda Sion Salvatorem* with its shifting clefs may predate the idea of voice "orchestration" as Nassarre and Marcos y Navas describe it. But whether or not the changing clefs reflects a *timbral* shifting between alto and tenor colors, the clef changes do seem to suggest—at the very least—that there is an *antiphonal* answering back-and-forth between two opposing choral groups. This conclusion is amply reinforced by other related or concordant versions of this setting. The same basic hymn setting appears in Santa Clara Ms. 3, although there are no clef changes and there has been an attempt to add utilitarian bar lines.[35] In the process, the scribe (Florencio Ibáñez) has changed his mind more than once, crossing out some lines and moving them laterally to one side or the other as he rethinks the metric structure. Interestingly, all of the *a* phrases are still intact, more or less, but the *b* phrases have all been crosshatched out, invalidating them as the requested phrases. So, is the piece even performable as it stands, and if so, what should be inserted to supplant the deleted material? The answer comes in a small folio sewn into this choirbook at this very location, a sort of musical "correction sheet" that repairs the botched *b* phrases and clarifies the forest of bar lines that had been crossed out and moved around.[36] It is in the handwriting of Pedro Cabot, and these small folios occur in several occasions. As he often does, Cabot updates the notational style from squared *canto de órgano* to regular modern notation, using a bass clef (but on the third line rather than the fourth), a time signature (3/4), and the note shapes that we use today. Although Cabot's notated example clarifies with laser precision any rhythmic ambiguities that had arisen in the *canto figurado* setting on the facing page, it still does not really indicate in any irrefutable way that antiphonal performance is desired.

The alternation of groups arises again as a valid consideration in other concordant versions of this particular *Lauda Sion Salvatorem*. The enormous Serra choirbook M.0612 presently housed at Stanford is one of the most impressive and magnificent books of the mission repertoire.[37] On folio 12v one finds *Lauda Sion Salvatorem* in exquisite *canto figurado* notation, with none of the erroneous cross-outs or misplaced bar lines that afflict the version in Santa Clara Ms. 3. But a careful inspection quickly reveals that only half of the piece is recorded here. It maps out the tune for phrase *a* and carefully writes out the words for verses 1, 3, 5, and 7 below the notes so that the text underlay will not be a problem. However, the musical phrase *b* is nowhere to be found, nor are the words for the even-numbered verses included anywhere. In short, Serra's choirbook gives us only *half* of the piece. As with many sacred settings in Serra choirbook M.0612, he implies an alternation of material between two performance groups but only provides the tune and text for one of the choirs. In this setting of *Lauda Sion Salvatoreum*, we have "team A" but need to scare up another source to suit up "team B."

That takes us back to an earlier suggestion regarding antiphonal performance and the use of changing clefs in Bancroft choirbook C-C-68:2. Given the context of Serra's manuscript and Santa Clara Ms. 3, we can reconfirm the hypothesis that *shifts in clefs in the Bancroft choirbook help indicate a shift in choirs* (and perhaps even a shift in vocal timbres).

Transposition in the "Spanish Style"

One of the most elusive aspects of clefs in Spanish sources of the seventeenth and eighteenth centuries regards transposition. It was a required skill of any professional keyboardist, harpist, or guitarist, and if we are to believe the major continuo players and theorists of the time, any player worth his salt could easily transpose and realize the appropriate harmonies at sight. Pablo Nassarre, Pedro Rabassa, Josef de Torres, and Francesc Valls all advocate the transposition down by a fourth of works in the Spanish style (but not the Italian).[38] Many *villancicos*—the ultimate "Spanish" genre of the Baroque—were obviously performed a fourth lower than written as evidenced by the harp parts that are pitched up a fifth or down a fourth from the notated vocal lines; two examples include Matheo Romero's "Ay, ojos suspendad, parad" and Cristóbal de San Jerónimo's "Al pan de los cielos."[39]

Beginning in the late seventeenth century, a G clef when used in "Spanish" pieces indicated transposition.[40] The three main Spanish baroque guitarists who discuss the art of accompanying are in agreement on this. Lucas Ruiz de Ribayaz harmonizes scales in his *Luz, y norte musical*, and when we encounter an F clef or C clef, there is no transposition. The G clef, by contrast, necessitates a lowering of the pitches by a fourth.[41] Sanz's explanation resembles Ribayaz's treatment. He reasons that if the range goes too high in the F clef, then the piece should be transposed down a fourth to accommodate the vocalist:

> Whenever the sopranos go very high in any composition using the G clef on the second line, the accompaniment on the guitar is transposing down a fourth for the comfort of the singer.[42]

Santiago de Murcia also addresses this point, placing the G clef in the context of the "old Spanish style." He suggests transposing up a fifth (which tonally leads us to the same key center as Ribayaz's and Sanz's instruction to transpose down a fourth):

> Deducing the treble part on the guitar with the G clef...transposed up a fifth...is the manner of composing with this clef in the Spanish style when it is used for melodies.[43]

Admittedly, transposition in California mission music is rare. Most texts are in Latin, void of any overt "Spanish" flair, and only rarely do we encounter a G clef that could suggest transposition—but several notable exceptions deserve attention. The jaunty "Cantar quiero un rato" written out by Juan Bautista Sancho is a semitheatrical work in which two characters banter back and forth in conversation. One might reasonably ask if this is one such work that is described by Torres, Sanz, and Murcia that—on the basis of its "Spanish" style—would call for transposition down a fourth.[44] We find two instances of a treble clef, perhaps hinting that transposition is needed. The "Duo para Domingo de Ramos, 'Altera autem'" is written for two voices using the treble clef, the first voice couched in a rather high tessitura, sometimes hovering around g' above the staff.[45] In no other composition in Sancho's hand does he write out a vocal line using this clef, nor do the majority of his manuscripts emphasize this high register. Again, he may expect the performers to transpose. Until the accompanying instrumental or continuo lines are found and used to check pitch level, it will be difficult either to confirm or to rule out the various options that present themselves.

A third example of possible transposition arises in the *Mass for St. Dominic*, as written out by Pedro Cabot in Santa Clara Ms. 1 and as found in Santa Inés Ms. 5 in which the sequence *In cœlesti Hierarchia* is set as a duet in parallel thirds in a march-like duet in cut time.[46] (See photo B-90 in appendix B online.) At first glance the work seems to be in G dorian, but significantly, both sources suddenly introduce the treble clef to notate this piece. This is peculiar. Although the treble clef crops up regularly in loose performance sheets that are unattached to a bound book, I can think of no other instance where a chant book makes this shocking shift to a G clef. Why did Cabot and the scribe of Santa Inés Ms. 5 feel compelled to do this? I would argue that the treble clef in this instance is mandating transposition down by a fourth, pushing the key center down to D dorian. This makes perfect sense tonally, in the context of performance, since the sequence will have to match up with the key center of the Alleluia that frames it. Customarily, a sequence follows on the heels of the Alleluia and its verse (in this case, in D dorian); a transposing clef would place the Alleluia and its accompanying sequence *In cœlesti Hierarchia* in the same key. Furthermore, this particular setting has a return to an "Alleluia" at the sequence's conclusion with its last stanza, "Apud curiam...." This final return to the words "alleluia" is a duet—just like the sequence—that gently ascends and descends in gentle, stepwise motion. Interestingly, this same contour had appeared at the end of the Alleluia's verse, "Pie Pater Dominice," but for some mysterious reason Cabot then reconsidered and vigorously scratched it out. Why did he write it out and then change his mind? The answer, of course, is that it would have been redundant, since the choir would have encountered the closing "alleluia" at the end of the sequence on the next page. The stricken one had become superfluous. There might be yet another reason that the G clef makes its sudden appearance in this instance. During the mission period, the G clef was commonplace for instrumental parts, but soprano vocal parts usually employed the C clef on the bottom line. Perhaps—through the use of the G clef—Cabot and the scribe of Santa Inés Ms. 5 are encouraging violins or flutes to double the vocal lines.

One more aspect of pitch transposition needs addressing. A letter from Narciso Durán sent to the Procurator of the Missions, Fray Juan Cortés, on January 7, 1821, indicates that the friar encountered a problem with his choirboys in that they had trouble singing sustained passages in the very high register. He therefore recommended tuning down to accommodate the distressed singers. In his letter, Durán requests that the Franciscan motherhouse in Mexico City send him an organ at the San José Mission, and he enumerates the qualities that this organ should have. After providing the desired physical dimensions, he then specifies that it should be tuned a whole tone lower than normal. He felt this would provide relief for his choirboys but would not generate such a relaxed string tension in the accompanying violins and cellos that there would be a problem.[47] This being the case, we can assume that Durán's choirs and orchestras sounded at least one step lower than was written on the page.

Alternatim Performance

At the missions, *alternatim* performance was an almost daily occurrence, in which a long text would be subdivided into alternating subsections or phrases that emphasized a contrast in style, texture, density, meter, or register as they bantered back and forth. For example, the odd-numbered verses of a Psalm could be sung as *canto llano*, whereas the even-numbered verses could be realized in the steady meter and harmonic richness of accompanied *canto figurado*. Or a hymn could be divided so that a small chamber ensemble performed delicate polyphonic phrases, and the full resources of the mission choir and orchestra responded in the full magnificent sonorities of Haydn-like splendor. The combinations are nearly endless, but in all these realizations two characteristics are always present: alternation and contrast.

The practice was so ubiquitous that certain texts (such as the Gloria or Credo) were nearly always divided at the same break points; in that way, the odd-numbered phrases could easily be replaced by another version of the same lines. It is a bit like having a wardrobe where variety is obtained through switching out items in varied combinations while trying to avoid a choice that would blatantly clash with the other clothing items selected for the day; if one is tired of one shirt, he can thumb through the closet to find a "new" one that seems agreeable or even elegant when worn with the slacks that have been chosen. Similarly, if a mission choir tired of singing the odd-numbered phrases of the Gloria in triple meter, it was a simple task to thumb through a chant book to seek out a "new" rendition in duple meter that would not clash with the even-numbered phrases that remained. With each new choice for each subsequent performance, the permutations kept the repertoire fresh and ever changing. The most dramatic visual proof of this practice is found in Narciso Durán's exquisite choirbook that he wrote out at the San José Mission in 1813. One folio has a *Dies irae* with musical flaps that can be raised and lowered so that one can select the musical phrase for the day at whim (see photos 2-1, 2-2, and 2-3).[48] One setting could be graphed as an alternation of phrases in the pattern *a-b-a-b-a-b-a*, and so on. But if we lower a flap, we could get a new phrase "c" covering the "b" material beneath, creating a rendition *a-c-a-c-a-c-a-c*, and so on. The top flap can be lowered, and we get even more permutations, depending on the position of the lower flap. And so this mix-and-match produces not one definitive version but instead a multitude of possibilities all based on the alternation of contrasting sonorities.

Brief mention should be made concerning the term *coro* as applied to these *alternatim* performances. The word *coro* (or "choir") is jotted down almost exclusively over single-melody passages, while the words *duo* and *a3* occur in the polyphonic passages. This strongly suggests that the phrases cast as single melodic lines are performed by the entire group in unison (accompanied by chords in the instrumental combo), whereas the counterpoint sections very likely are performed as chamber music with one vocalist per part. There is considerable evidence that very often

Photo 2-1 *Dies irae* (flaps up), the Bancroft Library, choirbook C-C-59, p. 69a. (Photo courtesy of the Bancroft Library, University of California, Berkeley.)

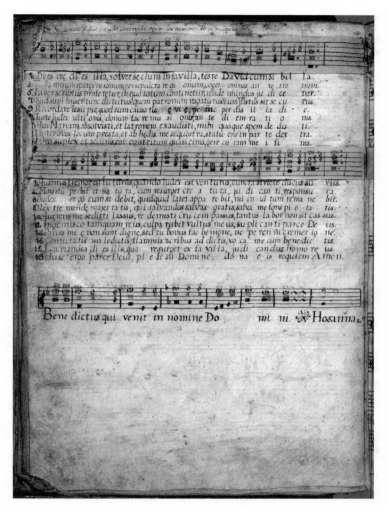

Photo 2-2 *Dies irae* (some flaps up, some flaps down), the Bancroft Library, choirbook C-C-59, p. 69b. (Photo courtesy of the Bancroft Library, University of California, Berkeley.)

sacred polyphony in Italy and the Hispano-American world was realized not by full choral resources but with one singer on each line; at the same time, plainchant was generally executed by the full choral resources.[49] The page, then, presents a visual impression that is counterintuitive to the actual sound that was echoing in the mission sanctuaries. The counterpoint *looks* richer, thicker, and heavier on the page due to the amount of ink on the paper, but the sonorities are not so calorie-laden, since the number of performers is few. The choir's notes, on the other hand, appear so small and paltry on the notated page, but the effect of their massive sound as they plunge in would be on a different scale altogether. Additionally, the choir's

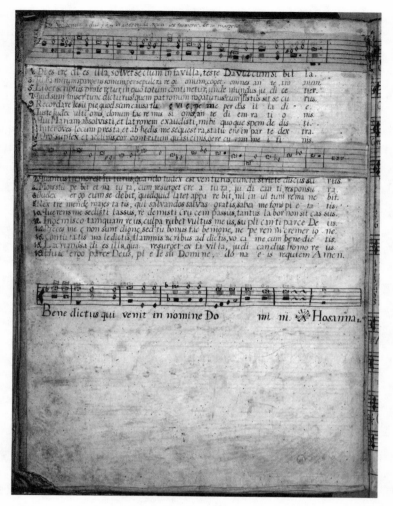

Photo 2-3 *Dies irae* (all flaps down), the Bancroft Library, choirbook C-C-59, p. 69c. (Photo courtesy of the Bancroft Library, University of California, Berkeley.)

homophonic passages *look* thin because the accompaniment is implied, not written. In short, the sonorities of the alternating sections are strikingly different, but there nevertheless is a sense of balance. The mass of the choir serves a sort of equalizing counterweight to the intriguing counterpoint of the soloists.

Other Notational Symbols

As with the *Dies irae* discussed earlier, the *Stabat Mater* on page 118 of the Durán choirbook at the Bancroft Library uses a small paper flap that covers up the four measures of the "amen" at the very end of the piece. By leaving the flap down and concealing this closing phrase, the singers instead bump up against the double bar that bounces them back to the beginning measures, where they then will proceed to sing each subsequent verse. In other words, the paper snippet serves as a graphic device denoting first and second endings. When it is left down, the first ending applies—and when it is lifted, the singers at last proceed forward to the closing "amen." Curiously, the *Dies irae* and the *Stabat Mater* that both use this flap innovation are transformed sequences. At their inception in the Middle Ages, both of them were built of paired phrases *a-a'*, *b-b'*, *c-c'*, *d-d'*, and so on, as we would expect of any medieval sequence. But as is often the case in California sources, sequences get a complete makeover. They are shaped and remolded into strophic hymns where the recurring musical material comes back—not as a lineup of paired phrases but as a long string of stanzas that all utilize the same musical mold over and over again. Granted, the stanza can be broken down into two contrasting musical components or phrases, but those two come back in exactly the same way, with only the words changing each time as we round the corner. These new hymnlike creations, therefore, have a pattern that could be graphed out as *a-b, a'-b', a''-b'', a'''-b'''*, and so on.

The Durán choirbook (manuscript C-C-59 in the Bancroft Library) has other quizzical features in its notation. With respect to the Lamentation setting, Durán explains that parentheses are inserted around optional material that can be excised; he is particularly concerned when passages float into the high register so that the stratospheric altitude gives the choirboys fits. As Durán explains, "And be it advised that wherever you see parentheses like this, { }, I'd say that you can omit the pitches that are contained inside, in the event that the boys are unable to reach up to the high notes."[50]

In three locations we find boxed-in measures in Durán's choirbook C-C-59 where borders frame the musical contents: (1) the Kyrie and Gloria to the *Misa de San Antonio*, (2) the Kyrie to the *Misa del quarto tono*, and (3) the Kyrie to the *Misa del sexto tono*.[51] One might surmise that the enclosed measures are a graphic variant of the parentheses, denoting a fragment that can be stricken at the performer's discretion. In each of these instances, the framed passages are not particularly high, so their register could not be the hazard or flaw that targeted them for possible deletion. With the respect to the *Misa de San Antonio* and the *Misa del quarto tono*, perhaps Durán has boxed in certain measures to make the phrases a bit shorter and not as complex for his novice performers. Significantly, no text is ever destroyed by leaping over the optional segment that is framed within the rectangle or the parentheses. And in no case is the juncture clumsy if one takes the shortcut; the phrases can be spliced together after excising the optional fragment as easily as train cars can rejoin after they have uncoupled and an internal boxcar has been removed. The Kyrie to the *Misa del sexto tono* presents a slightly different case; it has three iterations of "Kyrie eleison" in pleasant counterpoint, followed by a single statement of "Kyrie eleison" in *canto figurado* style. The same process transpires for the ensuing "Christe eleison." So unlike the previous two masses where the rectangles enclose mere fragments, the *Misa del sexto tono* captures entire, self-sufficient phrases. Durán does not explain his rationale, but I suspect it has to do with *alternatim* performance. As we have seen repeatedly, opposing textures or groups often alternated phrases in the mission performances—so this choirbook may have rectangles around *canto figurado* phrases to remind certain performers that they are to drop out at these locations and then are to rejoin the ensemble with the return of polyphony. Whenever these same compositions show up in other California sources—including the Bancroft choirbook's closest cousin, Santa Clara Ms. 4—there is not a boxed-in measure to be found. These "frames" seem to be a conditional afterthought, providing performance options as opposed to rigorous requirements for the piece's realization.

Instrumental Interludes: *Música, Toca,* and *Tocata*

In addition to the wealth of note shapes and clefs that the padres used to notate their musical repertoire, many other indications scattered across the manuscript pages tell us much about California music performance. In the large choral books, many of the selections intended for *alternatim* performance have inscribed at the ends of sung phrases the intriguing markings *música, toca,* or *tocata*. The theorists and musical sources of the era demonstrate that the instruction *música* marked onto the score denotes the temporary departure from plainchant to sonorities that incorporate instrumental accompaniment or even full-blown Baroque and Classical textures. Luis Hernández, in his definitive study of the sacred music at the Monastery of El Escorial, explains:

> When one mentions "*a música*" or simply "*música,*" it means nothing more than the music is not plainchant. Generally speaking, it further signifies that neither is the setting purely vocal nor is it the pure vocal polyphony of the Renaissance, but rather it is with instruments or with Baroque music.[52]

The application of this term to designate the need for instrumental accompaniment surfaces with great frequency in Psalm settings where a choir and organist exchange volleys. As Hernández elucidates, *alternatim* performance was most common on the feast days of greatest importance; on those supreme occasions, the trading off of phrases between the choir's plainchant and the organ's instrumental excursions prevailed in the first and third Psalms of each Nocturn in a Matins service. On days of lesser importance, this alternating style surfaced only in the first Psalm of each Nocturn, or in the second Psalms.[53] Similarly, the eighteenth-century theorist Martín de la Vera informs the reader that on important feast days, the five Vespers Psalms are all sung "*a música,*" with the choir alternating with the organ. He also allows for the insertion of *fabordón* in which the choir intones the Psalm verses, not in unison, but in pseudo-polyphony of chords that rise and fall, following the contour of the chant melody. The flipping back and forth between *fabordón* and instrumental *a música* heightens the dramatic sense and pageantry of the Vespers service.[54] One notch down in the liturgical hierarchy, according to de la Vera, are the Vespers services for Doubles or Commons in which the "special" performance features are applied to the first, third, and fifth Psalms as opposed to the whole kit and caboodle.[55] Martín de la Vera runs through these issues, stating:

> Vespers: it is the Divine Office or Hour that is celebrated with the greatest solemnity. In it, the organ, instrumental music, and *fabordón* play the largest role. All Vespers for a Prior, for a Vicar, a Rector, or Subvicar are done with instruments. The organ plays from the first Psalm onward in Vespers of the first order; it plays as well in the 1st, 3rd, and 5th Psalm during the feasts for major Doubles and those days from the Common of the Saints.[56]

The California mission manuscripts bear out the details as described by Martín de la Vera. Vespers services are few and far between, but when they do occur, they are for the primary feast of a mission's patron saint, such as the Feasts of Saint Joseph at the San José Mission, Saint Claire at the Santa Clara Mission, or Saint John the Baptist at the San Juan Bautista Mission.[57] Significantly, there are only three Vespers settings in the Durán choirbook, Bancroft choirbook C-C-59, but each of them incorporates the term *música* in its annotations for the Psalms, calling for instrumental usage and assuring a heightened sense of pageantry and splendor through the luxuriant sound of *alternatim* performance between plainchant and instruments.[58] Additionally, the lengthy Vespers service for Santa Clara found in Santa Clara Ms. 4 has five Psalms intended for *alternatim* performance: even though it does not explicitly state "*música*" here, it is implied that instruments would play on the even-numbered verses, given that the odd-numbered verses are set as four-voice single-staff polyphony in *fabordón* style.[59]

Another term found in mission sources, *tocata*, also calls for musical instruments. Historically, the word *tocata* developed from the root *tocar*, meaning "to touch" or "to play," as opposed to the root *cantar*, meaning "to sing." From the late Renaissance onward, *tocatas* (also called *tientos* or *fantasías*) explored the highly idiomatic capabilities of instruments; the ones that were realized on keyboard and plucked string instruments often alternated passages of rich, sonorous chords that inched forward with a discernible meter and rhythm, juxtaposed against wistful scale passages that could meander over the expansive range of the instrument, from high to low. Depending on the player's whim, the scale phrases could slow down with an ephemeral dissipation of energy or could accelerate forward with a rush of cascading runs or skyrocketing ascents. By the time of the mission period, *tocata* continued to designate a free-flowing instrumental piece, usually on the guitar, harp, or keyboard. Francesc Valls, in his treatise "Mapa armónico práctico breve resumen de las principales reglas de música," lumps together the terms *symphonia, concerto, tocata*, and *sonata*, stating that the *symphonia* is for two, three, or more instruments. He elucidates that the *tocata* or *sonata* is any instrumental piece in two parts: a treble and an accompaniment. Being a relatively conservative composer, he further laments the rather shallow aspect of modern Classical *tocatas* and sonatas, for in his view they did not have the rich counterpoint and solid craftsmanship of the Baroque predecessors.[60]

Clearly, then, the designation *tocata* in the California choral books instructs the vocalists that they are to hand over the ensuing phrase to instrumentalists before resuming their singing with the next line of text.[61] As we have seen, California music performance often highlighted a stark contrast between two alternating sonorities; in this case, the sonic flip-flopping between textures manifests itself in the shifting back and forth between voices and instruments.

Although instrumental *tocatas* or insertions are only rarely notated in the choirbooks—since they are the domain of the vocalists in a particular service—a few brief passages nevertheless do appear with that designation. In Santa Barbara, Document 2 has a brief instrumental prelude labeled "Tocata de La" (Tocata in A) at the inception of the *Misa chiquita* on page 75. The last sheet of the manuscript (p. [152]) is a free-flowing instrumental reverie labeled "Tocata."[62] This composition is notated in hollow, or "void," mensural notation on six-line staves: it bears the beautiful artistic design of Juan Bautista Sancho's *manu propria* that he drew on manuscripts and documents as his sign of ownership or possession. Additionally, there is a beautiful instrumental prelude on page *D* of Santa Clara Ms. 4 that commences the wistful Mass in A minor that follows. This mass is tucked into the added pages sewn into the binding between pages 119 and 121.

Specific music examples of *tocatas* may be rare, but the choirbook manuscripts in California are chock-full of references to *tocatas*; most often the term crops up in the context of concerted performance style, where voices and instruments faced off in a sort of antiphonal challenge. Close inspection of these settings reveals the common practice of providing the choir with the odd-numbered verses, and then surrendering the even-numbered phrases to the instrumental performers. Such is the case with the Magnificat in Santa Clara Ms. 4 and Bancroft choirbook C-C-59.[63] The same holds for Durán's fascinating rendition of the ancient sequence *Victimae paschali laudes*, whose text was authored by Adam of Saint Victor in the thirteenth century.[64] He sets only half of the textual lines, after which he places the word *música* to remind the vocalists that they are to pause while the "omitted" phrases are taken up by instrumental sonorities.[65] The *Te Deum* found in the Durán choirbook presents an intriguing variant of this practice as well.[66] He subdivides the lengthy text into two large sections. The first segment has odd-numbered phrases intoned by four-voice chords centered on D minor and in a nonmetric, rhythmically flexible rhythm; the even-numbered verses are to be played as "Musica de La, 4° T°" (Instrumental interludes on *A*, in mode 4). At the arrival of the text "Te ergo quae sumus," a completely new intonation formula arises, also in four-voice harmony and elastic rhythm; it emphasizes the tonal areas of D minor and a concluding E major, a refreshing change after the first section's exploration of D minor. As expected, the even-numbered verses are nowhere to be seen, since they are the obligation of instruments.

The word *toca* is used interchangeably with *tocata* or *música* in the California manuscripts.[67] For instance, the choirbook Santa Clara Ms. 4 employs the words

"Toca de ut" (Interlude in C) at the bottom of page 14 to prepare the performers for the next piece, *Veni Sancte Spiritus*, which is found on the ensuing page. Here again, only the odd verses are written out; at the end of each sung line we see the word *toca*, clearly indicating that it is the instruments that are to realize the missing even-numbered verses. The anticipatory reference of the "toca" on the preceding page could suggest that the instrumentalists who play the *música* perform an instrumental interlude here as a sort of prelude or *entrada* before the sung work. Although such a prelude was rarely written out in the chant books, the organist in Spanish cathedrals and churches commonly supplied an *entrada* in order to give the cantor the correct pitch to begin the chant.[68]

An abundance of Psalm settings in the Durán choirbook offer fascinating examples of alternating practice as well. For instance, the ambitious setting of *Vespers for the Feast of Saint Joseph, the Patron Saint of This Mission*, has a string of liturgical texts, all set in this antiphonal style.[69] As we would expect, the Vespers service opens with "Domine ad adjuvandum," but instead of a mediocre melodic shard, we get resonant block chords that intone the opening of this sacred service. Then we find a string of Psalms, all of which are set in a congenial battle of opposing forces, the voices versus the instruments. Each Psalm is prepared by the appropriate antiphon in monophonic plainchant; and this small tune also returns to close the Psalm and provide a sort of melodic border. These monophonic etchings frame the larger "Psalm."[70] In every instance, the choir sings the odd-numbered verses in four-part block harmonies that intone the chant—not in "melodic" intonation formulas but in homophonic chords that move forward in the same flexible rhythm as plainchant. Small annotations then inform the reader to select instrumental interludes, according to their mode or "key." For instance, the first Psalm, *Dixit Dominus (Psalm 109)*, replicates verses 1, 3, 5, 7 plus the Doxology, and then inserts a microscopic and smudged annotation instructing the performers to play "Musica de [Fa]" on the alternating sections. The even-numbered phrases of *Confitebor tibi Domine (Psalm 110)* are realized as "Musica de Vt o 5° t°" (Instrumental interludes in C, or mode 5). *Beatus vir (Psalm 111)* requires instrumental interludes in F ("Musica de Fa"). Moving forward, the fourth Psalm sets out the text for *Laudate pueri Dominum (Psalm 112)*, and its instrumental sections explore yet another key: "Musica de La" (Instrumental Interludes in A). And the fifth Psalm, *Laudate Dominum, omnes gentes*, returns to phrases in C ("Musica de Ut"). Several other *alternatim* settings follow on the heels of these five Psalms settings: the hymn *Te Joseph* abandons any shadow of the original chant tune from the Gregorian tradition and instead maps out melodic phrases in quadruple meter and in parallel thirds. At first glance, the manuscript presents the misleading clue that *alternatim* performance has been abandoned in lieu of a straight run-through, since the three lines of text under the hymn setting are labeled *1, 2,* and *3*. The numbering does represent the order that the choir will sing the text, because the words are actually drawn from verses 1, 3, and 5 of this beloved hymn. In truth, then, we can assume that the "missing" words have been delegated—once again—to an instrumental rendition. A much-needed sense of variety occurs here, however, since the ambling, free-flowing delivery of the choir's Psalm formulas has been replaced here by a marchlike duet in quadruple meter, couched almost entirely in parallel thirds. The "key" of the instrumental phrases centers on A ("Musica de La"). And the culmination of the Vespers service, the Magnificat, also explores an identical musical style. The choir sings a block-harmony formula for the odd-numbered phrases, and the even-numbered ones are delegated to the instruments. This gargantuan sacred service that explores melodic antiphons, Psalm verses in block harmonies, and instrumental interludes was clearly an extraordinary spectacle, one that would have been appropriate for the feast of the San José Mission's patron saint.

We can place this elaborate use of *tocas, tocatas*, and *música* in the centuries-old Spanish tradition of organ *versos* in which the keyboardist was given the even-numbered lines of extended texts such as Psalms and canticles that were then interpolated into the choir's realization of the plainchant. As Bernadette Nelson explains in her outstanding article "Alternating Practice in Seventeenth-Century Spain: The Integration of Versets and Plainchant in Psalms and Canticles":

> The most common function of the organ in liturgical worship in seventeenth-century Spain and Portugal was to alternate with plainchant—in particular with verses of Psalms, canticles, and hymns of the liturgical Offices, and with items of the Mass Ordinary. Most sources of seventeenth-century Iberian organ music include music designed specifically for this purpose, with alternatim versets for the Psalms and canticles forming the bulk of material.[71]

She elaborates that the organ normally was not allowed to intrude on the first verse or the Doxology, which therefore resulted in its usage on the even-numbered verses. The composition of organ *versos* was all the rage from the early Baroque well into the nineteenth century, as is evidenced by the quantity of them composed by Iberian artists such as Joan Baptista Cabanilles, Roque de Cõceiçáo, M. R. Coelho, Antonio Martín y Coll, Fray Frais [?] Coruba, Francisco Javier de la Fuente, Ramón Ferreñach, Gómez, Josef Lidón, Manuel Narro, Martínez, Joaquín Pastrana, José Prat, Padre Antonio Soler, and Josef Teixidor.[72] By the second half of the eighteenth century, *versos* expanded in size, stepping beyond the world of keyboard sources into the more expansive sonorities of symphonic *versos* for chamber orchestra. Some of the most elegant are the sets of *versos* composed by Ignacio de Jerusalem, the Mexico City chapel master in the mid–eighteenth century.[73] Although it is difficult to draw any verifiable conclusions until primary sources from the California missions are located, we nevertheless can surmise that Jerusalem's *versos* provide a model of music that could have constituted the mission repertory. We have already established that Jerusalem's masses were performed in California missions, and it would not be a stretch to include his *versos* as likely components of the mission repertoire.

In addition to *alternatim* performance, there is yet another context where the term *música* appears in California choirbooks. The immense volumes from Narciso Durán's scriptorium at the San José Mission lay out on a single staff all of the vocal lines that are to be executed, but the instrumental accompaniment is

largely anyone's guess. That there are instruments playing is evidenced by various works in the choirbooks with "blank" measures filled only with rests.[74] The
gaping holes make no sense aesthetically or musically speaking, but there would
not be the slightest distraction if this supposed "vacuum" were actually filled with
instrumental sounds. We encounter, then, performances where singers have to
coordinate their entrances and melodic lines with instrumentalists even though
those lines are not written out. A full score would certainly be helpful, and Durán
almost approximates this momentarily in the *Misa del sexto tono* with the occasional insertion of the word *música* under several passages.[75] He is courteously
marking the passing tones in the *acompañamiento* or continuo line as visual cues
for the singers; they can follow on and be better prepared for their next entrance.

That instruments were indispensable in mission music performance is well
confirmed by the terms *música, tocata*, and *toca* in the choirbooks and from other
irrefutable evidence. In fact, according to Durán, it was instrumental performance
in the liturgy that first piqued his interest and spurred him to seek high-quality
instruction at the Santa Clara Mission for his most talented choirboys. When they
came back from their studies, Durán tells us that the lamentable state of horrid
singing that had plagued the mission was rectified. He further explains that they
were then knowledgeable enough to label the instrumental interludes or *tocatas*
according to their key centers so that they could be inserted aptly into the chant
wherever they were needed. The plainchant's mode or *tono* had to match the
instrumental interlude's tonal emphasis, thus explaining the meticulous qualifiers
for his *tocata* and *música* instructions: "Musica en Ut," "Musica en La," "Toca en
Fa," and so on. Durán's passage from his preface to choirbook C-C-59 is worth
quoting in full for its clarity, humor, and insight:

When we arrived at this Mission [of San José], church singing was so piti-
ful that the *Asperges*, the only thing that the boys sang, had neither feet nor
head, and it seemed more of a howl than a song. Let's not even talk about
Masses; because if I were to tell you, almost without thinking about it, that
they didn't even know how to respond "amen," then you can figure out
the rest on your own. It is true that in some of the neighboring missions
they have been working on the singing, but since I did not think it was
necessary to send them away to learn—nor did I make the effort to teach
them myself—we were stuck in the same old rut. All of this stemmed from
the firm belief (that thank goodness has turned out to be false!) that the
young boys were completely incapable of entering into the art of singing.
But back then, some musical instruments had already come to the mission.
And observing a good deal of facility at playing them among the boys of
the neighboring missions, I began to get excited about sending some of
the boys from this mission to Santa Clara so that they might learn the first
rudiments, convinced that they would later be perfected here.

The success exceeded my first hopes; now that music was somewhat
rehabilitated—with the assignment of names to all the *tocatas* or instrumental interludes, and having organized them all by the mode to which

they belonged in order to match them quickly with the various modes of the chants—soon the sacred services were performed with more than a modicum of decency.[76]

Modes

During the mission period, there was not "one" mission style but many. As we have seen, the panorama of sounds, flavors, and effects encompassed everything from *canto llano* at one extreme to Haydnesque Classicism at the other. Similarly, the way in which pieces were identified with respect to their mode or key was equally broad and varied. Not surprisingly, the plainchant melodies drawn from medieval repertoire label each new selection by its mode, one of eight octave-species scale systems passed on from antiquity. But only rarely do the Spaniards actually employ the term *modo* for this context; instead, they use a rather slippery term, *tono*. The potential for confusion arises in that *tono* can also mean "whole step" or "half step," a point not lost on Baroque theorist Francesc Valls, who complains of the sloppy misapplication of *tono* to designate *modo*. In spite of Valls's valid admonition, it made no dent in the commonplace usage of *tono* as a modal identifier.[77] Nowadays freshman theory classes often give the down-and-dirty definition of the modes as octave scales that start on the different keys of the piano. That is only partially accurate. In truth, the mode conveys many other invaluable details that will help in performance. If one knows the mode of a work, then he or she can tell such things as the following:

a. the *final*, the last note upon which the melody will ultimately reside and the note that exerts the most gravitational tug on its neighbors;
b. the *tenor* of the piece, that is, the other important pitch (after the final) that tends to pull melodies toward it at the end of phrases;
c. the intervallic distance between each note of the scale and the placement of the various whole steps and half steps as one ascends or descends;
d. the location of the *final*, that is, whether it falls in the middle region of the register or if—on the other hand—it rests at the bottom so that melodies soar upward but never below; and
e. the *affect*, the actual physical power or emotive effect that the mode will have on the listeners.[78]

This last point is one often lost on modern scholars who are in a rush to ferret out instances of the modern major-minor system with its twenty-four major and minor keys at the exclusion of the coexisting modal system. They were not mutually exclusive. Even in the Classical era, the Spaniards in the Old World and the New World assumed that the modes held power; modes were not just part of a *musical* system but were part of a *belief* system as well, a kind of worldview that surely would have been imparted by the friars to their neophyte converts.

The eighteenth-century Spanish organist and theorist Pablo Nassarre explains in depth the emotive power of the modes, tracing his sources back to ancient times. He is a realist and up-to-date with respect to the hot new trends; he emphasizes that modern styles have not replaced chant and the power of the modes but have only added a new layer of possibilities to an old system that remains valid.[79] Many other authors such as Bernardo Comes y Puig delved into the emotions or *affections* elicited by the modes, mirroring much of the information found in Nassarre's pages. Significantly, these two authors shared much of the same worldview as our California friars, for both men were Franciscans and both were from eastern Spain—as were the bulk of the California padres.[80] It is worthwhile, then, to read through Nassarre's summaries regarding the modes, for they help to explain the context in which the California liturgy was performed.

Nassarre—like Boethius centuries earlier—argues that the harmony of the Heavens governs the lives we live and the music we make; the three entities of cosmos, humanity, and music all resonate in sympathy. The scale systems, then, are not mere patterns or pleasantries meant to entertain the ear but instead are part and parcel of cosmic law. And they have power. The eight heavenly planets are inextricably bound to the eight modes, and each reflects the personality of its companion. He elaborates:

> According to Cicero, the Stars exert influence over these eight modes, as they do over many other things in creation. The Sun has his dominion over mode 1; the Moon over mode 2; Mars over mode 3; Mercury over mode 4; Jupiter over mode 5; Venus over mode 6; Saturn over mode 7; and the Starry Sky exerts its influence over mode 8. Not only does each Planet have dominion over a mode, but likewise—just as the Planet influences various effects—so it is that the mode (over whom the Planet rules) similarly causes the same effects in the human condition through sympathy. I have already told many times of the interconnectedness that the harmonic proportions of the Heavenly Spheres has with the human body and with sounding music, through its complete similarity.[81]

He then takes up the power of each mode, one by one, and gives its profile:

> The Sun has power over mode 1, and just as the Sun is first among all of the Planets with regard to the benefiting of humankind, so it is that mode 1 is similar in its salutary effects. Thus, this mode infuses happiness and gravity: that is to say, that it expunges the sadnesses of the heart, without moving the heart to gaiety that we commonly call intemperate and frivolous, because this is sedate and modest contentment.... The Introit to the Mass that begins *Gaudeamus omnes* is in mode 1, having taken into account [this aspect] when it was composed. Since this mode and lyrics combined instill gladness, for which everybody becomes joyful in the Lord, no other mode will express this emotion any better than this one.[82]
>
> ....

Over mode 2, the Moon has its dominion. The effects of this Planet are the moving of one to tears of sadness, inspiring sleep and laziness, and exciting the vice of wretches.[83]

. . . .

The Planet Mars governs and rules mode 3: this Planet is the one that influences bad circumstances and inflames the heart to ire. It is terrible and frightening; and for those under its rule, these two aspects are particularly severe. It provokes arrogance and causes men to become liars and deceivers. It is against purity and has influence over all warriors. It foments rancor and malice. It excites impiety and complete cruelty.[84]

. . . .

The Planet Mercury has its influences over mode 4, also called Hypophrygian. This Planet has the authority to move one to weeping or to gaiety, to fury and to gentleness, to calmness and to ghastliness, to blandness and to strength. Although it has all good influences when by itself, when it joins up with Mars or another that exerts evil properties, it will have an influence similar to that other one with which it has hooked up—because with badness it is bad, and with goodness it is good.[85]

. . . .

By its very nature, the Planet Jupiter—which is in the fifth level of Heaven—is hot and moderately humid, for which qualities it is very wholesome in its influences, favoring human nature and nurturing it, purifying the pestilent airs. The year that it governs is very healthy. It causes very favorable conditions in the subjects over whom it has dominion, such as: the reconciliation of friendships, peace, mutual cooperation, calming reassurance, tranquility of spirit, benevolent kindnesses, and an inclination toward devotion.[86]

. . . .

The Planet Venus has its dominion over the Hypolydian mode, or mode 6: this Planet is the one with very beneficial powers. The effects that it causes are: heartfelt tenderness, piety, devotion, and an inclination for all things compassionate, the exercise of charity, an inclination for thankfulness, and the tendency to shed tears—out of loving kindness and out of devotion.[87]

. . . .

The Mixolydian mode is mode 7; over this mode the Planet Saturn exerts its rule, which is earthy and melancholic: its influences are the cause of hardships, hunger, afflictions, weeping, sighs, and all sorrow and melancholy.[88]

. . . .

Mode 8 is called Hypomixolydian. This mode is solemn and it engenders in the soul the following: spiritual joy, dutiful and subservient desires for eternal things, and a desire for the vision of our Maker and Creator. Saint Ambrose states that this mode—on account of its sweet mildness—is well suited for discreet men, for men who are keenly inventive, and for those who are well prepared. It has all those effects just mentioned, plus it brings about the same effects as Modes 1, 5, and 6. It is especially helpful in raising the heart to God, praising Him, and giving Him thanks for everything.[89]

Given these thumbnail sketches of modal personalities, we can see several good reasons why Durán may have chosen the melodic cores that he did when he standardized and reduced his whole chant repertoire to a handful of tunes. As Durán mentions, with the exception of Easter time, the Introits are all in mode 1 (associated with sedate joy and modest contentment) and are modeled on *Gaudeamus omnes*—the very chant that Nassarre mentions in conjunction with this mode. He provides an exception, however, for the Introits in Ash Wednesday and Holy Week, "setting those ones in mode 4, for that seemed to me more in keeping with the Spirit of the Church and the mysteries of those days."[90]

Indeed, the Introits used in Durán's manuscripts (Bancroft choirbook C-C-59, Santa Barbara Doc. 1, and Santa Clara Ms. 4) pertaining to the Passion depart from the *Gaudeamus omnes* contour that has shaped all the other Introits, and in each case their relationship to mode 4 is clarified in their titles with the ascription "Introito, 4° t°."[91] Similarly, the Communions *Qui meditabitur* for Ash Wednesday and *Pater si non potest* for Palm Sunday break all ties to the core mold (in mode 6) from which all of the others have been poured, and instead journey into mode 4.[92] This mode continues to dominate in the Easter season Offertories; *Exaltabo te Domine* for Ash Wednesday is couched in mode 4, as is *Dextera Domini fecit* from Maundy Thursday.[93] Durán's departure in Easter from his standardized melodies and one-size-fits-all approach makes the most sense when viewed through the prism of mode 4. This peculiarly ephemeral mode, according to Nassarre, embraces the world of opposites—of joy and weeping, of ghastliness and serenity, of gloom and ecstasy. There could hardly be a more appropriate combination of moods to encapsulate the depths of despair of the Crucifixion and the subsequent elation of the Resurrection. In short, Durán's comments about "the Spirit of the Church and mysteries of those days" are not a casual reference but a clear summation of the musical atmosphere in Holy Week, one steeped in mode 4. Significantly, with the singing of the Introit *Resurrexit et adhuc tecum* on Easter Sunday, Durán chooses to scuttle mode 4 and to return to his "normal" usage of the *Gaudeamus omnes* tune for Introits. It is that day, in Durán's view and those of his fellow believers, that goodness and stability are restored in heaven and earth, and as such, the return to "normalcy" with respect to his melodic models is significant and appropriate. Additionally, this "standardized" Introit tune that Durán reutilizes over and over and restores to primacy the prototypical melody from mode 1, a system that "infuses happiness and gravity . . . [and] expunges the sadnesses of the heart." And as we have seen, the Catholic cosmology held that mode 1 was governed by the sun, an image that the California friars certainly would have embraced as they sang "Resurrexit et adhuc tecum" at the sun's rising on Easter morning.

Durán's modal choices continue to reflect the way that music and theological belief were conjoined in California mission life. The clay for Durán's Alleluias and Communions is drawn from mode 6, associated with heartfelt tenderness, piety, devotion, compassion, charity, and thankfulness. If his choices were only a matter of whether or not something sounded "major" or "minor," then he could have chosen just as easily standard tunes in mode 7, which to modern ears sounds just as "major" as mode 6. But what would that imply? For Durán and the Franciscans trained in a worldview where chant was interconnected and where musical choices demonstrably shaped and affected the human spirit, a preponderance of tunes in mode 7 might endanger the very success of his evangelistic enterprise, eliciting the hazardous consequences of this mode, complete with "hardships, hunger, afflictions, weeping, sighs,...sorrow and melancholy." Just as Durán's choirbook ventured into the terrain of mode 4 for the Holy Week Introits, so it utilizes that same mode for the Communions during that season; similarly, as Durán returns to "normalcy" with the mode 1 pattern for the Introit on Easter Sunday, so he returns to normalcy with respect to the Communions on that same auspicious day.[94]

If modal theory was applicable only to plainchant in California, its use would merit little more than a paragraph or two and could be chalked up as a perfunctory nod to a timeworn tradition. Actually, the eight modes played a vital role in most of the *polyphonic* mission music as well—pieces in the *canto figurado* and *canto de órgano* styles habitually have modal designations as part of their titles. Granted, an occasional piece in *estilo moderno* reflected the modern major-minor system with its attendant keys to the exclusion of any reference or influence of the eight modes—but these "Classical-sounding" pieces were less pervasive in the California landscape. Browsing through the titles of compositions in the California repertoire, one encounters with great frequency the labeling of a piece with respect to its *tono*, or "mode." Some of the most beloved and performed pieces during the mission period were the *Misa del quarto tono (Mass in mode 4)* and *Misa del quinto tono (Mass in mode 5)*.[95] And this sort of modal designation to name a piece is typical of Spanish and Hispano-American music until the mid–nineteenth century. A preponderance of instrumental anthologies for guitar, harp, and organ use a work's mode as the essential feature of its title.[96] The guitar instructions and music collections of Gaspar Sanz, Francisco Gueráu, Antonio de Santa Cruz, Lucas Ruiz de Ribayaz, Santiago de Murcia, and Juan Manuel García Rubio are chock-full of works with names such as "Pasacalles del primer tono," "Preludio del quinto tono," and so on. These books deal primarily with the secular, including the rowdy and rambunctious, the danceable and theatrical; they are about as far away from chant as one could imagine. The important point here is that the modes were part of a *living* musical tradition that permeated every corner of musical life.

That being said, as soon as one crosses over from *canto llano* to any kind of harmonically based sonorities, one encounters discrepancies in modal usage that require explanation. If one examines the definitions of the modes as they appear in the speculative treatises pertaining to plainchant and then cracks open the books of the manuals made by guitarists, harpists, organists, and other

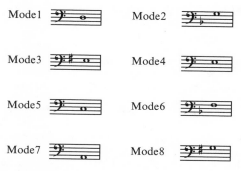

Figure 2-2 Modes as described by Marcos y Navas

practical performers, one encounters a substantial rift between the two systems. Granted, there are a few similarities between the medieval modes for plainchant and the newer modes used in polyphonic works, but it is imperative to keep in mind that their "finals" (their tonal centers) do not necessarily match up with each other. In addition, the newer modal system, which was developed largely by practicing instrumentalists in the 1600s, used key signatures—in conjunction with the "final"—to define any particular mode.[97] Thus, the modes as applied in Spanish polyphony were a sort of hybrid that reflected origins from the medieval modes but also incorporated other features drawn from an evolving major-minor tonal system.

One of the most concise but useful charts of the "new" modal system occurs in Marcos y Navas's *Arte, ó compendio general del canto-llano, figurado y órgano*, first published in Madrid in 1716 and then reissued almost continuously throughout the eighteenth century. As we have already established, many of the Franciscans owned a personal copy of this book, so we can safely assume that Marcos y Navas's modal system would have been familiar to many of them. In his section dealing with polyphony (*canto de órgano*), he draws out the following chart that clarifies the tonal center and key signature of each of the eight modes (see figure 2-2). The explanations of the modes offered by Santiago de Murcia, Antonio Ventura Roel del Río, Antonio Rodríguez de Hita, and Juan Miguel Urtasun de Yrarraga fall in line, more or less, with the properties graphed out by Marcos y Navas in his *Arte, ó compendio general*.[98]

Notes

1. For a good explanation of medieval notation and the way to read neumes, consult *The Liber Usualis with an Introduction and Rubrics in English*, ed. by the Benedictines of Solesmes (Tournai, Belgium: Society of St. John the Evangelist, Desclée, 1947), esp. ix–xxv; Richard Hoppin, *Medieval Music*, Norton Introduction to Music History (New York: Norton, 1978), 57–62; Willi Apel, *Gregorian Chant* (Bloomington: Indiana University Press, 1958; reprint in Bloomington: Midland Books, 1990), esp. 100–108; or the extensive chapter 4, "Notation," in David Hiley, *Western Plainchant: A Handbook* (Oxford: Clarendon Press, 1993), 340–401. It should be noted that in the breves written out by Juan Bautista

Sancho, the "squares" have a sag in the middle so that they appear more like little boats or smiling rectangles.

2. A brief explanation of music terminology is in order, since there is no universally accepted usage of terms with respect to California mission notation. I will use the terms "hollow notation" and "void notation" for hollowed notes that indicate plainchant performance with no implied rhythmic or metric value. The only difference between "regular" chant notation that employs solid note heads and void notation that employs hollow note heads is orthographic or visual: the two systems produce identical results in performance. "Mensural notation" or "white notation" also employs hollowed-out note shapes, but in this case the shape of the note head *does* indicate precise rhythmic durations and an underlying metric structure. Thus, hollow notation produces *canto llano*. White notation produces the rhythmically organized sounds of *canto de órgano* or *canto figurado*.

Some sources in Juan Bautista Sancho's hand utilize hollow notation to record several works in the *canto llano* style. Sancho utilizes hollow notation to write out the chant "Kirie tono 4to," in WPA folder 63, photo I-3, line 3: the piece then skips to line 6 for its completion.

More extensive examples are found in the *Artaserse Ms.* at the San Fernando Mission: this book is part of the collection discovered by John Koegel in 1991 at the San Fernando Mission Archive. Bill Summers treats the source in detail in his article "*Opera seria* in Spanish California: An Introduction to a Newly-Identified Manuscript Source," in *Music in Performance and Society: Essays in Honor of Roland Jackson*, ed. by Malcolm Cole and John Koegel (Warren, Mich.: Harmonie Park Press, 1997). Summers draws up an exceedingly useful catalogue of this extensive collection of manuscripts at the San Fernando Mission, providing each book or separate sheet with an identifying call number. He has shown that the large, bound volume in this miscellany is devoted primarily to the recitative ("A quali di tanti mali") and its succeeding aria ("Se del fiume altera l'onda"). Their texts are drawn from Pietro Metastasio's libretto *Artaserse*. Summers catalogues the entire book under the sigla "As-3." (See table 14.1 on p. 272 from Summers's article "*Opera seria* in Spanish California.") From here on, I refer to this book simply as the *Artaserse Ms.*

In this manuscript, Sancho uses hollow notation to write down the following chant melodies: "Yn medio Ecclesiae aperuit" and "Donum est confiteri Domini" (Introit for Mass of Doctors with the Psalm versicle), fol. 7v, lines 1 and 2; "Alleluia" and "Ynvita sua fecit" (Alleluia with its Psalm verse), lines 3 and 4; "Memoria ejus" (Offertory), lines 4 and 5; and "Dedit mihi donatus" (Communion), line 5. Other hollow-notation settings of chant in that volume include "Si queris miracula" (Responsory for the Feast Day of Saint Anthony), fol. 5v, lines 4–6; "Regina caeli laetare" (Antiphon for Holy Saturday), fol. 9v, lines 1 and 2; and "In manus tuas Domine" (Response at the end of Compline preceding the Canticle "Nunc dimittis"), fol. 14v, lines 8 and 9. The San Fernando Mission Archive also has several loose folios that contain a hollow-notation version of the chant *Salve Regina* (manuscript S-5), after which he shifts to a more traditional "black" notation for the remainder of the chant melodies, which include the "Regina caeli laetare," an "Alleluia," and "In manus tuas Domine" just mentioned with respect to the "white" notation versions in the *Artaserse Ms.*

3. For a color facsimile of a manuscript with red notes placed immediately above the black-noted lower part, consult Beryl Hoskin, *A History of the Santa Clara Mission Library* (Oakland, Calif.: Biobooks, 1961), color plate between pages 4 and 5, which reproduces fols. 89v–90 of Santa Clara Ms. 4.

4. See, for example, photo R-2 in folder 61 in the WPA collection at UC Berkeley, with its "Credo de Angeles" and also consult the *Lauda Sion Salvatorem* in manuscript S-2 in the San Fernando Mission in Los Angeles.

5. Two of the most striking examples are the "Credo Italiano" and *Veni Sancte Spiritus*, both of which are thoroughly discussed throughout the course of this book: for both of these selections, the notational idiosyncrasies of their various manuscript sources shed considerable light on performance practice during the mission period.

6. For facsimiles of this colored notation (black, red, hollow black, hollow red), consult the following photos as part of appendix B that is available online at the Oxford University Press Web site: B-5 through B-13; B-49 and B-50 from the San Fernando Mission; B-60 from the San Juan Bautista Mission; B-75 through B-79 and B-83; B-106, B-107, and B-109 through B-113. (B-5

through B-7, B-49, B-77, and B-111 and B-112 are printed in this text in black and white as photos 2-1, 2-2, 2-3, 6-2, 3-4, 4-3, and 4-2, respectively). Also consult Beebe and Senkewicz, *Lands of Promise*, 372, from Santa Clara Ms. 4.

7. For examples of note heads that are split in half, with the top and bottom halves being drawn in different colors, consult Santa Clara Ms. 2.

8. Charles Francis Saunders and J. Smeaton Chase cite two examples: "Santo Dios" and "Libranos Señor de todo mal" in the hand of Tapís at San Juan Bautista notated in four colors: yellow, red, white, and black. See Saunders and Chase, *The California Padres and Their Missions* (Boston: Houghton Mifflin, 1915), 369.

9. Owen da Silva, O.F.M., *Mission Music of California: A Collection of Old California Mission Hymns and Masses* (Los Angeles: Warren F. Lewis, 1941), 13. Depending on da Silva as their sources, other authors often repeat this attribution of colored notation to Tapís. See, for example, Beryl Hoskin, *A History of the Santa Clara Mission Library* (Oakland, Calif.: Biobooks, 1961), 43. For facsimiles of Tapís's writing, consult the following photos in appendix B available online: B-49, B-50, and B-51 from San Fernando; B-59 and B-60 from San Juan Bautista; and B-61 through B-65 from Santa Inés.

10. Consult Theodor Göllner, "Two Polyphonic Passions from California's Mission Period," *Yearbook for Inter-American Music Research*, vol. 6 (1970), 67–76; and William John Summers, "Orígenes hispanos de la música misional de California," *Revista Musical Chilena*, nos. 149–50 (1980), esp. 38–39; Summers, "The Spanish Origins of California Mission Music," in *Transplanted European Music Cultures: Miscellanea Musicologica*, Adelaide, Australia: Studies in Musicology, vol. 12, Papers from the Third International Symposium of the International Musicological Society, Adelaide, 23–30 September 1979, esp. p. 111

11. Göllner, "Two Polyphonic Passions," 70–71.

12. Manuscripts in the WPA collection at UC Berkeley that use metric "white" notation with "squared" note heads for settings of *canto figurado*—and all in the low register—include the "Credo de Angeles," folder 61, sheet R-2, and also the "Credo Mariano (vel imperiat) y Kyries compuestos con uniformidad al dicho Credo," folder 67, which actually contains a rhythmic setting for bass voice of the entire Mass Ordinary with a Kyrie, Gloria, Credo, Sanctus, and Agnus Dei. In addition, several selections in white mensural notation surface in folder 63, including "Credo de Jesus, tono 5to," photos I-1 and top of I-2; "Credo Ytaliano," photos I-2 and top of I-3; "Kirie tono 4to," photo I-3, line 3, but then skipping to line 6 (although this is in *canto llano* as opposed to metric *canto figurado*); "Gloria Todedana [*sic*]," photo I-3; "Quotiescumque manducabitis" (Communion for Corpus Christi), photo I-3, lines 7–8 (but this setting is *canto llano* in hollow notation with no metric underpinning); "Parisiense Gloria," photo I-3, an incomplete torso; and "tono 5to. Kyries à 3 voces," photo I-4. The San Fernando Mission Archive also has several pieces in metric white notation on loose folios (without an identifying catalogue number), including "Credo de Jesus à Duo, y unisono tono 5to" and "Sequencia, tono prim[e]ro, Lauda Sion Salvatorem," both of which are in Sancho's hand. There are even more instances where Sancho notates *canto figurado* with solid note heads in mensural "black" notation, including "Credo Artanense. Tono 5," folder 52; "Credo de la Trasportina," folder 53 (although the handwriting here does not exactly match Sancho's penmanship in the other folders, indicating that this might be another scribe's work); "Invtitatorium, tono 6 (Admirabile nomen Jessu)," folder 58, photos Y-1, Y-2, and top of Y-3, plus "Credo con versos alternando con el coro, 1ra vos," folder 58, photo Y-3, lines 4–5; "Kyries de Jesus. T° 5to," folder 61, photo R-12, lines 5–6 (although this is single-staff polyphony with both black note heads and "hollow" note heads); and "Kyries Dominicals," folder 68 (which has all of the movements for the mass: The scribe here is not Sancho, and interestingly, he chooses a peculiar hybrid notation that utilizes the "older" note shapes of breves and longs, while simultaneously employing "modern" quarter notes instead of semibreves).

13. Photographs of the Sancho manuscripts in the WPA collection visually look identical to the actual extant manuscripts in the San Fernando Mission Archive in Sancho's hand. There are so many similarities in the number of staves, the layout of the page, and so on, that it would seem most likely that the actual size of WPA sheets would be equivalent to those still found in San Fernando.

14. The "Credo de Angeles" is found on sheet R-2 of folder 61 in the WPA collection, beginning on staff 6 and continuing through staff 10 at the bottom of the page. The work does not end here, however, for Sancho ran out of room before finishing his copy work: he solves the problem by jumping up to the middle of staff 2 that previously had been vacant, and then scribbles in the last measures of the Credo to complete the job ("et vitam venturi saeculi, Amen, amen."). The Lamentation setting is a duet for two male voices (either basses or possibly tenors), and the text is lesson 2 from Matins for Holy Saturday, "Aleph, Quomodo obscuratum...." It actually begins on sheet R-1 and then continues on the verso side of the sheet, which is photo R-2 (the same sheet that contains the "Credo de Angeles").

15. Many of the manuscripts in the WPA collection in Sancho's hand are dated 1796 or 1797, when Sancho was still at the Convent de San Francesc in Palma. Although there is no signature, date, or ascription in folder 61 for these Lamentation settings, the handwriting is unmistakably that of Sancho. Furthermore, the headings for the Holy Saturday lesson (with its text, "Aleph, quomodo obscurtaum") are in *mallorquín* or Catalán—not Castilian—strongly suggesting that this, too, was written out by Sancho before he left for the Americas. Sheet R-1 has at its top the assignment to voice 1 with the heading "Primera veu Lamentacio â duo," and voice 2 on sheet R-3 has the heading "Segona veu Lamentacio â duo." Interestingly, the duet for Good Friday ("De Lamentatione...Heth, cogitavit Dominus") *does* have its voice designations in Castilian ("Voz primera" and "Segunda Voz"), not Catalán (see sheets R-5 and R-7, folder 61). This, too, is in keeping with Sancho in the brief period when he is preparing to leave his island home to embark on his missionary life in the New World. As his diary entries demonstrate, in the last years of the 1700s he would vacillate freely between Catalán (or Mallorcan) and Castilian, just as he does here in the Lamentations. Also, it should be noted that there are no dated writings by Sancho in Catalán after his arrival in Mexico and his subsequent move to California. For these reasons, the dating of this manuscript of the Lamentations almost certainly must be from around 1796 to 1798.

16. WPA folder 61, sheet R-12, line 5.

17. WPA folder 61, sheet R-12, beginning on line 5 and continuing through line 7.

18. For a facsimile of the "Credo de Jesus" in San Fernando manuscript S-1, consult photo B-125 in appendix B online. This same piece, labeled as "Credo de Jesus â Duo, y unisono tono 5to," appears in manuscript S-1 in the San Fernando Mission. It, too, is in Sancho's hand and is in metric "white" notation. A facsimile of this sheet is labeled B-52 in appendix B.

19. The San Fernando version of this piece similarly has an added voice at the phrase "Et incarnatus est...." In addition, there is a well-defined cross at the beginning and ending of this phrase; this symbol is used by Sancho and his contemporaries as a kind of "asterisk" intended to send you to another location for further comment. One can safely assume that there exists another sheet with these "crosses" with the appropriate "second voice." To find other examples of the "cross" being utilized as a sort of asterisk, consult Sancho's diary and also the setting of *Veni Sancte Spiritus* on p. 34 of Santa Clara Ms. 3.

20. For a facsimile of WPA folder 66, "Credo Italiano," consult photo B-127 in appendix B online.

21. As stated earlier in this book, the manuscripts themselves that had been at Stanford have been lost; only the photos taken by Sidney Robertson are extant (with the exception of the *Misa en sol* by Juan Sancho and the Serra choirbook M.0612, both of which are still in Stanford's possession, housed at the Greene Research Library).

22. Robertson's numbering of her photographs result in the following ascriptions: J-1 and J-2 pertain to the *acompañamiento* (or basso continuo). Photos J-3 and J-4 are the alto part. Photos J-5 and J-6 are the *baxo* or bass voice. J-7 and J-8 are a *coro* sheet that contains not only the *canto figurado* sections intended for performance by the choir but a few odds and ends on the staves that remained, including the soprano line in modern notation for a *Stabat Mater* in strophic form, and a duet setting of *¡O qué suave!*

23. All the missions had multiple printed copies of the *Missale Romanum* that covered this topic. For instance, this procedure along with the actual intonation formulas are found beginning on p. 238 of the *Missale Romanum ex Decr[etro] Sacr[osancti] Concilii Tridentini*... (Madrid: Typis Societatis, 1803), box 41, Hoskin 77, 1BM11–12, in the Santa Clara University Archives; and beginning on p. 208 of the *Missale Romanum ex Decreto Sacrosancti*

Concilii Tridentini... (Paris, 1826), box 70, Hoskin 82, 1BM14, in the Santa Clara University Archives. The Hoskin numbers are drawn from his helpful catalogue, *A History of the Santa Clara Mission Library* (Oakland, Calif.: Biobooks, 1961). In addition to the two *Missale Romanum* already mentioned, Hoskin cites several other copies of the *Missale Romanum* on pp. 72–73 of his catalogue, as items 76, 78, 79, 80, and 81.

24. Alfred W. Crosby, *The Measure of Reality: Quantification and Western Society, 1250–1600* (Cambridge: Cambridge University Press, 1997), 144.

25. Crosby places the invention of music notation in the center of main historical inventions or conceptual transformations, along with the invention of printing, the mechanical clock, double-ledger accounting, perspective drawing, and accurate map making.

26. For figure 2-1, the following sources were utilized. C clefs drawn from Santa Clara Ms. 3, p. 12; manuscript S-2, San Fernando Mission; WPA folder 59, photo P-2; WPA folder 63, photo I-1. F clefs drawn from Santa Clara Ms. 3, p. 12; choirbook C-C-59, p. 104; Baxo part from Sancho, *Misa en sol*, M.0573, box 1-1-1; WPA folder 60, photo N-2; WPA folder 74, photo B-1. G-clefs drawn from WPA folder 49, photo V-2; Tiple 2° part from Sancho, *Misa en sol*, in M.0573 at Stanford.

27. "P[regunta]. Usase la Clave de gesolreut en Canto Llano? R[espuesta]. No usa el Canto Llano, si solo de las Claves de fefaut y cesolfaut, que son Claves à proposito para vozes graves, ò baxas, las quales son las que siempre cantan el Canto Llano; y porque la Clave de gesolreut es para tiples, se usa solo en el Canto de Organo." Nassarre, *Fragmentos músicos repartidos en quatro* (Madrid: Joseph de Torres, 1700), vol. 1, facsimile ed., introduction by Álvaro Zaldívar Gracia (Zaragosa: Institución «Fernando el Católico» and Consejo Superior de Investigaciones Científicas [C.S.I.C.], 1988), 10. Nassarre provides a similar statement in his *Escuela Música según la práctica moderna, dividida en primera y segunda parte* (Zaragosa: Herederos de Diego de Larumbe, 1724); facsimile edition (Zaragosa: Institución «Fernando el Católico» and C.S.I.C., 1980), vol. 1, p. 105: "Advierto, que la [clave] de *gesolreut* no es necessaria para el Canto llano; y assi nunca se halla en èl, y solo sirve en el Canto de Organo, para vozes agudas, ù de tiples, que en el Canto llano solas dos, que son la da *cesolfaut*, y *fefaut*, se usan."

28. For more information on this conservatory, consult Miguel Bernal Jiménez, *La Música en Valladolid de Michoacán, México* (Morelia, Mexico: Ediciones de Schola Cantorum, 1962); Miguel Bernal Jiménez, *Morelia Colonial: El Archivo Musical del Colegio de Santa Rosa de Santa María de Valladolid, Siglo XVIII, Morelia Colonial* (Morelia, Mexico: Sociedad Amigos de la Música and Ediciones de la Universidad Michoacana, 1939); Robert Stevenson, *Renaissance and Baroque Musical Sources in the Americas* (Washington, D.C.: General Secretariat, Organization of American States, 1970), esp. 186–92; Stevenson, *Music in Mexico: A Historical Survey* (New York: Crowell, 1952), esp. 135 and 168. For further discussion of music schools in colonial Mexico, consult Gabriel Saldívar y Silva, with Elisa Osorio Bolio de Saldívar, *Historia de la música en México: Épocas precortesiana y colonial*), (Mexico City: Secretaría de Educación Pública, 1934; reprint, Mexico City: Ediciones Gernika and Secretaría de Educación Pública, 1987), esp. 171–86. My comparisons between the Conservatorio de las Rosas and the California missions can only be taken so far, since they are fundamentally different in their goals and their populations. An urban music school for the education of orphaned girls is not identical to an evangelizing institution for Native Americans in remote rural regions. Nevertheless, a case can be made that they share some overlap in purpose and style with respect to the genre *música moderna*.

29. "A ti mi Jesús amado" was composed by "Joh. Pérez" and dated 1763. Certainly, the author is none other than Joseph Benito Pérez, who was second organist at the cathedral in Orihuela, Spain, and who later petitioned for the post of chapelmaster at the Málaga Cathedral in 1788 upon the death of José Barrera. It is written for two sopranos, two violins, flute, and *acompañamiento* (meaning basso continuo).

Also in the archive of the Conservatorio de las Rosas is the exquisite "Jesús, mi dulce amor," dated 1767 and identified as a "Cantada a duo con violines, a los Dolores de N[uestr]a S[eñor]a, la S[agrad]a Virgen M[arí]a." It, too, is a duet for two sopranos, two violins, and *acompañamiento*. In a more exuberant vein is "Selebren los Astros. de Coloquios," also at the Conservatorio, written for three sopranos who are cast as stars who praise the birth of a new star in the firmament, an allusion to Jesus. A fourth soprano later enters singing the role of

Mercury. As with nearly every piece at the Conservatorio, it has a pair of accompanying violins and a basso continuo line.

30. "Aunque las partes son quatro, se dividen en dos extremos, y un medio, para el extremo alto, que es la parte del Tiple, corresponde de la clave de gesolreut, para el extremo grave corresponde la clave del baxo: y aunque las otras partes son dos, son medias entre los dos extremos, para las quales basta correspondiente una clave; pues segun en la linea, que estuviere situada, puede subir, y baxar en el continente de las cinco lineas todo lo que fuere necessario para Contraltos, y Tenores." Nassarre, *Escuela Música*, vol. 1, p. 223.

31. "La clave de *cesolfaut* para Tiples, se figura ordinariamente en la primera, para Contraltos en la segunda unas vezes, y otras en la tercera; para Tenores en la tercera, y otras vezes en la quarta, para baxos ordinariamente tambien se figura en la quarta, pero nunca en la primera; porque en los casos, que es necessario, por lo que ha de baxar, se figura la de *fefaut* en la tercera, que los signos estan en las mismas lineas, y espacios, y es mas razon se figure con la *fefaut*, que es mas propia de los signos graves, por estar situada en uno de ellos. Esta se pone tambien mas de ordinario en la quarta linea; pero en la quinta no es necessario, porque para que estè en la quarta, y si una vez, ù otra huviere de baxar mas, se suple, añadiendo una linea, ù dos para tales casos." Nassarre, *Escuela Música*, vol. 1, pp. 223–24.

32. "P. De qué voces usa la Música para la formacion de un quatro? / R. De tiple, contralto, tenor, y baxo. / P. Qué claves sirven á estos voces? / R. La de C sol fa ut en primera linea, ó raya sirve al tiple: en tercera al contralto; y en quarta el tenor; y la de F fa ut en quarta al baxo; y la de G sol re ut, siempre en segunda, á instrumentos altos, como al violin, oboe, &c." Francisco Marcos y Navas, *Arte, ó compendio general del canto-llano, figurado y órgano, en método fácil* (Madrid: Joseph Doblado, 1716), 359.

33. Folder 61 in the WPA collection at UC Berkeley has three full duets in Sancho's hand, each for a different vocal grouping and each for a different day during Holy Week. The first photos reproduce a duet for tenors, or maybe basses, as can be determined by the vocal range and also the choice of clef. Photos R-1 and R-2 are for the top vocal line, "Primera veu Lamentacio â duo," with the text "Aleph. Quo modo obscuratum" (which is lesson 2 for Holy Saturday. For the complete text and translation, see *Hours of the Office*, vol. 2, p. 1157). Photos R-3 and R-4 are for the other vocalist, "Segona veu Lamentacio â duo." Yet another duet is for a pair of sopranos. It begins with photos R-5 and R-6, bearing the title "Voz Primera â Duo" with the text "De Lamentatione Jeremie...Heth. Cogitavit Dominus" (which is lesson 1 for Good Friday; see *Hours of the Office*, vol. 2, p. 1133). Photos R-7 and R-8 have the other soprano for this duet, with the heading "Segunda Voz." The third duet is for a pair of tenors. Photos R-9 and R-10 are the sheet for the first voice, "Lamentaciõ â duo, Tenor 1ro," with the text, "Iod, Manum suam misit hostis" (which is lesson 3 for Maundy Thursday; see *Hours of the Office*, vol. 2, p. 1108). The accompanying second vocal line, with the heading "Lamentacion â duo. Tenor 2do," is found on photos R-11 and R-12. There are several works recorded on the "blank" staves of photos R-2, R-4, R-8, and R-12. Additionally, there may have been pieces notated on the bottom half of R-10, but clearly this portion of the sheet has been carefully removed, presumably to use as extra music paper for another work.

34. Choirbook C-C-68:2 in the Bancroft Library, pp. 67–68. In the Middle Ages, the text and musical phrases were grouped into paired phrases (*a-a', b-b', c-c', d-d'*, and so on), making it a sequence; in this choirbook's setting the rendition is actually strophic, since two phrases come back as an inseparable and recurrent grouping. Thus it resembles a hymn more than a medieval sequence. Thomas Aquinas's original text has been considerably abbreviated from twenty-four to eight verses. The San Juan Bautista Choirbook, ascribed to Estevan Tapís, has a nearly identical setting of *Lauda Sion Salvatorem* with the exception of a slightly modified gesture at closing cadences. See San Juan Bautista Ms. 1, p. 44 (plate 63 in WPA item 45). The San Juan Bautista Choirbook can be consulted in photographic facsimile as item 45 in carton 2 of the WPA collection at UC Berkeley.

35. Santa Clara Ms. 3, p. 48, beginning on line 5. For a facsimile of this sheet, consult photo B-95 in appendix B online.

36. The small sheet is folio *B* and is sewn in between fol. 46v (which can momentarily be regarded as a "p. 47") and fol. 48.

37. Serra choirbook M.0612 is an enormous book presently at the Cecil H. Green Library at Stanford University, filed under the title, "Mission Music: Choir Book, 1770–1784," call number M.0612 in Special Collections.

38. For a thorough treatment of transposition in the Spanish style, consult Rosa Isusi Fagoagoa, "Pedro Rabassa en la teoría musical del s. XVIII: Algunos aspectos sobre instrumentos y voces según 'su Guía para principiantes,'" *Revista de Musicología*, vol. 20, no. 1 (1997), esp. 412–14. Torres's treatment of transposition is particularly useful. Consult Joseph de Torres, *Reglas generales de acompañar, en organo, clavicordio, y harpa con solo saber cantar la parte, ò vn baxo en canto figurado* (Madrid: La imprenta de música, 1702), M.52, pp. 127–33, in the Biblioteca Nacional in Madrid. John Baron inadvertently gives examples of Spanish-style transposition in his discussion of solo songs from the early Baroque in Spain. He finds himself transposing the vocal line up a fifth for "Durmióse Cupido el son" in order to match the guitar chords; as already stated, this would have been a customary procedure in Spain (although Baron seems unaware of this standard—but idiosyncratic—practice of guitarists and vocalists in the "Spanish" style). See John Baron, "Secular Spanish Solo Song in Non-Spanish Sources, 1599–1640," *Journal of the American Musicological Society*, vol. 30, no. 1 (1977), esp. 36–38.

39. For the most perceptive and authoritative discussion of the *villancico* and aspects of performance practice, including transposition down a fourth due to *chiavette*, consult Paul R. Laird, *Towards a History of the Spanish Villancico* (Warren, Mich.: Harmonie Park Press, 1997), esp. 78–79.

40. See, for example, José Marín's "Pasacalle del 3° tono de 3 para este tono," in which the vocal line is written using a treble clef and Castilian text, but Marín supplies a tablature guitar accompaniment. The vocalist "appears" to be in D minor, but the guitar tablature places the guitar chords in A minor. However, if one applies the principles of a transposing G clef for "Spanish" pieces, everything works out splendidly. See Marín's piece as printed in John Baron and Daniel L. Heiple's *Spanish Art Song in the Seventeenth Century*, Recent Researches in the Music of the Baroque Era, vol. 49 (Madison, Wis.: A-R Editions, 1985), 23–24.

41. Lucas Ruiz de Ribayaz, *Luz, y norte musical para caminar por las cifras de la guitarra española, y arpa, tañer, y cantar á compás por canto de órgano* (Madrid: Melchor Álvarez, 1677), K.8.f.4. in the British Library, pp. 57–60. Another copy of *Luz, y norte musical* is in the archive of CENIDIM, Mexico City. Available in facsimile (Geneva: Minkoff Reprint, 1976).

42. "Pero quando los tiples en alguna composicion suben muy altos, usando de la llave de Gesolreut en segunda raya, se trasporta el acompañamiento en la Guitarra a la quarta baxo, por mas comodidad del Cantor." Gaspar Sanz, *Instrucción de música sobre la guitarra española; y método de sus primeros rudimentos, hasta tañerla con destreza* (Zaragosa: Herederos de Diego Dormer, books 1 and 2 published in 1674, and book 3 in 1697), section "Documentos y advertencias," pp. 1–2. For an excellent study of Sanz's tutor along with a complete facsimile, consult Luis García Abrines, ed., *Gaspar Sanz, "Instrucción de música sobre la guitarra española"* (Zaragoza: Institución «Fernando el Católico» de la Excma. Diputación Provincial and the Consejo Superior de Investigaciones Científicas, 1979).

43. "Para sacar la parte del tiple con la Guitarra...en la clave de Gsolreut...transportada quinta arriba...es la manera de componer sobre esta Clave al estilo de España, quando es para tonadas." Santiago de Murcia, *Resumen de acompañar la parte con la guitarra* (Antwerp: engraved in 1714 but released in Madrid in 1717), 35. For a thorough study and complete translation of Murcia's *Resumen de acompañar la parte con la guitarra*, consult my dissertation, "Santiago de Murcia: Spanish Theorist and Guitarist of the Early Eighteenth Century," 2 vols., Ph.D. diss., University of North Carolina, 1981; and Monica Hall, "The Guitar Anthologies of Santiago de Murcia," Ph.D. diss., Open University [England], 1983. Several facsimile editions exist, including one edited by Monica Hall (Monaco: Editions Chanterelle, 1980); and another with an introduction by Gerardo Arriaga (Madrid: Arte Tripharia, 1984). For a study of Murcia's life, consult the two aforementioned dissertations by Ms. Hall and by me, as well as my later publication *Santiago de Murcia's "Códice Saldívar No. 4": A Treasury of Guitar Music from Baroque Mexico*, 2 vols. (Urbana: University of Illinois Press, 1995).

44. "Ecos a duo, 'Cantar quiero un rato,'" WPA folder 50.

45. "Duo para Domingo de Ramos, 'Altera autem die que est post parasce.'" WPA folder 48.

46. Santa Clara Ms. 1 (pp. 1–2); Santa Inés Ms. 5 (pp. 55–56). Although Santa Clara Ms. 1 is now two folios bound together, its first folio bears the page number "53," indicating it had been part of a chant book at some point, not conceived of as an independent performance sheet.

47. "2° el tono del organo debe ser indispensablemente (sopena de no haber de servir), alomenos un buen punto entero mas baxo que los regulares de nuestros coros, porque los indios de esta mision tienen en general mal pecho para alcanzar y aguantar puntos altos. Mi parecer es que sea de un tono que comodam.^te pueda admitir el acompañamiento de violines sin haber de estirar violetam.^te las cuerdas." Addressed to "R. P. Procurador Fr. Juan Cortes" and signed "Fr. Narciso Duran. Mision del S.^r Sn Jose, 7 enero de 1821." Letter 30 in "Durán, Father Narciso. Transcriptions and Translations. Vault Ms. 17," California Historical Society.

48. Bancroft Library, choirbook C-C-59, p. 69. The permutations become even more varied if one allows insertions from the alternate sections of the *Dies irae* on p. 63 (a rhythmicized version of the recognizable plainchant setting) or p. 67 (where the odd phrases are written for two voices and the even phrases are for four). Note: there is a confusion in page numbers in this section of the choirbook. Consult my appendix A for a map to navigate through these pages successfully.

Some scholars have mistaken these "flaps" to be corrections that were meant to replace the material written on the main page below but have now become unattached. Generally speaking, that is a common occurrence in old documents—but that is not the case here on p. 69 (or on pp. 118 and 118bis in this same choirbook). A repair patch that later becomes detached from its host page inevitably leaves evidence that it was once affixed, such as (1) small traces of hardened glue; (2) the residual imprint of a page's image on the other where they had touched (but only in cases where one of them still had moist ink during the gluing process); or (3) some sort of surface damage as the once-glued surfaces separate from one another. Choirbook C-C-59 shows none of that. Instead, these flaps are in pristine shape with no evidence of ever having been glued. Furthermore, these flaps were *sewn* into the binding with exacting care so that they will move up and down precisely over the desired space. That is a painstaking and unnecessary process if the scribe only needed the flap to be an immovable replacement. If a bookmaker encounters a page full of mistakes at the time of binding, most often he simply *replaces* the entire error-ridden sheet rather create long replacement flaps for every notated measure of a particular piece; I can think of no instance in my research experience where a repair patch has been sewn into the binding rather than glued over the offending passage. In short, these strips are not "repair patches" but instead optional substitution flaps capable of altering a page's content at the will of the user.

49. For studies concerning the performance of polyphony with one vocalist on a part, consult Jean Lionnet, "Performance Practice in the Papal Chapel during the Seventeenth Century," *Early Music*, vol. 15, no. 1 (February 1987), 4–15; Luis Robledo, "Questions of Performance Practice in Philip III's Chapel," *Early Music*, vol. 22, no. 2 (May 1994), 198–220; and Richard Sherr, "Performance Practice in the Papal Chapel in the Sixteenth Century," *Early Music*, vol. 15, no. 4 (November 1987), 453–62. Apparently, this same system was the norm in the California missions.

50. "Y se advierte que donde esta; este parentesis { } / [tu]viese decir: que se pueden omitir las solfas que se contienen dentro, en caso que los muchachos / no puedan llegar á los puntos altos." Bancroft choirbook C-C-59, p. 96. The parentheses to which Durán refers are notated in his Lamentation settings. They occur in duet passages on pp. 77–81 and in solo passages on pp. 84–87. The same Lamentation setting is also set down in Santa Clara Ms. 4; the duet passages with parentheses occur on pp. 89–95, and the solo passages are located on pp. 97–98.

51. "Misa de S. Antonio 6° T°," pp. 50–52; "Misa [del] Quarto Tono a 4 VS," p. 122; "Misa a 4 Voces 6° T°," p. 137, Bancroft choirbook C-C-59. For a complete facsimile of the *Misa [del] Quarto Tono a 4 voces* (i.e., the *Misa del quarto tono*) consult photos B-8 through B-13 in appendix B online: A complete performing edition of this same mass is found in appendix D. Furthermore, of possible relevance is a "Misa de San Antonio" that John Koegel mentions in the context of the early mission music of Texas. If Koegel's "Misa de San Antonio" turns out to be the same mass by this name found in the California mission manuscripts, then we could surmise that this mass was possibly part of a "standard" mission repertoire that was promulgated by the

casa matriz, the Colegio Apostólico de San Fernando. After all, the Franciscans were active in both Texas and California, and their motherhouse of the Apostolic College supervised nearly every aspect of Franciscan life in both regions. See John Koegel, "Spanish Mission Music from California: Past, Present and Future Research," *American Music Research Journal*, vol. 3 (1993), 78–111, esp. 92.

52. "Cuando se dice «a música» or sencillamente *música* quiere decir sin más que no es a canto llano, aunque generalmente suele significar que no es a voces solas, o polifonía vocal pura del Renacimiento, sino más bien con instrumentos o la música del barroco." Luis Hernández, "Música y culto divino en el Monasterio de El Escorial durante la estancia en él de la Orden de S. Jerónimo," in *La Música en el Monasterio del Escorial. Actas del Simposium (1/4-IX-1992)*, Colección del Instituto Escurialense de Investigaciones Históricas y Artísticas, no. 2 (San Lorenzo de El Escorial, Spain: Estudios Superiores del Escorial and Ediciones Escurialenses, 1992), 103.

53. On p. 97 of his article "Música y culto divino," Luis Hernández states: "Los maitines eran cantados en fiestas de prior, vicariuo y subvicario y en algunas de hebdomadario. En las de prior era desde los primeros salmos. El órgano alternaba en el 1° y tercer salmo de cada nocturno, en las de prior de primero y segundo orden, y en el 2° los del tercero." He later continues to develop this theme on p. 107 and states: "Al igual que cuando se cantaba a canto llano, el coro alternaba con el órgano. Se cantaban de este modo el primer salmo de cada nocturno, o bien el segundo o el primero y tercero. Esto último tenía lugar en grandes festividades, teniendo en cuenta que algunas veces había salmos «a música.»"

54. Kenneth Kreitner devotes considerable attention to *fabordón* and its use in León Cathedral in Spain, drawing upon Document 3720 in the cathedral's archive. Kreitner explains the practice and cites the entire document in Spanish and in English translation. Of particular relevance is item 101, stating that the organist is "obligated to alternate with the singers, all the days that there is *fabordón* in Vespers ("que sea obligado alternar con los cantores todos los días que obiere favordon a las visperas en el primero y poster psalmo"). Items 105, 114, and 115 further explain the important feast days where *fabordón* would be required. See Kenneth Kreitner, "The Cathedral Band of León in 1548, and When It Played," *Early Music*, vol. 31, no. 1 (February 2003), 41–62, esp. 56–57. Luis Hernández gives profuse details concerning performance practice at the Royal Conservatory of El Escorial in the 1700s, providing the complete text of three manuscript instruction books for singing in the monastery (*Directorios del corrector del canto*). Each of the three provides copious information on the use of *fabordón* throughout the year, especially in the Psalms for Matins and Vespers services. On important feast days, such as the days in Holy Week, the instructions dictate that there is "música a 4" (four-voice polyphony, probably for instruments). The three manuscripts date from 1746, 1780, and 1804, and thus are perfectly suited for the time period in question. See Luis Hernández, *Música y culto divino en el Real Monasterio de El Escorial (1563–1837)*, II, transcription, introduction, notes and indices by Luis Hernández, Documentos para la Historia del Monasterio de San Lorenzo El Real de El Escorial, X., vol. 55 (Real Monasterio de El Escorial, Spain: Ediciones Escurialenses, [1993?]).

55. The most acclaimed people and events, of course, got their own specific day, with its attendant texts specifically for the occasion. But there were ways to deal with more general circumstances. Doubles occurred when a movable feast happened to fall on another important fixed date (such as having the Super Bowl fall on someone's birthday). It is an occasional occurrence as opposed to a yearly one. The Common of the Saints were those texts with music that could be applied to any old saint of a generic class such as the group of bishops, the group of martyred saints, the group of saints who did not die a martyr's death, female saints who were virgins, those were not, and so on. It was rather like a one-size-fits-all approach to the liturgy that allowed for considerable flexibility in accommodating the scores or even hundreds of feast days and liturgical celebrations. For a lucid and engaging explanation of the liturgical year and how to determine the order of each service and the various components, consult John Harper, *The Forms and Orders of Western Liturgy from the Tenth to the Eighteenth Century: A Historical Introduction and Guide for Students and Musicians* (Oxford: Clarendon Press of Oxford University Press, 1991). Valuable information is also found in Apel, *Gregorian Chant*; Hiley, *Western Plainchant*; and Hoppin, *Medieval Music*.

56. "Vísperas. Es la hora que se celebra con mayor solemnidad. En ella el órgano, la música y el fabordón tienen la mayor cabida. Todas las de Prior, Vicario, Rector y Subvicario son a música. El órgano toca desde el primer salmo en las de prior. En los dobles mayores y comunes también toca en 1°, 3°, y 5° salmo." Martín de la Vera, quoted in Hernández, "Música y culto divino," 98. Another remarkably useful source in navigating the liturgical year and the musical requirements for the various services is Javier Suárez-Pajares, *La música en la catedral de Sigüenza, 1600–1750*, 2 vols., Colección Música Hispana Textos, Estudios (Madrid: Instituto Complutense de Ciencias Musicales, 1998).

57. It is a recurring pattern in the gargantuan California choirbooks of immense physical scale and size to include the large Matins or Vespers service for the patron saint of that particular mission, and to intone all or most of the Psalms in those services using the polyphonic chanting formulas of *fabordón* and often annotated indications of "música"— requesting the performers to insert instrumental passages. The choirbook C-C-59 in the Bancroft Library was prepared by Narciso Durán while he was living at the San José Mission; he includes the "Domingo 3° después de Pascuas. Patrimonio del Señor San José Fiesta de Esta Misión. A Visperas" (Third Sunday after Easter. Feast for Saint Joseph, Patron Saint of this Mission. At Vespers), on pp. 20–24. The choirbook Santa Clara Ms. 4 was prepared (perhaps) by Narciso Durán for that particular mission with which he had the closest musical collaborations (as he clarifies in his preface to the choirbook C-C-59), and not surprisingly, he excises the elaborate service for San José that appeared in choirbook C-C-59 (since the Santa Clara Mission would not have made an elaborate affair about Saint Joseph's feast day) and instead includes the magnificent setting of Vespers for Saint Claire, replete with *fabordón*: "Día de Santa Clara, fiesta de esta Mission. A Visperas" (Day of Saint Claire, the Feast Day of This Mission. At Vespers)," pp. 23–28. For facsimile pages from Saint Claire's Vespers service, consult photos B-106 and B-107 in appendix B online. Margaret Cayward has suggested that Santa Clara Ms. 4 was written out by Father Viader of Santa Clara (as opposed to Narciso Durán). See Margaret Cayward, *Musical Life at Mission Santa Clara de Asís, 1777–1836* (Santa Clara: Santa Clara University Press, 2006), 4. Yet another source, the San Juan Bautista Ms. 2, "Supplement," includes a *fabordón*-influenced Matins settings for the Feast Day of Saint John the Baptist on pp. 41–48 of that choirbook, which are found as plates 192–99 in the photograph of that choirbook in WPA item 45. Also the end paper in that same choirbook has an index for another choirbook, now lost, that contains even more music for the Office (Vespers?) for the Feast Day of San Juan Bautista. That index is photographed as plate 136 in WPA item 45. Lastly, one can consult an exquisitely lettered piece in *fabordón* technique from San Fernando Ms. A320, by viewing photo B-50 in appendix B online.

58. The three Vespers in the Bancroft choirbook C-C-59 that use "música" for *alternatim* performance of its Psalms are "Vesperi autem Sabbati" (Vespers for Holy Saturday), p. 18; "Domingo 3° después de Pascuas. Patrimonio del Señor San José Fiesta de Esta Misión. A Visperas" (Feast for Saint Joseph, Patron Saint of This Mission. At Vespers), pp. 20–24; and Second Vespers for the Solemnity of San José (which can be determined through the opening antiphon, "Ascendit autem Joseph"), pp. 55–56.

59. "Día de Santa Clara, fiesta de esta Mission. A Visperas" (Day of Saint Claire, the Feast Day of This Mission. Vespers) Santa Clara Ms. 4, pp. 23–28.

60. "Es una composición desatada, y methodo libre y suelto, donde el compositor puede echar por donde quiere: sirve su uso para musica de Organo, Clavecimbalo, Arpa, Guitarra, ÿ qualquiera instrumento, que con el solo se pulsen, o se tañen tres, o quatro vozes. Las composiciones de Tientas, Resercaias, Simphonias, Concertos, Tocatas, ÿ Sonatas, pertenecen a este Estylo. / De algunos anyos a esta parte, se adulterá en el organo el methodo antiguo; pues la que antes era música trabajada, y solida en los Tientos Llenos, ÿ de Falsas; destreza de manos en los Partidos de mano drecha [*sic*] e izquierda; invencion de idea en las coreadas; mucha de la que se oye son Tocatas, y sonatas, cuya composicion consiste en dos vozes solas, que mas son un juguete que adula al oido, que Musica Magestuosa, que excite a la devocion, ni satisfaga al scientifico. / Entran también en este estylo las Symphonias, sonatas, ÿ Tocatas, que dezia (que en el tiempo presente casi son una misma cosa con diferentes nombres) de qualquiera instrumentos. La Symphonia es un concierto de tres, quatro, ō mas instrumentos, como Violines, Obuesses, Clarines, ÿ Flautas. Las Tocatas, o sonatas son por ordinario, de

una sola voz, con el accompañamiento." Francisco [Francesc] Valls, "Mapa armónico práctico breve resumen de los principales reglas de música," (Barcelona, 1742), M.1071 in the Biblioteca Nacional in Madrid, fols. 229–229v.

61. For representative examples in Santa Clara Ms. 4 of the designation "toca" or "tocata" to indicate an instrumental interlude, consult photos B-103 (the *Veni Sancte Spiritus*) and B-108 (*Dixit Dominus*). Both photos are available online as part of appendix B.

62. For a facsimile of Santa Barbara Doc. 2's "Misa Chiquita de La, y Tocata de La" and its subsequent "Tocata," consult photos B-76 and B-82 in appendix B online.

63. The instruction "tocata en fa" or "instrumental interlude in F" is found in the setting of the Magnificat, in Santa Clara Ms. 4, p. 28. Only the odd-numbered verses are written in the choirbook. The even-numbered lines are destined for the instrumentalists. On p. 29 of this same source, there is an instruction for instrumental performance: "An[tifon]a = Agnes &c. y luego tocata de ut" (Antiphon = Agnes etc. and later the instrumental interlude in C). Similarly, the Bancroft choirbook C-C-59 reproduces a Magnificat on p. 23 that reprints only the odd-numbered verses, implying the even-numbered ones are the domain of the instrumentalists.

64. "Victimae paschali laudes, Música de Ut. Sequencia. 5° tono" (Praise the Paschal Lamb, Instrumental Music in C, the 5th Mode), in choirbook C-C-59, p. 19; and "Música de ut. 5° t°. Sequencia. Victime Paschali laudes," in Santa Clara Ms. 4, p. 11.

65. Durán subdivides the text of *Victimae paschali laudes* differently than does Adam of St. Victor. In the traditional version as found in the *Liber Usualis*, 780, each of the pairs is of a different length than its neighbors; Durán takes the exceedingly long groupings and subdivides them into smaller pairs so that there is greater regularity in length. And he truncates the text, striking the last third of the piece. Whereas Adam of St. Victor's tune was monophonic plainchant in mode 1—which reminds modern audiences somewhat of D minor—Durán's tune is in the more optimistic key of C major. Furthermore, Durán's polyphonic texture and lilting triple meter depart from the asymmetric, undulating rhythmic flow of Adam of St. Victor's melody. As is often the case in California sources, the "duet" texture momentarily expands to richer three-part writing in several locations.

66. Te Deum a 4 Vs 5° y 4° T°... Vt y de La," Bancroft choirbook C-C-59, p. 119.

67. For examples that employ "música" as a term to indicate instrumental passages, consult photos B-4 (*Veni Sancte Spiritus* in Bancroft choirbook C-C-59) and B-77 (*Te Deum* from Santa Barbara Doc. 2). This latter photo is printed in black and white as photo 3-4 of this volume.

68. See Bernadette Nelson, "Alternating Practice in Seventeenth-Century Spain: The Integration of Versets and Plainchant in Psalms and Canticles," *Early Music*, vol. 22, no. 2 (May 1994), 241.

69. "Domingo 3° despues de Pascuas. Patrimonio del Señor San José Fiesta de Esta Misión. A Visperas," Bancroft choirbook C-C-59, pp. 20–24. The Vespers service includes the following selections: *Domine ad adjuvandum*; Antiphon 1, *Jacob autem genuit Joseph*, that frames Psalm 109, *Dixit Dominus*; Antiphon 2, *Missus est Angelus Gabriel*, that frames Psalm 110, *Confitebor tibi Domine*; Antiphon 3, *Ascendit autem Joseph*, that frames Psalm 111, *Beatus vir*; Antiphon 4, *Et venerunt festinantes*, that frames Psalm 112, *Laudate pueri Dominum*; Antiphon 5, *Et ipse Jesus*, that frames Psalm 116, *Laudate Dominum, omnes gentes*; the hymn *Te Joseph*; and the antiphon *Cum esset desponsata* that frames the singing of the Magnificat. There is an alternate antiphon, *Modicum et non videbitis*. Afterward, there are several other pieces in similar stylistic settings, presumably for Compline (?). They include the hymn *Sancte nobis Spiritus*; the antiphon *Missus est* that frames a greatly abbreviated setting of Psalm 118, part 3, *Legem pone mihi Domine*; and, lastly, the Response and Benediction *Constituent eum Dominum*.

70. It should be noted that the texts of the antiphons for the Feast Day of Saint Joseph match those that occur in the Gregorian tradition; they are readily found in the *Liber Usualis* on pp. 1444–45. The melodies, however, bear no resemblance at all. We see once again the reliance on a "Spanish" or Mozarabic chant tradition.

71. Nelson, "Alternation," 239.

72. For a discussion of the organ *verso* in Spain, consult Benjamin Lipkowitz, "The Villahermosa Manuscript: An Imported Source of Late Eighteenth-Century Spanish Keyboard Music," *Music in Spain during the Eighteenth Century*, ed. by Malcolm Boyd

and Juan José Carreras (Cambridge: Cambridge University Press, 1998), 207–13; Nelson, "Alternation," 239–59; Juan José Rey, "Manuscritos de música para tecla en la Biblioteca del Conservatorio de Madrid," *Revista de Musicología*, vol. 1, nos. 1–2 (1978), 221–33; José González Valle, "Liturgical Music with Orchestra, 1750–1800," in *Music in Spain during the Eighteenth Century*, 53–71, esp. 60–61; Theodore McKinley Jennings Jr., "A Study of 503 *Versos* in the First and Second Volumes of Antonio Martín y Coll's *Flores de Música*," 2 vols., Ph.D. diss., Indiana University, 1967, (University Microfilm Catalogue no. 68–2307), especially chap. 2, "Brief Summary of the Development of the Verset"; and Alfonso de Vicente, "La actividad musical en los monasterios de monjas en Ávila durante la edad moderna. Reflexiones sobre la investigación musical en torno al Monasterio de Santa Ana," *Revista de Musicología*, vol. 23, no. 2 (2000), 509–62, esp. 521.

73. For a discussion of Jerusalem's *versos*, consult Karl Bellinghausen, "El verso: Primera manifestación orquestal de México," *Heterofonía*, vol. 107 (July–December 1992), 4–10; and also my article "Hidden Structures and Sonorous Symmetries: Ignacio de Jerusalem's Concerted Masses in 18-Century Mexico" in *Res musicae: Essays in Honor of James Pruett*, ed. by Paul R. Laird and Craig H. Russell (New York: Harmonie Park Press, 2001), esp.141n25; and the entry "Eighteenth Century" that I wrote for the *Encyclopedia of Mexico: History, Society and Culture*, ed. by Michael Werner (Chicago: Fitzroy Dearborn, 1998). I also discuss the *versos* in my paper "The Apparition of the Virgin of Guadalupe and Her 'Reappearance' in the Choral Masterpieces of 18th-Century Mexico," presented at the annual meeting of the American Musicological Society (Phoenix, 30 October–2 November 1997) and at the annual convention of the College Music Society, Cleveland, 13–16 November 1997. A recording of Jerusalem's versos interpolated into the singing of plainchant in *alternatim* performance can be found on band 9 of the recording *Ignacio de Jerusalem, Matins for the Virgin of Guadalupe* (1764), performed by Chanticleer and Chanticleer Sinfonia, Das Alte Werke (Hamburg: Teldec, 1998), compact disc 0630–19340–2.

74. For examples of works that contain measures completely filled with rests, consult pages 97 and 114 in the Bancroft choirbook C-C-59.

75. The term "musica" is written under bass passing tones in "Misa a 4 Voces 6° T°" in the Bancroft choirbook C-C-59, pp. 137–39, esp. 138; and in another copy of the same work found in Santa Clara Ms. 4, pp. 132–34, esp. 133.

76. "Quando nosotros llegamos a esta Mision estaba el canto de la Iglesia tan atrasado, que el Asperges (unico que cantaban los mucha^s) [= muchachos] / ni tenia pies ni cabeza, y parecia mas ahullido que canto. No hablemos de Misas porque con decirle casi sin ponderar que no sabian / responder *amen* ya puedes hacer juicio de lo demas. Es cierto que en algunas Misiones vecinas se estaba organizando el canto; mas como / y no reconocia necesario enviarlos fuera para aprender, ni yo me meneaba para ensenarlos nos quedabamos del mismo modo. / Todo esto S° [= Sobredicho?/Santo Oficio?] originaba de la persuasion (que gracias al Sr. ha salido muy falsa) en que estaba de la impoten^te capacidad de los much^s / para entrar en el canto. Ya en este tiempo habian venido algunos instrum^tos de Musica: y yo observando bastante facilidad en los / muchachos de las Misiones vecinas en el manejo de ellos, empeze á animarme á enviar algunos desta á Sta. Clara para que apren-/ diesen los primeros rudim^tos persuadido que aqui desp^s se perfeccionarian. El exito exedio á mis primeras esperanzas: [] ya que / estubo medio habilitada la Musica, puestos Musica, puestos nombres á todas las tocatas, y divididas estas en los tonos á que pertenecen para aco-/ modarlas con prontitud a los varios tonos que ofrecen los santos, ya se hacian las funciones sagradas con una decencia mas que / mediana." The Bancroft Library choirbook C-C-59, fol. A.

77. Valls, "Mapa armónico," 26.

78. For a thorough discussion of modes, see Apel, *Gregorian Chant*, 133–78; Hiley, *Western Plainchant*, 454–77; and Hoppin, *Medieval Music*, 64–77.

79. "Hallanse ocho modos, ò tonos en la Musica, por medio de los que expressa sus afectos.... Aunque los Modernos no convienen en los nombres, y en el numero con los Antiguos, por causa de averse mudado la musica, y averse inventado variedad de partes, despues que en la antiguedad se escriviò; pero como el fundamento de la musica es el mismo, hada ha perdido, antes bien ha ganado." Nassarre, *Escuela Música*, vol. 1, chapter 18, "De los afectos que causan los ocho tonos," 75.

80. Nassarre was Aragonese, and Comes y Puig was Catalan. Of the 127 Spanish fathers who lived in California during the mission period, 22 were from Cataluña, 16 came from Mallorca, and 14 were from Aragón.

81. "Sobre estos ocho tonos tienen sus influencias los Astros, como sobre otras muchas cosas criadas, segun Ciceron. Sobre el primer tono tiene su dominio el Sol, sobre el segundo la Luna, sobre el tercero Marte, sobre el quarto Mercurio, sobre el quinto Jupiter, sobre el sexto Venus, y Saturno sobre el septimo, sobre el octavo tiene sus influencias el Cielo estrellado. No solo tienen el dominio cada Planeta sobre un tono, sino es que assi como aquel influye varios efectos, assi el tono, sobre quien domina, causa por la simpatia los mismos efectos en la naturaleza humana. Yà he dicho muchas vezes el enlazamiento, que tiene las proporciones armonicas de las Esferas, con las del cuerpo humano, y con las de la Musica instrumental por su total similitud." Nassarre, *Escuela música*, vol. 1, p. 75.

82. "El Sol tiene su dominio sobre el primer tono, que como es el primero entre todos los Planetas, en quanto à beneficiar al hombre; assi el tono primero es en sus efectos semejante. Y assi este infunde alegria, y gravedad: quiero dezir, que destierra las tristezas del corazon, sin mover à aquella alegria, que llamamos comunmente disoluta, ò liviana, porque es una alegria grave, y modesta.... El Introito de la Missa, que comienza *Gaudeamus omnes*, es primer tono, aviendo tenido la consideracion, quando le compuso, que como este tono infunde alegria, y la letra combi[na]da, à que todos nos alegremos en el Señor; ninguno otro expreßira [*sic*] el afecto mas bien, que este." Nassarre, *Escuela msica*, vol. 1, p. 76.

83. "Sobre el segundo tono, tiene su dominio la Luna. Los efectos de este Planeta son mover à lagrimas de tristeza, infundir sueño, y pereza, y excitar al vicio de miserables." Nassarre, *Escuela música*, vol. 1, p. 76.

84. "El Planeta Marte domina, y rige al tercer tono: es este un Planeta, que influye malas condiciones, enciende el corazon en ira, es terrible, y espantoso, son fuertes de condicion, sobre quienes domina, provoca à sobervia, y à ser mentirosos, y engañosos los hombres, es contra la pureza, tiene dominio sobre toda gente de guerra, fomenta los rencores, malas voluntades, excita à impiedad, y toda crueldad." Nassarre, *Escuela música*, vol. 1, p. 77.

85. "El Planeta Mercurio tiene sus influencias sobre el quarto tono, / (p. 78) llamando tibi Hipophrigio. Las influencias de este Planeta son mover à llanto, y alegría, à ira, y à mansedumbre, à apacibilidad, y terribilidad, à blandura, y fortaleza; aunque por si solo tiene todas las influencias buenas; pero si se junta con Marte, ù otro, que influye malas propiedades, las influirà semejantes à la de aquel, con quien se junta; porque con el malo es malo, y con el bueno es bueno." Nassarre, *Escuela música*, vol. 1, p. 77.

86. "El Planeta Jupiter, que està en el quinto Cielo, es de su naturaleza caliente, y humedo templadamente, por cuyas qualidades es muy benevolo en sus influencias, favoreciendo à la naturaleza humana, y beneficiandola, purificando los ayres pestilentes. Es muy saludable el año, que domina, influye muy buenas condiciones en los sugetos, sobre quien tiene dominio, como son reconciliacion de amistades, paz, concordia, sosiego, tranquilidad de animo, benevolencias, è inclina à devocion." Nassarre, *Escuela música*, vol. 1, p. 78.

87. "El Planeta Venus tiene su dominio sobre el modo Hipolidio, ò sexto tono: es este Planeta de influencias muy benevolas; pues los efectos que influye, son blandura de corazon, piedad, devocion, è inclinacion à toda cosa piadosa, y exercicio de caridad, à gratitud, y à lagrimas de ternura, y devocion." Nassarre, *Escuela música*, vol. 1, p. 79.

88. "El modo Mixolidio, que es el septimo tono,... Sobre este tono septimo tiene su dominio el Planeta Saturno, el qual es terreo, y melancolico: sus influencias son causar a trabajos, hambre, aflicciones, llantos, suspiros, y toda tristeza, y melancolia." Nassarre, *Escuela música*, vol. 1, p. 79.

89. "Llamaron al octavo tono Hipomixolidio... Es este modo grave, è influye en el alma alegría espiritual, servientes deseos de las cosas eternas, y de la vista nuestro hazedor, y creador. Dize San Ambrosio, que este tono por su suavidad conviene à los hombres discretos, de sutil ingenio, y bien acondicionados. Sus efectos son todos aquellos, que obra el primero, quinto, y sexto, y especialmente a lo que ayuda mucho es à levantar el corazon à Dios, alabandole, y dandole gracias de todo." Nassarre, *Escuela música*, vol. 1, p. 80.

90. "Los Introitos pues son primer tono, conformes ò á imitacion del *Gaudeamus*, que es el que he oido celebrar: a excepcion de los de Ceniza y Sema-/ na Santa, que me parecio mas

conforme al Espiritu de la Iglesia en los misterios destos dias; echarlos de 4° tono." Bancroft choirbook C-C-59, fol. 2.

91. In the Durán choirbook,manuscript C-C-59 at the Bancroft Library, the applicable Introits for Easter time—all of which are in mode 4—include *Miserere omnium Domine* for Ash Wednesday (p. 5), *Domine ne longe facias* for Palm Sunday (p. 9), and *Nos autem gloriari* for Maundy Thursday (p. 12). In all three cases, the texts match those from Gregorian sources; the melodies, however, depart completely from the Gregorian tunes (see *Liber Usualis*, 525, 590, 654).

92. The Communions *Qui meditabitur* for Ash Wednesday (p. 6) and *Dominus Jesus* for Maundy Thursday (p. 12) are both in mode 4. They have the same texts but different tunes than the corresponding Communions in the Gregorian liturgy. See *Liber Usualis*, 529, 657.

93. Offertories *Exaltabo te Domine* for Ash Wednesday (p. 6) and *Dextera Domini fecit* (p. 13) are both in mode 4; they have no melodic relationship to their corresponding texts in the Gregorian tradition. See *Liber Usualis*, 528, 656.

94. Yet another instance of the shift from mode 4 to mode 6 occurs with respect to the shift from the Tracts to the Alleluias. Of the three Tracts for Holy Week, two of them are in mode 4: *Deus, Deus meus* for Maundy Thursday (p. 10) and *Domine audivi* for Good Friday (p. 16). Thus, when the Tract is abandoned and replaced with the Alleluia again—all of which are in mode 6 in Durán's choirbook C-C-59—we make the same modal shift seen elsewhere with respect to other movements of the Mass.

95. See chapter 6 for a discussion of these pieces and their sources.

96. For a few important examples, consult Sanz, *Instrucción de música sobre la guitarra española*; Francisco Gueráu, *Poema harmónico, compuesto de varias cifras por el temple de la guitarra española* (Madrid: Manuel Ruiz de Murga, 1694); Ruiz de Ribayaz, *Luz, y norte mvsical*; Antonio de Santa Cruz, "Livro donde se verán pazacalles de los ocho tonos i de los trasportados," M.2209 in the Biblioteca Nacional in Madrid; Murcia, *Resumen de acompañar la parte con la guitarra*; Murcia, "Passacalles y obras de guitarra por todos los tonos naturales y acidentales," Add. Ms. 31640 in the British Library; Murcia, "El Códice Saldívar No. 4," manuscript in the personal collection of the heirs of Gabriel Saldívar, Mexico City; Juan Manuel García Rubio, "Arte reglas y escalas armonicas para aprender á templar y puntear la guitarra española de seis ordenes (1799)," M.1236 in the Biblioteca Nacional in Madrid; and "Libro de diferentes cifras de guitara [*sic*] escojidas de los mejores avtores año de 1705," M.811 in the Biblioteca Nacional in Madrid. For harp sources, consult Diego Fernández de Huete, *Compendio numeroso de zifras armónicas, con theórica, y práctica, para harpa de una orden, de dos órdenes, y de órgano* (Madrid: Imprenta de Música, 1702); "Cifras para arpa, de fines del siglo XVII a principios del XVIII. Procede de Avila," Ms. M.816 in the Biblioteca Nacional in Madrid; and the above-mentioned *Luz, y norte musical* by Ruiz de Ribayaz. And for important keyboard anthologies that identify numbers by their mode, consult "Flores de música obras y versos de varios organistas escriptas [*sic*] por Fray Antonio Martín Coll organista de San Diego de Alcalá, año de 1706," M.1357 in the Biblioteca Nacional in Madrid; "Huerto ameno de varias flores de mússica [*sic*] recogidas de muchos organistas por Fray Antonio Martín año 1708," M.1359 in the Biblioteca Nacional in Madrid; "Pensil deleitoso de suabes flores de mússica [*sic*] recogidas de varios organistas por F. Antonio Martín organista de S. Diego de la Ciudad de Alcalá año 1707. Estevan de Costa Salud," M.1358 in the Biblioteca Nacional in Madrid; Antonio Martín y Coll, "Ramillete oloroso. Suabes flores de mússica [*sic*] para órgano conpuestas por Fray Antonio Martyn año 1709," M.2267 in the Biblioteca Nacional in Madrid. Also see Francisco de Tejada's "Libro de música de clavi[i]címbalo del Sr. Dn. Francisco de Tejada. 1721," M.815 in the Biblioteca Nacional in Madrid.

97. In addition to the final and key signature, some of the practical theorists also provide cadential figures as a defining aspect for some modes, especially mode 4. Santiago de Murcia delves into them in his *Resumen de acompañar la parte parte con la guitarra*. I provide translations of Murcia's discussion and analyze his points in my dissertation, "Santiago de Murcia," esp. vol. 1, pp. 118–23, 129–32. Antonio Rodríguez de Hita and Juan Miguel Urtasun de Yrarraga replicate the cadential patterns as drawn out by Murcia. See Rodríguez de Hita, *Diapasón instructivo. Consonancias músicas, y morales. Documentos a los professores de música. Carta a sus discípulos* (Madrid: Viuda de Juan Muñoz, 1757), 24; and Urtasun de Yrarraga,

"Noble arte de música, tratado de composic[ió]n, compendio theórico, y práctico de ella," Mss. 14060/3 in the Biblioteca Nacional in Madrid, p. 36. Theodore Jennings also lucidly explains the cadence for mode 4 found in the music of Antonio Martín y Coll: he states, "The majority of the fourth-mode versets once more have the same or similar tonal schemes. All four *cantus firmi* among the fourth-mode versets are derived from the fourth psalm tone and exhibit an *A-minor* tonality with a closing half cadence on *E [major]*. There are 58 versets without *cantus firmi* but with similar tonal schemes, suited for use with the untransposed psalm tone." Jennings, "A Study of 503 Versos," 107.

98. Antonio Ventura Roel del Río covers the eight modes and explains verbally the musical aspects that Murcia maps out in a more graphic way. See Roel del Río, chapter 12, "De los Tonos y su Conocimiento," in *Institución harmónica, o doctrina musical, theórica, y práctica que trata del canto llano y de órgano* (Madrid: Herederos de la Viuda de Juan García Infazón, 1748), 231–35. In his chapter "Finales y conocimientos de los Tonos," Rodríguez de Hita runs through various possibilities for the modes, and they overlap largely with Murcia's chart. Since he offers a few other possibilities (mild variants from Murcia), I include in full the relevant text from de Hita's treatise. "Los finales de los tonos son: El de primero, DELASOLRE con diapason natural. El de segundo en ELAMI con un sustenido, ò en cosas de romance en GSOLREUT con un *Bmol*. El de tercero, en ELAMI como el segundo. El de quarto en ELAMI por diapason natural, y con final del baxo en quarta baxando, quinta subiendo, ò de segundo subiendo, ò baxando. El de quinto en ELAMI, como el tercero, ò en CESOLFAUT con el diapason natural. El de sexto; en FFAUT con un *bmol*. El de septimo en ELAMI, como el tercero, ò en DELASOLRE, como el primero, ò en la cuerda, que es ALAMIRE por lo comun, GSOLREUT alguna vez. El de octavo en DELASOLRE con un sustenido, ò en la cuerda, que es GSOLREUT. Otros finales de tonos accidentales, y transportados hay descendientes de estos, que los siguen en todo lo demas, y por eso no los pongo." De Hita, *Diapasón instructivo*, 24. Notably, de Hita's treatise held considerable sway through the rest of the eighteenth century and early nineteenth century. Juan Miguel Urtasun de Yrarraga copies out large chunks of de Hita's treatise, including his passage, in his "Noble arte de musica, tratado de composic[io]n," Mss. 14060/3 in the Biblioteca Nacional in Madrid, pp. 35–36. One of the most concise charts of this revised modal system appears in the *Resumen de acompañar la parte con la guitarra*, authored by the eighteenth-century guitarist, composer, and theorist Santiago de Murcia. The treatise was one of the most influential in the Spanish Empire on both sides of the Atlantic; its contents were copied by hand into many Mexican guitar anthologies, several of which made their way up to California (although it is unclear whether they arrived in the mission period or much later). On pages 10–11, Murcia lays out the finals and key signatures of the modes, and they closely match those in Marcos y Navas's explanation.

CHAPTER 3

Serra and the Introduction of Sacred Song

Veni Creator Spiritus, Salve, Te Deum,
and *Alabado*

Father Serra and the Founding of the San Fernando Mission, Baja California

Music played a central role in the daily life of "modern" California from its inception in 1769 and the founding of San Diego under the guidance of Junípero Serra up through the secularization of the missions and beginning of the "American" period in the mid-nineteenth century.[1] Music permeated most sacred and social gatherings; the singing of mass and songs of praise was an obligatory part of quotidian life, and social functions revolved around festive music making. The guitar was as necessary at a picnic as was the food, and weddings or baptisms were marked by pageantry, processions, and dancing—all of which were accompanied by the dulcet sounds of musical accompaniment.[2]

As Father Serra progressed forward on his trek northward to Alta California, he wended his way through the various missions of Baja California. On the 14 May 1769, he jots down in his diary the events as they transpired at the founding of the San Fernando Mission near Vellicatá, Baja California, detailing the manner in which he celebrated the holy feast of Pentecost in this remote outpost. One is struck by the martial pageantry of the service, where gunfire was as memorable as the singing, and by Serra's makeshift improvisations in patching together the necessary elements for the celebration of mass from the ad hoc resources at hand. He writes:

> In order to give Holy Communion to the captain and the soldiers, he [Father Fermín Francisco de Lasuén] had to come from Santa María to hear their confessions for them to make their Easter duty and in preparation for the expedition. They say that this Mass was the very first, for although in his trip the Jesuit Father Link had been here, as referred to in his diary, the soldiers who escorted him declared he did not celebrate at this

place. In this hut, then, was prepared an altar, the soldiers putting on their full accoutrement, leather jackets and shields, and with all the surroundings of holy poverty, I celebrated the Mass on that great day, consoled with the thought that it was the first of many to be continued permanently in this new Mission of San Fernando, thus founded that very day. While the celebration lasted, repeated discharges of firearms by the soldiers added to the solemnity: and for once the smoke of powder took the place of burning incense, which we could not use because we had none with us. And having no other candle than a stub I happened to have, and a small candle belonging to the Father, there was only one Mass, at which the Father assisted together with the soldier[s] in fulfillment of the obligation. After that we sang the *Veni Creator* [*Spiritus* in the 8th mode]. The congregation was made up of ourselves, the soldiers, and the Indian neophytes who came with us, while no gentile dared come near, frightened perhaps by so much shooting.[3]

Francisco Palóu, Serra's biographer, recounts the same event in language very similar to Serra's, but in passing he also alludes to the fact that they were lacking the organ and other instruments for accompaniment, clearly implying that the "expected" and most desirable performance would have been one in the *canto de órgano* or *canto figurado* traditions. His history informs us:

The following day, the 14 of May as has been established—and Whitsunday, the first day of Pentecost—the [mission] was inaugurated....And having sung the first Mass, he delivered a fervent speech on the coming of the Holy Spirit and the establishment of the mission. Having finished the Holy Office that was celebrated without any more lights than those of a small taper and another small stub of a candle, and since the shipments in which the candle wax was coming had not arrived yet, he [Father Serra] sang the *Veni Creator Spiritus*, making up for the lack of an organ and the other musical instruments through the continual shots of the troop, who fired continuously during the function. And the smoke of the gunpowder took the place of the incense that they did not have.[4]

Veni Creator Spiritus

Veni Creator Spiritus, the selection mentioned by name in both Serra's and Palóu's recollections of the day's events, was a cornerstone in the mission repertoire, performed at the founding of missions and other important occasions.[5] As will soon be seen, it was one of the pieces sung at the founding of the Carmel Mission in Monterey in 1770. In 1780, the mother institution of the Colegio Apostólico de San Fernando in Mexico City even codified this de facto tradition by requiring that the piece be sung the first evening at the founding of a new mission. With the friars singing its memorable strains, the men and women who assembled for the spectacle were to line up behind the Franciscans as they formed a procession.[6] The fact that very few mission sources jot down the melody is not terribly surprising, for the tune was quite catchy, repetitive, and known by all who grew up in Mexican and Spanish culture. If everyone already knows a melody—like the tune to "Yankee Doodle" or "Happy Birthday"—why squander valuable paper with scribbling down the obvious? As with all hymns (and unlike the other genres of plainchant), *Veni Creator Spiritus* is strophic in form: that is, a melody is mapped out in the opening stanza and then comes back over and over again, with this recurring tune accommodating each subsequent stanza of text. Memorization, therefore, is not much of an issue, and the fact that it is exceedingly easy to learn makes it ideal as an opening salvo for the attempted conversion of new souls by the friars; after two or three times through the loop, almost anyone can catch on and jump into the thick of things.

Although *Veni Creator Spiritus* is rarely notated in the extant mission sources, a sheet in choirbook C-C-68:2 at the Bancroft Library sheds considerable light on how the piece was executed under normal circumstances and how Serra and Palóu had to shift their expectations in the first days of the mission period.[7] A close examination of the melody shows it to be very closely modeled on the "standard" Gregorian melody of the Roman rite (dating from around the ninth century).[8] Each of the odd-numbered verses has the well-known tune notated above the appropriate lines of text, but all of the even-numbered lines are written out as text alone. The California source unmistakably implies that an *alternatim* performance style is required, where the standard tune is utilized for the odd-numbered stanzas, and some other style (probably a more complex setting in *canto figurado* or *canto de órgano*) cradles the text for the even-numbered stanzas. If we are to use the California settings of other semistrophic pieces as a model—for instance, the renditions of *Veni Sancte Spiritus, Dies irae, Lauda Sion Salvatorem, Victimae Paschali laudes, Vexilla Regis*—then we can gather that there was an alternation between contrasting textures between the odd- and even-numbered verses.[9] In the case of *Veni Creator Spiritus*, the standard melody is realized as *canto llano*; the opposing phrases would be drawn from a contrasting texture, accompanied by instruments. When Serra and Palóu founded the San Fernando Mission in Baja California, however, they did not have an organ or other instruments readily available—so they probably had to perform *Veni Creator Spiritus* not as a juxtaposition of different performance styles but as a repeated realization of the stanzas in plainchant with no recourse to instrumental accompaniment.

Serra and the Founding of San Carlos Borromeo Near Monterey

A little over six weeks after the makeshift ceremony at San Fernando in Baja California, Padre Serra and his fellow missionaries—along with the military commander, Gaspar Portolá, and his soldiers—trudged the final miles up from Vellicatá to arrive in San Diego in this new region of Alta California. This ragtag group of about seventy men fully expected to arrive at an already established base camp and fortifications, for according to the plan that was hammered out before departure, two ships were to sail from Baja California with troops and provisions who were to build the initial structures and prepare for Serra's arrival. But misfortune and mishap afflicted the voyages of both the *San Carlos*, which set forth from La Paz, Baja California, in January 1769, and the *San Antonio*, which sailed the following month. Both ships were blown off course and suffered a litany of adversities: by the time the ships arrived in San Diego, the crews were suffering from abysmal health and disease. Ninety men had manned the ships when they left port; only sixteen arrived in good health. One can only imagine the distress of Serra and company when they first caught sight of their comrades: they expected to find the beginnings of a new settlement and encountered instead more graves than reinforcements. Not surprisingly, then, neither Serra nor his biographer Palóu provides a detailed account of an opulent ceremony for the founding of the mission at San Diego—the padres were more concerned with the urgent necessities of stabilizing a very perilous and tenuous situation than with putting together an impressive pageant to attract new converts.[10]

In contrast, conditions had stabilized enough within the year that by the time of the founding of the next mission, San Carlos Borromeo de Carmelo near Monterey (also referred to simply as the Carmel Mission), a full-blown spectacle was planned for its inauguration on 3 June 1770. (See photo 3-1.)

In a letter to Father Juan Andrés, Serra renders a vivid account of the day's happenings in all its theatrical pageantry and splendor. Clearly, the intended audience was not confined to the friars and servicemen in attendance; the spectacle simultaneously was meant to attract and impress the Native Americans who would have been watching this peculiar assemblage that had ventured onto their shores. In his letter of 12 June, Serra delineates in minute detail each of the events:

Photo 3-1 Carmel Mission ("View of San Carlos Borromeo Mission"), by Henry Chapman Ford (1883), the Bancroft Library, BANC PIC 1963.002:0917:18-ffAL. (Photo courtesy of the Bancroft Library, University of California, Berkeley.)

The day came. A little chapel and altar were erected in that little valley, and under the same live oak, close to the beach, where, it is said, Mass was celebrated at the beginning of the last century. We came to the same spot at the same time from different directions, those from the sea and those from the land; we singing the divine praises in the launch, and the men on land, in their hearts.

Our arrival was greeted by the joyful sound of the bells suspended from the branches of the oak tree. Everything being in readiness, and having put on alb and stole, and kneeling down with all the men before the altar, I intoned the hymn *Veni Creator Spiritus* at the conclusion of which, and after invoking the help of the Holy Spirit on everything we were about to perform, I blessed the salt and the water. Then we all made our way to a gigantic cross which was all in readiness and lying on the ground. With everyone lending a hand we set it in an upright position. I sang the prayers for its blessing. We set it in the ground and then, with all the tenderness of our hearts, we venerated it. I sprinkled with holy water all the fields around. And thus, after raising aloft the standard of the King of Heaven, we unfurled the flags of our Catholic Monarch likewise. As we raised each one of them, we shouted at the top of our voices: "Long live the Faith! Love live the King!" All the time the bells were ringing, and our rifles were being fired, and from the boat came the thunder of the big guns.

Then we buried at the foot of the cross a dead sailor, a caulker, the only one to die during this second expedition.

With that ceremony over, I began the high Mass, with a sermon after the Gospel; and, as long as the Mass lasted, it was accompanied with many salvos of cannon. After taking off my chasuble after Mass, all together we sang the *Salve* in Spanish in front of the wonderful painting of Our Lady, which was on the altar. The Most Illustrious Inspector General had given us the picture for the celebration, but with the obligation of returning it to him afterward, as I will do when the boat sails.

As a conclusion to the liturgical celebration, standing up I intoned the *Te Deum Laudamus*; we sang it slowly, and solemnly, right to the end, with the verses and prayers to the Most Holy Trinity, to Our Lady, to the Most Holy Saint Joseph, patron of the expedition, to San Carlos, patron of this port, presidio and mission, and finally the prayer of thanksgiving.[11]

Just as we saw outside Vellicatá, Serra folds militaristic pageantry into the singing of mass with the rifle volleys and cannonades from the ships. The effect was meant to cause a ruckus, attract local interest, and perhaps even show off a bit and intimidate the local residents with the show of military might and overwhelming firepower. And we see again the central role of the song *Veni Creator Spiritus* in the founding of Monterey in 1770, just as at San Fernando near Vellicatá in May 1769.[12] (For a copy of *Veni Creator Spiritus* in a choirbook at the Carmel Mission, Serra's home church, see photo 3-2.)

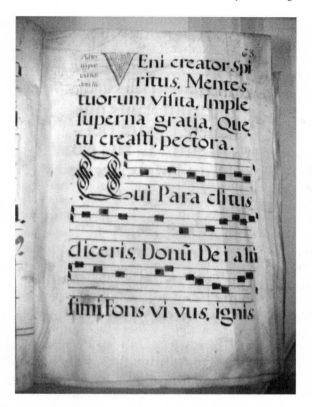

Photo 3-2 *Veni Creator Spiritus,* Carmel Mission Ms. 2, Antiphonary, Ms. 308.1955.46.139, fol. 4. (Permission to include this image courtesy of Carmel Mission; photo by the author.)

The singing of the *Salve* and *Te Deum* was part of the daily regimen of Spanish soldiers and sailors ever since the initial contact with the New World. Kristin Dutcher Mann quotes a fascinating account given by Father Juan María Ratkay, a Jesuit, of the sailors' routine on board ship in 1680—and it included the singing of mass in the morning and observance of the Laurentian Litany and the *Salve Regina* after sunset. She further delves into Jacob Baegert's account of the Jesuits and other passengers on board ship celebrating mass five times each day, as well as singing the Rosary at sunset plus the *Salve.* On the important Feast Day of Saint Peter and Saint Paul, they further sang the *Te Deum* during their 1750 voyage. In yet another California celebration involving military personnel, priests, and neophytes, and the singing of the *Te Deum*, we find it incorporated into the festive pageantry at the inauguration of Governor Pablo Vicente de Solá at Monterey in 1815.[13] In short, Serra's selection of core material was part of a broad and long-lasting tradition, not a personalized and idiosyncratic one.[14]

The *Salve*

Another piece mentioned by name at the founding of San Carlos Borromeo near Monterey was the *Salve*, a reference that merits careful scrutiny. Serra recalls that after the singing of mass, "all together we sang the *Salve* in Spanish in front of the wonderful painting of Our Lady, which was on the altar" (cantamos todos la salve en romance ante la bellísima imagen de Nuestra Señora que ocupava el altar). Each detail is noteworthy. First, we are told that it was not Serra himself who sang the piece, nor Serra and a few others—but *everyone*. Second, we observe that the *Salve* was not sung at mass but *after* it and specifically in conjunction with the veneration of the Virgin Mary. Third, Serra reveals that the whole group sang the *Salve* in a "romance" language—in this case, Spanish—not in liturgical Latin as one would expect of normal sacred functions. And last, Serra identifies the work by the abbreviated name, so short that he pruned it to a single word, *Salve*. In their translations of Serra's text, both Geiger and Tibesar assume the padre was referring to the famous antiphon *Salve Regina*, one of four antiphons to the Virgin that got farmed out during the last service of the day, Compline, through the various seasons to encompass the entire church year (the other three tunes being *Alma Redemptoris Mater*, *Ave Regina caelorum*, and *Regina caeli laetare*).[15] But this assumption is not explicitly confirmed by Serra, and I would argue that if one adopts this translation, one immediately is confronted by a series of irksome problems. The ancient antiphon *Salve Regina* is exquisitely gorgeous, but it is lengthy, with no literal repetitions of text or melody to hold one's place. It takes unexpected turns here and there that make memorization a dicey issue for a culture no longer steeped in the oral tradition. So I wonder, how is it that a hodgepodge of soldiers, friars, and neophyte converts from Baja California spontaneously launched into the *Salve Regina* by memory, with all its treacherous twists and turns, in a language that almost none of them spoke? The severity of the problem is borne out by one of the few extant manuscript sources from the mission period to contain the *Salve Regina*, a loose sheet in Juan Bautista Sancho's hand[16] that presently is found in the archive at the San Fernando Mission; it departs considerably from the standard Gregorian model as found in the plethora of chant books in Europe.[17] (See photo 3-3 for a facsimile of this sheet.)

Furthermore, it varies substantially even from the Franciscan version of the *Salve Regina* that had developed in the late thirteenth century and then continued with only microscopic variations in the printed Franciscan books of the sixteenth century and beyond.[18] It is as if Sancho were reminiscing and trying to recall the tune that he once sang long ago but had no "official" written model to help prune out the inadvertent discrepancies that had crept into his individualized version. Sancho was arguably the most accomplished musician of the period and a thoroughly trained Franciscan who would have sung Compline (and the four Marian antiphons) with regularity. If even Sancho veered off course in his recollections, how then could a group of soldiers who rarely sang Compline be expected to join in with any accuracy? Of course, it is entirely possible that Sancho is on the mark and is accurately recording the tune from another source, but one that is unorthodox

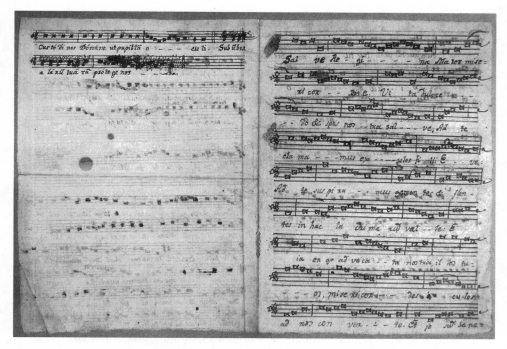

Photo 3-3 *Salve Regina* and Compline service, San Fernando Mission, Archival Center of the Archdiocese of Los Angeles, manuscript S-5. (Permission to include this image courtesy of the ACALA; photo by the author.)

in its contents. In that case, we are left with the same dilemma. How could this diverse grouping of peoples—who had radically different backgrounds—suddenly have joined together in the singing of a complicated melody if the melodic model for the Franciscan friars were an unorthodox and nonstandardized one?

The other California manuscripts provide scraps of clues that resolve these issues. One of the most commonly found text settings in mission sources is that of "Salve Virgen pura," which—significantly—is a Spanish text, short in duration, and downright catchy. All those features make it a likely candidate for the *Salve* that Serra described. Narciso Durán neatly records four settings of "Salve Virgen pura," and for each the text is identical:[19]

Salve Virgen pura,	Hail, pure Virgin,
salve Virgen Madre,	Hail, Mother-Virgin,
salve Virgen bella,	Hail, beautiful Virgin,
Reyna Virgen salve.	Virgin-Queen, hail![20]

Not only is the text accessible, but in each case the entire musical setting lasts but eight measures in a semipredictable and appealing four-part harmonization. The rhythmic substructure is also carved out of the same basic pattern. For the three settings in quadruple meter, the core two-measure pattern that surfaces for each phrase and line of text follows the pattern *short-short-short-short | long—long*. The one setting in triple meter has an equally simple pattern that recurs four times as well, running *long-short | long-short | long-short | loooong*.

Slight variants of this text and musical setting resurface in other locations, such as San Juan Bautista Ms. 1, on page 111 (plate 130 in WPA item 45). Its lyrics begin, "Dios te salve Reyna Maria" (May God save you, Mary-Queen), and the table of contents identifies this piece by the title "Salve Regina a 4 voces." This same tune and harmonic setting—in an abridged version—appear in an 1803 manuscript from the Convento San Francisco de Tarija in Bolivia, demonstrating that the Franciscans took this setting with them all across the Americas. Its importance in daily life is emphasized by the heading at the top of this musical sheet. It reads: "Salve, que se canta a tres vozes todos los días para dar principio a la Santa Misión" (The *Salve* that is sung in three-part harmony every day, in order to begin the day at the Holy Mission [of Tarija]).[21]

That the piece was a staple in mission life for well over a century and that it enjoyed fame in the rest of the Hispano-American world is borne out by several documents, such as the program for graduation ceremonies at the Sisters of Charity School in Los Angeles on 25 June 1858. Six sisters (three of whom were Spaniards) had arrived two years earlier, on 6 January 1856, and established a school for their young wards. They formed a choir from the 170 young ladies enrolled at their institution, and we can gather the breadth of their repertoire by the music they sang at their graduation, including such pieces as "Gaude Virgo," "Ave Sanctissima," W. W. Wallace's "It Is Better Far to Speak Softly," W. E. Hickson's "O Come, Come Away," and "Dios te salve María"—the same song that is written out (in a variant form) in San Juan Bautista Ms. 1.[22] Robert Stevenson provides a facsimile of the printed tune of "Dios te salve Maria" and four stanzas on page 59 of his article "Music in Southern California: A Tale of Two Cities." Yet another document reinforcing the wide dissemination of this song is the Yorba manuscript at the Bancroft Library.[23] Although written out in 1934, the preface to this volume provides a fascinating account of the booklet's contents and traces the heritage of its material back to recollections of Don Benancio de Ríos, who wisely began to scribble down the lyrics to the repertoire of the California missions in 1864 as taught to him by his aging father, Don Santiago de Ríos, who served as cantor at the San Juan Capistrano Mission from around 1840 to 1870.[24] Although the manuscript records no tunes whatsoever, the Yorba manuscript is particularly useful in reconstructing the complete text of the piece as it was passed down through successive generations in the missions.

In the Yorba manuscript, it is not much of a stretch from song number 15, "dios te salbe Maria" (Hail Mary), to song number 18, "dios te salbe bella augrora" (Hail Mary, beautiful Dawn). Even closer is song number 27; this third example from the genre appears in the table of contents, catalogued as "dios te salbe birgen pura," whose title departs just a smidgen from the Durán choirbook text for "Salve Virgen pura." The lyrics here, however, are not just a fleeting quatrain as they are in the Durán choirbooks but instead continue for a seemingly endless stream of subsequent stanzas. On the surface, the protracted length of the lyrics would argue against group performance for the reasons already presented; when would a group of gun-toting soldiers have the time to learn and rehearse such a gargantuan text? Fortunately, the engrossing preface to the Yorba manuscript explains exactly how this could be achieved. The head cantor would sing a line of a text, after which the assembled congregation would repeat the text in a subsequent response. Thus, if even *one* person had committed the whole song to memory and could lead the group through the forest of words, the entire group could wend its way successfully through to the end. The preface to the Yorba manuscript is of inestimable importance due to its references to the origins of the mission music literature and the richly descriptive detail concerning its performance in daily life. Its opening paragraphs explain:

Origin and History of these ancient chants of Mission San Juan Capistrano / Origen e historia de estos cantos

All of the chants in this manuscript are in their original form as taught to the *indios neófitos* of this mission from 1775 to about 1840 by the Franciscan padres.

Many of them were composed in ancient Spain, and some in Mexico after 1530.

Aside from those which the padres themselves chanted during the Rosary, after Mass, & after requiem Masses for the dead or during the *alabanzas* for the month of May (such as *Bella Augrora* [sic], *Despedida, & Benir Pecadores*) but which were also chanted by laymen, these chants of praise to the Heavenly beings and songs of the *velorios* (wakes), (such as *Abe Maria Beninísima, En la cria de un ojo de Agua*, etc.) were usually led by the official *cantor* or chanter of the mission.

The *cantor* would sing the opening verse, which all present would then repeat. Thereupon he would sing the second verse and so on, each time being answered in unison by the congregation with the chorus.

This custom is still in full effect among the *paisanos* of San Juan Capistrano, especially at the *velorios* or wakes, which begin at 8 PM and do not end until the singing of the *Alba* (*l alba*) the following dawn.[25]

It seems reasonable, then, that the performance of the *Salve* that Serra briefly notes in his letter of 1770 could have been handily achieved by using the model described in the Yorba preface and by the musical snippets that were certainly known in the various California missions, at least in the early 1800s and probably earlier. A simple eight-measure loop (such as those in the Durán choirbooks) could have been repeated over and over to accommodate a lengthy *Salve* text in Castilian, such as those in the Yorba manuscript. At the founding of Monterey and the San Carlos Borromeo de Carmelo Mission in June 1770, either Serra or some other friar with a good ear and capable memory could have offered each line of text, in the same way that pastors "line-out" spirituals or gospel tunes in African

American churches in the South. Just as the call-and-response singing of the American South allowed "regular" folks (not just conservatory-trained experts) to participate in a profoundly rewarding musical experience, so the songs from early California resounded with similar musical strains. In this repertoire described by Serra and clarified by the later Franciscan documents, we discover friars, soldiers, and neophyte converts joining together in a singing tradition where a worthy tune, a good cantor, and simple practice of follow the leader made congregational singing a practicality instead of an impossible obstacle.

Pedro Cabot writes out an even simpler, more utilitarian rendition of the *Salve* in Santa Barbara Mission Doc. 4B. Cabot's exquisite and laser-precise handwriting records the lengthy text, the three voices sharing a single staff, but there are only two musical phrases that serve as the core material from start to finish. They are actually more intonation formulas than "composed melodies," since the opening harmony can be reiterated multiple times as needed to accommodate extra syllables in any particular line. The rather static nature of the phrases and the circling back over familiar musical territory in seemingly endless loops would make this setting a prime candidate for the *Salve* that was passed by word of mouth among sailors, soldiers, neophyte converts, ranchers, and other "regular" citizens of California who learned their music through the oral tradition, not erudite notation that required extensive training to read and understand.

Yet another rendition of the *Salve* crops up in California sources, and its setting is much more "user-friendly" than the plainchant version found in the *Liber Usualis*. Santa Clara Ms. 3 records a folklike melody in *canto figurado* style; it marches forward in a sturdy duple meter in the key of A minor.[26] Its notation is approximate, not rigorous, and quite a bit of rhythmic fudging is necessary with respect to note values to ensure that there are not distracting hiccups or truncations in certain measures. Although its stolid character makes it inherently appealing, its length and lack of melodic phrase repetitions make it an unlikely candidate for the *Salve* performed at the founding of Monterey. In addition, its Latin text disqualifies it from consideration, since Serra clearly states it was in the vernacular.

The *Te Deum*

A few further comments concerning Serra's description of the founding of Monterey are in order. He concludes his brief portrait of the day's ceremonies with a reference to the *Te Deum*, some litanies, and a "song of thanksgiving." The *Te Deum*, also known as the Song of Ambrose and Augustine or the Hymn of Thanksgiving, was one of the staples of Catholic liturgy and was of great importance as the concluding piece of a Matins service. In Mexico, in fact, the *Te Deum* would have been one of the most beloved and well-known selections in religious performance, since Matins was as important in New Spain as opera was in Baroque Naples or oratorio in Baroque England. Matins, in truth, was *the* primary form of large-scale spectacle and entertainment in Baroque Mexico.[27] In this context, it is not surprising to see it occupy an equally critical place in the pageantry and cer-emonial spectacle of the California missions.

In fact, even in the earliest days of California's mission period, the *Te Deum* was sung on almost any occasion of great joy and celebration. When the over-land de Anza expedition eventually reached its California destinations in 1776, the ecstatic friars welcomed their friends with the exuberant singing of the *Te Deum*. Concerning their arrival at San Luis Obispo, we are told:

> Too excited and eager to await its slow pace, Fathers Caballer and Mugártegui went out on the road to meet the caravan. On its arrival Father Figuer, vested with a cope, bearing a censer, and with a broad smile on his face, was awaiting the pilgrims at the church door. Amid peals of mission bells and volleys of musketry the whole colony entered the tem-ple chanting the *Te Deum*, "and thus our arrival was a matter of great and mutual joy."[28]

Similarly, the de Anza party's arrival at Monterey was met with festive celebration. Pedro Font's diary entry for 11 March 1776 reads:

> The Commander and I and some few others set out from the presidio of Monterey at four in the afternoon and, at five, arrived at the Mission San Carlos de Carmelo—marked on the map with the letter G—having trav-eled one long league southwest by south. Here the fathers—there were seven of them—received us, singing the *Te Deum*, with the peals of bells, and great rejoicing.[29]

In Serra's account of the founding of Monterey, he too recalls how he intoned the *Te Deum*, and he implies that the assembled friars (and maybe soldiers) par-ticipated in the singing as well. He recounts, "As a conclusion to the liturgical cel-ebration, standing up I intoned the *Te Deum Laudamus*; we sang it slowly, and solemnly, right to the end."[30]

So where are the music sources that might clarify what notes Serra and his Franciscan brethren sang? If we are to consider the various extant settings for the *Te Deum* in the California sources, we find considerable variety in style and per-formance practice, and most of them would have been practical for realization in the context of this propitious day in 1770. The monophonic version that seems most consistent with the common *Te Deum* that had been used for centuries is the one recorded in Santa Clara Ms. 3.[31] It is not so much "melodic" as formulaic, with repeated notes for the bulk of a textual line and then a handful of recurring melodic gestures that are used to close off the various verses. It is not unlike the two formulas for the *Te Deum* found in the *Liber Usualis*—the "Solemn Tone" formula on pages 1832–34, and the "Simple Tone," which appears on pages 1834–36. Interestingly, the California manuscript is a *combination* of the "Solemn Tone" and the "Simple Tone" rather than being a pure and discrete version of one or the other. The repetitive aspect of intoning formulas would have made performance by Serra's entourage a snap. A few performance cues are suggested by the notation as well. The sudden shift to text in all capital letters at the section "TE ERGO QUAE SUMUS...SANGUINE REDEMISTI" corresponds to the portion of the *Te Deum* where the participants are expected to kneel.[32] As the singers removed themselves back to their seats or to a standing position, the text itself resumes normal capitalization procedures where only the first word of a phrase receives a capital letter.

Another more luxuriant but equally plausible candidate for the *Te Deum* as heard in 1770 is the "*Te Deum* for Four Voices in the Fifth Tone and the Fourth Tone (Te Deum a 4 Vs 5° y 4° T°)" recorded in multiple California manuscripts, including versions written out by Father Narciso Durán on page 119 of his choirbook C-C-59 at the Bancroft Library and pages 84–85 in Santa Barbara Document 2 (see photo 3-4).[33]

As the title states, it is harmonized for four voices, but as we have seen in the polyphonic Psalm-tone formulas at the missions, this is similarly a series of chords in a formulaic pattern that allows the vocalists to sing in a fluid, speechlike rhythm, and simply pour in the appropriate text. The harmonic mold is infinitely flexible, capable of accommodating the many varied lines of the *Te Deum* (in exactly the

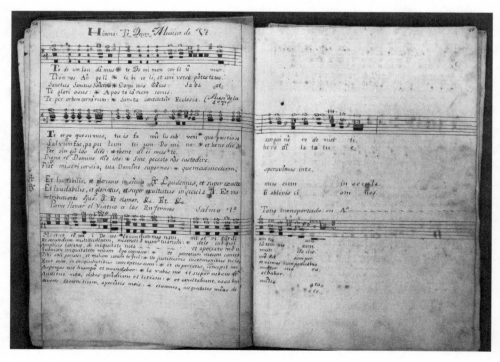

Photo 3-4 *Te Deum,* intoned in polyphony, Santa Barbara Mission Archive-Library, Document 2, pp. 84 and 85. (Permission to include this image courtesy of the SBMAL; photo by the author.)

same way that the monophonic formula of Santa Clara Ms. 3 works wonderfully in adapting to the mercurial changes in the text patterns). The Durán version only writes down the text for the odd-numbered verses. We can safely assume that this is yet another example of *alternatim* technique in which the odd-numbered verses are sung in the free-flowing rhythm of faubordon in polyphony, while the even-numbered verses are sung in another texture altogether, probably in intoned plainchant—such as the monophonic formulas and text found in Santa Clara Ms. 3—or in instrument interpolations that take the place of the excerpted verses. At the top of the page Durán writes down, "Vt y de La" (In *C* and in *A*) to facilitate finding instrumental passages in the key of C major or A minor that could then serve as appropriate substitutions for the even-numbered phrases without any jolting harmonic surprises. Like the Santa Clara Ms. 3 that had a visual cue of the division point where the performers knelt, so the Durán *Te Deum* also has a structural division at the point where the believers would genuflect before their Creator. At the line "Te ergo quae sumus," the old harmonic formula is discarded and a new one takes its place; it then is used as the mold for the subsequent phrases up through the end of the piece.

Yet another intriguing *Te Deum* surfaces in the Sancho materials in folder 77 of the WPA collection at the University of California at Berkeley, with the title page stating "*Te Deum* for Four Voices Alternating with the Voices of the Choir" (Te Deum a 4 voces alternando con las del coro) and immediately below it another subtitle, "*Te Deum* for Four Parts for the Use of Friar Jayme Pou. This passed into the possession of Father Friar Juan Bautista Sancho" (Te Deum â 4 del uso de Fr. Jayme Pou./ pasó al uso del Pᵉ Fr. juan Bau[tis]ta/ Sancho).[34] The folder contains four sheets for the four solo voices: a soprano, an alto, a tenor, and a bass. All phrases are in quadruple meter and strongly reflect mode 6 (as stated on the bass part), with a modern-sounding feeling of the key of F major. Whereas the other *Te Deum* versions we have considered set the odd-numbered verses, this particular rendition in WPA folder 77 has brief phrases, each slightly different from one another, that progressively wind through the even-numbered verses. As we have seen previously, polyphony was often performed one on a part in California mass settings, while the choir as a whole joined together for the monophonic *canto llano* or homophonic passages in *canto figurado*. Neither the intoned formula of Santa Clara Ms. 3 nor the four-part faubordon versions of the *Te Deum* already discussed make very compatible companions for the phrases in WPA folder 77; although the folder's even-numbered verses could be smoothly folded into the creases of the odd-numbered verses in the other *Te Deum* settings, their modes or "keys" are not really compatible.[35]

The *Alabado*

The last piece that Serra includes at the founding of San Carlos Borromeo de Carmelo was the *acción de gracias*, or "prayer of thanksgiving." Although not mentioned by its most common name, it is probably the beloved *Alabado* (song of praise) that was one of the most widespread genres of the period across Latin America. Upon rising at daybreak or retiring at dusk, no piece was more central to daily life in California than the *Alabado*. The first recording of an *Alabado* was made at the turn of the twentieth century by Father Alexander Buckler of Fernando Cárdenas of the Santa Inés Mission, better known by his nickname "Fernandito," when the singer was eighty-four. Charles Francis Saunders and J. Smeaton Chase describe the recording as metrically fluid and not at all regular—but it is hard to know whether it is a characteristic of the song itself or merely the flexibility of time that resulted from an octogenarian singer.[36]

Father Owen da Silva writes an engaging summary of the *Alabado* and provides critical information regarding the circumstances of the Fernandito recording. Da Silva states:

> Foremost among the old hymns is this one, the *Alabado*. It is mentioned in almost every historic account of California and the Southwest. It was sung by padre and soldier, colonist and neophyte, in church, at home, in the field, and on the trail. The padres often used it in place of the *Te Deum*.
>
> The hymn consists of twenty-four stanzas praising the Holy Trinity, the Blessed Sacrament, the Virgin Mary, the Angels and Saints....
>
> From Father Font we know that the *Alabado* was sung to the same tune at all the Missions. We believe that the present version [that da Silva prints in his volume] is the one referred to by that exact padre, and therefore, the original one. The late J. Smeaton Chase recorded it at Mission Santa Inés more than twenty-five years ago. The singer was Fernandito. We have also heard an old Edison home recording of Fernandito singing the *Alabado* at the home of Miss Mamie Goulet in Santa Bárbara. Miss Goulet and her uncle, the Rev. Alexander Buckler, were custodians of Old Mission Santa Inés for many years, and shortly before Fernandito's death in 1919, Miss Goulet was happily inspired to record the voice of the last of the Mission singers.[37]

One enigmatic segment of an *Alabado* appears in the Sancho materials of the WPA collection at the University of California at Berkeley.[38] The entire folio is a mishmash of musical ingredients, almost all of them small and fragmentary. This particular tidbit is written in the bass clef in triple meter in the key of F major; the five measures are written at the bottom of the page and upside down from the rest of the sheet's music (except for another brief excursion, "O dulcisimo jesu yo te doy mi corazon," on line 7). Its tune bears no perceptible relationship to the melody as sung by Fernandito and subsequently notated by da Silva, nor to the tune indicated by Robert Stevenson or by Saunders and Chase.[39] At one point in time there had been an *Alabado* in a choirbook at the San Juan Bautista Mission, but the book apparently has been lost, making it frustratingly impossible to compare it with the other notated versions of the *Alabado* to see how they correspond or differ.[40]

In all of the Hispano-American world, the *Alabado* was as much a part of daily life as sunrise or sunset. Leonardo Waisman's research on the Chiquitos missions of Paraguay during the eighteenth century demonstrates that the *Alabado* and Rosary were sung an hour before sunset at the evening service.[41] Philipp Segesser von Brunegg describes nearly the same tradition as practiced in Sonora and Arizona in the first half of the eighteenth century, clarifying that the end of the day was marked by the singing of the *Salve Regina*, the Rosary, the Litany, and the *Alabado*.[42] Texas, too, was part of this universal practice in the Hispano-American world. John Koegel informs us that the priest at Nuestra Señora del Rosario de los Cujanes (located near Goliad on the Gulf of Mexico in Texas) would call the converts together on Saturdays and lead them in reciting the Rosary and singing the *Alabado*.[43] Its popularity in that region has been long-lived. Anna Blanche McGill, writing in 1938, affirms that the *Alabado* and *Alabanza* were still sung throughout the Texas and the American Southwest.[44] Kristin Dutcher Mann provides a panoramic view of the *Alabado*'s usage, taking us to Dolores Mission in Sonora in 1687 and later presenting a strong case linking Fray Antonio Margil de Jesús's *Alabado* from the early 1700s with the one brought to California by Pedro Font and the de Anza expedition.[45] John Donald Robb, Thomas J. Steele, Vicente T. Mendoza, and Virginia R. R. de Mendoza also explore the *Alabados* that permeated the folkloric cultures of Mexico and New Mexico. Unfortunately, there is no irrefutable proof that would link the texts and tunes collected by Robb and Mendoza to mission period California. Nevertheless, it is quite possible that some of the versions that Robb and the Mendozas collected were transmitted to Alta California through the oral tradition even though they left no solid paper trail.[46]

In the missions of Baja California, the *Alabado* was sung several times at key moments of the day.[47] Using the writings of Miguel de Barco as source material, Harry Crosby details the ritual and regimen of daily events as they unfolded each day at the San José de Comandú Mission. From the rising of the sun until dusk, the *Alabado* was the most common recurring element marking the key points of the day, as Crosby relates:

> As the neophytes entered [the church after rising], they broke up and sat in four separate groups: men, women, boys, and girls. They joined in prayer and proclaimed the Blessed Virgin. The *Alabado* was sung, first by men, then by women, then by both. Singing was led by two neophyte women, Inés and Chepa, designated as *cantoras* (singers) and picked for strong voices and musical ability. At other times, the *cantoras* probably helped in teaching the young to sing.
>
> Worshippers whose work was needed to start the mission day rose from devotions and began their chores.... People who had no immediate duties stayed in church and took part in the daily Mass. That finished, they said prayers, sang the *Alabado* again, and went to take breakfast.[48]

Crosby then explores the various chores and tasks that occupied the men and women after breakfast and continues by describing the schooling of the children in sacred instruction, including the singing of the *Alabado* yet again:

At ten in the morning, the sexton again tolled the bells, and the boys and girls who were being prepared for catechism went to church. Segregated by sex, they chanted the catechism in unison, they sang the *Alabado*, which they were bade to perform "with proper feeling."

....

At midday, the bell was sounded anew, and all knelt, prayed to the Virgin, and sang the *Alabado* one time through. Then a noon meal was dished out....After the meal, everyone took a siesta until the hour of two, then work resumed. At five, the bell was tolled, and boys and girls again went to church to recite the *Angelus* and the catechism. At the end, they took turns singing the *Alabado*.[49]

The schedule as told by Miguel de Barco is reconfirmed by other writers familiar with activities in the Baja California missions. Father Sebastián Sistiaga captures the events of mission life at San Ignacio, Baja California, in 1744: "Daily, on arising, which is quite early, they direct their thoughts to Jesus Christ and His Most Blessed mother by singing the *Alabado* that the Spaniards recite."[50] Father Nicolás Tamaral relates the day's conclusion, a ritual that we have seen described by the other writers of the time:

After eating [the evening supper], all go to the church and, with the padre, recite the invocation and responses of the Rosary and Litany. This is done then and not before, because everyone is free of duties and able to pay full attention to his most important devotions. After chanting the Rosary and singing the *Alabado* in the church, all leave; the men with their temastián and the women with their temastiana, to totally separate places where they practice the catechism and then retire.[51]

Alta California was no different. Upon Serra's arrival in this new frontier, the *Alabado* was one of the first pieces he would teach at each new outpost. He taught this popular gem to the neophytes at the San Gabriel Mission in the 1770s, and Engelhardt tells us that as early as September 1773 the Native Americans at Rincón had learned the tune from Serra and his brethren.[52] Other padres taught the *Alabado* to new converts with equal vigor. The Franciscan Chronicler (writing between 1844 and 1850) explains that the *Alabado* as it was sung at the Santa Inés Mission had been taught to the neophytes at the Santa Barbara Mission by Father Lasuén.[53] Father Tapís also considered the work to be essential repertoire, as is evidenced by the multiple copies that exist in his hand.[54]

In one of the most graphic accounts of an early encounter between the Spanish newcomers and the native Californians, the chaplain on the *San Carlos*, Vicente de Santa María, details the various events of 23 August 1775 as the members of the ship and the Huimen and Huchiun peoples of the San Francisco Bay exchanged songs, dances, and ideas.[55] As with Serra's approach to first encounters, so the crew of the *San Carlos* used the attractive and theologically grounded aspects of the *Alabado* to begin the attempt at conversion. He writes:

Two reed boats were seen approaching in which were five Indians. As soon as the Captain was informed of this, he directed that signs be made inviting them aboard, to which they promptly responded by coming, which was what they wanted to do. Leaving their boats, they climbed aboard fearlessly. They were in great delight, marveling at the structure of the ship, their eyes fixed most of all on the rigging.... But what most captivated and pleased them was the sound of the ship's bell, which was purposely ordered to be struck so we could see what effect it had on ears that had never heard it. It pleased the Indians so much that while they were on board they went up to it from time to time to sound it themselves....

Throughout the time the Indians were on board, we tried to attract them to Christian practices, now having them cross themselves or getting them to repeat the *Pater Noster* and *Ave María*, now chanting the *Alabado*, which they followed so distinctly that it was astonishing with what facility they pronounced the Spanish.[56]

Immediately following the Spaniards' singing of *Alabado*, it was the Native Americans' turn to return the artistic gift with their own cultural offering. Vicente de Santa María tells of the chief's dancing on the ship's deck and reveals Santa María's insatiable curiosity in trying to learn as many Huimen and Huchiun words as he could from the afternoon's adventures. He continues:

The Indian chieftain, less reserved than the others, showed how much pleased he was at our warmth of feeling; more than once he took to dancing and singing on the deckhouse. I paid close attention to their utterances that correspond with their actions that their language went like this: *pire* means, in our language "sit down"; *intomene*, "what is your name?"[57]

The Franciscan chaplain continues with his thorough recollections of the days that followed; on one occasion he sails to shore in the launch in order to continue his developing relationship with the native residents and to delve further into their language and customs. On shore, the friar and native peoples once again exchange songs and dancing; interestingly, when Vicente de Santa María is asked to sing a song, it is the *Alabado* that comes to mind for the chaplain's performance. He depicts the scene by explaining:

As the Indians remained seated on the shore I could not bear to lose the rest of the afternoon when I might be communicating with them; so, setting out in the dugout, I landed and remained alone with the eight Indians so that I might communicate with them in greater peace. The dugout went back to the ship, and at the same time they all crowded around me and, sitting by me, began to sing with an accompaniment of two rattles that they had brought with them. As they finished the song, all of them were shedding tears, which I wondered at for not knowing the reason. When they were through singing, they handed me the rattles and, by signs, asked me also to sing. I took the rattles and, to please them, began to sing them the *Alabado* (although they would not understand it), to which they were most attentive and indicated that it pleased them.[58]

The fact that Vicente de Santa María could fit the *Alabado* into the steady rhythmic beat of the rattles implies a regularity of pulse and probably meter that is not evident in the elastic and irregular aspects of the Fernandito recording.

The Rosary is not nearly as prevalent in written sources as the *Alabado*, but that is owing largely to its life as part of the oral tradition rather than a written one. Nevertheless, a particularly beautiful setting of the Rosary appears on the final pages of Santa Barbara Document 1 and of the San Juan Bautista Manuscript 2, arranged for four voices in colored notation on a single staff—as is so typical of the California polyphonic repertoire. A single voice initiates the piece with the opening phrase "Dios te salve Maria," after which the other voices chime in at "llena eres de gracia." The gentle pulsation in quadruple meter makes it an easily memorized and fetching gem.[59]

That the *Alabado* and Rosary retained their importance in the daily routine of mission, rancho, and pueblo life in Alta California is well documented, beginning with Serra's and Palóu's descriptions of the founding ceremonies at each new mission and continuing up through the recollections of Antonio Coronel almost a century later. Palóu describes Serra's weekly habits in his *History of the Life and Apostolic Works of the Venerable Father Friar Junípero Serra*, indicating the *Alabado* and the recitation of the Crown of the Immaculate Conception of Blessed Virgin (i.e., the Rosary) were on the agenda every afternoon (at least during Lent, and Palóu may even imply that it was the expectation throughout the liturgical year). Palóu states, "Every Sunday during Lent he did not content himself solely with the doctrinal discussion during High Mass, but instead during the afternoon after the recitation of the Crown of the Immaculate Conception of the Blessed Virgin and the singing of the *Alabado*, he preached for them a moral sermon."[60] Palóu alludes to the critical role the *Alabado* occupied in Serra's activities during the Feast of the Immaculate Conception. Once again, the reciting of the Rosary and the singing of the *Alabado* are conjoined in the same celebration:

> The introduction to the devotion of Our Lady, Mother Mary—and especially with respect to her Immaculate Conception—was dedicated with the same care, especially making ready for celebrating her with the nine-day devotion, which the entire town attended. In addition, the Mass was sung on the day of this great festival, and he [Serra] preached the sermon, and afterward the *Gozos* [or sung poems] in honor of the Immaculate Conception were intoned. Every Sunday in the afternoon the Crown of the Mother of Mercy was said, finishing it with the *Alabado* and the poems of praise that were sung. And to better honor these praises, the Reverend Father placed an order from Mexico for a stunning statue of the most tender Lady,

placed on her platform, they paraded her through the town every Saturday evening, illuminated by lanterns while singing the Crown of Our Lady.[61]

Palóu's last statement highlights the importance of Marian processions on Saturday; the Hispano-American world had long celebrated Mass in honor of the Blessed Virgin on Saturdays, and California was simply another outpost venerating this Marian tradition.[62]

Engelhardt's description of activities at the San Antonio Mission reconfirms this pattern of a typical day with the reverberating strains of the *Alabado* and *Salve*—following the same regimen described by Serra and Palóu. After dawn, all would gather in the church, recite the Doctrine, and sing Mass. Then each neophyte and friar would go to his respective chores. At day's end, the bell was rung to announce the reconvening of all at the church, where they would sing the *Salve* and the *Alabado*.[63] Chroniclers of later life in California, such as Alfred Robinson and José del Carmen Lugo, reveal that whether *californios* were on the rancho or in the mission, the day's activities customarily drew to a close through the veneration of Mary.[64] This practice that Serra and his fellow friars had introduced in 1769 with the singing of the *Alabado* and the *Salve*, accompanied with the reciting of the Rosary, continued without interruption even through the turmoil and uncertainties of secularization and the Mexican period of the 1830s and 1840s. In his *Tales of California*, Antonio Coronel tells the reader of the family routine of singing the *Alabado* "in chorus" each morning, and other sacred hymns throughout the day:

> Religious education was observed in all homes. Before dawn each morning, a hymn of praise [i.e., the *Alabado*] was sung in chorus; at noon, prayers; at about 6:00 P.M. and before going to bed, a Rosary and another hymn [the *Salve*?]. I saw this on several occasions at balls or dances when the clock struck eight: the father of the family stopped the music and said the Rosary with the guests, after which the party continued. I saw the same thing sometimes at roundups, when the old men stopped work to pray at the accustomed hours, joined by all present.[65]

Alba (and *Alabanza*)

Yet another work closely related to the *Alabado*, serving more or less as a kind of substitute during the morning routine, is the *Alba* or dawn song. Ever since Owen da Silva's publication of the *Alba* in 1941, its beguiling melody and lyrics have made it one of the most often recorded and performed compositions from the mission period.[66] Although da Silva lops off the text after four stanzas, the invaluable Yorba manuscript preserves a total of twelve. When Don Benancio de Ríos wrote down the lyrics as recited to him by his old father, Santiago de Ríos, in 1864, in many instances he captured the *sound* of the words and syllables but misspelled or misunderstood the actual text.[67] De Ríos describes the singing of *velorios* or wakes that consume the entire night with music making until the rising of the sun and the singing of the *Alba*.[68]

So, what did the music sound like? Serendipitously, Ramón Yorba sang "El Alba" for Mrs. W. G. Hubbard, and that tune was subsequently published by Charles Francis Saunders and Father St. John O'Sullivan in their rather sentimental but informative *Capistrano Nights: Tales of a California Mission Town*. Between the lyrics (found in the Yorba manuscript at the Bancroft Library) and the tune (Ramón Yorba's tune found in *Capistrano Nights*), we have the critical elements for a convincing reconstruction of the *Alabado* as sung in the California missions.[69]

Saunders and O'Sullivan go on to tell of the *Alba*'s strains that filled the air on any given morning in California missions and towns. They provide several accounts of elderly Californians who remembered singing the *Alba* when they were tiny children earlier in the nineteenth century:

> Doña Balbineda, who was born here in the mission building, says that her mother remembered how the rough voices of the soldiers in the *cuartel*, or guardhouse, could be heard joining in it just as day broke; and Doña María has told me that when she was just a little girl on her father's ranch, it was the practice of the family to sing it every weekday morning *muy temprano*, as she expressed it, very early. At the first sign of light her father's voice resounded through the house, calling, "*Levántense, muchachos, y asiéntense á rezar*—rise, children, and sit up to pray!" Thereupon all the family would sit up in bed and repeat the angelus—*el angel del Señor anunció a María*— and as soon as this was concluded the *Alba* was started. There was no getting out of it; if any did not awake, they were made to awake; and the little María, who was the baby of the family, would thrust her head back into the pillow, immediately after prayer and song were ended, for another nap.[70]

Yet another moving account of this tradition is told by Don Antonio Colonel to Mrs. Helen Hunt Jackson, who published his recollections in 1883. Don Antonio ruminates:

> It was the custom of the town [Los Angeles] in all of the families of the early settlers, for the oldest member of the family—oftenest it was grandfather or grandmother—to rise every morning at the rising of the morning star and at once to strike up a hymn. At the first note every person in the house would rise, or sit up in bed and join in the song. From house to house, street to street, the singing spread; and the volume of musical sound swelled, until it was as if the whole town sang.[71]

Ms. Jackson further explains that the *Cántico del Alba (Morning Hymn to Mary)* and *Alabado* "were heard everywhere in California, in mission enclosures, from the courtyards of the ranchos, and in the streets of village and pueblo." She equates the *Cántico del Alba* with the "Morning Hymn to Mary." Saunders and O'Sullivan have a slightly different tack, equating the *Alabanza* (not the *Alba*) with the "Praises of

Mary." In short, many of these terms (*Alabado, Alabanza, Alba, Salve*) appear to have areas of overlap that cannot be divided by hard-and-fast, concrete walls of separation. In all of these, short melodies repeat to wend their way through a dozen or more stanzas. *Alternatim* performance would have provided an opportunity for varied sonorities. One of the priests told Saunders and O'Sullivan of an occasion at Serra's church (i.e., Carmel Mission), in which the children and adult cantors gave an ethereal performance of the "Alabanzas de Maria," alternating phrases antiphonally, the boy-sopranos calling out and the men-baritones answering. The vocal contrast must have been further enhanced by the physical separation of the two groups in the sanctuary. Saunders and O'Sullivan relate the story:

> The Father explained that there was to be a special service in the Serra church that evening, in which the children were to sing.... The church was dimly lit except where the candles lit up the beautiful altar. The service was short, made up in part of the singing of *Alabanzas de María*, or Praises of Mary, which consisted, as I remember, entirely of unaccompanied chants by the children, who sang alternately with chanters located in the body of the church, one group singing after another, the lovely music all the more appealing in the children's endearing treble. It was the devotion of *el Mes de Mayo*—the Month of May.

Notes

1. Much has been written on Serra, so a biographical summary here seems unnecessary. For those desiring more information on Serra's life, accomplishments, and personality, I refer the interested reader to two immensely rewarding books: Francisco Palóu, *Francisco Palóu's Life and Apostolic Labors of the Venerable Father Junípero Serra, Founder of the Franciscan Missions of California*, trans. by C. Scott Williams, introduction and notes by George Wharton James (Pasadena, Calif.: George Wharton James, 1913); and Maynard J. Geiger, O.F.M., *The Life and Times of Fray Junípero Serra, O.F.M., or The Man Who Never Turned Back (1713–1784)*, 2 vols. (Washington, D.C.: Academy of American Franciscan History, 1959).

2. Francis J. Weber has authored several important studies that help the scholar or interested reader to find primary source material regarding almost any aspect of past life in California, including some of the music traditions covered in this chapter. Weber provides a useful checklist of travelers who wrote firsthand accounts of their experiences in California, and many of those recollections describe musical events. See Weber, "The California Missions and Their Visitors," *The Americas*, vol. 24, no. 4 (April 1968), 319–36. Also, for those wishing to navigate through the available primary source material in California, Weber's research guide is particularly useful; consult "Archival Sources for the History of Religion in California. Part I: Catholic Sources," *Southern California Quarterly*, vol. 72, no. 2 (Summer 1990), 157–72.

3. "Para dar la comunión al capitán y soldados que desde Santa María havía ido a confessar para cumplimiento del annuo precepto, y prevenirse para la expedición; y se dize haver sido aquella la 1ª misa, por que ahunque estuvo allí en su viage el Padre Jesuíta Link como consta de su diario, dizen los soldados que lo acompañavan, que no celebró allí. En aquel xacal pues se dispuso el altar, se pusieron los soldados con sus cueras y adargas sobre las armas y con todos los asseos de la santa pobresa, celebré mi misa en aquel día tan grande con el consuelo de ser la 1ª de las que ya se havían de continuar, con la permanencia de aquella nueva Misión de San Fernando, que desde aquel día comenzava, la que mientras duró solemnizaron las muy repetidas descargas de las armas de los soldados, supliendo por esta vez los humos de la pólvora, por los de incienso que no podíamos ofrecer, por que no lo teníamos. Y como no havía

más cera que la que ardía que era un cabito de vela que me hallé y el cerillo del padre, fué por aquel día la misa única y la oyó el padre con los demás en cumplimiento del precepto. Después cantamos *Veni Creator Spiritus* de 3ª. El concurso lo hizimos nosotros, los soldados y los indios neófitos, que nos acompañavan, sin que asomase gentil alguno, quizás asustados con tantos truenos." Junípero Serra, *Writings of Junípero Serra*, edited by Antonine Tibesar, O.F.M., 4 vols. (Washington, D.C.: Academy of Franciscan History, 1955), vol. 1, pp. 60–61. Note that I have made two small corrections to Tibesar's translation of this passage. He incorrectly translates the term *soldados* as the singular "soldier" as opposed to the plural "soldiers" in the passage, "there was only one Mass, at which the Father assisted together with the soldier[s]," and he fails to address the numeral "3ª" after "Veni Creator." I strongly suspect the numeral was an "8" as opposed to a "3," since this sequence is in mode 8, and it was customary to identify a piece by its modal properties. This same event is covered in Geiger's *Life and Times of Fray Junípero Serra, vol.* 1, p. 218. Other sources thoroughly treating this founding include Rose Marie Beebe and Robert M. Senkewicz, *Lands of Promise and Despair: Chronicles of Early California, 1535–1846* (Santa Clara, Calif.: Santa Clara University; Berkeley: Heydey Books, 2001), 137–41; and Alexander Forbes, *California: A History of Upper and Lower California from the First Discovery to the Present Time… (1839)*, introduction by Herbert Ingram Priestley (San Francisco: John Henry Nash, 1937; reprint, New York: Kraus Reprint, 1972), 62–63.

4. "El dia siguiente, 14 de Mayo (como queda dicho) y primero de Pascua del Espíritu Santo, se dió principio á la fundación.…Y habiendo cantado la Misa primera, hizo una fervorosa Plática de la venida del Espíritu Sancto, y establecimiento de la Mision. Concluido el Santo Sacrificio (que se celebró sin mas luces que las de un cerillo, y otro pequeño cabo de vela, por no haber llegado las cargas en que venia la cera) cantó el *Veni Creator Spiritus*, supliendo la falta de Organo, y demás instrumentos músicos, los continuos tiros de la Tropa, que disparó durante la función; y el humo de la pólvora, al del incienso que no tenian." Francisco Palóu, *Relación histórica de la vida y apostólicas tareas del venerable Padre Fray Junípero Serra, y las misiones que fundó en la California Septentrional, y nuevos establecimientos de Monterey* (Mexico City: Don Felipe de Zúñiga y Ontiveros, 1787, facsimile ed. in March of America Facsimile Series, No. 49, ([Ann Arbor, Michigan]: University Microfilms, 1966), 70.

5. In the Roman rite, *Veni Creator Spiritus* is associated with the dedication of a church, which explains its importance in the founding days of the various missions.

6. For a thorough discussion of the 1780 code of regulations developed by the Franciscans at the Colegio Apostólico de San Fernando, consult chapter 22 of Geiger's *Life and Times of Junípero Serra*, esp. 166–67. Significantly, *Veni Creator Spiritus* had a long tradition of being used at the inauguration of new sacred worship spaces. For instance, the ceremony to open the new cathedral in Lima on 19 October 1625 began with the pealing of the bells, followed by a rendition of *Veni Creator Spiritus*. "Comenzó la orquesta a entonar el himno *Veni Creator* y después las letanías," and then they celebrated "con mucha mússica [*sic*] de canto de órgano." See Andrés Sas Orchassal, *La música en la Catedral de Lima durante el Virreinato*, vol. 1, *Primera Parte: Historia General*, Colección de Documentos para la Historia de la Música en el Perú (Lima: Universidad Nacional Mayor de San Marcos and Casa de Cultura del Perú, 1971), 28–29.

7. Choirbook C-C-68:2 in the Bancroft Library, p. 112bis. The handwriting and the gluing together of two sheets into single folios (as seen in this manuscript) match perfectly the handwriting and construction of Santa Clara Ms. 3; both of these choirbooks were prepared by Florencio Ibáñez.

8. The Gregorian model can be found in the *Liber Usualis*, 885–86.

9. It is worth noting here that California sources alter significantly the renditions of sequences that historically had been performed as paired phrases (*a-a', b-b', c-c', d-d'*, etc.) and instead couch the very same words but in strophic settings (*a-a'-a"-a"'-a""*, etc.). Some sources offer a variant of the strophic form where a contrasting pair of phrases come back repeatedly in *alternatim* style so that all of the odd-numbered phrases are set to a musical phrase *a* and the even-numbered phrases are set to a contrasting musical phrase *b*, resulting in the pattern *a-b, a'-b', a"-b", a"'-b"', a""-b""*, etc. Therefore, in California mission tradition, there is a marked similarity between "hymns" and "sequences," for the two genres can share structural features. In both cases, they usually alternate phrases between two opposing and contrasting phrases. For text settings in *alternatim* style, consult *Veni Sancte Spiritus* (Santa Clara Ms. 4,

p. 15; Santa Clara Ms. 3, p. 34; Bancroft choirbook C-C-82:2, p. 57; Bancroft choirbook C-C-59, p. 27; WPA folder 54); *Dies irae* (Bancroft choirbook C-C-59, p. 67); *Lauda Sion Salvatorem* (Bancroft choirbook C-C-82:2, p. 67; San Juan Bautista Ms. 1, p. 29 (plate 48 in WPA item 45); Santa Clara Ms. 3, p. 48 and pp. B–Bv; Serra choirbook M.0612, fol. 12v); *Victimae paschali laudes* (Santa Clara Ms. 4, p. 10; Bancroft choirbook C-C-59, p. 19); and *Vexilla Regis* (Bancroft choirbook C-C-59, p. 17).

10. For an excellent retelling of the events surrounding the early expeditions to California and the founding of the San Diego Mission, consult David J. Weber, *The Spanish Frontier in North America* (New Haven: Yale University Press, 1992), 243–44.

11. "Llegó el día, se formó capilla, y altar, junto a la misma barranquita y encino, todo immediato a la playa donde se dize haverse celebrado en los principios de la centuria passada. Veníamos a un mismo tiempo al parage por distinctos rumbos los de mar, y los [de] tierra, nosotros cantando en la lancha las divinas alabanzas, y los señores de tierra en sus corrazones.

Llegados y recibidos con repiques de las campanas colgadas del enzino, dispuesto todo lo necesario haviéndome revestido de alva y estola, incado con todos ante el altar entoné el hymno *Veni Creator Spiritus*, el qual concluído, e invocada por este medio la asistencia del Divino Espíritu para quanto ívamos a executar, bendixe sal y agua, y nos encaminamos todos a una cruz grande prevenida, y tendida en el suelo, la que entre todos levantamos, canté su bendición, la fixamos, y adoramos todos con ternura de nuestros corazones, roció con agua bendita aquellos campos, y levantado assí el estandarte del Rey del Cielo, se erigieron los de nuestro cathólico monarca, celebrándose uno y otro con altas vozes de *Viva la Fe Viva el Rey*, que acompañavan, repiques de campanas, y tiros de fusileria, y cañones del barco.

Luego hizimos al pie de la cruz el entierro de un diffunto marinero calafate el único que ha muerto en este barco en esta 2ª expedición.

Y concluydo comensé la missa cantada, que llevó después del evangelio su sermón y toda fué muy acompañada de cañonasos. Concluída y despuesta la casulla cantamos todos la salve en romance ante la bellísima imagen de Nuestra Señora que ocupava el altar y la dió el Ilustrísimo Señor Visitador General para esta función *cum onere* de debolvérsela después, como lo haré assí que marche el barco.

Y para conclusión, puesto en pie, entoné el *Te Deum Laudamus*, que pausada, y solemnemente seguimos hasta su fin que se dió con los versos y oraciones de la Santíssima Trinidad, de Nuestra Señora, del Santíssimo San Joseph, patrón de la expedición, San Carlos, que lo es de este puerto, presidio y misión y la de acción de gracias."

The core of this translation is by Antonine Tibesar, from his *Writings of Junípero Serra*, vol. 1, p. 169. However, in a few instances Tibesar slightly alters Serra's original statements, painting a slightly different picture of the event. In these specific locations, I have made the following modifications and alterations to Tibesar's core.

In Serra's letter, he observes, "Veníamos a un mismo tiempo al parage por distinctos rumbos los de mar, y los [de] tierra." Serra does not limit himself to *two* directions, as Tibesar translates, and the term *rumbos* does not limit the procession to only *one* path from the sea and *one* path from the land, but instead implies that there are several directions simultaneously, i.e., *those* from the sea and *those* from the land. Tibesar's translation depicts an almost linear event, whereas Serra's text allows for clusters of events to have been occurring from multiple angles. I therefore have changed Tibesar's text from "Two processions from different directions converged at the same time on the spot, one from the sea, and one from the land expedition" to "We came to the same spot at the same time from different directions, those from the sea and those from the land."

In the ensuing paragraph, Serra continues "Y levantado assí el estandarte del Rey del Cielo, se erigieron los de nuestro cathólico monarca, celebrándose uno y otro con altas vozes de *Viva la Fe Viva el Rey*." The passage in question states that there is one flag for the King of Heaven, but *several* for the King of Spain. This latter reference "*los* de nuestro cathólico monarca" is unmistakably plural. I therefore have altered Tibesar's translation from "And thus, after raising aloft the standard of the King of Heaven, we unfurled the flag of our Catholic Monarch likewise" to "And thus, after raising aloft the standard of the King of Heaven, we unfurled the flags of our Catholic Monarch likewise." The potential for a more impressive and colorful display is allowed by Serra's original description, for the unfurling of multiple flags (not just two) to the accompaniment of cannon shots and the volleys from their rifles could have been prolonged and more spectacular in effect.

I made several other changes to Tibesar's translation to clarify Serra's musical observations. Near the end of the quoted passage Serra observes, "Concluída y despuesta la casulla cantamos todos la salve en romance ante la bellísima imagen de Nuestra Señora." Tibesar translates the phrase as "all together we sang in Spanish the *Salve Regina*, in harmony, in front of the wonderful painting of Our Lady." Nowhere is there a mention of "harmony," so I have removed this qualifier. Also, Serra does not mention the "Salve Regina" but instead only the "Salve." There are other possibilities. I therefore have translated Serra's original designation of "la salve en romance" as "the *Salve* in the Spanish language" without any potentially misleading additions to either harmony or the Marian antiphon *Salve Regina*.

Tibesar also departs slightly from Serra's original when translating the passage "entoné el *Te Deum Laudamus*...con los versos y oraciones de la Santíssima Trinidad." Tibesar translates the passage as "I intoned the *Te Deum Laudamus*;...with the responses [*sic*] and prayers to the Most Holy Trinity." Tibesar's decision to translate *versos* as "responses" is a misleading alteration. The latter term has its own variable meanings, indicating structural aspects and also performance practice, whereas *versos* merely implies the verses of the text. I therefore have replaced Tibesar's "responses" with "verses" in the appropriate location.

Before abandoning the discussion of this passage, it should be noted that Maynard Geiger provides another useful translation in his study, *The Life and Times of Junípero Serra*, vol. 1, pp. 247–48. It is meritorious and fluid, and in some instances is more accurate that Tibesar. For instance, Geiger captures the ambiguity regarding the varied directions of the initial approaches from land and sea instead of lining them up in singular directions as Tibesar does. Also, Geiger captures the sense of Serra's text with respect to the flags of the monarch, as opposed to a single flag for the monarch. Even Geiger's translation, though, has a few limitations that should also be addressed. He completely expunges the passage concerning the burial of the soldier with no indication that there has been material removed from the excerpt. He similarly alters the reference to the "Salve" to "Salve Regina" and in so doing makes a clarification based on assumptions rather than evidence. He translates "imagen de la Virgen" as a "statue" of the Virgin as opposed to a "painting," which is Tibesar's interpretation of the word *imagen*. The Spanish term *imagen* can designate either; until further evidence is unearthed, it is wise to remain open to the possibility that Serra used either a painting or a sculpture at this mission's founding. Serra's text itself remains frustratingly ambiguous on this matter. Geiger states that they intone the *Te Deum*, "observing the pauses." In actuality, Serra's use of the adjective *pausada* refers to the measured and deliberate way that the work was sung, not the actual inclusion of "pauses." Thus, when Serra explains "entoné el *Te Deum Laudamus*, que pausada, y solemnemente seguimos hasta su fin," he is stating, "I intoned the *Te Deum Laudamus* that we sang and continued until its end in a solemn and *deliberate* manner."

12. The Carmel Mission possesses a fragment of an extremely old missionary Antiphonary with *Veni Creator Spiritus*. It is tempting to imagine this possibly being the source from which Serra and his followers sang at the founding of Carmel Mission. See photos B-43 and B-44 in appendix B, available online.

13. "On the following day, about twenty priests, with their president, were in attendance at the church to chant a *Te Deum*, assisted by thirty Indian musicians [i.e., instrumentalists] collected from the different musicians, together with an equal number of singers. Governor Sola, escorted by the late governor and all the officers of the staff and garrison, walked to the temple, and amidst the salutes of the artillery of the fort, and of the cavalry here stationed, partook in the solemn services, which ended with an eloquent and appropriate sermon by Fray Vicente." Hubert Howe Bancroft, *California Pastoral, 1769–1848*, vol. 34 of *The Works of Hubert Howe Bancroft* (San Francisco: San Francisco History Company, 1888), 421–22. Larry Warkentin provides an abbreviated summary of this same event (placing the year in 1815, whereas Bancroft places it in 1816) in "The Rise and Fall of Indian Music in the California Missions," *Latin American Music Review*, vol. 2, no. 1 (1981), 50. Warkentin provides the added information that the musicians were led by the neophyte "*José el Cantor*, the favorite pupil of Florencio Ibáñez."

14. Ratkay's account reads: "The sailors and soldiers were aroused from their sleep, and the mate set the sails. Then followed mass, or at least a morning prayer. At nine o'clock a bell

announced breakfast.... After breakfast chocolate was served to those who desired it, and then the passengers did whatever they pleased.... At four in the afternoon dinner was eaten in the same manner as breakfast. After sunset the signal was given for evening prayer, which included the singing of the Laurentian Litany and the *Salve Regina*." Baegert's description of Saint Peter's and Saint Paul's feast day reads, "All people took communion, by which devotion the captain and other gentlemen gave a good example for the common man. In the evening, some cannons were fired while singing the *Te Deum*." Quotation from Kristin Dutcher Mann, "The Power of Song in the Missions of Northern New Spain," Ph.D. diss., Northern Arizona University, 2002, 50–51.

15. For a discussion of these four Marian antiphons, consult John Harper, *The Forms and Orders of Western Liturgy from the Tenth to the Eighteenth Century: A Historical Introduction and Guide for Students and Musicians* (Oxford: Clarendon Press of Oxford University Press, 1991), 132–33, 274–75; Richard Hoppin, *Medieval Music* (New York: Norton, 1978), 104–5; and the *Liber Usualis*, 273–76.

16. Since Sancho does not always sign his music, a few words pertaining to his handwriting are in order, since several scribal idiosyncracies can help identify unlabeled sheets as being his work. The sheet with *Salve Regina* at the San Fernando Mission is catalogued by William Summers as manuscript S-5 (see Summers, "*Opera seria* in Spanish California: An Introduction to a Newly-Identified Manuscript Source," in *Music in Performance and Society: Essays in Honor of Roland Jackson*, ed. by Malcolm Cole and John Koegel (Warren, Mich.: Harmonie Park Press, 1997), 276). At the end of the *Salve Regina*, Sancho draws his distinctive "double bar" that he often uses to mark the conclusion of a work, where rows of small semicircles protrude to the right of the double bar, with the first row having five of these circles, and with each progressive row having one fewer semicircle than the previous one. The drawing resembles a pyramid of stacked oranges that has been glued together and then turned on its side so that the "peak" of the pyramid points to the right. Other Sancho manuscripts with this pyramid-like double bar at the conclusion of the work include the following works in the WPA folders of the University of California at Berkeley: WPA folder 58, "Admirabile nomen Jessu"; WPA folder 61, "Lamentatio a duo"; WPA folder 64, "Misa de quinto tono"; WPA folder 66, "Credo Italiano a duo"; WPA folder 69, "Missa de los Angeles"; and WPA folder 72, "Missa de Requiem." There are other sources at the San Fernando Mission—in addition to the aforementioned *Salve Regina* in Sancho's hand—that contain his recognizable handwriting. Manuscript S-1-5 has jotted down on its sheets a mass that begins with a "Kyrie Clasichs" and the "Gloria simple": Sancho draws his distinctive pyramid-like double bar to conclude this composition. It should also be noted that Pedro Cabot uses this same pyramid-like drawing at the conclusion of "O Christe mundi Salvador" in WPA folder 60.

17. Manuscript S-5 at the San Fernando Mission has been folded to make a small booklet consisting of two smaller folios, a total of four pages, and it contains the music for Compline, as described and clearly mapped out by Jerome Roche, "Musica diversa di Compietà: Compline and its Music in Seventeenth-Century Italy," *Proceedings of the Royal Musical Association*, vol. 109 (1982–83), 60–79, esp. 62. See also Harper, *The Forms and Orders of Western Liturgy*, 82–83. The *Salve Regina* was widely known in the Gregorian tradition (see *Liber Usualis*, 276). For further annotations concerning the construction of manuscript S-5 at the San Fernando Mission, consult appendix A available online, which also provides information regarding the similarities (or lack thereof) of these chants to those in the Gregorian tradition. Observe that manuscript S-5 at San Fernando has a strong connection to Santa Clara Ms. 3 (fols. 55v–56v). For this Compline service, both manuscripts share melodies not matching Gregorian models. One of the main points of interest here concerns the role of Pedro Cabot in his collaboration as a scribe with two of the central figures in California mission music; we find Cabot interpolating material into the Compline service for both the San Fernando manuscript S-5 (where Juan Sancho is the scribe) and Santa Clara Ms. 3 (where Ibáñez is the principal scribe).

18. The definitive authority on the *Salve* and its performance in the New World, Robert J. Snow, provides a summary of its history in the Franciscan monasteries and publications, supplying the tunes as they appear across the Hispanic world, and none of them match the tune that Sancho has written down. See Snow, *A New World Collection of Polyphony for Holy Week*

and the Salve Service "*Guatemala City, Cathedral Archive, Music MS 4.*" (Chicago: University of Chicago Press, 1996), esp. 68–74.

19. Durán writes out the "Salve Virgen pura" in Bancroft choirbook C-C-59, p. 73, Santa Barbara Doc. 1, p. 171, and Santa Clara Ms. 4, pp. 67 and 68. (See photo B-114 in appendix B online for a facsimile of p. 68.) Other California manuscripts contain related material, including Santa Barbara Doc. 2, p. 87, and folder C at Santa Barbara, where Maynard Geiger twice wrote out the stanzas for this song.

20. Although the Castilian word *salvar* means "to save" or "to rescue," in this context it actually means "hail," derived from the phrase "Dios te salve, María, llena de gracia," meaning "Hail, Mary, full of grace." See *Diccionario moderno español-inglés, English-Spanish Larousse*, ed. by Ramón García-Pelayo y Gross and Micheline Durand (Paris: Ediciones Larousse, 1979), 374. This text was also known as the *Alabanza*, according to Charles Francis Saunders and Father St. John O'Sullivan. They base their analysis and discussion on the recollections of Doña María, who grew up in the mission period. She recalls that this hymn was sung on Sundays in honor of the Blessed Virgin as a substitute for the singing of the *Alba* that began the other days of the week. See Saunders and O'Sullivan, *Capistrano Nights: Tales of a California Mission Town*, illustrated by Charles Percy Austin (New York: Robert McBride, 1930), 155–57.

21. A color facsimile of this "Dios te salve Reyna madre" can be found on p. 93 of Lorenzo Calzavarini's *Breve guía histórica, artística y cultural del Convento San Francisco de Tarija (en el IV Centenario de su fundación, 1606–2006)* (Santa Cruz, Bolivia: Editorial Centro Eclesial de Documentación, 2006).

22. For information concerning the Sisters of Charity School graduation, consult Robert Stevenson, "Music in Southern California: A Tale of Two Cities," *Inter-American Music Review*, vol. 10, no. 1 (Fall–Winter 1988), esp. 58–59.

23. The Bancroft Library, Ms. C-C-73/108c. "Copia del manuscripto Ramón Yerba [*sic*]. Cantos de la Misión." The last name should read "Yorba" and is in fact spelled correctly throughout the bulk of the document. Hereafter, I abbreviate this source as the "Yorba manuscript."

24. The pedigree of the Yorba manuscript, Ms. C-C-73/108c, is worth retelling, as recorded in the preface to his volume (pp. 1–7). I provide the entire text as item C-5 in appendix C online under the section for the Bancroft Library.

25. Preface to the Yorba manuscript, Ms. C-C-73/108c in the Bancroft Library.

26. Santa Clara Ms. 3, fols. 56v–57.

27. For a discussion of the Matins service in the context of Mexican society in the Baroque and Classical eras, consult my entry "Eighteenth Century" for the *Encyclopedia of Mexico: History, Society and Culture*, ed. by Michael Werner (Chicago: Fitzroy Dearborn, 1998). I address the importance of Matins in Mexico as the central theme in "The Apparition of the Virgin of Guadalupe and Her 'Reappearance' in the Choral Masterpieces of 18th-Century Mexico," paper presented at the annual meeting of the American Musicological Society, Phoenix, 30 October–2 November, 1997, and at the annual convention of the College Music Society, Cleveland, 13–16 November 1997. Further relevant information can be found in my article "Hidden Structures and Sonorous Symmetries: Ignacio de Jerusalem's Concerted Masses in 18th-Century Mexico," in *Res musicae: Essays in Honor of James Pruett*, ed. by Paul R. Laird and Craig H. Russell (New York: Harmonie Park Press, 2001), 135–59. For treatment of the *Te Deum*, consult Harper, *The Forms and Orders of Western Liturgy*, 83–84, 90, 93, 270–71; and the *Liber Usualis*, 1832–37.

28. Herbert Eugene Bolton, *Anza's California Expeditions: An Outpost of Empire* (Berkeley: University of California Press, 1930), vol. 1, pp. 367–68.

29. "Salimos de dicho Presidio de Monterey el Sʳ Comandante, yo y otros pocos â las quatro de la tarde, y â las cinco llegamos â la Mission de San Carlos del Carmelo senalada en el mapa con la letra G. haviendo caminado una legua larga con el rumbo al sudoeste quarta al sur. Aqui nos recibimos los Padres que eran siete cantando el tedeum, con festivos repiques y singular alegria." Pedro Font, *The Anza Expedition of 1775–1776: Diary of Pedro Font*, ed. by Frederick J. Teggart, Publications of the Academy of Pacific Coast History, vol. 3, no. 1 (Berkeley: University of California Press, 1913), 60–61.

30. See note 11 for the entire quotation.

31. Santa Clara Ms. 3, fols. 83–84v.

32. See the instructions in the *Liber Usualis*, 1833 and 1836.

33. There are several concordant versions of this setting of the *Te Deum* in faubordon technique in which the same formulaic harmonic pattern is used to accommodate the rhythmic and textual variants of the odd-numbered lines of this text. This model was clearly well known, given its common recurrence across California. For concordant versions of the same musical and textual setting, consult Bancroft choirbook C-C-59, p. 119; Bancroft choirbook C-C-68:1, fols. 30v–31; Santa Clara Ms. 4, p. 122; Santa Barbara Doc. 2, pp. 84–85; and Santa Barbara Doc. 10, fol. 1.

34. See photo 5-9 in chapter 5 for a facsimile of the title page of WPA folder 77, "Te Deum a 4 voces alternando con las del coro."

35. The monophonic formula in Santa Clara Ms. 3 is in transposed mode 2 with an emphasis on A (sounding a bit like A minor to modern ears). The jumps between modes 6 and 2 (or the keys F major to A minor) are not entirely satisfactory or fluid. Similarly, Durán clarifies that the interpolated passages need to be either in C major or A minor, and the sixth mode (or "F major") of WPA folder 77 does fill the bill.

36. The history of this recording and notated transcription of it is found in Charles Francis Saunders and J. Smeaton Chase, *The California Padres and Their Missions* (Boston: Houghton Mifflin, 1915), 372–74.

37. Owen da Silva, O.F.M., *Mission Music of California: A Collection of Old California Mission Hymns and Masses* (Los Angeles: Warren F. Lewis, 1941), 120.

38. For the five-measure fragment of the *Alabado* in the Sancho materials, consult the WPA collection at the University of California at Berkeley, folder 68: photograph W-2, staff 6; and photograph W-4, staff 13 (for this image, the sheet must be rotated 180 degres because the passage is written upside down). For extra stanzas of lyrics that can be supplied to these tunes, consult folders A, C, F, and G of lyrics copied out by Father Maynard Geiger, O.F.N., that are stored in the "Music" filing cabinet at the Santa Barbara Mission Archive-Library.

39. For the notated version of the *Alabado*, consult da Silva, *Mission Music of California*, 112–13; Saunders and Chase, *The California Padres*, 373–74; and Stevenson, "Music in Southern California," 55.

40. The reference to the *Alabado* is found on an index that is now an end paper for another source, Manuscript 2 at the San Juan Bautista Mission. We can ascertain what works had been included (even though the book is not extant) by examining the index for that work. The relevant page can be found as plate 136 in the photos of the San Juan Bautista sources in the bound volume, item 45 in the WPA collection at the Department of Music of the University of California at Berkeley.

41. Leonardo Waisman, "¡Viva María! La música para la Virgen en las misiones de Chiquitos," *Latin American Music Review*, vol. 13, no. 2 (1992), 214.

42. Koegel, "Spanish and French Mission Music," 25–26.

43. Ibid., 33.

44. McGill goes on to develop her points further, including the continued practice of mission music by the Tigua Indians near El Paso. See Anna Blanche McGill, "Old Mission Music," *Musical Quarterly*, vol. 24, no. 2 (April 1938), 188–89.

45. See Kristin Dutcher Mann, "The Power of Song in the Missions of Northern New Spain," Ph.D. diss., Northern Arizona University, 2002, 175–83, esp. 180.

46. See John Donald Robb, *Hispanic Folk Music of New Mexico and the Southwest: A Self-Portrait of a People* (Norman: University of Oklahoma Press, 1980), 612–43; and Vicente T. Mendoza, *Panorama de la Tradicional de México*, Instituto de Investigaciones Estéticas, Estudios y Fuentes de Arte en México, no. 7 (Mexico City: Universidad Nacional Autónoma de México, 1984), esp. 39–40. After the main body of the text he provides musical examples (on unnumbered pages) of the *Alabado*; see nos. 30–35. In addition, plate 20 at the back of the book is a facsimile of the single sheet "Alabado dispuesto por el R. P. Fr. Antonio Margil de Jesús..." published in a bilingual edition by Federico Gómez de Orozco, Mexico City, in the early 1700s. The lyrics presented here of Margil's *Alabado* make no appearance in California manuscripts. Mendoza provides another exhaustive study of the *Alabado* providing specific tunes and texts. See Vicente T. Mendoza and Virginia R. R. de Mendoza, *Estudio y clasificación de la música tradicional hispánica de Nuevo México*, Instituto de Investigaciones Estéticas, Estudios de Folklore, no. 5 (Mexico City:

Universidad Autónoma de México, 1986), 30–51. The flourishing of the *Alabado* in New Mexico through the centuries is the subject of Thomas J. Steele's *The Alabados of New Mexico*, ed. and trans. by Thomas J. Steele (Albuquerque: University of New Mexico Press, 2005). He provides many texts in Spanish and English translation, but no melodies are included.

47. One of the most comprehensive discussions of mission life at the San José de Comundú Mission in Baja California is found in Harry Crosby, *Mission and Colony on the Peninsular Frontier, 1697–1768*, published in cooperation with the University of Arizona Southwest Center and the Southwest Mission Research Center (Albuquerque: University of New Mexico Press, 1994), esp. 237–39. John Koegel also delves into this material in his indispensable article, "Spanish and French Mission Music in Colonial North America," *Journal of the Royal Music Association*, vol. 126 (2001), esp. 29. A third scholar, Francis J. Weber, provides a thorough explanation and insightful observations concerning mission life in "Jesuit Missions in Baja California," *The Americas*, vol. 23, no. 4 (April 1967), esp. 414–15.

48. Crosby, *Mission and Colony*, 238.

49. Ibid., 238–39. A comparison of this account of mission life in the Jesuit missions of Baja California with that of Miguel de Barco and with yet another by Pablo Tac during his youthful days in the Franciscan missions of Alta California in the 1820s reveals a nearly identical regimen. For an exploration of Tac's life story and fascinating recollections from Mission San Luis Rey, consult Beebe and Senkewicz, *Lands of Promise and Despair*, 329–40, esp. 335–36.

50. Beebe and Senkewicz, *Lands of Promise and Despair*, 95.

51. Crosby, *Mission and Colony*, 239.

52. Stevenson, "Music in Southern California," 40 and 55. On p. 55, Stevenson provides a facsimile of a print containing the music and lyrics; it differs completely from the version notated in da Silva's *Mission Music of California*, 112–13.

53. Rev. Francis J. Weber, *Readings in California Catholic History* (Los Angeles: Westernlore Press, 1967), 20–21.

54. Saunders and Chase, *The California Padres*, 369.

55. The lengthy account of Vicente de Santa María is well worth reading in its entirety and is chock-full of fascinating details on a wide variety of subjects. It is reproduced in Beebe and Senkewicz, *Lands of Promise and Despair*, 177–85.

56. Ibid., 181.

57. Ibid.

58. Ibid., 184.

59. Santa Barbara Doc. 1, pp. 178–79; San Juan Bautista Ms. 2, p. 44 (plate 196 in the photos of this source as part of item 45 in the WPA collection). The text runs, "Dios te salve Maria, llena eres de gracia, el Señor es contigo, bendita tu eres entre todas las mugeres. Y bendito es el fruto de tu vientre, Jesus. Gloria Patri et Filio et Spiritui Santo."

60. "Todos los Domingos de Quaresma no se contentaba con la Pláctica Doctrinal de la Misa mayor, sino que á la tarde, después de rezada la Corona de María Santísima, y cantado el Alabado, les predicaba un Sermon Moral." Palóu, *Relación histórica de... Serra*, 30. The "Corona de María Santísima" to which Palóu refers is the prayer written around 1628 by San José de Calasanz. It contains twelve acclamations of "Hail Mary" reflecting the twelve graces bestowed by the Trinity (four by the Father, four by the Son, and four by the Holy Spirit). The imagery is based upon the passage in Revelation by John the Evangelist: "And there appeared a great wonder in heaven; a woman clothed with the sun, and the moon under her feet, and upon her head a crown of twelve stars" (Rev. 12:1). For information on the Crown of the Immaculate Conception of the Blessed Virgin, consult "Devoción a María, Corona de las Doce Estrellas [i.e., the Crown of the Immaculate Conception]," by San José de Calasanz (ca. 1628), *Devocionario Católico*, http://www.devocionario.com/maria/corona_estrellas.html (accessed 4 August 2004). There are many iconographic depictions of Mary with her crown of twelve stars, the *Stellarium*, associated with the Conception. See Suzanne L. Stratton, *The Immaculate Conception in Spanish Art* (Cambridge: Cambridge University Press, 1994). With respect to this imagery's relevance as seen in Mexican music of the time, see Drew Edward Davies, "The Italianized Frontier: Music at Durango Cathedral, *Español* Culture, and the Aesthetics of Devotion in Eighteenth-Century New Spain," Ph.D. diss., University of Chicago, 2006, esp. chap. 5 (UMI Microfilm No. 3206320).

61. "Con igual cuidado se dedicó á introducirlos en la devocion de Maria Srá. Nuestra, y con particularidad á su Purísima Concepcion inmaculada, previendose á celebrarla con la Novena, á que asistia todo el Pueblo; y en el dia de esta gran festividad se cantaba la Misa, y predicaba el Sermon, y despues se entonaban los Gozos de la Purísima Concepcion. Todos los Domingos por la tarde se rezaba la Corona á la Madre de Misericordia, concluyendola con el Alabado ó con los Gozos que se cantaban. Y para mas aficonarlos el V. Padre pidió de México una Imagen de bulto de la dulcísima Señora, que puesta en sus andas, la sacaban en Procesion por el Pueblo todos los Sabados de noche, alumbrando con faroles, y cantando la Corona." Palóu, *Relación histórica de... Serra*, 32.

62. The association of Saturday Mass with veneration of the Virgin Mary is seen across the Americas. For instance, this relationship as practiced in the Chiquitos missions of Paraguay is explored in Waisman, *¡Viva María!* 214.

63. Fr. Zephyrin Engelhardt, O.F.M., *Mission San Antonio de Padua: The Mission in the Sierras*, Missions and Missionaries in California, New Series: Local History (Ramona, Calif.: Ballena Press, 1972), 35,

64. Alfred Robinson provides a snapshot of the evening activities at Mission San Luis Rey, including the supplication to the Virgin. Consult Robinson, *Life in California: A Historical Account of the Origin, Customs, and Traditions of the Indians of Alta-California*, foreword by Joseph A. Sullivan (Oakland, Calif.: Biobooks, 1947), esp. 17. José del Carmen Lugo's memoirs of his life on a rancho near Mission San Antonio include his recollections of evening prayers and the reciting of the Rosary. See "1840s: Life on a California Rancho [by] José del Carmen Lujo," in Beebe and Senkewicz, *Lands of Promise and Despair*, 434–42, esp. 434.

65. From Antonio Colonel's *Tales of California* from the 1840s, quoted in Beebe and Senkewicz, *Lands of Promise and Despair*, 448.

66. da Silva, *Mission Music of California*, 111, 120.

67. Yorba manuscript, Ms. C-C-73/108c, song 16, with the title "lla biene lalba [= Ya viene el alba]. The text proceeds: "[1] lla biene lalba, rallando el dia, daremos grasias, abe maria [Ave María] / [2] bendita sella [= bendita es ella], la lus del dia, i el angel bello, que vos lEnbia / [3] Cantemos todos, Con eficasia, nasio maria, llena de grasia / [4] digamos todos, en alta bos, nasio maria, madre de dios / [5] nasio maria, nasieron flores, nase el refujio, de pecadores / [6] nasio maria, para consuelo, de pecadores, i lus del sielo / [7] bella grandesa, no quiso ber, la sierpe cruel, de lusifer / [8] la sierpe fea, llora sus penas, maria le pone, fuertes cadenas / [9] biba Jesus, biba maria, lla quin selebran, en este dia / [10] biba Jesus, biba maria, biba tanbien, la lus del dia / [11] Cantemos todos, Con alegria, digamos todos, Ave Maria / [12] lla bien lalba, rallando el dia, daremos gracias, abe maria / Amen."

68. "This custom is still in full effect among the *paisanos* of San Juan Capistrano, especially at the *velorios* or wakes which begin at 8 PM and do not end until the singing of the *Alba (l alba)* the following dawn." Yorba manuscript, Ms. C-C-73/108c, p. 1.

69. Saunders and O'Sullivan, *Capistrano Nights*, 157; Yorba manuscript, Ms. C-C-73/108c, song 16.

70. Saunders and O'Sullivan, *Capistrano Nights*, 153–54.

71. Helen Hunt Jackson, "Echoes in the City of the Angels," *Century Illustrated Monthly Magazine* (1883), 196, reprinted in Howard Swan, *Music in the Southwest 1825–1950* (San Marino, Calif.: Huntington Library, 1952), 92.

CHAPTER 4

Sacred Celebration

Song, Sequence, Dance, and Pageantry

SACRED MUSIC IN the missions was not a static, monolithic re-creation of medieval plainchant transplanted from Europe, as some previous authors have implied, but instead was a pluralistic combination of voices and instruments, of liturgy and spectacle, of styles and functions—and even of cultures—in a new blend that was nonexistent before the friars and soldiers made their way to the remote frontier of Alta California. Nor was the music exclusively rudimentary, simplistic, or uninteresting, as some scholars have imagined, based on the unspoken assumption that the neophytes were perpetual "beginners," incapable of reaching European standards. Competency in singing and playing was the expected norm at all the missions, and in some locations technical accomplishment by the neophyte musicians ascended to the heights of skilled virtuosity.[1] Nor was the mission repertoire a smorgasbord of hors d'oeuvres, as might be suggested by a quick visual perusal of the various scraps of melody that are scribbled here and there, seemingly void of any larger or more capacious context. The musical tidbits are presently dispersed among many archives and libraries, but if one takes the trouble to assemble them, decipher their clues, and then place these orphaned scraps in their proper context, one can successfully re-create a vision of a mission feast day, complete with its fusion of music, dance, theatricality, and ceremony that would have been meaningful for friar and convert alike. Nor was the relationship between the friars and the neophytes a singular one, where the padres did all the teaching and the neophytes did all the learning; in many instances, it is clear, the path connecting them ran in both directions simultaneously. In some missions, Native American dance and musical traditions were allowed to continue and contributed to mission worship in various ways, as long as they were not flagrantly heretical.

Gozos or Songs of Praise

Mission choirbooks and numerous loose sheets record songs in Spanish that were intended to accompany important feast days during the year. Most of them are strophic, built on repeated musical elements, making them easy for the larger congregation to sing (unlike some of the complex mass settings in Latin that would have been relegated exclusively to the expert musicians). Several songs in this style are identified as *gozos* or praise songs, such as the *Gozos de la Purísima* and *Gozos al Señor San José*.[2] The lyrics to the *Gozos de la Purísima* begin with the following words:

> *Para dar luz inmortal, siendo vos alva del día…*
> In order to give eternal light, you being the new dawn of day…

This opening line is also adopted for the *Gozos al Señor San José*:[3]

> *Para dar luz inmortal, siendo esposo de Maria…*
> In order to give eternal light, you being the husband of Mary…

Structurally both the *Gozos de la Purísima* and *Gozos al Señor San José* share many of the same musical features. (See figures 4-1 and 4-2. For a facsimile reproduction of the *Gozos al Señor San José*, consult photo B-110 available in appendix B online.) Visually on the page, things first appear to be a mishmash of text and tangled instructions. If one takes the time to follow the indicators, however, both of these works actually turn out to be strophic, folklike structures emphasizing four-line stanzas. The typical *gozos* setting adheres to the following pattern. First, we hear an introduction built of two brief phrases; the first, or "antecedent," phrase (*A*) sets things in motion with rich choral polyphony in *canto de órgano* style. The second, or "consequent," phrase (*Rx*) is cast as a single melodic thread in *canto figurado* style. This particular line assumes great importance later as the *gozos* unfolds, for it recurs at the end of each subsequent stanza, serving as a type of returning refrain line.

The stanzas that follow the introduction and that constitute the body of the work are all forged in identical fashion to each other (except that the text changes in each ensuing stanza). The first two lines of the lyrics are set to the same music (making an *a-a'* pattern).[4] The music for this *a* phrase cadences on the "tonic," the tonal center of gravity, providing a sense of stability early on in each stanza. The next phrase *b* embarks on a new, fresh melodic line that cadences on the "dominant" of the key, conveying a feeling of unresolved suspense in the middle of the stanza.[5] Then, each stanza takes us back to the "tonic," with its restatement of the refrain line (labeled by Durán as *Rx*, meaning "response" or "refrain").

After the long stream of four-line stanzas, we have a brief conclusion. In this way, the larger formal structure has a sort of elegant balance and symmetry; just as there had been a brief two-phrase introduction to set things in motion, so there is a two-phrase coda to tie things up. The concluding gesture of a *gozos* first presents a single line of text that is poured into the *a* melody contour: it is followed immediately by the final, concluding appearance of the response *Rx*. The introduction and the coda are both built of the same shape, *a-Rx*. Musically speaking, therefore, they are twins—we end as we had begun. The complete shape of a typical *gozos* (including the settings seen in figures 4-1 and 4-2) resembles the pattern as shown in figure 4-3.

Figure 4.1 *Gozos de la Purísima,* "Para dar luz inmortal siendo vos alva del día

si lo di-ce la em-ba-xa - da, del mi-nis-tro Ce-les-tia[l].

* parallel 5ths & octaves

D.S. al Fine

** perhaps should be changed
from "a" to "G."

Para dar luz inmortal siendo Vos alva del dia Sois concebida Maria sin pecado original.	To give immortal light, since You are the dawn of the day You were conceived, Mary, without original sin.
Ave sois Eva trocada sin el ve de aquella pena como os dira gratia plena quien os busca maculada si lo dice la embaxada del ministro Celestial Sois concebida Maria sin pecado original.	You are Eve transformed into "Ave" without the stigma of that sin, as the sinner who seeks you will say 'gratia plena' to you, if the emmisary from the Celestial ministry says it. You were conceived, Mary, without original sin.
Como la culpa traýdora a el sol no pudo mirar tampoco pudo aguardar que amaneciese la aurora pues huýe de vos Señora este nocturno animal. Sois concebida Maria sin pecado original.	As the traitorous temptor couldn't look upon the sun, neither could it endure the coming of dawn, so this nocturnal animal flees from you, Lady. You were conceived, Mary, without original sin.
Sois de la harina la flor para pan sacramentado que nunca tuvo salvado la massa del Salvador si para formarse amor la previno candeal. Sois concebida Maria sin pecado original.	You are the wheatmeal for the sacramental bread; . for the dough of the Savior would never have been saved if love had not provided white wheat for its creation. You were conceived, Mary, without original sin.
Dice que sois toda hermosa en sus cantares un Dios no hallando macula en Vos para ser su amada Esposa a cancion tan misteriõsa repitan con goso igual. Sois concebida Maria sin pecado original.	A God says in his songs that your are beautiful, and finding you without sin, you are his beloved Wife. Let all repeat such a mysterious song with equal joy. You were conceived, Mary, without original sin.
Ya la Yglesia militante celebra con atencion que sois en la creacion pura limpia y radiante en aquel primer instante punto fisico y real. Sois concebida Maria sin pecado original.	Already the militant Church celebrates with attention that you were created pure, clean, and radiant in that first physical and real instant. You were conceived, Mary, without original sin.
Para defender Escoto en Paris esta opinion hizo antes oracion a vuestra Ymagen devoto y vos le admitis el voto con milagrosa señal. Sois concebida Maria sin pecado original.	Before defending this opinion in Paris, Escoto first offered a devout prayer to your image, and you granted him the vote with a mysterious sign. You were conceived, Mary, without original sin.
En la religion sagrada de San Francisco hallareis el titulo que teneis de Virgen Inmaculada Y por esso es tan realsada quanto humilde es su saýal. Sois concebida Maria sin pecado original.	In the Holy religion of Saint Francis you will find that you hold the title of Immaculate Virgin, and for this reason it is as exalted as its robes are humble. You were conceived, Mary, without original sin.
Pues pudo elegiros tal, el que para Madre os cria Sois concebida Maria sin pecado original.	So He could choose you, He who created you to be His Mother You were conceived, Mary, without original sin.

Figure 4-1 *(continued)*

Modal features are reinforced in both of these *gozos* in figures 4-1 and 4-2. The *Gozos de la Purísima* is in mode 6 (as Durán's title explicitly announced in choirbook C-C-59). The final of mode 6 is the pitch F, and the tonal center of secondary importance is C, both of which become the destination points for the various phrases in these *gozos*. Although the mode for the *Gozos al Señor San José* is not explicitly identified in the work's title, it can be ascertained nevertheless as being in mode 7 through its key signature and tonal centers. As we saw in chapter 2, a piece whose key signature possesses no sharps or flats, that emphasizes A minor, and that sometimes gravitates toward E is identified as being in Mode 7.[6] However, the work emphasizes the descending Phrygian cadence, a feature that the Spaniards associated with the presence of Mode 4.[7] Yet another genre from the mission era that utilized the Phrygian cadence to build its phrases was the *fandango,* California's most popular dance.

Before the rise of the *fandango,* the *folía* had been all the rage in Baroque Spain and Italy. Its chord progression and rhythmic features bear a particularly

Figure 4-2 *Gozos al Señor San José,* "Para dar luz inmortal siendo esposo de María"

Para dar luz inmortal siendo Esposo de Maria
Sois Jose el claro dia en pureza angelical.

To give immortal light, being the Husband of Mary
You are Joseph, the clear day in angelic purity.

Ave sois Angel trocado por vuestra innocente vida
estando vuestra alma unida al autor de lo criado
siendo de Dios tan amado inmenso es vuestro caudal.
Sois Jose el claro dia en pureza angelical.

You are transformed into an angel by your innocent life;
since your soul is united with the author of the Child,
being so beloved of God, your fortune is immense.
You are Joseph, the clear day in angelic purity.

Sois Arcangel illustrado en los misterios de Dios
siendo el deposito vos, de los del Verbo encarnado
no es mucho si a vuestro lado teneis al Sol immortal.
Sois Jose el claro dia en pureza angelical.

You are an Archangel enlightened in the mysteries of God:
since you are the depository of the Word incarnate,
it is not much if at your side you have the immortal Sun.
You are Joseph, the clear day in angelic purity.

Sois trono pues a Dios Niño vuestros brazos recibieron
y en dulce abrazo se unieron con tiernisimo cariño
gozad Jose del armiño desta flor celestial.
Sois Jose el claro dia en pureza angelical.

You are a throne, since your arms received the Christ Child
and they came together in sweet embrace with the tenderest affection;
enjoy, Joseph, the ermine of this celestial flower.
You are Joseph, the clear day in angelic purity.

Sois Dominacion tan pura que el Reŷ de tierra ŷ Cielo
sujeto estuvo en el suelo a vos siendo criatura
grande fue vuestra ventura gozadla siempre eternal.
Sois Jose el claro dia en pureza angelical.

Such pure governance are you that the King of Heaven and Earth
when he was an infant on the floor was subject to you;
great was your fortune: enjoy it for ever and ever.
You are Joseph, the clear day in angelic purity.

Sois Principado dichoso pues en nuestro corazon
reŷnais sin contradiccion con imperio amorozo
aquel sera venturoso que os sirviere leal.
Sois Jose el claro dia en pureza angelical.

Your are a lucky Prince, since in our heart
you rule without contradiction in loving governance;
whoever serves you loyally will be fortunate.
You are Joseph, the clear day in angelic purity.

Sois Potestad pues el nombre solo de vuestra Persona
en el Ŷnfierno aprisiona al enemigo del hombre
no es mucho que al mundo asombre potestad general.
Sois Jose el claro dia en pureza angelical.

You are powerful, as your name alone
imprisons in Hell the enemy of man:
it is not much that your general power should surprise the world.
You are Joseph, the clear day in angelic purity.

Sois Serafin abrazado en la llama del amor
pues el mas que el dolor desta vida os ha llevado
nuestro corazon elado haced incendio total.
Sois Jose el claro dia en pureza angelical.

You are a Seraphim embraced in the flame of love
since that, more than the sorrow of this life, has carried you:
make of our frozen heart a burning fire.
You are Joseph, the clear day in angelic purity.

Pureza tan virginal dice en un ave maria.
Sois Jose el claro dia en pureza angelical.

Such virginal purity, in an "Ave Maria," says:
You are Joseph, the clear day in angelic purity.

Figure 4-2 (*continued*)

Structural form of a *gozos*

Intro	Stanza 1	Stanza 2	Stanza 3	Stanza 4		**Coda**
a-Rx	*a-a'-b-Rx*	*a-a'-b-Rx*	*a-a'-b-Rx*	*a-a'-b-Rx*	...	*a-Rx*

Figure 4-3 Structural form of a *gozos*

strong resemblance to the *Gozos al Señor San José*.[8] The first measure of the *gozos* opens with a quarter rest followed by two quarter notes on A minor, which then thrust forward to an E-major harmony; in like fashion, the *folías* in its formative years opens with a quarter rest and two strums on an A minor, proceeding to E. And if one reverses the order of the *gozos'* phrases (so that we first hear phrase *b* and then phrase *a*), it becomes evident that the order of the chords in the *folía* and the *gozos* is almost identical. (See figure 4-4.) Musically, the two works are siblings. The *order* of the phrases may have been switched, and the rhythms may need a few minor adjustments, but the strong family resemblance of their *harmonic* makeup is striking.

An aspect that can appear puzzling at first is the casual disregard for the "rules" regarding voice-leading in both the *Gozos de la Purísima* and the *Gozos al Señor San José*. Ever since the early Renaissance, parallel fifths and parallel octaves were strictly off-limits, yet they crop up here like weeds.[9] Another general principle is to avoid the doubling of voices with the same melody for extended periods. Renaissance and Baroque treatises were in unanimous agreement that the independence of each vocal line was the desired goal. Yet once again, the *gozos* have neighboring voices duplicate each other for two, three, or four notes in a row before parting their separate ways. One possible explanation for these "forbidden infractions" may have to do with the vestiges of an antiquated tradition of semi-improvised polyphony such as parallel organum or the parallelisms of *fauxbordon*. On the other hand, it is possible that they were not looking back to an ancient past but that they simply *liked* the rough-hewn, rugged edges of the sonorities and their raw appeal. Regardless of the historical origin of these *gozos,* they became part of the American experience during the mission period. I propose that the Franciscan fathers of California were much like William Billings, who was active at the same time in New England: these American musicians on both sides of the continent

Figure 4-4 Harmonic progressions of *folías* and *gozos*

knew what they wanted, were repelled by anything that was overly prim or prissy, and at times seemed attracted to strong, gutsy music that appealed to their congregations.[10]

Gozos and pageantry were intertwined. In his biography of Father Serra, Palóu observes the role of the *gozos* in the Feast Day of the Conception and on Saturday's liturgy specifically dedicated in honor of the Virgin; he states, "On the day of this great festival the Mass was sung, and he [Serra] preached the sermon, and afterward were intoned the *gozos* or poems in honor of the Immaculate Conception." Palóu then describes the magisterial procession of the Virgin's statue, placed on her platform, which was paraded through town every Saturday evening.[11] A procession outside the confines of the mission church presented the performers with certain logistical problems such as the necessity of singing something that was easily put to memory—traipsing across a courtyard or cloister while reading music from a colossal choirbook such as the Bancroft Library's choirbook C-C-59 or Santa Clara Ms. 4 would have been clumsy.[12] The music written down in these choirbooks, however, shows that the material could have been easily memorized, for a variety of reasons. There are structural, melodic, harmonic, modal, and folk-like features that collectively helped to make memorization a snap. The formal structure is strophic, so once the musical core is learned, it is simply a matter of filling in the new words with each new loop. Although the textures are in a constant state of flux as the phrases alternate between monophony and polyphony, a rock-solid unifying element bonds the two textures together: the single strand of melody in the response *Rx* is identical to the tenor line of the contrapuntal stanzas. Thus, the same core melody returns for each phrase, without fail, regardless of the accompanying texture. As we have already seen, the harmonies of the phrases are nearly identical—and thus easily learned. Only their cadences differ, but even here the strong modal features would have felt "normal" and automatic to anyone trained in this singing system (as the neophytes were). As the vocalists neared a cadence, they could have been on modal "cruise control"; for the native converts to sing along with the *Gozos al Señor San José* would be no more difficult than a modern blues guitarist joining in to riff on a twelve-bar blues progression.

At the other end of the spectrum stylistically, yet within the same category of *gozos,* or songs of praise, are the *Gozos y antífona de San Joseph* in folder 56 of the WPA collection at Berkeley and the fragment of a *Gozos a duo de San Miguel* in the *Artaserse Ms.* at the San Fernando Mission.[13] The *Gozos y antífona de San Joseph* opens with the text "You are a saint, without equal" (Pues sois sancto sin igual). Similarly, the *Gozos a duo de San Miguel* begins, "You are an Angel, superior among the heavenly hosts" (Pues sois Angel superior entre los coros del cielo). At first blush, these incipits seem unrelated to the other *gozos* that we just discussed, which begin with a different opening line, "Para dar luz inmortal." However, similarities begin to surface among these four selections if we compare their *response* lines (*Rx*) as well as their opening incipits. (See figure 4-5.)

The similarities between these lines are hardly coincidental. The genre of the *gozos* is partially defined by a prominent use of the formulaic opening "*Sois...*" (You are...) in the same way that fairy tales have a cliché opening, "Once upon

Incipits and response lines (*Rx*) for a *gozos*

"Pues <u>sois</u> sancto sin igual"	Incipit to *Gozos y antífona de San Joseph*	WPA, folder 56
"Pues <u>sois</u> Ángel superior"	Incipit to *Gozos a duo de San Miguel*	As-3, fol. 10
"<u>Sois</u> José, el claro día"	*Rx* to *Gozos al Señor San José*	C-C-59, p. 98
"<u>Sois</u> concebida de María"	*Rx* to *Gozos de la Purísima*	C-C-59, p. 121

Figure 4-5 Incipits and response lines (*Rx*) for a *gozos*

a time, in a land far, far away...," or in the same way that folk songs often utilize a standardized opening to produce the aura of a new beginning: "'Twas early one morning..." or "'Twas early, early in the month of May...."

In all likelihood, it was friar Juan Bautista Sancho who brought the *Gozos y antífona San Joseph* and the *Gozos a duo de San Miguel* to California. The cover page for the former bears the ascription "*Gozos* and antiphon beginning 'Joseph, etc.,' in praise of the Patriarch Saint Joseph; for the sole use of Friar Juan Bautista Sancho, Religious Observant, in the year 1796," revealing the source to have been in the private library of Juan Sancho when he was in charge of musical activities at the Convent de Sant Francesc in Palma de Mallorca.[14] The *Gozos a duo de San Miguel* can also be connected to Sancho in at least a peripheral way, for the only extant example of this composition in California is the version that is hastily scrawled out in Sancho's hand in the *Artaserse Ms.* at the San Fernando Mission.

Musically speaking, the *Gozos y antífona de San Joseph* in WPA folder 56 could hardly be more different in style and effect from the previous *gozos*. It is a duet for two sopranos and basso continuo accompaniment and is constructed in the same form as the eighteenth-century *villancicos* that constitute a substantial percentage of the repertoire in cathedrals of the Hispano-American world. The *villancico* was a sacred genre that admitted secular music styles into the sacred temple. Whatever popular sounds one heard on the street or the countryside were admitted into the cathedral in *villancico* performance. Moreover, unlike the normal components of Catholic liturgy where Latin was the norm, *villancicos* were inevitably in the regular everyday speech of the community. Thus, in a sacred performance incorporating *villancicos* one might hear strummed guitars accompanying a soloist pretending to be a ruffian *jaque* singing the rowdy *jácaras* from around the campfire, followed by a group of ladies pretending to be Gypsies and singing in an Andalusian accent as they lull the baby Jesus to sleep, followed by a group of choristers pretending to be Angolans from Africa bringing the Christ child gifts and singing in a mishmash of Spanish and Africanisms from the Cuban barrios, and so on. Paul Laird, the recognized authority on the *villancico*, rightly argues that it was the single most important genre in sacred music of seventeenth-century and early eighteenth-century Spain.[15] By the time the missions were in full swing, however, the *villancico* was receding from the cultural landscape across the Hispanic world, which accounts in part for the paucity of *villancico* examples found in the mission archives. Additionally, the affectionate depiction of ethnic caricatures and comic provincial stereotypes, which was the bread and butter of the *villancico*'s appeal, would have made little sense to Native Americans whose experience with

Europeans would have been limited to a handful of Franciscan fathers and a few dozen soldiers—an exceedingly narrow sampling.

Since the *villancico* tried to capture the feeling of the common man, it based its structure on folk music where improvised couplets (or *coplas*) were inserted between an *estribillo* or recurring refrain that would come back, over and over. The *estribillo*'s text never changed, so all participants generally joined in to give a spirited delivery of this refrain—and then each individual could take a turn (or two or three or four turns, depending on the poet's wit and ingenuity), making up some clever *coplas* on the spot that would amplify the theme that was being addressed. In actuality, the *villancico* manuscripts in Spanish and Mexican cathedrals nearly always have the *coplas* texts written out rather than improvised, which would have required the chapel musicians to dream up texts with the facility of the street poets upon whose skills the *villancico* is modeled. The pseudo-spontaneity is therefore prearranged. Nevertheless, the folkloric structure remains intact where a full-bodied *estribillo* sung by the full ensemble alternates with groups of *coplas* that are sung by vocal soloists. The design of the *Gozos y antífona de San Joseph* with its opening line, "Pues sois sancto sin igual," is cut from this folklike structural pattern. A group refrain comes back repeatedly, and the three vocalists each get their turns with a seemingly endless stream of *coplas* that are supposed to sound as if they were spontaneously whipped up in the fervor of the moment. The tenor voice is given *coplas* numbers 1, 4, 7, and 10; the second soprano is given *coplas* 2, 5, 8, and 11; and the first soprano is given numbers 3, 6, 9, and 12. The three voices take their turns in a round-robin that follows the order illustrated in figure 4-6.

The *estribillo* cheerily drifts along as a duet, the two sopranos combining their melodies in parallel thirds, with occasional sixths or even a diminished fifth whenever a dominant-V chord is implied. The tenor jumps into the flow halfway through the *estribillo,* thickening the texture a bit. Whenever he sings, he doubles the continuo melody, and his text matches the sopranos' lines so that all three vocalists enunciate the same words together. The tenor's role is a bit superfluous in the *estribillo,* but he becomes indispensable during the *coplas* passages, where he is expected to shine.

Unlike the carefully notated and complete *Gozos y antífona de San Joseph,* the *Gozos a duo de San Miguel* found on folio 10 of the *Artaserse Ms.* is problematic. Measures are often crossed out and overwritten so that the intended melodic lines are hard to decipher. Sancho jotted down a soprano part on lines 1 through 3 (all in triple meter) and then a second soprano part on lines 4 and 5 that has a quizzical passage in duple meter that cannot be reconciled easily with the first soprano's material. We can assume that the work was strophic in its central section, where

Villancico form as seen in "Pues sois sancto sin igual"

Figure 4-6 *Villancico* form as seen in "Pues sois sancto sin igual"

the *coplas* would spill forth a series of stanzas. There undoubtedly was a refrain, since at one point Sancho draws the sign of a cross: scribal practice in seventeenth- and eighteenth-century Mexico and Spain utilized the shape of a "cross" or a "#" to indicate a leap to another location, rather like a *D.S. al segno* indication in today's music.[16] Unfortunately, none of the text after verse 1 is recorded, so we cannot tell how the words or subject material unfolded. There is no *acompañamiento* to steer us through the harmonies, and to exacerbate the problems, the second soprano's music peters out, evaporating into blank nothingness. All told, this intriguing fragment lacks much of the material necessary for a satisfactory reconstruction of the work.

When Sancho moved from his island home of Mallorca to California, he brought with him several works with Spanish lyrics; he wrote out the *Gozos y antí- fona de San Joseph* in 1796, and the subsequent year he wrote out yet another ver- nacular-texted piece, the "Ecos a duo" in folder 50 of the WPA collection.[17] Rather than being a *villancico* with its *estribillo* and *coplas,* along with the attendant alter- nations in texture between the group of musicians and the soloists, this composi- tion is more of a vignette in question-and-answer format: it unfolds as a sort of play where an inquisitive soul happens upon an enchanted cave. He calls out into the darkness and hears a mysterious "echo" in response. In trying to ascertain the true identity of this mountain nymph who answers his questions with enigmatic responses, he plies her for information with twenty-five queries in a smorgasbord of dialects and languages. His first questions are in Castilian, but in the middle of stanza 12, the conversation shifts to Latin. Several stanzas later, the interrogation continues with a linguistic tour of the Europe continent; through the course of their banter, the lady of the enchanted cave answers back in Greek, Valencian, and Tuscan. He racks his brain for something more obscure. "Do you know that noble language from Mallorca?"—and she answers in flawless Mallorquín, "Esta, esta, millor que totas!" (Oh this one, this language is better than all of them!). He con- tinues down the same road, "Well, I see you can answer in many languages, but how is your Portuguese?" She nails that one as well, "Essa, essa, hablar deseo" (Oh, that one, I really want to speak that one). In amazement and exasperation at her pro- digious linguistic talents, the gentleman finally asks, "Oh beautiful nymph, is there any other language or word that you know how to speak?" to which she answers, "Sure, I speak *all* of them!" At last, he gives up, stating that he does not want to tire her out any more and gives her his blessing, "May you go with Christ."[18]

The Feast of San José inspired some of the most tantalizing literature from the missions, including the *Gozos y antífona de San Joseph* and *Gozos al Señor San José* already discussed in this chapter. A third composition for Joseph in the vernac- ular—and the most beguiling of the lot—appears in most of the mission choir- books, titled *Dulce Esposo de María* (María's Gentle Husband).[19] (See figure 4-7. For a facsimile reproduction of this piece, consult photo B-109 available online in appendix B.)

As with most of the vernacular tunes in choirbooks, it is a duet fashioned almost exclusively of parallel thirds, but at the conclusion of major cadences, the texture thickens from two voices to four. The "modern" sound of the work is contradicted, or at least concealed, by the antiquated appearance of the choirbook notation, with its blockish breves and chunky semibreves. If one glances at the page without taking the trouble to sing through the line, then he might expect to hear a serene Renaissance motet by Palestrina or fluid chanson by Josquin—what a surprise, then, when the notes of *Dulce Esposo de María* are realized as actual *sound,* to hear a work engendered in the late Baroque or early Classical eras. The melody opens dramatically in D minor with a breezy ascent by thirds before tumbling downward with a large leap; except for this opening gesture, all the subsequent phrases are launched by a robust dotted rhythm that propels each one forward. The ends of

Figure 4-7 *Dulce Esposo deMaría*

* Originally, the notes in this
measure were a third higher.

Figure 4-7 (*continued*)

phrases, on the other hand, often absorb rather than generate energy with surface
motion that is less incisive. In the middle section of the piece, unstressed cadences
and tender "sigh figures" abound. This middle section sounds even more seraphic
due to its modulation to the relative major, F major, that serves as the perfect foil
to the intense D minor that begins and ends the work.

Although Latin was the central language for worship within the mission walls,
outside its doors the expectations changed, especially during processions or the
singing of devotional hymns apart from mass.[20] Certain feast days enjoyed special
treatment, with important vernacular songs in Spanish. As we have seen, during
the Feast of San José and the Feast of the Conception the voice of the mission
converts sang out with Spanish songs of praise in their *gozos*. Another important
feast was that of the Blessed Trinity, celebrated on Friday, Saturday, and Sunday
after Pentecost. Central to its celebration is the text of the Angelic Trisagion, and

** Originally, the rhythmic
value was equivalent to a
dotted half with no rest.

Dulce esposo de María	Sweet Husband of Mary
y de Jesús fiel tutor,	and faithful tutor of Jesus
amparadme en la agonía	help me in my dying
y entregad el Alma mía	and place my soul
en las manos del Señor.	in the hands of the Lord.
Si tuviera en aquel día	If on that day I have
a vuestra esposa a mi favor,	Your Wife in my favor,
con tan buena compañía	with such good company
de Jesús y de María	as Jesus and Mary
saldré siempre vencedor.	I will always prevail.
En el tranze de la muerte	In the trance of death,
sed José mi protector,	may Joseph be my protector
en aquel combate fuerte	in that fierce combat
yo no temo mala suerte	I will fear my fate no more
siendo vos mi defensor.	with you as my defender.
Para muerte tan preciosa	For such a precious death
en los ojos del Señor,	in the eyes of the Lord,
pedit [sic] vos a vuestra esposa	request from Your Wife
una vida fervorosa,	a fervent life,
fé, esperanza y mucho amor.	faith, hope and great love.
Si tuviera a vuestro lado	If at Your side You have
a Jesús mi Redentor,	Jesus my Redeemer,
me asino [sic] de su costado	I'll place myself by his side,
y gozozo [sic] y confiado	and happy and confident
daré el alma al Criador.	I'll give my soul to my Creator.

Figure 4-7 *(continued)*

its recurrence in mission manuscripts reveals it to have been one of the big hits of the era.[21] The core of the California setting consists of three main choral responses, each of which would have been repeated numerous times. The first of these, labeled "Trisagio 1° a 4 voces," is introduced by the larger group singing, "Santo Dios, Santo fuerte, Santo inmortal, ten misericordia de nosotros" (Holy God! Holy strong one! Holy immortal one, have mercy upon us); it is set in four-part harmonization, all notated in the single-staff colored notation associated with the California mission books. The second Trisagion slims down to a two-voice texture, and historically its phrase is repeated a total of nine times with the text, "Santo, Santo, Santo, Señor Dios de los Ejércitos: llenos están el cielo y la tierra de vuestra gloria" (Holy, holy, holy Lord, God of hosts: Heaven and earth are filled with Thy glory). The third Trisagion is *villancico*-like with a recurring *estribillo,* "Santo, Santo, Santo es Dios de verdad" (Holy, holy, holy is the Lord of Truth), that separates a series of stanzas or *coplas*.[22] This structure bears a strong structural resemblance to another piece—the "Gozos en el Trisagio de la augustísima Trinidad"—that is often associated with the closing moments of this liturgy and that similarly has stanzas with the returning refrain "Ángeles y Serafines dicen: Santo, Santo, Santo" (Angels and Seraphim proclaim, "Holy, Holy, Holy").[23] That the "Gozos en el Trisagio de la augustísima Trinidad" was part of the standardized repertoire in California is documented with its presence in the Yorba manuscript at the Bancroft Library; back in 1864, the aged Don Santiago de Ríos sang the most important mission songs for his son Don Benancio de Ríos, and the younger musician wrote out the "Trisagio, Angeles y serafines" as part of the celebration as selection number 10 of the twenty-eight works written out in this mission collection.[24] Its refrain is the same as that of the "Gozos en el Trisagio de la augustísima Trinidad." Other concordant versions of Trisagions crop up elsewhere, reconfirming their importance.

Durán writes out two of the Trisagions, "Santo, Santo, Santo, Señor Dios de los Ejércitos" and "Santo Dios, Santo fuerte" on pages 71 and 73 respectively of choirbook C-C-59. In New Mexico, the Trisagion has continued in the oral tradition all the way to modern times, as is evidenced by Dr. F. M. Kercheville's recording of a group of Native Americans singing the now-familiar text, "Santo, Santo, Santo, Señor Dios de los Ejércitos," although the setting does not match the one notated in the Durán choirbook C-C-59.[25] John Donald Robb, who performed groundbreaking work with folkloric culture of New Mexico, further jots down the lyrics "¡O pan del cielo admirable!" as sung to him by Tranquilo Lujan in 1951; this is a vernacular paraphrasing of the Latin versicle and response in Durán's choirbook C-C-59 that immediately precedes the singing of "O Sacratissimo cuerpo de Jesús" and then "Santo, Santo, Santo, Señor Dios de los Ejércitos."[26]

A related composition directed toward the Blessed Trinity, "Santo Santo Santo Señor," was written out by Juan Sancho on folio 9 of the *Artaserse Ms.* It is in common time (C) with a C clef on the bottom staff. The phrase begins in duet texture in parallel thirds, but as phrases march toward their cadences, occasionally the texture fills out in denser four-part chords.

Of the various written music books preserved from the mission era, the *Artaserse Ms.* has some of the most plentiful and intriguing examples of Spanish-texted songs. (Consult appendix A online for a table of contents for this source.) The *gozos* for the most revered feast days constitute a sizable portion of this repertoire, but there are also several political songs proclaiming loyalty to the Spanish Crown. Juan Sancho and Pedro Cabot, the two fathers whose handwriting is clearly distinguishable, generally choose to write out the polyphonic voices on a single staff where two voices float along, locked arm in arm as their melodies rise and fall in parallel thirds.

Procession and Pageantry

Corpus Christi: The Body of Christ

If one races through the tiny scraps of music paper in the mission archives, devoid of any larger context, it would be hard to discern the extent to which the Franciscan friars and the Indian converts engaged in religious ceremonies of elaborate splendor and magnificence. The melodic snippets are so tiny—but they were employed in spectacles of impressive grandeur. That processions were essential for the friars in their zeal to convert new followers to Christ is evident in the Franciscan music book *Musica Choralis Franciscana, tripliciter divisa* (1746) that lays out all one needs to know for the singing of chant. After explicating the basics of chant notation and of the modes, it delves into the singing of strophic hymns (a repertoire that is abundant in California mission books) and then devotes enormous attention to processions. In fact, the entire book 3 of this three-volume work is devoted exclusively to them.[27] The written record is clear: major celebrations occurred throughout the liturgical year on the important liturgical days such as Christmas, Ash Wednesday, Maundy Thursday, Good Friday, Holy Saturday, Easter, Pentecost, the Feasts of Saint Michael, Saint Francis, Saint Claire, and Saint Joe, the Assumption of the Virgin, and so on.[28] Although one could select any of these days to get a sense of the theatricality and display that surrounded these celebrations, I have chosen to examine the Feast of Corpus Christi as a fitting example of elaborate spectacle that was part of life in the California missions.

The Feast of Corpus Christi celebrates the miracle of Communion in which the Catholic faithful believe that the bread and wine on the altar become—quite literally—the sacrificial body and blood of Christ. The sacrament of Communion (often called the Eucharist) had been a cornerstone of the Christian church ever since the Last Supper, when Christ broke the bread and poured the wine for his disciples, asking that in the future they continue to reenact this meal in remembrance of him. It was not until the thirteenth century that the church designated a specific day on the liturgical calendar (sixty days after Easter, the Thursday after Trinity Sunday) specifically to commemorate the Eucharist, largely on the urging of Juliana of Liège. She had been receiving visions of a full moon with a darkened or hollow center that she interpreted to mean that there was a "hole" in the church calendar since Communion did not have its own specifically designated celebration. In the year 1246, the bishop and synod in Liège established a formal feast for Corpus Christi in their local region, but it was not until 1264 that Pope Urban IV (previously Archdeacon Jacques Pantaleón of Liège) elevated Corpus Christi to its present status as a first-class feast to be celebrated by the universal church.[29] Urban IV asked one of the church's great theologians and writers, Thomas Aquinas, to compose the liturgy for this feast day: historically, he has been credited with composing such marvels as the sequence *Lauda Sion Salvatorem* and the exquisite hymns *Verbum supernum prodiens, Pange lingua, Sacris solemniis, O salutaris,* and *Tantum ergo.*[30]

One of the most engaging accounts of the Corpus Christi ceremony and procession in the hinterlands of northern Mexico and the remote Californias is provided by Francisco Palóu in his life of Junípero Serra. In chapter 7, which explores Serra's missionary life in the Sierra Gorda of northern Mexico, Palóu recounts how Serra used the Feast of Corpus Christi to attract a large following of converts; although the reminiscence deals with Serra's work in northern Mexico— before his later years in Baja and Alta California—we can safely surmise that Serra's mode of operation was not significantly altered when he changed geographic locations. Palóu tells us:

> It was with no less care that this Servant of God [Father Serra], managed to attract his children to the worshipful devotion of the Holy Sacrament. He instructed them to prepare the path where the procession of Corpus Christi would pass and to adorn it with decorations [arches?] made of branches. Four Chapels were formed with their respective altars, so that the Eucharist bread and wine of our Sacrificed Lord would be placed on them. And at each one of them—after the singing of the corresponding antiphon, [Psalm] verse, and prayer—an Indian youth would stop and recite a poem in honor of the Divine Sacrament, which caused devotion in everyone and softened their hearts. Of these, two poems were in Castilian and the other two were in the Pamé language of the local Native Americans. Upon the return to the Church, Mass was sung and the sermon preached on this Most Holy Mystery.[31]

Several aspects of this paragraph are noteworthy: (1) the importance of a procession in conjunction with this feast; (2) the creation of arbors or "decorations made of boughs" on the path of the procession; (3) the use of four altars, each with its own musical veneration and prayers; (4) the placement of the procession *before* mass—instead of *after* it, as is now the custom; and (5) the use of Castilian Spanish and Pamé—regular, everyday languages that would have been easily understood by the participants (as opposed to liturgical Latin, which would have been used within the confines of the sanctuary itself). Serra's deliberate usage of Pamé, in particular, reveals his attitude regarding worship to be largely inclusive and practical, as opposed to elitist or inflexible. (For a photo of a sacred procession at California's San Juan Bautista Mission—although not necessarily for Corpus Christi—see photo 4-1, as well as photo B-25 available online.)

The primacy of pageantry and processions as essential features of the Feast of Corpus Christi dates back to its inception.[32] One of the dramatic elements of the pageant is the elevation of the Host (the Communion bread and wine), an aspect that resembles closely the pre-Christian agricultural celebrations where bounteous crops and foods were raised up before the Deity in ceremonial gratitude. In the sixteenth century, the Council of Trent further advocated processions during Corpus Christi, and many of the church's most intriguing and distinctive "additions" arose in the context of these parades. In England, one finds the *cycle dramas* in which short skits are mounted that explain the history of the cosmos, beginning with Genesis and continuing up to the end of time at doomsday. Other places in Europe insert minidramas along the parade route, the short skits recounting the

Photo 4-1 San Juan Bautista Mission by Edward Vischer (1862), the Bancroft Library, BANC PIC 19xx.039:29-ALB. (Photo courtesy of the Bancroft Library, University of California, Berkeley.)

lives of the saints or religious miracles. Floats and costumed personages representing allegorical themes are commonplace. For many centuries, Corpus Christi parades in Spain and its American colonies have included gargantuan characters of wood or papier-mâché—such as *gigantes* (larger-than-life giants) or *cabezudos* (large figures with colossal and often grotesque heads, frequently painted in vibrant colors). In Seville, the dance of the choirboys (*los "seis"*) before the altar in the cathedral during Corpus Christi marks one of the most ancient and reverent traditions of sacred, liturgical dance.[33]

Although the Corpus Christi procession varies in some details through the ages and with slight variants depending on geographic locations, certain features recur with predictable frequency. The general outline can accurately be summed up as follows:

> After the Mass on Corpus Christi, all kneel and sing *O Salutaris Hostia.* The Host is incensed, and carried under an *ombrellino* (an umbrella-like canopy) to the *baldacchino,* a rectangular tent-like canopy that is rather like a Jewish *chuppah.* Then the procession forms, led by the Crucifer (the acolyte who carries the processional Cross), who is flanked by acolytes carrying candles. Then follow members of religious associations and orders, children strewing rose petals in the path of the Blessed Sacrament (they are customarily dressed in their First Communion clothes), clergy, and then two thurifers who incense the path. Then comes the Blessed Sacrament, carried at eye-level by a priest (with his hands veiled) in a monstrance,

under the *baldacchino*, all flanked by torchbearers. The people walk behind. Usually four stops are made, and at each come Gospel readings, prayer, the singing of *Tantum Ergo* and a Benediction of the Blessed Sacrament. After the last stop, all process back to the church and sing the Divine Praises.[34]

Samuel Edgerton gives a lucid description of the Corpus Christi pageantry as it flourished in the Old and New Worlds, brought to the many indigenous peoples by the wandering mendicant friars. He summarizes:

> Corpus Christi processions included religious theatrical performances (called *autos*), and portable palanquins (called *andas*) with live actors or posed mannequins representing holy stories, all accompanied by music-playing and costumed dancers. As the Corpus Christi procession moved through the streets of each community, sedge grass, boughs of poplar and pine, and flowers in abundance would be strewn in its path. The celebrants often paused for benediction at the four "stations" strategically located around the town, at which the Gospels were recited and *autos* presented. The Host itself was carried aloft in a hooded monstrance, often decorated with gilded rays, thus replicating the sun.[35]

The use of flowers, rose petals, or tree boughs to adorn the path has historically been a prevalent feature of the Corpus Christi procession. As Francis X. Weiser explains, "The houses along the route of the procession are decorated with little birch trees and green boughs. Candles and pictures adorn the windows; and in many places, especially in Latin countries, the streets are covered with carpets of grass and flowers, often wrought in beautiful designs."[36] Flowers had long occupied a central role in American Indian worship, and the Franciscans utilized this motif to great success in their attempts to convert native populations to the Christian faith.[37] The sixteenth-century historian Motolonía gives a fascinating accounting of the Corpus Christi procession in the New World as early as 1538 as celebrated by the Tlaxcalans. Already one sees the primacy of nature's abundance as part of the procession's adornments: "The entire road was covered with sedge grass and reeds and flowers, while someone kept strewing roses and carnations, and many kinds of dances enlivened the procession. On the road there were chapels with their altars and retables well adorned, for resting during the procession."[38] As Motolonía continues his recollection, he emphasizes the use of other biological decorations—flowered triumphal arches, branches of pine boughs, sedge, strewn rose petals and roses, bulrushes—all in the context of sacred processions of the new Native American converts.[39] In one place he elaborates, "There were ten large triumphal arches which were very neatly fashioned.... The space for the procession was marked off by medium-sized arches, set about nine feet apart. There were by actual count one thousand and sixty-eight arches of this kind.... All the arches were covered with roses and flowers in different colors and shapes."[40] In late eighteenth-century Mexico, flowers continued to adorn the path of Corpus Christi processions; Maynard Geiger paints a colorful picture of the Mexico City celebration as it took place on 10 June 1773 in which "the procession went from the Cathedral along Calle Tacuba over a carpet of flowers."[41] Serra and the other friars who eventually found their way to California certainly participated in these processions: for months or years, each of them lived in Mexico City, studying and preparing for their future life as missionaries at the motherhouse of the Franciscan friars in that same city.[42] It is not a stretch, then, to see Serra continue with nature's themes when he takes the Corpus Christi celebration to the Californias: as Palóu recounts, Serra had the parade route lined with "decorations made of branches."

Serra's Celebration of Corpus Christi in Monterey, 1770

Upon Serra's arrival in California, one of his first major religious celebrations was that of Corpus Christi at the founding of Monterey on 6 June 1770.[43] He writes a lengthy and exuberant letter to Inspector General Joseph de Galvez, giving a meticulous account of the festivities. He had hoped to celebrate the feast day with respectful elegance but resigned himself to the disappointing realization that there were no "special" items on board the ships that could help make the service less Spartan. Serendipitously, the night before Corpus Christi, one of the shipmates was looking for medical supplies and opened up a crate that was full of unused lanterns, the perfect items to make the procession a bit fancier. Soon the sailors came across another crate, similarly stuffed with lamps that were brand-spanking new. He further paints a graphic picture of how the makeshift church (the recently completed storehouse) was adorned from top to bottom with flags. Just as Palóu had described the decorations made of boughs, so we find that recurring element arising here as well. The service must have been boisterous, given the bell ringing and gunfire. Among many other details, Serra provides clues as to the parade route; once again, it was a "square," a geometric feature that reminds us of the four altars put forth in Palóu's summary. Serra places the singing of "hymns and sacred songs" in the context of the procession before mass and also after mass, following on the heels of Communion. Serra tells his story:

> We were preparing to celebrate the Feast and Procession of the Most Blessed Sacrament that day. And now I can say that in point of fact we did celebrate it, and with such splendor that it might have been gazed upon with delight even in Mexico.
>
> . . . .
>
> A monstrance indeed we had, but the rest we were without. And if angels did not bring what we needed, at least it came as dew from heaven. On opening a big packing case on board ship, believed to contain medical supplies they were looking for, it turned out to be full of brand-new glass lanterns of whose existence nobody had the least idea.
>
> Gratified by the find, we were now content. Whereupon a sailor told us he had seen, below, another case, twin to this one, and that the first had had

lanterns, so might the other too. Orders were given to bring it out immediately; and it turned out just as was expected.

All this happened the evening before the feast.

. . . .

The lanterns provided with sockets and shafts to be carried on high are six in number—fine big ones. The hand lanterns, of superior workmanship, number three. Two of these with wax candles were put near the monstrance; the six, with their poles stuck in the ground, on each side of the altar. On the altar itself were placed the six big silver candlesticks that came from Loreto, along with their stands and a Missal [sic] stand[44] of the same material. In between, we put smaller candlesticks. For the lanterns, both big and small, Don Juan Pérez provided tallow candles. They all were lighted throughout the high Mass, the sermon and the procession—and not a breath of air stirred.

The men from the ship got ready the church—the middle of the storehouse, which had already been finished. They decorated it with signal flags, and the ceiling was covered in the same way. It was done in such a tasteful manner that in me it excited devotion. The space, or square, in which the procession was to take place was cleaned up, and hung with green branches forming arches under which we walked. Bells were rung, guns were fired, hymns and sacred songs were sung—everything went off in fine fashion and could not have been improved upon. And so you see we did not do things by half-measures at all—especially as it is a matter that concerns the honor of God.

The wonderful painting of Mary, Most Holy, belonging to Your Most Illustrious Lordship, was hung right in the middle and above the monstrance of her Most Holy Son. And there Our Lady stood on guard over the church, whilst her Most Holy Son passed along through those untilled fields in the Sacrament which I carried in my unworthy hands.

When the procession was all over, the Sacred Host was divided into smaller parts to be given in Holy Communion to those who were ready to receive it. And thus with the addition of many more hymns of praise the solemnity came to an end. There was only one thing wanting to make our happiness complete—that Your Most Illustrious Lordship could have seen the festivities, even though it were only to peep through a window.[45]

Several salient features in Serra's account merit further exploration: (1) he was deeply concerned with providing the Corpus Christi celebration with magnificent splendor; (2) candles and lanterns were essential elements; and (3) even at the earliest celebrations of mass in California, Serra brought with him a stand from Loreto to hold some sort of liturgical book to be used during mass.

Serra's letter underscores that illumination was central to the grandeur and resplendent spectacle of the whole celebration. Motolonía, like Serra, includes candles in his description of the 1538 commemoration of Corpus Christi: "The Most Holy Sacrament was carried in procession, together with many crosses and with platforms bearing the images of Saints....There were many banners of the Saints, among them the Twelve Apostles attired in their insignia. Many of those who took part in the procession carried candles."[46] From our modern perspective, where, for a penny and the simple flick of a light switch, one can illuminate a room for an hour, it is easy to forget how overwhelmingly impressive—and exorbitantly expensive—it was during the mission period to provide man-made light. For example, the budget detailing the total expenses for the Festival of San Pedro Arbués, celebrated every 16 September in Mexico City by the Tribunal of the Inquisition during the late seventeenth and eighteenth centuries, shows that the cost of candle wax exceeded all the other expenses combined. For the same cost as for the candle wax, the Confraternity of San Pedro de Arbués was able to purchase vast numbers of bouquets and lilies, bonfires, carpets for the chapel, a newly commissioned drama each year that included the construction of a stage in the cathedral and the performance itself, and—of course—music that included the rehearsal and performance by the Mexico City Cathedral choir and its chapelmaster. Similarly, if we look at opera house expenses in the eighteenth century—such as those incurred at the Teatro di San Carlo in Naples—we discover that candle wax was so pricey that it totaled more than costs of the musicians and staging combined.[47] In this context, Serra's preoccupation with special lighting and his euphoria at finding two cartons of lanterns designed for processions make perfect sense.[48] It also explains California's economy during the mission period: a relationship between candles and cattle provided the foundation of California's wealth in the first decades of the nineteenth century. It was not the meat products that provided monetary value and a source for hard currency at the missions, but the tallow gained by boiling animal carcasses. With a viable cattle industry one could make candles, a necessity and invaluable treasure for providing artificial illumination.[49] All told, if we consider the musical and liturgical goals of the friars, the practical exigencies they confronted in trying to create radiant and ceremonial majesty, and the natural resources that they had close at hand, we can see why the candles and lanterns were such a major aspect of the Corpus Christi procession in California.

Serra's account for Corpus Christi celebrations at Monterey in 1770 also describes that on the altar was a "stand made of silver." We could rightfully ask, "What was on that stand?" Though he does not specify its use, there are two likely choices—either it held the small-scale Missal for the officiating priest, or it held the enormous, communal choirbook (the Gradual orAntiphonary) used by the friars to sing the chants of the Mass Proper or even Ordinary. Fortunately, Stanford University owns a huge choirbook known as the "Serra Choirbook" that possibly was the Gradual used by the choir on that auspicious occasion.[50] This book meets all the criteria needed to place it in that context. It is gargantuan, measuring fifty-six by thirty-nine centimeters and thus could have been read by a large assemblage. The binding was built to last—even in the toughest environments—with two thick boards wrapped in cowhide leather as its covers. The modern paper attached to its front outside cover states, "Gregorian Chant / book used by the / Very Rev. Frai Junipero Serra O.S.J. / to teach the indians of / San Carlos in Carmelo Valley /

during the years of his Mission / from 1770–1784 / Presented / by Father Angelo D. Casanova Vic. For. / P. P. of Monterey / to / Mrs. J. L. and Governor Stanford / Monterey July 1888." If this paper is accurate, it places the choirbook in the possession of Serra during his lifetime and furthermore places it in Monterey at the date of its founding in 1770 up until 1888, at which time it was gifted to the Stanfords. Supposedly, Father Casanova gave this choirbook and other manuscripts to the Stanfords in gratitude for their help in the public drive to rebuild the roof at Carmel Mission, which had caved in due to years of neglect and disrepair. Through Casanova's persistence, the new roof was finished in 1884.[51]

With respect to the choirbook, it is unclear who wrote the explanatory paper glued to its cover. Perhaps this is Casanova's personal annotation or a comment from someone with firsthand knowledge of Casanova's bequest. Unfortunately, there is no documentary evidence reconfirming a putative connection between Serra and this manuscript. At the same time, the musical styles captured in the choirbook were common from the late 1600s up to the mid-1800s, and there is nothing in the choirbook that refutes the hypothesis that the volume belonged to Serra. In the end, then, we can consider the link between the Serra choirbook M.0612 and Father Serra as at least plausible (but not proven beyond doubt).

Could this book have been the one that was on the altar, resting on the "stand made of silver," that Serra describes? It is possible, but even if it were a small Missal that was on Serra's altar stand, rather than this huge tome, there still would have been need of a Gradual in use *somewhere* in the sanctified space where they celebrated Corpus Christi Mass. In short, the anecdotal story concerning the altar stand is not a determining factor as to whether or not this book would have been used at the founding of Monterey. A more critical aspect to consider would be the book's potential functionality and relevance to the Feast Day of Corpus Christi.

If one thumbs through its pages, lo and behold, we come across the service of Corpus Christi (how convenient!). We first have the critical elements for the Proper for this feast on folios 11 through 13 (including the Introit, Alleluia, Sequence, and Communion), after which we find two settings of the Mass Ordinary on folios 14 through 15 (top) and on folios 15 (bottom) through 18 (including the Kyrie, Gloria, Sanctus, Agnus Dei), either of which fits acceptably with the Corpus Christi Proper. (See appendix A online for a detailed list of these contents). So, we return to the intriguing question, "Was this Gradual used by Serra in 1770 at the founding of Monterey?" A credible case could be made in its favor, for if the prefatory paper affixed to the choirbook is true, then we can connect this book to Father Serra, to Monterey, to the year 1770, and to the Corpus Christi liturgy—the sacred music sung on that occasion.

Music for the Corpus Christi Procession

Several hymns have long served as the preeminent core of the Corpus Christi procession, especially *Pange lingua, Sacris solemniis,* and *Verbum supernum prodiens,* all three of which historically have been attributed to Saint Thomas Aquinas.[52] Additionally, each of these three hymns has important subcomponents that serve as freestanding sacred songs in their own right. The last stanzas of *Sacris solemniis* constitute the beloved *Panis angelicus (Bread of Angels)* that is often performed as its own separate entity. Similarly, the closing stanza of *Verbum supernum prodiens* is excerpted as the *O salutaris,* a staple at the beginning of each Communion celebration (not just at the Feast of Corpus Christi). The *Pange lingua* hymn concludes with the stanzas *Tantum ergo sacramentum* and *Genitori genitoque* that are heard every day in closing moments of Communion at mass; the latter stanza bears a link not only to Saint Thomas Aquinas (as the putative composer of the hymn) but also to Adam of Saint Victor, whose hymn for Pentecost is the unmistakable model for much of the same text.

This triptych of hymns, *Pange lingua, Sacris solemniis,* and *Verbum supernum prodiens,* arises with regularity in the California sources. Durán's enormous mission book C-C-59 preserves two of them: a simple monophonic setting of the *Pange lingua* and a more sonorous four-voice rendition of *Sacris solemniis.*[53] Both Juan Bautista Sancho and Felipe Arroyo de la Cuesta jot the *Verbum supernum prodiens* down in a cursory way in their large sheets where they scribbled down the greatest hits of their respective missions.[54] The fragmentary mission choirbook C-C-68:2 in the Bancroft Library preserves the three processional hymns in the same order as they appear in the traditional Roman rite. In this California manuscript, the melody for each hymn is written out in a barless triple meter using typical *canto figurado* notation, denoting a rhythmic, homophonic setting with an implied improvisatory chordal accompaniment.[55] Significantly, the *alternatim* performance that is normally so pervasive in California performance practice—especially for settings of lengthy texts—is not evident here. Repeatedly in mission sources, we see long strophic texts being snipped apart and divided into alternating phrases so that only the text for the odd verses or only the even ones is supplied at any given location. In the case of these three hymns, however, the complete text is carefully inscribed below the melodic contour.[56] Perhaps the performance conditions surrounding an outdoor procession would preclude antiphonal or alternating performance. Performers who are on the move and in ever-shifting spatial configurations would be in a fundamentally more difficult performance situation for antiphonal or responsorial performance than they would be from their customary sedentary positions within the sanctuary walls.

Vernacular renditions of these hymns also surface in California sources. The choirbook at San Juan Bautista offers both the *Sacris solemniis* and the *Pange lingua* in versions translated into Castilian.[57] Additionally, Arroyo de la Cuesta's recording of *Verbum supernum prodiens* is on a sheet chock-full of Native American texts; it is conceivable that some of these—including the ones in immediate proximity to the *Verbum supernum prodiens*—are translations of these hymns to the local Salinan or Chumash dialects.[58] For both the Spanish texts and the putative Indian ones, their presence in a Corpus Christi procession would resonate with Palóu's description of Serra celebrating this feast with his neophytes. Just as Serra had used both Castilian and Pamé for the prayers in the Sierra Gorda of

Mexico, it would make sense that this same practice continued when the friar laid the foundation for sacred music making in Alta California. It bears noting that vernacular texts were utilized frequently when the religious celebration took place outside, rather than inside, the sanctuary walls.

A prevalent feature of the Corpus Christi procession is its "fourness": Palóu describes the "four Chapels...with their respective altars" and the singing of praises and recitation of prayers at each of the four. As has already been seen, this aspect of "fourness" appears as a defining feature in many portrayals of the Corpus Christi procession. W. J. O'Shea explains the association of the four stops of the processions with nature; he states, "In Germany it became associated with the processions for good weather, which explains the practice of celebrating Benediction four times en route, given toward the four corners of the earth, each preceded by the singing of the four Gospels."[59] One of the more spectacular examples of "fourness" in New World celebrations appears in Motolonía's detailed description of the Corpus Christi procession celebrated by the Tlaxcalans in 1538: "[The procession] had one very striking thing. At each of four corners or turns that the road made, there was constructed a mountain and from each mountain there rose a high cliff. The lower part was made like a meadow, with clumps of herbs and flowers and everything else that there is in a fresh field; the mountain and the cliff were as natural as if they had grown there."[60] Furthermore, Edgerton shows that the physical march to the four stations during Corpus Christi resonated with Native American converts, largely because their native religions had similarly centered on the *quincunx* and its four sides.[61] The Franciscans, therefore, elaborated upon the *quincunx* and took advantage of its implications to achieve their own missionary purposes.[62] It is not surprising then, that some of the most exquisite and inspired music from the California mission repertoire appears as groupings of Castilian songs for the Corpus Christi procession, and—significantly—they normally come in groupings of four, possibly intended to correspond to the four "stations" and altars along the parade route. It is also noteworthy that the texts are Spanish (not Latin), once again showing the use of the vernacular in outdoor devotions, just as Palóu had described.

The Corpus Christi procession was known all across the California landscape, as evidenced by the many manuscript sources that devote considerable attention to this music.[63] The most "complete" sources for Corpus Christi in California include four hymns—*¡O qué suave!; ¡O pan de vida!; ¡O Rey de corazones!;* and *¡O sacratissimo cuerpo de Jesús!*[64] The order does not seem to be rigidly fixed, but since *¡O qué suave!* is often followed immediately by *¡O pan de vida!,* one might wonder whether there is some significance to this prescribed order of these two songs.[65] In figure 4-8, I provide translations for the hymns found in Durán's choirbook C-C-59, a version that is representative of the Corpus Christi celebrations as they are written out in other California mission manuscripts.

This repertoire is extraordinary in the mission choirbooks. Not only are the hymns in Spanish (a relatively uncommon occurrence), but stylistically three of them (*¡O qué suave!; ¡O pan de vida!;* and *¡O Rey de corazones!*) are amazingly

Lyrics and translations for the songs on the Feast Day of Corpus Christi.

(*Letras para las Estancias del día de Corpus*)
Durán, choirbook C-C-59 at The Bancroft Library

1. ¡O qué suave! (p. 70)]

¡O qué suave y dulce estáis,
altísimo Dios de amor!
Cuando muy fino
ocultáis con la nube el resplandor

Enciéndase y arda en mi corazón,
mi amante Divino, mi rey,
mi dueño y Señor,
pues al incendio puro de tu dulce amor.

1. Oh, how gentle!

Oh, how gentle and sweet you are,
exalted Lord of love,
when—with a cloud—you
so delicately hide your brilliant splendor.

Let it ignite and burn in my heart,
my Divine love, my King,
my Lord and Master,
in the pure fire of your sweet love.

2. ¡O pan de vida! (p. 70)

¡O pan de vida! ¡O Dios, O Dios!
O fragua del altar!
Haced que os sepa amar (fol.71)
con digno amor de Vos!

2. Oh Bread of Life!

Oh Bread of Life! Oh Lord, Oh Lord!
Oh, forge of the altar!
Let me know how to love
with a worthy love of You!

3. ¡O Rey de corazónes! (p. 71)

1ʳᵃ

¡O Rey! ¡O Rey de corazónes!
Delicias del Criador!
Tus prendas y fñezas
cautivan mi aficion.
[Refrain]
¡Que luz! ¡Que esplendor!
Sois todo, amor,
mi dulce corazon.

3. Oh King! Oh King of hearts!

1ˢᵗ * *Extra text from Santa Clara Ms. 3*

Oh King! Oh King of hearts!
Delights of the Creator
Your garments and finery
captivate my passion.
[Refrain]
What light! What splendor!
Love, you are everything,
My sweet heart.

2ᵃ

Espinas pentrantes
te dan corona atroz,
porque te saludemos
Rey martir de dolor.
¡Que luz! ¡Que esplendor! ...

2ⁿᵈ

Piercing thorns
give you an atrocious crown,
so we greet you,
King, Martyr of Pain.
What light! What splendor! ...

3ʳᵃ

Amor de la vida,
el que murió de amor,
y el que entre fuego y nieve,
su amor Sacramentó.
Que luz! Que ardor ...

3ʳᵈ

Love of Life—
he who died of Love—
and he that between fire and ice
gave his love as a sacrament.
What light! What ardor! ...

Figure 4-8 Lyrics and translations for the songs on the Feast Day of Corpus Christi. (*Letras para las Estancias del dia de Corpus.*) Durán, choirbook C-C-59 at The Bancroft Library.

4ta   4th

Esas llamas pregonan con tierna,   Those flames proclaim with a
y ardiente voz,   tender, ardent voice
que estáis enamorado,   that all of you are in love
con Divina pasión.   with Divine passion.
Que luz! Que ardor...   What light! What ardor! ...

5ta   5th

¡Ay amor estremado!   Oh, extreme Love!
¡Ay! si pudiera yo,   Oh! If only I could
a costas de un martirio,   at the cost of a martyrdom
curar tanto dolor.   cure so much pain.
Que luz! Que ardor...   What light! What ardor! ...

**[R] Panem de caelo, presitisti eis   Bread from heaven
alleluya.(p. 71)   Alleluia**
[Versicle with Response]   [Versicle with Response]
V. Panem de caelo, presitisti eis.   Thou hast given them bread from heaven.
Alleluya (intoned)   Allelulia (intoned)
Rx. Omne delecta mentum, in de   Having within it all
habentem.   sweetness.
Alleluya (intoned)   Allelulia (intoned)

4. ¡O sacratissimo cuerpo de Jesús !   4. O most blessed body of Jesus!
"Para alzar la hostia"   ["for the elevation of the Host"]
= "O sacratísimo cuerpo"   "O most blessed body" used with the Host
& a lower text "Para alzar el caliz"   {"for the elevation of the Chalice"]
"O preciosísima sangre"   "O most blessed blood" used with Chalice.

¡O sacratissimo cuerpo de   O most holy body of
Jesús sacramentado!   Jesus made sacrament!
En esa sagrada Hostia.   In that holy Host,
con fe viva te adoramus   we adore You with living faith.
O preciossisima Sangre,   O most precious blood
por nos en la Cruz vertida!   spilled for us on the Cross
En esse Caliz sagrado   In this holy Chalice
te adoramos con fe viva.   we adore you with living faith.

5. Trisagio, compas de 4 (p. 71)   5. Trisagion, in quadruple meter
Santo, Santo, Santo   Holy, Holy, Holy,
Señor, Dios de los exercitos,   Lord, God of Hosts,
llenos están los cielos y   Heaven and earth are
la tierra de vuestra gloria   full of your glory.
Gloria al Padre, Gloria al Hijo,   Glory to the Father, Glory to the Son,
Gloria al Espiritu Santo.   Glory to the Holy Spirit.

Figure 4-8 (*continued*)

modern and up-to-date, steeped in the *galant* style of the eighteenth century. On the other hand, *¡O sacratissimo cuerpo de Jesús!* is rather chunky and so fraught with parallel octaves and fifths that one cannot imagine that it was written by the same creative mind as any of the other three. *¡O qué suave!* and *¡O pan de vida!* are both graceful duets, with the two voices wafting along in parallel thirds. *¡O Rey de corazones!* similarly concentrates largely on duet texture in parallel thirds, but inserted into this texture are also rich, four-voice homophonic passages. These three pieces may look ancient and old-fashioned to the naked eye, given their antiquated notation conventions, but once one actually plays through them, one is struck by the aesthetic grace of eighteenth-century Classicism. They may not sound exactly like Mozart, but they are clearly a product of the same cultural milieu. For instance, the wide rhythmic variety reminds one more of Haydn than of Handel: steady quarter notes can be followed by sixteenths and asymmetric patterns; smooth rhythms give way to dotted ones or even to triplets; cadences arrive at their destinations with the prototypical "sigh figure" that points more toward Classical rather than Baroque aesthetics.

Although there is no notated time signature, one cannot fail to miss the implied shift in meter midway through *¡O qué suave!*—the work begins in triple meter with accents on both the first and the second beat of each measure, a gesture reminiscent of the stately sarabande. At the midpoint, and without warning, the composition suddenly launches forward in duple meter at the words "Enciéndase y arda en mi corazón" (Ignite Yourself and burn in my heart). (See figure 4-9. For facsimile reproductions, consult photo 4-2 in this chapter and photos B-112 and B-99 in appendix B that are available online.)

One finds a major bipartite subdivision as well in the structure of *¡O Rey de corazones!;* in the Durán choirbook C-C-59 the scribe even places asterisks at the beginning and end of this second section to mark out its borders in a graphic way. In eighteenth-century Spain and France, asterisks were sometimes used to indicate the repetition of a final phrase or section as a *petite reprise*.[66] The organizational division of this piece is even more obvious in the small sheet written out by Pedro Cabot and sewn into the binding of Santa Clara Ms. 3 after folio 47; although there is no music on the page, Cabot writes out the text for five stanzas of *¡O Rey de corazones!*, making it the most complete source with regard to lyrics. At the end of each stanza there is a distinctive symbol :)) that directs the performer to the same symbol at the bottom of the page (beginning with the words "¡Qué luz! ¡Qué ardor!" Clearly, these words begin the refrain that is to follow each of the five stanzas. Cabot also provides us the favor of inserting dynamic markings of *fuerte* (loud) and *piano* (soft) above the appropriate sections in the refrain. This sheet is one of the very few in California sources with dynamic markings. The refrain to *¡O Rey de corazones!* surfaces in slightly different realizations in the various sources that present an intriguing puzzle through their discrepancies. The Durán choirbook C-C-59 has the refrain's exclamations repeated ("¡Qué luz! *¡Qué luz!*" and "¡Qué esplendor! *¡Qúe esplendor!*"), with each antecedent statement being performed by a duet that is then echoed by the richer, five-voice harmonization of the entire vocal ensemble. Curiously, the version copied into Santa Clara Ms. 4 has the

Figure 4-9 *¡O qué suave!*

echoes chopped out completely: we are left with a single statement of each phrase. A duet proclaims "¡Qué luz!" that is then answered by a four-voice exclamation of "¡Qué esplendor!" The choral texture has been trimmed a bit as well, for the highest-sounding voice in the Durán choirbook C-C-59 is absent in this Santa Clara source. Pedro Cabot's lyric sheet in Santa Clara Ms. 3 has the repeated phrases as we find them in the Durán choirbook C-C-59—with one small exception. The second phrase group sings the words "¡Qué ardor!" instead of "¡Qué esplendor!"

Figure 4-9 (*continued*)

Obviously, the dynamic markings penned by Cabot make sense only if the phrases are repeated, enabling there to be a contrast between answering phrases. (See figure 4-10. For a facsimile reproduction, consult photo 4-3 in this chapter and photos B-111 and B-81 in appendix B that are available online.)

Although there is no such graphic marker at the midpoint of *¡O pan de vida!*, there is a clear phrase break before the text "Haced que os sepa." At this juncture, the music crisply announces this new line with jaunty dotted rhythms. It might be

Figure 4-9 (*continued*)

Photo 4-2 *¡O que suave!* in Santa Clara Ms. 4, p. 66. (Permission to include this image courtesy of the Santa Clara University Archive; photo by the author.)

Figure 4-10 *¡O Rey de corazones!*

surmised that this second half (like the second halves of its neighboring hymns) could be repeated a second time if the performers so desired.

Several rhythmic idiosyncrasies arise in these three pieces that could easily stump the modern performer if he or she is not forewarned. Bar lines, for instance, often feel like they are displaced. Normally, we expect an "upbeat" to *precede* the bar line and then have the downbeat fall on the first beat of any given measure; but in these three *galant*-sounding pieces, the upbeat frequently

Figure 4-10 (*continued*)

occurs immediately *after* the bar line, with the downbeat falling in midmeasure. This curiosity is not as rare as it might seem; several guitar tablatures from the early eighteenth century use this unorthodox system of having the anacrusis or upbeat fall immediately after the bar line.[67] Several items in the California mission manuscripts—such as the widely disseminated *Misa de la Soledad* or the "Benedicamus Domino" at the San Antonio de Padua Mission—similarly shift the downbeat's location.[68] For the song *¡O qué suave!*, the "misplaced bar lines" begin at the second section ("Enciéndase y arda el corazón!"). With respect to *¡O Rey de corazones!*, the rhythmic glitch occurs at the beginning of measure 5; there is a missing half rest at the beginning of this bar that needs to be inserted

Figure 4-10 (*continued*)

to rectify any rhythmic confusion that otherwise would arise. Similarly, a glitch needs reparations in measure 12 of *¡O pan de vida!* If one changes the quarter rest to an eighth and shortens the following entrance of the vocalists (singing the pitches A and C on the syllable "del") from a quarter rest to an eighth in value, then the rhythmic displacement for the next three measures will be corrected. Once again, we see the anacrusis on the word "O" written immediately *after* the bar line at measure 14 instead of *before* it, as we would normally expect. The "normal" rhythmic features are restored beginning at measure 16 and continuing until the final measure, where the first pitch should be elongated by the length of a quarter note.

Figure 4-10 (*continued*)

The Spanish hymn *¡O qué suave!* for Corpus Christi is one of the central pieces in the California mission repertoire.[69] It is found in several of the mission choirbooks, such as Santa Clara Ms. 4 (p. 60) and the Durán choirbook C-C-59 (p. 70). In addition, Juan Bautista Sancho—the magnificent musician active at the San Antonio Mission near present-day King City—copied out the tune in several locations. Sancho jotted down the first portion of *¡O qué suave!* on several "blank staves" at the bottom of the sheets of the *Credo italiano a duo con el coro* (as found in WPA folder 66, photo J-7, line 8, and photo J-8, lines 7 and 8). These measures in WPA folder 66 get us only halfway through the work, but Sancho *finished* it in yet another folder in the same WPA collection. He took

Photo 4-3 *¡O Rey de corazones!* in Santa Clara Ms. 4, p. 65. (Permission to include this image courtesy of the Santa Clara University Archive; photo by the author.)

the blank staves left over from *Lamentatio a duo* in the WPA folder 61, photo R-8, lines 7–9, and then recorded the duple-meter portion of *¡O qué suave!* beginning with the text "Enciéndase y arda en mi corazón." Thus if we consult *both* folder 66 and folder 61, we have a complete rendition of the piece's vocal lines written out by Sancho.

It is possible that *¡O qué suave!* was composed in Spain and then transported to the New World. After all, folder 66 with its fragmentary beginning to *¡O qué suave!* bears Sancho's title page for a *Credo italiano* that he dates as 1796—a year when he was still directing music activities at the Convent de Sant Francesc in Palma de Mallorca. Of course, Sancho could have brought this *Credo italiano* from Mallorca to California and only later notated *¡O qué suave!* once he had arrived in the New World. The jury is still out. Another shred of evidence possibly linking this repertoire with the Balearic Islands and Cataluña is the watermark found on the sheets in choirbook C-C-68:1 (a manuscript that preserves two of these hymns, *¡O qué suave!* and *¡O pan de vida!*). If one looks through almost any sheet in this source, one sees plainly the watermark "CATALUÑA" in capital letters. This watermark is rarely found in California sources, indicating that it was not generally distributed as "blank" paper for the friars' use. We can assume, therefore, that the owner of this source was probably either Catalan or at least familiar with the Catalan music repertoire. Unfortunately, the presence of this watermark still does very little to clarify where this choirbook was conceived. It could have been written out in Spain or the New World, as long as the scribe had some contact with Cataluña and its paper industry.

An alluring signpost in one score for *¡O qué suave!* guides us toward the possible inclusion of percussion in these hymns. The fragmentary choirbook C-C-68:1 has the intriguing annotation *golpe*, or "strike," written above each appearance of the word *amor*.[70] It intimates some sort of percussive effect, but if that is the case, this choice of text expression on the word "love" is an enigmatic one. It should be noted, though, that the three successive *golpes* occur on the strong downbeat of each successive measure—at least if we apply the rule already discussed in which the strong beat can actually *precede* the measure line. If we accept and apply this notational anomaly, then the striking of a drum or other percussive instrument would fall on downbeats and provide an incisive edge to the metric rhythm. Also, observe that the scribe in this choirbook has scribbled the word *compás* (meaning duple or quadruple meter) right below the word *golpe*, but then has summarily crossed the word out. Perhaps *compás* was intended to forewarn the performer of the meter change from triple to duple in the middle section of this piece, but the scribe then reconsidered the usefulness of the indicator, since the metric shift had already occurred a few measures earlier.

Although there is no "orchestral score" for the three tunes *¡O qué suave!; ¡O pan de vida!;* and *¡O Rey de corazones!,* it is nevertheless clear that they were performed with instrumental accompaniment. The choirbook settings of *¡O Rey de corazones!* have full measures of nothing but rests, and it is unimaginable that the piece simply grinds to a halt every three or four bars. The logical assumption is that the instruments filled these spaces with related thematic material and figuration while the voices rested. Similarly, there are obvious air pockets sprinkled through *¡O qué suave!* and *¡O pan de vida!* Given the *galant* stylistic features of their graceful and varied melodic contours, it seems most appropriate to support these lines with a typical *galant* orchestral sound of the time: a pair of violin lines and a basso continuo grouping of a cello and a chordal instrument or two (such as baroque harp or baroque guitar).

The fourth member of the Corpus hymns, *¡O sacratissimo cuerpo de Jesús!,* exhibits different characteristics than the other three (see figure 4-11). Two lines of text appear below the staff, one for the elevation of the Host and the second for the elevation of the Communion chalice. This four-voice homorhythmic setting exhibits none of the *galant* features of the other three Corpus hymns. Its brevity also sets it apart from its companions. There are only two phrases: the first one descends to a half-cadence on the dominant chord, C major, that is approached by using a Phrygian descent (F–Eb–Db–C) that reminds one of Spanish flamenco guitar music; the second phrase arrives back at the tonic, F, through conventional iterations of tonic, subdominant, and dominant harmonies and repetitions of a V-to-I cadence. The bass vocalist sometimes crosses over the tenor line; but if a cello or some other instrument doubles the bass voice—and at a lower octave, at least occasionally—then any confusing chord inversions can be averted. There is a rugged and nonconformist beauty to this hymn's voice-leading. Much like the anthems of William Billings that sounded on the East Coast of North America at the same time that this repertoire sounded in the West, this hymn similarly shuns the niceties of "proper" counterpoint and carves out its phrases in a rough-hewn fashion. Parallel fifths and parallel octaves pop up as frequently as dandelions; and like dandelions, some might consider these voice-leading "errors" to be weeds, whereas others might perceive them to be flowers.

Figure 4-11 *¡O sacratissimo cuerpo de Jesús!*

Inside the Mission Walls at Corpus Christi

The Mass for Corpus Christi

Returning to Palóu's account of Father Serra's celebration of Corpus Christi, we are reminded that after the procession took place outside, the participants reentered the church to celebrate mass: "Upon the return to the Church, Mass was sung and the sermon [was] preached on this Most Holy Mystery." Not surprisingly,

Figure 4-12 *Sacris solemniis*

* In the manuscript, at mm. 5, 11, & 17, there is no sharp before the alto's
   c, but a sharp is needed in order to avoid a cross relation with the
   bass's *C-sharp*.

** The alto's final note in measures 5, 11, & 17 is a *B*. It can be
   harmonized easily enough with a B-diminished chord. However, it is
   plausible to think this pitch is in error. If we replace it with a *B-flat* we
   get "Alternative Version 1" written out below, and if we use an *A* we
   get Alternative Version 2."

Alternative Version 1   Alternative Version 2

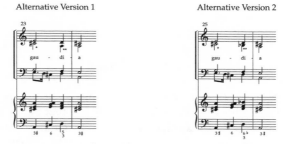

Figure 4-12 (*continued*)

the liturgy for Corpus Christi Mass is readily found in many California mission
manuscripts.[71] The three Durán choirbooks (C-C-59 at the Bancroft Library, Santa
Clara Ms. 4, and Santa Barbara Doc. 1) are nearly identical in their content: all of
them contain the mass's Introit (*Cibavit eos*), the sequence *Lauda Sion Salvatorem*,
and the Communion (*Quotiescumque manducabitis*). Rather than using the tunes
for the Introit and Communion as found in the standard Roman rite, these three
mission choirbooks—as always—use Durán's "generic tunes" for both the Introit
and the Communion.[72] Even though these three volumes are close siblings, choirbook C-C-59 contains an additional work not found in the others: the hymn *Sacris
solemniis* for the Corpus Christ procession appears on page 30 in a single-staff,
four-voice setting that includes all seven stanzas of text. (See figure 4-12. For a facsimile reproduction, consult photo B-75 in appendix B that is available online.)

Two of the most comprehensive sources for Corpus Christi Mass are Santa Clara
Ms. 3 and Choirbook C-C-68:2 at the Bancroft Library. As has been mentioned
previously, these two sources were written out by Florencio Ibáñez in exquisite

hand-lettered script. Everything one needs to realize the Mass Proper appears in their pages: the Introit, Alleluia, the sequence *Lauda Sion Salvatorem*, the Offertory, and the Communion. These two sources supply *canto llano* and *canto figurado* melodies that change appropriately from piece to piece rather than conform to the "standardized" tunes that Durán reiterates in his three large choirbooks. Much of the plainchant in Santa Clara Ms. 3 and choirbook C-C-68:2 draws upon traditional Gregorian chant.[73] In addition, both of these manuscripts have their own "bonus" contributions beyond the core of the Mass Proper. Santa Clara Ms. 3 records the processional hymn *¡O Rey de corazones!* and choirbook C-C-68:2 has the three Latin processional hymns for Corpus Christi (*Pange lingua, Sacris solemniis,* and *Verbum supernum prodiens*) written out after the Communion—just as we find in the Roman rite. This location just after the mass's conclusion implies that the processional hymns in Latin accompanied a Corpus Christi procession if it took place *after* mass.[74] On the other hand, the Spanish processional hymns that we have already discussed (*¡O qué suave!; ¡O pan de vida!; ¡O Rey de corazones!;* and *¡O sacratissimo cuerpo de Jesús!*) appear to have been positioned *before* the mass, at least according to Palóu's description of the Corpus Christi liturgy as celebrated by Father Serra.

Lauda Sion Salvatorem

One of the cornerstones of the Feast Day of Corpus Christi is the inspiring sequence *Lauda Sion Salvatorem.*[75] From its inception as genre, the "sequence" most typically followed on the heels of the Alleluia at high Mass. Its structure was based on paired phrases, although oftentimes the first phrase that set things in motion was a musical orphan that had no companion. As a piece advanced forward through time, then, the listener would hear a stream of "new" pairs, each possessing its own distinctive melodic material. The structure therefore resembled the shape *a-a', b-b', c-c', d-d',* and so on. In short, a sequence with its procession of ever-changing musical pairs could be compared to the pairs of animals that marched into Noah's ark—a long string of different species marching along, two by two, in boundless variety yet exquisite symmetry. Through the centuries, however, the sequence underwent several transformations: by the time of the California mission period, the pattern of paired phrases was largely scrapped in favor of semistrophic patterns where two contrasting musical units alternate back and forth in a pattern that could be mapped out *a-b, a'-b', a"-b", a'''-b''',* and so on. The various settings of *Lauda Sion Salvatorem* in the mission repertoire—and there are many—exemplify this latter template of alternating *a* and *b* phrases. In none of the settings do we have two stanzas of text in a row set to the same music, thus obliterating any resemblance to the "pairs" of a medieval sequence structure.

There are three basic versions of *Lauda Sion Salvatorem* that circulated in the California mission repertoire, none of them using the "original" melodic material from antiquity. The three Durán choirbooks present a polyphonic setting that glides along in duet texture with an occasional expansion to three voices at cadences. A second version—that circulated widely—presents a single melodic line in *canto figurado* style that strolls along in a jaunty triple meter. A third version found at the San Fernando Mission in Juan Bautista Sancho's handwriting lays out yet another *canto figurado* setting in triple meter, but this one is built of motivic cells or building blocks, a handful of which are arranged and reordered to fabricate each of the phrases.

The polyphonic duet version is molded from three different phrases, each in triple meter with a pair of voices sauntering along in parallel sixths or thirds until their inevitable cadences on a C-major harmony.[76] (See figure 4-13. For facsimile reproductions of this piece, consult photos B-73 and B-104 available online in appendix B.) At cadential points the rigorous parallelisms evaporate in lieu of cursory contrary motion and the temporary insertion of a third voice to the textural mix. The composition's formal structure is puzzling. As we have firmly established, *alternatim* performance was the norm, so most settings in California sources present either the odd-numbered verses or the even ones. But here the original twenty-four verses of the medieval sequence have been trimmed down to ten, with no transparent or obvious pattern. The three phrases and their stanzas are as follows: phrase *a* sung to verses 1, 3, and 9; phrase *b* sung to verses 11, 14, and 17; and phrase *c* sung to verses 19 and 21. Under normal circumstances, if we apply a simple alternation between odd and even stanzas, all the phrases line up in numerical order (1, 2, 3, 4, 5, 6, etc.), but that is not the case here. In this particular version we encounter large potholes in *Lauda Sion Salvatorem*'s lyrics; what happens to other missing stanzas is rather a mystery. Perhaps they are merely stricken; another solution would be an instrumental rendition of the missing phrases, as implied by the work's instruction "con música a la misma," or "with instrumental music in the same key."[77]

The second version of *Lauda Sion Salvatorem* was chiseled from only two phrases in *canto figurado*, the single melodic line traversing an exceedingly wide melodic range with frequent leaps of an octave or rising fourth—in truth, it sounds and feels more like a bass instrumental line that has been texted than it does a breezy soprano air.[78] It begins and ends in A minor with a major excursion to the nearly related key of C major in the middle of each phrase. The two phrases alternate between the *a* and *b* phrases, but in each of the mission sources, the work is cut short after only six or seven verses (rather than plodding along through all twenty-four). Serra choirbook M.0612 at Stanford provides verses 1, 3, 5, and 7, followed immediately by a brief "alleluia" that pulls things to a close.[79] Similarly, the choirbook C-C-68:2 truncates the text after verse 7 and its culminating "alleluia." In the same way, Santa Clara Ms. 3 cuts the piece off after only four verses (although there might be a missing page in this location—there is no concluding "alleluia" to tie up loose ends). And the alternate version of the sequence written out by Pedro Cabot onto a small sheet and sewn into Santa Clara Ms. 3 contains only six verses. (See photo B-95 in appendix B for a photo of this sheet.) The fact that several blank staves fill out the rest of the sheet would indicate that his trimming of the text down to six verses was willful, since there was plenty of space to continue.[80]

Juan Bautista Sancho wrote out a third version of *Lauda Sion Salvatorem* in D minor on a loose sheet that also contains a "Kiries clasiches," a Mass Ordinary

Figure 4-13 *Lauda Sion Salvatorem,* three-phrase version, Santa Clara Ms. 4

setting that undoubtedly came from his native Mallorca.[81] After all, the Kyrie's title is written in *mallorquín,* not Castilian. (For a facsimile, consult photo 1-8 in chapter 1. Also see photo B-53 in appendix B online.) There are no other known exemplars of this particular version of *Lauda Sion Salvatorem;* it clearly did not have the widespread dissemination and appeal of the *canto figurado* setting already discussed. Given the provenance of the "Kiries clasiches" setting on this manuscript sheet, and considering there are no duplicates of Sancho's version, one might suppose that this particular version might also be from Sancho's native island, not a core melody from the broader repertoire. Continuing the trend of alternating performance, Sancho writes out the text and tune only for the odd-numbered phrases. The even-numbered ones could have been poured into the same melodic molds as used for the odd-numbered phrases, or more likely, Sancho could have inserted the *b* phrases using contrasting textures (such as instrumental interludes or different-sized vocal groupings). The polyphonic setting found in Durán's C-C-59 and the Santa Clara Ms. 4 does not really provide any usable material for the missing *b* phrases, since their emphasis on C major would make clumsy companions with the D-minor phrases in Sancho's manuscript. On the other hand, Sancho could have mined his *b* phrases for the even-numbered stanzas from the well-known *canto figurado* setting ("Version 2") already discussed. If they are transposed from A minor to D minor, those *b* phrases can be dropped into place without a hitch. Unlike the other California manuscripts, Sancho's setting ambitiously drives ahead from start to finish with no detours and no vacuous extractions: every one of the odd-numbered phrases of text shows up for duty. Musically, this is one of the most beguiling settings due to its cohesive unity. Sancho forges nearly every phrase from a handful of recurring motives. The first phrase stands alone (as is so often the case even in the medieval sequence), but all the remaining phrases share the same chromosomes to their musical DNA. He has four different opening gestures, a standardized middle "core" that carries the bulk of the phrase, and then two recurring cadences—one drawing us to the dominant and the other to tonic. By shuffling elements and swapping out different components, Sancho builds every one of his phrases. (See figure 4-14 for a graph of the various components as they appear in Sancho's copy of *Lauda Sion Salvatorem*.)

Two Prominent Gems of California Liturgy

Dies irae

As with any village or township, in the missions the cornerstones of life—birth, baptism, marriage, and death—were celebrated or commemorated appropriately with music. Sadly, death was a frequent visitor, largely because of the inability of Native Americans' immune systems to combat European-borne diseases. The services related to death and burial are elaborate and consume wide swaths of paper in the mission choirbooks.[82] In fact, only Holy Week commands more attention in the music sources. One of the most deeply moving of these sorrowful funeral pieces was the ancient sequence *Dies irae,* a work most often ascribed to Thomas of Celaeno, the confidant, biographer, and friend of Saint Francis.[83] This original version from the Middle Ages is a sort of structural hybrid, maintaining the paired phrases expected of a medieval sequence yet exhibiting aspects of strophic form by grouping the phrases into three large "stanzas" of repeated

Figure 4-14 *Lauda Sion Salvatorem* as copied out by Juan Bautista Sancho. (Translation from www.chanted.com/lyrics)

material. All told, the phrase structure follows the pattern: *aabbcc—aabbcc—aabbcde*. The ancient plainchant version is preserved more or less intact in Santa Clara Ms. 4, an exceedingly rare instance of a sequence that preserves its medieval roots instead of evolving into a metric or polyphonic transfiguration.[84] It should be noted, however, that the medieval sequence had entirely new melodic material for its last two phrases, numbers 18 and 19; in this California manuscript, however, the piece returns to its previous melodic material. The end result is the pattern *aabbcc—aabbcc—aabbccb* instead of the original sequence's structure of *aabbcc—aabbcc—aabbcde*.

The traditional melodic contours of the *Dies irae* serve as the basis for a rhythmicized setting that emerges in the California mission repertoire; a few notes

Figure 4-14 (*continued*)

are excised, but the rest of the tones are poured into a repeated triple meter of *long-short, long-short, long-short,* and so on.[85] This metric conversion into *canto figurado* style arises in the Durán choirbook C-C-59, but it also tinkers around with melodic substitutions on the last phrases—similar to what we saw in the plainchant revision in Santa Clara Ms. 4. But unlike that latter source, the Durán rendition strides forward into a "new" phrase *d* (maintaining its fealty to the medieval structural model), but then chooses to rebound to the familiar *b* phrase to close off the work. As a result, we end up with the modified phrase pattern, *aab-bcc—aabbcc—aabbcdb.*

Lauda Sion Salvatorem
Sequence for Corpus Cbristi

1. Lauda, Sion, Salvatorem,
Lauda ducem et pastorem
In hymnis et canticis.
Quantum poses, tantum aude:
Quia major omni laude
Nec laudare sufficis.

Sion, lift thy voice and sing:
Praise thy Savior and thy King;
Praise with hymns thy Shepherd true:
Dare thy most to praise Him well;
For He doth all praise excel;
None can ever reach His due.

2. Laudis thema specialis,
Panis vivus et vitalis
Hodie proponitur;
Quem in sacrae mensa coenae
Turbae fratrum duodenae
Datum non ambigitur.

Special theme of praise is thine,
That true living Bread divine,
That life-giving flesh adored,
Which the brethren twelve received,
As most faithfully believed,
At the Supper of the Lord.

3. Sit laus plena, sit sonora,
Sit iucunda, sit decora
Mentis iubilatio.
Dies enim solemnis agitur,
In qua mensae prima recolitur
Huius institutio.

Let the chant be loud and high;
Sweet and tranquil be the joy
Felt to-day in every breast;
On this festival divine
Which recounts the origin
Of the glorious Eucharist.

4. In hac mensa novi Regis
Novum Pascha novae legis
Phase vetus terminat.
Vetustatem novitas,
Umbram fugat veritas,
Noctem lux eliminat.

At this table of the King,
Our new Paschal offering
Brings to end the olden rite;
Here, for empty shadows fled,
Is reality instead;
Here, instead of darkness, light.

5. Quod in coena Christus gessit,
Faciendum hoc expressit
In sui memoriam
Docti sacris institutis,
Panem, vinum in salutis
Consecramus hostiam.

His own act, at supper seated,
Christ ordained to be repeated,
In His memory divine;
Wherefore now, with adoration,
We the Host of our salvation
Consecrate from bread and wine.

6. Dogma datur Christianis,
Quod in carnem transit panis
Et vinum in sanguinem.
Quod non capis, quod non vides,
Animosa firmat fides
Praeter rerum ordinem.

Hear what holy Church maintaineth,
That the bread its substance changeth
Into Flesh, the wine to Blood.
Doth it pass thy comprehending?
Faith, the law of sight transcending,
Leaps to things not understood.

7. Sub diversis speciebus,
Signis tantum, et non rebus,
Latent res eximiae:
Caro cibus, sanguis potus;
Manet tamen Christus totus
Sub urtaque specie.

Here in outward signs are hidden
Priceless things, to sense forbidden;
Signs, not things, are all we see:-
Flesh from bread, and Blood from wine;
Yet is Christ, in either sign,
All entire confessed to be.

Figure 4-14 (*continued*)

8. A sumente non concisus,
Non confractus, non divisus
    Integer accipitur.
Sumit unus, sumunt mille;
Quantum isti, tantum ille:
    Nec sumptus consumitur.

They too who of Him partake
Sever not, nor rend, nor break,
But entire their Lord receive.
Whether one or thousands eat,
All receive the selfsame meat,
Nor the less for others leave.

9. Sumunt boni, sumunt mali:
Sorte tamen inaequali,
    Vitae vel interitus.
Mors est malis, vita bonis:
Vide, paris sumptionis
Quam sit dispar exitus.

Both the wicked and the good
Eat of this celestial Food;
But with ends how opposite!
Here 'tis life; and there 'tis death;
The same, yet issuing to each
In a difference infiite.

10. Fracto demum Sacramento,
Ne vacilles, sed memento,
Tantam esse sub fragmento,
    Quantum toto tegitur.
    Nulla rei fit scissura,
Signi tantum fit fractura,
Qua nec status nec statura
    Signati minuitur.

Nor a single doubt retain,
When they break the Host in twain,
But that in each part remains
What was in the whole before;
Since the simple sign alone
Suffers change in state or form,
The Signifed remaining One
And the Same forevermore

11. Ecce panis Angelorum,
Factus cibus viatorum,
    Vere panis filiorum,
Non mittendus canibus.
In figuris praesignatur,
Cum Isaac immolatur;
Agnus Paschae deputatur,
Datur manna patribus.

Lo! upon the Altar lies,
Hidden deep from human eyes,
Angels' Bread from Paradise
Made the food of mortal man:
Children's meat to dogs denied;
In old types foresignified;
In the manna from the skies,
In Isaac, and the Paschal Lamb.

12. Bone Pastor, panis vere,
Jesu, nostri miserere,
Tu nos pasce, nos tuere,
Tu nos bona fac videre,
    In terra viventium.
Tu, qui cuncta scis et vales,
Qui nos pascis hic mortales,
Tuos ibi commensales,
Cohaeredes et sodales,
Fac sanctorum civium. Amen

Jesu! Shepherd of the sheep!
Thy true flock in safety keep.
Living Bread! Thy life supply;
Strengthen us, or else we die;
Fill us with celestial grace:
Thou, who feedest us below!
Source of all we have or know!
Grant that with Thy Saints above,
Sitting at the Feast of Love,
We may see Thee face to face. Amen

Figure 4-14 (*continued*)

Florencio Ibáñez's Santa Clara Ms. 3 reflects the same core elements as Durán's choirbook C-C-59, but with a few significant alterations. The same three melodic phrases appear in both books, but the Santa Clara choirbook switches phrases *b* and *c* so that they appear in the reverse order: that is, what had been phrase *b* in choirbook C-C-59 is now utilized as the *c* material. Like the plainchant model of the *Dies irae* that became ensconced into the Roman rite, Santa Clara Ms. 3 launches into *new* melodic territory at the last two phrases of the sequence (phrases *d* and *e*)— but it makes no referential nod to the Roman rite's melodic contour. Instead, this version, as it appears in Santa Clara Ms. 3, meanders into truly new melodic terrain, not replicating the well-known tune as practiced in the Gregorian tradition.

Several versions of the *Dies irae* in the mission manuscripts supply a cornucopia of substitute sections that can be mixed and matched, swapped and exchanged.[86] One spare proxy that can fill in for the *a* phrases in the *Dies irae* is a polyphonic phrase found in Santa Clara Ms. 4.[87] Set in F minor or F dorian, the phrase is arranged for four voices in quadruple meter, all voices plodding forward in steady half-note motion (in other words, in a constant flow of breves). After this single phrase, the scribe instructs the singers where to find the other necessary material: "Quantus tremor &c., como en la otra prosa pag. 79," or "For the next verse of the sequence *Quantus tremor,* and the remainder of the lyrics, refer to page 79." As we have already noted, the *Dies irae* on page 79 is in meterless plainchant.

The most dramatic example of music substitution occurs in Durán's choirbook C-C-59. He writes out the core to this sequence twice: once on pages 67 and 68 with a few cross-outs and errors; and again, a few pages later, where small snippets of paper are glued into the choirbook that can be folded back to remove—or be pushed down to include—variant versions of each phrase.[88] (See photos B-5 through B-7 in appendix B online and photos 2-1 through 2-3 in chapter 2 along with the accompanying explanation.) Interestingly, no matter what option the performers adopt, the structural underpinning will always be that of two alternating phrases (*a-b-a-b-a-b,* etc.), scrapping entirely the three-phrased frame of the original *Dies irae* (i.e., the pattern, *aabbcc—aabbcc—aabbcde*).[89] Durán builds rich textures, flipping between duet texture and a full-bodied quartet. He explains this give-and-take in his instructional advice, at three locations, each specifying that "this sequence is sung by alternating between a verse in duet texture with another set in four-voice texture, according to the numbers in the margin."[90]

Veni Sancte Spiritus

One of the jewels of California polyphony is the graceful and richly varied setting of the sequence *Veni Sancte Spiritus* for Pentecost. This church feast day was of immense importance in the mission year. Falling on the fiftieth day after Easter Sunday (its name derived from the Greek word *pentekoste,* or "fiftieth"), it commemorates the coming of the Holy Spirit to the Apostles who appeared to them in the "upper room" as flaming tongues of fire.[91] We have already examined Serra's absorbing description of the Pentecost celebration on 3 June 1770 at

Monterey—although this occasion saw the inclusion of the hymn *Veni Creator Spiritus,* a *Salve,* and the *Te Deum,* with no mention of the sequence *Veni Sancte Spiritus.*[92]

As with most sequences, *Veni Sancte Spiritus* is preceded in the mass by the singing of the Alleluia. For Pentecost, the Alleluia's Psalm verse has a very similar text, beginning with the same three words and then continuing, "Veni Sancte Spiritus, reple tuorum corda fidelium, et tui amoris in eis ignem accende" (Come, O Holy Ghost, fill the hearts of Thy faithful and kindle in them the fire of Thy love).[93] Several contrasting versions of *Veni Sancte Spiritus* circulated in California; no known copies of the original plainchant are extant in mission manuscripts.[94]

The three Durán choirbooks (C-C-59 at the Bancroft Library, Santa Clara Ms. 4, and Santa Barbara Doc. 1) preserve a version that is fundamentally a duet in texture.[95] (See figure 4-15, and for facsimiles, consult photos B-4 and B-103 in appendix

Figure 4-15 *Veni Sancte Spiritus,* duet texture

B that is available online.) All three sources, however, add voices as the phrases continue and build toward a cadence, in much the same way that a chef adds flour to thicken a sauce: the density increases, but the core flavor is not really changed. In the Santa Clara source the adjustment in texture is modest, with a third voice joining in only at the cadences' resolutions. Choirbook C-C-59 and Santa Barbara Doc. 1, on the other hand, quickly add sonorities, at first emphasizing trio voicings and then becoming even fuller with a fourth voice. (In C-C-59, the final sonority expands further to notate a fifth voice!) It should be noted that the number of notated voices is a bit deceiving, since there is extensive voice doubling. In truth, usually only three different pitches are resounding at any given moment. None of these choirbooks places numerals in front of the stanzas to keep track of the text, but if one compares the lyrics jotted on the page with the "complete" sequence *Veni Sancte Spiritus,* he will find only the odd-numbered stanzas.[96] Once again, we can safely assume that the friars and their congregations sang in *alternatim* style. This theory is reinforced by the instructions and annotations in the margins. Before the Alleluia (that leads without pause into the sequence *Veni Sancte Spiritus*), Durán instructs the choir: "Alla. 5° T° Musica de Vt" (Alleluia, Mode 5, Music in C major). As has already been observed, the use of the term *música* in this context indicates that instrumental interludes are to take the place of the missing even-numbered stanzas.[97] To avoid any performance missteps, Durán assures us of his intentions twice more on this same page. On the heels of the Alleluia and above the sequence he writes, "Musica la misma solfa que la Sequencia, o de Ut" (the instrumental music is in the same *solfege* or key as the Sequence, that is to say, the key of C). And right after the final cadence and last words of the verses, he writes down the reminder "Música" (Instrumental music).

The most tantalizing setting surfaces in Santa Clara Ms. 3.[98] (For a facsimile of Santa Clara Ms. 3's *Veni Sancte Spiritus,* see photo 1-6 in chapter 1 and photo B-94 in appendix B available online. For a transcription, consult figure 4-16.) Perhaps the most alluring aspect of the piece is its spellbinding combination of three contrasting styles, each of which enjoyed an essential role in mission liturgy: it begins in meterless plainchant or *canto llano* with the opening Alleluia; as it embarks on the sequence *Veni Sancte Spiritus,* the texture shifts to *canto figurado* to a swaying triple meter; and this texture in turn broadens with the ensuing phrase in *canto de órgano* or *estilo moderno,* depending on how one realizes the implied instrumental accompaniment. The disparate ingredients to this polymorphous piece are sprinkled across the page (and sometimes crossed out and relocated). A bit of detective work and explanation is in order.

At first glance, the setting of the Alleluia is rather straightforward. The scribe—probably Fray Florencio Ibáñez—copies out the tune in unexceptional chant notation that would not have raised any eyebrows. His performance instructions, however, are another matter. The first advice he provides in Latin: neatly printed above the Psalm verse "Veni Sancte Spiritus, reple tuorum," Ibáñez writes; "hic Flectuntur genua" (Here, all kneel). That is traditional practice at the Alleluia verse during the Feast of Pentecost.[99] Below the staff at this location is an elaborate cross, a near duplicate of which appears in the left-hand margin. The cross is a sort of

"Alleluia and *Veni Sancte Spiritus*,"
Santa Clara Ms. 3

Edited by & with instrumental
parts composed by Craig H. Russell

Santa Clara Ms. 3, p. 34

hic Flectuntur genua (Here, all kneel)

Al - - le - - - - lu - ia. Ve - - - - ni Sanc - te

Spi - - ri - tus re - ple tu - o - rum cor - da fi - de - li - um,

et tu - i a - mo - ris in e - is ig - nem ac - - - - cen - de.

Sequentia
Tono 2do

Voice

[1] Ve - - ni Sanc - te Spi - ri - tus, Et e - mi - te
[3] Con - - so - la - tor op - ti - me, Dul - cis hos - pes
[5] O lux be - a - tis - si - ma, Re - ple cor - dis
[7] La - - va quod est sor - di - dum, Ri - ga quod est
[9] Da tu - is fi - de - li - bus, In te con - fi -

Continuo

coe - li - tus lu - - - cis tu - ae ra - di
a - - ni - mae, Dul - - ce re - fri - ge - ri
in - - ti - ma, Tu - o - - - rum fi - de - li
a - - ri - dum, Sa - na quod es sau - ci -
den - - ti - bus, Sa - - crum sep - te - na - ri

† Estarán arrodillados todos todo el tpõ qᵉ la Tambora haga un ruido como el cañon gᵈᵉ del organo.
All will kneel here for the whole time until the drum makes a ruckus like the big metal organ stop of the organ.

Figure 4-16 "Alleluia and *Veni Sancte Spiritus*," Santa Clara Ms. 3. (Translation from www.chanted.com/lyrics and www.arvopart./composition_text.php?id=46)

footnote, the symbol referring us to the advice written at the side—and the advice is revelatory. We read:

Everyone will kneel here for the whole time that the drum makes a ruckus like the big metal organ stop of the organ (*Estarán arrodillados todos todo el tpõ qᵉ la Tambora haga un ruido como el cañon gᵈᵉ del organo*)

** A sharp originally was
notated but has been
erased.

Figure 4-16 (*continued*)

This is shocking. One would have to look for an eternity in European chant books to find any reference to drums as an accompaniment to plainchant! That detail is bursting with far-reaching implications. The drum is the most essential element for indigenous worship in the Americas: its inclusion here hints at a mutual accommodation between two contrasting and sometimes conflicting cultures that come together in this Pentecost service to worship their single Creator. The *Veni Sancte Spiritus* incorporates the most sacred elements from both peoples. Of course, the Franciscans do not make a fuss about this and draw attention to this unorthodoxy when writing back to Spain. If they were to report this sort of detail to their superiors, some stuffy official could accuse the friars of blasphemous heresy. Therefore, they conveniently skipped any potentially explosive or offensive details when writ-

Figure 4-16 (*continued*)

ing their reports and filling out their forms. Granted, the Franciscans were "true believers" in the faith, but they were also realists, and some were rather open-minded. It is meaningful that a core element of Native American worship had not been completely expunged from sacred life in the California missions but instead was incorporated into the singing of mass.[100] The performance advice is simultaneously bold and inviting. Don't politely tap the drum in passive lethargy; make a ruckus.

The hodgepodge of handwriting, corrections, and cross-outs on page 27 of Santa Clara Ms. 3 provide an intriguing window into performance practice at the missions. We have just discussed the peculiarities regarding plainchant in the verse of the Alleluia. The ensuing phrases also have their riddles whose solutions are

Figure 4-16 *(continued)*

revealing. After the Alleluia, Ibáñez moves forward with the "Sequencia. 2do tono"
(Sequence in the 2nd mode) and writes out the first phrase of *Veni Sancte Spiritus*
in antiquated *canto figurado* notation with squared-off breves, semibreves, and
minims. The second phrase of the sequence follows, "Veni, veni Pater pauperum,"
and at this point things get interesting. The manuscript has two layers of information written on top of each other, providing two different musical settings of this
phrase. The older one is barely visible underneath the revision and shows the signs
of attempted and largely unsuccessful erasure. With a little care, both versions
can be divined and understood, in the same way that an archaeologist can dig

Alleluia and *Veni Sancte Spiritus*
Alleluia and Sequence for Pentecost

Alleluia:

V. Veni Sancte Spiritus,
reple tuorum corda fidelium:
et tui amoris in eis ignem accende.

Alleluia:

(Verse) Come, Holy Spirit,
fill the hearts of your faithful:
and ignite the fire of your love within them.

Sequentia

Veni, Sancte Spiritus,
et emitte caelitus
lucis tuae radium.

Veni, pater pauperum,
veni, dator munerum
veni, lumen cordium.

Consolator optime,
dulcis hospes animae,
dulce refrigerium.

In labore requies,
in aestu temperies
in fletu solatium.

O lux beatissima,
reple cordis intima
tuorum fidelium.

Sine tuo numine,
nihil est in homine,
nihil est innoxium.

Lava quod est sordidum,
riga quod est aridum,
sana quod est saucium.

Flecte quod est rigidum,
fove quod est frigidum,
rege quod est devium.

Da tuis fidelibus,
in te confidentibus,
sacrum septenarium.

Da virtutis meritum,
da salutis exitum,
da perenne gaudium, Amen, Alleluia.

Sequence

Come, Holy Ghost, send down those beams,
which sweetly flow in silent streams
from Thy bright throne above.

O come, Thou Father of the poor;
O come, Thou source of all our store,
come, fill our hearts with love.

O Thou, of comforters the best,
O Thou, the soul's delightful guest,
the pilgrim's sweet relief.

Rest art Thou in our toil, most sweet
refreshment in the noonday heat;
and solace in our grief.

O blessed Light of life Thou art;
fill with Thy light the inmost heart
of those who hope in Thee.

Without Thy Godhead nothing can,
have any price or worth in man,
nothing can harmless be.

Lord, wash our sinful stains away,
refresh from heaven our barren clay,
our wounds and bruises heal.

To Thy sweet yoke our stiff necks bow,
warm with Thy fire our hearts of snow,
our wandering feet recall.

Grant to Thy faithful, dearest Lord,
whose only hope is Thy sure word,
the sevenfold gifts of grace.

Grant us in life Thy grace that we,
in peace may die and ever be,
in joy before Thy face. Amen. Alleluia.

Figure 4-16 (*continued*)

down and uncover several levels of buried foundations of buildings that had been covered over long ago. At the lowest level, the oldest setting that Ibáñez wrote out is a duet that travels along in parallel thirds with no apparent sense of meter or rhythm. Of course, a rhythmic realization in a consistent meter could have been imposed and passed along through the oral tradition, but there is nothing on the page to indicate such a rendition. Fortunately, we have a concordant version of this piece that helps considerably in rescuing from oblivion the ghostlike images in Santa Clara Ms. 3. The choirbook C-C-68:2 contains the same piece in very similar notation; its *b* phrase at "Veni, veni Pater pauperum" matches its twin as the "erased" version in Santa Clara.

In revising the composition to produce his "second version," Ibáñez inked over the discarded erasures and wrote out a single melodic line in *canto figurado* notation. Unlike the meterless void of the older, abandoned setting, this newer version of the *b* phrase skates along in the same ebullient triple meter as the opening *a* phrase ("Veni Sancte Spiritus") that set the sequence in motion. In short, the initial rhythmic drive and energy is not only maintained: it is heightened. Ibáñez's small jottings to the side of the staff at this new phrase provide essential information. He writes "Tono 2do," reaffirming the key of the work as a whole, and at the top of staff he inserts the phrase "2ª voz / Duo" (2nd Voice of a Duet). At first blush, this may seem confusing, for we have only the "2nd voice." Where is the first? Fortunately, the two bottom staves of the page have the truant "1ʳᵃ voz" written out by another scribe, Pedro Cabot. The two voices have the same text and—when combined— give us the lovely parallel thirds of a dulcet and well-blended duet.

Not only has the handwriting shifted from one scribe to another, but also the notational conventions leap from antiquated to modern. Ibáñez had been using the squared note heads of *canto figurado;* Cabot's writing brings us forward to the "rounded" note shapes of half notes, quarter notes, and eighth notes. That notational shift further implies a journey from the strummed chords of *canto figurado* to the instrumental currency of *estilo moderno* and contemporary Classicism. Significantly, Juan Bautista Sancho writes out the same "revised" version of *Veni Sancte Spiritus* that we find on page 27 of Santa Clara Ms. 3, and Sancho writes it out exclusively using "modern" notation: he summarily skips the plainchant section of the Alleluia and its verse. Since Sancho was the most "hip" of the friars when it came to being up-to-date with musical fashion, it is noteworthy that he copies out the *Veni Sancte Spiritus* into his free sheets for his use: it implies that this piece fell into the orbit of "modern-sounding" Classicism that so enthralled this Mallorcan padre. A performance of this sequence as it resounded in the California missions would demand some sort of *galant* or Classical accompaniment.

As we have seen so often in California sources, the written page (taken out of its larger cultural context) can be misleading when it comes to lyrics and text underlay. At first glance, one might think that *Veni Sancte Spiritus* is a rather short, through-composed ditty. That is the impression one would get if he were to consider only the Santa Clara Ms. 3 and Sancho's copy in WPA folder 54. Both sources write out only two verses of the original ten associated with this medieval text. The performance conventions in California strongly suggest that the piece should continue forward: the first musical phrase *a* is applied to all the odd-numbered verses, and the second phrase *b* to the even-numbered ones. In so doing, we arrive at that recognizable pattern *a-b-a-b,* and so on. Not only does that pattern conform to countless other examples in this mission frontier, but we find the proof in the pudding in choirbook C-C-68:2. This choirbook's version of *Veni Sancte Spiritus* is a close sibling to the two other sources, but it takes the trouble to write out each of the ten stanzas over the next three pages. All the odd verses have the same music, and the music for all the even-numbered verses matches as well.

We could continue on and on, exploring the many wonders of other feast days with their attendant hymns, sequences, songs of praise, and so on. The journey down that path, although pleasant, would merely lead us to the same destinations and only underscore further what we have already established. So let us move on to the next tasks that *do* remain—the study of Fray Juan Bautista Sancho and of the mass. This genre in California represents some of its most varied, resplendent, and virtuosic repertoire. And Sancho represents one of the most versatile and technically adroit musicians on the West Coast, developing his talents as teacher, interpreter, conductor, and—perhaps—composer. Sancho's impressive accomplishments at the San Antonio Mission are not an encyclopedic view of everything that happened in all twenty-one of the California missions between 1769 and 1848. His story is but one among many. However, sometimes a narrowly focused snapshot tells us something that sweeping generalities cannot; an examination of Sancho's life and music can tell us much about the human experience in California during the early nineteenth century. Let us begin.

Notes

1. For a discussion of past scholarship—both its contributions and its limitations—consult the introduction to this volume.

2. "Gozos de la Purisima q⁰ se cantan [todos los] Sabados 6° T° Compas de 4" (Praises for the Immaculate Conception that are sung on every Saturday, in mode 6 and quadruple meter), Durán choirbook C-C-59, p. 121. "[Gozos] al Sr. Sn. José que se cantan los días 19 de Todos los meses. Compás de [3]" (Praises for San José that are sung on the 19th of every month, in Triple Meter), Durán choirbook C-C-59, p. 98. From here onward I abbreviate these two works as *Gozos de la Purísima* and *Gozos al Señor San José,* respectively.

The most important study of *gozos,* or praise songs, is Joan Carles Gomis Corell's "Los Gozos marianos en la Comarca del Campo de Morvedre: Estudio histórico y documental," *Revista de Musicología,* vol. 25, no. 1 (June 2002), 251–81. He explores countless of these songs, including the "Gozos a la Purisima…," for which he provides a facsimile of a lyric sheet printed in Valencia in the eighteenth century. A comparison reveals these lyrics to be the same as those used in the California settings, beginning with the line "Para dar luz inmortal" and having as its important response, "Ave sois, Eva trocada."

Several California sources include a version of *Gozos de la Purísima,* including choirbook C-C-59, p. 121. On this page, after the word *cantan,* there is a blotch that severely hampers reading the next words; the amount of space accommodates about ten letters, and similar titles for *gozos* in the Durán manuscript utilize the words "todos los." Also, as we have seen previously, the Hispano-American world generally celebrated Mass for the Virgin on every Saturday ("todos los Sabados"). There is a concordant version of the same music with a variant of the text in Santa Clara Ms. 4, p. 64. The Durán choirbook records a total of eleven stanzas, whereas Santa Clara Ms. 4 includes only seven; many of the same stanzas appear in both, but not necessarily in the same order. There also is a third concordant version on fols. 34v–37 of the choirbook fragment C-C-68:1 in the Bancroft Library. Its version precisely matches the music and the first seven stanzas of text as they appear in the Durán choirbook, C-C-59. The latter source, however, continues with five additional stanzas. Juan Sancho also wrote out a portion of this work as found on photo J-8 in folder 66 of the WPA collection. It is hastily written out, perhaps intended to be more of a reminder than an actual formal performance part. The fragment bears no title or identifier of any kind, but it contains the bass line and some of the tenor line for the *Gozos de la Purísima* as notated in other California manuscripts. Sancho's fragment records the incipit phrase and text "Para dar luz inmortal, siendo vos alva del día." Then it skips the response (*Rx*) and goes directly to the first stanza of the verses: "Ave sois eva trocada, sin elve de aquella pena."

3. In the Durán choirbook C-C-59 on p. 98, we find the relevant incipit "Para dar luz inmortal" as the opening lyrics for the *Gozos al Señor San José*. There are torn edges to the sheets in this choirbook, thus removing the beginning and ending words of the title; nevertheless, the title can be ascertained by its identification in other sources, and the meter can be determined through context even though the torn edge has removed the "3" that must have been there when the title was written out. This same piece is found in Santa Clara Ms. 4, on p. 63. (For a facsimile reproduction of this sheet, consult photo B-110 available in appendix B online.) The incomplete choirbook fragment in the Bancroft Library, C-C-68:1, has a concordant version of the *Gozos al Señor San José* on fols. 20v and 40v. In this manuscript, the creator tried to avoid the distracting "ghost" images of bleed-through (where the writing on one side of the page is visible on the other due to dark ink and thin paper) by pasting together two sheets and thus making each folio twice as thick. The added thickness would assure that no image would show through from the back side. Unfortunately, some of the double sheets have become unglued so that the two sheets are no longer firmly attached—subsequently, when this book was sewn together again (apparently in a failed restoration), some sheets have been lost or relocated to other regions of the volume, so that "companion sheets" can be widely separated from each other. Such is the case with the *Gozos al Señor San José;* fol. 40v had originally been on the left side of a pair of sheets that read straight across from left to right, and the recto or right side had been fol. 20v. Taken together, these two sheets originally had been the facing pages.

For a recording of the *Gozos al Señor San José,* "Para dar luz inmortal," consult the CD release *Mission Road,* Chanticleer and Chanticleer Chamber Ensemble, directed by Joseph Jennings and with artistic consultant Craig H. Russell (Claremont, Calif.: Warner Classics and Jazz and the Rhino Entertainment Company, 2008).

4. Observe that the melody and harmony at the beginning of any stanza is the same that we heard as the "antecedent" phrase in the introduction. They both are made of the same core *a* material.

5. I use the terms "dominant" and "tonic" here primarily to help the modern listener "hear" the way these phrases function. There is a kind of tension when the first phrase resides on the "dominant" that is then resolved on the subsequent phrase's arrival on the "tonic." Technically, however, this piece is modal (see chapter 2), and a more rigorous use of terms would substitute word "tenor" for "dominant" and would replace the word "tonic" with the term "final."

6. See the section "Modes" in chapter 2.

7. See, for example, the modes and cadences found in Santiago de Murcia's *Resumen de acompañar la parte con la guitarra* (engraved in Antwerp, 1714; released in Madrid, 1717), 10.

8. For a thorough discussion of the historical and musical features of the *folías,* consult Aurelio Capmany, "El baile y la danza," in *Folklore y costumbres de España,* dir. F. Carreras y Candi (Barcelona: Casa Editorial Alberto Martín, 1943–46), vol. 2, pp. 167–418, esp. 220; Maurice Esses, *Dance and Instrumental "Diferencias" in Spain During the 17th and Early 18th Centuries,* 3 vols., Dance and Music Series, No. 2 (Stuyvesant, N.Y.: Pendragon Press, 1992), esp. vol. 1, pp. 636–48; Richard Hudson, "The *Folia* Dance and the *Folia* Formula in Seventeenth-Century Guitar Music," *Musica Disciplina,* vol. 25 (1971), 199–221; Hudson, "The Folia Melodies," *Acta Musicologica,* vol. 45 (1973), 98–119; Hudson, *The Folia, the Saraband, the Passacaglia, and*

the Chaconne: *The Historical Evolution of Four Forms That Originated in Music for the Five-Course Spanish Guitar,* Musicological Studies and Documents, No. 35, American Institute of Musicology (Stuttgart: Hänssler-Verlag, 1982); Craig H. Russell, *Santiago de Murcia's "Códice Saldívar No. 4": A Treasury of Guitar Music from Baroque Mexico,* 2 vols. (Urbana: University of Illinois Press, 1995), esp. vol. 1, pp. 55–57; and John Ward, "The Folía," *Kongressbericht der Internationalen Gesellschaft für Musikwissenschaft, 5 Kongress,* Utrecht, 1952 (Amsterdam: International Musicological Society, 1953).

9. Parallelisms also arise with frequency in the *canto figurado* masses, as will be seen in chapter 6.

10. Wallace McKenzie discusses the prevalence of open fifths and parallel fifths and octaves in the *Sacred Harp* tradition that swelled in importance in the late eighteenth and nineteenth centuries. See MacKenzie, "Anthems of the *Sacred Harp* Tunesmiths," *American Music,* vol. 6, no. 3 (Fall 1988), esp. 251–54.

11. "Palóu, *Relacion historica de...Serra,* 32. For a more complete text and translation, consult note 61 in chapter 3.

12. While discussing performance pertaining to a parade or procession, we probably should consider the possibility that the participants could read from small personal copies that were portable rather than having them read collectively from one large book. The fact that mission archives and libraries preserve many large choirbooks but no portable copies of these *gozos* argues against the "personal copy" theory.

13. "Gozos y aña...del Patriarca San Joseph," in folder 56 of the WPA collection. This folder contains the photos for four different performance parts: "Tiple 1ro â Duo," "Tiple 2. â Duo," "Tenor," and "Acompañamiento para los Gozos, y Aña del P^{ca} [Patriarca] San Joseph." Its opening line of text reads, "Pues sois Sancto sin igual." William John Summers gives the designation "manuscript As-3" to the *Artaserse* manuscript at the San Fernando Mission (hereafter abbreviated as the *Artaserse Ms.*). The "*Gozos* a duo" for San Miguel is found on fol. 10, lines 1–5. See Summers, "*Opera seria* in Spanish California: An Introduction to a Newly-Identified Manuscript Source," in *Music in Performance and Society: Essays in Honor of Roland Jackson,* ed. by Malcolm Cole and John Koegel (Warren, Mich.: Harmonie Park Press, 1997), 274.

14. "Gozos y aña *Joseph &c.* / del Patriarca San Joseph: / Del uso de Fr. Juan Bautista / Sancho Reg^{so} Obse^{te} / Año 1796." Photo F-1 of the title page in folder 56 of the WPA collection. When Sancho inserts the ex libris "del uso de," he is doing so in the tradition of Franciscans who took a vow of poverty and were not allowed to "own" anything. This statement affirms that he had daily access to an item, but his "possessions" remained the property of the order—he was merely assigned them for his use.

15. See note 67 in chapter 1 for a list of important scholarship pertaining to the *villancico*.

16. See, for example, *Veni Sancte Spiritus* in Santa Clara Ms. 3, p. 34; the personal journal by Juan Bautista Sancho at the Bancroft Library, manuscript C-C-73:16, fol. 3 recto; the last rites in a Native American language, written out by Juan Bautista Sancho, preserved at the Bancroft Library, manuscript C-C-73: 17, on p. 3. In addition, this practice was commonplace in the Mexico City Cathedral. Ignacio de Jerusalem habitually used a variant of the cross to indicate *D.S. al segno*. See, for example, the following works from his *Maitines para Nuestra Señora de Guadalupe* (1764), all found in the manuscript source, E814, Ct., Leg.C.c.9 and C.c.10, Am0605–0606: "Invitatorio i Himno â 4 con VVs. Trompas i Baxo a N[uestra] S[eñora] de Guadalupe" (Sancta Maria dei genitrix); Responsorio 3° (Quae est iesta quae processit); Responsorio 6° (Elegit et sanctificavi). The Responsory N°3 "Quae est ista quae processit" appears in yet another manuscript in the Mexico City Cathedral: "Motete 3° del 2° Nocturno para los Maitines de N^a S^a de Guadalupe [1765] (Quo [*sic*] est ista quo processit sicut sol)," stating that this was used as the procession for the Matins for the Apparition of the Virgin (Para la Procesion de la Aparision), AM0511. The crosshatch "#" also shows up in Jerusalem's Responsorio 4° para los *Maytines de la Asuncion de Nuestra Señora* (Et vidente eam filae Sion), in Leg. C.c.6.

17. "Ecos a duo" with the opening line, "Cantar quiero un rato," folder 50 in the WPA collection, twenty-five verses for two voices. Photo z-1 is a cover sheet written in Juan Bautista Sancho's hand: "Ecos a Duo. / del uso de Fr. Juan Bautista Sancho. / Reg[ligio]so Observä[n]te. / 1797."

18. Stanza 19: Inquisitive Soul: "Sabes tu de Mallorca, la lengua noble, que remate la fiesta?" / Nymph of the Cave: "Esta, esta, millor que totas." Stanza 22. Inq. Soul: "Y pues en tantas lenguas, hablarte veo, saber la Portugueza?" / Nymph: "Essa, essa, hablar deseo." Stanza 23. Inq. Soul: "Hablarás por ventura, O Ninfa bella, otra lengua ô vocablo?" / Nymph: "Hablo, hablo, en todas lenguas." Stanza 24. Inq. Soul: "Mas no quiero cansarte, queda con Christo, que has echado el resto. / Nymph: "Hesto, hesto, hasta por dicho."

19. *Dulce Esposo de María* is found in several California sources, including "Letra al Ss^mo P^a S^r S[n Jos]é..." in Durán choirbook C-C-59, p. 56; Santa Clara Ms. 4, p. 62 (for a facsimile, consult photo B-109 in appendix B online); San Juan Bautista Ms. 1, p. 110 (plate 129 in WPA item 45); and Bancroft C-C-68:1. For this latter source, only the verso page of the work is extant. In C-C-68:1 the works read across the open book from the left page (which is a verso side of a sheet) straight across to the right page (which is a recto side). In this instance, the accompanying recto side that *should* be on the right is missing and instead we find the beginning of *¡O qué suave!*—which is another work for San José. With regard to the five stanzas of text, the middle stanza number 3 in the Santa Clara Ms. 4 is moved from its "middle position" and then placed as the last stanza in the rendition found in the Durán choirbook C-C-59.

For a recording of *Dulce Esposo de María,* consult the CD *Mission Road* by Chanticleer and Chanticleer Chamber Ensemble.

20. It is also possible that nonliturgical hymns—that is, those texts that were not explicitly part of the Mass Ordinary or Proper—might have been performed inside the mission as well. This is a point in need of further investigation.

21. See "Trisagio a la Santísima Trinidad," http://www.terra.es/persona12/andresja/trisagio. htm#ofrecimiento; and "Angelic Trisagion," http://www.catholic-forum.com/saints/pray0201. htm (accessed 19 August 2004).

22. The choirbook at San Juan Bautista (Ms. 1) has the following works for the Feast of the Blessed Trinity: *Trisagio 1° a 4 voces,* "Santo Dios, Santo fuerte," p. 102 (plate 122 in WPA item 45); *Trisagio 2° a 2. Voces,* "Santo, Santo, Santo," p. 102 (plate 122); and *Trisagio 3° para adorar a la SS. Trinidad* that begins with the *estribillo,* "Santo, Santo Santo es Dios de verdad," after which the first stanza of *coplas* begins: "Todo el orbe cante con gran voluntad," p. 105 (plate 125 in WPA item 45).

23. For the entire text of this service of the Blessed Trinity, consult the Web site, "Trisagio a la Santísima Trinidad" cited in note 21, or "Trisagio a la Santísima Trinidad," found at http://www. churchforum.org/info/Manual_de_Oraciones/Trisagio_Sma_Trinidad.htm (accessed 24 March 2006).

24. Ms. C-C-73/108c, "Copia del manuscripto Ramón Yerba. Cantos de la Misión," selection no. 10. The Bancroft Library, Ms. C-C-73/108c. "Copia del manuscripto Ramón Yerba [*sic*]. Cantos de la Misión," selection no. 10. The last name should read "Yorba" and is in fact spelled correctly throughout the bulk of the document. Hereafter, I abbreviate this source as the "Yorba manuscript."

25. A transcription of the recording made by F. M. Kercheville's of Native Americans in New Mexico singing the "Trisagio a la Santissima Trinidad" with the text, "Santo, Santo, Santo, Señor Dios de los ejércitos..." is included in the excellent study of New Mexican folk music made by Vicente T. Medoza and Virginia R. R. de Mendoza. See their *Estudio y clasificación de la música tradicional hispánica de Nuevo México,* Instituto de Investigaciones Estéticas, Estudios de Folklore, no. 5 (Mexico City: Universidad Autónoma de México, 1986), esp. p. 58, song no. 8.

26. See John Donald Robb, *Hispanic Folk Music of New Mexico and the Southwest: A Self-Portrait of a People* (Norman: University of Oklahoma Press, 1980), 696; and Durán's choirbook C-C-59, p. 71.

27. MUSICA / CHORALIS / FRANCISCANA, / TRIPLICITER DIVISA, / IN / MEDULLAM / CANTUS GREGORIANI, / SIVE EJUSDEM / PRINCIPIA GENERALIA; / IN / CANTORALE / TONORUM COMMUNIUM, / IN PROVINCIA / FF. MIN. RECOLL. / COLONIENSI USITATORUM / ET IN / PROCESSIONALE / ROMANUM ET ORDINIS. / COLONIAE AGRIPPINAE, / Anno M.DCC.XLVI. UC University of California, Berkeley, Music Library, t M2148.8.P7 C6 1746 Case X. The end paper shows the book was owned by F.

Bonacurae Adelsech in 1758. The next annotation indicates that Adelsech died on 20 September 1818 and that the book then passed into the possession of Friar Xavier Oswald.

28. That processions were also indispensable aspects on "secular" occasions is further evidenced by such events as the magnificent parades and festivities associated with the inauguration of Governor Pablo Vicente de Solá in 1815 at Monterrey. Bancroft spells out the activities in great detail, and the week's events involved more than 2,000 people! See Hubert Howe Bancroft, *The Works of Hubert Howe Bancroft*, vol. 34, *California Pastoral, 1769–1848* (San Francisco: San Francisco History Company, 1888), 420–24.

29. For a summary of the Feast of Corpus Christi and its historical background, consult Francis X. Weiser, S.J., *Handbook of Christian Feasts and Customs: The Year of the Lord and Liturgy and Folklore* (New York: Harcourt Brace, 1952), 259–64; W. J. O'Shea, "Corpus Christi," in *New Catholic Encyclopedia* (New York: McGraw-Hill, 1967), vol. 4, pp. 345–47; R. S. Hoyt, "Thomas Aquinas, St.," in *New Catholic Encyclopedia*, vol. 14, pp. 102–15; and Nelly Sigaut, "Procesión de Corpus Christi: La muralla simbólica en un reino de conquista Valencia y México-Tenochtitlán," in *México en el Mundo Hispánico*, ed. by Óscar Mazín Gómez Zamora (Michoacán: El Colegio de Michoacán, 2000), vol. 1, pp. 363–405.

For Web sites, consult: "Corpus Christi," http://www.fiestasiesta.co.uk/fiestas/corpus_cristo. html; "Corpus Christi," http://www.haverford.edu/engl/eng1301/corpuschristi/corpus_christi. html; "Corpus Christi Hymns," Catholic Culture, information drawn from Francis X. Weiser, S.J., *Handbook of Christian Feasts and Customs* (New York: Harcourt, Brace, 1958), http://www. catholicculture.org/lit/activities/view.cfm?id=1081; "Corpus Christi Processions," Catholic Culture, information drawn from Francis X. Weiser, S.J., *Handbook of Christian Feasts and Customs* (New York: Harcourt, Brace, 1958), http://www.catholicculture.org/lit/activities/view. cfm?id=1087; "Dictionary of Eucharistic Terms," the Real Presence Association, http://www. therealpresence.org/eucharst/pea/define.htm; "Eucharistic Adoration," http://www.kensmen. com/catholic/eucharisticadoration.html; "The Eucharistic Devotion of St. Thomas Aquinas," Warren H. Carroll, Ph.D., in association with Eternal World Television Network, http://www. ewtn.com/library/DOCTRINE/TAEUCHDV.TXT (all sites accessed 28 June 2005).

30. Although Saint Thomas Aquinas was long held to be the composer of the glorious liturgy for Corpus Christi, R. S. Hoyt explains that a more accurate description of his role in creating that liturgy was that of compiler and editor. As a basis for his views Hoyt quotes Saint Thomas's first biographer, William of Tocco: "[Thomas] wrote the Office of Corpus Christi at the command of Pope Urban, in which he expounded all the ancient forms of this sacrament and compiled the truths that pertain to the new grace." See R. S. Hoyt, "Thomas Aquinas, St.," in *New Catholic Encyclopedia* (New York: McGraw-Hill, 1967), vol. 14, pp. 102–15, esp. p. 106.

31. "No fue menor el esmero con que el Siervo de Dios procuró atraher á aquellos sus hijos á la devocion del Santísimo Sacramento. Instruyólos á que preparasen y adornasen con enramadas el camino por donde habia de transitar la Procesion del Corpus: formabanse quatro Capillas con sus respectivas Mesas, para que en ellas posase el Señor Sacramentado, y despues de cantada en cada una la correspondiente Antífona, Verso y Oracion, se paraba un Indio (de corte edad) que recitaba una Loa al Divino Sacramento (de las quales, dos eran en Castellano, y las otras dos en el idioma Páme, nacional de ellos) que enternecian y causaban devo/cion á todos; y resituidos á la Iglesia, se cantaba la Misa, y se predicaba el Sermon de este Sacrosanto Misterio." Palóu, *Relacion historica de...Serra*, 31–32. Serra's desire to use music as a prime vehicle of conversion is all part of a long tradition of missionary work in the New World. Lourdes Turrent explores these aspects in her book *La Conquista Musical de México*, prologue by Andrés Lira (Mexico City: Fondo de Cultura Económica, 1993). She concisely sums up this point: "No hay duda de que la música fue el medio para atraer a las indígenas a la nueva religión y que las escuelas anexas a los monasterios fueron el camino más útil para iniciar su conversión. En ellas, los frailes aprendieron lengua indígena y fomentaron el desarrollo de la música que tan útil les había sido en los primeros años de evangelización." See Turrent, *La Conquista Musical*, 128.

32. Kristin Dutcher Mann provides an excellent summary of the Corpus Christi procession, explaining its pageantry and its centrality to the culture of Mexico and the Southwest in her chapter "Corpus Christi in the North and Central Mexico" from her dissertation, "The Power of Song in the Missions of Northern New Spain," Ph.D. diss., Northern Arizona University,

2002, 202–13. Also consult the Web sites "Corpus Christi," http://www.haverford.edu/engl/eng1301/corpuschristi/corpus_christi.html; and "Corpus Christi Processions," http://www.catholicculture.org/lit/activities/view.cfm?id=1087.

33. The definitive authority on sacred dance in Seville's cathedral is Lynn Matluck Brooks, who—through the generosity of a Fulbright Grant in 1978–79—wrote her dissertation on the subject, a study that paved the way for her more recent contribution, *The Dances of the Processions of Seville in Spain's Golden Age,* Teatro del Siglo de Oro: Estudios de literatura, 4, dir. by Kurt and Roswitha Reichenberger with Evangelina Rodríguez and Antonio Tordera (Kassel: Edition Reichenberger, 1988). In chapter 2, "Religious and Processional Celebrations: The Corpus Christi Prototype" (43–90), she presents the dazzling spectacle in all its details, including the parades with banners, crosses, dances, floats, bell ringing, music, and so on—plus the other celebrations such as tournaments, masques, and bullfights. In chapter 3, "The Church Sponsored Dances: *Los Seises,*" Brooks provides a fascinating description of liturgical dance by the choirboys known as the *cantorcicos* or *los seises* (91–122). Also, consult the Web sites "Corpus Christi," http://www.fiestasiesta.co.uk/fiestas/corpus_cristo.html; and "Corpus Christi," http://www.haverford.edu/engl/eng1301/corpuschristi/corpus_christi.html.

34. "Eucharistic Adoration," http://www.kensmen.com/catholic/eucharisticadoration.html.

35. Edgerton, *Theaters of Conversion,* 64.

36. Weiser, *Handbook of Christian Feasts and Customs,* 262.

37. "Corpus Christi Processions," Catholic Culture, «http://www.catholicculture.org/lit/activities/view.cfm?id=1087».

38. Fray Toribio Motolonía, *Motolonía's History of the Indians of New Spain,* trans. with annotations by Francis Borgia Steck, O.F.M. (Washington, D.C.: Academy of Franciscan History, 1951), bk. 1, chap. 15, on p. 152. Original text: "Todo el camino estaba cubierto de juncia, y de espadañas y flores, y de nuevo había quien siempre iba echando rosas y clavelinas, y hubo muchas maneras de danzas que recogijaban la procesión. Había en el camino sus capillas con sus altares y retablos bien aderezados para descansar, a donde salían de nuevo niños cantores cantando y bailando delante del Santísimo Sacramento." Fray Toribio de Benavente Motolonía, *Memoriales o Libro de las cosas de la Nueva España y de los naturales de ella… con inserción de las porciones de la "Historia de los Indios de la Nueva España" que completan el texto de los Memoriales,* edited and with critical study by Edmundo O'Gorman, Serie de historiadores y cronistas de Indias, no. 2 (Mexico City: Universidad Nacional Autónoma de México and Instituto de Investigaciones Históricas, 1971), 99–100. The Jesuit friar José Cardiel describes the Corpus Christi processions in the mid-1700s in his "Breve relación de las misiones de Paraguay": his account resembles Motolonía's summary very closely—even though his eyewitness account occurred well over two centuries later. For Cardiel's explanation, consult Piotr Nawrot's *Indígenas y cultura musical de las reducciones jesuíticas. Guaraníes, Chiquitos, Moxos,* vol. 1, Colección: Monumenta Música 1, Festival de Música Renacentista y Barroca Americana, Misiones de Chiquitos, Asociación Pro Arte y Cultura, Santa Cruz de la Sierra, Misioneros del Verbo Divino (Cochabamba, Bolivia: Verbo Divino, 2000), esp. 21–22.

39. Edgerton, drawing upon Motolonía's writings, emphasizes the use of nature in the Tlaxcalan elebration of Corpus Christi. See Edgerton, *Theaters of Conversion,* 64 and 211, especially the details provided on p. 306nn48, 51, and on p. 321n7. Original text: "Estaban diez arcos triunfales grandes muy gentilmente compuestos;…en la parte de en medio había veinte pies de ancho; por ésta iba el Sacramento y ministros y cruces con todo el aparato de la procesión…y de éstos había por cuenta mil y sesenta y ocho arcos….Estaban todos cubiertos de rosas y flores de diversas colores y manera." Motolonía, *Memoriales,* 100.

40. Motolonía, *Motolonía's History of the Indians of New Spain,* bk. 1, chap. 15, pp. 152–53.

41. Maynard J. Geiger, O.F.M., *The Life and Times of Fray Junípero Serra, O.F.M., or The Man Who Never Turned Back (1713–1784),* 2 vols. (Washington, D.C.: Academy of American Franciscan History, 1959), vol. 1, p. 370.

42. For a thorough accounting of the friars' lives, including their preparations for missionary life in Mexico City, consult Maynard Geiger, O.F.M., *Franciscan Missionaries in Hispanic California 1769–1848: A Biographical Dictionary* (San Marino, Calif.: Huntington Library, 1969).

43. Some authors incorrectly merge and commingle two different celebrations that took place in Monterey on different days, only three days apart (3 and 6 June 1770), and some

writers confuse the dates of actual ceremonies with the dates that Serra describes them. Those dates do not necessarily coincide. To put things in order and rectify any lingering confusion, here is a summary of the sequence of events. Serra arrives in Monterey on his boat, the *San Antonio* (also called *El Príncipe*), on 31 May 1770. The following day (1 June), Serra meets with Father Crespí and military personnel who had already arrived there through a land expedition. On that same day, Serra invites everyone to celebrate mass in the near future. Serra states, "On meeting, I issued an invitation to all, for the day after tomorrow—a Sunday and the Feast of Pentecost—to participate in the celebration of the first Mass, and the erection of the standard of the Most Holy Cross in that country." Those religious festivities (the raising of the cross, celebration of mass, and inauguration of Mission San Carlos Borromeo), then, occurred on 3 June—a date that Serra reiterates in his letter to Inspector General Joseph de Gálvez dated 2 July 1770. In that same letter, Serra explains that he and the other friars, soldiers, and sailors celebrated Corpus Christi just three days later on 6 June. He explains, "All these details I described, at some length, in my letter of the 6th of last month [June], taken by the couriers who left here on the most solemn Feast of Corpus Christi. The couriers must have reported by word of mouth if it was not written in some of the letters from the men who had finished their letter-writing later than I, that we were preparing to celebrate the Feast and Procession of the Most Blessed Sacrament that day. And now I can say that in point of fact we did celebrate it, and with such splendor that it might have been gazed upon with delight even in Mexico." Consult Antonine Tibesar, O.F.M., *Junípero Serra: Writings of Junípero Serra*, 4 vols. (Washington, D.C.: Academy of Franciscan History, 1955), vol. 1, pp. 169, 183.

44. In this location, Antonine Tibesar translates the word *atril* as "missal stand [*sic*]." A Missal is the book that the priest uses to intone the necessary texts during mass; a Missal stand, therefore, is small in scale. In contrast, a Gradual or Antiphonary is a book of huge dimensions from which the choir sings; a stand for a Gradual or Antiphonary can be quite large. Unfortunately, Tibesar's addition of the adjective "missal" here introduces a level of specificity that is not present in Serra's original account. I will return to this point later, but for now I want to establish that Serra's *atril* could be *any* kind of "stand"—small or large—and we do not know whether it held a Missal, a Gradual, or something else altogether. See Tibesar, trans., *Writings of Junípero Serra*, entire passage in vol. 1, pp. 182–87.

45. Tibesar, trans., *Writings of Junípero Serra*, vol. 1, pp. 182–87. Tibesar provides Serra's original Spanish, which reads:

"Hívamos a celebrar fiestta y proseción [*sic*] del Santísimo Sacramento en tal día; yo ahora digo que en efecto assí se executtó, y berdaderamentte con tal lucimiento que pudo mirarse con gustto aún en México....

Ésta [una custtodia] ya teníamos, pero lo demás que nos falttava sí no lo trageron los Angeles al menos a nosottros se nos hizo como llovido, habiendo un caxón grande a bordo que les parecía de medicamenttos que buscaban, se halló ser de faroles de vidrio sin esttrenar, de que nadie tenía noticia.

Conttenttos con el hallazgo y ya satisfechos, dixo un marinero, que havía vistto avajo otro caxón como aquél, y que si éstte havía salido de faroles puede que el otro fuesse lo mismo; se mandó sacar luego, y se halló serlo también.

Y esto fué la víspera de la festividad.

....

Los faroles de llevar en altto, o con baras bien grandes y lindos son 6; los de mano muy presiosos, son 3; los 2 de ésttos, con sus belas de cera se pusieron juntitos a la custodia; los 6 en sus baras clavadas en el suelo a los lados del alttar; sobre éstte, los 6 blandones de platta grandes benidos del Loreto con sus palabreros, y atril de lo mismo, a los que se intterpolaron otros candeleros menores; para los faroles grandes y ciriales apresttó belas de cebo Don Juan Pérez; todo ardió en toda la missa cabttadam sermón, y proseción sin una pisca de aire.

La iglesia la formaron los del barco vajo el techo del medio agamacén [almacén] que ya esttaba concluído, con las banderas de la barias potencias su cielo de lo mismo y tal hermosura que hastta a mí me cuasava devoción. El círculo, o quadragécimo [quadrángulo] que havía de andar la proseción se limpió, y adornó con ramas verdes que formavan calles, repiques, truenos, imnos, y cánticos de alavansa: todo parece que iva como si nos pagasen (como suele decirse) que claro esttá no son viveres que se hechan en saco roto, siendo cosas tan del divino cultto.

La hermosa imagen de María Santísima (que es de Vuestra Señoría Illustrísima) ocupava el lugar medio sobre la custtodia de su Santísimo Hijo, y quedó la Señora guardando la iglesia mientras andava passeando esttas inculttas tierras Su Santísimo Hijo sacramenttado en mis indignas manos.

Acavada la prosezión se dió de comunión la sagrada ostia hecha partículas a los que quedavan prevendios [*sic*] para comulgar; y con estto y con nuebos cántticos de alavansa se concluyó la función a la que sólo faltó para consuelo de todos el que Vuestra Señoría Ilustrísima la huviesse podido mirar siquiera por una benttanica."

46. Motolonía, *Motolonía's History of the Indians of New Spain,* bk. 1, chap. 15, p.152. Original text: "Iba en la procesion el Santísimo Sacramento y muchas cruces y andas con sus santos. . . .Había muchas banderas de santos. Había doce apóstoles vestidos con sus insignias: muchos de los que acompañaban la procession llevaban velas encendidas en las manos." Motolonía, *Memorias,* 99.

47. The expenses of the Teatro di San Carlo are discussed in Anthony R. Del Donna, "Production Practices at the Teatro di San Carlo, Naples, in the Late 18th Century," *Early Music,* vol. 30, no. 3 (August 2002), 429–45. For the 1781–82 opera season, the budget for musicians was 1,516.10 ducats, and staging material ran to 479.84 ducats—whereas wax consumption and lighting ascended to 2,766.57 ducats. Other years reflect similar trends. Consult table 2 on p. 433 of Del Donna's "Production Practices."

48. The primary source for the Festival of San Pedro Arbués is found in the Archivo General de la Nación (AGN), Ramo de Cofradías y Archicofradías, Tomo 17, expediente 2, hojas 73–312, 1688–1741, «México Sr Sn Pedro de Arbues.» This document contains the budgets for the Festival of San Pedro de Arbués celebrated by the Tribunal of the Inquisition every year on 16 September in Mexico City. For a discussion of the AGN documents and their relevance to this festival, see my articles "Rowdy Musicians, Cofraternities and the Inquisition: Newly Discovered Documents Concerning Musical Life in Baroque Mexico," *Revista de Musicología,* vol. 16, no. 5 (1993), *Actas del XV Congreso Internacional de Musicología,* 2801–13, esp. 2802–3, plus footnotes 8–10; and "Musical Life in Baroque Mexico: Rowdy Musicians, Cofraternities and the Holy Office," *Inter-American Music Review,* vol. 13, no. 1 (Fall–Winter 1992), 11–14.

49. In the 1840s, businessman and traveler Josiah Belden places the price for hides at 2 pesos each and tallow at 1.5 pesos per *arroba* (an *arroba* equaling about 25 pounds). Antonio María Osío has observations regarding the tallow trade, setting the price at 10 *reales* per *arroba.* Alfred Robinson explains the rationale for the mass slaughter of the missions' herds at the moment the missions were secularized by the Secularization Act of 17 August 1833. The friars wanted to obtain as much liquid wealth as fast as possible in order to distribute the funds to the Native Americans who soon would be on their own. The friars were concerned about the well-being of their wards during this radical transition, so they sought the only real source for quick cash they could find—the tallow from their cattle. Many others discuss this mass slaughter, although many assign different motives to the friars for this drastic action. See the following sources: Josiah Belden, *Josiah Belden, 1841 California Overland Pioneer: His Memorial and Early Letters,* edited and with an introduction by Doyce B. Nunis Jr. (Georgetown, Calif.: Talisman Press, 1962), 56; Antonio María Osio, *The History of Alta California: A Memoir of Mexican California,* translated, edited, and annotated by Rose Marie Beebe and Robert M. Senkewicz (Madison: University of Wisconsin Press, 1996), 118–19, 198; Alfred Robinson, *Life in California: A Historical Account of the Origin, Customs, and Traditions of the Indians of Alta-California,* foreword by Joseph A. Sullivan (Oakland, Calif.: Biobooks, 1947), 100–101; Angustias de la Guerra Ord, *Occurrences in Hispanic California,* translated and edited by Francis Price and William H. Ellison (Washington, D.C.: Academy of American Franciscan History, 1956), 31–32; Edwin Bryant, *What I Saw in California, Being the Journal of a Tour, by the Emigrant Route and South Pass of the Rocky Mountains across the Continent of North America, the Great Desert Basin, and through California, in the Years 1846, 1847* (Minneapolis, Minn.: Ross and Haines, 1967), 444; Bancroft, *California Pastoral,* 230.

50. "Mission Music: Choirbook, 1770–1784," San Carlos Borromeo Basilica (Carmel, California), sometimes referred to as the "Serra Choirbook," Stanford University, Green Research Library, SPEC COLL M.0612. I refer to this source with the abbreviated citation, Serra choirbook M.0612.

51. See California Missions Resource Center, "The Wrong Roof at the Right Time," http://missionscalifornia.com/stories/roof.htm (accessed 27 August 2007). A photograph of Joseph Strong's painting of Father Angelo Casanova with him leading worship at Mission San Carlos Borromeo is provided in James A. Sandos's *Converting California: Indians and Franciscans in the Missions* (New Haven, Conn.: Yale University Press, 2004), 151.

52. Many liturgical books, including those in the possession of the friars during the mission period, hold these three hymns as central repertoire in the Corpus Christi procession. For example, in San Juan Bautista Mission there is a published *Rituale Romanum Pauli V. Pont. Maximi. Jussu Editum...cum cantu Toletano* (Toledo: Typography of the Benedictine Order and the Typographorum Bibliopolarumque Regni, 1787), and as expected, it gives the three big hymns for Corpus on pp. 347–50. In order, they are *Pange lingua, Sacris solemniis,* and *Verbum supernum prodiens.* Each is set in metric *canto figurado.* These three hymns in the same order and same *canto figurado* style appear in choirbook C-C-68:2 (pp. 70–72). The Roman rite traces out the order of selections and instructions for the procession in the Feast of Corpus Christi (e.g., consult the *Liber Usualis* starting on p. 950); it begins, "The Procession: as the Priest leaves the Altar, the Cantors intone the hymn *Pange lingua.*" The next pieces that the cantors are instructed to sing (see p. 952) are the *Sacris solemniis* and *Verbum supernum prodiens.* Additionally, the chapel can sing yet another hymn, *Salutis humanae Sator.* This latter hymn, however, has failed to enter the liturgy with the same overwhelming impact as the previous three hymns by Thomas Aquinas. For thorough descriptions (written in the mid-1700s at the monastery or El Escorial) of the performance requirements for mass, for the hours, and procession in Pentecost, consult the *Directorios del director del canto* as presented verbatim in Luis Hernández's *Música y culto divino en el Real Monasterio de El Escorial (1563–1837), II,* transcription, introduction, notes & indices by Luis Hernández, Documentos para la Historia del Monasterio de San Lorenzo El Real de El Escorial, X., vol. 55 (Real Monasterio de El Escorial, Spain: Ediciones Escurialenses, [1993?]), esp. 54–55, 140–42.

53. The hymn *Pange lingua* applies to the processions on both Maundy Thursday in Holy Week and also Corpus Christi; in Durán's choirbook C-C-59, then, it is not surprising to find a version of the *Pange lingua* in the context of "Jueves Santo" (Maundy Thursday) on p. 13. Immediately before the music there is the preface "En la Proces^n se canta," indicating that "for the Procession the *Pange lingua* is sung." Its text is similar to the standard one as found in the *Liber Usualis* on pp. 950–52 and 957–59, but it is missing stanza number 4 that begins, "Verbum caro, panem verum." Its melody, however, resembles neither Gregorian model. Instead, its melodic contour is very close to another well-known model—the rhythmic *canto figurado* setting that circulated widely throughout Spain and its colonies in both published and manuscript sources. For instance, this *canto figurado* setting of the *Pange lingua* surfaces in choirbook C-C-68:2, p. 70 and also the *Ritual Romanum Pauli V. Pont. Maximi....Manuali Toletano* (Toledo: Typography of the Benedictine Press and Bibliopolarumque Regni, 1787), a book found in the California missions—such as San Juan Bautista. Unlike the widely circulated *canto figurado* version, the Durán choirbook C-C-59 expunges any discernible metric or rhythmic features. Given the widespread popularity of the *canto figurado* setting, however, one might surmise that the California friars and neophytes nevertheless sang it in triple meter.

The *Sacris solemniis* in choirbook C-C-59 (p. 30) is in four-voice polyphony with all parts sharing the same six-line staff, the four voice lines following their respective parts through the use of different-colored note heads, a notational system used repeatedly by Durán and numerous other friars in the California missions. It is notable that *all* seven stanzas are copied onto the page; in a sense, this self-sufficient setting makes it possible to perform from start to finish in a direct way, without necessarily having to impose the *alternatim* style that so often pervades the California mission style. Santa Barbara Doc. 2 has a very similar rendition on p. 65 (see photo B-5 in appendix B online). Santa Clara Ms. 4 also presents a slightly different four-voice setting of the *Sacris solemniis* on p. 132. Even though the *Sacris solemniis* is in a different location in Santa Clara Ms. 4, its context is nevertheless clearly that of Corpus Christi, given that the preceding piece is *¡O sacratissimo cuerpo de Jesús!*—a piece that is one of the four hymns sung in the Corpus Christi procession. Like the *Sacris solemniis* in choirbook C-C-59, it too is homorhythmic, with all four voices sharing a single six-line staff in colored notation, although the choice of keys differs—Santa Clara Ms. 4 selects C major, whereas choirbook C-C-59's setting is in F major. As we have seen repeatedly with respect to California sources, if we encounter only the odd-numbered stanzas on a single page, then we can safely assume that *alternatim* performance is expected, whereas the presence of the complete text in a single location makes direct performance a possibility. Since the setting of *Sacris solemniis* in Santa Clara Ms. 4 jots down *only* the first stanza of text, we cannot determine with certainty which of the two styles—*alternatim* or direct—was expected. However, given the enormous similarities between this version and the one found in choirbook C-C-59, one might reasonably guess that the direct performance style of choirbook C-C-59 would transfer nicely to its close musical cousin in Santa Clara Ms. 4.

54. Juan Bautista Sancho's handwriting is evident on the sheets preserved in WPA folder 68. The *Verbum supernum prodiens* is recorded in chant notation (albeit with hollow note heads and only with the incipit of the text) on line 12 at the bottom of photo W-4. Felipe Arroyo de la Cuesta at Mission San Juan Bautista similarly wrote down a hodgepodge of material on some large sheets, much like his contemporary Juan Bautista Sancho at Mission San Antonio de Padua. Arroyo de la Cuesta's version of *Verbum supernum prodiens* is present in the photos of WPA folder 78, but the photostatic reproductions have deteriorated so badly it is nearly impossible to make out the contents with much specificity. Nevertheless, when Sidney Robertson made the folders of the contents for the music department at the University of California at Berkeley, she habitually wrote in the manila folder containing the photos a summary of contents; it is there one can read more plainly that the manuscript that she helped photograph contains the *Verbum supernum prodiens.*

55. "Pange lingua gloriosi. Processio Corpus Christi" (p. 70); "Sacris solemniis" (p. 71); "Verbum supernum prodiens," Ms. C-C-68:2 in the Bancroft Library.

56. As has been previously noted, the intoned version of *Pange lingua* on p. 13 of the Durán choirbook C-C-59 does omit *one* verse (no. 4), but that still does not alter the fact that *alternatim* performance is avoided here.

57. "Hymno Sacris Solemniis traducido al Castellano, se canta como el anter[io]r" with the opening text "Altísimo Señor"; and "Hymno Pange lingua traducido al Castellano" with the opening text "Canta lengua al glorioso," San Juan Bautista Ms. 1, p. 109 (plate 128 in the facsimile of this choirbook in WPA item 45).

58. The WPA folder 78 contains multiple photostatic copies of a single sheet written in the hand of Felipe Arroyo de la Cuesta, a friar active at Mission San Juan Bautista. Although it is hard to make out any "Verbum supernum prodiens" on the highly deteriorated photos of Arroyo de la Cuesta's manuscript, this chant melody was surely readable on the original, since Sidney Robertson makes reference to it on the manila folder that she used to contain the photographs. On the photos of manuscript one can barely make out the text and tunes for the following works in Native American languages: "A tolomeya," beginning at the midpoint of staff 3; "E me-e me-e me-e me," beginning immediately after the two measures of another work that begin that staff 4; and "Ena ina-a, a lo lo a ya," midpoint of staff 4 and continuing onto staff 5.

59. O'Shea, "Corpus Christi," *New Catholic Encyclopedia,* vol. 4, p. 365.

60. Fray Toribio Motolonía, *Motolonía's History of the Indians of Spain,* translated and edited by Elizabeth Andros Foster, Documents and Narratives Concerning the Discovery and Conquest of Latin America, No. 4 (Berkeley: Cortés Society of the Bancroft Library, 1950), 103. Original text: "Una cosa muy de ver: tenían en cuatro esquinas o vueltas que se hacían en el camino, en cada una su montaña, y de cada una salía su peñón bien alto; y desde abajo estaba hecho como prado, con matas de yerba y flores, y todo lo demás que hay en un campo fresco, y la montaña, y el peñón tan a el natural como si allí hubiera nacido." Motolonía, *Memorias,* 100.

61. Edgerton, *Theaters of Conversion,* esp. 58–59.

62. Edgerton goes to great lengths to develop the "fourness" of architecture and pageantry in the conversion of Native Americans by the mendicant holy orders. See his *Theaters of Conversion,* esp. 55–59.

63. The Spanish-texted *Letras para las Estancias del día de Corpus (Songs for the Stations of the Feast Day of Corpus Christi)* are found in the following California manuscript sources: C-C-59 at the Bancroft Library, pp. 70–71; C-C-68:1 at the Bancroft Library, fols. 25–26v; Santa Barbara Doc. 2, pp. 140–43 (for facsimile reproductions of these pages, consult photos B-79 through B-81 in appendix B that is available online); Santa Clara Ms. 3 (only "O Rey de corazones! Delicias del Criador") on p. C between pp. 47 and 48 (for facsimile reproduction, see photos B-96 and B-96b in appendix B); Santa Clara Ms. 4, pp. 65–68 (for facsimile reproductions of these pages, consult photos B-111 through B-114 in appendix B); San Fernando Ms. A320, pp. 15–18 (fols. 8v–10); San Juan Bautista Ms. 1, pp. 103–4 (photos 123–24 in WPA item 45); San Juan Bautista "Lost" Choirbook on pp. 27–33 (information for the contents of this "lost" choirbook found in the index, still extant, on photo 136 in WPA item 45); and lyrics for Corpus Christi hymns, WPA folder 75. For a detailed listing of the contents in these sources consult appendix A.

64. The four main Spanish hymns sung during the procession of Corpus Christi. That they are intended to accompany the elevation of the Communion Host and Chalice is clarified by the recurring reference in their titles "para alzar la Ostia y Caliz" or simply "para alzar." Some of the locations of these four hymns in California sources are as follows:

¡O qué suave!: in choirbook C-C-59 at the Bancroft Library, p. 70; Santa Clara Ms. 4, p. 66; WPA folder 66, photos J-7 and J-8; the second part of *¡O qué suave!* that begins in duple meter and with the words "Enciéndase y arda en mi corazón," found in WPA folder 61, photo R-8; choirbook C-C-68:1 in the Bancroft Library, fols. 25 and 26v.

¡O pan de vida!: in C-C-59, pp. 70–71; Santa Clara Ms. 4, pp. 66–67; C-C-68:1, fol. 26v.

¡O Rey de corazones!: in C-C-59, p. 71; Santa Clara Ms. 4, p. 65; San Juan Bautista Ms. 1, p. 124; Santa Clara Ms. 3, additional sheet that I label as "C" (after p. 47). Text only, for the five verses. Labeled "fuerte, piano, fuerte, piano" at the ending.

¡O sacratissimo cuerpo de Jesús!: in C-C-59, p. 71 (in F major) and also alternate version on p. 73 (in C major); Santa Clara Ms. 4, p. 65 (in F major) and also alternate version on p. 132 (in C major); C-C-68:1, fol. 18v.

Durán's choirbook C-C-59 includes a detail regarding intoned responses that are overlooked in the other sources. This source includes the intoned response "Panem de caelo…" immediately after *¡O Rey de corazones!* and before *¡O sacratissimo cuerpo de Jesús!.* This same choirbook alludes to this same intoned response by scribbling the single word "Panem" immediately after *¡O pan de vida!* and just before *¡O Rey de corazones!* Although this small detail is nowhere to be found in the other manuscripts, we can safely assume this was the intoned response that was used to close off each of the four Corpus Christi hymns in this liturgical procession and celebration.

Other tunes for the elevation of the Communion Host occur in the mission choirbooks, although not necessarily in the specific context of the Corpus Christi feast day. These titles include the following:

Altissimo Señor, que supisteis juntar [?]. In choirbook C-C-59, p. 72, there are five stanzas to this hymn neatly printed out. Its instructions ("Letra para desp[ue]s de alzar al Tono del Sacris. Pag. 30") show that it is intended to be sung immediately after the elevation of the Host and that it is to be sung to the music for the hymn *Sacris solemniis* found on p. 30—a setting that records four polyphonic voices on a single staff, a texture often found in the California sources. Similarly, Santa Clara Ms. 4 prints out the lyrics for this hymn on p. 65.

Ave verum corpus. The San Juan Bautista choirbook (Ms. 1) includes the "Ave verum corpus" with the subtitle "Letra para la elevada de la Hostia y del Caliz, à duo, Tono 6" (p. 123). (The *Ave verum corpus* is also written out by Felipe Arroyo de la Cuesta, WPA folder 78.) After the *Ave verum corpus,* the San Juan Bautista choirbook then continues with two more pieces on p. 123 meant to accompany the elevation of the Communion Host and Chalice ("Otras dos Letras para el mismo fin"): *O dueño sacramentado* and *O Jesus dulce*. This latter work (*O Jesus dulce*) has many stanzas of text written out in the Yorba manuscript, Ms. 73/108c in the Bancroft Library (selection no. 7).

In addition, WPA folder 75 contains photos of a single sheet, badly damaged, with some of it clearly torn off and missing, with writing on front and back. It contains ten numbered stanzas of song lyrics but with no musical notation. The annotation (by Sidney Robertson?) at the beginning of the folder labels the tune "O gloria nave [*sic*] y dulce" when in fact it is the familiar "O qué suave y dulce estáis…" that begins *¡O qué suave!* The sheet at one time was clearly in the possession of Pedro Cabot but written out by his brother Juan Cabot. It reads: "Al Serv[ici] o / Al Ill[ustrísimo] N[uestro] P[adre] Dn. Pedro Ca;/bos [*sic*], M[aes]t⁻ro de la Mis[ió]n de/ S[an] Antonio./ Del P[adre] Juan / Cabot" (for the use of Our Most Illustrious Father, Don Pedro Cabot, Master of Mission San Antonio. [Written out] by Father Juan Cabot). The sheet's verso side bears the ascription "[Al] Servi[ci]o / [del Go]bern[ad]or de la Alta / [California] Monterrey" (For the Service of the Governor of Alta California, Monterrey). Sadly, the rest of this ascription is on the portion of the sheet that is now missing.

65. The connection between these two hymns is further suggested by the way they are notated in C-C-68:1. There is no double bar or other indication separating the end of *¡O qué suave!* and the beginning of *¡O pan de vida!*

66. For a discussion of the *petite reprise* and the usage of asterisks to indicate these repeated sections, consult the preface to volume 2 of my book *Santiago de Murcia's "Códice Saldívar Nº4": A Treasury of Secular Guitar Music from Baroque Mexico,* 2 vols. (Urbana: University of Illinois Press, 1995), vol. 2, pp. xiv–xv.

67. For examples of displaced bar lines where the downbeat or emphasized pulse of the measure is *before* the barline, consult the "Zaravanda Francese" and "Tironan arietta" on fol. 15 of Stefano Pesori, *I Concerti di chitarriglia di Stefano Pesori. Vna dvce virtute regontvr omnes* [Verona: Andrea and Frat. Rossi, n.d.], K.1.g.16, in the British Library. Also, several examples can be found in the anonymous baroque guitar manuscript "Libro de diferentes cifras de guitara [*sic*] escojidas de los mejores avtores año de 1705," M.811 in the Biblioteca Nacional in Madrid, such as "Marizápalos" (pp. 23–27) and "Zarabanda" (p. 46). This latter example is particularly worthy of scrutiny, since it is a rather close reworking of the "Zarabanda francesa" in Sanz's *Instrucción de música sobre la guitarra española* (Zaragosa: Herederos de Diego Dormer, 1674, and book 3 in 1697), bk. 1, plate 12. The bar lines have been shifted from Sanz's original: whereas Sanz has the downbeats fall after the bar line, the revised version in M.811 has the downbeats precede the bar line. This same manuscript M.811 has several scribal hands; the last guitarist to write in the book includes three works that fluctuate in their treatment of the bar line, sometimes having the stressed pulse to the left of the bar and at other times to the right. See "Languilla" on p. 152 of M.811 (new hand); "La Chamberga" (p. 153) and "La Gaita" (p. 153). For a comparison with a "regular" guitar setting of "La Chamberga," consult Santiago de Murcia, *Códice Saldívar No. 4*, fols. 51–51v, and for Murcia's setting of "La Gaita," consult fols. 40v–42v.

68. The rhythmic shifts in the *Misa de la Soledad* are discussed in chapter 6. Similar shifts surface in the third "Benedicamus Domino" from the enormous Antiphonary at the Mission San Antonio (p. 107). No friar ever etches out the "rules" for this sort of metric displacement, but in these California cases one sees the shifts occur most often in the context of phrase endings. If one finishes the phrase and puts in an intuitive and implied rest to close it off (even though the rest is not visually marked), the phrases inevitably unfold in a natural way and often end up sounding "symmetric" or balanced.

69. For a recording of *¡O qué suave!,* consult the CD *Mission Road* by Chanticleer and Chanticleer Chamber Ensemble.

70. During its setting of *¡O qué suave!,* choirbook C-C-68:1 in the Bancroft scrawls *golpe* above the word *amor* at the phrase "pues, al incendio puro de tu dulce *amor,* de tu dulce *amor*." See fol. 26v, lines 2 and 3. When inserted into a modern revised score, the *golpe* accents occur at the beginnings of measures 38, 40, and 41. There is another instance of the word *golpe* being applied to a musical score but in a very different context: Santiago de Murcia writes the word "strike" or "hit" into his guitar tablature setting of the African American *cumbé* for a thrillingly

rhythmic and exhilarating effect. Consult my edition *Santiago de Murcia's "Códice Saldívar N⁰4*," vol. 2, pp. 47–48, 188–91. I provide a discussion of the *cumbé* in vol. 1, pp. 69–77.

71. Relevant sources that contain selections for the Mass Proper of Corpus Christi include the following: C-C-68:2 at the Bancroft Library (also includes three hymns for the procession), pp. 66–72; C-C-59 at the Bancroft Library (based on Durán's "standardized," reusable melodies, and this source includes a concluding hymn "Sacris solemniis" for the procession) pp. 28–30; Santa Barbara Doc. 1 (based on Durán's "standardized," reusable melodies), pp. 120–23 (but incomplete; a page has been torn out); Santa Barbara Doc. 5, p. 4 (fol. 2v); Santa Barbara Doc. 16 (only the Introit, and based on Durán's "standardized," reusable melody for the Introit), p. 3; Santa Clara Ms. 3 (based on the version in Vicente Pérez's *Prontuario*), fols. 46–48v, and two inserted sheets between pp. 47 and 48 that I label as fols. *B* and *C*; Santa Clara Ms. 4 (based on Durán's "standardized," reusable melodies), pp. 17–18; San Fernando Mission (only the sequence "Laud Sion Salvatorem" for Corpus Christi), loose sheet S-2, staves 4–9; Santa Inés Ms. 1, pp. 35–36; Serra choirbook M.0612, fols. 11v–13; San Juan Bautista Ms. 1, pp. 43ff. (photos 62ff. in WPA item 45); and WPA folder 63 (only "Quotiescumque manducabitis," the Communion for Corpus Christi), on photo I-3, staves 7–8. For specific details concerning these mass settings, consult appendix A online.

72. For an explanation of these "standardized" reusable tunes, see the section on *canto llano* found in chapter 1 and notes 40–43.

73. In Santa Clara Ms. 3, Corpus Christi melodies that are drawn from Gregorian models include the Introit "Cibavit eos" on p. [47] (*Liber Usualis,* 1282); the Alleluia on p. [47] (*Liber Usualis,* 944); and the Communion "Quotiescumque manducabitis" on fol. 48v (*Liber Usualis,* 950). The Offertory "Sacerdotes Domini" on fol. 48v, however, bears no resemblance melodically to the version in the *Liber Usualis* on p. 949, although their texts are the same. The same holds true for choirbook C-C-68:2.

74. The order of the procession with respect to mass is worth examining. The "normal" procedure is to have mass first and to consecrate the bread and the wine as the veritable body and blood of Christ. In that way, the holy miracle of Christ is paraded through the town. As W. J. O'Shea explains, the procession "is to follow the Mass and the Host used for it should be consecrated at the Mass. . . . The Host carried in the procession is the Body of Christ, who gives himself as food to associate us in His sacrifice. The procession is thus put in the context of the Mass and is a prolongation of it." See O'Shea, "Corpus Christi," *Catholic Encyclopedia*, vol. 4, p. 365. Willi Apel's detailed study of chant tradition also places the procession after the mass, as does the *Liber Usualis*. See Willi Apel, *Gregorian Chant* (Bloomington: Indiana University Press, 1958; reprint Bloomington: Midland Books, 1990), 11; and *Liber Usualis,* 950.

75. Technically, the Corpus Christ feast did not have a sequence assigned to it as part of the standard liturgy until the reforms at the Council of Trent in the sixteenth century. By assigning it the sequence *Lauda Sion Salvatorem*, the council put it in the elite class of Easter and Pentecost. The emphasis on Corpus Christi was one of the main aspects of Tridentine reforms. See John Harper, *The Forms and Orders of Western Liturgy from the Tenth to the Eighteenth Century: A Historical Introduction and Guide for Students and Musicians* (Oxford: Clarendon Press, 1991), 160–61.

76. The polyphonic version of *Lauda Sion Salvatorem* is found in Durán's choirbook C-C-59, p. 29; Santa Barbara Doc. 1, p. 122; and also in the Santa Clara Ms. 4, pp. 17–18. This particular setting constitutes half of the music for *Lauda Sion Salvatorem* as sung by Chanticleer in *alternatim* performance style on their most recent CD, *Mission Road*. The other half of the phrases are drawn from Juan Bautista Sancho's *canto figurado* setting of *Lauda Sion Salvatorem*.

77. For a discussion of instrumental interpolations as indicated by the term "música," consult the section "Instrumental Interludes: *Música, Toca, and Tocata*," in chapter 2 and notes 52 and 53.

78. This second version of *Lauda Sion Salvatorem* with a single melody in *canto figurado* style is found in the following sources: Choirbook C-C-68:2, pp. 67–68; San Juan Bautista Ms. 1, p. 44 (photo 63 in WPA item 45); Serra choirbook M.0612, fol. 12v; Santa Inés Ms. 1, p. 27 (but for the sequence we find "Lauda Sion Salvatoris, Jesu nomen et amoris") and on p. 36; Santa Clara Ms. 3, a version on fol./p. 48, and also a version on the insert sheet in Pedro Cabot's hand in that same source, fol. *B*. This version was also part of the standard repertoire in the Mexican

Cathedral tradition, as evidenced by its recurring presence in the cathedral's large choirbooks. See, for example Choirbook 4-1-6, film 72 of the Mexico City Cathedral, also fol. 64v; and Choirbook 2-1-2, film 47 of Mexico City Cathedral, from "In feste Pentecostes ad Vesperas," fol. 64v. For a discussion of *alternatim* performance as related to clefs and music notation, I refer the reader to the section "*Alternatim* Performance" in chapter 2.

79. Though not a California source, Choirbook 2-1-2 in the Mexico City Cathedral (fols. 64v–65v) has a version of *Lauda Sion Salvatorem* utilizing the same melody. It similarly uses exactly four of these *a* phrases for the hymn *Lauda Sion Salvatorem* in Choirbook 2-1-2 of the Mexico City Cathedral, fols. 64v–65v. The four *a* phrases are followed by a concluding plainchant gesture, "Amen, Alleluia," much like the closing "Alleluia" in Serra choirbook M.0612. This California source systematically takes every other stanza, resulting in verses 1, 3, 5, and 7. Choirbok 2-1-2, however, leaps around a bit more, taking the texts from verses 1, 5, 14, and 17. (One can find the "standard" order of the verses as they appear in the Roman rite by consulting the *Liber Usualis,* 945–49.)

80. For the two versions of *Lauda Sion Salvatorem* in Santa Clara Ms. 4, consult fol./p. 48 (on this sheet the *b* phrases are crossed out, but the *a* phrases are left intact), and also consult sheet *B-Bv* for Cabot's alternate version.

81. See manuscript sheet S-2 in the San Fernando Mission Archive of the Archdiocese of Los Angeles, in San Fernando, California. This source provided half of the phrases for Chanticleer's performance of *Lauda Sion Salvatorem* on their latest release, *Mission Road.*

82. In the Durán choirbook C-C-59 he includes the following: "Vigilia de diffuntos" (Vigil of the Dead), pp. 57–61; Requiem Mass for the Dead, pp. 62–64; "Entierro de Adultos" (Burial Service for Adults), pp. 64–66; another "Missa de Requiem a 4 voces...compás a 4" (Requiem Mass for the Dead for four voices...in quadruple meter), pp. 67–69 and another unnumbered sheet that I paginate as pp. *E* and *F*. Santa Clara Ms. 4 includes the following: "Vigilia de Difuntos" (Vigil of the Dead), pp. 69–77; Requiem Mass for the Dead, pp. 77–81; "Entierro de Adultos trasportado en fa" (Burial Service for Adults, transposed to F), pp. 81–84; "Missa Solemne de Difuntos" (Solemn [Requiem] Mass for the Dead), pp. 84–86. Santa Clara Ms. 3 includes the following: Requiem Mass for the Dead, pp. 1–10; "Vesp. Def." (Vespers for the Dead), fols. 57v–61; Matins for the Dead, fols. 61v–75v; Burial Service for Adults, fols. 75v–76v. In addition, three folders in the WPA collection contain music for the Requiem Mass or burial service. WPA folder 54, photo Q-2, contains the Second Lesson for the Office of the Dead: "[Lec]ción Seg. de Difuntos ad libitum" [?] with the opening text "Tedet Animam meam." WPA folder 72 contains photographs of a Requiem Mass in the hand of Juan Bautista Sancho. Its title page reads, "Missa de Requiem à3 voces/ et Laboravi â 3./ Es del uso de Fray Juan Bau[tis] ta/ Sancho Diaconos y Religioso/ Observante./ Año 1796" (Requiem Mass for 3 Voices and a Laboravi for 3 voices. This is for the use of Friar Juan Bautista Sancho, Deacon and Religious Observant, in the Year 1796). Without question, this Sancho manuscript provides the most "modern" and erudite settings in California for the Requiem or burial services. WPA folder 73 is in a different hand entirely and is so error-ridden that it is almost impossible to restore, given the notational misunderstandings. The last portion of this manuscript contains the recitative "O qué humilde" and aria "Grande fue la agonía." Fortunately, there is a concordant version of this recitative and aria in the *Artaserse Ms.* in the San Fernando Mission Archive, As-3, fol. 1. The San Juan Bautista Ms. 1 has the "Missa defuntorum" (Mass for the Dead), on plates 73–77, pp. 54–58, and the "Vigilia Defunctorum" (Vigil of the Dead), on plates 77–83. pp. 58–64. Santa Barbara Doc. 1 has the "Misa de Requiem a 4 voces" (Requiem Mass for the Dead in 4 parts), pp. 53–59; "Matins for the Dead," pp. 54–59 (this service begins in "midstream" because the choirbook is missing pp. 60–67, where the Matins had clearly begun); "Vigilia de Difuntos" (Vigil of the Dead), pp. 68–69; "Misa de Requiem a canto llano" (Requiem Mass in plainchant), pp. 69–79; "[Maitines para el] Entierro de Adultos" ([Matins for the] Burial for Adults), pp. 80–97.

83. Some authors have called into question Thomas of Celaeno's role as composer of this sequence (or at least of the composer of the whole work), since some of its elements appeared beforehand. Even if certain details had existed previously, Thomas can be credited with recrafting the disparate elements—and perhaps composing some of it—into the masterful version that has come down to us today. See J. Szövérffy, "Dies irae," in *The*

Catholic Encyclopedia, vol. 4, pp. 863–64. Also consult the Web site "Dies irae," in H. T. Henry's *New Catholic Encyclopedia*, http://www.newadvent.org/cathen/04787a.htm (accessed 7 July 2005).

84. Santa Clara Ms. 4, p. 79.

85. Several of the rhythmic *canto figurado* versions of *Dies irae* appear in California sources: Durán choirbook C-C-59 at the Bancroft Library (transposed up a minor third), p. 63; Santa Inés Ms. 1 (same as C-C-59 but not transposed), pp. 42–43; and San Juan Bautista Ms. 1, p. 55 (photo 74 in WPA item 45). The choice of transposition in C-C-59 is consistent with Durán's practice of transposing almost every melody so that the tonic is F instead of D. See the section *"Canto llano"* in chapter 1 and note 44. Obviously, the transposition up by a third requires the frequent insertion of accidentals to preserve the proper disposition of half steps and whole steps of the melody.

Another *canto figurado* setting (that is closely related but not identical to the version mentioned above) is based on the *canto figurado* setting as published in Vicente Pérez Martínez's *Prontuario del cantollano gregoriano* (Madrid: Julian Pereyra, 1799 and 1800), vol. 2, pp. 690ff. (For a facsimile, consult photo B-88 in appendix B that is available online.) With only minor revisions, the *Prontuario* version is copied into Santa Clara Ms. 3 (pp. 3–6). (For a facsimile of the Santa Clara Ms. 3 version, see photo B-92 in appendix B.) This particular setting of the *Dies irae* appears again as the model for Santa Inés Ms. 5 (pp. 34–38). However, this latter version is incomplete; the only phrases notated in Santa Inés Ms. 5 are "Dies irae... sibilla." / "Quātus tremor... discusurus." / "Tuba mirum... ante tronum." / "Lacrymosa... homo reus." / "Huic ergo... Amen."

Santa Clara Ms. 4, p. 79 has a peculiar setting of the *Dies irae* that conceivably could be either *canto llano* or *canto figurado;* there are no bar lines, and if mensural notation rules are applied, the most consistent meter would be duple. A *canto figurao* interpretation, however, turns out to be inconsistent if forced into one meter all the way through.

86. Some settings of the *Dies irae* that offer polyphonic phrases alternating two-voice with four-voice texture, usually in conjunction with implied *alternatim* performance, include choirbook C-C-59 at the Bancroft Library, p. 67; Santa Barbara Doc. 1, p. 57; and Santa Barbara Doc. 2, pp. 14–15. Yet another polyphonic setting of the *Dies irae* is found in the "Missa de Requiem, a 3 voces, 1796" in Sancho's hand, preserved in folder 72 of the WPA.

87. Santa Clara Ms. 4, p. 85.

88. At the bottom half of page 67 of Durán's choirbook C-C-59, he writes out the *a* phrase (applicable to the odd-numbered verses) in a duet version, but it is so heavily blotched that it is almost impossible to read. At the top of page 68 he continues with the *b* phrase (applicable to the even-numbered verses); it is crafted for four voices rather than two, and it appears Durán has second thoughts. For some inexplicable reason, at the end of the lyrics he begins correctly with the fragmentary "18. Hu"—but then he stops short. The text should read "Huic ergo...," but he has cut the word "Huic" in half and discarded letters "ic" along with the remaining text for this verse. On page 67 he refers the reader or performer to the "corrected" version of this composition, as it is found on page 69. Note: there is a muddle with respect to the pagination at this point. Consult my appendix A for a precise explanation of the contents on the ensuing sheets, including p. 69 with the foldable flaps.

89. This alternation of *a* and *b* phrases is applicable to both versions of the sequence in choirbook C-C-59, whether one adopts the blotchy and crossed-out phrases on pp. 67–68 or the multifarious variations of the sequence available on page 69.

90. On the half sheet that folds over on top of page 67, Durán writes out the instructions: "Sequencia Pag. 69 alterna a duo y quatro voces según los números de la margen" (The sequence as found on page 69 alternates duet textures with four-voice texture, according to the numbers in the margin). If one lifts up this half sheet to reveal the bottom of page 69, one finds a very similar annotation: "Nota: esta Sequencia se canta alte[r]natibamente un verso a duo y otro a quatro según los números de la margen" (Note: this sequence is sung by alternating between a verse in duet texture with another set in four-voice texture, according to the numbers in the margin). To reinforce the desired sonorities, Durán advises the choir yet again at the top of page 69 by titling the work, "Sequencia a duo y a 4 alternada según los numeros a la margen."

91. For a discussion of Pentecost, its origins, and the manner of its celebration, consult Weiser, *Handbook of Christian Feasts and Customs,* 246–54. The depiction of the Holy Ghost's visitation to the disciples is described in the second chapter of the *Acts of the Apostles.*

92. For a detailed examination of this Pentecost celebration in Monterey, consult the section "Serra and the Founding of San Carlos Borromeo Near Monterey" in chapter 3 and note 11.

93. Translated in "Traditional Catholic Prayers: Come O Holy Ghost," Society of Saint Pius X, District of Great Britain. Web site http://www.sspx.co.uk/prayers.php?id=130.

94. For one beautiful setting of *Veni Sancte Spiritus,* consult the *canto figurado* version as written out by Estevan Tapís in San Juan Bautista Choirbook 1, pp. 41ff. A facsimile is found in appendix B online under the heading "B-59."

95. Durán choirbook C-C-59, p. 27; Santa Barbara Doc. 1, p. 27; and Santa Clara Ms. 4, p. 15.

96. One can find the traditional setting as practiced in the Roman rite by referring to the *Liber Usualis,* 880–81.

97. For clarification of the term *música* and its relationship to instrumental performance practice, consult the section "Instrumental Interludes: *Música, Toca,* and *Tocata,*" in chapter 2.

98. A second related (but not identical) setting of *Veni Sancte Spiritus* occurs in choirbook C-C-68:2, pp. 57–59. This setting is in the antiquated notation of *canto figurado* but lacks the bar lines found in Santa Clara Ms. 3, p. 27. In addition, its *b* phrase is different from the *b* phrase in Santa Clara. Both versions develop parallel thirds, but the contours are not identical and choirbook C-C-68:2 has no discernible meter. Close scrutiny of Santa Clara Ms. 3 reveals, however, that *originally* it had the same *b* phrases as C-C-68:2. The scribe, probably Florencio Ibáñez, had second thoughts; he erased (as well as he could) the older nonmetric phrase and replaced it with another. A less-complete but nevertheless informative copy of this same *Veni Sancte Spiritus* is found in WPA folder 54, photo Q-1. This page has the first part of the piece ("Veni Sancte Spiritus…") written out on line 10, the last staff on the page. Immediately above it on staves 6–9 we find the second part of the piece ("Veni, veni Pater pauperum…") as a duet: the two parts are written in score format, with one part aligned correctly above the other. In other words, the highest-sounding part occupies lines 6 and 8, and its lower companion is written out on lines 7 and 9. All melodies are in bass clef.

For a recording of the Santa Clara Ms. 3 setting of *Veni Sancte Spiritus,* consult Chanticleer's most recent CD, *Mission Road.*

99. For instance, consult the *Liber Usualis,* 880, and one finds the words "Here all kneel" printed above this very same verse.

100. Many of these same features of mutual accommodation arise in Samuel Y. Edgerton's indispensable book *Theaters of Conversion.* He elucidates how the missionaries and the Native American peoples together "negotiated" their artistic creations in the field. He explains how the friars in the Yucatán used arches and vaults in their architecture to appeal to the Native Americans' association of caves with the holy and the sacred. He states: "By deploying the European masonry vault so ostentatiously in the Yucatán, they hoped to remind the Indians that the cavernous Christian church was not dissimilar in meaning as well as form from their natural sacred grottoes and thus ease their resistance to the new religion" (92). He develops the theme expansively, later illustrating how the Yucatán experience migrated to New Mexico—where the missionaries had built churches over sacred kivas (a sort of sunken, manmade cave in the shape of a circle). See pp. 275–78, esp. p. 278. In short, the friars did not try to vanquish all traces of Native American worship but instead adapted indigenous customs and beliefs for their own evangelical purposes. Furthermore, Edgerton explains that the Franciscans took care *not* to report back to Spain that their new converts were sometimes continuing with their old traditions such as visiting their ancestral sacred caves. Such a report back to church authorities might have raised eyebrows. Instead, the friars chose to look the other way (p. 90). All of this runs parallel to what we hear in the *Veni Sancte Spiritus* from the Feast of Pentecost in California. At the height of worship in the mission, a drum resounded to accompany the Alleluia; one has to think that the Franciscans were trying to *remind* their converts of this sacred connotation of the traditional Indian drum rather than stamp it out—in the same way that they tried to *remind* the neophytes of the cave, now metamorphosed into the Christian church.

Francis F. Guest illustrates that tolerance and acceptance (at least initially) of Native American practices was official policy of the Franciscans as articulated in the Manual of Pastoral Theology, authored by Montanegro in 1754. Guest explains the manual's thesis: "One should not be hasty about detaching them [the Native American converts] from the religious rites and ceremonies to which their tribal tradition had long accustomed them. If these religious practices did not involve a clear and open violation of the divine law, they should be tolerated until, little by little, the Indians were weaned away from ancient forms of worship." See Francis P. Guest, O.F.M., "An Inquiry into the Role of the Discipline in California Mission Life," *Southern California Quarterly,* vol. 71, no. 1 (Spring 1989), 3.

CHAPTER 5

Juan Bautista Sancho

Tracing the Mallorcan Connection

AMONG THE FRIARS active in the California missions, few rival (and none sur-
pass) Juan Bautista Sancho y Literes in their musical expertise, breadth of repertoire, and adroit craftsmanship. The laudable choir and orchestra he established
on his arrival at the San Antonio de Padua Mission in 1804 proved capable of
performing elaborate and complex compositions, and Sancho is responsible,
more than any other individual, for introducing into California the "modern"
sounds of the *galant* and of Classicism. Fortunately, we have a relative abundance of performance parts (either as existing manuscripts or as photos of
sources now lost) penned by Sancho that provide us with a more specific and
detailed representation of the musical life in California missions than do the
generalized comments made in nineteenth-century diaries and letters by visitors to the area. His performance parts, used by the neophyte musicians at the
San Antonio Mission, as well as numerous separate papers with tunes and lyrics
(more or less equivalent to condensed "lead sheets" in popular music), illustrate
the repertoire, styles, and sonorities of California mission music. Furthermore,
Sancho's signed and dated manuscripts help to trace the origins of certain works
in the mission repertoire—which in turn illuminates the cultural relationships
between his native Spain (where he received his initial musical training) and the
missions in the New World (where he spent his mature life teaching the neophytes everything from *canto llano* to *estilo moderno*). He was as engrossed with
learning as with teaching, as can be seen in his essays that exhibit a fascination
with Native American music and language. He wrote about the musical instruments and singing of native peoples and became fluent enough to translate Latin
and Spanish texts in the local indigenous languages (presumably Mutsun and
Salinan). Evidence suggests that he might have been the composer—not merely
the scribe—for some of the concerted works that we find in his hand. Even if
we move the title of "composer" to the side as unproven, Sancho's indisputable
accomplishments as interpreter, pedagogue, conductor, and arranger are at such

a level that he must be considered as one of the main musical figures of North America in the nineteenth century.

Remarkably, Sancho's role and importance have largely escaped notice until fairly recently. Robert Stevenson and Alfred Lemmon have shed considerable light on mission music of the Americas, but their spotlight never narrowed its beam on Sancho. William Summers first brought attention to Sancho's impressive output and adroit musical skills in more than a dozen articles that sparked interest in the scholarly community. John Koegel took the next leap in mission research with his discoveries of "lost" or unknown works—dozens of them either written out or possibly composed by Sancho—as well as his prolific scholarly essays and monographs that have broadened our understanding. Antoni Pizà has engendered several projects on both sides of the Atlantic focused on Sancho's life and music. The Mallorcan priest and genealogical sleuth Antoni Gili has ferreted out hundreds of details regarding Sancho's family tree through decades of painstaking work in the parish archives of Artà, Sancho's birthplace. The Los Angeles–based group Zephyr issued a charming and sometimes lush recording of Sancho's *Misa de los Angeles,* and Grant Gershon with the Los Angeles Master Chorale, Juan Pedro Gaffney with the Coro Hispano de San Francisco, and John Warren with the New World Baroque Orchestra have all been impassioned advocates for his music. In spite of all their efforts, however, most music lovers and California scholars are oblivious to his name, yet alone his music. To fill in some of these holes, let us begin with Sancho's life.

Juan Bautista Sancho i Literes: Family History and His Life in Artà

Near the charming town of Artà, at the far eastern coast of Mallorca, lies the ranch land of "Sos Sanchos," where the Sancho family prospered for centuries. If one climbs the steps to the top of the hill in Artà and gazes northward from the church of Sant Salvador, one gets a full panoramic view of the countryside, including "Sos Sanchos" (see Photo B-136 in appendix B online). The one parish church in town (the Església parroquial d'Artà) is a stolid stone structure nestled into the village streets below Sant Salvador (see photo B-133 online). The baptismal font sits inside the parish entrance; its basin was made in 1672, and a century later Pere Josep Sanxo i Nicolau and Margarida Lliteres Llinas brought their newborn son, Juan Bautista Sancho, to be christened into the Christian faith. As a youngster, Sancho received his education at the Convent Franciscà de Sant Antoni de Pàdua, which is situated down at the foot of the rising hill in Artà, to the southwest of Sant Salvador and the Església parroquial (see photo B-134 online).

The untiring and fastidious researcher Mosen Antoni Gili has uncovered so much genealogical documentation in the Església parroquial d'Artà that he can now trace Juan Bautista Sancho's lineage directly back by eighteen generations to the fourteenth century and can provide some familial linkage to the thirteenth century.[1] (For a detailed family tree of Sancho's heritage, based on the research of Mosen Gili, see figure 5-1.)

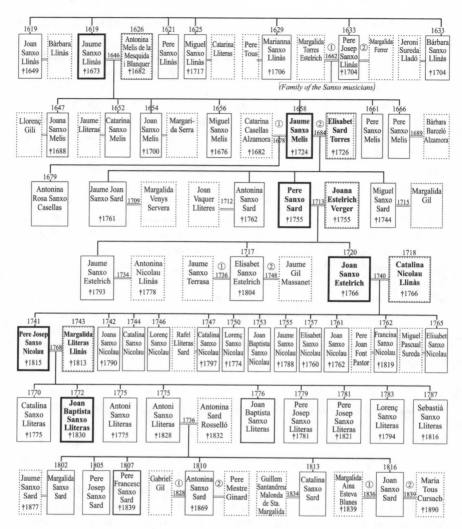

Figure 5-1 Sancho's family tree. Based on newly uncovered documentation by Mosen Antoni Gili y Ferrer

Juan's parents, Pere Josep and Margarida, took their marriage vows on 28 September 1768 (see Photo B-135 online).[2] Two years later, Margarida gave birth to their first child, Catalina, and two years after that, they had their first son, "Joan Baptista Sanxo Lliteras" (our friar-musician). Juan Bautista's baptismal registration in the Església parroquial bears the given name "Joan Baptista" and date 1 December, 1772 (see photo 5-1, that is also available online as photo B-136).[3] Later in life, as Sancho moved from Mallorca to the wider Spanish world, he used the

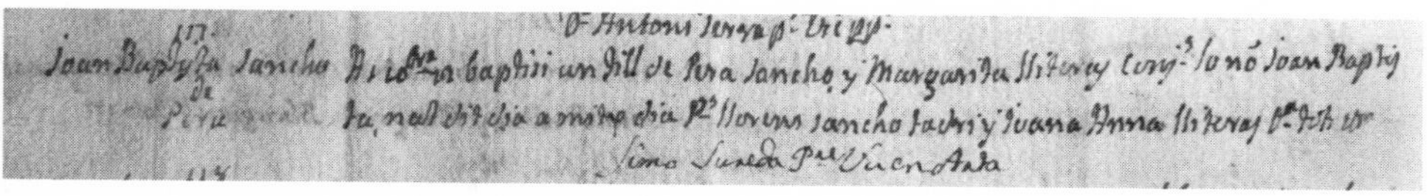

Photo 5-1 Baptismal registration of Juan Sancho, Església parroquial d'Artà, *Bautismos, 1764–1796,* fol. 48, no. 117. (Photo by the author.)

Castilian equivalent of his name, "Juan Bautista Sancho y Literes," and it is in this form that we recognize him in California documents.

Following 1772, the biographical documents become muddled in perplexing confusion, for Mosen Gili has located a *second* baptismal registry dated 24 November 1776, for a "Joan Baptista Sanxo Lliteras," born to the *same* parents in the same parish.[4] He posits that the first child with that name must have died, and then the couple bestowed the name yet again on an infant who survived to adulthood—and became the friar who moved to California.[5] This theory does accommodate the curious presence of two baptismal registrations four years apart, but it is problematic as well. If we accept the theory that a child was born in 1772 with the given name "Joan Baptista Sanxo Lliteras," but died before the age of three, why is there no record of a death or burial? Was the parish priest simply forgetful or sloppy? Unlikely. It was canonic law for the priest to register the death within a day: failure to do so was not simply a matter of paperwork—it was a mortal sin to fail in this recording function.[6] Also, if Sancho were born in 1776, when he took the Franciscan habit in 1791 he would have been only fifteen years old (instead of the expected eighteen). If the novitiate were born in 1772, however, the math works perfectly. Sancho became a presbyter in 1796; the normal age of becoming a presbyter would be twenty-four; again, the year 1772 would be a much more plausible birth year. In addition, the obituary by Pedro Cabot written at the San Antonio Mission in California is precise. Cabot states that he administered the last rites to Sancho on 7 February 1830, and then Cabot kindly offers the statement that Sancho had lived fifty-seven years, two months, and seven days. When we do the math, it comes out to be a birthday of 1 December 1772—the exact date specified in the first baptismal registry.

However, the 1772 birth date also has unexplained holes. If our friar were born in 1772, how can we explain his parents giving birth to another son four years later and giving that child exactly the same name of "Juan Bautista Sancho"? One possible explanation for the mystery has been offered by Astrid Russell: perhaps the friar Sancho was actually born in 1776, but he willfully pretended to be his deceased older brother who must have died at childbirth or soon thereafter. By "adopting" the earlier birth date of 1772 instead of 1776, Juan Bautista would have the distinct advantage of being regarded as the firstborn son of the Sancho family—a position of privilege that would have brought with it high social esteem and many legal rights. In the end, the situation is fraught with contradictions or unresolved mysteries. Until further evidence surfaces, the birth year remains an open question.

In Mallorca, two career paths presented themselves as highly attractive to aspiring youths: monastic orders and musical careers. This latter profession lured and occupied many members of Sancho's extended family; that surname arises with regularity in the musician rosters, beginning as early as the fifteenth and six-teenth centuries, when Esteve Sanxo appears in payment records as a reputable organist.[7] "Pere Sancho" made a name for himself as a professional musician at the music chapel of the Confraternity of Saint Cecilia in the Royal Palace, receiv-ing ten *lliures,* both in 1736 and again in 1737, for his service.[8] This name resembles that of Sancho's great-grandfather Pere Sanxo i Sard, who was born sometime after 1684 (the date of his parents' wedding) and who died in 1755.[9] One might ask if Sancho's great-grandfather and this musician at the Royal Palace were one and the same, for the dates are certainly appropriate. Until further evidence surfaces, however, this link between Sancho's direct bloodline and this esteemed musician must be viewed as conjectural.

During Juan Bautista Sancho's lifetime, other members of his extended family rose to prominence in Palma. Antoni Sancho Sacrer appears on a musician's roster for 1776 and 1781.[10]

Few Mallorcan musicians in the late 1700s matched in renown or musical prestige Jaume Sancho Melis, Juan Bautista Sancho's cousin.[11] Jaume, like Juan Bautista, was a native of Artà. Having left his hometown for Palma, Jaume achieved fame as a composer, professor of music, violin virtuoso, and music director. His name crops up as early as 1768 as an artist in the employ of the Royal Chapel and in conjunction with the Convent de Sant Francesc in Palma. Eventually, he won the meritorious post of chapelmaster for the See of Mallorca from 1793 to 1803 (substituting for Mestre Llorens).[12] Concurrently, Juan Bautista Sancho resided in Palma at the Convent de Sant Francesc, also carving out a name for himself as a laudable musician.

Several other musicians with the Sancho surname—but with only remote family ties to the branch of the family from which Juan Bautista sprang—ascended to highly honored positions in Mallorcan musical circles. Between 1793 and 1803, Miquel Sancho i Vicens (1767–1840) worked his way up the ladder at the See of Mallorca until being named interim chapelmaster at the Palma Cathedral in 1803 and 1804; his artistic skills proved worthy, so his position was made permanent in 1804. He served in this capacity as "Master and Director of Music for the Music Chapel for the See of Mallorca" until his death.[13] Miquel's son, Joaquim Sancho i Canyellas (1798–1886), was deemed the "Mallorcan Haydn" due to his legacy as pianist, professor, and composer.[14] The noble tradition extends up to the modern era with musicians such as the highly respected Antoni Sancho i Nebot in the twentieth century.[15] Modern-day music scholars Antoni Gili i Ferrer and Llorenç Vich Sancho can both trace their origins through various branches of this musical Sancho heritage.[16]

In addition to the missionary heritage, Sancho pursued another branch of his Mallorcan patrimony—that of friar. Ever since the Mallorcan friar Antoni Llinàs i Massanet founded the Apostolic College of the Holy Cross (Colegio Apostólico de Santa Cruz) in Querétaro, Mexico, in 1683, a flood of young Mallorcan men inspired by their fellow countryman took up the challenge of missionary work in the New World. Llinàs's efforts spread Christianity across the Sierra Gorda in Mexico, and his *colegio* in Querétaro engendered the next *casa matriz,* or mother-house, in Mexico City—the Colegio Apostólico de San Fernando. Founded on 15 October 1733, this Franciscan institution later supervised and governed the chain of twenty-one missions that dotted the coastal regions of Alta California. In the ensuing decades, dozens of Mallorcan friars left their island home to reside at the Colegio Apostólico de San Fernando and its satellite missions that it governed; they left with little more than a few manuals and tools, a sense of adventure, and the determination to live faithful and purposeful lives. The musical legacy of Mallorca is equally impressive. During Sancho's lifetime, for example, the musical training in Palma was akin to that at the Juilliard School or Peabody Conservatory today. Several of the most celebrated musicians in the Royal Chapel in Madrid—such as the spectacular guitarist and composer Francisco Gueráu, his brother Gabriel Gueráu, and the acclaimed composer and cellist Antonio Lliteres—received their musical training in Mallorca.[17]

Not surprisingly, Sancho took on the monastic mantle of Llinàs, Serra, and his Mallorcan predecessors who devoted themselves to missionary evangelization. On 17 May 1779, the eight-year-old was confirmed in the Christian faith.[18] He entered the Convent de Sant Francesc as a novitiate on 9 February 1791.[19] He professed his solemn vows the ensuing year.[20]

One of the richest fonts of information concerning Sancho's life is the heart-felt obituary that Pedro Cabot authored at Sancho's death. Cabot summarized the accomplishments of his lifelong friend, stating, "He was the son of Pedro Sancho and his wife Margarita Lliteras, and was baptized in the Villa de Artà, Isle and Diocese of Mallorca, on 1 December 1772. He received the habit of our Fr. Saint Francis in the royal convent of the City of Palma, on 9 February 1791, and on concluding the year of the novitiate, made the solemn profession in the said convent." Cabot provides a window from which to view Sancho's gestatory years at the Convent de Sant Francesc: "On being ordained priest, and having the faculties of a confessor and preacher, he exercised said ministries for some years in the Province. He would, on account of the lack of a Vicario de Coro, direct the chant by his strong and agreeable voice, and gave complete instruction in plainchant [*canto llano*] as well as in figured music [*canto figurado*]."[21]

Sancho's Diary and His Life in Palma

Cabot's overview of Sancho's life can be put in clearer focus using Sancho's "diary," a tiny but invaluable booklet that I discovered at the Bancroft Library in Berkeley.[22] In the fall of 2005, I was shuffling through the random mishmash of folders, identified as "mission miscellany" in the Bancroft Library under the call number C-C-73, and I stumbled upon a tiny four-page pamphlet whose first sheet contained printed papal bulls in miniature type. The library catalogued the pocket-size booklet as "Fragment from printed book of Papal Bulls, 1631 with mss. notes, 1772–1804."[23] A snippet of the title page has been torn off, but nonetheless one can decipher

Photo 5-2 "y â la Nueva Califᵃ llegue," the Bancroft Library, Ms. C-C-73:16, Diary of Juan Bautista Sancho, fol. 1. (Photo courtesy of the Bancroft Library, University of California, Berkeley.)

"SUM[ ]A BULLÆ SS. D. N. Urbani VIII…data Romæ die 25. Januari i anno 1631," hence supplying the "1631" date used by the Bancroft Library in cataloguing this item. If one turns the page, the flip side of this folio reveals another papal bull, "CONSTIT[ ]IO SS. D. N. INNOCENTII PAPÆ XII.…" My heart began to race, however, when I noticed—scribbled near the bottom of the first page—the annotation that read: "y â la Nueva Califᵃ llegue dia 15 de Agˢᵗᵒ de 1804" (and I arrived in New California the 15th day of August 1804). (See photo 5-2, that is also available online as photo B-15.)

It struck me that this script resembled Sancho's handwriting in every detail. As I continued to turn the pages, the evidence mounted, until I came across the definitive proof of Sancho's authorship. On folio 3v, he jotted down his ex libris: "Este Diurno es del simple uso del P. Fr. Juan Bautista Sancho Religˢᵒ Obs." (This Diary is for the sole use of Father Friar Juan Bautista Sancho, Religious Observant). (See photo 5-3, that is also available online as photo B-16.) This indisputable proof confirmed my initial hope; this microscopic pamphlet served Sancho as a kind of personal diary. His first entry concerns his novitiate as a Franciscan

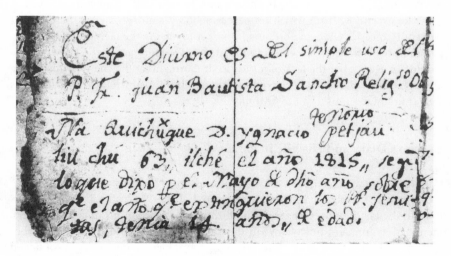

Photo 5-3 "Este Diurno es del simple uso del P. Fr. Juan Bautista Sancho," the Bancroft Library, Ms. C-C-73:16, Diary of Juan Bautista Sancho, fol. 3v. (Photo courtesy of the Bancroft Library, University of California, Berkeley.)

in Palma in 1791, and his scribbled entries continue up through 1815, when he was firmly ensconced as a friar at the San Antonio Mission in California.[24]

The booklet contains a hodgepodge of entries written in two or three different hands on a variety of themes, usually religious in nature. Clearly, this pocket-size booklet was passed from owner to owner, most likely between friars at the Convent de Jesús or Convent de Sant Francesc in Palma, and Sancho was the last in the chain to use this hand-me-down. The petite manuscript served as a sort of memory album, where Sancho would inscribe annotations on days of personal accomplishment or momentous occasions, such as his vows as a novitiate or his departure for the New World. Perusing this document, we get a privileged view of Sancho's heartfelt goals and psychological instincts. Out of the many events that he experienced, when he chose to include an event in his diary, we get a momentary glimpse of his passions and value judgments. Entries correspond to those occasions he desired to commemorate as life-altering and quintessential, and his decisions reveal a man of subtle self-awareness and introspective reflection.

Occasional gaps appear between consecutive entries—sometimes spaced apart by a few years—but when he does pick up the quill again, he captures the immediacy and passion of the moment. Just as Sancho journeyed to new lands and continents, so his diary undergoes a linguistic journey as well. At first, he

Photo 5-4 "Nota" and "Altre nota," the Bancroft Library, Ms. C-C-73:16, Diary of Juan Bautista Sancho, fol. 4v. (Photo courtesy of the Bancroft Library, University of California, Berkeley.)

jots down his thoughts in Mallorquín (a version of Catalán). As he readies to embark for Cádiz, his language begins to meld together Castilian with Catalan in a sort of linguistic alloy of the two—much like the merging of English and Spanish into "Spanglish" in modern Southwestern culture. By the time he sets foot in Mexico to begin his missionary life, he has completely abandoned his regional dialect in favor of Castilian, the universally adopted "standard" for the Spanish friars of the mendicant orders. The linguistic metamorphosis continues upon his arrival in California, until Native American language eventually supplants his Castilian usage.

Sancho customarily provides the date and the critical summary of each occasion. Since the entries were jotted down on different days, sometimes years apart, one sees pronounced differences in the width of the pen nib and shade of ink. Curiously, the entries of Sancho's diary do not appear on consecutive pages in an obvious chronological order but instead are sprinkled around in various locations—wherever he encountered free space left over from the writings made by the book's previous owners. The first entry, in fact, occurs on the *last* page of the booklet. (See photo 5-4, that is also available online as photo B-17.)

After inscribing his initial comment at becoming a novitiate in 1791, the remaining "empty" space is sufficient for him to trace out four more entries in microscopic cursive writing that take us up to 1803, when he set foot on Mexican soil. His diary entries explain:

Note:

Day 9 of February of the year 1791, I took the [Franciscan] habit [as a novice], I, Friar Juan Bautista Sancho.

And I took the Order of Presbytery on the 17th day of December of 1796, and I said my first mass on the 27th of this same month.

And on the 20th of July of the year 1798 I was examined to become a Confessor for the first time by Bishop Bernat Aodat y Crespi.

Another Note:

I departed from Artà for the Colegio de San Fernando on the 23rd of February of 1803, the first day of Lent.

And having left the Port of Cádiz, on the 20th of June 1803, I arrived at the said Colegio de San Fernando [near Mexico City] on the 9th of September of the same year.[25]

The haphazard arrangement of material—a seemingly random positioning determined by the unused, "free space" that was available—can be rearranged in the correct chronological order that Sancho had recorded his entries. Leaving the opening entries on fol. 4v (dated 1791 and 1796), we can turn to folio 3, where we find a list of items associated with the Hours of the Divine Office that Sancho recited in Palma in 1797. The entry reads:

In the year 1797, in the Convent de Jesús, outside the cloister walls, [the friars] sang 29 Offices or Requiem Masses on the Day of the Dead, which is the 2nd day of November, and they were sung in succession.[26]

Interestingly, we find a sort of chart with the names of honored saints lined up on the left side as if they were part of a "to-do" list—and each name is stricken out, perhaps indicating that this saint's feast day had been faithfully executed at the appropriate time in the liturgical year.[27] This list of Offices and Requiems entered into the booklet in 1797 at the Convent de Jesús in Palma is followed by two concise insertions made back in his native Artà.

And in Artà in the year 1801, a quantity[?] of 27 of them
And for the year 1802, 21 Offices.[28]

Sancho's entries depict various aspects of his life in Mallorca before he settled in the New World. While still in his island homeland, he was actively performing various priestly duties in Artà in 1801 and 1802. His annotations describe further ecclesiastical activities in Palma at the Convent de Jesús; several friars who eventually set down roots in California had strong ties to this prominent monastic center.[29] Junípero Serra and Francisco Palóu, the inaugural founders of the mission chain in Alta California, took their first steps as friars in the Convent de Jesús; Serra entered the Franciscan order there in 1730, as did Palóu nine years later.[30]

Other Mallorcan friars whose careers were initiated and forged at that monastic institution before emigrating to California include Francisco Dumetz (who joined the order in 1751), as well as Buenaventura Sitjar (taking his vows in 1758) and Luis Jayme (joining in 1760).[31] Antonio Jayme and Jerónimo Boscana subsequently followed in those footsteps: Jayme entered the Convent de Jesús on 7 December 1774; and Boscana joined on 4 August 1792.[32] Sancho almost certainly became acquainted with Boscana while still in Mallorca, for they joined the order almost simultaneously and then pursued very similar career paths for the next ten years. Sancho set sail from Cádiz for Mexico's Colegio Apostólico de San Fernando on 20 June 1803, and Boscana's ship left port for Mexico that same summer. Once transplanted to Alta California, the two men devoted their lives to mission evangelization for the next quarter century and died within a year of each other. Their respect for and fascination with Native American culture and indigenous languages were heartfelt and highly visible. In his book *Chinigchinich*, Boscana explored the customs and rituals of the Acjachemen Nation who resided in the region surrounding the San Juan Capistrano Mission, and Sancho delved into the Native American lifestyles and observances in the detailed *Interrogatorio* of 1814 that he coauthored with friar Pedro Cabot. When forced to work inside due to inclement weather, Sancho spent countless hours translating catechisms and other sacred texts into the vernacular dialects of the indigenous peoples who inhabited the lands surrounding the San Antonio Mission.[33]

Without question, the monastic center that exerted the clearest influence on Sancho as a young man was the Convent de Sant Francesc—the place where he entered the order as a novitiate and subsequently took his full vows into the

Franciscan Order. Almost every Mallorcan friar who relocated to California, at one time or another spent formative years within the orbit of this venerated monastic center.[34] If one exits the imposing cathedral and strolls through Palma's cramped but enchanting streets to the convent, the narrow passageways suddenly burst open into a small city square, presenting an exquisite, unrestricted view of the monastery. (See photo 5-5, that is also available online as photo B-142.)

The simple, straightforward design aptly captures the unassuming, humble spirit of Saint Francis himself with its unadorned, sturdy facade and single, circular window above the entrance. This architectural simplicity greatly resembles the convent of Sant Antoni de Pàdua, the Franciscan center in Artà where Sancho first attended grammar school as a child. When one passes through the imperious doors into the sanctuary, the restrained and simple is transformed into the magnificent and ornamental. The awe-inspiring church organ is surrounded by a casement of florid carvings befitting the ornate trills and mordents that must have emanated from its ranks of glimmering pipes in the late eighteenth century—a time when Sancho almost certainly directed musical performances from the organ bench. If one proceeds through the nave toward the altar and exits through the

Photo 5-5 Façade of the Convent de Sant Francesc, Palma de Mallorca. (Photo by the author.)

doors to the right, he or she will chance upon the cloister with its gracile columns and luxuriant gardens. (See Photos B-143, B-144, and B-145 online.) Sancho's diary records his multifarious activities at Sant Francesc (as does Cabot's obituary of Sancho); these two sources mention his acquired skills as preacher, priest, and confessor—plus his impressive service at Sant Francesc as music director.

Sancho's diary mentions in passing his musical contributions at Sant Francesc, but the music manuscripts Sancho wrote out while there show the extent of his salient musical expertise. Additionally, Pedro Cabot's obituary of Sancho describes the artistic abilities and duties of his lifelong friend when they had been in Palma together: "He would, on account of the lack of a Vicario de Coro, direct the chant by his strong and agreeable voice, and [he] gave complete instruction in plainchant *[canto llano]* as well as in figured music *[canto figurado]*." This passage not only praises Sancho's vocal skills but also sheds light on the convent's music chapel hierarchy; without any official *maestro de capilla,* apparently Sancho's duties encompassed those of a music educator and choir director.[35] Certainly, Sancho's professional music experiences as music director at Sant Francesc in the 1790s readied him for his music duties at the San Antonio Mission in the ensuing decades. Few of the other California friars (except possibly Florencio Ibáñez) had such extensive or occupational music training.[36] His musical resources at the Convent de Sant Francesc must have been accomplished and versatile if we are to judge by the impeccable musical standards set in Mallorca by eighteenth-century virtuosos such as Francisco and Gabriel Gueráu, Antonio Lliteres, and Sancho's putative cousin, Miquel Sancho i Vicens. While residing at the Convent de Sant Francesc in Palma in the 1790s, Sancho meticulously wrote out numerous music manuscripts that he later packed into his luggage for his move to the San Antonio Mission in California in the early 1800s. Sancho signed many of these sheets and even recorded the date of completion. Although the original sheets are lost, photographs of these treasures are nevertheless extant and can be consulted at the Department of Music of the University of California at Berkeley. These invaluable photos and their contents will be addressed shortly.

While still in Palma, Sancho sketched out a concise chart of the Matins service; on folio 2v of his diary, he clarifies the various times that the service should begin, depending on the season of the year. During the short daylight hours of midwinter, he promotes a starting hour of around 2:30 A.M.; as the months pass, however, the longer days cause him to adjust the starting time to progressively later hours. By June and July at the height of midsummer, the starting hour for Matins has pushed forward all the way to 3:45 A.M.[37] Sancho then instructs the choir to avoid the sin that results from the casual changing around of the Hours of the Divine Office and stipulates various considerations with respect to worship at Franciscan institutions.[38] He spells out advice on the order of the liturgy at the bottom half of folio 3.[39]

Music Sources in Sancho's Hand from the Convent de Sant Francesc

Unfortunately, the archives of the Convent de Sant Francesc no longer preserve manuscript sources from the late eighteenth century, making a study of its influence on the California mission repertoire exceedingly difficult. However, through several lucky twists of fate, we do have sufficient clues preserved in California archives that make it possible to reconstruct a path connecting Sant Francesc to the music known across the California landscape. Juan Bautista Sancho had copied out piles of music sheets while still at the Mallorcan convent—many are dated and signed. The story of how these papers made it to the Franciscan missions and how their contents were rescued from oblivion bears retelling. The Carmel Mission (San Carlos Borromeo Mission) had fallen into dreadful disrepair by the late 1800s, and Father Angelo Casanova mustered support for its rebuilding. Jane Lathrop Stanford (wife to Governor Stanford) helped procure the financial resources for the reconstruction of the roof that had fallen into rubble; her efforts and donation were so appreciated by Father Casanova that he bestowed on her a sizable quantity of mission papers, among them an impressive stack of more than forty compositions written out in Sancho's hand; Father Owen da Silva described these documentary assets in his groundbreaking study of mission music, *Mission Music of California* (1941).[40] Unfortunately, with the exception of Serra choirbook M.0612 and the *Misa en sol*, no trace of these irreplaceable treasures has been seen for the last thirty years.[41] The first scholar to draw attention to their inauspicious disappearance was Bill Summers in 1977, but the imaginative sleuthing of John Koegel led to the rescue of their contents—in the form of photographs that had been taken in the 1930s as part of the Work Projects Administration Folk Music Project.[42] The goal at the time was to preserve anything that could be construed as "folk music." Although these manuscripts had very little to do with actual "folk music" in the oral tradition, we are blessed that the photographers were mistaken in their assessment and therefore turned their lens to these sheets nevertheless. It is through this well-meaning "mistake" that we now have preserved at the University of California at Berkeley a large carton that is brimming with black-and-white facsimiles of these "lost works."[43] From the photos we can glean several dates inscribed by Sancho onto the title pages, such as the *Missa de los Angeles,* the *Gozos y antífona de San Joseph* and the *Missa de Requiem a 3 voces* (all dated 1796); and the "Ecos a duo" (dated 1797).[44] John Koegel's detective work led him to yet another gold mine of Sancho-related sources at the Archival Center of the Archdiocese of Los Angeles at the San Fernando Mission.[45] Several other gems in Sancho's hand surface at the Santa Barbara Mission Archive-Library.[46] Taken together, the primary sources in these archives present evidence of a California tradition indebted to the performance trends at the Convent de Sant Francesc in Palma; furthermore, these sheets reveal previously hidden secrets about Fray Juan Bautista Sancho's formative years as musician and friar at Sant Francesc before setting sail for the Americas.

Of the various materials written out in Sancho's hand, the most important is the carton of photographs collected as part of the Work Projects Administration (later called the Works Progress Administration) and presently owned by the University of California at Berkeley. Their contents include the following:

WPA folder 50. "Ecos a Duo. / del uso de Fr. Juan Bautista Sancho. / Reg[ligio]so Observā[n]te. / 1797" (A Duet of Echoes, for the sole use of Friar Juan Bautista Sancho, Religious Observant, 1797). Modern notation. (See photo B-121 online.)

WPA folder 52. "Credo Artanense" (Credo from Artà). Significantly, this title specifically mentions Sancho's hometown of Artà. One finds at the bottom of sheet Aa-2 the annotation "Día 21 de Maio cerca las once de la n[oc]he acabo de escrivirlo" (The 21st of May, at about eleven o'clock at night, I have just finished writing this). Mensural black notation, i.e., *canto figurado*. (See photos 5-6 and 5-7, that are also available online as photos B-123 and B-124.)

WPA folder 56. "Gozos y antiphona San Joseph" (Poem and antiphon in honor of Saint Joseph). Text: "Pues sois sancto sin igual" (Well, you are a saint without equal). Its title page reads: "Gozos y añ[tifon]a Joseph &c. / del Patriarca San Joseph:/ Del uso de Fr. Juan Bautista/ Sancho Re[li]g[io]so Obs[er]v[an]te/ Año 1796." Modern notation.

WPA folder 58. "Invitatorium, Admirabile nomen Jessu, tono 6" (Invitatory in mode 6, Admirable name of Jesus). Its title page reads, "Este pliego es del/ uso de Fr. Juan/ Sancho" (This sheet is for the sole use of Friar Juan Sancho). The bottom of sheet Y-3 has the annotation, "Jesus, Maria, y Joseph. 1796. Esto es del uso de Fr. Juan Sācho" (Jesus, Mary, and Joseph, 1796. This is for the sole use of Friar Juan Sancho). Mensural black notation, i.e., *canto figurado*.

WPA folder 61. "Lamentatio a duo" (Lamentation duet), and the "Encierro a duo tono 2do" (Communion duet in mode 2). Modern notation.

WPA folder 64. "Kyrie a2" "Gloria a2" and "Credo a2" in "tono 5to." Modern notation.

WPA folder 66. "Credo Italiano, a duo con el coro (1796)" (Italian Credo, alternating duet sections with choral ones, 1796). In this folder, the "duo" sections are in modern notation. The "coro" sections make a shift to *canto figurado* notation and are to be performed in metric homophony. "Kyris [*sic*] t[on]o 2°," "Gloria," "Sanctus," Agnus Dei," plus "¡O que suave y dulce estais!" (Oh how smooth and sweet you are!) on sheets J-7 and J-8. A "Stabat Mater" appears on sheet J-8, plus we find some fragmentary parts for the *Gozos de la Purísima* ("Para dar luz inmortal" (In order to give eternal light) and "Ave sois eva trocada" (Bird, you are Eve transformed) on sheet J-8.

WPA folder 69. "Missa de los Angeles â 4 voces, 5to tono; y/ Credo Dominical 6to tono del/ simple uso de Fr. Juan Bautista Sancho/ Re[li]g[io]so Observante i Diacono./ 1796" (Mass of the Angels for 4 voices, in mode 5, and the Credo for Sundays in mode 6, for the sole use of Friar Juan Bautista Sancho, Religious Observant and Deacon,

1796). Modern notation. (See photo 5-8, that is also available online as photo B-128.)

WPA folder 70. "Misa de 5to tono â 4 voces del P[adre]./ Fr. Juan Bau[tis]ta Sancho" (Mass in mode 5 for 4 voices by Father Friar Juan Bautista Sancho). This *acompañamiento* part is meant to go with the music for folder 65, the *Misa en sol* (but here in folder 70 we find only the *acompañamiento* for the Gloria and the Credo movements). Modern notation.

WPA folder 72. "Missa de Requiem, a 3 voces, 1796." Has title page: "Missa de Requiem â3 voces/ et Laboravi â 3./ Es del uso de Fray Juan Bau[tis]ta/ Sancho Diaconos y Religioso/ Observante./ Año 1796."

Photo 5-6 "Credo Artanense," WPA folder 52, photo Aa-1. (Photograph courtesy of the Department of Music and Music Library, UC Berkeley.)

Photo 5-7 "Día 21 de Maio cerca las once de la noche" (last page), WPA 52, photo Aa-2. (Photograph courtesy of the Department of Music and Music Library, UC Berkeley.)

Photo 5-8 "Missa de los Angeles â 4 voces" (cover page), WPA folder 69, photo G-1. (Photograph courtesy of the Department of Music and Music Library, UC Berkeley.)

These ascriptions reveal several new tidbits of information. They indicate that Sancho became a deacon before he was ordained into the priesthood in 1796, as clarified in WPA folder 69, "...del simple uso de Fr. Juan Bautista Sancho, Religioso Observante i Diacono, 1796" (...for the sole use of Friar Juan Bautista

Sancho, Religious Observant and Deacon, 1796), and in WPA folder 72 in a similar statement in which Sancho is referenced as "Diaconos [sic] y Religioso Observante." Sancho writes out the "Credo Artanense" in WPA folder 52, a nostalgic reminiscence of his hometown of Artà. Another sheet (in different handwriting) refers to this same Credo: "Credo 5to tono, a 4 voces, alternando con el Credo Artanense" (Credo in the 5th tone for 4 voices, alternating with phrases from the Credo Artanense).[47] Additional papers in this stack—that was once probably in Sancho's possession—were written out by other scribes and explicitly link their source material to the Convent de Sant Francesc or the surrounding geographic area. Catalan words crops up with regularity, such as *tible* (soprano), *baix* (bass), *segona* (second), *veu* (voice), and *regulat* (regular). Such regionalisms hint at their provenance; surely Sancho gathered these papers together while sill in Mallorca, before his adventures in New Spain, where Castilian was the prescribed norm.[48]

The WPA folders mention two other Franciscans in addition to Sancho. The *Te Deum* setting in WPA folder 77 has a title page with an ex libris for Friar Jayme Pou and a clarification that it then passed to Juan Bautista Sancho for his usage, presumably after Pou's death. The setting itself is musically engaging with its alternation of metric, polyphonic phrases with contrasting lines of plainchant. The cover reads: "Te Deum â 4 del uso de Fr. Jayme Pou. / pasó al uso del Pᵉ Fr. juan Bau[tis]ta/ Sancho" (*Te Deum* in 4 parts for the sole use of Friar Jaume Pou. It passed into the possession of Father Friar Juan Bautista Sancho).[49] (See photo 5-9, that is also available online as photo B-131.)

Photo 5-9 *Te Deum* (title page), WPA folder 77, photo X-1. (Photograph courtesy of the Department of Music and Music Library, UC Berkeley.)

A little digging turns up confirmation of two "Jayme Pous" who were living in Palma concurrently with Sancho, either of whom might have been the previous owner of the *Te Deum* that Sancho brought to California. Mosen Antoni Gili mentions a "Jayme Pou" who became a deacon and lector of philosophy. Born in Llucmajor in Mallorca, the friar died at the early age of twenty-three in Palma on 8 July 1794.[50] Another possible candidate is "Jayme Ignaci Pou." In the burial records at the Arxiu del Regne de Mallorca, I came across the interment of "Jayme Ignaci Pou" on 21 November 1797.[51] This latter individual has a tangential link tying him to Sancho's birthplace; Fray Jaume Ginard, one of the officials who signed Pou's burial certificate, had served as guardian at the Convent de Artà.[52] For either of these candidates, their death dates of 1794 or 1797 allow for the possibility that Pou's manuscript passed to Sancho's hands while he was still serving at the Convent de Sant Francesc.

In addition to "Jayme Pou," another name arises in the context of these manuscripts. Folder 64, whose contents consist of Sancho's "Misa de 5to tono" (Mass in Mode 5), has inscribed at the top of the soprano sheet: "Tono 5° interpolando, digo, ô alternando con los Kyries â 4, voces del P. Vic. Torres" (Mass in mode 5, interpolating—that is to say—alternating with the Kyries for 4 voices, by Fr. Vic. Torres).[53] Who is this "Fr. Vic. Torres"? The numerous abbreviations in Sancho's annotation present multiple paths in the pursuit of this mystery man. Unfortunately, I have found no documentation for a "Victor Torres," but if we consider that "Vic" might be a surname—rather than an abbreviation for "Victor"—then several candidates arise. Unfortunately, I have found no documentation for a clergyman or friar named "Victor Torres." But if we consider that "Vic" (or "Vich") might be a surname—rather than the abbreviation for "Victor"—then several possible candidates arise. Three friars with the *apellido* "Vich" are found in the same interment records as Jayme Ignaci Pou: either Juan Ramon Vich, Antoni Vich, or Bartomeu Vich could turn out to be the padre "Vic. Torres" mentioned in WPA folder 64.[54] Another theory argues that "Vic." could signify a truncated version of "vicario" or "vicar." Fray Bonaventura Torres, active as a religious cleric at the Convent de Sant Francesc during Sancho's residency, could fulfill this description of "padre" and "vicario."[55] There is a sporting chance, therefore, that he could be our "Father and Vicar Torres."

Taken together, then, the photos of the WPA collection (not to mention the manuscripts at the San Fernando Mission) have denotative indicators linking the original folios to Mallorca in the late eighteenth century. The abundance of music pages written out in Sancho's distinctive handwriting, the dating of several autographs in 1796 and 1797 (while Sancho was in Palma), the allusions to Mallorcan friars on several cover pages, and the inclusion of Catalán vocabulary all evince a cultural connection between the Balearic Isles and the California coast at the turn of the nineteenth century. They further spotlight the extent to which one of the friars—Juan Bautista Sancho—nurtured his skills within sight of the Mediterranean and then later used his artistry and acquired repertoire to pour a "new" musical foundation near the distant shores and rolling hills of California, halfway around the globe.

New Horizons: Sancho's Departure for the New World

As we know from his diary, Sancho spent the beginning of the nineteenth century in Artà, performing his clerical obligations as priest and friar. The next entry in his diary must have been particularly exhilarating yet heartrending, as he bids farewell to his parents and loved ones upon striking out for the New World. The "Altre Nota" at the bottom of folio 4v preserves the moment: "I departed from Artà for the Colegio de San Fernando on the 23rd of February of 1803, the first day of Lent." The next citation continues with his disembarkation and subsequent arrival: "And having left the Port of Cádiz, on the 20th of June 1803, I arrived at the Colegio de San Fernando [near Mexico City] on the 9th of September of the same year."

Sancho shoved off for Mexico with his lifelong friend and fellow friar, Pedro Cabot, at his side. Cabot paints the scene as the two brothers set sail from Cádiz on 20 June 1803, "on the *San Miguel* alias *Sagrada Familia* and arrived in Vera Cruz, Mexico, in August and finally arrived at San Fernando College, September 9."[56] Seven weeks passed before they safely arrived in Mexico City, having made the transatlantic voyage to Veracruz and ensuing land trek to the Mexican capital. Sojourners from Iberia were required to obtain a sort of passport for passage to New Spain, and from this document we discover a verbal "photograph" of Sancho's imposing stature and features; he was "tall, swarthy, with dark hair, gray eyes, a large, thick nose, thick beard, and bushy eyebrows."[57] These two fast friends began their studies together at the Colegio Apostólico de San Fernando— the training school for Franciscans who were schooled in every aspect of missionary work and evangelization. The reach of the mendicant orders extended to the most far-flung territories of the Spanish Empire, and in 1804 no region seemed more remote—or more desirable—to the friars than the frontier expanses of Alta California.

Sancho's postings in his pocket diary provide a wealth of informational nuggets that help rectify many misconceptions we have had concerning his life. Muddled confusion has surrounded the date of Sancho's maiden voyage from Spain. Engelhardt and Bancroft set forth the reliable date of 1803 for Cabot's and Sancho's departure.[58] But in one of his few missteps, Father Geiger incorrectly placed the journey in 1802; understandably, almost everyone after him has followed in his wake, committing the same momentary error.[59] The ramifications of this correction are noteworthy, for we now see that Sancho and Cabot were at the apostolic college for only a few months, not nearly two years as previously believed.[60] They had scarcely arrived and taken a crash course in missionary survival skills before they had packed their bags and set out once more to face new horizons and unknown challenges—this time, in Alta California.

Geiger observes that Sancho had volunteered for missionary work in California no later than 22 December 1803. That date is in accordance with Bancroft's statement that the Mallorcan friar actually departed Mexico City for the California outback the following February 1804, arriving safely in port at Monterey on 4 August 1804.[61] We get a glimpse of their actual route from Geiger, who explains that Sancho and Cabot arrived in Guadalajara and then soon left on 23 April, as the two brothers forged ahead toward their ultimate destination.[62] Yet again, there is a nagging inconsistency between the generally accepted date for Sancho's arrival at Monterey on 4 August and the 15 August date articulated by Sancho himself in his diary entry: "And I arrived in New California the day of August 15, 1804." Geiger and Bancroft must have based their conclusions regarding Sancho's arrival on some documentary evidence, but to our frustration, they do not clarify their primary source.

Sancho's Years of Service in Alta California

Father Junípero Serra trekked inland from the coast in 1771 to a spot nestled into one of the folds of California's coastal range and there, by the oaks and fields of an idyllic valley, established the third of the California missions, San Antonio de Padua.[63] Cabot and Sancho wound their way through those same mountain passes in 1804 to begin their new life at this budding village and religious center. Another Mallorcan, Buenaventura Sitjar, had already spent years laying the groundwork for this sprouting community, and these friars—together with the diligent sweat and hard work of the native Californians—succeeded in building a wondrously vibrant and prosperous community.[64] In short order, the mission enjoyed rapid growth in light industry and agricultural production, as seen in the creation of textile manufacture, a mill, shoe shops, carpentry shops, smithy shops, expanded lumber storage, a tannery, and a complex irrigation system. As the population skyrocketed, dormitory and small apartments were rapidly added to the mission complex to accommodate the housing demands of the mission's 2,000 residents.[65]

The sanctuary that had been cobbled together in the late 1700s no longer sufficed for the burgeoning population, so the friars and neophytes began building a new chapel to meet their growing needs. They poured the foundation for a new church in 1810; the walls were completed in 1811; work progressed throughout 1812; and the finishing touches were dispatched in 1813. To the present day, the "new" mission's appealing appearance and enchanting architecture make it one of the jewels in the entire mission chain. (See photo 5-10, also found online as photo B-21. In addition, consult photos B-41, B-42, and B-147 through B-153, of the San Antonio Mission in appendix B online.)

Production of both livestock and crops was bounteous and plentiful. For example, in 1824 animal husbandry was so efficient that the livestock inventory rose to include 6,000 head of cattle, 9,000 sheep, 28 goats "de pelo," 1,070 horses, 34 mules, 2 burros, and 77 pigs. Farming and horticulture generated a superabundance of food for the dining table and storehouse: the crop storerooms of 1824 were almost spilling over with 1,355 *fanegas* of wheat, 90 of corn, 44 of beans, 308 of barley, and 52 of chickpeas and other vegetables.[66] Agriculture—especially farming—depended on an irrigation system that was remarkably well engineered. Frances Weber explains, "Installation of the intricate series of aqueducts

Photo 5-10 "Mission of San Antonio de Padua," by Henry Miller (1856), the Bancroft Library, BANC PIC 1905.00006-B (no. 22 of 38). (Photo courtesy of the Bancroft Library, University of California, Berkeley.)

in the next decade (1790s) increased the material fortunes of the mission considerably, so that by 1830 the entire valley was one giant vineyard stretching as far as the eye could see."[67] At its inception, only a handful of people lived on-site at the San Antonio Mission, but it soon blossomed into a small town. Within a decade after its founding, more than a thousand converts were residing in the mission complex, "the largest number of neophytes contained at any one of the mission chain" in those early years.[68] The population fluctuated a bit but generally averaged around 1,000 permanent residents.[69] The statistics graphed out by Robert Hoover in his article "California Mission Economic Development" bear out evidentially that the San Antonio Mission had devised a fecund agricultural infrastructure.[70] This is especially true for the years 1805 through 1823—the time period when Cabot and Sancho were fully immersed in the planning, supervising, and building of the mission's agglomeration of buildings and production systems. In summary, the inventive planning, hard work, and shared labor by friar and indigenous neophyte alike produced a flourishing society that was economically self-sufficient and culturally robust. The trite postcard image of native Californians as lazy do-nothings in a pastoral Eden where work is neither necessary nor rewarded is sheer fiction, completely unsupported by the historical record.[71]

The San Antonio Mission, then, was not so much a single house of worship surrounded by oaks and open fields as it was an energetic, bustling community, defined by its plenteous light industry, enterprising horticulture, ambitious animal husbandry, stimulating musical environment, pious worship ranging from the quotidian to the ceremonial, and occasional dose of zestful social entertainment. At the center of nearly all these activities stood Juan Bautista Sancho. Contemporary compatriots describe him as a tireless worker who loved nothing more than rolling up his sleeves and physically digging into a work project. At Sancho's death, his steadfast friend Pedro Cabot writes a touching obituary in which he describes his Franciscan brother with these words:

> Fr. Sancho was animated by a good spirit and healthy intentions in his deliberations. He worked a lot, in the spiritual realm as well as the earthly. His constancy was particularly noteworthy. This good Father and exemplary model to missionaries knew how to combine both occupations (of the spiritual and temporal)—for he would be seen working away in the manufacturing craft shops and in the fields, enduring the greatest heat and most extreme cold with stoic suffering—but without forgetting to minister to the sick who needed to be cured of their pains, by administering the Holy Sacraments with complete punctuality to those who were close to death and in dire need, and without leaving those nearby in need for lack of expert religious advice. He would accomplish this without ceasing his manual labor, all the while reprimanding vices and animating all to virtue.
>
> The supposed "rest" that he took on those days when the weather was poor and he could not go outside consisted of him composing catechism instructions, and he was greatly aided in this task by the good knowledge he had of the local Native American languages. In this occupation (of translating catechisms), very often he would lose track of time and miss lunch or dinner altogether! If he observed that I was lending him a hand, it seemed to him that he was not doing anything at all, since he was not doing everything by himself.
>
> As an example, I will tell of a time ten years before his death, a time when God was stretching out his life. He was still recuperating and without any strength after a grave illness. Seeing that he was returning so soon to his strenuous, hardworking lifestyle, I said to him, "Padre, it is not time yet; leave this work alone and wait until you have more strength." He responded with his typical simplicity and inborn candor, "If I have food to eat, I should work." This is proof that he was a declared enemy of laziness.[72]

Cabot is not the only friar to hold Sancho in high esteem. In 1817 Friar Sarría praises him, stating: "In its [San Antonio's] spiritual development he [Sancho] is justly considered as one of the best among the missionaries because of his constancy, zeal, application, activity, and industry in the development of buildings together with his knowledge of the language of the mission."[73] Friar Payeras lauds the Mallorcan friar in 1820 with similar enthusiasm: "His merit corresponds with his great application and efficacy in every branch of the ministry, and his aptitude is for a complete missionary and for one or the other offices in the Order."[74]

During the eighteenth and early nineteenth centuries, most European societies (and their colonial extensions) practiced corporal punishment as an unexceptional necessity; beatings were a regular occurrence. Sancho's behavior reflects the attitudes of his era. Bancroft recounts one situation in which the friar habitually doled out a beating to a young boy:

> When the mission San Antonio was in charge of fathers Juan Cabot [*sic;* it was Pedro Cabot] and Juan B. Sancho, the latter directed agricultural operations, and also attended to the music, the mission having a good orchestra. He always kept near his person a handsome Indian boy named Josafat, who was charged to give timely warning of the venomous ants abounding in that region. Nevertheless, the padre was often bitten, and then Josafat received a whipping at the hands of the mestizo, Antonio Rosas....These facts were obtained from Josafat himself in 1847, when he was still living in San Antonio at an advanced age.[75]

The portrait of Sancho painted here by Bancroft is multifaceted and complex. On the one hand, we see Sancho's discomforting readiness to resort to the lash (an attitude typical of the era); on the other hand, we simultaneously see Sancho in the hands-on role of agricultural supervisor, spearheading activities himself from the field. He was an outdoorsman, not a complacent, indoor do-nothing.

Bancroft often tends to underscore negative aspects of the friars' attitudes, and his perspective may have been a factor in the selection of the previous story and its telling. Cabot, understandably, is a much more sympathetic biographer, and his obituary for Sancho portrays a completely different mind-set and approach for interaction with the mission populace. According to Cabot, Sancho never failed "to minister to the sick who needed to be cured of their pains...administering the Holy Sacraments (or Last Rites) with complete punctuality to those who were close to death and in dire need." He continues, stating that when bad weather forced Sancho inside, he would pass the time translating sacred texts and catechisms into the local native dialects. Recently, documentation has surfaced confirming Cabot's description of Sancho's acumen as translator: while thumbing through a hodge-podge of various items at the Bancroft Library, I discovered a single sheet with the opening words "Mos antiquus tote Hispanæ"—that is folded in the middle so that it becomes a four-page booklet (much like a folded greeting card). It turns out to be a translation of the last rites into a Native American language, all etched out in Juan Bautista Sancho's beautiful script.[76] The lettering is exquisite, and the pages are circumscribed with an elegant, pristine border that reflects meticulous care and craftsmanship. The Bancroft Library presently identifies this source as "*Protesta de la fee p^a el S^{to} Viatico,* text in Indian dialect, H. H. Bancroft Collection." The *Santo Viático* (or, in Latin, *Viaticum*) signifies the "Food for the Journey," that is, the Communion given when death is imminent.[77] The *Protesta de la Fee* refers to the *Confiteor Deo* (the "Confession of Faith") that one finds early in this solemn rite.[78]

Even though this manuscript bears no signature or attribution, my analysis of the handwriting confirms this to have been written out by Juan Bautista Sancho.

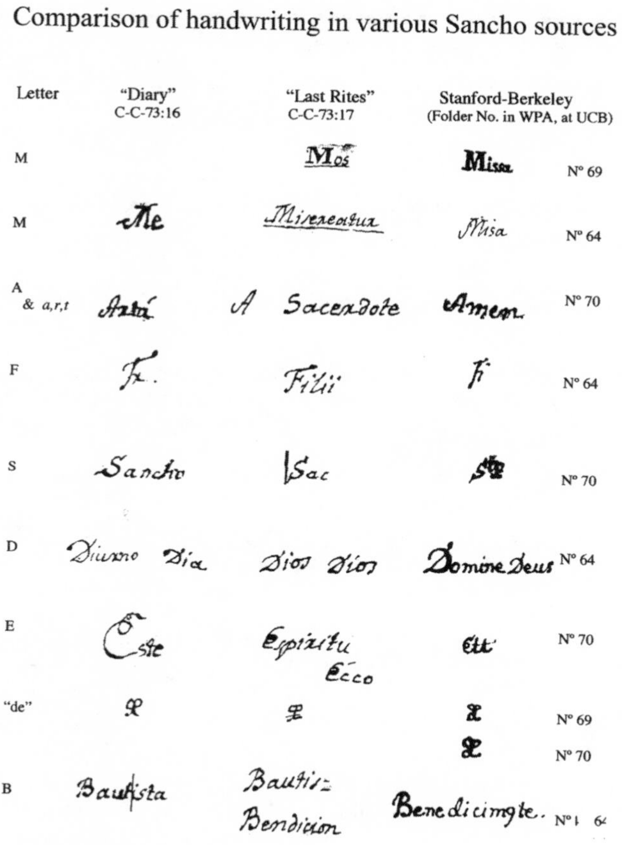

Comparison of handwriting in various Sancho sources

Letter	"Diary" C-C-73:16	"Last Rites" C-C-73:17	Stanford-Berkeley (Folder No. in WPA, at UCB)
M		*Mos*	*Missa* Nº 69
M	*Me*	*Misereatur*	*Misa* Nº 64
A & a,r,t	*Auti*	*A Sacerdote*	*Amen.* Nº 70
F	*F.*	*Filii*	*F* Nº 64
S	*Sancho*	*Sac*	*S* Nº 70
D	*Diurno Dia*	*Dios Dios*	*Domine Deus* Nº 64
E	*Este*	*Espiritu* *Ecco*	*Ett* Nº 70
"de"	*de*	*de*	*de* Nº 69 *de* Nº 70
B	*Bautista*	*Bautis-* *Bendicion*	*Benedicimgte..* Nº 1 64

Figure 5-2 Comparison of handwriting in various Sancho sources

The many manuscripts in his hand that were photographed as part of the WPA collection, the burial records from San Antonio that constituted part of Sancho's duties, and Sancho's entries in his diary all show similarities in their writing idiosyncrasies that match hand-in-glove with the writing of the "*Protesta de la fee pª el Sᵗᵒ Viatico*" or last rites (see figure 5-2 and photo 5-11).[79]

Sancho and the "Oath of Loyalty"

While Sancho, Cabot, and their fellow residents at the San Antonio Mission were laying the cornerstone for their new sanctuary in 1810, a new governmental foundation was simultaneously being poured in Mexico. Gunshots set off the Mexican War for Independence in 1810, and the dust did not settle until Mexico's successful separation from Spain in 1821. Under Agustín Fernández de San Vicente's supervision, the Mexican flag ascended the flagpole in Santa Barbara in 1822; Mexico

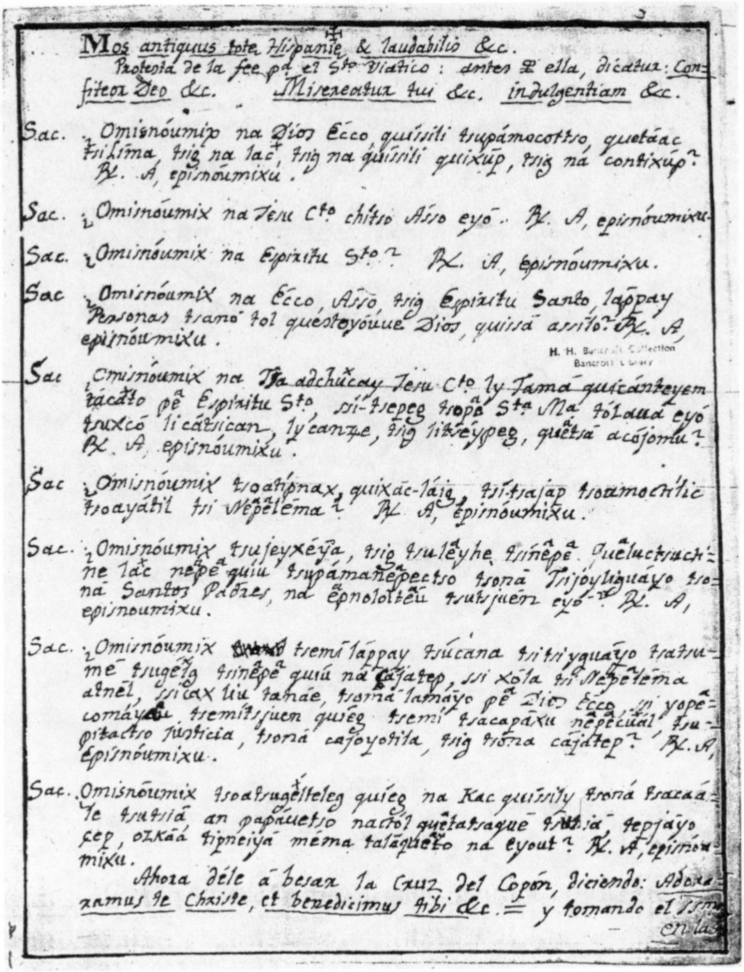
Mos antiquus totæ Hispaniæ & laudabilis &c.
Protesta de la fee pª el Sto Viatico: antes d̄ ella, dicatur: Confiteor Deo &c. Misereatur tui &c. indulgentiam &c.
Sac. ¿Omisnóumix na Dios Ecco quisili tsupámocottso, quetáac tsilima, tsig na lac, tsig na quisili quixup, tsig na contixup? R. A, episnóumixu.
Sac. ¿Omisnóumix na Jesu Cto chitso Asso eyo. R. A, episnóumixu.
Sac. ¿Omisnóumix na Espiritu Sto? R. A, episnóumixu.
Sac. ¿Omisnóumix na Ecco, Asso, tsig Espiritu Santo, lappay Personas tsano tol questoyóuue Dios, quisa assilo? R. A, episnóumixu.
...
Ahora dele a besar la Cruz del Copon, diciendo: Adoramus te Christe, et benedicimus tibi &c. = y tomando el ... en las

Photo 5-11 "Mos antiquus totæ Hispanæ," Sancho's translation of the last rites, the Bancroft Library, Ms. C-C-73:17, fol. 1. (Photo courtesy of the Bancroft Library, University of California, Berkeley.)

confirmed a new constitution in 1824; and Alta California now fell under Mexican, not Spanish, jurisdiction.[80] This plunged the mission system into uncharted waters, and the loyalties of the friars appeared murky to the new Mexican authorities. Nearly all of the Franciscans had been born in Spain, and it was feared that they still might see themselves as subjects of the Spanish Crown; their views toward the new Mexican government were untested. As a result, Mexico City issued a stream of decrees in the 1820s, demanding each of the Spanish padres swear an oath of loyalty to the newly constituted government. Governor Echeandía, on 3 June 1826, ordered the military commanders at the four presidios in Alta California to travel up and down the territory, securing sworn oaths of fealty to Mexico. The results were mixed. Echeandía summarizes the outcome: nineteen friars dissented and remained Spanish loyalists. Felipe Arroyo de la Cuesta and Narciso Durán were among the defiant padres.[81] Cabot and Sancho finessed the situation. They reaffirmed their identity as Spaniards—refusing to break their previous loyalty oath to Spain and its king—but in the same breath, they assured the Mexican authorities that they would not stir the waters of discontent and, furthermore, would obey all Mexican laws and decrees. Echeandía sums up their stance, stating:

> Fr. Felipe Arroyo de la Cuesta: age 49 years old; he took the oath [of allegiance] in 1826, but now claims loyalty to the King of Spain.
>
> ....
>
> Fr. Pedro Cabot: 49 years old: good health and strict religious conduct; refused to take the oath because he had sworn fidelity to Fernando VII, but he will obey the authorities.
>
> Fr. Juan Bautista Sancho: 57 years of age; health not good; agrees with Fr. Cabot.
>
> ....
>
> Fr. Narciso Durán: age 51 and 11 months; good health; he declined to swear allegiance.[82]

Clearly, the governor had fallen short in his goal of obtaining sworn allegiance from every friar. In spite of that frustration, he had tested the waters and encountered tolerance and even goodwill toward the Mexican regime. He saw no reason to pursue expulsion of the Spanish padres as had been mandated by his superiors. His report urged the fledgling government to view with broad-minded indulgence the padres' noncompliance. Besides, they were critical stabilizing elements in the region and had been responsible for much of California's growth. He explains his case:

> There are twenty-one missions, but only three Mexican friars; the others are Spaniards, who by their industry have placed the missions in a state of actual wealth. If unhappily the missions should be deprived of these Fathers we should see the population in a lamentable condition for want of subsistence.[83]

Echeandía's counsel delayed any rash punitive action, but in the 1830s the implementation of secularization set in motion a series of calamitous events that Echeandía had predicted. Many Spanish friars were evicted; without their stewardship, even the most prosperous missions fell into ruin. Mission populations plummeted, and once vibrant communities withered away into a ghostly shadow of their previous incarnation.

Sancho's political leanings as a faithful Spaniard are seen in the works that he chose to write down in his music notebooks. For example, he jots down a mishmash of "loyalist" pieces in the "empty" spaces of the *Artaserse Ms.* On folio 11v, he touts the heroism of the Spanish in the face of Napoleon's French invaders.[84] (See photo B-48 in appendix B online.) The lyrics exclaim:

Warlike Spain, wave your banner
against the odious power of vile Napoleon!
Hear his crimes, listen to the treason!—
yes, the treachery with which the world's face
has been covered in horror.
To arms, to arms, Spaniards!
Death to Napoleon, and long live
King Fernando, our Homeland, and Religion![85]

Continuing later in this anthology, we find "Quando Fernando se ausenta," which exhibits similar patriotic feelings. (See photo 5-12, also available online as photo B-46.)

Whenever King Fernando is absent, Spain sighs, "alas, alas!"
And thus, between anguished grief and yearnful longing,
        she raves in delirium "alas, alas!"
Oh my misery, woe is me! When will he come back? Alas,
    alas, alas![86]

Photo 5-12 "Quando Fernando se ausenta," San Fernando Mission, Archival Center of the Archdiocese of Los Angeles, *Artaserse Ms.*, As-3, fol. 5v. (Permission to include this image courtesy of the ACALA; photo by the author.)

The sonorous parallel thirds of this song—written out on a single staff, with an F clef, in duple meter—typify the *californios'* fascination with these vocal duets.[87] The size of the note head denotes the appropriate voice: the larger ones are sung by the lower voice, while the "added" upper voice is indicated by smaller notes (that can shrink so small in some sources as to become microscopic dots). In the ensuing song, "Si queris mirácula más error calimitar," Sancho switches writing styles; he abandons the "modern" note heads and rests in exchange for the "hollow" or "void" notation so prevalent with *canto figurado* tunes. This latter homophonic setting—a Responsory text for Saint Anthony—would have been a conspicuous highlight at San Antonio's feast day. How fitting, then, that we find a version written out in the hand of Sancho, the prominent music director at the San Antonio Mission.[88]

Continuing through the *Artaserse Ms.*, we encounter yet another patriotic anthem proclaiming nationalistic fervor and devotion to King Fernando VII. The Spanish monarch's adversary, Napoleon, is vilified: "Long live Fernando! Death to Napoleon! May Spain triumph! And may the war end!"[89] When all this evidence is considered, then, we perceive Sancho's loyalty to Spain, the church, and the king as remaining untarnished and unweakened throughout his life; in the face of persistent and aggressive pressures to accommodate the shifting political winds, he remained imperviously stalwart.

Music Making at the San Antonio Mission

In 1814, Sancho and Cabot graphically depict musical activities at their mission as part of an extensive *Interrogatorio (Questionnaire)* intended to scrutinize and evaluate various aspects of mission life. The secretary of foreign relations, Don Ciríaco González Carvajal, had mandated that the California padres provide detailed answers to thirty-six questions; this charge was sent to the Bishop of Sonora, who then required the father-president of the California missions, Father José Señan, to implement the survey, consolidate the responses, and pass them back up to the supervising authorities.[90] All the missions complied, although the report from La Purísima Mission has been lost, and, obviously, no reports were issued from the two missions that had not yet been established: the San Rafael Mission (founded 1817) and the San Francisco Solano Mission (founded 1823). Father Señan bundled the responses together into his official report on mission life on 11 August 1815.[91]

The friars' responses vary in length and detail, and many approach the task with widely disparate perspectives. Some were steeped in a Eurocentric outlook, whereas other friars reveled as well in aspects of native Californian customs. On 26 February 1814, Sancho and Cabot craft a response that delves into the "indigenous" as much as the "imported." These two friars were captivated by native music systems and local instruments. This presents yet another example of their inclusive attitude and open-minded curiosity. As we have already seen, Sancho had become fluent in Native American languages; he became enchanted by their music traditions as well. Sancho and Cabot's submission to the *Interrogatorio* paints a fascinating portrait of musical life at their mission:

Question 32 regarding Music:

The neophytes have a lot of musical talent, and they play violins, cello, flutes, horn, drum, and other instruments that the Mission has given them [implying that there were even more kinds of instruments available and that they collectively constituted a full orchestra]. From their pagan days they preserve a flute, which they play like a recorder. It is entirely open-ended from top to bottom. It measures five palms in length, but others measure no more than three palms. It can form eight pitches with perfection. They perform various instrumental numbers, almost all in the same meter, the majority of which are happy. It normally has eleven holes, but sometimes there are more and sometimes fewer. They have another string instrument that is nothing more than a bow made out of a stick, which is then strung with animal gut; and it creates a single note. They have no other instruments. They have many songs, of which some are used to accompany their dances, while others are separate and independent. Not being professional musicians we are not able to send [notated] examples of these songs, but we do know that they sing using different terminal pitches and with different scale systems. These scales go up and down, using the intervals of seconds, thirds, fourths, fifths, and also octaves [but not employing the intervals of sixths or sevenths]. [In their traditional music, the Native American converts] *never* sing independent polyphonic lines; but in the unique cases when many sing together, some of them sing an octave higher. Almost all of their songs are happy, but they have some that are partially sad. In all of these said songs, they do not tell a story or make a clearly discernible point: instead, they only use isolated words, naming birds or familiar place-names, et cetera. And from their ancient past, they have always sung these songs and used the two aforementioned instruments. The Indian converts sing Spanish lyrics perfectly, and they easily learn every kind of singing that is taught to them, *canto llano* or plainchant as well as the metric singing of *canto figurado* [and accompanied by instruments]. Also, they can successfully perform as a choir, or even pull off the singing of a polyphonic Mass with separate, independent melodic lines—as long as there are the necessary performance parts. In all this they are aided by a clear voice and good ear that they all have, both men and women alike.[92]

Their account merits careful scrutiny. We discover that San Antonio could boast of an orchestra, as evidenced by their complete music inventory. As discussed in chapter 1, we know that the instrument distribution at San Antonio was top-dominated, a hallmark of the Classical orchestra sonority; in addition, the full gamut of colors heard in any European city or New World capital would have been readily available to the friars, as evidenced by the equipment requisition lists spelled out in Mexico City.[93]

William Summers provides an instrument list at San Antonio from 1842 that replicates that of a small Classical period orchestra: "four new violins, another old one, one large member of the violin family called a bass, one drum, four flutes, another new one, a French horn, a clarion trumpet, two triangles, one choir book with ten or eleven masses."[94] This collection is remarkably complete with respect to its size and distribution of timbres, in spite of the ravaging effects of secularization that had produced confiscation and even looting. Miraculously, the orchestra described by Sancho and Cabot in 1814 remained intact, more or less, up through 1842. As articulated in chapter 1, the Spanish orchestra in the late eighteenth century customarily had for a musical foundation four to five violins; a pair of flutes, oboes, or horns; and a few low-sounding instruments such as cello, bass, and bassoon. Significantly, the concerted masses now preserved at the Archival Center of the Archdiocese of Los Angeles require these same performance resources, and they would have been readily available at the San Antonio Mission.[95] In addition, intermingled in this pile of concerted music written in a Classical aesthetic, we find an assortment of loose sheets written in Sancho's hand plus the intriguing *Artaserse Ms.* that contains operatic excerpts and Sancho's insertions—all indications that the *estilo moderno* and Classicism resonated in the San Antonio Mission chapel at a time when Sancho was at the helm.[96]

The description of musical life found in Cabot's and Sancho's answers to the "Questionnaire" addresses a plethora of musical styles. Their opening sentences of the *Interrogatorio* (taken together with their instrument inventories and concerted music manuscripts) make clear that the *estilo moderno* was a critical element of mission life and was in step with the Classical stylistic trends sweeping Europe and the Americas.

But the modern style only constituted a slice of the larger pie; these Franciscan brothers spell out the importance of *canto llano* and *canto figurado* in daily life: "The Indian converts sing Spanish lyrics perfectly, and they easily learn every kind of singing that is taught to them, *canto llano* or plainchant as well as the metric singing of *canto figurado*." Performance practice in the missions, then, consisted of options and variety, not monolithic singularity. Cabot's and Sancho's description in the *Interrogatorio* further establishes a fact that the music papers themselves do not prove—that the California manuscripts were meant to facilitate *performance*. Were it not for their comments to the "Questionnaire," we might have mistakenly regarded the orchestral, concerted pieces in San Fernando as mere library copies for consultation.

Sancho's Death

Near the end of his life, Sancho suffered terribly from a tumorous growth in his thigh. Pedro Cabot gives an account of his dear friend's painful affliction in Sancho's obituary:

> For these last ten years, Sancho has endured them full of pain, without question caused by his daily chores and tasks, because according to the medical specialists who have observed his ailments and afflictions, they

were caused by the mass of blood that they said had been brought to boil. At last, at the end of this past November, completely possessed by the malady that was an inflammation of the thigh that burst out with pus at the knee, and that years before had started to become abscessed along with a constant fever, he surrendered himself to immense pains that he suffered for more than two months—during which time he confessed several times, taking the Holy Viaticum as his duty, and he took the most Divine Sacrament [of Communion] out of devout habit. And on the 7th of this present month I administered the Holy Unction, and on the following day at about three in the morning, with him being completely conscious and aware—in spite of the exceedingly high fever—God called his soul to Himself in order to reward him (as we might come to believe) for so many Apostolic accomplishments. And we can judge his death as happily blessed, not only for his poverty, but for his disinterest in the material things of this world, and for his ardent zeal for Religion and the spread of the Catholic Faith—to which he dedicated himself throughout his entire life, in both word and deed. And on the 9th (the same day that he took the habit of Our Holy Father Saint Francis, having served in the Order 39 years, and having lived 57 years, 2 months, and 7 days), I buried him as secular clergy [?] in the presbytery of this church on the Evangelical side [i.e., before the altar, and to the congregation's left], in the tomb closest to the center, with the bodies of the late Reverend Fathers Pujol and Sitjar remaining between the wall and the said Father Sancho. And so that it might be formally established wherever it has been required or might be so required, I sign here, at this mission of San Antonio de Padua on 11 February 1830. Friar Pedro Cabot.[97]

Exploring Two Representative Musical Examples

The "Credo Artanense"

Under Sancho's artistic guidance, the sonorities filling the sanctuary at the San Antonio Mission must have been diverse and richly multifarious, extending from the straightforward and uncluttered (ideal for new converts unfamiliar with European expectations of "tastefulness" and "refinement") to full-fledged Classicism (demanding technical virtuosity and gracile finesse that is achievable only through years of practice and study). In this context, it is appropriate to examine two dissimilar works—the "Credo Artanense" and the *Misa en sol*—to explore them in some depth and penetrate their musical secrets. In addition, a thorough probing of these two examples can provide discoveries that can be applied in a broader sense to the mission repertoire as a whole. The unassuming "Credo Artanense" serves as a valid model for understanding the accompanied *canto figurado* that permeated the mission manuscripts and choirbooks. At the other end of the spectrum, the elegant *Misa en sol (Mass in G)* unfolds with the harmonic daring, imaginative phrasing, rhythmic vigor, and melodic embellishment that are indicative of the *estilo moderno* at the turn of the nineteenth century.[98] These two seemingly opposite works actually turn out to be musical cousins, for the Credo from the sophisticated *Misa en sol* incorporates half of its phrases from the older and more clear-cut "Credo Artanense." In this one movement, the two settings share many identical musical "chromosomes."

The photos of the "Credo Artanense" are found tucked into WPA folder 52; certainly, Sancho must have learned this jaunty tune as a youth growing up in his native Artà (see photo 5-6). Initially, the ancient-looking notational conventions of squared-off rectangles and diamonds resemble plainchant—at least superficially—but closer inspection demonstrates Sancho to be scribbling down this foot-tapping Credo in mensural *canto figurado* notation. The tune first sets out as a single melodic line until reaching the text "Et incarnatus est" (and was made incarnate), at which point the melody divides into two streams, requiring a minimum of two vocalists. With the expansion of textural resources at this particular moment, the sonorities become slightly richer and more sensual—providing an audible sense that Christ came to earth by taking *human* form. The music thus becomes more sumptuous, carnal, and luxuriant in order to appeal overtly to the pleasure-seeking *human* ear. This lapse into the partially hedonistic is short-lived as the melody is trimmed back to a single line (but with implied accompaniment). As the text moves forward to the Crucifixion, Christ's journey from the carnal back to the Divine is echoed here by the music's journey from sensual polyphony to chaste homophony. On one other occasion the melody splits into two. At the words "Et expecto resurrectionem mortuorum" (I look for the resurrection of the dead), a crisp, singular line captures the spotless modesty of the Divine as it glides heavenward (*resurrectionem*), but entering the realm of death (*mortuorum*), the intrusive sounds of polyphony disrupt this chaste simplicity. Just as the mortal world decays in corruption, sensuality, and eventual death, so the musical phrase that depicts death momentarily descends into a duet of sensually pleasing polyphony.

By the early Renaissance, recurring word painting metaphors within the Credo's text had become accepted conventions: sensual polyphony reflected humanity's hedonistic flaws, and accompanied monody depicted the unblemished simplicity of the divine. Similarly, Louise Stein compares the associative metaphors of different vocal styles in Spanish Baroque theater and concludes that uncluttered recitative was attributed to the domain of the Gods. In contrast, sumptuous polyphony or foot-tapping arias, on the Spanish stage, depicted the sensual, decadent world of man.[99] California was no different in its rhetorical-musical traditions. Shifts in texture abound in the Credo settings in mission manuscripts throughout the late eighteenth and early nineteenth centuries. For example, WPA folder 67 contains a "Credo Mariano (vel imperiat)" that sets out initially in a single melodic thread, but at the line "Et incarnatus est de Spiritu Sancto ex Maria Virgine; et homo factus est" (and was incarnate by the Holy Spirit, born of the Virgin Mary, and was made man), it sprouts into three-voice chords—the same polyphonic metaphor applied to this line of text in the "Credo Artanense." In this latter setting, *mortuos* resounded in counterpoint to reflect its power over man's realm, not God. The "Credo Mariano" takes a slightly different tack, depicting the abyss of death not through polyphony but by plunging downward into the lowest register of the piece. California is chock-full of similar applications of this musical word painting. At first glance, the "Credo Dominical" found on sheet W-3 of WPA folder 68 appears to be a single-line *canto figurado* melody from start to finish. No clue would hint at a polyphonic excursion, for we see only one notated line. But another folio (photo W-1) contains an additional contrapuntal line—a "musical island"—that has no connections to any surrounding material on its sheet. We discover that it actually should be conjoined with the main melody on sheet W-3.[100] When reunited, these two melodies intertwine in a musical macramé of independent filigree (not the lockstep parallel thirds seen frequently in mission duet settings). Significantly, this detour into polyphony happens on the text that tells of Christ's *human* form: "Et incarnatus est...et homo factus est." This musical-rhetorical gesture is nearly identical to the word-painting of the same line in the "Credo Mariano" and the "Credo Artanense": in all three instances, God's "humanity" takes on the allure of polyphony. Yet again, we encounter a splendid example of this metaphor in the "Credo Italiano." A solitary phrase with the heading "1ra voz â Duo" (First voice for the duet) is scrawled onto an isolated staff, almost like an afterthought, on the back cover of the alto part. If we take this orphaned fragment, "Et incarnatus est...et homo factus est," and combine it with the music for "coro" inside the folder at the same line of text, we fashion a winsome duet. The "first voice" floats above the "coro" line in parallel thirds. In summary, these California Credo manuscripts share a rhetorical norm: they use duet or three-voice textures to embody man's mortality and attraction to sensual passions; they highlight God's humble chastity and "oneness"—immune to tempting distraction—with the pure directness of monophony or frill-less homophony.

Not only do these Credo settings utilize changes in texture to portray human fallibility, but they often use changes in meter for an identical purpose. The word painting depends on the long-established notational traditions, dating back to the late Middle Ages, in which pulse groupings of three were called "perfect" for they reflected the "three-ness" and perfection of the Holy Trinity. Duple groupings, on the other hand, were seen as "imperfect," since they lacked the extra pulse that would be needed in order to "perfect" them. Incorporating this rhythmic metaphor, the "Credo Artanense" begins and ends in "perfect" meter, but it shifts from triple to duple meter—from the "perfect" to "imperfect"—at the line "and was incarnate by the Holy Spirit, born of the Virgin Mary, and was made man" in order to portray man's imperfect incompleteness. In identical fashion, the *Misa en sol*'s Credo and the *Misa de los Angeles*' "Credo Dominical, 6to tono" explore the same symbolic gestures; these settings waft along in triple meter until arriving at the line portraying Jesus' time on earth when he took on human form. The single line, "Et incarnatus est...et homo factus est," marches forward in duple mensuration. At the ensuing line proclaiming Jesus' Resurrection ("et resurrexit"), triple meter is restored—since God's form is once again "perfected."

The "Credo Artanense" employs other expressive musical gestures to spotlight the essence of the text. In describing that Jesus "descended down from heaven" (descendit de caelis), the melodic line sinks downward for eight measures. A falling melodic line aptly portrays the lowering of Christ's body into the grave at "passus et sepultus est" (he died and was buried). The ecstasy of the Resurrection, "et resurrexit tertia die" (and on the third day he rose again), is driven home by an exalted ascending line. Later, the melody spirals upward to reflect the soaring imagery at "Et ascendit in caelum" (and He ascended into heaven) and "et expecto resurrectionem…" (and I look for the resurrection…). Many other Credo settings explore similar word painting devices.

The "Credo Artanense" in WPA folder 52 bears no signature, but the handwriting is unmistakably that of Juan Bautista Sancho. At the end of the piece, he scribbled out the date and hour of completion: "Día 21 de Maio cerca las once de la n[oc]he acabo de escrivirlo" (The 21st of May, at about eleven o'clock at night, I have just finished writing this). We can surmise that Sancho's task here was probably one of copyist, not composer; the tune is almost a replica of the *baix* (or bass vocal line) from the "Credo à duo, 5. tono" (Credo as a duet in mode 5).[101] (See photo 5-13, also available online as photo B-122.) The "Credo à duo" in WPA folder 51 contains a *tible*, or soprano line that is absent from Sancho's rendition of the "Credo Aratanense." It is unclear, however, whether Sancho had originally written

Photo 5-13 "Baix, Credo à duo," WPA folder 51, photo c-2. (Photograph courtesy of the Department of Music and Music Library, UC Berkeley.)

out this *tible* line as well (in which case, it is now missing), or whether Sancho felt that the Credo's text could be performed sufficiently well by the bass voice alone and thus saw no need to scribble out an "optional" soprano part.

The "Credo à duo" and several other works in the WPA collection sometimes use Catalán words (*baix, tible, regulat,* etc.), hinting that Sancho acquired these sheets in Mallorca before leaving for his life in the New World, where Castilian, not Catalán, was the expected norm. As we have already seen from his diary, Sancho gradually abandoned his native tongue and adopted, bit by bit, the more universally accepted Castilian.

A detailed examination of the calligraphy found in the "Credo à duo" and "Credo Artanense" shows radically different writing conventions. In Sancho's autograph, he employs squared-off breves and diamond-shaped semibreves associated with *canto figurado* style. The "Credo à duo," on the other hand, sets the same core tune but uses the rounded shapes of modern notation with its elliptical whole notes and half notes. Its text lettering reminds me of manuscript sources from the early or mid-1700s. Taken together, the evidence suggests that this Credo melody was an old standard, and that the "Credo à duo" was written out long before Sancho copied out his version (the "Credo Artanense").

Another discrepancy between these two manuscripts should be noted. The "Credo Artanense" is complete from start to finish and is performable as it stands. The "Credo à duo," however, presents only the odd-numbered phrases, clearly implying that *alternatim* performance is expected. To realize this Credo in a live setting, one would have to supply the "missing" even-numbered lines by drawing upon other source material (be it memorized or notated), and then alternate between the odd- and even-numbered phrases, much like the teeth of two interlocking gears that alternate their cogs and spaces. Alternating performance style is explicitly mentioned in the soprano part's heading: "Credo à duo, 5. tono, alternando con el Credo Regulat" (Credo in a duet setting, in mode 5, alternating with the "regular" Credo). Unfortunately, this sheet gives no inkling as to what the "regular" Credo entails and where its music might be found; most likely, it is one of the well-known plainchant settings from antiquity or one of the single-voice *canto figurado* settings distributed throughout the mission chain.[102] In any case, the sonic contrast between the even-numbered phrases (probably *canto llano* or *canto figurado*) and the soprano-bass pairing of the odd-numbered phrases would have been quite captivating and alluring. It should be emphasized that the realization of this "Credo à duo" in California worship was more a collection of performance options than it was a rigidly formalized and predetermined composition.

Returning to Sancho's version of this Credo (the "Credo Artanense" in WPA folder 52), we find all of the necessary phrases except for the initial line, "Credo in unum Deum." Sancho saw no pressing need for its inclusion, since he would have intoned that incipit himself, setting the Credo on its course. In writing out the piece, Sancho blocks off major divisions of the phrase structure by drawing visual barriers, consisting of double bars with a forest of crosshatching. By circumscribing these predetermined phrase boundaries, he also assists anyone wishing to alter the setting through some sort of *alternatim* performance; the prepackaged blocks of texts are ready for removal and replacement.[103] Notably, in California sources that call for *alternatim* performance, there often is one voice that participates in *both* of the contrasting textures—as opposed to being confined to only the even or odd phrases; this "shared" part that threads its way back and forth between the two alternating textures is most often the bass voice, not the tenor, alto, or soprano.[104] Not surprisingly, the complete text of the Credo as found in the "Credo Artanense" maps out each phrase in the bass clef (hinting at its "shared" ambivalence and ability to partake in both of the antiphonal groupings).

The Misa en sol

One of the most entrancing works in the California repertoire is the *Misa en sol* (presumably by Sancho); its stylistic features exhibit a remarkable familiarity with contemporaneous developments in Europe and the music centers of the New World.[105] The two sopranos in the Kyrie and Gloria are *galant* in their melodic filigree. They have tremendous variety in their rhythmic note values, even within the same phrase (making them more Classical than Baroque). Half notes give way to dotted eighths. Steady quarters become disrupted by racing sixteenths. Rests are frequent and break up the linear shapes into clearly articulated phrases. The sigh figures, the graceful appoggiaturas, the refined ornaments, and the luminescent texture all are stylistically compatible with the *galant* and Classical aesthetic. The Gloria requires both vocal refinement and florid virtuosity: its text does not unfold in one singular gesture but is divvied up into separate, free-standing movements—much like the Classic masses of Ignacio de Jerusalem, Matheo Tollis de la Rocca, or Joseph Haydn. The Gloria's sections provide the listener with a varied palette of contrasting meters, tempos, key centers, and emotional colors. The *Misa en sol* avoids the nervous barrage of rapid-fire chord changes that one encounters in the high Baroque. Instead, its harmonic rhythm ambles along at a more leisurely pace; as with other works in the *galant* style, a change from one chord to the next can occupy the space of measures rather than a furtive pulse or two. The clarity of the tonal center is usually hammered home by frequent and extended statements of the defining tonic, subdominant, and dominant chords. The translucent textures, harmonic daring, and breathless articulations of the Sanctus and Agnus Dei remind one more of Mozart and Schubert than of Bach and Schütz. (See figure 5-3.) In short, this composition leaves no impression of a cultural backwater or the wild frontier but instead exudes a sense of the *galant* or Classicism that would have been at home in the major churches of Mexico City, Rome, or Vienna.

Father Owen da Silva's *Mission Music of California,* first released in 1941, appends a brief catalogue of works by Sancho at Stanford University; the *Misa en sol* and the Serra choirbook M.0612 are the only two of that collection that have not disappeared. How fortunate that this inspired composition was among the few at Stanford that has not vanished. A rebirth of interest in the *Misa en sol* has followed on the heels of several reconstructions of the score, first by Harold C. Schmidt, whose edition premiered on 7 April 1991, during Stanford's centennial

Edited by & with instrumental parts
composed by Craig H. Russell

Agnus Dei

from the *Misa en sol*

Juan Bautista Sancho

Figure 5-3 Agnus Dei from the *Misa en sol*

celebrations; second, through the many performances by John Warren and the New World Baroque Orchestra using Warren's own edition; and third, by my own reconstruction (which can be found in appendix D on the Oxford University Press Web site).[106]

The authorship of the *Misa en sol* is not firmly established: there are few sources, and none bear a signed ascription by the composer. However, a mounting stack of evidence supports the theory that Juan Bautista Sancho composed this

© Craig H. Russell, 2004

Figure 5-3 (*continued*)

mass while living at the San Antonio Mission. For starters, the *Misa en sol* manuscript at Stanford was initially part of the large stack of Sancho materials donated
by Father Casanova to Jane Lathrop Stanford in 1888 and later was filmed as part of
Work Projects Administration Folk Music Project in 1938.[107] In addition, the Credo
from the *Misa en sol* has as its foundation the "Credo Artanense"—a melody from

© Craig H. Russell, 2004

Figure 5-3 (*continued*)

Sancho's birthplace (and he is the only California friar to hail from this charming hamlet). Actually, the *Misa en sol* does not borrow all of the "Credo Artanense" but instead retains only the *canto figurado* phrases for the even-numbered verses. For the odd-numbered verses that have been snipped out and removed, Sancho inserts new phrases in lush four-part harmony. The Credo's soprano and bass sheets to the *Misa en sol* describe these alternating textures: "Credo in Mode 5, for 4 voices, alternating with the Credo from Artà."[108] Given the isolated location of Artà, the paucity of California friars who would have known this village's tunes, and the limited number of friars capable of composing four-part settings, Sancho surfaces as the most likely candidate as this work's composer. But the door must be left open for another reasonable possibility; conceivably, this "alternating" Credo was composed by some other native son of Artà, and Sancho merely learned it and copied it while still in Mallorca and then embarked to the New World with this polished "Credo in Mode 5, for 4 voices, alternating with the Credo from Artà" in his backpack.

As I observed earlier, the handwriting of Stanford University's manuscript copy of the *Misa en sol* bears no resemblance to Sancho's distinctive script or notational habits. On the surface, that would tend to undermine a case favoring Sancho as the work's author. However, a meticulous comparison of the exquisite lettering and music idiosyncrasies of this source with the gorgeous, laser-precise writing of his bosom friend Pedro Cabot proves them to be identical in their writing conventions and handiwork. For example, the Smithsonian Institution acquired a prayerboard from the San Antonio Mission, signed "P. Cabot" and dated 1817, whose script replicates that of the *Misa en sol* in almost every detail.[109] Unmistakably, they are created by the same hand. (See figure 5-4 and photo 5-14, identified as photo B-115 online, and photo 5-15, identified as photo B-117 online. In addition, consult photos B-116 and B-118 in appendix B online.)

Using the prayerboard as a guide, we can compare its writing conventions with other mission sources and track down dozens of manuscripts in Cabot's exacting

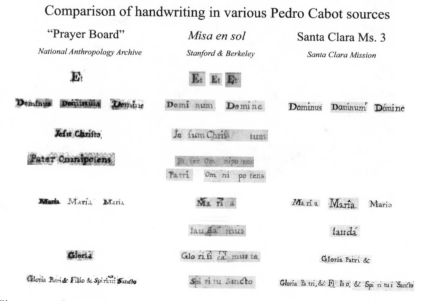

Figure 5-4 Comparison of handwriting in various Pedro Cabot sources

Photo 5-14 Smithsonian prayerboard, recto side, the Smithsonian Institution National Anthropological Archives, "Prayerboard with Liturgy Written in Spanish 1817," Ms. 1082. (Photograph courtesy of the Smithsonian Institution.)

Photo 5-15 *Bajo* part, 1st page of the Credo, *Misa en sol,* in Stanford University, M.0573. (Photograph courtesy of Stanford University.)

hand.[110] In all of these scribal examples, Cabot shows himself to be a consummate professional, not some unskilled inkslinger.[111] In the end, the presence of Cabot's manuscript copy of the *Misa en sol* actually reinforces the theory that Sancho is the composer. Both friars were staunch companions and spent almost their entire adult lives at each other's side. It would be only natural for them to collaborate— Sancho as author and Cabot as scribe.

Admittedly, the case for Sancho's authorship would be even stronger if we were to find a copy in his own hand; fortunately, that is the case with respect to the Credo movement. In the WPA collection at Berkeley, folders 64 and 70 contain photos of Sancho's autograph for a Credo in mode 5. The title page in folder 70 reads: "Misa de 5to tono a 4 voces del P. Fr. Juan Bauta Sancho" (Mass in Mode 5 for 4 Voices by Father Friar Juan Bautista Sancho). The entire Credo can be completed by inserting the homophonic *canto figurado* phrases of the "Credo Artanense" (in folder 52) between these polyphonic passages (located in folder 64). If we use *alternatim* technique to weave together the interlocking phrases from these two manuscript sources—both of which are in Sancho's hand—we get an elegant, finished fabric of varied sonorities. Cabot's and Sancho's end products are the same, but the two brothers take slightly different notational roads. Sancho's rendition necessitates flipping back and forth between two neighboring manuscripts. Cabot preserves the alternating textures by interspersing the *canto figurado* phrases between the contrapuntal ones, but he has written them out on a single sheet, progressing straight from start to finish.

Trying to ascertain the performance resources and stylistic expectations in the *Misa en sol* can be difficult, given the seemingly contradictory information that can be mined from folder 64 in the WPA collection. The first mystery we confront has to do with the number of vocalists that is required. Someone (probably Sidney Robertson) has penciled in commentary on the cover of folder 64, classifying this mass as a two-voice work in duet texture. Repeatedly, we see the penciled annotation "a2" after each movement's title: "Mass. Kyrie (tono 5to) à 2 / Gloria (tono 5to) à 2 / Credo (tono 5to) à 2." This denotation is derived from the only extant vocal parts in the folder, "Tiple 1ᵒ" and "Tiple 2º" (Sopranos 1 and 2). In spite of this logical conclusion designating this as a duet mass, Sancho sends us down another path altogether: his title for the accompaniment part specifies a four-voice texture (*a 4 voces*).[112] We can speculate that there had once been two vocal lines sounding below the sopranos to round out the four-part texture. This supposition is confirmed by the Stanford University copy of the *Misa en sol*'s Credo; its polyphonic phrases are all crafted in four-part harmony, and the top two lines replicate the two soprano voices in WPA folder 64.[113] From this evidence we can deduce that the penciled annotation "a2" designating a duet texture is erroneous; the lower vocal parts have gone missing, at least with respect to WPA folder 64's setting of the Credo.

The next thorny issue in folder 64 confronting the music sleuth concerns authorship of the Kyrie. The inscription at the top of the Kyrie reads: "Tono 5° interpolando, digo, ô alternando con los Kyries â 4,, [*sic*]voces del P. Vic. Torres."[114] From this title, Bill Summers posits that there might have been a friar-composer, Vic Torres, active at Palma's Convent de Sant Francesc and that Sancho made his own copy of his colleague's work. Another possibility presents itself if we translate that inscription as saying, "Mass in mode 5, interpolating—that is to say, alternating—with the Kyries for 4 voices by Father Vic Torres." This could infer that the Kyrie found in folder 64 is not actually Torres's composition at all but is instead a collection of phrases that alternate *with* Torres's four-voice setting. Presently, folder 64 contains no trace of a four-part phrase, so we can presume that Torres's quartet either is lost or was preserved elsewhere. As we established in chapter 2, one of the main traits of the mission style was its affinity for dramatic contrasts in sonority. Just as the Baroque concerto grosso juxtaposed the small concertino group versus the full orchestral tutti resources, so the mission settings of long texts could alternate opposing textures—measured polyphony versus free-floating plainchant, strummed homophony versus flamboyant "modern style," and so on. In this particular Kyrie jotted down in WPA folder 64, Sancho has written out several homophonic phrases, but we really have only "half" of the piece.[115]

The other interlocking phrases (presumably Torres's four-voice creation) would supply the missing ingredients for completion.

Sancho's manuscript references the "four-voice Kyrie by P. Vic. Torres" without clarifying this individual's identity. From the citation alone, it is difficult to ascertain whether "Vic" is an abbreviation of a first name or is part of a surname; in either case, it is intriguing to wonder if "Vic. Torres" is one of the three "Vichs" or "Bonaventura Torres" who were all Franciscan friars active in Palma in the 1790s, the same time that Sancho resided there.[116] If one of them turns out to be our musician, it is not a stretch to suppose that Sancho and "Padre Vic. Torres" actually knew each other as abbots at the Convent de Sant Francesc, maybe even sharing in the Kyrie's creation as collaborators. A personal connection between two Franciscan brothers would easily explain the presence of this obscure composer's works in California, a rather isolated corner of the Spanish Empire.

Questions of attribution crop up with respect to the Gloria in WPA folder 64 as well as its Kyrie. More accurately, there is not one, singular Gloria as much as there are two different but complementary settings; the "Gloria [del] 5to tono" covers the odd-numbered phrases ("Et in terra pax bonae voluntatis," "Benedicimus te," "Glorificamus te," etc.), and the "Gloria Espacio" applies to the even-numbered phrases ("Laudamus te," "Adoramus te," "Gratias agimus tibi," etc.).[117] If we sew together these phrases in alternating fashion, we wend our way through the entire Gloria text. The odd-numbered passages are slightly more substantial and assiduous than the even-numbered ones, and they bear a striking resemblance to the four-part passages in the *Missa de los Angeles* that Sancho wrote out while still in Palma. However, the even-numbered passages are cut from a different cloth. They are more relaxed and succinct and seem to have been drawn from an older inveterate model. The same music surfaces in WPA folder 63 under the title "Parisiense Gloria."[118] If Sancho were the composer of this Gloria, it would be hard to explain why he chose to call it "Parisian," since he never traveled to France or expressed any infatuation with French taste. However, several mission manuscripts affix a "Parisian" provenance to particular selections, and this specific "Parisiense Gloria" would be but another Mass movement in that long-standing tradition.[119]

To summarize our conclusions up to this point regarding WPA folder 64, we might reasonably attribute several works to Sancho as their probable (or at least possible) creator: the homophonic Kyrie (that traded phrases back and forth with the polyphonic Kyrie of "P. Vic. Torres"); the odd-numbered phrases of the "Gloria [del] 5to tono"; and the odd-numbered phrases of the polyphonic Credo (that alternated phrases with the *canto figurado* tunes in the "Credo Artanense").

Before leaving the issue of authorship, another issue must be addressed relating to Sancho's title pages and colophons. The sheets that were photographed in the WPA collection often bear Sancho's annotation, "*del uso de* Juan Bautista Sancho" (*for the use* of Juan Bautista Sancho). At the very least, this heading assures us that Sancho had these papers at his disposal, and the ex libris might be intended to identify the composer as well—but there is nothing that explicitly pins that down. For the caption in folder 70, Sancho prints out, "Misa de 5to tono à 4 voces *del* P. Fr. Juan Bautista Sancho" (Mass in Mode 5 for 4 voices *of* Father &

Friar Juan Bautista Sancho). Spanish writers and composers occasionally used *de* (rather than *por*) as a way of assigning authorship.[120] That could be the case here. If Sancho is referring to himself as the creator of the "Misa de 5to tono â 4 voces," then it would not be a stretch to imagine him as the *Misa en sol*'s creator given the other circumstantial evidence pointing in that direction. In the end, however, ambiguity remains.

One elusive issue surrounding the *Misa en sol* concerns its overall style and implied instrumental accompaniment. The full bars of rest in all of the vocal parts confirm the presence of instruments during those measures to fill in the vacant space—so what did they do?[121] Was the music preconceived or improvised? What sorts of instruments were played, and in what style? Were these passages notated, and if so, where is the music written out? An examination of the extant vocal parts is critical if we are to select an appropriate instrumental vessel to support them. As noted previously, the vocal lines are clearly shaped in the mold of *galant* and Classical ideals: the tunes are chock-full of "sigh" figures, graceful ornamentation, shifting surface rhythms, clear phrase structure, and frequent rests that create hierarchical division points. Though virtuosic, the work exudes a sense of clarity and refinement—the very core of the Classical aesthetic. Therefore, the accompaniment must also be Classical if the sounds are to "match" and be historically congruent.

As we have seen earlier in this chapter and in chapter 1, the core orchestral sonorities for the *galant* and Classical styles in Spain and its American colonies consisted of two violin sections (Violins I and II), plus the *acompañamiento* realized by a cello or cellos, a contrabass, a bassoon, and some chordal instruments to flesh out the sonorities with improvised chords.[122] To this foundation, pairs of woodwind or brass could provide a few dashes of color and sonorous depth. The San Antonio Mission had a full stock of these instruments, and to imagine that the neophytes there merely used their instrumental resources to double the vocal melodies would be beyond the realm of credibility. Assuredly, they supplied something steeped in the *galant* and Classical aesthetic that resembled the pervasive trends of the time—especially those spreading throughout New Spain. That they had access to Classical orchestral models is verified by the presence in California of masses by Ignacio de Jerusalem and Francisco Javier García Fajer, both of whom exhibit the instrumental vigor and luminous orchestration reminiscent of Joseph Haydn.

The fetching duet movements in the *Misa en sol* fit right in with the huge corpus of contemporaneous compositions in Spain and Mexico written for a pair of sopranos; typically, the vocal duet is supported by two violins plus an *acompañamiento* (basso continuo). Several representative examples of these two-voice settings can be found in Morelia's Conservatory of the Roses (in works such as "Jesús mi dulce amor" and Joseph Pérez's "A ti mi Jesús amado") or in Joseph de Nebra's alluringly sublime *Miserere*.[123] All said, we can surmise that Sancho's *Misa en sol* was probably supported by an instrumental scaffolding consisting of a pair of violins plus figured bass, and possibly winds or horns in pairs. Furthermore, if we scrutinize any accompanying parts in this Classical *estilo moderno* from the late 1700s and early 1800s, we can see that the instruments nearly always had independent, highly idiomatic lines that propelled the piece forward with vigor and technical figuration—sawing away in carbon copies of the vocal lines was exceedingly rare.

That instruments played along here is irrefutable, but finding the actual sheets from which they played presents a mystery—where are they? One plausible answer for *canto figurado* would be that they were improvised on the spot; in this style, the underlying chords are usually straightforward, and the phrase lengths are compact. Improvised accompaniments would be a piece of cake. But for the *estilo moderno* (to which the *Misa en sol* belongs), its extended architectural structures, complex harmonies, subtle modulations, expansive phrases, and generally plentiful number of performers (often grouped into sections such as "Violin I" and "Violin II") necessitate that the instrumental passagework be composed. And that brings us back to the question, "Where are the actual performance parts?" Fortunately, at least the Credo's *acompañamiento* line for the *Misa en sol* is retrievable, for Sancho wrote out a continuo line for this Credo as part of the "Misa de 5to tono" (the photograph for this sheet is located in WPA folder 70; see photo B-130 online).[124] This makes yet a third component of the *Misa en sol* that is found in Sancho's handwriting, the other two being the *canto figurado* rendition of the "Credo Artanense" (folder 52) and the four-voice passages of the "Credo de 5to tono" (folder 64). No one knows the whereabouts of the upper violin parts that played along together with Sancho's figured bass line, but that problem afflicts almost every concerted piece in the California repertoire. García Fajer's and Jerusalem's masses are missing much of their instrumental dressing.[125] Therefore, it is not surprising that the presumed violin parts and continuo line for the *Misa en sol* (and maybe wind and brass parts as well) are not preserved in any known archival repository.

Compositionally, the *Misa en sol* is both well-wrought and dazzling, showing a level of craftsmanship not automatically assignable to a friar's standard musical training. Granted, for all Franciscans the singing of Mass and the Divine Office (Matins, Vespers, etc.) was a primal obligation, literally "God's work." In addition, the mendicant orders promoted music education and performance as tools of conversion in the New World, even in the earliest years of the Encounter. One cannot help but be impressed with the indefatigable efforts of Pedro de Gante and his choir school for neophytes in Mexico City during the early sixteenth century.[126] But the erudite aspects of the *Misa en sol* is not generic music making, attainable by just anyone with intermediate music skills. No, whoever authored this mass was a seasoned professional who had a thorough grasp of the rules of harmony, counterpoint, and the most up-to-date trends of Classicism and the *galant*. If we make a roster of potential candidates active in California who could fit these requirements, the list is short. A stellar nominee would be Narciso Durán. As music educator, choir director, and codifier of the mission repertoire, he is unsurpassed. But claims that he crafted original compositions are dubious.[127] The most stellar ethnomusicologist would have been Felipe Arroyo de la Cuesta at the San Juan Bautista Mission, but he was completely enchanted with Native American traditions, not so much with the "refinements" of Eurocentric Classicism. Father Esteban Tapís also makes the list of highly skilled musicians, but he left no hint that he composed works from scratch. His accomplishments spring up elsewhere. Other than Sancho, the most well-versed in the music arts would have been Florencio Ibáñez. His professional credentials are impressive.[128] He earned the high rank of chapelmaster on several occasions and unquestionably was cognizant of contemporary fads. He necessarily was schooled in the compositional craft; any chapelmaster worth his salt would have been able to pen an original *villancico* or Vespers Psalm at a moment's notice. In spite of Ibáñez's obvious qualifications, he is not the most likely composer of the *Misa en sol*. It would be hard to explain why Ibáñez would include an affectionate remembrance to Artà (as we find in the Mass's Credo), and all of the Mass's components in California are written out by Sancho or Cabot—not a single ingredient appears in Ibáñez's scribal handwriting.

One final prospect needs to be explored before we finish our detective work. It is possible that the Mass was conceived by a Mallorcan musician other than Sancho—but someone who would have known Artà firsthand and was therefore predisposed to pay homage in a musical composition. In this theory, Sancho's function would be that of copyist and transporter, dashing off his own duplicate of the work while still in Palma and then carrying it with him to the New World. Palma, after all, was a vibrant musical center with a dozen musicians capable of writing a top-notch, musically informed mass.[129] We have already confirmed that in the 1790s Sancho made a habit of copying out works for his personal use; the *Misa en sol* might fall within that category of copied—but not "original"—work.

So the conundrum remains: Is Sancho's function that of composer or merely scribe while still in Mallorca? A stronger case can be made for the former. First, we have to account for Pedro Cabot's gorgeous manuscript copy of the *Misa en sol* at Stanford. Cabot wrote out many musical manuscripts while in California—as evidenced by their presence at Stanford University, Santa Clara Mission, Santa Barbara Mission, San Fernando Mission, and the University of California at Berkeley.[130] However, not a single one appears to have been created prior to his departure from Palma. In this context, we can assume that the *Misa en sol* was the fruit of Cabot's labors while he was at the San Antonio Mission, and there could hardly be a more rewarding task for him there than to write out a mass created by his dearest friend and fellow friar, Juan Bautista Sancho.

Moreover, a comparison of the main phrase for "quoniam tu solus" in the *Misa en sol* and that same text phrase as found in California's *Misa de San Antonio* (also known as the *Misa Solemne*) shows them to be identical twins.[131] They are cast in identical rhythms and melodic contours. Only the key center has been altered (see Figure 5-5). The *Misa de San Antonio* was a ubiquitous and constituent setting in the California mission repertoire, known all along the mission chain, yet there is no known concordant version in Spain (including the Balearic Islands). I would propose, then, that the California mission repertoire was a critical element in the composer's imagination when he crafted the *Misa en sol,* and that the incorporation of the "quoniam tu solus" tune—either consciously or unconsciously—into the *Misa en sol*'s Gloria decidedly reinforces a California connection. In the search for this Mass's creator, no other friar fills the bill as persuasively as Juan Bautista Sancho.

"Quoniam tu solus" in California manuscripts

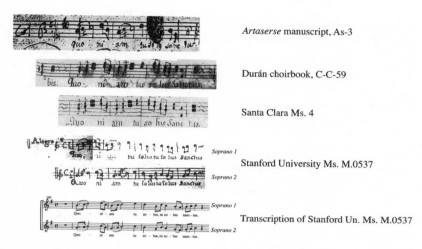

Artaserse manuscript, As-3

Durán choirbook, C-C-59

Santa Clara Ms. 4

Stanford University Ms. M.0537

Transcription of Stanford Un. Ms. M.0537

Figure 5-5 "Quoniam tu solus" in California manuscripts

If we are to summarize the case favoring Sancho as the probable composer of the *Misa en sol,* we find the following supporting evidence: (1) the multiple sources of this work and its related component materials were all part of Sancho's manuscript collection that he brought to the San Antonio Mission in the early 1800s; (2) the most complete version of the mass is in the handwriting of Sancho's fast friend and Franciscan brother at San Antonio Mission, Pedro Cabot; (3) at the University of California at Berkeley, WPA folders 52, 64, and 70 contain the musical ingredients—written out in Sancho's own distinctive script—for the *Misa en sol*'s Credo; (4) the mass references Artà and even includes a melody from this remote hamlet that was Sancho's birthplace; (5) Sancho inscribes a heading on the mass's Credo, "*del* P. Fr. Juan Bau[tis]ta Sancho" (*of/by* Father Friar Juan Bautista Sancho), that could be interpreted as his claim to authorship; and (6) the passage "quoniam tu solus" in the *Misa en sol* replicates nearly every aspect of this same phrase in the *Misa de San Antonio,* a mass beloved in the California missions but not well known beyond California's shores. Taken separately, these clues are not overwhelming or definitive, but if they are bound together into one probative, cogent case, they are rather convincing. Out of the many friars active in California during the early 1800s, Juan Bautista Sancho rises as the most plausible (even probable) creator of the resplendent *Misa en sol.*

Notes

1. For a complete description of Sancho's extended family and a rigorous reconstruction, consult Antoni Gili [y Ferrer], "Els Sanxo de Artà" (The family Sancho of Artà), in Antoni Pizà, William J. Summers, Craig H. Russell, and Antoni Gili Ferrer, *J. B. Sancho: Compositor pioner de*

Califòrnia, edited and coordinated by Antoni Pizà (Palma de Mallorca, Spain: Universitat de les Illes Balears, Servei de Publicacions i Intercanvi Cientific, 2007), 241–314. A condensed version of Gili's family tree can also be found reproduced in my article "Fray Juan Bautista Sancho: Tracing the Origins of California's First Composer and the Early Mission Style," *Boletín: Journal of the California Mission Studies Association,* pt. 1 in vol. 21, no. 1 (2004), 71.

2. Marriage registration of Pere Josep Sancho i Nicolau and Margarida Lliteres Llinas: "Pera Joseph Sancho, fadri, Margalida Lliteras V^a, A 28 7bre—68 ... [on the 28th of September, 1768...," Església parroquial d'Artà, *Matrimonios,* 1755–1837, fol. 23, no. 20. Note: alternate spellings in some documents include "Pera" for "Pere," "Margarita" for "Margalida" or "Margarida," and "Sanxo" for "Sancho."

3. Baptismal registration of Joan Baptista Sancho: "Joan Baptista Sancho de Pera, A 1 10bre— 72, baptisi un fill de Pera Sancho y Margarita Lliteras y conj^s lo nó Joan Baptis/ta, nat dit dia a mitg dia, P^s Llorens Sancho Fadri y Joana Anna Lliteras D^n toti ett / Simo Sureda P^{re} Vú en Artá" (Joan Baptista Sancho, son of Pera: on the 1st of December 1772, I baptized a son of Pera Sancho and Margarita Lliteras whom they named Joan Baptista, born on this day at noon. Godparents: Llorens Sancho Fadri and Joana Anna Lliteras, etc. / [signed by] Simo Sureda, Padre Vu in the town of Artà). Església parroquial d'Artà, *Bautismos,* 1764–1796, fol. 48, no. 117.

4. For a complete citation, see Gili, "Els Sanxo de Artà," 265, with a facsimile of the document on p. 314. No matter which year we accept (1772 or 1776), we can now rectify several erroneous statements in the published literature concerning Sancho's birthdate: Hubert H. Bancroft mistakenly places the date a month later on 1 January 1773, and Maynard Geiger muddies the issue further by stating Sancho was born in 1791—an impossibility, for that would mean that Sancho would have been less than a year old when he took his vows as a Franciscan. See Hubert Howe Bancroft, *The History of California,* 7 vols. (San Francisco: History Company, 1884–90), vol. 2, p. 621n17; and Maynard Geiger, O.F.M., "Documents: Reply of Mission San Antonio to the Questionnaire of the Spanish Government in 1812 Concerning the Native Culture of the Indians," *The Americas,* vol. 10, no. 2 (October 1953), 211. In another publication, however, Geiger gives the correct (or at least probable) birthdate of 1 December 1772, as does Fr. Zephyrin Engelhardt in his book on Mission San Antonio. See Maynard Geiger, O.F.M., *Franciscan Missionaries in Hispanic California 1769–1848: A Biographical Dictionary* (San Marino, Calif.: Huntington Library, 1969), 223; and Zephyrin Engelhardt, O.F.M., *Mission San Antonio de Padua: The Mission in the Sierras,* (Ramona, Calif.: Ballena Press, 1972), 109.

5. See Gili, "Els Sanxo de Artà," 255, 285, and 302–3.

6. I wish to thank William Summers for bringing this critical point to my attention in a personal conversation in New York in April 2007.

7. *Gran Enciclopèdia de Mallorca,* vol. 16, ed. by Pere A. Serra Bauzà, Consell Insular de Mallorca and Banca March (Palma de Mallorca: Promomallorca, 1991), 14.

8. "4-IV-1736, Pere Sanxo, receptor de la capella de la Confraría de Santa Cecília, fundada en el Palau Reial, rep 10 lliures," and "1737, Pere Sanxo, receptor de la Música Vella, olim de la seu, rep 10 lliures." Arxiu del Regne de Mallorca (ARM), Document C-1588, cited in Gili i Ferrer, "Contribució a la historia musical de Mallorca," 103.

9. See Gili, "Els Sanxo de Artà," 308.

10. "Antoni Sancho Sacrer, firm de Orde y en presencia del P. Jaume Frontera, capellar de St Antoni 1776." "Lo abax firmal [firmat?] Fr. Fran^{ch} Ferrer P^{dor} del Sr Syndich del Rl. Conv^t de St Fran^{ch} deu se com el dit Sr Syndich ha rebut de los sobreposats de ditas confrarias j mans De ses Pre^{dors} Antoni Sanxo y Juan Montaner y Canellas, cent trenta nou lliuras de nou sous y 10 d^s q la mesada de vail [?] del als 30 Abril 1781. 139 L 19 P. 10. Fr. Franch Ferrer." Both citations found in the Arxiu del Regne de Mallorca (ARM), "Llibre de recibos del Sr. Sindich Sachristia y Musicos comensant 1737 fins 1781," book C-1015, fols. 181v and 190v. If Antoni Sancho Sacrer is related to Juan Bautista, it is probably only remotely, since the surname "Sacrer" is not found on the detailed family tree graphed out by Mosen Gili. See Gili, "Els Sanxo de Artà," 306–8.

11. Jaume Sancho Melis was Juan Bautista's first cousin, once removed. Jaume was the son of Juan Bautista Sancho's first cousin, Miquel Sancho Torres, and his spouse, Antonio Anna Vicens Horrach. Miquel, in turn, was the son of Pere Josep Sancho Llinàs—a younger brother to Jaume Sancho Llinàs, Juan Bautista's father. See Antoni Gili i Ferrer, Rosa de Aguilar Morales, and Llorenç Vich Sancho, "Una família de músics: Els Sancho," *Estudis Musicals.*

XIII Simpòsium i Jornades Internacionals de l'Orgue Històric de les Balears & XIII Trobada de Documentalistes Musicals (Palma and Búger: Fundació ACA–Centre de Recerca i Documentació Històrico-Musical de Mallorca, 2006), 130 and 154. In this article, these three authors provide the birth date of 1743—as does the *Gran Enciclopèdia* (p. 15). Joan Parets i Serra et al., in their *Diccionari*, give the birth year as 1742. See Joan Parets i Serra, Pere Esterlich i Massuti, and Biel Massot i Muntaner, *Diccionari de compositors mallorquins (segles XV–XIX)*, Centre de Recercca i Documentació Històrico-Musical de Mallorca (Palma de Mallorca: Conselleria d'Éducació i Cultura, Govern Balear, Edicions Cort, 1987), 11.

12. The ARM contains the following entries: "Llibre de recibos del Sr. Sindich Sachristia y Musicos comensant 1737 fins 1781," book C-1015: "Jaume Sancho, Resp^r de la Capella a R^l errebut dels sobrepossatz de la purissima consep° del R^l Convent de S^t de Sr Franc^h, 1768," fol. 163v; "Jo Jaume Sancho Resp^r de la Capella R^l errebut dels sobrepasat de la purissima consep° del R^l Convent de St Franc^h deuit lluiras y sinc sous ço es 2 per la Musica & t de rres días 2L5& per la Musica del Bon Pastor 6 Ll per la Musica del 3 Maig y 3 Ll per la Musica intro 8^m del P. Pr Antoni 2 Ll per la Musica dels 8 Crio^l y 3 Ll per la Musica als 2 agost 1768 a conp^t fins als 21 p^tre 1768 son ___ 18L5," fol. 163v; and "Jaume Sancho, Resep^r de la Capella R^l, 1769," fol. 166v.

13. "Miquel Sanxo Vicenç...Mestre i director de música (1804–40) de la capilla de la Seu de Mallorca," *Gran Enciclopèdia*, 15. This source gives Miquel's birthplace as Palma, but Parets and his coauthors describe his birthplace as being Artà. "Miquel Sancho i Vicens...fou Mestre sustitut de Cipela de la Seu de Mallorca 1803–1804," Parets et al, *Diccionari*, 110–11. For more information regarding Miquel Vicens Sancho, consult Gili i Ferrer et al., "Una família de músics: Els Sancho," 133–35, and the entry "Sancho Vicens, Miguel" by María González Peña and Luiz and Joan Company Florit found in the *Diccionario de la música española e hispanoamericana* directed and coordinated by Emilio Casares Rodicio (Madrid: Sociedad General de Autores y Editores, 2002), vol. 9, p. 697.

14. Consult Gili i Ferrer et al., "Una família de músics: Els Sancho," 135–37. See also *Gran Enciclopèdia*, 14. Parets and his coauthors observe that Joaquim was held in high esteem, having received the nickname the "Haydn mallorquí." Parets et al, *Diccionari*, 109.

15. Parets et al, *Diccionari*, 110.

16. Both scholars have provided invaluable work, but their most recent contribution (coauthored with Rosa de Aguilar Morales) is probably the most important. See their "Una família de músics: Els Sancho," for it continues in copious detail, straightening out the tangle of biographical data that surrounds the Sancho family through the ages.

17. The spellings are not uniform: "Gueráu," "Grau," "Grao" and "Literes," "Lliteres," "Litteres." The definitive study of Spanish music in the eighteenth century, including the works of Literes and the Gueráus, is Antonio Martín Moreno, *Siglo XVIII*, vol. 4 of *Historia de la música española*, series directed by Pablo López de Osaba (Madrid: Alianza Editorial, 1985). I discuss many aspects of the music of Literes and Francisco Gueráu in *Santiago de Murcia's "Códice Saldívar N°4": A Treasury of Secular Guitar Music from Baroque Mexico*, 2 vols. (Urbana: University of Illinois Press, 1995). A major study of Literes's life is that by Nicolás A. Solar Quintes, "Antonio Literes Carrión y sus hijos (Nuevos documentos para su biografía)," *Anuario musical*, vol. 5 (1950), 169–89. For specific material on Literes, also consult the following: Carmelo Caballero, "El manuscrito Gayangos-Barbieri," *Revista de Musicología*, vol. 12, no. 1 (1989), 131–32; Pere Esterlich i Massutí, "Antoni Lliteres i Carrió, Músic Barroc," *Palau Reial* [published by the Consell Insular de Mallorca in Palma], vol. 1, no. 7 (January 1987), 20–24; Antoni Gili i Ferrer, "El músico mallorquí Antoni Lliteres," *Lluc.* no. 801 (1997), 12–16; Nicolás Morales, "Real Capilla y festería en el siglo XVIII: Nuevas aportaciones para la historia de la institución musical palatina," *Revista de Musicología*, vol. 22, no. 1 (1999), 175–208; Antonio Martín Moreno, "El compositor mallorquín Antonio Literes (1673–1747)," *Tesoro sacro musical*, vol. 643 (1978), 24–26; Antonio Martín Moreno, "Cantada sola de Reyes con vs. y obue *Ha del rústico* (1710) de Literes," *Tesoro sacro musical*, vol. 643 (1978), 1–24; and Judith Ortega, "La Real Capilla de Carlos III: Los músicos instrumentistas y la provisión de sus plazas," *Revista de Musicología*, vol. 23, no. 2 (2000), 418.

For studies of Francisco Gueráu or Gabriel Gueráu, consult the following: Gerardo Arriaga, "Francisco y Gabriel Gueráu, músicos mallorquines," *Revista de Musicología*, vol. 7, no. 2 (July–December, 1984), 253–99; Louis Jambou, "Documentos relativos a los músicos de la segunda mitad del siglo XVII de las capillas reales y villa y arte de Madrid sacados de su Archivo de Protocolos," *Revista de Musicología,* vol. 12, no. 2 (1989), esp. 488–89; Janis Stevenson, "A Transcription of *Poema Harmónico* by Francisco Guerau for Baroque Guitar," M.A. thesis, San Jose State University, 1974; Brian Jeffery, introduction to and translation of Francisco Gueráu's *Poema harmónico,* 1694 (London: Tecla Editions, 1977); and M. June Yakeley, "New Sources of Spanish Music for the Five Course Guitar," *Revista de Musicología,* vol. 19, nos. 1–2 (1996), esp. 279–81. Several archives containing important works by Francisco Gueráu include the New York Hispanic Society, the Biblioteca del Montestir in Montserrat, the Real Monasterio de San Lorenzo El Escorial, the Biblioteca de Cataluña in Barcelona, and the Biblioteca Nacional in Madrid.

18. Geiger, *Franciscan Missionaries,* 223; Antoni Gili i Ferrer, "Evangelitzadors Artanencs al Nou Món," in *Congrés Internacional d'Estudis Històrics Les Illes Balears i Amèrica* (Palma, Mallorca: Gener, 1992); 139.

19. Geiger, *Franciscan Missionaries,* 223; Engelhardt, *San Antonio,* 109; Gili, "Evangelitzadors," 139; Bancroft, *History of California,* vol. 2, p. 621n17.

20. Geiger claims the date of his solemn vows was 10 February 1792, but he gives no documentary record that states that day specifically. He is probably extrapolating forward one year (the customary probationary time) from the date 9 February 1791, when Sancho entered the novitiate (a date that is documented in several locations). Nevertheless, it is unclear whether the vows would have been on 9 or 10 February. See Geiger, *Franciscan Missionaries,* 223.

21. "Juan Bautista Sancho, Ministro de esta Mision de Sn. Antonio / de Padua; hijo de Pedro, y de Margarita Lliteras: fue bautizado / en la Villa de Artá, Ysla, y Obispado de Mallorca; el dia prime-/ro de Diziembre de 1772; Tomó el habito de N. P. Sⁿ Franᶜᵒ / en el Real Convento de la Ciudad de Palma, el dia 9, de Febrero / del 1791, y concluido el año del Noviciado hizo solemne profesion / en dicho Convento. Ordenado de Sacerdote; gran ordenanzas [?] de Confe/sor, y Predicador, exercito dichos Ministerios por algunos años en / la Provincia: supliendo en falta del Vicario del Coro, la direcion / del canto por su fuerte, y agradable voz, y dio instruccion completa,/ tanta en el canto llano, como figurada." Original text available in a photocopied facsimile, *Deaths: Mission San Antonio 1819–1872,* vol. 2, at the Santa Barbara Mission Archive-Library, burial record no. 3499, fols. 49–50. The passage in question is found on fol. 49. Translation by Engelhardt, *San Antonio,* 109.

22. Bancroft Library, Ms. C-C-73:16, "Fragment from printed book of Papal Bulls, 1631 with mss. notes, 1772–1804." I wish to thank Jordi Puig-Suari (professor of aeronautical engineering) for his generous assistance in translating the Catalán passages in Sancho's diary.

23. The diary is tiny, measuring 9.3 by 15.2 centimeters.

24. Some explanation of the manuscript's dates is called for, especially with respect to the Bancroft Library's catalogue description: "Fragment from printed book of Papal Bulls, 1631 with mss. notes, 1772–1804." All three years—1631, 1772, and 1804—are incorrect. The text for Urban VIII's papal bull was publicly disseminated in 1631, but this document is unmistakably a later reissue, as can be gathered by the flip side of the same sheet; there we find printed yet another papal bull by a different pope altogether, Innocent XII, who served as pope from 1691–1700. The bottom of that papal bull has the identifying phrase "Ex debito: Die 28 Augusti 1694." The booklet, therefore, cannot be any earlier than 1694. It seems likely that this small sheet was printed even later in the early or mid-1700s, given the fact that the first handwritten entry in this booklet is dated 1771.

The Bancroft Library catalogue asserts the earliest "manuscript note" is from the year 1772—but that assumption is slightly off the mark. It is true that the year "1772" is clearly written on fol. 4v in Juan Sancho's handwriting, immediately below a horizontal line that divides the page in half. But that is because he is telling us his *birthday,* not the date that he is making his entry: "Naci â 1 de[ciembre] sobre de 1772" (I was born on the first of December in the year 1772). In truth, the earliest entry is at the top of this same page by one of the booklet's previous owners. It states: "Die 31 Janer de 1771 feren lectors el P. Lector Mir el P. Simoner el P. Paleron, el P. Arbona, y Fr. Canals Diara...." (On the 31 of January 1771, the lectors were Father Mir, Father Simoner, Father Palerón, Father Arbona, Friar Canals Diara).

Similarly, the last entry is misstated in the Bancroft Library catalogue as being from 1804. In truth, at the bottom of fol. 3v there appears a brief passage dated 1815; it seems to be in a mixture of Castilian and native languages. The hand closely resembles Sancho's writing and very well might be his entry. The text reads: "Na Quichuque D. Ygnacio Tenorio Petjau liu chú 63 ilché el año 1815 seg u lo que dixo p[or] el Mayo de dhô año sobre qᵉ el año qᵉ extinguieron los ppˢ jesuitas, tenia 14 años de edad."

25. "*Nota*. Dia 9 de Febrer de lo Añy 91 vax pendrer lo habit yo Fr. Juan Bapᵗᵃ Sancho. y vax pendrer el Orde de Presbiterad Dia 17 de Dezembra de 1796 y vax dir 1a 1ᵃ Missa. Dia 27 del matex Mes. Y Dia 20 de juliol del Añy 1798 vax ser examina[t] de Côfessor la 1ʳᵃ vegade per el Bisba Bernat Aodat y Crespi. *Altre nota*. Me vaig pertir de Artá per el Collegi de S. Fernãdo dia 23 de Fabrer [*sic*] de 1803, 1ʳ dia de Quaresma. Y haviendome partido del puerto de Cadiz dia 20 junio de 1803; llegue al dicho Colegio de Sⁿ Fernando dia 9 septᵇʳᵉ del mismo año." Fol. 4v, about halfway down the sheet continuing to the end. Notice the gradual shift from Catalán to Castilian.

26. "Lo añy 1797 en el Conᵗ de Jesus *Extra Muros,* cantaren 29 Oficis o Misas Requiem Dia de los Mors qᵉ es Dia 2 Noᵇʳᵉ et erat sucsesive." Fol. 3, upper right quadrant.

27. The names that are notated and then crossed out are "Sᵗᵉ Joanne de Capistrano, Sᵗᵉ Jacobe de Alarchia, Sᵗᵉ Francisce Solane, Sᵗᵉ Didace, Sᵗᵉ Paschalis, Sᵗᵉ Petre Regelale, Sᵗᵉ." Fol. 3, upper left quadrant.

28. "Y en Artá en cãtid[ad] (there is a smudge here), Lo añy 1801: 27. y lo añy 1802. 21 Ofici." Fol. 3, upper right quadrant, immediately below the entry mentioned in note 26.

29. Geiger (*Franciscan Missionaries,* 175) gives the full title of the convent as being Convento de Santa María de los Ángeles de Jesús, and gives the geographic location of the Convent de Jesús as being outside the walls of Palma. See Geiger, *Franciscan Missionaries,* 126, 128, 175.

30. Ibid., 175, 239.

31. For a summary of Luis Jayme's life, consult ibid., 128–29.

32. For a summary of Antonio Jayme's life, consult ibid., 126–27. Bartolomé Gili's life is covered by Geiger on pp. 106–8.

33. For a concise summary of Boscana's life, consult ibid., 29–32. For a modern edition of Boscana's treatise, see the Friar Gerónimo Boscana, *Chinigchinich: A Natural Historical Account of the Origin, Customs, and Traditions of the Indians of the Missionary Establishment of St. Juan Capistrano, Alta-California,* [trans. by Alfred Robinson], (Oakland, Calif.: Biobooks, 1947).

34. Some of the California padres who spent time in the Convent de Sant Francesc include Juan Vicente Cabot, Pedro Cabot, Juan Crespí, Bartolomé Gili (who was to become the organist at the Convent de Sant Francesc), Luis Jayme (who studied for the priesthood at the Convent de Sant Francesc), Francisco Palóu (who became a Franciscan at the Convent de Jesús but who then studied with Serra at the Convent de Sant Francesc), Miguel Pieras, Antonio Ripoll, Mariano Rubí, Juan Bautista Sancho, Serra (who joined the Franciscan order at the Convent de Jesús but later became a major figure at the Convent de Sant Francesc), and Buenaventura Sitjar (who became a Franciscan at the Convent de Jesús but left for Cádiz and then the New World from the Convent de Sant Francesc). For the connections between the Convent de Sant Francesc and the above-mentioned friars, consult Geiger, *Franciscan Missionaries,* 32, 34, 51, 106, 128, 175, 196, 207, 210, 223, 239, 245.

35. Technically, Cabot does not place Sancho at the rank of "Maestro de Capilla," a position that would have required rigorous public examinations among different applicants, the winner of which would have obtained the post. Nevertheless, this passage clearly states that he had a leadership role that surpassed that of a mere *chantre,* or head singer of plainsong. For a discussion of the requirements for obtaining the post of chapelmaster, consult the following: José Artero, "Oposiciones al Magisterio de Capilla en España durante el siglo XVIII," *Anuario musical,* vol. 2 (1947): 191–202; José Martín González, "Oposiciones al Magisterio de Capilla de la Catedral de Valladolid durante el siglo XIX," *Revista de Musicología,* vol. 14, nos. 1–2 (1991): 511–34; Judith Ortega, "La Real Capilla de Carlos III: Los músicos instrumentistas y la provisión de sus plazas," *Revista de Musicología,* vol. 23, no. 2 (2000): 395–442; Immaculada Quintanal, "Enrique Villaverde: Importancia de la capilla de música de la Catedral de Oviedo en el siglo XVIII," *Revista de Musicología,* vol. 1, nos. 1–2 (1978): 124–90, esp. 136; and Robert Stevenson, *Spanish Cathedral Music in the Golden Age* (Berkeley: University of California Press, 1961), 29. Also, mention should be made of William Summers's outstanding and detailed discussions of Sancho's musical prowess. In one article, he credits Sancho as being the chapelmaster at

Sant Francesc during the years 1794–97; see Summers, "*Opera seria* in Spanish California: An Introduction to a Newly-Identified Manuscript Source," in *Music in Performance and Society: Essays in Honor of Roland Jackson*, ed. by Malcolm Cole and John Koegel (Warren, Mich.: Harmonie Park Press, 1997), 282. In another, he supplies a starting date of 1795 instead of 1794 for Sancho's employment at Sant Francesc; see Summers, "Recently Recovered Manuscript Sources of Sacred Polyphonic Music from Spanish California," *Ars Musica Denver*, vol. 7, no. 1 (1994), 14. That Sancho was at Sant Francesc in 1796 and 1797 can be gathered from several signed sheets by Sancho, but I have found no primary documentation for the earlier dates of 1794 or 1795. Nevertheless, Summers's dating has to be either on the mark or extremely close, since we do know Sancho professed at the institution in 1792.

36. Ibáñez earned the post of chapelmaster at the Convento de Nuestra Señora de Jesús in Zaragoza, and later at the Franciscan Convent de Catalayud, both of which had music making of the first rank. With Ibáñez's move to Mexico, he became the chapelmaster at the Colegio de San Fernando—the very institution that served as the motherhouse for all of the California missions and their missionaries. See Geiger, *Franciscan Missionaries*, 124–25, 223–25; Summers, "Sancho: The Preeminent Musician of Alta California," in Antoni Pizà et al, *J. B. Sancho: Compositor pioner de Califòrnia*, 26, 46, and 99; Summers, "New and Little Known Sources of California Mission Music," *Inter-American Music Review*, vol. 11, no. 2 (Spring–Summer 1991), 21; Summers, "Orígenes hispanos de la música misional de California," *Revista Musical Chilena*, nos. 149–150 (1980), 46n27; and Owen da Silva, O.F.M., *Mission Music of California: A Collection of Old California Mission Hymns and Masses* (Los Angeles: Warren F. Lewis, 1941), 22. Other friars, such as Durán, Tapís, and Arroyo de la Cuesta, were clearly musically inclined, but there is no evidence of comparable professional training in the musical arts.

37. "En El Sabado de los S^tos. Par[a]rezar los Maytines." (There is a hole in the page that leaves off letters in the middle words.) Continuing: "En Enero y Deciembre; â las 2 y med[ia]." (The page is trimmed here and therefore the last letters are missing.) "En Febrero y 9bre; â las 2 y 3 qûrte [*sic*]. En Marzo y Octub^re; â las 3. En Abril y 7bre; â las 3 y quarto. En Mayo y Agosto; a las 3 y media. En junio y julio; â las 3 y 3 quarte." Fol. 2v, middle of sheet.

38. "Invertir el orden de las Horas Cano^cas sin [?] causa; solo es pecado venial." "Nota: qñdo en el Coro se dexîa ô se [pa?]rra alguna cosa, ha de rezar despues del *fidelium animæ misericor:* &c. ahora iii y despues *Pater noster,* &c." Fol. 2v, bottom third of sheet.

39. Nota: / Per guañar la indul/zenc-ia de Porciuncula bas:/[te r]ezar el P[ater] N[oster] y A[tifona] / [y Glo]ria tres vegades y / [p]regar per la concordia / de los Principes Christia[no] s / extirpacio de las heré/gites &c. y dèu precehir [*sic*] / la cómunio, y se adver/tex q^e la comunio baste q^e / se prega, en qualsevol / part, no es precis, com / alguns pensan que se / hage de prenda en / las Iglesias Franciscanas / y es probable q^e si ni ha al/guns qui no poden pren/ da la communio y poden / fer les demes diligencias / se los pot comutar la / cõ/muniò p el et Confesion / en altre obra piadosa / y axi guañar la indu[lzencia] / y lo mismo cõ aquellas / personas q^e por su poca / edad no comulgan to/davia. Ferraris xv jubi/leum, ant. 2." Fol. 3, bottom half. This long exposition of liturgy in some ways is in keeping with the religious tenor of the other entries, even those not made by Sancho. The top half of fol. 3v—done in the same hand as the scribal work on fol. 2—has a detailed attempt to calculate the age of the universe based on theological references in the Bible. "La sentencia de Ch^te ano de la Cre/acion del mundo cinco mil dos cientos / treynta y tres, fue intimada p pilatos. / Dia 25 de Março. Desde el Dia q^e / Fonch criat Adan, Fins â la Encar/nacio del Di[vi]ño verbo, passáren 5199 / y añadint los 9 Messos, que estigué en / el Ventre Virginal de Maria, y 33 q^e / visque, fan los sinch mil docents / trenta y 3, y los tres mesos &c. ut / Mistica ciudad de Dios 2 p^te lib. / 6 cap 21."

40. da Silva, *Mission Music of California*, esp. 23, 127–28.

41. The *Misa en sol* is presently found at the Cecil H. Green Library at Stanford University, filed under the author "Juan Sancho" and the citation "Mass in G (Mission Music), ca. 1795," M.0573 in Special Collections. Frustratingly, only the vocal parts are extant. No trace exists of the instrumental lines. The Green Library at Stanford has one other extant mission source mentioned by da Silva, although not in the context of the Sancho collection. It is the oversized and elegant choirbook brought to California by Father Junípero Serra, under the citation "Mission Music: Choirbook, 1770–1784," San Carlo Borromeo Basilica (Carmel, California), M.0612 in Special Collections. From here onward, I refer to this source as Serra choirbook

M.0612. Mention should be made of photographic copies (of poor quality) of both sources that are available at the music department of the University of California, Berkeley, as part of the collection made for the Work Projects Administration in 1937 and catalogued under the citation "WPA Folk Music Project. Items 45–87, Box 2 of 12. California Folk Music Project Records, ARCHIVES WPA CAL 1." From here onward, I refer to this collection with the abbreviation "WPA." The photos of California mission music are stored in box 2. WPA folder 65 contains photos of the Sancho *Misa en sol,* and WPA folder 47 contains photos of Serra choirbook M.0612. For consultation of these sources, prior notice should be sent to the Music Library, since it normally stores the WPA collection at the Northern Research Library Facility in Richmond.

42. See the previous note for a complete citation of the WPA Folk Music Project that took place as part of the WPA. Except for the two sources already cited (Sancho's *Misa en sol* and Serra's choirbook), the materials at Stanford described by da Silva have not been seen since he authored his book *Mission Music of California* in 1941. Bill Summers first discovered they were missing in 1977, and subsequent trips to Stanford by Summers, John Koegel, John Warren, and me have failed to resurrect the missing items. In 1990, however, Koegel discovered that there were photographic copies of these resources made as part of the WPA Folk Music Project operated by the WPA in the 1930s. He informed me of his exciting discovery in a letter dated 1 January 1991. Koegel also notified Bill Summers, who has summarized the history of these manuscripts and the details of Koegel's work and contributions. For a discussion of Koegel's discovery of these photos, consult the following articles by Summers: "Sancho: The Preeminent Musician," 27–28, 48–49, 70; "*Opera seria* in Spanish California," 270; "Orígenes hispanos," 43; "Recently Recovered Manuscript Sources," *Ars Musica Denver,* 14n9; "Recently Recovered Manuscript Sources of Sacred Polyphonic Music from Spanish California," *Revista de Musicología (RdM),* vol. 16, no. 5 (1993), 2844–46, esp. n13; "The Spanish Origins of California Mission Music,"*Transplanted European Music Cultures: Miscellanea Musicologica,* Adelaide, Australia: Sudies in Musicology, vol. 12, Papers from the Third International Symposium of the International Musicological Society, Adelaide, 23–30 September 1979, 116. Also, Summers provides an invaluable description and catalogue of the contents in this collection in the aforementioned works; he provides the cursory list as presented by da Silva and then immediately supplies a much more detailed breakdown of the individual works found in the various folders.

43. In 1937, Sidney Robertson wrote a letter explaining the WPA photography project and provided many pages of handwritten annotations relating to the photography sessions. For the complete text of Robertson's letter and a mapping out of the WPA contents in their entirety, consult the entry for folder 46 in the WPA, in appendix A online in conjunction with this book.

44. These works are found in the following folders in the WPA collection at Berkeley: *Missa de los Angeles* (WPA folder 69); "Gozos y antiphona San Joseph" (WPA folder 56); *Missa de Requiem a 3 voces* (WPA folder 72); and the "Ecos a duo" (WPA folder 50).

45. Once again, John Koegel discovered a huge stack of uncatalogued mission music, this time at the Archival Center of the Los Angeles Diocese at Mission San Fernando in 1991. He generously shared his discovery with William Summers and with me; we both have published studies on these manuscripts. For a thorough catalogue of the contents in this collection, consult Summers's "*Opera seria* in Spanish California," table 14.1, pp. 271–76. For a discussion of the works for choir and orchestra—which I have shown to be the work of Ignacio de Jerusalem and Francisco Javier García Fajer—consult my articles "Hidden Structures and Sonorous Symmetries: Ignacio de Jerusalem's Concerted Masses in 18th-Century Mexico," in *Res musicae: Essays in Honor of James Pruett* (New York: Harmonie Park Press, 2001), 135–59; "The Mexican Cathedral Music of Ignacio de Jerusalem: Lost Treasures, Royal Roads, and New Worlds," *Actas del XV Congreso de la Sociedad Internacional de Musicología* (Madrid, April 1992), published in the *Revista de Musicología,* vol. 16, no. 1 (1993), 99–134; "New Jewels in Old Boxes: Retrieving the Lost Musical Heritages of Colonial Mexico," *Ars Musica Denver,* vol. 5, no. 2 (Spring 1995), 13–38; and "Newly-Discovered Treasures from Colonial California: The Masses at the San Fernando Mission," *Inter-American Music Review,* vol. 13, no. 1 (Fall–Winter 1992), 5–10. I have established that the *Mass in F* at Mission San Fernando is actually Ignacio de Jerusalem's *Missa a 4 in F* (Legajo D.b.14 in the Mexico City Cathedral). I have encountered a concordant version

of the *Mass in D* at Mission San Fernando; it corresponds to García Fajer's *Missa del Españoleto* (Legajo D.c.9 in the Mexico City Cathedral). For a thorough treatment of García Fajer and his music, consult Juan José Carreras López, *La música en las catedrales durante el siglo XVIII, Francisco J. García «El Españoleto», 1730–1809* (Zaragoza: Diputación Provincial Institución «Fernando el Católico», 1981). In addition, there is a study and score of Jerusalem's *Polychoral Mass in G* that exists in an incomplete set of parts in the Santa Barbara Mission Archive-Library, by George A. Harshbarger, "The Mass in G by Ignacio de Jerusalem and Its Place in the California Mission Music Repertory," D.M.A. diss., University of Washington, 1985. This *Polychoral Mass in G* exists in at least two concordant versions: Legajo D.b.15 in Mexico City and Legajo 70 in the Puebla Cathedral.

46. See, for example, Documents 2, 5, and 24 at the Santa Barbara Mission Archive-Library.

47. Photo A-4 in WPA folder 65.

48. For instance, the "Credo à duo" in WPA folder 51 is written for a *baix* and a *tible,* the Catalán words for a bass voice and a soprano. In addition, the soprano part has on its first page the title and instruction "Tible, Credo à duo 5. tono, alternando con el Credo Regulat." In WPA folder 61, we find the terms "Primera *veu* lamentacio a duo" on sheet R-1, and "*Segona veu* Lamentacio a duo," on sheet R-3. WPA folder 73 is also probably of Catalán or Mallorcan origin, given its peculiar spelling of soprano as *tipble.*

49. William Summers suggests that this work is *by* Pou based on the title page, but I think this conclusion is yet to be finalized. The phrasing actually states that it is for Pou's *use* (but that does not necessarily equate with being composed by him). See Summers, "Recently Recovered Mission Manuscript Sources," handout for convention of the International Musicological Society, Madrid, 1992, p. 13.

50. See Gili, "Els Sanxo de Artà," 256, 287, and 304. On p. 256 he cites as his primary source "Necròlogie franciscà. MONTI-SION DE PALMA."

51. The burial record reads, "Dia 21 9bre de 1797 muri es torn del Morcat Jaume Ignaci Pou fill de Sebastia y de Marg^ta Farregut, de 6 mesos." The column by this entry has the identifying label "Pou / Jaume / Pigota / empeltado." The entry is found in the ARM, "Llibre de enterros de Albats comensant dia 14. Janer de lo añy 1783. Finit als 13 Juliot 1808," book C-1019, fol. 67.

52. The connection to Fray Jaume Ginard is made evident by the title page in this burial registry (book C-1019) that begins: "Llibre de enterros de Albats comenzant el dia 14. Janer de 1783 … y sacristá el R. P. Fr. Jaume Ginard Pred^r Jub^t y Ex-Guardia de los Convents de Artá y de Llummajor. Finit als 13 Juliol 1808."

53. Actually, the title of this mass does not appear in this folder, but since the vocal lines here in folder 64 match the continuo lines supplied in folder 70, we can determine the title from the latter. Folder 70 has the titled page that states: "Misa de 5to tono de 4 voces del P. Fr. Juan Bau^ta Sancho" (Mass in mode 5 for 4 voices by Father Friar Juan Bautista Sancho).

54. Juan Ramon Vich (fol. 7), Antoni Vich (fol. 7), and Bartomeu Vich (fol. 91), found in ARM, "Llibre de enteros de Albats," book C-1019.

55. Bonaventura Torres appears on fol. 79 of the burial registry, ARM, "Llibre de enteros de Albats," book C-1019.

56. Geiger, *Franciscan Missionaries,* 34–35.

57. Ibid., 224. Also briefly discussed in Richard E. Ahlborn, "The Mission San Antonio Prayer and Song Board," paper presented at the California Mission Studies Association Conference, Mission San Antonio de Padua, February 1993, published in *Southern California Quarterly,* vol. 74 (Spring 1992), reprinted as *The Mission San Antonio Prayer and Song Board* (Northridge, California: Padre Press, 1993), 13.

58. Bancroft states Sancho embarked from Cádiz on 20 June 1803, arriving at the Colegio de San Fernando in September; his lengthy footnote for Sancho's biography does not break itself down into individual statements and attributions, so it is very hard to discern his source of information. See Bancroft, *History of California,* vol. 2, p. 621, fn 17. Also see Engelhardt, *San Antonio,* 109.

59. Geiger provides a departure date from Cádiz as 20 June 1802 on the *San Miguel* or *Sagrada Familia* and an arrival in Vera Cruz, Mexico, in August. See Geiger, *Franciscan Missionaries,* 224. That Geiger knew the correct date of 1803 is clear from his description of the same voyage on pp. 34–35, so we can suppose the mistake on p. 224 is merely a typo, but one

that has lived on scholarly research. Using Geiger as their main source, Gili, Summers, and Ahlborn—and I as well—have repeated the incorrect departure year as being 1802. See Gili, "Evangelitzadors," 139; Summers, "Recently Recovered Mission Manuscript Sources," handout for IMS, 11; Summers, "Orígenes hispanos," 46n27; Summers, "Recently Recovered Manuscript Sources," *Ars Musica Denver,* 224n19; Ahlborn, "The Mission San Antonio Prayer and Song Board," 13; Craig H. Russell, handout for the invited lecture "Joan Sanxo: El genioso milagro musical en las misiones de California," Simposium de Documentalistas Musicales, 27–28 November 1999 (Artà, Mallorca); Russell, handout for "Joan Sanxo—Tracing the Origins of California's First Composer and the Early Mission Style," annual meeting of the College Music Society (Santa Fe, New Mexico, 16 November 2001).

60. Again, the authors mentioned in note 59 who had followed Geiger's typographical error (myself included) have developed their theories believing Sancho was in the metropolitan center of Mexico City for an extended period.

61. Geiger, *Franciscan Missionaries,* 224; Bancroft, *History of California,* vol. 2, p. 621n17. Nearly all subsequent authors have used the dates supplied by Geiger and Bancroft, with the exception of da Silva's volume, which provides the erroneous year of 1803 rather than 1804 for Sancho's arrival in California. Da Silva, *Mission Music of California,* 23.

62. Geiger, *Franciscan Missionaries,* 35.

63. Among the small party in attendance were Fathers Junípero Serra, Miguel Pieras, and Buenaventura Sitjar (who lived until 1808, so he was present at San Antonio while Sancho and Cabot were in their initial years there). Not all authors are in agreement as to the founding date. Most have correct details, such as Monsignor Francis Weber and Paul C. Johnson, who state it was established on 14 July 1771. See Francis J. Weber, *Readings in California Catholic History* (Los Angeles: Westernlore Press, 1967), 10; Paul C. Johnson, ed., *The California Missions: A Pictorial History,* historical and architectural consultant, Harry Downie, photography by Philip Spencer (Menlo Park, Calif.: Sunset, 1964), 101. Engelhardt claims it was founded a year earlier, stating that the first Mass in honor of Saint Anthony was celebrated on 14 July 1770. See Engelhardt, *San Antonio,* 3–4, 103ff. George Wharton James agrees with Weber, giving the founding year as 1771, but he states the day was 17 July as opposed to 14 July. See George Wharton James, *The Old Franciscan Missions of California,* new ed. (Boston: Little, Brown, 1925), 104–5.

64. The definitive studies of life at Mission San Antonio are those authored by Robert L. Hoover, whose Mission San Antonio Archeological Field School has met every summer since the mid-1970s. The handouts from those summer research findings provide copious detail of the construction projects, their nature, and when they were completed. For some of Hoover's important work, consult "California Mission Economic Development," handout for the Mission San Antonio Archeological Field School (San Luis Obispo, Calif.: author, 1982); "Message from the Director," no. 23 (August 1999), for the Mission San Antonio Archeological Field School (San Luis Obispo, Calif.: author, 1999); "Mission San Antonio de Padua Indian Barracks Chronology," handout for the Mission San Antonio Archeological Field School (San Luis Obispo, Calif.: author, 1976); "Mission San Antonio Research Design," handout for the Mission San Antonio Archeological Field School (San Luis Obispo, Calif.: author, post-1983); review of Robert H. Jackson and Edward Castillo, *Indians, Franciscans, and Spanish Colonization: The Impact of the Mission System on California Indian, Ethnohistory,* vol. 14, no. 2 (Spring 1996), 352–54; "Some Models for Spanish Colonial Archaeology in California," *Historical Archeology,* vol. 26, no. 1 (1992), 37–44; and "A Window on the Past: Mission San Antonio de Padua," *The Way of St. Francis,* vol. 7, no. 3 (May–June, 2001), 15–22. For a comprehensive study of Mission San Antonio, consult Engelhardt, *San Antonio.* Summers provides a brief but good summary of life at Mission San Antonio in his article "Recently Recovered Manuscript Sources," *RdM,* 2846. Da Silva and Bancroft assign much of the credit for San Antonio's prosperity to Sancho's efforts and guidance. See da Silva, *Mission Music of California,* 23; Bancroft, *History of California,* vol. 2, p. 621n17; Hubert Howe Bancroft, *The Works of Hubert Howe Bancroft,* vol. 34, *California Pastoral, 1769–1848* (San Francisco: San Francisco History Company, 1888), 203. Geiger offers the opinion that San Antonio was particularly lucky to have together the three Mallorcans Buenaventura Sitjar, Pedro Cabot, and Juan Bautista Sancho. See Geiger, *Franciscan Missionaries,* 224. There is also a readily accessible history of San Antonio Mission that contains

a useful chronology of construction projects and a general overview of the various friars at San Antonio and their lives. See Beatrice [Tid] Casey, *Padres and People of Old Mission San Antonio,* reprint in King City: Casey Newspapers in conjunction with Franciscans of San Antonio, 1976 of (King City: The Rustler-Herald, 1957).

65. Among other accomplishments during Sancho's and Cabot's years at San Antonio, Engelhardt (in *San Antonio*) lists the following construction projects: 1805, new houses of adobe and tile roofs for the Native American family dwellings, water ditch begun; 1806, water power mill, more adobe homes built; 1808, structure to store lumber, ditch for irrigation dug, tannery with four tanks, half of the garden enclosed; 1809, twenty-five new houses for the neophytes, water ditch that was begun in 1805 is now completed; 1810, thirty-one new houses built, horse power mill constructed for grinding wheat, foundation for new church is laid; 1811, adobe walls for new church are eight yards high, construction of community kitchen; 1812, church almost completed, new tannery, hut for seed storage in garden is finished; 1813 new church is finished, old church destroyed to build quarters for Cabot and Sancho; 1814, their quarters completed, granary built and a hennery; 1815, huge structure finished that contained shops such as a weaving room, carding and spinning room, shoe shop, smithy shop for iron implements, leather working, carpentry, and a stable; etc. Similar construction projects continue throughout Sancho's lifetime. See Engelhardt, *Mission San Antonio*, 3–29.

66. Every year each mission had to send in a report, giving its inventory of livestock and crops in storage. The accounting for the missions in 1824 is available in facsimile in Arthur Danning Spearman, S.J., *The Five Franciscan Churches of Mission Santa Clara, 1777–1825* (Palo Alto, Calif.: National Press, 1963), 52bis. The measuring unit of the *fanega* was equivalent to either 22.5 or 55.5 liters, depending on the locale. It is unclear which value should be applied in California during this period. See *Diccionario moderno español-inglés, English-Spanish Larousse,* ed. by Ramón García-Pelayo y Gross and Micheline Durand (Paris: Ediciones Larousse, 1979), 430; and also María Moliner, *Diccionario de uso del español*, vol. 1 (Madrid: Editorial Gredos, 1979), 1281.

67. Weber, *Readings*, 10. Weber then gives the sobering account of the missions' destruction, observing, "The downfall of the missions was swift and by 1843 the whole compound was a mass of ruins."

68. Ibid.

69. In 1805 there were 1,296 neophytes at the mission. By 1817 there was a slight drop to 985 residents. In 1830 the padres record 650. After secularization, the population continued to drop. In 1834, it sank to 567, and by 1839 the numbers plummeted to a paltry 270 registered inhabitants at the mission. See James, *The Old Franciscan Missions*, 106–7; Hoover, "A Window on the Past"; and Summers, "Recently Recovered Manuscript Sources," *Ars Musica Denver*, 14. The figures for 1817 are in the Bancroft Library, Ms. C-C-69, Mariano Payeras, "Noticias de las misiones," report to the Superiors of the Colegio de San Fernando de México of the Missions of California, H. H. Bancroft Collection 35073. For a discussion of Figueroa and the confiscation of Mission San Antonio during secularization, consult Engelhardt, *San Antonio*, 57–60.

70. Hoover, handout, "California Mission Economic Development." Hoover further delves into the engineering feats of the residents (with the construction of reservoirs and aqueducts) and the planting of orchards and crops so that San Antonio enjoyed a "constant food surplus" in his outstanding article "A Window on the Past," esp. 18–19.

71. This oft-repeated view of an idyllic Eden populated by lackadaisical inhabitants began back in the nineteenth century with writers such as Alexander Forbes, Captain Frederick William Beechey, and Hubert Howe Bancroft. Their views on early California and its culture reflect the attitudes of his era, complete with unflattering stereotypes and prejudices regarding Hispanic and Native Americans. For a discussion of these historical attitudes and the shadow cast on California scholarship, consult my introduction.

72. "Animado, el P. Sancho del espiritu bueno, y una sana intencion / en sus deliberaciones; trabajo mucho tanto en lo espiritual, como en lo temporal, y lo particular la constancia, con que este buen Religioso y / exemplo de Misioneros, sabia unir ambas ocupaciones; se le veia en / los trabajos de fabricas y campo aguantando los mayores calores, y ex-/tremados frios con todo sufrimiento, sin olvidar enfermos, como de-/bian curarse su[s] dolencias, administrandoles con toda puntualidad los / S^tos Sacramentos sin que los que estaban cerca caresiecen de pla-/ ticas

ex periciales [?] sin dejar de trabajar de manos, reprehendiendo vicios,/ y animado â todos a la virtud. El descanso que romaba [tomaba?] de dia quando / por mal tiempo no podia salir de casa era componer catecismos, ayu-/ dandole el suficiente conosimiento que poseya del idioma / des [*sic*] estos naturales; en cuia ocupacion muchas veces se le pasava la / hora de comer ô cenar. Si observaba, que yo le daba la mano, le parecia / que el nada haçia, porque no lo hacia solo todo: en recuerdo dice, que / 10 años antes de morir, tiempo en que Dios le alarga la vida, despues / de un[a] grave enfermedad, convaleciente aun y sin fuerza, viendo la que tan pronto volvia a su vida laboriosa, le dije: Padre, no es tiempo,/ deje eso, aguarde tener mas fueras: me respondio con su acostum-/brada sencillez ê innata naturalidad: Si tengo de comer, debo trabajar,/ prueba de que era enemigo declarado de toda ociosidad." *Difuntos que se asientan, en esta Mision de Sn Antonio de Padua de esta Nueva California,* manuscript book of burial records at San Antonio de Padua, available in facsimile at the Santa Barbara Mission Archive-Library, *Deaths. Mission San Antonio 1819–1872,* vol. 2, entry 3499 on fols. 49–50.

73. Geiger, *Franciscan Missionaries,* 224.

74. Ibid.

75. Bancroft, *California Pastoral,* 203. Whipping was an everyday aspect of eighteenth- and nineteenth-century life, both in the Americas and in Europe. Sancho's resorting to this act, although unacceptable by modern standards, was nevertheless a regular occurrence in the cultural context of the age. For a thorough discussion of corporal punishment in the missions and daily life in Europe and the Americas, consult Francis P. Guest, O.F.M., "Cultural Perspectives on California Mission Life," *Southern California Quarterly,* vol. 65, no. 1 (Spring 1983), 1–65; and Guest, "An Inquiry into the Role of Discipline in California Mission Life," *Southern California Quarterly,* vol. 71, no. 1 (Spring 1989), 1–68.

76. Bancroft Library, University of California, Berkeley, Ms. C-C73:17. Each page in this document measures 15.8 by 21.5 centimeters.

77. For a complete explanation of the last rites in both Latin and English, consult the Web sites "Extreme Unction," http://www.kensmen.com/catholic/unction.html; and Patrick Morissroe, "Communion of the Sick," trans. by Michael T. Barrett, *The Catholic Encyclopedia,* vol. R ([New York?]: Robert Appleton, 1908), online edition by K. Knight, 2003, http://www.newadvent.org/cathen/04174a.htm (both sites accessed 8 May 2004).

78. For information concerning the text and order of events in the last rites as prescribed in this document, consult Russell, "Fray Juan Bautista Sancho: Tracing the Origins," 100–101; and Russell, "Juan Bautista Sancho: Tracing the Origins of California's First Composer of the Early Mission Style" in Antoni Pizà et al, *J. B. Sancho: Compositor pioner de Califòrnia,* 108, 145, and 179.

79. The burial records at San Antonio de Padua are available in facsimile at the Santa Barbara Mission Archive-Library. *Deaths: Mission San Antonio 1819–1872,* vol. 2. For a more detailed discussion of Sancho's calligraphy and its essential defining features, consult Russell, "Fray Juan Bautista Sancho—Tracing the Origins," 101; and Russell, "Juan Bautista Sancho: Tracing the Origins of California's First Composer," 109, 145–46, and 180.

80. Consult Rose Marie Beebe and Robert M. Senkewicz, *Lands of Promise and Despair: Chronicles of Early California, 1535–1846* (Santa Clara, Calif.: Santa Clara University; Berkeley: Heydey Books, 2001), 313ff.; Angustias de la Guerra Ord, *Occurrences in Hispanic California,* trans. and ed. by Francis Price and William H. Ellison (Washington, D.C.: Academy of American Franciscan History, 1956), 9–10; and Auguste Duhaut-Cilly, *A Voyage to California, the Sandwich Islands and around the World in the Years 1826–1829,* trans. and ed. by August Frugé and Neal Harlow (Berkeley: University of California Press, 1997), 191–92nn8, 9.

81. Fr. Zephyrin Engelhardt, "Upper California," vol. 3 of *The Missions and Missionaries of California,* pt. 2, *General History* (San Francisco: James H. Barry, 1913), 244, 269–73; Engelhardt, *San Antonio,* 55.

82. Engelhardt, "Upper California," 270–72.

83. Ibid., 273–74.

84. This manuscript book is part of the collection discovered by Koegel in 1991 at the Archival Center of the Archdiocese of Los Angeles at the San Fernando Mission. William Summers has shown that the main work in this manuscript is an aria from the Metastasian libretto *Artaserse.* Summers catalogues this source as "As-3" in table 14.1, page 272, of his article "*Opera seria* in Spanish California: An Introduction to a Newly-Identified Manuscript Source,"

in *Music in Performance and Society: Essays in Honor of Roland Jackson,* ed. by Malcolm Cole and John Koegel (Warren, Mich.: Harmonie Park Press, 1997). From here on, I refer to this book as the *Artaserse Ms.*

85. "España de la guerra trémola su pendón / contra el poder ynfame del vil Napoleon. / Sus crímenes ohid, escuchad la traición, / si la traición con qᵉ â la Faz del mundo / se ha cubierto de horror! / ¡A la guerra, a la guerra, españoles! / Muera Napoleon, / y viva el Rey Fernando, la Patria y Reli[gi]ón." *Artaserse Ms.,* fol. 11v, staves 1–4.

86. "Quando Fernando se ausenta, España suspira, ay ay ay, ay ay ay / y entre cõgojas y ancias asi delira, ay ay ay / Infelice de mi ay si, cuando vendra por si, ay ay, ay ay ay ay." *Artaserse Ms.,* fol. 5v, lines 1–3.

87. This efficient notation system of writing duet textures on a single staff permeates nearly all of the choral books in California that use "squared" mensural notation where the note heads are squares and diamonds. Sancho's notated example of "Quando Fernando se ausenta" in the *Artaserse Ms.* has a slightly modified notational style where modern quarter notes and half notes are stacked up. This practice recurs as well, particularly with selections written down by Sancho in the *Artaserse Ms.,* including: "O que humilde escuchas te [*sic*] al paraninfo," fol. 1, line 2; "Grande fue la agonía," fol. 1, line 3; "Fratres, fratres sobrii es tote," fol. 4v, lines 1, 3, 5; "Domine ad adjuvandum," fol. 5, line 1; Doxology ending, "et in saecula seculorum, Amen," fol. 5, line 5; "Marcha Suiza," fol. 6v, lines 1–2; "En lo frondoso de un verde prado," fol. 7, lines 1–2; "Para vuestro Pueblo," fol. 8, lines 1–3; "¡O mi Dios! ¡O mi Dios! sin ausentáis," fol. 8v, lines 8–9; "Santo, santo, santo, Dios de los exercitos," fol. 9, lines 1–5; and "Ten mi bien, mi amor, misericordia," fol. 10v, lines 1–3. In addition, there are at least two instances of this same procedure in the hand of Sancho's compatriot and friend Pedro Cabot. One example in Cabot's hand is "Si milagros buscas," found in the *Artaserse Ms.* on fol. 6, lines 1–4. Another example of single-staff polyphony using quarter notes and half notes in Pedro Cabot's handwriting is found in "In caelesti Hierarchia," Santa Clara Ms. 1, fol. 1, lines 8–9. For a discussion of the different numbering systems used for identifying the four mission music sources at Santa Clara University, consult appendix A on the Oxford University Press Web site in conjunction with this book.

88. *Artaserse Ms.,* fol. 5v, lines 4–6. This work, "Si queris miracula," appears in a concordant version in WPA folder 76. It bears the title "Responsoriũ[m] D[on] Antonii Patronini constans ex 3 vocibus" (Responsory for Patron Saint Anthony, consisting of 3 voices) which clarifies its association with the Feast Day of Saint Anthony. The folder contains photos for four different performance parts: there are the three voice lines (soprano, alto, bass) plus a separate accompaniment line that resembles the vocal bass line once in a while but not always. Also, it should be observed that sometimes the soprano (*tiple*) line has two notes stacked above each other, over the same word, an unmistakable indication of *divisi* at those points where two vocal lines split. In truth, then, the folder is a kind of five-part setting with at least *two* sopranos (since there are glimpses of *divisi* passages), alto, bass, and accompaniment. A comparison of the chant melody from the *Artaserse Ms.* and the soprano line of the version in WPA folder 76 reveals that the tune was carefully preserved in the modern polyphonic setting but given a clearly metric rendition. Summers has suggested that "Si queris miracula," found in WPA folder 76, might have been composed by Sancho while he was at San Antonio Mission, observing that it would have been appropriate for the Feast Day of San Antonio de Padua, celebrated every year on 13 June. See Summers: "Recently Recovered Manuscript Sources," *Ars Musica Denver,* 22–23; "Recently Recovered Manuscript Sources," *RdM,* 2851; and "Sancho: The Preeminent Musician," 28, 49–50, 71. This is a possibility, but his case would be strengthened if this work were notated in Sancho's handwriting, and unfortunately neither the musical idiosyncrasies nor the text script matches Sancho's notational habits. I offer another possibility—that this polyphonic setting was brought by Sancho from the Franciscan Convent of San Antonio in Artà where he had done his youthful studies, or perhaps simply from the Convent de Sant Francesc in Palma (which surely would have honored Saint Anthony's feast day with special music and other celebrations). I think a Mallorcan provenance is more likely than a California one. For the complete text in both Latin and English, consult the Web site: "Si quaeris, Antyfona-Antiphone, Doî W. Antoniego Padewskiego—To St. Anthony of Padua," 11 May 2002, http://www.rosaryhour.net/Siqueaeris.html (accessed 9 May 2004).

89. *Artaserse Ms.*, fol. 12v, line 1 and last half of lines 4 and 5. "Viva Fernando, Napoleon muera, Triunfe España y cēse la guerra." This work is also a duet (in triple meter), but it is notated on two staves rather than one, both staves using bass clef. The upper melodic line is notated twice on the page, the first time in an unadorned fashion (line 1) and a second time with some added ornamentation in dotted rhythms (the last half of line 4). Both Koegel and Summers have previously dug into the political ramifications of this work and placed it in the context of Sancho's life. Also, Koegel supplies a transcription of the work. See Koegel, "Spanish Mission Music," 89–90; Summers, "*Opera seria* in Spanish California," 274.

90. The complete friars' responses to this questionnaire have been translated and published by Maynard Geiger, O.F.M., and Clement W. Meghan in *As the Padres Saw Them: California Indian Life and Customs as Reported by the Franciscan Missionaries 1813–1815*, Santa Barbara Bicentennial Historical Series, No. 1, series editor, Doyce B. Nunis Jr. (Santa Barbara, Calif.: Santa Barbara Mission Archive-Library, 1976). The original documents of the *Interrogatorio* are housed at the Archive of the Archdiocese of Monterey, presently under the guidance Father Carl Faría. He is starting to organize and update the filing system but as of yet has been unable to locate an old "call number" for these sources. Regrettably, I have been unable to consult the original texts, since their whereabouts have not been precisely indicated by the previous archivists. Fortunately, photocopies of many of these reports are presently housed at the Santa Barbara Mission Archive-Library: the folders with facsimiles of the reports generally include a typescript in English translation of the Spanish original (apparently made by Father Geiger). One can consult the reports from the following missions: La Purísima, San Antonio, San Carlos Borromeo (Carmel), San Fernando, San Gabriel, Santa Inés, San Juan Bautista, San Luis Obispo, San Miguel, Santa Barbara, and Santa Cruz. Several reports are missing in the folders of photocopies in the Santa Barbara Mission Archive-Library. Those missions without copied reports include San Buenaventura, San Diego, San Francisco, San José, San Juan Capistrano, San Luis Rey, Santa Clara, and Soledad.

91. Engelhardt, *Upper California*, 16.

92. "32 [*sic*; should be 33]. Tienen mucha inclinacion á la Musica, y tocan violines, violon, flautas, trompa, tambora, y otros instrumentos que la Mision les ha dado; de su Gentilidad conservan una flauta, la que se toca como la dulce, está toda abierta de arriba á bajo, tiene 5.. qt^{as} de largo, (otras tienen como 3.. qt^{as} no mas) forma 8. puntos con perfeccion, tocan varias tocatas casi todas de un mismo compás, las mas son alegres; tiene 11.. agujeros, otras mas, ó menos. Tienen otro instrumento de cuerda, que se reduce á un arco de palo, al que se la amarra un nervio de animal, y forma un punto; y no tienen mas instrumentos. Tienen muchas canciones para cantar en sus bayles, y fuera de ellos tambien; mas por no ser Musicos de profesion, no podemos mandar exemplar de ellas; pero si conocemos, que cantan por varios terminos, y tienen varios tonos; suben y bajan, ya segundas, ya terceras, ya quartas, ya quintas, ya octavas; y nunca cantan á voces, si solamente quando cantan muchos juntos, algunos van octava alta. Las canciones, las mas son alegres, tienen algunas de tristes en parte: en todas las dichas canciones, no forman proposicion alguna, solo usan palabras sueltas nombrado Aves, lugares de sus tierras, etc. y desde su gentilidad, siempre las han usado, ê igualmente los dos referidos instrumentos. Las letrillas en castilla las cantan por perfeccion, y aprenden con facilidad todo canto, que se les enseña, asi llano, como figurado; y desempeñan un coro, una Misa â voces, mas que sean papeles obligados; á todo esto les ayuda las [*sic*] voz clara, y el buen ohido que tienen todos, asi Hombres como Mugeres." Santa Barbara Mission Archive-Library, *Interrogatorio (Questionnaire)* or "Preguntas y Respuestas," 26 February 1814, Mission San Antonio, "Al R. P. Presid^{te} Fr. José Señan." Observe that in Mexican and Spanish documents of the eighteenth century there often are two slashes or two dots after numerals that are measurements. I have preserved them in the previously quoted passage. Several authors have translated the above-cited passage in their studies. The entire text of this document is reprinted along with an accompanying translation in the article by Maynard Geiger, O.F.M., "Documents: Reply of Mission San Antonio to the Questionnaire of the Spanish Government in 1812 Concerning the Native Culture of the Indians," *The Americas*, vol. 10, no. 2 (October 1953), 211–27. Owen da Silva also translates most (but not all) of this document and without supplying the original Spanish text in his *Mission Music of California*, p. 5. A translation that in many ways is closely related to da Silva's version appears in Engelhardt's *San Antonio*, 38–39. Unfortunately, the previous authors' lack of familiarity with

eighteenth- and nineteenth-century music terminology has caused some substantial errors that have crept into their work and conclusions.

93. For a full discussion of the size and instrumentation of the Classical orchestra, especially in the context of the Spanish style and that of Spain's colonies, consult chapter 1, esp. the section "The Mission Performance Styles in the Americas" and note 87. Also, see item C-4 in appendix C to this book, containing the document Archivo General de la Nación: Número de Registro 53860, Grupo Documental 8, Archivo de Hacienda, Número de Soporte, 283.

94. "San Antonio de Padua, 1842, 4 violines nuevos, 1 idem viejo, 1 idem grande llamad bajo, 1 tambor, 4 flautas, 1 idem nueva, 1 trompa, 1 clarin, 2 triangulos, 1 libro de coro ya viejo con 10 u 11 misas. Original inventories are in the SBMAL." Quotation from Summers, "The Spanish Origins of California Mission Music," 123n7.

95. John Koegel discovered these remarkable mass settings at the Archival Center of the Archdiocese of Los Angeles in the San Fernando Mission. William Summers and I are both of the opinion that these manuscripts at one time had been at Mission San Antonio in the personal effects of Juan Bautista Sancho. I discuss these works in chapter 7.

96. For extensive treatment of the Jerusalem masses in the California missions consult my articles "The American Baroque: Recovering the Lost Musical Treasures of the New World," in *Creative Journeys* (Eugene, Ore.: Oregon Bach Festival, 1996), 53–56; "Hidden Structures and Sonorous Symmetries," 135–59; "The Mexican Cathedral Music of Sumaya and Jerusalem: Lost Treasures, Royal Roads, and New Worlds," paper presented at the XV Congreso de la Sociedad Internacional de Musicología, Madrid, April 1992, published in the *Revista de Musicología*, vol. 16, no. 1 (1993), 99–134; "Newly-Discovered Treasures from Colonial California: The Masses at the San Fernando Mission," paper presented at the thirty-fifth annual meeting of the College Music Society, San Diego, California, 29 October–1 November 1992, revised version in *Inter-American Music Review*, vol. 13, no. 1 (Fall–Winter 1992), 5–10. I have edited and published the Kyrie and Gloria from Jerusalem's *Mass in* F at the San Fernando Mission plus another mass in that collection, the *Polychoral Mass in D*—that I attribute to Jerusalem—through my publishing house: Russell Eds., 541 Lilac Drive, Los Osos, CA 93402. Both full scores and piano-vocal reductions are available. The *Polychoral Mass in D* was recorded in spectacular fashion by Chanticleer on the compact disc *Mexican Baroque: Music From New Spain*, Chanticleer and Chanticleer Sinfonia, directed by Joe Jennings (Hamburg: Teldec, 1994), Teldec 4509-9333302. In addition, a study and score of Jerusalem's *Polychoral Mass in G* that exist in an incomplete set of parts in the Santa Barbara Mission was written by George A. Harshbarger, "The Mass in G by Ignacio de Jerusalem" (see note 45 of this chapter). This mass was recorded on *México Barroco*, vol. 1, "Ignacio Jerusalem y Stella & Francisco Delgado," Schola Cantorum and Conjunto de Cámara de la Ciudad de México, dir. by Benjamín Juárez Echenique (Mexico City: Urtext Digital Classics, 1994), Urtext, UMA 2001. Also consult Summers, "*Opera seria* in Spanish California."

97. The original passage is found in the Santa Barbara Mission Archive-Library, *Deaths: Mission San Antonio 1819–1872*, vol. 2, fols. 49v–50. "Estos 10, / ultimos años los vivio lleno de dolores, causados sin duda, de sus faenes / y tareas porque segun los facultativos, que en varios tiempos observa-/ren sus dolencias y achaques eran causados de la masa de la sangre / que; decian tenia quemada. Por fin a ultimos de Noviembre del proxi-/mo pasado poseido enteramente del mal, que fue una inflamacion / en un muslo qᵉ se le rebento en podre en la rodilla, y que de años antes/ se le estaba formando postema, con una fiebre constante se rendio â / tantos dolores los que toleró, con todo sufrimiento por mas de 2 me-/ses, en cuya intervalo se confeso varias veces, a mas del Sᵗᵒ Viatico / por precepto, se recibió el Divinisimo por devocion: y el Dia 7 de este / presente mes administré la Sᵗᵃ Vncion y el dia siguiente / como â las tres de la mañana con el mayor conocimiento, â pesar / de la calentura tan fuerte, llamo Dios para si a su A.ma [Alma], para / premiarle, como podemos pensar tantas tareas Apostolicas: / ptre[?] dichosa podemos juzgar su muerte, tanto por su pobreza, como por / el desprendimiento de las cosas del mundo; ardiente zela de la Religion / y aumento de la fé catholica, como lo acredito toda su vida en obras, / y palabras: y el dia 9, dia en que recibió el habito de N. S. P. S. Franᶜᵒ / y cumplia 39 años; y 57, 2 meses y 7 dias de edad; le a sepultura secular[?] / en el presbiterio de esta Yglesia al lado del evangelio, en el sepulcro / mas al centro, quedando los cuerpos de los finados RR. PP. Pujol, y Sitjar; / entre la pared y dicho P. Sancho. Y para que conste donde convencia, ô / pueda convenio; lo firmo en esta mision de Sn Antᵒ

de Padua en / 11 de Febrero de 1830. / Fr. Pedro Cabot." There is also a different translation by Engelhardt of this passage and the rest of the obituary in Engelhardt's *San Antonio*, 110–11.

98. Juan Bautista Sancho, "Mass in G (Mission Music), ca. 1795," Cecil H. Green Library, Stanford University, M.0573 in Special Collections. "Credo Artanense," folder 52 in the WPA collection. For a complete recording of the *Misa en sol*, consult the CD *Mission Road*, Chanticleer and Chanticleer Chamber Ensemble, directed by Joseph Jennings and with artistic consultant Craig H. Russell (Claremont, Calif.: Warner Classics and Jazz and the Rhino Entertainment Company, 2008). The performance edition is my reconstruction (with newly composed instrumental parts to replace the ones that have been lost); this edition is found as appendix D found online at the Oxford University Press Web site.

99. Louise K. Stein, *Songs of Mortals, Dialogues of the Gods: Music and Theatre in Seventeenth-Century Spain*, Oxford Monographs on Music (New York: Clarendon Press and Oxford University Press, 1993). It should be observed, however, that Stein emphasizes that rhythmic flexibility for a natural speech rhythm is part of the "divine" effect, and that particular aspect does not correspond closely to the mission style.

100. This "orphan material" on photo W-1 is scribbled onto an available staff at the bottom of the page that previously had been "blank" after the conclusion of the previous piece.

101. "Credo a duo 5° tono, alternando con el Credo regulat," photo c-2 in WPA folder 51.

102. With regard to *canto figurado* settings of the Credo, there are several folded into the Mass Ordinaries at the end of Francisco Marcos y Navas's *Arte, ó compendio general del canto-llano, figurado y organo, en método fácil* (Madrid: Joseph Doblado, 1716). Many extant copies of this publication are found in mission archives (consult chapter 1, esp. note 1). Given the friars' thorough familiarity with this publication, it is possible that one of Marcos y Navas's Credos was in fact the "regular Credo" that is referenced in the "Credo a duo," WPA folder 51. For an anthology of the most common plainchant settings of the Credo (semistandardized tunes that had been widely disseminated before the mission period), consult the *Liber Usualis, with an Introduction and Rubrics in English*, ed. by the Benedictines of Solesmes (Tournai, Belgium: Society of St. John the Evangelist and Desclée, 1947), 64–73 and 90–94.

103. Spaniards often used double bars to mark off blocks of music that could then be interchanged, replaced, rearranged, and so on. For a discussion of this practice, consult Craig H. Russell and Astrid K. T. Russell, "El arte de recomposición en la música española para la guitarra barroca," *Revista de Musicología*, vol. 5, no. 1 (1982), 5–23; and Craig H. Russell, "Santiago de Murcia: Spanish Theorist and Guitarist of the Early Eighteenth Century," 2 vols., Ph.D. Diss., University of North Carolina, 1981.

104. The bass voice part notates both the chant and the polyphonic passages in the Stanford copy of the *Misa en sol;* the "Credo Italiano, a duo con el coro (1796)," WPA folder 66; and the "Missa de Requiem, a 3 voces, 179," WPA folder 72. In these cases the "alternation" is between textures but not necessarily between different groups of performers who are in opposition antiphonally.

105. See note 41 of this chapter for complete citations of the *Misa en sol* and Serra choirbook M.0612. Fortunately, photographic copies of the other works previously at Stanford still exist as part of the WPA collection at the University of California, Berkeley. For a detailed history of the WPA photos, their creation by Carleton Sprague Smith and Sidney Robertson in 1937, and their rediscovery by Dr. John Koegel in the early 1990s, consult "Music Department, University of California, Berkeley, WPA Folders," in appendix A that is available online at the Oxford University Press Web site in conjunction with this publication. Bill Summers has frequently mentioned the depth of quality in the *Misa en sol* and is largely responsible for the awakened interest in this work—especially given the fact that it is glossed over as a mere citation in da Silva's *Mission Music of California* and therefore has escaped attention from the wider public. See Summers, "Recently Recovered Manuscript Sources," *RdM*, 2849.

106. The information concerning Harold C. Schmidt's reconstruction of the mass and his 1991 performance is found on the Stanford Library Web site, "Socrates," in the long display for Juan Bautista Sancho, "Mass in G (mission music), ca. 1795," M.0573. John Warren and the New World Baroque Orchestra are some of the most ardent and hardworking advocates for California mission music, performing regularly across the state. They have done much to further the public's knowledge of the "García Manuscript" (also known as the Eleanor

Hague manuscript) preserved at the Braun Research Library of the Southwest Museum. Another staple in their repertoire is Sancho's *Misa en sol,* which they play annually at Mission San Antonio and elsewhere. Their performance at the annual meeting of the California Missions Studies Association in San Luis Obispo on 13 February 2004 was a highlight of the conference. One can obtain access to Warren's transcribed score of Sancho's *Misa en sol* and a videotape of their 1999 performance at San Antonio Mission by consulting Cecil H. Green Research Library, Stanford University, Special Collections, M1100. The New World Baroque Orchestra can be reached at New World Baroque Orchestra, P.O. Box 2121, Paso Robles, CA 93447–2121.

107. For a discussion of Casanova's gift of manuscript materials to the Stanford Library and of the WPA materials, see my entries "Stanford University, M.0612, 'Serra Choirbook'" and "Music Department, University of California, Berkeley, WPA folders," as part of appendix A that is available online at the Oxford University Press Web site in conjunction with this book.

108. The title on the soprano page, sheet A-4, identifies the work as "Credo 5to tono â 4 voces, alternando con el Credo Artanense" (Credo in Mode 5, for 4 voices, alternating with the Credo from Artà). Similarly, the title on the bass page, sheet A-8, identifies the work as "Baja â 4 voces 5to tono, alternando con el Credo Artanense."

109. Richard E. Ahlborn discusses this prayerboard in "The Mission San Antonio Prayer and Song Board" (see note 57 of this chapter). He states that it came from Mission San Antonio to the Smithsonian via Alexander S. Taylor, who sold various mission artifacts to the museum in the early 1850s; the Smithsonian's 1860 report lists the prayerboard among its holdings.

110. Several sources have numerous pages in Cabot's hand. Consult the various tables of contents in appendix A available online at the Oxford University Press Web site in association with this book, especially the contents for the WPA collection at UC Berkeley; the *Artaserse Ms.* at the San Fernando Mission; and Santa Clara Ms. 3. In addition, I compare the writing idiosyncrasies of Cabot (and Florencio Ibáñez) in my article "Fray Juan Bautista Sancho: Tracing the Origins of California's First Composer and the Early Mission Style," *Boletín,* vol. 21, no. 2 (2004), 21–24; and also in "Juan Bautista Sancho: Tracing the Origins of California's First Composer," 121, 158, 191, and 233–38.

111. Ahlborn observes that Cabot was known for "his work as a scribe." See Ahlborn, "The Mission San Antonio Prayer and Song Board," 14. Mention must be made of the difference between Cabot's cursive script (which can be seen in the baptismal and burial registries from Mission San Fernando) and his printed script, which he uses for music manuscripts and the prayerboard in the Smithsonian.

112. It is on the *acompañamiento* or basso continuo line (found on photo Ab-1 in WPA folder 70) where Sancho states that the Credo is for four voices. Above the top staff he writes the title, "Misa de 5to tono â 4 voces del P./ Fr. Juan Bau[tis]ta Sancho." Also, there are problematic issues involving the number of actual voices required for the Kyrie in WPA folder 64. I will deal with the continuo line and the Kyrie setting later in this chapter.

113. Although the two top parts match in both settings, the second voice is labeled an alto in the Stanford copy.

114. Quotation taken from the Kyrie on sheet L-3, WPA folder 64. Summers discusses the possible attribution of this work to Vic Torres and was the first to point out a plausible connection between "Vic Torres" and the Convent de Sant Francesc in Palma. Consult his articles "Recently Recovered Manuscript Sources," *RdM,* 2850; and "Sancho: The Preeminent Musician," 29, 50–51, 72.

115. To avoid potential confusion, I should address the penciled description on the outside of folder 64 in the WPA collection that titles the work as a "Kyrie (a2)." This is a simple mistake where the cataloguer has jumped to the conclusion that each of the movements was a duet, since the settings of the Gloria and Credo occupy considerable space for the two vocalists. A careful reexamination of the manuscripts reveal, however, that only one soprano includes the Kyrie.

116. See note 54 for a discussion of these three individuals who share the same last name "Vich." See note 55 for a discussion of Bonaventura Torres. These are found on pp. 92–93 of the first part of my article "Fray Juan Bautista Sancho: Tracing the Origins of California's First Composer," which appeared in volume 21, no. 1 (2004) of the *Boletín.*

117. Folder 64 of the WPA collection has two different but interlocking Gloria settings. The odd-numbered verses ("Et in terra pax...," "Benedicimus te," etc.) are titled *Gloria 5to to[no]* and occur on pages L-4 (tiple 1ro) and L-7 (tiple 2do). The even-numbered verses ("Laudamus te," "Adoramus te," etc.) are titled *Gloria Esp[aci]o* and occur on pages L-3 (tiple 1ro). For the *Gloria Espacio*, there is no extant part for the second soprano (tiple 2do).

118. The even-numbered verses of the "Gloria Esp[aci]o" found on L-3 of folder 64 are concordant with the "Parisiense Gloria" on sheet I-3 of folder 63 (the relevant portions found at the very bottom of the page). For the version in folder 63, Sancho unfortunately ran out of space and had to leave off copying with the phrase "propter magnam gloriam...."

119. Several works in mission manuscripts refer to this title. A "Credo Parisiense à duo 6° tono" is found on plate 93, p. 74, of Mission San Juan Bautista, Ms. 1 (Mission Music, ascribed to Padre Estevan Tapís), 16" x 12," 112 parchment leaves, red and black notes. In addition, there is a "Credo Parisiense" on fols. 16v–18v of the Serra choirbook M.0612 at Stanford (For a complete citation, consult note 41.) Da Silva provides a complete transcription of Serra's "Credo Parisiense" and a facsimile of fol. 17v. Black-and-white photographic facsimiles of both manuscripts can be found in the WPA collection at Berkeley. San Juan Bautista Ms. 1 is identified as item 45, and Serra choirbook M.0612 is folder 47.

120. If one peruses the *Catálogo Musical de la Biblioteca Nacional de Madrid*, several patterns become clear. The preferred manner of ascribing authorship in Spanish publications is through the unambiguous terms *por* (by); *compuesto por* (composed by); *dadas a luz* (published or brought to light); or *su autor...* (its author...). However, the following authors have the preposition *de* instead of *por* in their publications: *Diapason Instructivo... Carta a sus discipulos de Don Antonio Rodríguez de Hita* (Madrid: Viuda de Juan Muñoz, 1557 [*sic*; should be 1757]); *Arte de Mvsica, theorica y practica, de Francisco de Montanos* (Valladolid: Diego Fernandez de Cordoua y Obiedo, 1592); and Tomás de Iriarte's *Colección de obras en verso y en prosa de D. Tomás de Iriarte* (Madrid: Benito Cano, 1787). French publications follow similar practices with their preference for *par* rather than *de*. Only the Italians seem to have employed the preposition *di, da, dell'* (of) with frequent regularity. In the Madrid *Catálogo Musical* a large number of Italians are listed who use *di* to designate authorship, such as Giovanni Maria Artusi, Filippo Bonani, Antonio Carbonchi, Giovanni Battista Doni, Fabio Colonna Linceo, Giovanni Battista Granata, Vincenzo Manfredini, Aurelio Marinati, Pietro Pontio Parmegiano, Vicenzo Riqueno, and Chioseffo Zarlino da Choggia. Spaniards who had their works published in Italy often followed the Italian convention of using *of* instead of *by*, as can be seen in the following: Diego Ortiz's treatise, *Il primo Libro de Diego Ortiz Tolletano, Nel qual si tratta delle Glose sopra le Cadenze* (Rome: Valerio and Luis Dorico, 1555); Stefano (Esteban de) Arteaga's *Le Rivoluzioni del Teatro Musicale Italiano dalla sua origine fino al presente. Opera di Stefano Arteaga Madridense* (Bologna: Carlo Trenti, 1785); and Tomás de Iriarte's *La Musica Poema di D. Tomasso Iriarte* (Venice: Antonio Curti Q. Giacomo, 1789). Interestingly, the Madrid and Mexico City printings of Iriarte's *La Musica Poema* use the preposition *por* instead of *de* that we see in the Italian release: *La Musica Poema por D. Tomás Yriarte* (Madrid: Imprenta Real de la Gazeta, 1779) and (Mexico City: Felipe de Zuñiga y Ontiveros, 1785). See Higinio Anglés and José Subirá, *Catálogo Musical de la Biblioteca Nacional de Madrid* (Barcelona: Consejo Superior de Investigaciones Científicas and Instituto Español de Musicología, 1946–51).

121. The Gloria's opening and final movements both have an empty measure at their outset, and the Gloria's "Gratias agimus tibi" delays two measures before the sopranos enter. The beginning of the Sanctus has five full bars of rest. The Agnus Dei, similarly, begins with two empty measures in the vocal parts.

122. Since Santa Barbara was the only mission with a functioning organ, the baroque guitar and harp would have been the standard chordal instruments used to fill in the harmonies of the *acompañamiento* or basso continuo line at the California missions. For more extensive information on guitar and harp continuo accompaniment, consult note 82 in chapter 1.

123. If one examines the catalogues for archives in Spain and Latin America, one comes across many works for two sopranos plus chamber accompaniment. Some of the works that stylistically resemble the *Misa en sol* would include Joseph Pérez's "At ti mi Jesús amado" (1763) for two sopranos, two violins, flute, and basso continuo. Pérez was second organist in

Orihuela, Spain. A manuscript copy of the work is preserved at the Conservatorio de las Rosas in Morelia, Mexico, and a recording will soon be released by the early music ensemble Ramo de Flores. Pérez's melody is nearly identical to the "Qui tollis peccata mundi" in the Gloria to Joseph de Nebra's *Polychoral Mass in G* (a copy of which is found in the Mexico City Cathedral Archive under the call number E9.2 / C2 / LEG C.c.32 / AM0652.). Modern edition available: Jaime González Quiñones, *Villancicos y canatas mexicanos del siglo XVIII*, Monumentos de la Música Mexicana, series 1, nos. 3–9 (Mexico City: Escuela Nacional de Música, 1990), 92–108. Another duet at the *conservatorio* is "Jesús mi dulce amor" (1767) for two sopranos, two violins and continuo. Ignacio de Jerusalem's Responsory No. 7 (with the text "Felix namque") from his *Maitines para la Virgen de Guadalupe* is also a duet for two sopranos plus chamber orchestra; its early Classical features are cut from the same cloth as Sancho's *Misa en sol*. These three aforementioned works are available in performing editions through Russell Editions (www.russelleditions.com). One of the most gorgeous works of the eighteenth century is José de Nebra's *Miserere* that is now preserved in Zaragoza Cathedral. It features two sopranos, alternating concerted movements with plainchant settings. There is a spectacular recording by Al Ayre Español under the direction of Eduardo López Banzo: *José de Nebra, Miserere and excerpts from "Iphegenia en Tracia,"* BMG and Deutsche Harmonia Mundi, 2001, CD 05472-77532-2.

124. Actually, folder 70 contains the continuo for two movements (the Gloria and the Credo) from the mass in folder 64, the "Misa de 5to tono." Only the Credo corresponds to the music of the *Misa en sol*; the Gloria from folder 64 is a completely different setting than the one in the *Misa en sol*. Sheet Ab-2 of folder 70 has the heading: "Acop^{to} de la gloria 5to tono. â 4. voces. y el Credo tambiẽ â 4. voces." There is a rare copying error in measure 1 of the Gloria, where the entire passage is written a third too low; the error is rectified by measure 2.

125. At the Archival Center for the Archdiocese of Los Angeles, the continuo line is missing from García Fajer's *Mass in D,* Jerusalem's *Mass in F,* and the "anonymous" *Polychoral Mass in D* (that I attribute to Jerusalem on stylistic grounds). Additionally, the Violin I part is absent from Jerusalem's *Mass in F*; the Violin II part, however, is still extant. The chuckholes afflicting the extant parts of Jerusalem's *Polychoral Mass in G* at Santa Barbara are even more severe; only four vocal parts are still in their possession. See note 86 of chapter 7.

126. For a thorough discussion of de Gante and his pedagogical role in sixteenth-century Mexico, see Samuel Y. Edgerton, *Theaters of Conversion: Religious Architecture and Indian Artisans in Colonial Mexico*, photographs by Jorge Pérez Lara (Albuquerque: University of New Mexico Press, 2001), esp. 38–39, 111–19; Robert M. Stevenson, *Music in Mexico: A Historical Survey* (New York: Crowell, 1952), 19, 34–35, 52–58, 62, 83, 264; and da Silva, *Mission Music of California*, 3–4.

127. In the preface to his choirbook C-C-59, Durán makes it clear that he is "practical" in his approach and is not professionally trained; nowhere does he imply he composed. Father Owen da Silva argues that the most probable composer of the *Misa Viscaína* and the *Misa de Cataluña* was Narciso Durán, but the evidence is shaky or problematic. See chapter 6, esp. the section "Narciso Durán as Compiler (Not Composer)" for a discussion of Durán's putative authorship of the central California mission repertoire.

Summers has called into question da Silva's view. Drawing upon the recent research of Jon Bagüés Erriondo, Summers presents the finding that the *Misa Viscaína* is actually by Martín de Crucelaeguí. See Summers, "The *Misa Viscaína*," 134; Jon Bagüés Erriondo, *La música en la Real Socieda [sic] Bascongada de los Amigos del Pais* (Donastia–San Sebastián: Izarberri, 1990), vol. 1, pp. 88–92.

128. For Ibáñez's music pedigree, see note 36 of this chapter.

129. For example, Mallorca's native sons were highly sought after at the most prestigious institutions of the time, such as the Royal Chapel in Madrid. For information concerning the Mallorcan-born masters Francisco Gueráu, Gabriel Gueráu, and Antonio Literes, see note 17 of this chapter.

130. For the examples of musical pieces in Cabot's handwriting, consult notes 87 and 110. Also consult appendix A (for it lists those works that are written out in his hand) and appendix B (that contains actual facsimiles). Both appendices are available online at the Oxford University Press Web site in conjunction with this book.

131. The phrase "Quoniam tu solus sanctus, tu solus altissimus, Jesu Christe" is found in the *Artaserse Ms.* in the San Fernando Mission on fol. 14, line 8. It is a direct quotation from the *Misa de San Antonio* in the Durán choirbook, identified as "Choir book in Gregorian form: ms., 1813 / by Fr. Narciso Durán for use of the neophytes of Mission San Jose," choirbook C-C-59 at the Bancroft Library at UC Berkeley, p. 51, line 12. This is concordant with the same line as written down in the *Missa Solemne 6 t°* in Santa Clara Ms. 4 (which is Manuscript No. 1 in both the Hoskins and Spearman books). The phrase in question is found on p. 52, lines 8–9.

CHAPTER 6

Music for the Mass

A Spectrum of Artistic Invention

OF ALL THE genres, the mass holds the privileged role as the artistic and spiritual core of the California repertoire.[1] The number of pages devoted to mass settings constitutes three or four more times the amount of all the other genres added together, and the breadth of stylistic variety is breathtaking. Some of them are simple and repetitive, the perfect vehicle for beginners thrust into a newly introduced culture; others are virtuosic, elegiac, and sublime—representing some of the most worthy artistic achievements from our American past. Some meander in timeless fluidity; others push forward in rhythmic excitement and infectious glee. They explored in depth and incorporated all the textures of the mission style: plainchant or *canto llano;* polyphonic vocal arrangements or *canto de órgano* (also called *música a voces*); single-line vocal melodies in a steady meter with strummed chordal accompaniment or *canto figurado;* and the concerted modern style, or *estilo moderno,* that interweaves fully independent instrumental threads with voices into sonorities that sound almost Mozartean.

In addition to the panorama of contrasting textures, several other aspects of the mission masses merit further consideration (and will be dealt with in this chapter). A careful comparison of the melodies in disparate sources across California proves that there was a standardized repertoire of mass settings that was spread from mission to mission, regardless of the musical expertise or inexperience of any individual padre at any specific location.[2] The normative core contains such stalwarts as the introspective *Misa del quarto tono* and its ultrapopular "Gloria simple"; the hypnotic *Misa del quinto tono* (also known as the *Misa de Cataluña*), with its pulsations of homorhythmic chord changes; the two-voice *Misa de la Soledad* with its conspicuous thematic unity; and the erudite and sophisticated *Misa Solemne.*

It is not just the core repertoire that proves to be fascinating, but also the *way* it was written down. The order of items can be meaningful: at times, the location of a Mass Ordinary in a choirbook can imply a functional association with a particular day or occasion. The layout in some manuscripts also proves to be well conceived and organized—often with groupings of Ordinary settings into "threes." In each of his choirbooks, Narciso Durán parcels out three rudimentary Ordinaries for four voices and always glues the same three together as an inseparable trio. Similarly, three duet settings of the Ordinary crop up in Durán's choirbooks; they line up in the queue in the same order.

The themes that have permeated our discussion in previous chapters maintain their importance here as well in the context of Mass settings: word painting enhances the passions and subtleties of the Mass's text; *alternatim* performance provides a seemingly infinite opportunity for reinvigorating the missions' musical environment with ever-changing permutations and new combinations; and instruments supported the vocal soloists and ensembles in nearly all the settings that will be discussed. A "choirbook" contains vocal information, not surprisingly, but it would be horribly mistaken to imagine this repertoire as a cappella driven simply because the instrumental parts are not written into a vocal manuscript. Like two lifelong friends who can complete each other's sentences, so it was between the instruments and voices of the mission churches. The task at hand, then, is to track down "orphaned" instrumental parts in lonely folders and restore them to their vocal families, or—in the worst case—try to build a usable instrumental framework for these masses that would be in the spirit and cultural expectations of the mission style.

Standardized Repertoire

The flow of plainchant in the mass consisted of several different streams of material. The first of these, Gregorian chant (or the "Roman rite"), provides much of the music, but it was not the only current. Another channel flowed from Toledo, inspired by the attempted revision of "Mozarabic" or "Old Hispanic" chant that was initiated by Cardinal Cisneros in the early 1500s. As I suggested earlier in chapter 1, some of the repertoire may have been from a Franciscan tradition, issuing forth from the motherhouse of the Apostolic College of San Fernando in Mexico City. Yet another source of chant in the California mission books had its headwaters in the desire to simplify the liturgy. Instead of drawing upon the enormous sea of melodic invention in the Roman rite, several friars diverted a few of those tunes and used them to create a small pool of reusable melodies.[3] One of the friars to establish a simplified and reduced melodic core for singing Mass was Narciso Durán. He diverted a small rivulet of three or four tunes, and from this trickle he could navigate through the entire liturgical year.[4]

Narciso Durán as Compiler (Not Composer)

Before continuing further with a discussion of the mass settings in California, we need to address the messy issue of "authorship" as formulated by Father Owen

da Silva. His contribution, *Mission Music of California,* has served as the foundation and initial inspiration for nearly every subsequent scholar and enthusiast of
mission music (including me!). Overall, da Silva is on the mark, and the value of
his publication cannot be overstated. Unfortunately, though, the few blemishes in
da Silva's study have been repeated over and over, generally unchallenged, taking
on a life of near-biblical truth through the process of echoing repetition.[5] (One
dramatic exception to the follow-the-leader approach has been William John
Summers, who has made numerous corrections and set us straight on many occasions.)[6] One flaw that has entered the scholarly literature as "truth" is da Silva's
assertion that Father Narciso Durán composed the *Misa de Cataluña, Misa Viscaína, Misa de Requiem,* and a sizable proportion of the California mission repertoire. Since a house of cards has been built upon his claim, it is high time that we
examine the assertion and question the evidence, point by point, that he offers to
support it. Da Silva makes his case:

> For the present there is good reason to hold that the *Misa de Cataluña,* the
> *Misa Viscaína,* and possibly other masses and some of the Mission hymns,
> are the work of Padre Narciso Durán. In fact, the present collection of Mis-
> sion music was made under this hypothesis. . . .
>   The works themselves point to a man such as Father Durán; a practical
> man gifted with musical talent, and especially a sense of melody, but one
> who was unacquainted with the laws of conventional harmony. This would
> explain the unusual leading of voices, the occasional consecutive octaves
> and fifths, and the abrupt modulation in the hymns.[7]

Taking his first criterion, "a practical man gifted with musical talent," we
could include at least twenty other friars (and maybe even fifty) in that pool of
candidates—but that does not even address the wider possibility that the works
might be written elsewhere. If we include all the musicians who possessed a "sense
of melody" and were active in the Spanish Empire over a few centuries, the pool of
candidates becomes an ocean. In truth, the first "clue" does little to narrow things
down. Nothing yet points directly toward Durán. Da Silva's next point, regarding unorthodox voice leading, is a bit perilous. If we were to search for someone
"unacquainted with the laws of conventional harmony," we would have to include
most of the population. Again, things do not really point in any specific direction
toward an identifiable individual. Of course, if we actually had one or two pieces
signed by Durán or confirmed to be his creations, we could make a comparison
and perhaps ascertain some of his individualized compositional tendencies. Since
we have not even a single signed work by Durán, however, we are left grasping at
sweeping generalities.

Da Silva continues with his case, stating that "there is the local tradition which
ascribes these works, in particular the *Cataluña,* to Father Durán." This clue, unlike
the previous ones, has specificity: it does point in the direction of Durán. However,
a healthy dose of caution is justified. Statements that are passed down through the
oral tradition can take on all sorts of embellishments and added details. Again, it

would help if Durán or the other friars (or the visitors and travelers, for that matter) ever mentioned his compositional interests. We are left instead largely with hearsay from individuals who were alive long after the writing down of the mission choirbooks and manuscripts.

Da Silva's strongest point concerns a letter dated 15 April 1858, written to Father Gonzales Rubio of the Santa Barbara Mission by Rev. Edmondo Venisse. Writing from Copiapó, Chile, Rev. Venisse inquires:

> Well, now, what I would like to know is whether Father Narciso Durán is the author of these masses (*de Cataluña,* the *Biscaína,* the Requiem Mass, and another that has no name and which Father José gave me in San Gabriel). If he is the author of the masses, he must also be the author of the songs, for the musical style is the same, and what is more, many of the songs are nowhere found printed (except the words). In California I asked various Spaniards if they knew them, or if they had heard them in Spain; all responded negatively, and Very Rev. Bishop Amat, who asked me for a copy of them all, told me that they were composed in California by the missionaries themselves. Father Sebastian, once *cura* in Los Angeles, and now *soto cura* in Copiapó, tells me that they are the work of Father Narciso Durán, who has a nephew in Santiago.[8]

Venisse's words supply very little concrete information and are more inquisitive than they are clarifying—the *asking about authorship* is not really the same thing as *confirming it.* Nearly every other comment is problematic or erroneous. First, Venisse is correct that the masses and songs in the California repertoire share some general stylistic similarities, but there is enormous variety as well (as we have already discussed). The repertoire as a whole is too broad and varied to be the handiwork of a single person. Even if we group together the selections that *do* share stylistic features with the *Misa de Cataluña* and *Misa Viscaína,* there is nothing that distinguishes Durán as that privileged artist.

An implied argument supporting Da Silva's thesis concerns geography: Narciso Durán was born in Castellón de Ampurias, diocese of Gerona, Cataluña, in 1776, and it would be logical for a native son to honor his homeland with a mass named *Misa de Cataluña.* But it would helpful if Durán actually *called* it the "Misa de Cataluña." He does not. Instead, the three choirbooks in Durán's hand call this work the "Misa de 5° tono a 4 voces" (Mass in Mode 5 for 4 Voices).[9]

Nevertheless, Durán *is* affiliated with Cataluña, and one can connect a thread between the *Misa de Cataluña* and Durán's place of birth. But what of the *Misa Viscaína?* If we were to use geographic location as the main link connecting the Catalonian Narciso Durán to the *Misa de Cataluña,* we should probably do the same to link a friar from the Bay of Biscay to the *Misa Viscaína*—and there are several candidates. In fact, it is exactly this point that Ignacio Omaechevarría, Jon Bagüés Erriondo, and Bill Summers bring forward in their scholarship that questions Durán's authorship of the *Misa Viscaína* and instead attribute it to the Basque friar Padre Martín de Cruzelaegui.[10]

The last fallacious element of Venisse's statement and da Silva's argument concerns the proof of authorship. Bill Summers and Grayson Wagstaff have stated (and restated) that the Requiem in Durán's choirbooks (and one of the three pieces mentioned by Venisse and da Silva by name as being Durán compositions) is actually a four-voice reworking of the three-voice Requiem in Juan Bautista Sancho's hand, signed and dated by him in 1796, when Sancho was still at the Convent de Sant Francesc in Mallorca (years before his departure for the New World).[11] Clearly, this work is *not* by Narciso Durán while living in the California hinterland. As we have just seen, the attribution of the *Misa Viscaína* to Durán is problematic, at best. And the third work mentioned, the *Misa de Cataluña,* also is an unlikely candidate, for the following reason. The opening statement of the "Kyrie eleison" from Sancho's *Misa de los Angeles*—dated 1796—is identical to the music for the "Christe" section in the *Misa de Cataluña.*[12] Therefore, a central core to the *Misa de Cataluña* (as with the Requiem) was resounding in Mallorcà in the 1790s, decades before Durán was writing out the same musical material in his choirbooks in California.

In short, the three pieces mentioned by name as "Durán compositions" in the writings of Edmondo Venisse and Owen da Silva are more directly associated with other individuals (Sancho certainly, and perhaps Cruzelaegui). Durán neither signs any works as original compositions nor mentions an interest in composing—even though the introduction to his choirbook C-C-59 is exhaustive in scope. In this context, it seems a far stretch to laud Durán as a major composer of the corpus of California mission music.

That being said, it would be a huge mistake to underestimate Durán's contributions to the musical environment in which he lived. No friar left more extensive and revealing writings about music performance and music education in the missions than Durán. His three choirbooks—although they do not contain original compositions—nevertheless constitute the richest and most invaluable anthologies of music from the mission period. Travelers' accounts of Durán's orchestra and choir are plentiful and show that he was triumphant as a music educator and choir director.[13] Removing one gem (that of "composer") from his musical crown does not diminish its beauty or luster.

Mass Ordinaries for Specific Occasions

Three "Easy" Quartet Settings for Mary

In our previous discussion of standardized repertoire, we saw three main stylistic streams that flowed through the California missions. Most of those crosscurrents and forks explained earlier are seen in settings of the Proper. On any given day, it was during the Proper of the Mass (as opposed to the Ordinary) where *Californians* partook in the singing of plainchant. The matching up of a musical piece with its respective day is an indelible, obligatory part of the Proper: the Introit, Alleluia,

Offertory, and Communion are permanently glued to their attendant days in the church calendar, and each text is wed to its context, referring to the day's unique theme.[14] An Offertory for the Feast of Saint Claire would not pop up haphazardly on Saint Joe's day. How bizarrely unsettling it would be to sing "The Old Rugged Cross" on Christmas morning, or "I'm Dreaming of a White Christmas" on the Fourth of July, or "Away in a Manger" on Easter Sunday! The song should match the occasion. In exactly the same way, a setting of the Mass Proper has to match its context. If one turns the pages of California choirbooks that contain Mass Propers, he or she will traipse through the year chronologically, matching up the same services as they would pop up in sequence on the calendar.

Whereas the Proper was generally set afloat in meterless *canto llano*, the Ordinary brought into the mission a torrent of other sonorities—the mellifluous harmonies of *canto de órgano*, luxuriant orchestral accompaniments of *estilo moderno*, and surging cascades of harmonies in *canto figurado*.[15] The Ordinary's relationship to events in the calendar year presents a less obvious situation than the Proper's. The unvarying and rather generic texts of the Kyrie, Gloria, Credo, Sanctus, and Agnus Dei make them flexible and reusable on any day of the year, since the immutable lyrics do not refer to any "special" biblical reading or sermon. The Mass Ordinary is rather like a pair of tube socks in a sporting goods store that prominently advertises, "one size fits all."

Although the lyrics to the Ordinary have nothing affixing them to a certain feast day, it can be surmised that several specific *musical* settings of it were attached to particular occasions, as can be gathered by several clues: annotations in their titles; the names of neighboring works in close proximity; the physical layout of choirbooks and other manuscripts; and the verbal descriptions of the mass and feast days by the mission padres.

Rather than have all the Ordinaries huddled together in one place, some choirbooks intersperse them between Proper settings for specific days or religious seasons. This placement in the choirbooks may not be random: it might indicate a linkage between the Ordinary's music and the dates or seasons implied by the Proper on the adjacent pages.[16] Furthermore, several choirbooks bond together Mass Ordinaries into groupings of three. Narciso Durán puts forth a threesome of simple-sounding Mass Ordinaries for four voices: the *Misa Sabbatina*, the *Misa del sexto tono*, and the *Misa Ligera*.[17] Each mass of the triptych moves along in facile, easy rhythms. Each of the three is forged from a unifying phrase or formula that pervades all the movements. The texts are complete, running straight through from start to finish—without the inevitable potholes that arise in *alternatim* performance.[18] Instead of bantering between two contrasting textures, as is more often the case in California performance practice, these three Ordinaries set a consistent texture that plows ahead, undaunted, with no whiff of flip-flopping sonorities.

Another similarity binds these three "easy masses" together—an association with the Blessed Virgin Mary. Durán labels the first of them as "Misa Sabbatina ō de la Virgen 1ʳ Tono" (Mass for Saturdays or for the Virgin, in Mode 1). This appellation makes perfect sense given our snapshots of mission life, for characteristically,

Mary was the central devotional focus every Saturday.[19] Palóu recounts how Father Serra and his Indian converts took "a stunning statue of the most tender Lady, placed on her platform, [and] paraded her through the town every Saturday evening, illuminated by lanterns while singing the Rosary."[20] The linkage of this Mass to Mary is reinforced by the canon that follows on the heels of the Agnus Dei. Titled "Canon a la Virgen 1° T°," with the opening lyrics, "Virgen divina, virgen sagrada," its voices go round and round in a three-phrase loop, eventually running through six stanzas of text that exuberantly extol Mary's virtues. After the canon, Durán returns to settings of the Mass Ordinary with the *Misa del quarto tono*. Obviously, the canon is the odd man out. It makes no sense as an "orphan" and gains significance only when we see this Marian canon as *part* of the *Misa Sabbatina,* the mass that the *californios* associated specifically with the Blessed Virgin. (See figures 6-1 through 6-3. For a facsimile of the "Canon a la Virgen, consult photo B-14 in appendix B online.)

Not only does their physical location in choirbook C-C-59 imply that this Ordinary and the canon are tied together, but there are musical features as well that tie the knot. Nominally, the *Misa Sabbatina* is cast in mode 1, but from the get-go one is struck by its ambivalent major-minor duality. In fact, we have barely set out before the introspective "minor" feel of mode 1 is obliterated. After a mere one-and-a-half measures, an F sharp flips the harmony from minor to major. Just like a pancake poured on a griddle, the phrase is cooked on one side and flipped over to cook equally on its other side. Likewise, D minor and D major share an equal number of pulses (six each) before moving through a string of V-to-I progressions that reach a rather sunny half cadence on F major. We expectantly await our return to the more solemn D-minor home chord, but instead land smack dab on D major to tie things off.

This wobbly vacillation between minor and major—between earnest solemnity and more hopeful geniality—also characterizes the canon for the Virgin Mary associated with this Mass. The title for "Virgen Divina, Virgen Sagrada" advertises it to be in mode 1, but the opening D-minor harmony is immediately converted into D major by the same eager F sharp that had jumped into the *Misa Sabbatina*'s phrases. Moreover, the conflicted duality of our minor-major pancake also applies to the canon; the harmonic underpinning oscillates, spending exactly half of its time in D minor and the other half in D major. Furthermore, the joyous ending of the canon's phrases matches the joyous endings of those from the *Misa Sabbatina*. In short, this Mass for the Virgin and its companion canon are matched up perfectly, not only by their liturgical context but by musical features as well.[21]

The quartet settings of the Ordinary continue with two more in this triptych— the *Misa del sexto tono* and *Misa Ligera*. Many of the same features arise here as with the previous *Misa Sabbatina*. The *Misa Ligera* marches its way through all of the movements with cloned phrases made from the selfsame clay. Only once does it whittle down its texture (at the "Qui tollis" in the Gloria). A core set of phrases is utilized in the *Misa del sexto tono* to build four of the five movements (the odd man out is the Credo). In fact, three main building blocks are recycled—one at the beginning, one in the middle, and one at the end—and when they reappear in a new movement, they preserve their respective locations. Beginnings remain as beginnings, the middle core stays put in the midsection, and the identical ending closes each movement.[22] New material and connective elaborations can be tucked in between these three fundamental components. For the threesome of quartet masses the texts run from start to finish without interruption. Unlike the *Misa Sabbatina* and *Misa Ligera*, with their consistent full-bodied texture,

Figure 6-1 "Canon a la Virgen"

1. Virgen Divina, Virgen Sagrada,
   Virgen hermosa, Virgen suave.
   Vos sois el amparo que siempre buscamos
   Y nuestras ansias son siempre encontraros.

2. Pues soys tan buena, pues soys tan Santa,
   pues soys tan linda, pues soys tan blanda.
   De vos esperamos muerte suave,
   Y despues della por siempra gozaros.

3. Vuestra dulzura, vuestra fragrancia,
   vuestra ternura, vuestra abundancia.
   Todo nos promete que nuestra demanda
   Será oida por pura gracia.

4. La Santa Iglesia, de Dios os llama,
   de pecadores, piadosa Madre.
   Pues llenad de gracias ó buena Madre,
   A quien os llama con confianza.

5. La misma Iglesia, con voz suave,
   por llena de gracia, gustoza os clama.
   Pues con gran deseo y consonancia,
   Os invocamos los desterrados.

6. Pues Virgen Santa, Hija del Padre,
   Madre del Hijo, Paloma Santa.
   Pues a ti suspiramos con grandes ansias
   En esta valle, gimiendo y llorando.

Divine Virgin, Holy virgin,
Beautiful Virgin, tender Virgin,
You are the help that we are always seeking,
And we are always yearning to find you.

You are so good, you are so Holy,
You are so beautiful, you are so gentle.
From you we can hope for a peaceful death,
And after that to please you forever.

Your sweetness, your fragrance,
Your tenderness, your bounty,
All promise that our request
Will be heard through your pure grace.

Sinners of the Holy Church of God
Call upon you, compassionate Mother.
Fill with grace, O good Mother,
Those who call upon you in faith.

The same Church, with a quiet voice,
Filled with grace, calls you with pleasure,
Because with great yearning and harmony,
We exiles invoke you.

Holy Virgin, Daughter of the Father,
Mother of the Son, Sacred Dove.
We sigh for you with great longing,
Crying and wailing in this valley.

Figure 6-1 (*continued*)

the *Misa del sexto tono* offers *alternatim* phrases for the Kyrie, Gloria, and Credo. Often in California manuscripts, one finds half the phrases for a piece in one place and the opposing phrases in another; it is the performer's job to interweave the phrases from two locations into one body, much like folding together your hands by interlocking five fingers from your right hand with five on your left. This setting is slightly different in that respect, conveniently providing one-stop shopping for the four-voice phrases and the contrasting *canto figurado* lines that are interpolated between them.

A final unifying feature interjoins these three masses—adoration of Mary. In the Durán choirbook C-C-59, we find Marian songs appended after the Agnus Dei. The *Misa Sabbatina* tacks on the catchy "Virgen Divina, Virgen Sagrada," a unique canonic gem in the mission repertoire. At the tail end of the *Misa del sexto tono*, Durán writes out two four-voice settings of the strophic song "Toda hermosa eres María" (Mary, You are all-beautiful). This hymn resembles in texture, content, and

Figure 6-2 Sanctus from the *Misa Sabbatina*

Figure 6-2 *(continued)*

function another vernacular hymn for the Virgin with almost the same title. "Eres toda hermosa" (You are all-beautiful), surfaces in conjunction with the Mass for the Seven Dolours of the Blessed Virgin Mary and like its cousin, "Toda hermosa eres María," wafts along in graceful triple meter. Both of these hymns initiate each new stanza in a call-and-response between a single voice and answering choir.[23]

The trio of "easy" masses is not the only musical material conjoined to the veneration of Mary. The more complex *Misa del quarto tono* and *Misa del quinto tono* (*"de Cataluña"*) have Marian associations as well. For example, the same setting of "Toda hermosa eres María" that is affixed to the *Misa del sexto tono* in choirbook

Edited by & with an instrumental
accompaniment composed by
Craig H. Russell.

Agnus Dei
from the *Missa Sabbatina*

Choirbook C-C-59, p. 133

Figure 6-3 Agnus Dei from the *Misa Sabbatina*

C-C-59 is hitched to the back of the *Misa del quarto tono* in Santa Clara Ms. 4.[24]
Similarly, the Marian hymn "Eres toda hermosa" that we find secured to the Mass
for the Seven Dolours of the Blessed Virgin Mary in choirbook C-C-59 is hitched to
a beautiful Mass in C major that is sewn into the binding of Santa Clara Ms. 4.[25] This
latter Mass in C major is in the same vein as the triptych of quartet masses already
discussed. The four voices move in easily memorized and repetitive rhythms. No
solo interpolations interrupt the texture. Thematic unity and core phrases permeate

each movement; they are almost photo duplications of each other except for the differing texts. And like the threesome of similar masses already discussed, it too is affiliated with Mary, as suggested by two bits of evidence: (1) the location of the mass in the choirbook and (2) thematic references to other Marian songs.

To make my case, I first need to explain the physical layout of Santa Clara Ms. 4. As one thumbs through this choirbook (pp. 116–19), we find a lineup of Proper texts for female saints in the typical standardized order that we do in *Liber Usualis* (pp. 1209–41) or any Gradual. Maintaining the orthodox sequence of presentation, there comes the Proper for the Dedication of a Church, which then leads directly into the Feasts of the Blessed Virgin Mary. It is here, tucked between the Dedication of the Church and Feasts of the Blessed Virgin, that we find an intriguing insertion: sewn into the binding are eight unnumbered pages (i.e., four folios) of a completely different paper type right after the Common of the Dedication of the Church. These "bonus" sheets contain two homophonic settings of the Ordinary for four voices, one in C major and the next in A minor. When the "regular" paper type and pagination return, we pick up where we left off to finish "Quam olim" from page 119. It then immediately delves into the polyphonic Marian hymn "Eres toda hermosa" that we had seen in choirbook C-C-59 to conclude the Mass for the Seven Dolours of the Blessed Virgin Mary. Next in line is the Ordinary titled *Misa del quarto tono,* with its companion hymn "Toda hermosa eres Maria." Finally, the triumvirate of four-voice Marian Masses polishes things off. The order of pieces, then, is mapped out in figure 6-4.

"Female" mass settings in Santa Clara Ms. 4

Propers are in canto llano; Ordinaries are in single-staff polyphony.
The page numbers "A" through "H" are my reference citations and
do not appear in the manuscript itself.

Choirbook, numbered pages

Proper for a Virgin Martyr	pp. 116-17
Proper for a Virgin, not a Martyr	p. 118
Proper for a Female Saint, neither a Virgin nor a Martyr	pp. 118-19
Proper for the Dedication of a Church	pp. 119-20

Inserted Sheets

Mass Ordinary in C major	pp. A-D
Mass Ordinary in A minor	pp. D-H

Choirbook, numbered pages

(Conclusion of Proper for Dedication of a Church)	p. 121
"Eres Toda Hermosa," single-staff polyphony, strophic	p. 121
Te Deum, single-staff, 4-voice intoned formula	p. 122
Mass Ordinary: *Misa del quarto tono*	pp. 123-27
"Toda hermosa eres Maria" single-staff polyph., strophic	p. 128

[Triptych of Marian Ordinaries]

Mass Ordinary: [= *Misa Sabbatina o de la Virgen*]	p. 130-32
Mass Ordinary: [= *Misa del sexto tono*]	pp. 132-36
Mass Ordinary: *Missa Ligera*	pp. 137-40

Figure 6-4 "Female" mass settings in Santa Clara Ms. 4.

This huge swath of material from pages 116–40 is knit together with a common theme—the celebration of "female" divinity. We begin with women saints, move to the motherchurch, and then proceed to the Blessed Virgin Mary. Some of the Ordinary settings are explicitly tied to Mary as well with the annexation of supplemental Marian songs. This choirbook postfixes "Toda hermosa eres Maria" to the *Misa del quarto tono,* and "Eres toda hermosa" follows on the heels of the Dedication of a Church (another "female" religious image). In another choirbook (C-C-59) we just saw the triptych of Marian Ordinaries affixing these same two hymns as a postscript to the Agnus Dei. I would argue, therefore, that the *reason* that Durán choose to insert the four sheets with the Mass Ordinaries in C major and A minor at this location was due to their association with the feminine imagery and the adoration of Mother Mary.

That argument is reinforced by melodic references as well. As with nearly every Ordinary in this family of settings, the Mass in C major builds all its movements using a handful of adaptable, recurring phrases. For each of the "major-sounding" members of these settings (that is, the Mass in C major, plus the F major focus of the *Misa del sexto tono* and *Misa Ligera*), they relinquish their sunny major tonality with a modulation to the relative minor at the line "Qui tollis peccata mundi" (Thou who takest away the sins of the world) in the Gloria. This reminds one of other examples of word painting in California masses where sin, despair, or man's flawed fallibility are reflected in musically audible ways.[26] The somber excursion into minor modality does that perfectly in these three Mass settings.[27] The Mass in C major plunges into the a sobering A minor to convey the worldly angst of the "sins of the world."

These notes have yet another meaning, however. In addition to the rather glum mood that captures the text's intent, any *californio* would have heard another beloved but mournful piece lurking in the background—the *Stabat Mater*. This hymn describes Mary's agony at the foot of the cross as her son expires before her eyes. Durán writes out polyphonic settings of the *Stabat Mater* twice in choirbook C-C-59, once in his section from the Mass for the Seven Dolours of the Blessed Virgin Mary (p. 118) and earlier in Maundy Thursday of Holy Week (p. 15).[28] That latter setting matches exactly the "Qui tollis" phrase from the Mass in C major. (See figure 6-5.)

This melodic reference would not have raced by, unnoticed, in an ephemeral whiff. The Californians *knew* this melody. After all, the California *Stabat Mater* is strophic in structure (unlike the paired phrases of the original, ancient version). As a result, the tune goes around the block and keeps coming back and back with each new stanza of text (and there are *lots* of them). Undoubtedly, then, the neophytes would have known this tune as well as Methodists know Charles Wesley's "O God Our Help in Ages Past" or "All Hail the Power of Jesus' Name." Thus, when the Mass in C major suddenly quotes this exact phrase in the middle of its Gloria, the California padres and converts would have simultaneously seen in their mind's eye the image of Mary, weeping for her dying son. In short, this musical tie to Mary reinforces the bridge to Marian feasts we saw arise from the manuscript's layout.[29]

Shared phrase between the "Qui tollis" and the *Stabat Mater*

Figure 6-5 Shared phrase between the "Qui tollis" and the *Stabat Mater*

Three "Intermediate" Duet Settings for Holy Week

In the same way that Durán grouped together three straightforward, quartet set-tings for the Ordinary, so he grouped together a threesome of Ordinary settings for two voices that share common features. For both of the Durán choirbooks, the *Misa de la Soledad, Misa Viscaína,* and *Misa de San Antonio* (also called the *Misa Solemne*) are the only two-voice Mass settings in the entire tomes.[30] The duet feature alone is enough to bond them together as fraternal confreres, since the other polyphonic Ordinaries are arranged for four or more voices. Each of the three is in mode 6 (or F major). Textually, each is reasonably complete; that is, they avoid the potholes and piecemeal components that one sometimes finds in manuscripts that are providing only half of the ingredients for an *alternatim* performance.

In almost all the sources, the *Misa de la Soledad* and *Misa Viscaína* have the shorter, truncated texts for the Sanctus and Agnus Dei, unlike the "complete" and through-composed *Misa de San Antonio/Solemne.*[31] (However, the two Santa Barbara Mission choirbooks [Docs. 1 and 2] do include a "Benedictus" section to the *Misa de la Soledad's* Sanctus—the other sources of this mass, on the other hand, crop off the piece after the "Hosanna.") The abbreviated texts for the Sanc-tus and Agnus Dei do not really present a performance problem. In the Sanctus it is assumed that one can sing the "Pleni sunt caeli" as written and then return—retexting the phrase with the unwritten but implied "Benedictus qui venit." In fact,

Santa Barbara Document 1 even writes the necessary "Benedictus qui venit" above the larger "Pleni sunt caeli" of the *Misa Viscaína*'s Sanctus, thus expunging any ambiguity of how to realize the complete text.[32] A similar text substitution works handily in the Agnus Dei. One repeats the main phrase three times but the last time through merely swaps the closing words "miserere nobis" with "dona nobis pacem." Problem solved. Most Hispano-American sources do not even bother to instruct the performers of the substitution, since it was seen as automatic. Santa Clara Ms. 4 confirms this tradition: Durán courteously adds the reminder by writing the words "dona nobis pacem" in small letters above the larger font of the words "miserere nobis." This also holds true for Santa Barbara Documents 1 and 2.

This trilogy of duet Masses sound radically different stylistically and explore entirely different sonic landscapes. They get harder as they go along. The *Misa de la Soledad* moves in predictable, synchronized motion in all the voices, striding forward in simple rhythms of breves and semibreves (transcribed as half notes and quarter notes). Stepwise motion in parallel thirds is the rule. Organically, the same musical genetic code engenders every phrase. Stepping upward to an intermediate-level piece, the *Misa Viscaína* already confronts the listener with textural variety not seen in the previous piece. Solo lines in *canto figurado* interlock with those for two parts, mostly in parallel thirds. The unswerving, rigorous persistence of cloned phrases in the *Misa de la Soledad* are contrasted with more forgiving and varied ones in the *Misa Viscaína*. That is not to say the piece has been patched together with odds and ends. There are sweeping phrases that get reutilized, so there is a filial resemblance between all five movements, but not with the clockwork regularity of *Soledad*. Clearly, the second of these masses would require more rehearsal time. The third one in the set, the *Misa de San Antonio*, is the most complex by far, requiring virtuosic performance skills and artistic subtlety. Like the other two, generally its voices sway and skip in parallel thirds, but here the surface rhythms are mercurial and ever changing. At one moment they are unrushed and poised, and at the next they are dashing forward in dotted rhythms, rapidly plummeting, gliding to repose, or twittering in frisky ornamentation. Its phrases pull to closure with sigh figures and unstressed cadences. In short, this Mass reflects contemporary Classicism and would have required well trained, diligent, and refined performers. Taken as a whole, then, these three duet masses progress from easy, to intermediate, to advanced.

One of the aspects that these masses share is their probable performance during Semana Santa, or Holy Week. The grouping of these three in the choirbooks reflects fundamental features seen in Father Palóu's description of Holy Week as celebrated by this friar and Serra in the missions of the Sierra Gorda (and subsequently in Alta California). Palóu informs us:

Holy Week was celebrated with all the ceremonies of our Mother Church. On Palm Sunday the procession was celebrated and beginning on that day and every day thereafter the Passion was recited, in which each of us had to take double part because there were but two of us. The same with regard to the Matins of the three days. On Holy Thursday, the Eucharist was put in the place prepared for it and both on that day and on Friday, and on Saturday as well, all the other ceremonies were performed according to custom. In addition to these he added several processions which he was wont to terminate with a sermon. On Thursday, after having washed the feet of twelve of the oldest Indians and eaten with them, he proceeded to the sermon of "washing the feet," and at night made the procession with the image of the Christ Crucified in the presence of all the people. On Good Friday he used to preach in the morning on the Passion, and in the afternoon the Descent from the Cross was represented with the great vividness by manner of a lifelike figure which he had ordered made for the purpose and which had hinges. He handled the subject in his sermon with the greatest devotion and tenderness. The body of Our Lord was placed in a casket and then used in the procession of the Holy Burial. It was afterward placed upon an altar which he had also prepared for this purpose and at night another procession was made in honor of Our Lady of Solitude [Nuestra Señora de la Soledad], and then the day was finished with a special sermon on this subject. On the Saturday following, all ceremonies belonging to the day were observed, the water was blessed and the converts who had been instructed and prepared for it were baptized. Very early on Sunday morning the procession of Our Risen Lord took place, which was celebrated by means of an image of the Lord and another of the Most Holy Virgin. On returning to the church High Mass was sung and the Venerable father would preach about this Sovereign Mystery.

By means of these most holy exercises the great tenderness of devotion of the converts was greatly increased and by the use of them the Holy Week was yearly more and more celebrated, the word going out among the peoples in the vicinity, composed of Spaniards, and causing many of them to come to take part in the service, being attracted by what they heard said concerning the extreme devotion of the Indians; and when they had once witnessed the ceremonies they would return from year to year, moving from their homes to the Mission where they remained until the Holy Week had passed.[33]

Palóu's almost cinematic description matches up beautifully with the music preserved in the Durán choirbooks, especially C-C-59 at the Bancroft Library. Nearly all the elements are present, such as the music for the distribution of the palms and parade on Palm Sunday, the processional music on Maundy Thursday with the image of Christ on the cross plus the tune to accompany the washing of the feet, the hymns *Pange lingua* and its response *Crux fidelis* (Faithful Cross) and *Vexilla Regis prodeunt* (most likely to accompany the descent from the cross), the enormous setting of Good Friday's Matins and Lauds, and the critical moments on Holy Saturday and Easter Sunday, complete with a polyphonic rendition of *Victimae paschali laudes* with instrumental insertions.[34] The missing component from these pages would be the Ordinary settings needed for

Mass on these days. It seems more than likely that the triumvirate of the *Misa de la Soledad, Misa Viscaína,* and *Misa de San Antonio/Solemne* would serve as "special" settings needed for Good Friday, Holy Saturday, and Easter Sunday. While detailing events on Good Friday, Palóu tells us, "At night another procession was made in honor of Our Lady of Solitude [*Nuestra Señora de la Soledad*], and then the day was finished with a special sermon on this subject." Would it not seem appropriate to match up the *Misa de la Soledad* with the events in her honor on Good Friday?

As Holy Week moves forward, after Good Friday would come Holy Saturday; if we continue taking the duet masses in order, we move from Friday's *Misa de la Soledad* to the *Misa Viscaína.* The ordering suggests that this latter mass and Holy Saturday are conjoined. This supposition is confirmed on page 18 of the choirbook, where Durán maps out the day's chants. For Holy Saturday's Kyrie, he supplies the plainchant melody of the *Kyrie de Angeles* (from Mass VIII in the *Liber Usualis*), one of the few *canto llano* tunes that was central to worship in all the missions.[35] With the ensuing Gloria, however, he departs from the monophonic chants in Mass VIII and instead prints out the cursory instruction "Gloria Vizcaína," a reference that bounces us all the way to the *Misa Viscaína* in our triumvirate of duet masses. In other words, the connection between Holy Saturday and the *Misa Viscaína* is explicit. The final association of our third day (Easter Sunday) with our third mass (the *Misa de San Antonio/Solemne*) is a logical one, but not confirmed by any ascription. Nevertheless, the stylistic features of this mass ordering would make perfect sense. The easier *Misa de la Soledad* would prepare the way on Good Friday; the more intriguing *Misa Viscaína* would build in intensity toward the following day; and the exquisitely ornamented and captivating *Misa de San Antonio/Solemne* would provide the musical climax needed to reflect the culmination of Holy Week and the church year—Christ's Resurrection on Easter Sunday. The *Misa de San Antonio* may have done "double-duty," selected as the special mass on Christmas as well, as indicated by the abbreviated instruction in Santa Barbara Doc. 1 (p. 154), where it states: "Christmas day, the birth of our Lord Jesus Christ, 25 of December, use the 3rd Mass, and the Introit is *Puer natus est nobis* found on page 98 of this choirbook" (Dia de Navidad de Ns. S. J. C. 25 de Diciembre. 3ª Misa. Puer p. 98).

Misa de la Soledad

Musically, the *Misa de la Soledad* traipses along in strict parallel thirds, only abandoning them on rare occasions for a few fifths, sixths, or octaves. The melodic contours could hardly be more straightforward or unexceptional; they are like the gentle hills of the Piedmont, rising, falling, and then reversing direction, but never attaining any great peaks or valleys. This Mass would not be mistaken for a Pulitzer Prize–winning masterpiece, but it surely had its utilitarian merits in the outback of Alta California. The repetitive phrases would be easily memorized by a small village of new converts unfamiliar with European traditions.

The notation of the *Misa de la Soledad* can be misleading to modern performers if they assume that bar lines reflect metric stress, where the downbeats fall on "beat one" immediately after the bar line. (See photo 6-1, a color version of which is identified online in appendix B as photo B-72.) In the *Misa de la Soledad,* each measure is filled with the necessary two or four beats, but the "downbeat" can be an illusory phantom, appearing almost anywhere. The math works out, but the accents do not.[36] It seems strangely odd and unpredictable that phrases come back as repetitions later in a movement and are identical in every respect—except that their rhythms often are shifted over a pulse within the metric structure, so that a phrase's reappearance is out of sync with its original model. Right out of the starting gate we slam smack-dab into this problem: the first and second statements of the words "Kyrie eleison" end with the same closing gesture, but they are unmistakably off-kilter. (See figure 6-6.)

For those unfamiliar with the notational conventions of the mission choirbooks, this wobbly shifting of phrasing, back and forth across the bar line, can seem haphazard and sloppy. But what first seems to be haphazard actually turns out to be rational and systematic. In truth, one need only *add an implied rest* at the end of a line of text, and in so doing the added half measure of implied silence both separates neighboring phrases from each other—literally providing a bit of breathing room—and also establishes natural and intuitive phrase lengths. Without the implied rests, all the phrase lengths are divvied up into unpredictable and bizarre fractions. Consider, for example, the "raw"

Photo 6-1 Kyrie from the *Misa de la Soledad,* Santa Barbara Mission Archive-Library, Document 1 (Durán Choirbook), p. 9. (Permission to include this image courtesy of the SBMAL; photo by the author.)

Staggered phrases in the Kyrie
from the *Misa de la Soledad*

Choirbook C-C-59, fol. 43

Figure 6-6 Staggered phrases in the Kyrie from the *Misa de la Soledad*

structure of the phrases in the Kyrie where no rests have been inserted. (See figure 6-7.)

Frankly, that structure is peculiar and clumsy to sing. But if we now add a pause (i.e., a half-note rest) at the end of each phrase, just as we do when speaking, everything works out quite naturally. The quizzical fractions in the phrase lengths vanish. Additionally, identical phrases now line up in a parallel way: that is, their downbeats and upbeats coincide with respect to the bar line instead of being staggered. (See figure 6-8 for the "revised" version of the Kyrie, incorporating the needed rests.)

The textual divisions that require pauses in the Kyrie, Sanctus, and Agnus Dei are not very tricky to determine, since the texts are short and the options are few. Ascertaining the divisions of the Gloria and Credo, however, can be problematic, since there is a multitude of ways that one could chop up the text. So the question arises, How do we know where the performers in California paused and added the implied rests? Fortunately, the mission manuscripts tell us exactly where those division points are. The *canto figurado* settings of the Gloria and Credo were chopped up, ready to use in an *alternatim* performance setting. Those grammatical components are standardized in California: they had to be, because if one is flipping back and forth between two opposing textures, one has to make sure that an inserted component will function once it is plugged into the larger whole. It is like replacing a water pump on an old Ford. If one were to seek a replacement

Phrase structure (*without* rests) in the Kyrie, *Misa de la Soledad*

where a "pulse" is equal to a breve in the original notation and equal to a half note in my transcription.

Text:	Kyrie	Kyrie	Kyrie	Christe	Christe	Christe	Kyrie	Kyrie	Kyrie
Pulses:	5.5	4.5	2.5	2.5	4.5	2.5	2.5	4.5	7.5

Figure 6-7 Phrase structure (*without* rests) in the Kyrie, *Misa de la Soledad*

Kyrie
from the *Misa de la Soledad*

Choirbook C-C-59, p. 43
Santa Clara Ms. 4, p. 41

Figure 6-8 Revised version of the Kyrie from the *Misa de la Soledad*

part, then all of those water pumps that one would find (the official ones sold at the dealership, the inexpensive knockoffs made in Macao, the rebuilt ones at the local garage, and even the used ones scavenged from the junkyard) are going to be *the same size*. That is a requirement: otherwise the part will not fit and the car will not run. In the same way, the *californios* cut apart the Gloria and the Credo in the same standardized way, time after time, and they swapped out replacement parts week after week, Mass after Mass. Therefore, the neophytes would have known backward and forward where the text was to be divided. Moreover, with respect to the *Misa de la Soledad,* they would have automatically added the rests at those same junctures. If one actually takes that into account when realizing a modern score, all the phrases line up neat and tidy and reflect an exceedingly cohesive phrase structure between the different movements of the Mass. Refer to figure 6-9 for a chart of the Gloria's division points.

This mass is one of the most unified and tightly knit with respect to its phrasing. With the exception of the Credo, all the movements are woven from the same melodic threads. The most common one consists of two half notes, followed by four quarters, and then a half note or two to tie off the rhythmic string. Another recurring pattern is a descent of four half notes. The directions of the ups and downs can vary slightly, but the rhythmic cohesion is nearly universally

Division points in the Gloria

A division point or break occurs after every change from bold font to regular and vice versa.

Gloria in excelsis Deo.
Et in terra pax
hominibus bonae voluntatis.
Laudamus te.
Benedicamus te.
Adoramus te.
Glorificamus te.
Gratias agimus tibi
propter magnam gloriam tuam.
Domine Deus, Rex caelestis,
Deus Pater omnipotens.
Domine Fili unigenite Jesu Christe.
Domine Deus. Agnus Dei, Filius Patris.
Qui tollis peccata mundi,
miserere nobis.
Qui tollis peccata mundi,
suscipe deprecationem nostram.
Qui sedes ad dexterman Patris,
miserere nobis.
Quoniam tu solus sanctus.
Tu solus Dominus.
Tu solus altissimus,
Jesu Christe.
Cum Sancto Spiritu,
in gloria Dei Patris.
Amen.

Glory to God in the highest. [can be intoned]
And on earth peace
to men of good will.
We praise you.
We bless you.
We adore you.
We glorify you.
We give you thanks
For your great glory.
Lord God, heavenly King,
God the Father Almighty,
Lord Jesus Christ, the only-begotten Son.
Lord God, Lamb of God, Son of the Father.
Who takes away the sins of the world,
have mercy upon us.
Who takes away the sins of the world,
receive our prayer.
Who sits at the right hand of the Father,
have mercy upon us.
For you alone are holy,
You alone are Lord.
You alone, O Jesus Christ,
are most high.
Together with the Holy Spirit,
in the glory of God the Father.
Amen.

Based on the "Gloria Dominical," WPA folder 68, "Gloria espacio," WPA folder 64, "Gloria pastoril," WPA folder 55, "Gloria simple," WPA folder 55, "Gloria Toledana,"WPA folder 63, "Gloria tono 5°,"WPA folder 64.

** Also in Santa Barbara Doc. 17 & Doc. 24.

Figure 6-9 Division points in the Gloria

observed. (See figure 6-10 for an illustration of thematic unity in the *Misa de la Soledad.*)

Misa Viscaína

The subsequent mass in the Holy Week trilogy, the *Misa Viscaína,* is bound together in cohesive unity through recurring passages from its two distinct and contrasting textures: (1) the soloistic *canto figurado* lines, and (2) the duet passages in parallel thirds. The Kyrie, Gloria, and Credo are expansive and indulge in *alternatim* style.[37] (For a facsimile of the Kyrie from this mass, consult photo B-71 in appendix B online.) They begin with an unpretentious single thread of *canto figurado* melody that is replicated in each of the three movements' incipits except for the change in text and a few minor adjustments to accommodate an extra syllable here and there. The last two movements (the Sanctus and Agnus Dei) are so brief that *alternatim* performance is not a viable possibility; they are over in a

Thematic unity in the *Misa de la Soledad*

Figure 6-10 Thematic unity in the *Misa de la Soledad*

blink with no time to flip-flop between solo tunes and duets. These two instead concentrate exclusively on duet texture. These movements are likewise fused to the Kyrie, but with different solder than the Gloria and Credo. The entire setting of the Agnus Dei is drawn from the extended, sweeping passage in duet texture in the Kyrie (mm. 22–36)—and it serves as well to form the central core of the Sanctus (mm. 10–24). The final cadential gesture of this phrase (mm. 34–36 of the Kyrie) is also mirrored in the Gloria (mm. 19–21) and the Credo (mm. 56–59, 124–26,

146–48). Ultimately, it is this cliché cadence that most strongly cements these five movements together.

Drama and text expression momentarily step forward out of the otherwise homogeneous mood. The Gloria shines a floodlight on the Messiah's importance at the words "Je-su Chri-sti" by descending from a high peak in slow, dramatic articulation of each syllable in dotted half notes (dotted breves). This same gesture recurs later in the Gloria and yet again in the Credo in the description of the Lord's descent "from heaven." The opposite mood is elicited later in the Credo. A shift to F minor from the optimistic F major—coupled with a severe slowing of the surface rhythms—conjures up an almost tragic mood at the Credo's line "et homo factus est" (and was made man). The somber feeling is heightened by the change to a more ponderous tempo just measures earlier, with the instruction to play "muy despacio" (very slowly). This shift in emotional climate at the description of mankind is commonplace in the Credo settings sung in Alta California.

Misa de San Antonio (Misa Solemne)

The fancier *Misa de San Antonio/Solemne* differs considerably from the previous two masses in its rhythmic variety and hierarchy of rests and pauses; whereas the *Misa Viscaína* has not bothered to write a single rest, the *Misa de San Antonio* has them peppered throughout, and of different values. Again, this concern with articulation and the role of silence to clarify phrasing and structure is a Classical feature. The jagged dotted rhythms in the Kyrie, plus the variety of surface rhythms and swooping cadential descents in the Gloria, place this mass closer to the realm of *estilo moderno* than *canto figurado*. Unlike the other masses in the California repertoire, this one has the most dancelike qualities. The Kyrie could almost be a gavotte, the Gloria resembles a minuet (but with several meter changes and shifts in character), and the Sanctus plus Agnus Dei conjure up the march. With the exception of the Credo in the habitual *alternatim* style, the other movements are through-composed and completely texted.[38] The Sanctus contains a Benedictus with its own, fresh musical material, and the Agnus Dei covers new musical terrain for each of its three phrases, rather than simply repeat the same phrase three times. That an instrumental accompaniment supported the vocal lines is once again self-evident; there are measures filled with silence in the choirbooks, showing the singers where to wait out the small orchestra fills. The parentheses in the *Misa de San Antonio* occur in florid and difficult passages. Although Durán explains this notational idiosyncrasy by stating the singers have the option of not singing in these boxed-in measures, one might suppose the violins and vocalists are doubling a good deal of the time; the fiddles would forge ahead, and the singers could catch them at the pass.

Martín de Cruzelaegui, Possible Composer of the Misa Viscaína

Before abandoning the three "duet masses" entirely for other musical settings, it would be worthwhile to return momentarily to the *Misa Viscaína* with respect to its possible authorship. For years, the *Misa Viscaína* has been attributed— problematically—to Father Narciso Durán.[39] More recently, Ignacio Omaeche- varría has proposed that the *Misa Viscaína* is actually the fruit of Basque composer and friar Martín de Cruzelaegui (also spelled "Cruzelagui," "Crucélegui," "Cruce- laegui," "Cruzalaegui," and "Cruzealaegui"). His proposal was later taken up by Jon Bagüés Erriondo and William Summers in their revealing publications.[40]

Cruzelaegui is a fascinating—but overlooked—composer who was active in the late 1700s in Mexico City.[41] The Basque scholar Bagüés Erriondo has tracked down Cruzelaegui's baptismal registration in Elgoibar, Guipozcoa (Spain), dated 19 Feb- ruary 1737, and identifying his parents as "Francisco Crucelegui" and "Josepha de Ascarraga."[42] Maynard Geiger tells us that Cruzelaegui took the Franciscan habit on 12 November 1759 in the province of Cantabria and that "he was evidently in charge of the choir at San Fernando."[43] Bagüés Erriondo discovered the document establishing Cruzelaegui's arrival at that institution on 29 May 1770, along with a fellow Basque friar, Pablo de Mugártegui. Cruzelaegui was still at San Fernando in 1772, appearing on the list of friars-in-residence in that year, and he authored a mass (seen by Geiger) in 1774 while he was still at the Apostolic College.[44] He published a rousing *Laudate Dominum* in 1775 that identifies Cruzelaegui as the organist at this same institution.[45] In 1784, Cruzelaegui petitions the Royal Basque Society of Friends of the Country to be recognized with the title of Professor of Music.[46] Tom Stanford places Cruzelaegui in the circle of Father Serra's friends, and apparently Cruzelaegui was one of the adjudicators who recommended Aren- zana for the post of chapelmaster at Puebla Cathedral in 1791.[47] His works are substantial, both in compositional sophistication and in number, and they crop up in the Mexico City and Puebla cathedrals in manuscripts dating from the middle to late 1770s, as well as in the holdings at the Centro Nacional de Investigación, Documentación e Información Musical (CENIDIM) in Mexico City. Most of the Cruzelaegui manuscripts at this latter institution originally were in the possession of the Convento Santísima Trinidad in Puebla.[48]

Since Omaechevarría set in motion the credible theory that Cruzelaegui com- posed the *Misa Viscaína,* his argument bears careful examination. Omaechevarría explains:

> Fray Martín de Crucélegui [was] himself a Franciscan friar, a native of Elgoibar, a notable musician, the Vicar of the Choir of the [Apostolic] College of Missionaries of San Fernando in Mexico, without question the author of the work called *Misa Viscaína* that was sung a lot in the Califor- nia missions—as is proven by the copies of it that are preserved today in the mission archives—and that Father Owen da Silva assigns authorship, without justification, to Father & Friar Narciso Durán. Although the *Misa de Cataluña* and other works can be attributed to him [*sic*], this is certainly not the case with the *Misa Viscaína....*
>
> And having touched upon this theme, I have to mention as an aside that they once again began to sing this famous *Misa Viscaína* in several California churches, reedited by the North American Franciscans. It must

have arrived in California by way of Father Mugartegui who was in frequent correspondence with Father Crucélegui at the time that he was composing music at the Missionary College of San Fernando in Mexico and when Crucélegui was accompanying Father Junípero Serra in the California missions.

It was no mere accident that among the friars attached to the Royal Basque Society of the Friends of the Country—practically from its inception—there were included the musicians Friar José de Larrañaga and Friar Martín de Crucelegui. And with that, I am going to answer those who might ask for specifics about the musical compositions of Father Crucelegui. He was, I remind everyone, a Vicar of the Choir—or Chapel Master— of the Missionary College of San Fernando in Mexico City, to which order the California missionaries all belonged. The illustrious North American researcher Maynard Geiger discovered in Mexico a mass composed by him, that he neither acquired nor copied and that no one knows where is to be found. Might we not issue a call from here directed to the Mexican that might possess this treasure that he tell us about it and describe it for us?

For my part, I am of the opinion that this mass is none other than the *Misa Viscaína* which one finds copied out in the mission archives across California and that has come to be revived in our own time. I do not find plausible reasons that a mass composed by Friar Narciso Durán might be classified as "a mass from Biscay." On the other hand, it would be strange that a mass composed by Friar Martin de Crucelegui (friend to Father Mugartegui in Mexico City's Apostolic College of San Fernando) would not make it to California.[49]

In many respects, Omaechevarría's thesis that affixes the *Misa Viscaína* to Cruzelaegui resembles in at least three ways the argument that Owen da Silva makes in attaching the *Misa de Cataluña* to Durán. Their arguments share some of the same inconclusive elements. For example: (1) there is no signed autograph identifying the composer, (2) no one at the time ever clarifies or mentions authorship, and (3) the geographic loyalty to one's homeland is used as a pillar of attribution. In this context, I find Omaechevarría's confident assertion that "Fray Martín de Crucélegui was *without question* [emphasis added] the author of the work called *Misa Viscaína* that was sung a lot in the California missions—as is proven by the copies of it that are preserved today in the mission archives" as overstepping the evidence itself. Actually, the number of copies proves next to nothing; it demonstrates only that the Franciscans drew upon a standard model, but we have no clue yet as to who engendered that first original creation. Granted, Crucélegui was from Basque country, but so were other musicians and friars in Mexico and California, and it is wise to remember that there are hundreds (or even thousands) of candidates from Vizcaya itself that would fit the bill. It is a very real possibility that the work actually is *from* Vizcaya and was then transported to the New World by the network of Franciscan friars. In short, we might be jumping the gun a bit if we summarily assign the *Misa Viscaína* to Crucélegui as the *only* possible author.

On the other hand, Omaechevarría's case is much stronger than da Silva's—especially given Cruzelaegui's impressive track record as a composer. Whereas no primary document mentions Durán as a composer, that is not the case with Cruzelaegui. Mexican archives are peppered with his music, and we have biographical data firmly establishing this Basque friar's musical pedigree.

Bill Summers (who accepts Omaechevarría's case) observes the discrepancy between the style of Cruzelaegui's published *Laudate Dominum* and the *Misa Viscaína* and tries to reconcile them. He observes that the friar might be adjusting his style from fancier to easier depending on his goals and the performance skills of the musicians. Summers states:

> The composition of the *Misa Viscaina,* also identified in some California sources as the *Misa 2a a 6° tono (Misa secunda á sexto tono),* must reflect Crucelaegui's desire to produce part music of a very different nature, music that could be taken to the missions which would be intelligible to and performable by his confreres first of all, and also serve as a work that would produce musical results consistent with the performance goals of parish churches in Spain and the New World. Quite clearly, Crucelaegui was capable of composing works that reflected the most elaborate cathedral traditions. His task as a faculty member of the Apostolic College was to assist with the primary work of all missionaries, the propagation of the Catholic religion through the regular celebration of the sacred rites of the Church.[50]

Summers then adds another potential Franciscan friar to the mix—Francisco Rouis at the Apostolic College.[51] At the Archive of the Archdiocese of Los Angeles (at the San Fernando Mission in California), there is a loose sheet with a Credo; it ends with a signature, "Fran[cisco] Rouis." Summers presents the possibility, therefore, that this Credo was an original composition by the friar Francisco Rouis living in Mexico City during the mission period. Although this is plausible, I offer another possible explanation. Perhaps this signature designates ownership of this sheet (as opposed to proof of composition). We have seen several examples of an ex libris in mission manuscripts, such as the copy of the *Misa de Cataluña* by Pacífico Capéñaz (written out in 1841 but appearing in California manuscripts in the first two decades of the nineteenth century); Santa Barbara Document 1, with a signature of ownership by "Cera" and Juan Mariner; and yet another ex libris by Mariner in Santa Barbara Document 15.[52] This latter document's title page reads, "Lamentacion Primera / para el Miercoles. / Del P. Fr. Juan Mariner"; judging from this wording and signature, one might think that this was created by the padre from scratch, but when one turns the page to sing the work, one finds the intoning of plainchant—hardly a "new" composition by Mariner. In addition, we have already seen numerous manuscripts signed by Juan Bautista Sancho, some of them probably "original" and some of them merely copied out from other sources but "owned" by this friar. In short, I am cautious in accepting that Rouis is a composer until further evidence surfaces to support that assumption.

Misa del quinto tono (Misa de Cataluña)

One of the most beloved works on the West Coast was the *Misa del quinto tono,* written in four-voice polyphony on a single staff as was so common in California manuscripts.[53] The five movements share a common bond in a mutually shared cadential phrase; it appears first as the closing measures of the Kyrie, but it then gets used and reused as the service unfolds. Another unifying gesture audibly leaps from the texture; the basso continuo line that sets in motion the "Domine Deus" of the Gloria is the same bass line that is sung to launch us into the Agnus Dei.[54] (See photo 6-2, a color version of which is available online as photo B-49.)

Most of the *Misa de Cataluña*'s features fall within the locus of typical mission practice. The Kyrie and Sanctus are slight variants of each other; their opening moments present a catchy, soldierly phrase built of dotted rhythms that defines the tonic of C major and marches to new harmonic terrain with each successive phrase (to the dominant G major and a return back to the home C major).[55] The middle section of the Kyrie declaims the text "Christe eleison" in bold, unadorned rhythms with no detours or frilly diversions in sight. Here, one can imagine the raw energy

Photo 6-2 Kyrie and first part of Gloria from the "Misa Catalana, Tono 5" (*Misa de Cataluña*), San Fernando Mission, Archival Center of the Archdiocese of Los Angeles, Ms. A320, pp. 1-2. (Permission to include this image courtesy of the ACALA; photo by the author.)

of the martial rhythms sung in the previous phrases as continuing in the unwritten instrumental accompaniment. This hunch is confirmed in a serendipitous instance where we still have fragments of the instrumental performing parts.

This extant evidence pops up, unexpectedly, in a completely different mass setting—the *Misa de los Angeles* in the hand of Juan Bautista Sancho. If one takes the trouble to piece together a score from the parts tucked into WPA folder 69, he or she will find that the opening statement of "Kyrie eleison" from Sancho's *Misa de los Angeles*—dated 1796—is identical to the music for the "Christe" section in the *Misa del quinto tono [Misa de Cataluña]*. (See figure 6-11.) The ramifications of this are many. For one, this correspondence argues against Owen da Silva's well-meaning but erroneous assertion that the *Misa de Cataluña* is the handiwork of Padre Narciso Durán.[56] There was no possible way for Sancho and Durán to have been in any personal contact in the Americas until sometime after 6 June 1806, the date of Durán's arrival in California, yet Sancho is writing out the music for this Kyrie in 1796 while at the Convent de San Francesc in Palma. Of course, several other possibilities could explain the occurrence of this same musical phrase in Sancho's *Misa de los Angeles* and Durán's manuscripts. Perhaps both of these Franciscans knew this setting before leaving for the New World. That Sancho knew it while still in Mallorca is irrefutable; for Durán to have learned it while in his native Gerona, Cataluña, seems highly likely. Durán took his vows as a Franciscan in Gerona, was ordained there, and continued his religious functions in Gerona before departing Cataluña for Mexico in 1803 to begin his life as a missionary.[57] For the *Misa de Cataluña* to be circulating in the 1790s as part of the Franciscan repertoire both in Durán's native Gerona and in nearby Mallorca where Sancho was simultaneously serving would not be much of a stretch. I suggest that the *Misa de Cataluña* is exactly that—a mass from Cataluña, its authorship unknown—and

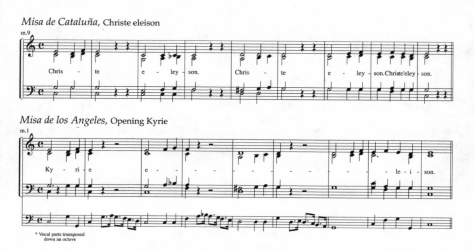

Misa de Cataluña, Christe eleison

Misa de los Angeles, Opening Kyrie

* Vocal parts transposed
down an octave

Figure 6-11   Similar phrases in the *Misa de Cataluña* and the *Misa de los Angeles*

that both of these friars knew the work without having had any direct personal contact until years later. Attributing it to Durán as an original composition, who had no known musical training at this time, is highly unlikely. In addition, there is no hard proof either confirming or refuting the possibility that Sancho was its author. As things stand presently, we can demonstrate with certainty only that it was known in Spain in the 1790s and that it was a smash hit in California in the early 1800s.

Instruments played a major role in the *Misa de Cataluña*'s Gloria and Credo that undoubtedly did more than double vocal lines: the full measures of rests are a dead giveaway that instrumental figuration of some sort filled up the vacant spaces in the vocal writing. There are even some instrumental cues in the Gloria where the continuo line is notated before the voices enter.[58] The choirbook score has the bass and tenor lines cross often, creating odd harmonic inversions: again, if we factor in a continuo line that is sounding lower than these voices (doubling the vocal bass line an octave lower), then all the harmonies work out splendidly.

The text expression effectively captures subtle aspects of the lyrics. The implied tempo at the beginning of the Gloria is probably allegro, or at least moderato, but explicitly slows to *despacio* at "qui tollis peccata mundi" (he who taketh away the sins of the world). The martial rhythm at "Quoniam tu solus sanctus" (You alone are Holy) is extremely similar to the opening of the Gloria: we might assume that we return to a brisker tempo at this juncture. The "Amen" has a moment of antiphonal counterpoint between the tenor-bass combo versus the sopranos and altos (much like some of the colonial fuguing tunes or Sacred Harp singing). The Credo traces through its text in *alternatim* performance—the norm for this movement in the California mission style. A more sullen mood is conjured up at the Credo's "Et incarnatus est" by a shift from C major to A minor and from triple to duple meter. As we have seen many times already, man's sin and frailty are captured by the "two-ness" of duple meter, for each measure lacks the critical third pulse that would associate it with the Trinity. When we sing of God, we sing of the Three-in-One (and musically, with three pulses in one measure). Humankind, however, is lacking perfection and therefore is portrayed in twos. At "Et incarnatus est" we also a shift from C major (or, technically, mode 5) to what "sounds" like A minor to our ears. In truth, the phrases weave back and forth between the poles of E major and A minor, but the cadence point each time is on E major. The gravitational center is E, not A minor. In the proper modal context, this turns out to be mode 4. At the words "ex Maria Virgine" (born of the Virgin Mary), mode 4 is firmly cemented as the voices plod downward in parallel fifths and octaves in the Phrygian cadence that defines mode 4 by descending chords: A minor-G-F-E.[59] We saw in chapter 2 that this mode, influenced by the planet Mercury, can "move one to weeping or to gaiety, to fury and to gentleness, to calmness and to ghastliness, to blandness and to strength."[60] The ambivalent experience of Christ as a suffering, perishable man and—on the other hand—triumphant, immortal God is thus portrayed by the transient dualities of mode 4, coupled with the "humanness" of God explained at "et incarnatus est."

With the Credo's next lines of text explaining the Crucifixion and Resurrection, we once again have a metric shift from the incomplete "two-ness" of duple meter to the more perfect triple meter to portray Jesus' journey from mortal flesh to triumphant redemption. The resurrection confidently restores the exuberant C-major harmonies of mode 5, that is basically maintained through the end of the movement, with the exception of fleeting allusions to mode 4 and its A-minor and E-major fluctuations; these passing moments occur on mortuos" (the dead), and "in remissionem peccatorum" (and in the remissions of sins). Again, these harmonies provide more than simple harmonic variety; they conjure up mode 4 to subtly underscore the mortality of humankind.

Misa del quarto tono

In the California repertoire, we often see the four-voice settings of the Ordinary subdivided into two families of movements: the Kyrie, Sanctus, and Agnus Dei are often pulled together with shared material, and the longer Gloria and Credo constitute the other grouping. Such is the case with the *Misa de Cataluña,* and to some extent that organizing principle functions as well in the *Misa Viscaína.* A third mass in this vein is the *Misa del quarto tono* that was as central to the California mission repertoire as any other single piece.[61] Its Kyrie, Sanctus, and Agnus Dei are poured from the same mold, with only a few adjustments here and there to reconcile the text's declamation to the underlying triple meter. (For a facsimile of this complete mass, consult photos B-8 through B-13 in appendix B online.)

The Gloria and Credo are studies in textural change; there is an element of *alternatim* performance style, with sonorities changing at the same elemental division points we discussed earlier in the context of the *Misa Ligera,* but here there is a more vibrant palette of colors.[62] In addition to the full four-voice homophonic passages and the soloistic *canto figurado* phrases, we also see plenty of duets and trios, and the voices that make up these smaller ensembles are ever-changing. Instead of having two different textures or timbres flip back and forth between them, in this Mass's longer movements nearly every combination of voices and groupings shows up. The Durán choirbook C-C-59 develops this palette even further, sometimes adding a fifth voice to the large, full-bodied sections.[63] Not only do the number of independent melodic lines shift perpetually, but the "weight" of the vocal resources also undergo changes. Sometimes a single melodic line will be labeled "coro," and at other times "solo" or "solo tiple." Clearly, the full choral resources will have a heavier and more rotund sonority than the clearly etched line of a single soprano. There are also four-part passages that are to be sung by "todos" (everybody) and other four-part passages with no advice to steer the way. As discussed in chapter 2, these polyphonic passages were very likely the domain of soloists with one-on-a-part, unless marked otherwise. With the choirbook indication "todos," the piece can shift from full four-part harmony by the soloists and then shift to the even richer sound of the whole choir realizing the chords. Furthermore, the different colors of note heads or the use of "hollow" notes as opposed to "filled" ones can indicate that different voice types are to sing the different lines. In a sense, then, the *Misa del quarto tono* "orchestrates" the mass by using the full gamut of contrasting vocal timbres.[64] Sancho's rendition of this piece, however, shrinks the whole texture down to three vocalists, and the reduction is forced to ignore all the timbral subtleties found in the larger choirbooks where a larger and more varied performing force was utilized.

Quite possibly it is associated with the Mass for the Seven Dolours of the Blessed Virgin Mary, as suggested by the neighboring "Toda hermosa eres Maria."[65] The origins of its Gloria show the union of two different "family trees," one from Toledo in central Spain and the other from Cataluña. The thinner solo lines in *canto figurado* that accompany the even-numbered text snippets ("Laudamus te," "Adoramus te," "Gratias agimus tibi," etc.) possibly are from Toledo, since this is the Gloria written out in Serra's choirbook in the context of the "Misa Toledana, Quarto tono, punto alto."[66] The polyphonic section's genealogy is Catalan, as indicated by several clues. Folder 55 in the WPA collection contains the music for the odd-numbered verses ("Et in terra pax," "Benedicimus te," "Glorificamus te," etc.) in its mass titled *Misa simple*. Significantly, the same sheets of music have written on their flip sides a setting of a *Gloria pastoril, 5° tono,* and for the soprano part it indicates the performer as "tible 1," a Catalan spelling as opposed to the Castilian cognate *tiple*.[67] Reinforcing this regional association, the version of the *Misa simple* preserved at the San Fernando Mission (and written out in the hand of Juan Bautista Sancho) utilizes its Gloria from a *Misa simple*—and its Kyrie is titled "Kyrie Clasichs â 2. tono 4to." The terminology "Clasichs" is Mallorquín or Catalán.[68]

We are fortunate to have an extant instrumental part for the *Gloria simple* that is the polyphonic core of the *Misa del quarto tono*. Folder 55 in Berkeley contains vocal parts (for "tiple" and "baxo") but further includes the "Acompanyamento para el Organo." As with so much of the WPA materials that were originally the personal collection of Fray Juan Bautista Sancho, we can guess that they were prepared *before* Sancho's departure for the New World—hence the reference to the "órgano," an instrument not readily available in the missions. As with almost any basso continuo line for choral works, it most frequently doubles and reinforces the vocal "baxo" line—but not always. We find a model for the brief instrumental introductions before some of the sections.[69] Unfortunately, the notated upper-register parts (if there were any) are no longer extant.

Notes

1. There is no need to go through the various movements and elements of the Mass here, since it is easily found elsewhere. See John Harper, *The Forms and Orders of Western Liturgy from the Tenth to the Eighteenth Century* (Oxford: Clarendon Press of Oxford University Press, 1991), especially chap. 3, "The Liturgical Year and Calendar" (pp. 45–57), and chap. 7, "The Mass" (pp. 109–26). Also recommend is Richard Hoppin, *Medieval Music* (New York: Norton, 1978), esp. the section "The Liturgical Year and the Church Calendar" (pp. 51–56) and chap. 5, "The Roman Mass" (pp. 116–43).

2. For obvious reasons, I cannot explore *every* mass in this "core" repertoire, not to mention all the masses that fall outside it. This chapter deals with representative examples.

3. For example, the scribe for Santa Barbara, Doc. 7 took the tune for the "Statuit ei Dominus" and recycled it for nearly every text at Mass; its melody serves as the Introit, Alleluia verse, Offertory, and Communion, all on the same day. For each successive day in the liturgical

year, he reused this same melody yet again to set the text for that particular day's Mass Proper. Similarly, one basic Alleluia melody is reused over and over. Obviously, if only two recurring melodies are used to celebrate Mass, it would only be a matter of days before new converts were able to join in. In my opinion, the most likely creator of Document 7 was either Estevan Tapís or José Viader.

4. For information regarding Durán's standardization of plainchant tunes in his choirbooks, see the section *Canto llano* in chapter 1 and especially notes 40–43.

5. Owen da Silva was the first to credit Narciso Durán as the primary composer of the California mission repertoire, followed afterward by the influential article by Sister Mary Ray Dominic and Joseph H. Engbeck Jr. in which they take the theory one step further, ruminating that Durán incorporated elements from native California in his compositions. See Father Owen da Silva, O.F.M., *Mission Music of California: A Collection of Old California Mission Hymns and Masses* (Los Angeles: Warren F. Lewis, 1941), esp. 14–15, 117–18; and Mary Dominic Ray and Joseph H. Engbeck, Jr. *Gloria Dei: The Story of California Mission Music* (Berkeley: University Extension, University of California, 1975), esp. 3. As subsequent scholars mined da Silva and Dominic and Engbeck for information, this vein of enthusiasm for Durán-as-composer continued to spread and grow. See Maynard Geiger, O.F.M., *Franciscan Missionaries in Hispanic California 1769–1848: A Biographical Dictionary* (San Marino, Calif.: Huntington Library, 1969), 69; Joseph Halpin, "A Study of Mission Music Located at Mission Santa Clara de Asís," M.A. thesis, San Jose State College, 1968; Beryl Hoskin, *A History of the Santa Clara Mission Library* (Oakland, Calif.: Biobooks, 1961), esp. 44n20; Kristin Dutcher Mann, "The Power of Song in the Missions of Northern New Spain," Ph.D. diss., Northern Arizona University, 2002, esp. 239; Francis Price, "Letters of Narciso Durán from the Manuscript Collections in the California Historical Society Library," *California Historical Society Quarterly*, vol 37, no. 2 (June 1958), 97–99; James A. Sandos, *Converting California: Indians and Franciscans in the Missions* (New Haven, Conn.: Yale University Press, 2004), esp. 137–38; and Howard Swan, *Music in the Southwest 1825–1950* (San Marino, Calif.: Huntington Library, 1952), 86–87.

6. William Summers was the first to really scrutinize the issue of Durán's putative authorship and arrives at a different conclusion. He states: "Da Silva also suggested, though never stated outright, that the polyphonic mass ordinary settings in Durán's choirbook may have been composed by him. Their titles, *Misa de Cataluña, Misa Viscaina,* etc., may in da Silva's mind have reflected the nostalgia Durán felt for Spain. What seems to be the case, though, is that this polyphonic music for the Mass was probably not composed by Durán, but reflected Durán's very energetic eclecticism in searching out useful music for his Native American choirs." See Summers, "The *Misa Viscaina:* An Eighteenth-Century Musical Odyssey to Alta California," in *Encomium Musicae: Essays in Memory of Robert J. Snow,* ed. by David Crawford and G. Grayson Wagstaff, Festschrift Series, No. 17 (Hillsdale, N.Y.: Pendragon Press, 2002), 134.

7. Da Silva, *Mission Music of California,* 14.

8. Ibid., 15.

9. "Misa de 5° T° a 4 voces, compás de 4" (Mass in mode 5 for 4 Voices, in Quadruple Meter), choirbook C-C-59 in the Bancroft Library, pp. 112–16; "Misa de 5° t°. Compás de 4 a 4° voces," in Santa Clara Ms. 4, pp. 57–62; "Misa de 5° t° a 4 Vs," Santa Barbara Doc. 1, pp. 41–52. It is not until the distorted rendition of this piece written out by Pacífico Capénaz in 1841 that this mass was identified as the *Misa a 4 vozes de Cataluña.* Santa Barbara Doc. 3, "Misa a 4 vozes de Cataluña / Nuevamente hago y firmo, / hoy dia 1° de Di^bre de 1841 / Pacífico Capénaz".

10. Jon Bagüés Erriondo, *La música en la Real Sociedad Bascongada de los Amigos del País,* Ilustración musical en el País Vasco, [Tomo] I, Colección Ilustración Vasca, Tomo II (Donastia–San Sebastián: Departamento de Cultura del Gobierno Vasco and Real Sociedad Bascongada de los Amigos del País, 1990), 88–89, 268; Fr. Ignacio Omaechevarría, "Los Amigos del País y los Frailes de Aranzazu," and "Los Frailes de Aránzazu en la Edad de Oro de las Misiones de California," *Misiones Franciscanas,* no. 429 (1964) 278–79, cited in Bagüés Erriondo, *La música en la Real Sociedad Bascongada,* 88n87, and bibliography on p. 268; William J. Summers, "The *Misa Viscaina,*" 135–37; and Summers, "*Opera seria* in Spanish California: An Introduction to a Newly-Identified Manuscript Source," in *Music in Performance and Society: Essays in Honor of*

Roland Jackson, ed. by Malcolm Cole and John Koegel (Warren, Mich.: Harmonie Park Press, 1997), 271.

11. Summers identified the Requiem in Durán's choirbooks as a reworking of Sancho's Requiem in "Spanish Music in California 1769–1840: A Reassessment," Manuscript 912 in Santa Barbara Mission Archive, *Report of the Twelfth Congress of the International Musicological Society, Berkeley, 1977* (Kassel: Bärenreiter, 1981); and Summers, "The *Misa Viscaina*," 134. Grayson Wagstaff also reconfirms this point, acknowledging Summers's research as the basis for his argument, in his perceptive article "Franciscan Mission Music in California, c. 1770–1830: Chant, Liturgical and Polyphonic Traditions," *Journal of the Royal Music Association*, vol. 126 (2001), 62, 77. The Sancho manuscript to which they refer is found in the folder of photographs in the WPA collection at the Department of Music of the University of California, Berkeley, WPA folder 72, "Missa de Requiem, a 3 voces, 1796." This manuscript has the title page "Missa de Requiem â3 voces/ et Laboravi â 3./ Es del uso de Fray Juan Bau[tis]ta/ Sancho Diaconos y Religioso/ Observante./ Año 1796." Its movements include "Requiem eternam dona eis Domine," "Et tibi reddetur," "Kyrie eleyson," "Domine Jesu" (Offertorio, & a clef change, lower to alto voice), "Laboravi in gemitu (Motete â 3)," "Quantus tremor est futurus," "Rex tremendae majestatis," "Querems me se disti," "Lacrimosa dies illa," and "Pre Jesu Domine." The Durán Requiem to which they refer is found in several choirbooks, including "Missa de Requiem a 4 voces...compás a 4," in choirbook C-C-59, pp. 67–69, and 67bis, p. E. p. Ebis, p. Ebis2, p. F; "Misa Solemne de Difuntos a 4 voces, compás de 4," in Santa Clara Ms. 4, pp. 84–86; "Misa de Requiem a 4 voces," in Santa Barbara Doc. 1, pp. 53–59 (although the sheet containing pp. 55–56 is missing from the choirbook, as are the sheets containing pp. 60–67 that almost certainly would have paralleled the material found in both C-C-59 and Santa Clara Ms. 4).

12. WPA folder 69, "Missa de los Angeles â 4 voces, 5to tono; y/ Credo Dominical 6to tono del/ simple uso de Fr. Juan Bautista Sancho/ Re[li]g[io]so Observante i Diacono./ 1796."

13. Two such individuals are Alfred Robinson and Sir George Simpson; their accounts of music activities are intriguing and reveal a vibrant and accomplished musical establishment at the San José Mission and Santa Barbara Mission under Durán. See Sir George Simpson, *Narrative of a Voyage to California Ports in 1841–42. Together with Voyages to Sitka, the Sandwich Islands and Okhotsk. To which are added: Sketches of Journies across America, Asia, and Europe. From the Narrative of a Voyage around the World*, edited, corrected, and with a foreword by Thomas C. Russell (San Francisco: Private Press of Thomas C. Russell, 1930), esp. 128–29; and Alfred Robinson, *Life in California: A Historical Account of the Origin, Customs, and Traditions of the Indians of Alta-California*, foreword by Joseph A. Sullivan (Oakland, Calif.: Biobooks, 1947), esp. 52–53, 71–72.

14. In general, the mission choirbooks include only some movements from the Proper: Introits, Alleluias, Communions, and sometimes Offertories. Gradual movements are exceedingly rare. Exceptions include "Christus factus est," Gradual for Maundy Thursday, found in choirbook C-C-68:1, fol. 6v, and in Santa Clara Ms. 3, p. 30. That latter choirbook also includes the Gradual for the Mass for the Dead, "Requiem aeternam," p. 2.

15. Ordinary settings in *canto llano* are rare in California manuscripts. It should be emphasized that many California sources for the Mass Ordinary look like they are plainchant settings but are not. Instead, most turn out to contain *canto figurado* settings or *canto figurado* snippets intended for insertion in *alternatim* settings. When actual plainchant does crop up, it is often in conjunction with Lent, Holy Week, Requiem masses, or burial services. The most frequent plainchant settings from the Ordinary are the Kyrie "fons bonitatis" and Kyrie "de Angelis" as found in the *Liber Usualis, with an Introduction and Rubrics in English*, ed. by the Benedictines of Solesmes (Tournai, Belgium: Society of St. John the Evangelist and Desclée, 1947) on pp. 19 and 37. Hereafter I refer to page numbers in the *Liber Usualis* with the prefix "L.U." Consult the following:

C-C-68:2. "Kyrie," last unnumbered folio [Ev] (Kyrie "fons bonitatis," in L.U.19).
C-C-59. *Ash Wednesday:* "Kyrie," p. 5; "Sanctus," p. 6. *Palm Sunday:* "Kyrie Dominicales 1° t°," p. 10 (Kyrie "Orbis factor," in L.U.46); "Credo Dominical," p. 10 (Credo I, in L.U.64). *Good Friday or Holy Saturday:* "Kirie eleyson, 5° t°,"

p. 18 (Kyrie "de Angeles," in L.U.37). *Mass for the Dead:* "Kirie eleyson," p. 62
(L.U.1807).

Santa Clara Ms. 4. *Ash Wednesday:* "Kyrie," p. 4; "Sanctus," p. 6. *Mass for the Dead:*
"Kirie eleyson," p. 78 (L.U.1807). *Burial for Adults:* "Kirie eleyson," p. 84.

WPA collection. Folder 61, "Kyries. Tono 4to un punto alto," and "Kyries de Jesus,
t[on]o 5to," on photo R-12. Folder 63, "Kirie, tono 4to," photo I-3 (Kyrie "fons
bonitatis," in L.U.19). Folder 74, "Kirie semple [*sic*] 7° 8° [tonos], photo B-1;
"Sanctus," photo B-4, "Agnus Dei," photo B-4. Folder 79, "Kyrie" copied by
Arroyo de la Cuesta (Kyrie "de Angeles," in L.U.37).

Serra choirbook M.0612. *Mass in Mode 6:* "Kyrie eleyson," fol. 14; "Sanctus," fol. 14v;
"Agnus Dei," fol. 15. *Missa Toledana, Quarto Tono, Punto Alto:* "Kyrie eleyson,"
mode 4, fol. 15, "Sanctus" mode 2, fol. 16; "Agnus Dei," mode 1, fol. 16v.

San Juan Bautista Ms. 1. "Kyrie eleyson," p. 65 [photo 84 in WPA item 45], (Kyrie "de
Angeles," in L.U.37).

16. An association between some masses and particular feast days is demonstrable, but that
does not confine those masses solely to those days. Some flexibility in usage is assumed.

17. Several choirbooks contain these three masses grouped in the following manner.
Choirbook C-C-59: "Misa Sabbatina ō de la Virgen 1ʳ Tono" (Mass for Saturdays or for the
Virgin, in Mode 1), pp. 131–36; "Misa a 4 Voces 6° Tº" (Mass for 4 Voices in Mode 6), pp. 137–40;
"[Misa Ligera] (Uncomplicated Mass)," pp. 141–44. Santa Clara Ms. 4: [Misa Sabbatina ō de la
Virgen], pp. 130–32; [Misa a 4 Voces 6° Tº], pp. 132–36; and "Misa Ligera," pp. 137–40. In addition,
the "Missa Sabbatina o de la Virgen. 1ʳ tono" is found in Santa Barbara, Doc. 2, pp. 143–50, and
yet another copy of it is located (without title) in Santa Barbara, Doc. 21A, fols. 1–1v. The title
"Misa Ligera" has several connotations. The term "ligera" can indicate "light, facile, effortless,
smooth, uncomplicated, straightforward, simple." The Santa Clara choirbook gives "Ligera" as
part of the title to the third mass, and choirbook C-C-59 leaves the mass untitled. However, this
latter source uses the term "ligera" can indicate e in the Gloria movement. There had just been
an excursion to new material in D minor at "Qui tollis peccata mundi" that bore the marking
"Despacio." With the return of the original musical material that introduced the movement—
but now at the words "Qui sedes ad dexteram Patris"—choirbook C-C-59 provides the new
instruction "ligera." We might assume that this description of "simple, light, effortless" would
also apply to the work's beginning, since the musical material is the same.

18. Although the text runs forward with no internal deletions, it should be observed that the
Sanctus and Agnus Dei are set in their truncated, abbreviated form as is so often the case in the
Hispano-American sources of the late Baroque and Classical periods. The Sanctus is cut short
before the "Benedictus qui venit," and the Agnus has no reference to the last phrase, "dona nobis
pacem." It is assumed, however, that the choir simply sings the text "dona nobis pacem" over the
same notes that they had used for "miserere nobis." Also, the incipits of the Gloria and Credo
are intoned rather than set as polyphonic phrases. Thus, the first *polyphonic* phrase in the
Gloria begins "et in terra pax." Similarly, the choir enters the Credo by singing polyphonically at
the line "Patrem omnipotentem."

19. The dedication of Mass to Mary is a long-standing tradition and one that was practiced
in the missions of South America as well as in North America. Fray Francisco Xarque, a Jesuit
friar in Paraguay, writes in 1687, "On every Saturday, at daybreak, a polyphonic Mass for the
Blessed Virgin is sung by the whole music chapel, with the entire village in attendance" (Todos
los Sabados al amanecer, se canta Missa de Beata Virgine, a canto de organo, con la Capilla,
y assiste todo el Pueblo). See Piotr Nawrot's *Indígenas y cultura musical de las reducciones
jesuíticas. Guaraníes, Chiquitos, Moxos,* vol. 1, Colección: Monumenta Música 1, Festival de
Música Renacentista y Barroca Americana (Cochabamba, Bolivia: Verbo Divino, 2000), 16.

20. For more information on Saturday Mass for the Blessed Virgin, see the discussion of the
Alabado in chapter 3, especially the latter pages of that section, and notes 60–62.

21. Although the title, *Misa Sabbatina ō de la Virgen,* clearly associates this Mass Ordinary
with Mary in choirbook C-C-59, this same work is untitled in Santa Clara Ms. 4. Also, that
particular choirbook follows the Agnus Dei with *¡O sacratissimo cuerpo de Jesús!* and *Sacris
solemniis* which would place it in the context of Corpus Christi. Apparently, Corpus Christi

functions and Marian ones shared some of the same Mass settings; there are other examples as well, such as the *Misa del quinto tono* (also known as the *Misa de Cataluña*). Evidence for a *Corpus Christi* affiliation with the *Misa de Cataluña* is as follows: Choirbook C-C-68:1 in the Bancroft Library begins with a mass on its first eight folios. The Gloria for this mass is drawn from the *Misa de San Antonio* (choirbook C-C-59, p. 50), also known as the *Misa Solemne* (Santa Clara Ms. 4, p. 50)—and this mass is explicitly associated with Easter. If we continue in the liturgical year past Easter, we arrive at Corpus Christi. Significantly, the subsequent mass in choirbook C-C-68:1 (fols. 9–18v) is the widely disseminated one known across California as the *Misa del quinto tono* or the *Misa de Cataluña*. Since this mass follows on the heels of Easter's *Misa Solemne*, it would make sense for the *Misa de Cataluña* to be associated with the main feast after Easter—that of Corpus Christi. This theory is reinforced by the placement of three polyphonic Corpus Christi hymns (*¡O sacratissimo cuerpo de Jesús!*, *Sacris solemniis*, and the *Gozos de la Purísima* ("Para dar luz inmortal") on the ensuing pages immediately after the *Misa de Cataluña* (fols. 18v–20v). These hymns would complete the Corpus Christi feast day; they would be used in the outdoor procession of the Host, immediately after the celebration of the Mass of Corpus Christi. Evidence for a *Marian affiliation* is as follows: in Santa Clara Ms. 4 (p. 57), the *Misa de Cataluña* is followed by *Dulce Esposo de María, Gozos al Señor San José* ("Para dar luz inmortal . . . esposo de María"), *Gozos de la Purísima* ("Para dar luz inmortal . . . alva del día"), *¡O sacratissimo cuerpo de Jesús!*, *¡O Rey de corazones!*, *¡O qué suave!*, *¡O pan de vida!*, *Trisagio*, and four settings of *Salve Virgen pura*—all material that is associated both with Corpus Christi and with Marian feasts.

22. The "standard" opening phrase in the *Misa del sexto tono* occurs in the Kyrie, mm. 1–10; and Sanctus, mm. 1–10. The recurring "middle" phrase occurs in the Kyrie, mm. 18–23; Gloria, mm. 16–21; and Sanctus, mm. 11–16. The cliché "ending" phrase occurs in the Kyrie, mm. 34–44; Gloria, mm. 125–35; Sanctus, mm. 21–31; and Agnus Dei, mm. 16–26.

23. "Eres toda hermosa, Letra a la SS. Virgen," choirbook C-C-59, p. 120.

24. The version of "Eres toda hermosa" in Santa Clara Ms. 4, p. 128, is a slight variant of the hymn as it appears in choirbook C-C-59, p. 120. The latter source sometimes adds a few more voices. As has been observed earlier, the "added" voices in C-C-59 may not go up and down in exactly the same way that the other voices do at any given moment, but usually the "added" voices end up doubling *pitches* that are already sounding. The difference between the two choirbook versions, therefore, would be hardly distinguishable to the ear.

25. This untitled Mass Ordinary in C major is found in Santa Clara Ms. 4, unnumbered pages *A–D* immediately following p. 120; a concordant version is found in the small booklet of five folios, Santa Clara Ms. 2, without any appended hymns.

26. For a discussion of word painting in the *canto figurado* settings of the Credo, see chapter 5, especially the section that analyzes the "Credo Artanense" and notes 99–100.

27. The two major-mode masses of the triptych both make excursions into minor modality, especially in order to express the more despondent or world-weary references to sin, or of man's fallibility. Minor-mode emphasis occurs in the following locations. *Misa del sexto tono:* Gloria: "Qui tollis peccata mundi, suscipe deprecationem nostram," mm. 72–85; Credo, "consubstantialem Patri" (D minor), mm. 54–58; "Et incarnatus est" (D minor), mm. 80–83; "judicare vivos et mortuos" (F minor), mm. 141–45; and "et vivificantem" (D minor), mm. 156–61. *Misa Ligera:* This mass's core structure vacillates between phrases in F major and D minor. As a result, many areas in D minor are simply part of the "regular" phrasing and not intended to incorporate word painting. However, when *new* musical material and phrasing occur in a minor modality, it is clearly intended to convey the melancholic and somber text, such as in the Gloria's "Qui tollis peccata mundi," mm. 46–59, and the Credo's "Et incarnatus est," mm. 58–66.

28. Yet another book that connects a polyphonic setting of the *Stabat Mater dolorosa* with the Mass for the Seven Dolours of the Blessed Virgin Mary is San Juan Bautista Ms. 1, plate 53, p. 34. The "lost" San Juan Bautista Choirbook had a "Stabat mater dolorosa: à 2 y à 4 voces" on p. 66. Unfortunately, that source is no longer extant. Only the index is preserved as plate 136 in WPA item 45.

29. It should be noted for the *Stabat Mater* on p. 118 of choirbook C-C-59, which comes near the end of the Mass for the Seven Dolours of the Blessed Virgin Mary, there are flaps with new "replacement" music measures glued over the original musical staves, concealing from view the

original musical material. It is possible that this "original" musical setting matched the *Stabat Mater* seen on p. 15 (which is also the tune that we find referenced in the Gloria of the Mass in C major). If this is the case, then we would have an even stronger tie between the Mass in C major and a putative association with Mary.

30. At least four choirbooks group together the three duet masses. Choirbook C-C-59 contains "Misa de la Soledad a duo 6° T° y Compás de 4" (Mass of [Our Lady] of Solitude, for two voices in mode 6 and in quadruple meter), pp. 43–46; "Misa Vizcaina a dos voces, Compas de tres 6° T" (Mass from Biscay [or "Basque Mass"], for two voices, in triple meter and mode 6), pp. 46–50; and "Misa de S. Antonio 6° T°" (Mass of San Antonio in mode 6), pp. 50–55. Santa Clara Ms. 4 contains "Misa de la Soledad a duo. 6 t° Compás de 4," pp. 41–45; "Missa Viscaina. Compás de 3. 6° t°," pp. 45–50; "Missa Solemne. 6 t°" (Solemn Mass in mode 6 [= the same piece as choirbook C-C-59's *Misa de San Antonio*]), pp. 50–55. Santa Barbara Doc. 1 contains "Misa Viscaina, 6° T°," pp. 1–8; "Misa de la Soledad," pp. 9–18; "Misa de S. Antonio 6° tono," pp. 18–29. Santa Barbara Doc. 2 is missing the first half of its original contents, beginning in midstream at p. 108. This page begins with the "solus Dominus" of the Gloria in the *Misa de la Soledad* (continuing, pp. 108–11) and is followed by the *Misa de San Antonio* (pp. 111–18). We can safely assume, therefore, that the *Misa Viscaína* was copied into the previous pages of this manuscript that are now missing (probably around pp. 100–106). The "Tapís choirbook" at San Juan Bautista (San Juan Bautista Ms. 1) includes the *Misa Viscaína* under the title "Misa 2ª a duo, 6° tono" on pp. 69–73 (photos 88–92 in WPA item 45), but the preceding mass is "Misa 1ª a duo, 6° tono," another duet mass in mode 6, but it does not match any of the masses in the aforementioned choirbooks. The third mass in San Juan Bautista Ms. 1 is the monophonic "Misa 3ª De Angelis. Tono 5," the plainchant Mass VIII in the *Liber Usualis,* pp. 37–40. Mention should also be made of the fragmentary and error-ridden version of an untitled Gloria in choirbook C-C-68:1 at the Bancroft Library, fols. 2v–3.

31. In Hispano-American sources it was common in the Sanctus to excise the text "Benedictus que venit in nomine Domini." Frequently, the Agnus Dei would notate only a single statement, "Agnus Dei qui tollis peccata mundi, miserere nobis."

32. The writing of mnemonic aids also occurs in the *Misa Ligera* of Santa Clara Ms. 4, where "substitute" words are written in small letters either above or below the main text to prompt the singer. In the Sanctus of the *Misa Ligera,* "Benedictus qui venit ..." is inscribed below the "Pleni sunt caeli" (p. 140). Similarly, the words "Dona nobis pacem" from the Agnus Dei are written tidily below the line "miserere nobis" (p. 140). In another example from Santa Clara Ms. 4 in which a musical phrase is recycled with a new line of text, the Introit "Guadeamus omnes in Domino" during the Feast of the Assumption (p. 32) has two alternate texts written below the main one so that the tune can be applied to the Feast of Saint Francis and for All Saints' Day. The words "Beatæ Mariæ Virginis de cujus assumtio" are written in large letters, and they are destined for the Feast of the Assumption. Under those words—written in small letters—we see "beati Patris Franciscii Solemnitate" (for the Feast of Saint Francis) and "Sanctorum omnium de quorum" (for All Saints' Day). The same type of substitution happens in the Durán choirbook C-C-59, p. 35, where he supplies the Franciscan text underneath the text for the Assumption.

33. "La Semana Santa la celebraba con todas las ceremonias de nuestra Madre la Iglesia: El Domingo se hacia la Procesion de Ramos, y asi en este dia, como en los siguientes se cantaba la Pasion, (haciendo uno o dos Papeles, porque no eramos mas de dos) y tambien los Maytines del Triduo: El Jueves se colocaba el Depósito en el Monumento, y tanto en este dia como el Viernes y Sabado se practicaban todas las demas ceremonias y formalidades de costumbre. A mas de ésto añadia varias Procesiones que acaba con algun Sermon ô Plática El Jueves, despues de haber labado los pies á doce Indios de los mas viejos, y comido con ellos, predicaba el Sermon de Mandato, y á la noche hacia la Procesion con una Imagen de Christo Crucificado con la acompañamiento de todo el Pueblo. El Viernes por la mañana predicaba de la Pasion, y á la tarde se representaba con la mayor viveza el descendimiento de la Cruz, con una Imagen de perfecta estatura, que para el efecto se mandó hacer de goznes; y predicando de este asunto con la mayor devocion y ternura, se colocaba al Señor en una Urna, y se hacia la Procesion del Santo Entierro. Poniase despues en un Altar que para este efecto se hallaba preparado, y á la noche se hacia otra Procesion de nuestra Señora de la Soledad, que se concluia con una Plática

de este asunto. El Sabado se hacian todas las ceremonias pertenecientees á este dia, se bendecia la Fuente, y bautizaban los Neófitos que habia instruidos y dispuestos para ello. El Domingo muy de mañana salia la Procesion de Jesus resucitado, la qual se hacia con una devota Imagen del Señor, y otra de la Santísima Virgen, y vueltos á la Iglesia se cantaba Misa, y predicaba el V. Padre de este Soberano Misterio.

Con tan devotos exercicios, no pudo menos que imprimirse una tie[r]na y grande devocion en aquellos Neófitos, y con ella se disponian á celebrar anualmente la Semana Santa, y corriendo la voz por los Pueblos de la cercanias que habitaban Españoles, venian estos á practicar lo mismo, atrahidos de lo que oían decir de la devocion de aquellos Indios; y luego que lo experimentaron, se acostumbraron á concurrir todos los años, mudandose á la Mision, hasta que pasaba la Pasqua." Francisco Palóu, *Relacion historica de la vida y apostolicas tareas del venerable Padre Fray Junipero Serra, y las misiones que fundó en la California Septentrional, y nuevos establecimientos de Monterey* (Mexico City: Don Felipe de Zúñiga y Ontiveros, 1787), facsimile edition, March of America Facsimile Series, No. 49, ([Ann Arbor, Mich.]: University Microfilms, 1966), 30–31. Translation by C. Scott Williams in *Francisco Palóu's Life and Apostolic Labors of the Venerable Father Junípero Serra, Founder of the Franciscan Missions of California,* trans. by C. Scott Williams, introduction and notes by George Wharton James (Pasadena, Calif.: George Wharton James, 1913), 29–30.

34. In choirbook C-C-59 the Holy Week Mass Propers occur on pp. 8–19. It goes through the important final days of the week in detail: Palm Sunday (including what is sung during distribution of the palms and the procession), pp. 8–12; Maundy Thursday (including the *Pange lingua...mysterium* for the Procession, the *Mandatum novum do vocis* during the washing of the feet, and the polyphonic *Stabat mater dolorosa,* probably sung in the evening's procession), pp. 12–15; Good Friday (with reference to singing *Stabat Mater* plus the new hymns *Pange lingua...certaminis* with the response *Crux fidelis* [in polyphony] and *Vexilla Regis prodeunt* [both hymns probably accompanying the procession]), pp. 16–17; Holy Saturday, including music for Vespers (with the explicit incorporation of instrumental performance), p. 18; Easter Sunday (including a polyphonic rendition of *Victimae paschali laudes* with instrumental insertions), p. 19. Good Friday is also given special attention, with its Matins appearing on pp. 75–92 and its Lauds on pp. 92–98.

With respect to choirbook C-C-59, it is worth considering the context of the hymns *Pange lingua... certaminis* along with its polyphonic response, *Crux fidelis,* and *Vexilla Regis prodeunt,* both of which occur on Good Friday. In standard liturgical practice *Pange lingua... certaminis* is from Matins and *Vexilla Regis prodeunt* is sung during Vespers. But we do not have the neighboring music for Vespers or Matins written out at this location. Why? A clue is provided a few pages earlier, where *Pange lingua...mysterium* that occurs just a few pages before that is tied explicitly to the *procession* on Maundy Thursday. Given the "fancier" treatment of these pieces here (in *alternatim* performance, in polyphony, or both), it seems most logical that the other pieces in an "elevated" style were meant for the special occasion of the procession. In this instance, the texts are particularly fitting. *Vexilla regis* proclaims, "The standards of the King appear, the mystery of the Cross shines out in glory...." There could hardly be a text more evocative of the processions with banners and the cross as described by Serra and Palóu on religious occasions. Similarly, the response *Crux fidelis* with its "outdoor" imagery would have been graphically realistic: the words exclaim, "Faithful Cross, tree that is alone in its glory among all other trees...." Again the text would be perfectly suited for the neophytes who paraded out of the mission through the surrounding trees with the cross held high.

In Santa Clara Ms. 4 some of the same material appears, in particular, the Mass Propers for Holy Week: Palm Sunday, pp. 6–7; Maundy Thursday, pp. 7–8; [Good Friday, not indicated], Holy Saturday (including Vespers), p. 9; Easter Sunday, pp. 10–11. Good Friday Matins is found on pp. 86–103 and Good Friday Lauds on pp. 103–5. This source does not contain all the "bonus" material such as the hymns that appear in choirbook C-C-59 and that would be needed to complete the Holy Week pageantry as described by Palóu.

35. For an explicit reference to the "Kyrie de Angeles" or the inclusion of its music, consult choirbook C-C-59, "Kirie eleyson. Sabado Santo después de las Letanías se canta Kiries de Angeles. 5° t°," p. 18; the Kyrie de Angeles in the hand of Felipe Arroyo de la Cuesta in folder 79

in the WPA collection; "Misa 3ª de Angeles. 5° tono," in San Juan Bautista Ms. 1, p. 73 (which is plate 92 in WPA item 45). It is also likely that Sancho interpolated phrases from this chant in *alternatim* performance in his "Missa de los Angeles â 4 voces, 5to tono; y/ Credo Dominical 6to tono del/ simple uso de Fr. Juan Bautista Sancho/ Re[li]g[io]so Observante i Diacono./ 1796," folder 69 in the WPA.

36. We have already seen the enormous flexibility in bar line placement with regard to *¡O qué suave!* and *¡O Rey de corazones!* See the discussion of bar lines in the section "Music for the Corpus Christi Procession" in chapter 4.

37. Father Owen da Silva includes a complete edition of the *Misa Viscaína* in *Mission Music of California*, 57–74. San Juan Bautista Ms. 1 has a version that coincides with da Silva about 90 percent of the time in the Gloria and Credo, but there are important variances. The Sanctus and Agnus Dei are completely different. A few comments regarding da Silva's editorial decisions are in order. In da Silva's edition of the Credo, the music accompanying "Crucifixus etiam pro nobis" (mm. 97–110) is completely different than that found in choirbook C-C-59, Santa Clara Ms. 4, and the San Juan Bautista Ms. 1. Also da Silva has included a setting of the Sanctus's "Benedictus qui venit" (p. 73) that is not found in these three choirbooks or in the Santa Barbara Mission Music Choirbook (Doc. 1). Da Silva cites four manuscripts as his sources: "There are two copies of the Mass at Mission Santa Bárbara, one at Mission San Juan Bautista, and one at the Bancroft Library, Berkeley" (da Silva, *Mission Music of California*, 118). Since the aforementioned "Benedictus qui venit" is found neither in the choirbook C-C-59 at the Bancroft, nor in Mission San Juan Bautista, nor in Santa Barbara Doc. 1, it must have been obtained from the remaining Santa Barbara manuscript—a source with which I am not familiar. He states that his modern edition is in the original keys, but he transposes the Sanctus up a step from F to G. He has inadvertently deleted measure 5 from the Sanctus.

Da Silva ascribes the mass's authorship to Narciso Durán (See da Silva, *Mission Music of California*, pp. 14–15, 118), but no known source attributes this work to Durán. Without question, Durán played an important role in the musical life of mission period California, but there is no evidence that he composed or received prior musical training that would prepare him with that skill. Durán describes his own musical abilities as those of a novice. Refer to chapter 1 for a discussion of Durán's musical training and musical skill.

38. In two of the sources, the Credo for the *Misa de San Antonio/Solemne* is placed in a slightly different location—coming after the Agnus Dei—as opposed to the *Misa de las Soledad* and *Misa Viscaína*, where the Credo is folded between the Gloria and Sanctus. In choirbook C-C-59 the Credo is titled "Credo Recoleto 5° T° a Duo, Compás de 3" (pp. 53–55); Santa Clara Ms. 4 contains the same Credo as "Credo 5 t°" (pp. 53–56). In Santa Barbara Doc. 1, however, the Credo for this mass (titled "Credo recoleto a duo 5° tono") *is* inserted between the Gloria and Sanctus (pp. 23–27).

39. As we have already seen, this linkage of Durán to this composition began with da Silva, *Mission Music of California*, 14–15, 118.

40. Bagüés Erriondo, *La música en la Real Sociedad Bascongada*, 88–89, 268; Fr. Ignacio Omaechevarría, "Los Amigos del País," and "Los Frailes de Aránzazu," *Misiones Franciscanas*, 278–79 (cited in Bagüés Erriondo, *La música en la Real Sociedad Bascongada*, 88n87, and bibliography on p. 268); Summers, "The *Misa Viscaina*," 135–37; and Summers, *Opera seria*, 271. See note 10 for complete citations.

41. Cruzelaegui's name rarely appears in the studies of eighteenth-century music in Spain, Mexico, or the New World, in spite of his importance and the competent craftsmanship of his music. For instance, there is no entry for Cruzelaegui in the most recent edition of *The New Grove Dictionary of Music and Musicians* (London: Macmillan, 2001). He is mentioned, however, in the *Diccionario de la Música Española e Hispanoamericana*, 10 vols., directed by Emilio Casares Rodicio, adjunct directors, José López-Calo and Ismael Fernández de la Cuesta (Madrid: Sociedad General de Autores y Editores, 2000), vol. 4, p. 206, in an entry by Jon Bagüés Erriondo.

42. Bagüés Erriondo, *La música en la Real Sociedad Bascongada*, 90.

43. Maynard Geiger, O.F.M., "The Internal Organization and Activities of San Fernando College, Mexico (1734–1858)," *The Americas*, vol. 6, no. 1 (July 1949), 7, 12–13.

44. Bagüés Erriondo, *La música en la Real Sociedad Bascongada*, 90; Geiger, "Internal Organization," 7, 12–13.

45. Miguel Alcázar, Jesús Estrada, and E. Thomas Stanford include a complete facsimile of this work in their anthology *Periodo Virreinal*, Series 3 (Antología), vol. 1 of *La Música en México*, series ed. by Julio Estrada (Mexico City: Instituto de Investigaciones Estéticas and the Universidad Autónoma de México, 1987), 75–99. This work is also covered in Lincoln Spiess and Thomas Stanford's *An Introduction to Certain Mexican Musical Archives*, Detroit Studies in Music Bibliography, No. 15 (Detroit: Information Coordinators, 1969).

46. The original petition reads: "7ª. El Padre Martín de Cruzelaegui Capellán que ha sido del señor [José Antonio de] Areche, ha manifestado en su viaje por las Americas grandisimo celo por los aumentos de la Sociedad: y asi pudiera pensar la Junta en conseguirle Título de Profesor por la Clase de Músico." Document discovered by and quoted by Bagüés Erriondo, *La música en la Real Sociedad Bascongada*, 88.

47. "El autor [del *Laudate Dominum*], quien era amigo de fray Junipero Serra, escribió esta obra siendo organista del colegio mencionado [Colegio Apostólico de San Fernando en México], donde se señala su actividad desde 1775." Stanford, commentary on Cruzelaegui's *Laudate Dominum* in *Periodo Virreinal*, 75. See also Bagüés Erriondo, *La música en la Real Sociedad Bascongada*, 9; Spiess and Stanford, *An Introduction to Certain Mexican Musical Archives*.

48. The following citations have been drawn by combining and coordinating the information from four main sources: (1) Thomas E. Stanford, *Catálogo de los Acervos musicales de las Catedrales Metropolitanas de México y Puebla de la Biblioteca Nacional de Antropología e Historia y otras colecciones menores* (Mexico City: Instituto Nacional de Antropología e Historia, Gobierno del Estado de Puebla, Universidad Anahuac del Sur, Fideicomiso para la Cultura México/USA, 2002); (2) Thomas Stanford, "Catalogue for the Archivo de Música Sacra Iglesia Metropolitana México, D.F.," unpublished typescript catalogue of the microfilm collection of the Mexico City Cathedral music archive prepared by Thomas Stanford with technical operator Oscar Arzate Huete, available for consultation in the Museo Histórico de Antropología, Mexico City; (3) Thomas Stanford, "Catalogue for the Archivo de Música Sacra de la Catedral de Puebla," unpublished typescript catalogue of the microfilm collection of the Puebla Cathedral music archive prepared by Thomas Stanford with technical operator Oscar Arzate Huete, available for consultation in the Museo Histórico de Antropología, Mexico City; and (4) my own observations and annotations taken at the Mexico City Cathedral. For those longer citations bearing the more modern "AM" ascription at the citation's end, I personally examined the work and have added pertinent referential information. Robert Stevenson's earlier catalogue of Mexican cathedral holdings still merits consultation, even though it has been largely supplanted by Stanford's more recent published contribution. See Stevenson, *Renaissance and Baroque Musical Sources in the Americas* (Washington, D.C.: General Secretariat, Organization of American States, 1970).

Mexico City

Vísperas para la Preciosisima Sangre de Nuestro Señor Jesu Christo, which can be subdivided into "Dixit Dominus (1775)," Leg. C.c.14, no. 1; "Beatus vir" (1775), Leg. C.c.14, no. 2; "Laudate Dominum" (1775), Leg. C.c.13; "Hymno [Hymnus ad Vesperas]," Leg. C.c.15, no. 2; "Magnificat" (1775), Leg. C.c.13, no. 2.
Maitines para la Preciosisima Sangre de Nuestro Señor Jesu Christo, which can be subdivided into "Christum Dei Filium. Invitatorium" (1775), C2, E13.15, Leg. D.d.15, AM1217; "Gratificavit nos Deus. Resp° [Primero]" (1775), C2, E13.15, Leg. D.d.15, AM1218; "Non corruptilibus. R[esponsori]o S[egund]o, Prec. Sangre" (1775), C2, E13.15, Leg. D.d.15, AM1219; "Christus Peccata Nostra. R°3°" (1775), C2, E13.15, Leg. D.d.15, AM1220; "Ipse Est Caput. R°4°" (1775), C2, E13.15, Leg. D.d.15, AM1221; "Cum Essentis Aliquando, [Responsorio 5°] (1775), C2, E13.15, Leg. D.d.15, AM1222; "Dignus es Domine. R° 6°" (1775), C2, E13.15, Leg. D.d.15, AM1223; "Passus est Christus. R°7°" (1775), C2, E13.15, Leg. D.d.15, AM1224; "Invitatur ad Paradisi. R°8°" (1775), C2, E13.15, Leg. D.d.15, AM1225; "Te Deum," Leg.

C.c.15, no. 1; "Sanguis olim victimarum," E13.16, Leg. D.d.16, AM1229; "Himno e Ynvitatorio. Preciosᵃ Sangre," E13.16, Leg. D.d.16, AM1230; and "Maytines al Preciosimi Sanguinis" [= earlier Responsories, Leg. D.d.16. AM1231].
"Terceto al Nacimiento del Niño Dios, Navidad" (1774).
"Yste Confessor," Leg. C.c.15, no. 3.
"Motete a 3 con vns" (1779), Leg. C.c.16, no. 1.

Puebla Cathedral

"Laudate Dominum," G major.
"Sequencia, Stabat Mater Dolorosa," C minor.

CENIDIM (previously from Puebla, Convento Santísima Trinidad)

Invitatorio, Himno y ocho Responsorios...para la Festividad de la Preciosisima Sangre de Nuestro Señor Jesu Christo (1775), Puebla Cathedral
Maitines, Sangre de Cristo, E-flat major.
Misa a solo de sexto tono.

49. Omaechevarría's original text reads:
"Fr. Martín de Crucélegui, asimismo Franciscano, natural de Elgoibar, músico notable, Vicario de Coro en el Colegio de Misiones de San Fernando de Mexico, autor sin duda alguna de la llamada '*Misa vizcaina,*' que se cantó mucho en las Misiones de California, según lo prueban las copias que guardan todavía los archivos misionales, y que el P. Owen da Silva atribuye sin razón al Padre Fr. Narciso Durán, al que se deben sí la '*Misa Catalana*' [sic] y otras composiciones, pero no seguramente la '*Misa vizcaína*'....
Y una vez que tocamos este tema, debo advertir entre paréntesis que otra vez se ha comenzado a cantar en algunas iglesias de California esta famosa '*Misa vizcaina,*' reeditada por los Franciscanos noretamericanos, la cual debió de llegar a California por mediación del P. Mugartegui, que tuvo frecuente correspondencia con el P. Crucélegui, mientras este componía música en el Colegio de Misiones de San Fernando de Mexico y aquél acompañaba a Fr. Junípero Serra en las Misiones californianas.
No fue pura casualidad que entre los frailes agregados a la Sociedad casi desde el principio hubiera músicos Fr. José de Larrañaga y Fr. Martín de Crucelegui. Y con esto voy a contestar a quien me pide datos sobre las composiciones musicales del P. Crucelegui. Fue, vuelvo a recordar, Vicario de Coro—o Maestro de Capilla—del Colegio de Misiones de San Fernando de México, a cuya plantilla pertenecían los Misioneros de California. El ilustre investigador norteamericano P. Meynard [sic] Geiger halló en México una Misa compuesta por él, que no recogió ni copió y que no se sabe a dónde habrá ido a parar. ¿Podrá servir la llamada que se dirige desde aqui para que el mexicano que posea este tesoro nos dé cuenta de él y nos los describa?
Por mi parte, opina que es la '*Misa vizcaina*' de la que se han encontrado ejemplares en los archivos misionales de California y que se ha vuelto a reeditar en nuestro tiempo. No encuentro razones plausibles para que a una Misa compuesta por Fr. Narciso Durán se le calificara de '*Misa vizcaina.*' En cambio, sería extraño que la Misa compuesta por Fr. Martin de Crucelegui, el amigo del P. Mugartegui, en San Fernando de Mexico, no llegara a California."
Found originally in Omaechevarría, "Los Frailes de Aránzazu," 278–79; Spanish quotation and citation in Bagüés Erriondo, *La música en la Real Sociedad Bascongada,* 88–89.
50. Summers, "The *Misa Viscaina,*" 135.
51. Ibid.; Summers, *Opera seria,* 271.
52. Juan Mariner (b. 24 September 1743 in Vilaplana, Cataluña) was a Franciscan active in California from 1785 until his death on 29 January 1800. For a brief biography, see Geiger, *Franciscan Missionaries,* 145.
53. "Misa de 5° T° a 4 voces, compás de 4" (Mass in mode 5 for 4 Voices, in Quadruple Meter), choirbook C-C-59, pp. 112–16; "Misa de 5° t°. Compás de 4 a 4° voces," in Santa Clara

Ms. 4, pp. 57–62; the untitled mass in choirbook C-C-68:1, fols. 9–18v; "Misa de 5° t° a 4 Vs," Santa Barbara Doc. 1, pp. 41–52 (this setting includes a "Benedictus" in the Sanctus movement, not found in the other settings except for Santa Barbara Doc. 2); "Misa 5° T° a 4 Vs. Compas a 4," Santa Barbara Doc. 2, pp. 127–33 (this setting contains a "Benedictus" for the Sanctus movement; for a facsimile of the opening movement, see photo B-78 in appendix B online); Santa Barbara Doc. 23, incomplete copy of this mass (missing the Kyrie and beginning of the Gloria on p. 3 with "Rex caelestis"), pp. 3–8; Santa Barbara Doc. 3, "Misa a 4 vozes de Cataluña / Nuevamente hago y firmo, / hoy dia 1° de Di^bre de 1841 / Pacífico Capéñaz" (a version of the mass with the third voice missing, leaving voices 1, 2, and 4 (see photo B-183 in appendix B online). Perhaps it is stricken because in the other versions it often crosses *below* the "bass" and confuses the harmony. Also, the dotted rhythms have been smoothed out into even eighths. The repetition of phrases in the Sanctus has been altered to a single statement of each phrase, unlike the other versions of this mass setting); Santa Inés Ms. 1, "[Misa 5° T° a 4 Vs.]," pp. 48–52; San Fernando Ms. A320, "Misa Catalana. Tono 5. à 4 voces," fols. 1v–6 (numbered pp. 1–10). In addition, da Silva mentions extant copies at the Mission San Juan Bautista. Da Silva, *Mission Music of California*, 117–18. One has to assume that the copy in Mission San Juan Bautista was a separate folder, since it appears neither in the Tapís choirbook at that mission nor in the "Suplemento" choirbook. Nor does it appear in the "Indice" that is affixed to the back of the "Suplemento" for a now-lost choirbook. Da Silva provides a complete edition of the *Misa de Cataluña* that has served the musical community well for over half a century as one of the few windows into California's past that was readily obtainable by modern music lovers. See da Silva, *Mission Music of California*, 37–53. A few corrections or editorial comments are needed, however, to rectify a few problems: all of the movements were initially in mode 5 (C major). All of my following comments are in the context of the original tonal centers. There is a measure full of rests in the Gloria (m. 62) that da Silva deletes. Similarly, he has deleted some of the rests before "miserere nobis" in the Agnus Dei. The "amen" at the end of the Gloria should be sung twice, since the choirbooks actually write out the repeat. The "Rx de ut" (Response in C) and the "amen" at the end of the Agnus Dei in the original manuscripts have been scrapped in da Silva's version. The voice crossing of the tenor and bass is often ignored. The upper voices are transcribed by da Silva in the treble clef, thus separating the soprano and alto combination from the tenors and basses by more than an octave. We end up with a pair of very low voices and a pair of very high ones. In truth, they are all in close position (basses, baritones, and tenors), bumping elbows in the same octave. Da Silva changes the Phrygian cadence in mm. 88–90 of the Credo. Da Silva smoothes out the dotted rhythms of the Kyrie and Sanctus. He has truncated the phrases of the Sanctus; they should be exactly like those in the Kyrie.

54. Gloria, mm. 22–23, 26–27; Agnus Dei, mm. 1–4.

55. Da Silva smoothes out the dotted rhythms and makes them all even eighth notes. The choirbooks, however, are in agreement and present them as dotted rhythms. Also, da Silva excises the repetitions of phrases in the Sanctus that are an indispensable part of the movement. By retaining them, one replicates exactly the same music heard in the Kyrie.

56. Da Silva, *Mission Music of California*, 14–15, 117.

57. For a summary of Narciso Durán's life, consult Geiger, *Franciscan Missionaries*, 68–75. For Durán's early years in Cataluña, consult p. 68.

58. See, for example, the section "Domine Deus" in the Gloria, mm. 22–23, 26–27.

59. See mm. 87–90 of the Gloria. For clarification of the musical and associative aspects of mode 4, see the section "Modes" in chapter 2.

60. For Nassarre's original text and a complete citation, consult chapter 2, esp. note 85.

61. This mass has been beautifully reconstructed in a performance edition by the musicologist and choir director Keith Paulson-Thorp, who has performed it widely with his choir from the Santa Barbara Mission. The mass occurs in various sources with similar titles, including "Misa Quarto Tono a 4 VS [= Voces]" (Mass in Mode 4 for Four Voices), choirbook C-C-59, pp. 122–27; "Missa 4° t°," Santa Clara Ms. 4, pp. 123–27; "Misa a 4 Vs. 4° T°," Santa Barbara Doc. 1, pp. 30–42; and "Misa de 4° T°" (only the Kyrie and portions of the Gloria), Santa Barbara Doc. 21B, fols. 1–1v; and "Misa a 4 Vs. 4° T°," Santa Barbara Doc. 2, pp. 118–26. Each of these sources brings something of particular value that is often lacking in the others. Santa Clara Ms. 4 has short runs that are certainly the cues for the continuo lines.

See the following measures: Kyrie, m. 7; Gloria, mm. 5, 71, 75, 111, and 113; Credo, mm. 6, 10, 149, 178, 182, and 200; Sanctus, mm. 7 and 24. The Santa Barbara manuscript sources include plainchant that is interpolated into the Kyrie. Santa Barbara Doc. 1 has a different voice sing the "Genitum non factum" in the Credo (see m. 55); this same choirbook also uses tiny dots to add polyphony in this movement. See the Credo's sections "factum" (mm. 57–58); "Virgine" (mm. 92–93); and "Filio" (mm. 173–74). The *canto figurado* sections in the Gloria are set as part of the "Missa Toledana" in Serra choirbook M.0612 at the Green Research Library at Stanford, fols. 15v–16. The text in this Gloria include phrases "Laudamus te / Adoramus te / Gratias agimus tibi," and so on. The other phrases in polyphony that would interlock with the ones found in Serra choirbook M.0612 are found in WPA folder 55, photos D-1, D-3, and D-5. They include two voice lines plus the basso continuo part. They are labeled "Gloria Simple. 4° tono, tiple Primero" (photo D-1); "Gloria Simple. 4. tono Baxo" (photo D-3); and "Gloria simple 4° t. Acompanyamento para el Organo" (photo D-5). The text for WPA folder 55 begins with "Et in terra pax" and continues "Benedicimus te / Glorificamus te / Dominus Deus," and so on. Also, the Archive of the Archdiosene Library of Los Angeles at the San Fernando Mission contains some loose sheets in Sancho's hand with a trio version of this same Gloria seen in WPA folder 55. Sheet S-3 contains the "Tiple 1ro â 3, Gloria simple." Sheet S-2v contains the "Tenor â 3. Mi[ssa] Simple." Sheet S-1v contains the "Bajo â 3. Mi[ssa] Simple." Summers discusses these sheets and this mass briefly in his article "*Opera seria* in Spanish California," esp. 275–76.

62. See figure 6-9 for a chart of the Gloria's division points.

63. An expanded five-voice texture arises at several locations in choirbook C-C-59, including the end of the Kyrie (p. 122); several sections in the Credo, such as "Et ex Patre natum" (p. 124), "Confiteor unum" (p. 126), and "Et vitam venturi" (p. 126); the Sanctus (p. 126); and Agnus Dei (p. 127).

64. See chapter 2, especially the section "*Misa 'de Jesús'* and the *Misa Italiana*," for a discussion of note heads and the orchestration by the note head, plus the soloistic nature of the polyphony.

65. As we discussed earlier in this chapter, "Toda hermosa eres Maria" is a vernacular-texted hymn associated with the Mass for the Seven Dolours of the Blessed Virgin Mary. This work and the other attendant materials for the Mass for the Seven Dolours of the Blessed Virgin Mary immediately precede the *Misa del quarto tono* in choirbook C-C-59 (pp. 117–21). In Santa Clara Ms. 4, "Toda hermosa eres Maria" comes immediately after the *Misa del quarto tono* (pp. 128–29).

66. Serra choirbook M.0612, fols. 15–18.

67. WPA folder 55, photo D-1 contains the "Gloria simple. 4° tono. tiple Primero." Its flip side appears in photo D-2 and contains the "Gloria pastoril. 5 tono. tible 1."

68. Archive of the Archdiocese of Los Angeles in San Fernando, sheets S-1 and S-2. See Summers, *Opera seria*, 275.

69. There is a four-measure introduction to the section "Deus Pater omnipotens" and a two-measure introduction to the section "Domine Deus."

CHAPTER 7

Classical Masses for Voices and Orchestra by Ignacio de Jerusalem and García Fajer

Ignacio de Jerusalem y Stella: Biography

Born in Lecce, Italy, on 3 June 1707, to violinist Matteo Martino Gerusalemme (Jerusalem) and Anna Curzio Stella, Ignacio de Jerusalem grew up in a richly musical environment, becoming a masterful violinist.[1] He moved to Spain early on, and with his wife, Antonia Sixto, began raising a family: their daughter Isabel was born in the Spanish enclave of Ceuta on the coast of North Africa around 1738, and Antonia gave birth to their son Salvador in Cataluña in 1739.[2] Jerusalem applied for passage to the New World (along with his family) in 1743, and the musicians Antonio Saul, Paolino dell'Anno, and Nicolás Pierro spoke in favor of his application. All their testaments identify them as residents of Cádiz—the hot spot for musical theater in Spain at the time—and we can safely assume that the Jerusalem family had moved to this port city in the early 1740s. Antonio Saul (b. 1703) was five years older than Jerusalem and had known Ignacio since their childhood days in Italy, dating back to at least 1718, when Jerusalem was not yet a teen. A member of the Marine Battalion, Saul had collaborated with Jerusalem back in Naples and also Cádiz. Similarly, the younger Paolino dell'Anno (b. 1710), who was employed as a musician in the Zamora Regiment, had known Jerusalem from around 1719 and had worked with his compatriot in several different kingdoms. The oldest of the three, Nicolás Pierro (b. 1700), had met Jerusalem only recently, around 1735, but had joined with him on several functions and music gigs.[3]

Jerusalem and several other artists had been recruited in 1742 for the journey by Don Josef Cárdenas, the chief administrator of the Royal Hospital of Indigenous Citizens, as part of Cárdenas's efforts to entice the brightest and best musicians to join the musical resources of the Coliseo, the impressive and newly renovated theater that was the center of drama and musical theater in the Mexico City. The Royal Hospital was a charitable institution devoted to the unfortunate and destitute, much like the Ospedale della Pietà in Venice where

Vivaldi had penned hundreds of enthralling compositions; it received its funding through the profits of productions mounted at the Coliseo, Mexico City's important "Broadway theater." During the eighteenth century it underwent several renovations and transformations. A rather shabby wooden structure, referred to in the eighteenth century as the Antiguo Coliseo (Old Theater), was situated on the Avenue of the Holy Spirit (Callejón del Espíritu Sancto) and Ravine Street (Calle de la Acequia, that later was renamed the "street of the Old Theater"). It was rebuilt in 1725 but was then destroyed in midcentury. Under Cárdenas's stellar stewardship of the Royal Hospital and Coliseo, construction began in 1752 on a new, more stolid theater made out of stone, situated on Girl's College Street (calle del Colegio de Niñas)—and later renamed Theater Street (calle del Coliseo). Costs for the Nuevo Coliseo (also called the Teatro de México and Teatro Principal) mounted to between 18,000 and 20,000 pesos, and construction reached completion by 25 December 1753; announcements in the press proclaim the doors opened to the drama *Mejor ésta que estaba (Better This One Than the One That Was)*.[4]

In order to boost profits and more handily meet the fiscal exigencies of the Royal Hospital, Cárdenas had requested permission to go to Cádiz in search of fresh talent, the assumption being that more enthralling artists would be a big draw and improve ticket sales and subscription income. He embarked for Spain in 1742, and his successful recruiting trip in Cádiz gathered together an impressive assemblage of actors and musicians, the culminating star being Ignacio de Jerusalem.[5] The eighteenth-century account of the Royal Hospital, titled *Prólogo a las constituciones y ordenanzas para el régimen y gobierno del Hospital Real* and published by Felipe de Zúñiga y Ontiveros in 1778, tells us:

> That which elevated the Coliseo Theater to an outstanding level was the dedication of Don Josef Cárdenas, Administrator of the Royal Hospital of Indigenous Citizens, and honorary bookkeeper of the Royal Tribunal of Accounts. In 1742 he received permission from His Majesty to recruit some talented individuals in Cádiz for this Coliseo, and in that year and the following he signed Josef Ordóñez and his wife Isabel Gamarra with their two daughters Vicenta and Josefa, of whom the latter later became a highly reputed actress of the theater. She married the celebrated Panseco. He also hired: Juan Gregorio Panseco, a native of Milan, a musician of the naval battalions and outstanding on the violin, violoncello, and transverse flute; Josef Picado from the Duchy of Milan, outstanding on the violin, hunting horn, and a dancing master; Juan Bautista Arestin, an outstanding Frenchman on the violin and violoncello; Gaspar and Andrés Espinosa, who played the transverse flute, hunting horn, oboe, and violin; Benito Andrés Preibus, who had the same abilities as the others and was from the port of Santa María; Francisco Rueda and his wife Petronila Ordóñez, appointed to the theater in Barcelona—the husband being outstanding on violin and hunting horn, and the wife being a famous actress and excellent singer who accompanied herself magnificently on violin and guitar; and

lastly, the celebrated musical composer, Don Ignacio de Jerusalem, a native of the city Lecce in the kingdom of Naples, who was later Chapelmaster in this Holy Cathedral [of Mexico City]. *The Viceroys attended a Matins service composed by Jerusalem that was performed on Maundy Thursday of 1753 before a larger-than-numerous gathering that had assembled to hear it"* (italics added).[6]

Having arrived in Mexico City, Jerusalem immediately became a fixture in musical life in the viceregal capital city, not only working for the theatrical productions in the Coliseo but also branching out into sacred compositions for the Mexico City Cathedral. On 27 May 1746 he petitioned the cathedral to admit his son Salvador as a member of its elementary school (the Colegio de Infantes). The school promptly accepted the application, commenting that Jerusalem was serving as the music master of the Coliseo and as such "is very intelligent in all aspects of music, composition, and counterpoint," and that "through love of his son, he would show up as well—and the school's children would be able to benefit greatly."[7] Their assessment of his prodigious skills is laudatory. According to Estrada, the Cathedral's Actas del Cabildo for 15 July 1746 states:

And talking about his great facility on the violin and his profound knowledge of music, he is the only composer from this city or even in Spain that there has been [to have them in such abundance]....That he played violin in the orchestra should not damage his case for admittance into the Cathedral chapter, and Don Joseph de Cárdenas will not hinder his case, in spite of what has been legally notarized.[8]

They put together an attractive package for Jerusalem, praising his qualities as violin virtuoso (for which they were prepared to pay him 300 pesos annually) and apt music educator (for which they mustered another 200 pesos to be music teacher to the Colegio de Infantes where Ignacio's son was in attendance). As part of his duties, they also require that he compose *villancicos* for the annual feasts of Saint Peter, the Assumption of the Virgin, the Virgin of Guadalupe, and any other major feasts when he is asked.[9]

Jerusalem's ascendancy in prestige and fame in the capital city set him on a collision course with the de facto head of the cathedral's music chapel, the ineffectual Domingo Dutra. He had been at the helm ever since 1739 in the aftermath of Manuel de Sumaya's hasty departure from the post in order to follow his dear friend and dean of the cathedral, Tomás Montaño, to Oaxaca after the latter's appointment as archbishop in this southern city. Granted, Sumaya would be a hard act to follow—how does one take up the reins of a Bach or a Handel? Nevertheless, Dutra's skills were mediocre at best, and in his ten years trying to hold things together at the cathedral, there is not an instance where he truly distinguished himself as a master musician. For Dutra, Jerusalem's arrival in the cathedral was disastrous, for he was suddenly confronted with Jerusalem's prodigious and transparent talent. Within three months he became despondent and fell ill, requesting a leave of absence. The cathedral chapter, which liked Dutra personally, consented and softened the blow by naming him officially as the chapelmaster "ad interim" in 1746 while simultaneously attributing Dutra's illness and sullen melancholy to jealousy of the immensely gifted Jerusalem, whom the cathedral had just recently hired.[10]

The documents for the next three years show Jerusalem in rather mundane affairs, requesting more funds for his clothing allowance and complaining that some of the cathedral musicians are double-dipping and therefore are not showing up for work. Estrada tells us Jerusalem requests 100 pesos for a vestuary allowance on 31 July 1746, and that his dress was typical clerical attire of soutane and surplice ("en sotana y sobrepelliz, traje muy clerical"). Jerusalem's displeasure with his colleagues caused him to lodge the complaint: "Several musicians are absent [from their cathedral posts], having been contracted by other bards or stage performers to participate with their company in a gig at the Church of Jesus of Nazareth." On 19 July 1748 he goes back to the cathedral chapter pleading for an additional 150 pesos to purchase new clothes (and is granted 100), lamenting that he is "in the state of complete nakedness."[11]

By 1749, the cathedral chapter is left adrift with no sense of direction, due to Dutra's persistent melancholy. The chapter acts tell us "Domingo Dutra—due to unavoidable necessities and other matters—does not take care of anything, for which the chapel finds itself without governance."[12] Two of the principal players in this unfolding drama, González and Santos, move to have Dutra pushed into retirement and suggest that Jerusalem assume the soon-to-be vacated post of "interim" chapelmaster. When Jerusalem got wind of the impending shake-up, he jumped the gun and submitted his application early for the *oposiciones* that had yet to be announced.[13] Jerusalem was merely anticipating the customary process for selecting a new chapelmaster; ever since the 1500s, *oposiciones* (i.e., exams and contests to demonstrate competence in various areas such as language skill, theological grounding, compositional facility, knowledge of counterpoint, etc.) were used as a way to winnow down the field of applicants and actually select a new director of music. The *oposiciones* were, in effect, a sort of trial by combat where the chief candidates went head-to-head to prove their breadth of knowledge, artistic skill, facile adaptability, and compositional prowess.

The contest itself was delayed, for a variety of reasons. The chapter thought it premature and slightly rude for Jerusalem to be submitting his application before the new job opening was even announced and publicly declared, and the chapter had its hands full at the moment trying to resolve a critical shortage of soprano voices—a dilemma they solved by soliciting four boy castrati from Naples. With their attention turned once again to the lack of a viable chapelmaster, they finally agreed to schedule the *oposiciones* for 30 June 1750. The jury consisted of Manuel Herrera, Joseph González, plus Martín Vázquez, and surprisingly, there was only one finalist—Ignacio de Jerusalem. Once the *oposiciones* commenced, he was handed several thorny tasks that would test his mettle and speed as a composer. He was given the antiphon "O Emanuele Rex" and instructed to "take the Gregorian melody so that it could be employed as a cantus firmus in a four-voice, contrapuntal composition, with the soprano carrying the plainchant tune, and with a deadline of twenty-four hours to complete the task."[14] The next test involved the writing of a concerted *villancico* for voices and instruments to the lyrics "A la milagrosa escuela," where the various solfege syllables were supposed to be matched to their corresponding pitches.[15] That is, using the system of note identifiers, the word "sol" for sun would call up the pitch G, the possessive adjective "mi" would conjure up the pitch E, the definite article "la" could produce an A, the syllable "re" results in a D, and so on. Sure enough, we hear the solfege syllables accurately proclaimed from the opening measures with the A's and E's resounding appropriately on the words "A *la mi-la*-gro-sa escuela."[16] Soon thereafter, we hear a steady scalar ascent in canonic imitation as the text enunciates, "do-re-me-fa-sol." The couplets (*coplas*) inserted in between statements of the refrain are even more impressive, with almost every available syllable landing smack-dab on a solfege syllable. If one takes into account the vocal elision where the words "el hace" smooth out to become "e-*la*-ce" or where the text "la regla" can be heard almost as "*la re*(g)*la*," we discover that Jerusalem has hammered every note appropriately with the syllable matching its solfege syllable—no easy task. He had to compose an orchestral vessel to support the predetermined notes of the text and somehow make it sound natural and effortless. And he succeeds. If we take the entire *coplas* text and underscore where there is a one-to-one correspondence between the pronounced syllable and the note that accompanies it, we find an impressive display of clever text realization:

> *Sol-fa la sol fa* de Pedro
> Es *la re-gla* del primor
> Pues sólo el-*ha*-ce *mi-la*-gros
> *Re*-petidos en su voz.[17]

This sort of sound puzzle was actually a common quiz for *oposiciones,* as can be gathered by the ingeniously clever "Solfa de Pedro" that Manuel de Sumaya dashed off in the 1715 *oposiciones* for the Mexico Cathedral chapelmastery that he handily won over his worthy (but unsuccessful) opponent, Francisco de Atienza.[18] The text for Jerusalem's contest bears remarkable similarities to Sumaya's test piece as well. Both make frequent references to the "Solfege system of Pedro" and obvious references to the ascending notes of the scale, trills and warbling, the use of sharps and flats (using the "bland" and "hard" hexachord system of sight-singing that was the core for singing instruction at the time), the singing in counterpoint, and then the subsequent coming together of all the voices. As far as poetic artistry is concerned, both texts are more or less gobbledygook, but they succeed splendidly with their purpose—to provide the composer with a slew of highly graphic word images and the inclusion of musical concepts so that the contestant can show off his command of music theory and colorful "word painting" skills. This point is relevant to the extant masses by Jerusalem found in California archives. As will be seen shortly, Jerusalem took care to encapsulate and then express the subtleties of the mass's text in his concerted settings. He exhibited a certain flair for text expression even in his examination piece for the Mexico City chapelmastery, and that aspect followed him throughout his compositional career.

Remarkably, the jury was dissatisfied with Jerusalem's submissions! So they requested yet another work from him to prove his pliant compositional ability. This time they handed him the Vespers antiphon "Iste Sanctus pro lege Dei sui," demanding that he run through the gauntlet of compositional techniques; he was to write "passages in running counterpoint, fugues, canons, 'forced' passages [i.e., in double time or at a rapid pace?], suspensions, and whatever other contrapuntal devices that can be made, so that it might be generally recognized that he understands them and is able to compose using these techniques."[19] Undaunted, Jerusalem dove into the contest yet again, meeting the deadline as always, this time complying with the committee's demands by authoring a four-voice setting, cradled by a small chamber ensemble that consisted of first and second violins, plus a basso continuo. The jury heard the work on 10 July 1750, and they were stumped. They fired questions at him right and left, and all sorts of disputes erupted—but both the jury and Jerusalem got stymied by the language barrier. When an answer was not forthcoming or was off the mark, it was nearly impossible to tell whether the obstacles arose from lack of knowledge or lack of understanding by the various parties.[20] The jury's assessments were confused and lukewarm. One vacillating, but somewhat sympathetic, jurist wrote:

> It certainly has been very hard for us, and was hard for us again today, to form an accurate assessment of how broad his understanding and competency extends. Jerusalem defended himself sparingly and got tripped up in his explanations and his polyphonic voice leading; but we also saw with what agility and expediency he addressed and dispatched whatever questions we posed to him. With pen in hand, he instantaneously wrote down and formed solutions on staved paper to whatever we told him to do.[21]

This judge certainly ended up casting his vote in favor of the Italian composer, but a contrary opinion was explained by another committee member:

> Since I have issued my judgment in the said examination—as my sacred and sworn duty—to fulfill my obligation and state whatever I believe to be true, and in order to have a clear conscience, I say a cathedral chapelmaster should be a compendium of musical abilities: in such a way that a master knows the things that others ignore, and the master ignores what others know—and I cannot verify those skills in Jerusalem.[22]

A perusal of Jerusalem's examination piece "A la milagrosa escuela," and his later works, leaves one in a quandary as to why the jury was perplexed or dissatisfied with his craftsmanship. In truth, his consummate understanding of voice leading, music theory, and composition was spectacular, but his avant-garde, *galant* characteristics placed him on the cutting edge of the new trends that were to sweep Europe and the Americas—and those attributes had not yet become ensconced in the cathedral's expectations. Quite frankly, the young whippersnapper must have confused the older generation who were expecting a Baroque aesthetic instead of the new surge toward Classicism that was to come.

The committee eventually decided in favor of Jerusalem's appointment, but with some members in open opposition. Even those in favor could not muster much enthusiasm in their job offer, sounding almost desperate in their statement that there was no other applicant for the post and for the time being there was no viable alternative for a composer residing in Mexico! Hardly a vote of supreme confidence. Nevertheless, with the majority in favor and with the support of the archbishop, Jerusalem was offered the position on 3 November 1750, and he held that job until his death on 16 December 1769.[23]

Jerusalem's duties as the new post of chapelmaster were varied: in 1750 he comments that he has composed a new *Te Deum*, a *Salve*, and a *Miserere* and requests that he be paid for his instructing the children of Colegio de Infantes. He had at least two private students, presumably on violin, but a listing also arises of two pupils studying horn with the maestro. The 1750s got off to a bumpy start for our musician; to kick things off, he contracted typhoid fever, and his wife, Antonia, felt compelled to ask the cathedral chapter for aid during his convalescence.[24] They assented and contributed 150 pesos to the Jerusalem family. Another problem raised its head in the early 1750s when Jerusalem complains that other musicians are usurping his privileges as chapelmaster. Whereas he had been counting on substantial sums (between 150 and 200 pesos annually) from funerals, professions, and other honors that sprang from his duties as head of the Mexico City cathedral music establishment, artists from other churches such as the Merced, Santo Domingo, and San Francisco, and even independent mulattoes with no ecclesiastical affiliation whatsoever, were siphoning off these lucrative opportunities, much to Jerusalem's consternation.[25] However, not all was frustration. His Matins service for Maundy Thursday in 1753 drew an immense audience, including the viceroy and his vicequeen.[26] We know he had fallen behind in his composition duties, since his petition in 1754 to have one of his children professed as a Carmelite friar in Puebla was put on hold by the perturbed clerics in the Mexico City Cathedral trying to hold Jerusalem accountable for his lethargic pace in composing a promised mass that was to be modeled in the style of José de Nebra.[27] The relationship between Jerusalem's music and his desire to follow the trend-setting José de Nebra is not a trivial one. Nebra was the principal organist at the Royal Chapel and the convent of Descalzas Reales in Madrid in the mid–eighteenth century, and he was without rival as a theater composer in Spain, a role that certainly influenced and intrigued Jerusalem. Both artists shared a passion for exploring both theatrical and church genres.[28]

Jesús Estrada's research on Jerusalem's life shows that the 1750s continued to be a rocky decade for Jerusalem, with three major issues plaguing the composer: a lawsuit brought against him by Joseph Calvo at the Coliseo, a disintegrating marriage, and the newly arrived composer Matheo Tollis della Rocca, whose presence in the cathedral chapel apparently irked Jerusalem, at least initially. Even though Jerusalem was still under contract to supply all the music for the Coliseo's productions—in exchange for the hefty salary of 800 pesos annually—he had been remiss in his duties.[29] The Coliseo's renter, Don Joseph Calvo, eventually was forced to take legal action in desperation. In his civil suit he alleges that Jerusalem was already paid 557 pesos and 4 reales of his salary but had shown up only for a total of three months and nineteen days, far short of his contract's expectations. The complaint was passed on from the civil to the church authorities, where the cathedral was asked to make restitution to Calvo by paying the 255 pesos and 6 reales (apparently for the work for which Jerusalem had already been paid but never performed).[30] One document suggests that he and his wife may have even drawn off more funds from the theater: "The money that he received from the Coliseo, 400 pesos, he earned in monthly payments of his salary, and the other 400 pesos his wife removed in goods and merchandise from the store of Mister Calvo." The situation must have looked bleak for our poor musician, suffering from the fiscal exigencies of the lawsuit. Jerusalem begs the chapter not to make restitution by docking his pay: "Yes, it is certainly true that I earn the income of 800 pesos [from the cathedral]; nevertheless, by taking away from me the money to pay off my debt, my salary is not enough for me to make a living." Continuing with his litany of financial burdens, Jerusalem complains that his pay has been docked for those occasions when he failed to show up for work at the cathedral school. Moreover, as the coup de grâce, he laments that he is so penniless, "I cannot even afford to pay either my copyist or poet for my composition." Estrada does not tell us whether or not Jerusalem ended up having to sacrifice part of his pay, but it is clear that the whole hullabaloo ended up with Jerusalem being dismissed from his post at the Coliseo.[31]

Another storm cloud was on the horizon as well, involving Jerusalem's home life and the disintegration of his marriage. Antonia, Jerusalem's wife, had just solicited the cathedral chapter for a portion of her husband's salary in order to assist (or reimburse?) her brother, with whom she was now residing—obviously demonstrating that the couple had become estranged and were no longer living under the same roof. This did not sit well with the disgruntled cathedral chapter. Jesús Estrada accurately observes that Jerusalem was somewhat of an "outsider" to begin with, since he was a secular apostate (i.e., a layman) as opposed to a cleric. Although he was under no obligation to take clerical vows or to join a religious order in order to hold the chapelmastery, he nevertheless *was* required "to live a well-ordered and respectable life"—and his suffering marriage fell short of meeting that expectation.[32]

Perhaps the biggest flap in Jerusalem's life, though, had to do with the hiring of Matheo Tollis de la Rocca.[33] He was a talented keyboardist and remarkable composer who benefited enormously from the enthusiastic support of the Vicequeen Doña María Luisa del Rosario de Ahumada y Vera, Marquesa de las Armarillas. She was the wife (and niece!) of Viceroy Don Agustín de Ahumada y Vallalón. When the royal couple arrived in Mexico City on 1 November 1755, they were greeted by a parade worthy of Caesar, the city decked out in banners and torches. For days the city was abuzz with regal festivities such as parties, bullfights, and musical extravaganzas.[34] Shortly after their arrival, the vicequeen exercised her clout to try to have de la Rocca installed as organist in the cathedral. In an unprecedented move, she tries to circumvent the normal employment process (that would entail an initial job announcement, the solicitation of applicants, and then the careful procedure of selection through *oposiciones* and deliberations by the chapter); she writes to the archbishop, who in turn pleads her case on behalf of Tollis de la Rocca before the cathedral chapter. The archbishop's petition identifies Tollis de la Rocca as "master of the harpsichord and organ, and a professional composer for churches and cathedrals."[35] Taken aback by the external pressure, the chapter stalled for time, claiming (correctly) that the post of organist was already occupied—and they simply did not know where to place this unsolicited applicant. After eight months of foot-dragging by the chapter, the archbishop finally pressed for a live audition where Tollis could demonstrate his prowess at the keyboard. The music chapel convened to hear him perform on 24 September 1757, and during the reunion of cathedral musicians the topic of Jerusalem's laziness in complying with his duties became a hot issue. The chapelmaster Jerusalem was reproached for failing "to compose that which he is required to do." When all was said and done, Tollis de la Rocca was voted into their ranks, "to substitute and make up for the absences of the noncompliant chapelmaster at the choir school, and as organist or keyboardist during the singing of arias," and was granted a salary of 300 pesos for his keyboard playing and an additional 200 pesos as the second chapelmaster. It must have stung Jerusalem when the chapter specifically singled out Tollis's laudable personal qualities—his "promptness, his honor and good judgment with which he responds to all that he has been charged to accomplish"—the very traits that Jerusalem had been condemned for lacking.[36]

We have already seen the chapter's repeated frustrations with Jerusalem's laxity in showing up for work at the chapel's *escoleta* (singing school for young lads), but we can also surmise that his negligence extended to his conducting duties as well, as can be gathered from Jerusalem's complaint to the chapter in 1757 where he bemoans that "Don Francisco de Selma has been beating time and directing the choir without any right to do so...and this stigmatizes and tarnishes me, for it is only I who has the privilege to conduct."[37] The sudden hiring of Tollis de la Rocca was probably just the barb needed to prod Jerusalem back into action. The competition with this new "threat" seemed to do him good. He was justified in his fear that Tollis's talents might dethrone him as the city's star composer and that Tollis might encroach further on the unchallenged privileges and perks of the chapelmaster unless he actually started doing his job with true vigor. Jerusalem starts to reclaim his waning prestige, pointing out that he had won his post through long-running, established procedures—that involved grueling exams and meticulous scrutiny of his qualities by his peers—whereas Tollis was thrust into their midst as second-in-command without any test whatsoever.

Estrada tells of Jerusalem's foolish and failed attempt to finger Tollis with the blame for Jerusalem's failure to write music in honor of Queen María Bárbara of Bragança.[38] Jerusalem states that he had been denounced as having refused to write anything in the queen's honor—unless he were paid to do so—and that the trumped-up charge was patently untrue. The impugnation of his character was, according to Jerusalem, a scheming plot of intrigue cooked up by Tollis to discredit him. Jerusalem's argument failed miserably and instantaneously, for the cathedral's *chantre* stepped forward to flatly contradict Jerusalem's testimony. In fact, the *chantre* revealed that he had *personally* informed Jerusalem that the chapelmaster was obligated to compose music for this occasion and that this mandate was even documented and legally notarized! To make matters even worse, the *chantre* then testified that he had no other recourse than to turn to Tollis de la Rocca in desperation, "so that he would arrange some sheets of some performance parts of a Bassani mass, so that we could count on having music for the memorial services that we had to produce."[39]

Jerusalem unquestionably had his back to the wall, having his credibility squashed and his personal flaws paraded before his colleagues. The next chapter in this minidrama is oddly fascinating. He finally consents to compose the music for the queen's memorial service, but in exchange for this concession he requests three favors of the cathedral chapter, the most dramatic demand being his second, in which he throws down the gauntlet and challenges Tollis de la Rocca to a musical duel to prove who is the better musician. Estrada quotes the three favors made by Jerusalem:

> 1st: that Tollis not be permitted to usurp the functions of chapelmaster through self-promoting encroachment, and that only through sickness or absence of the appointed chapelmaster may he govern the music chapel.

> 2nd: that it be recognized by a titular musician whether Tollis de la Rocca or Jerusalem is more expertly qualified in the art of composition, or which of them is more suited for the chapelmastery. The two shall be enclosed in a room without recourse to any instrument at all, and they shall make do with nothing but pen and ink in their tasks. Rocca is to craft a piece using an antiphon from plainchant [as a *cantus firmus*]; and he is to give me the difficulties that he demands that I follow in my piece... and later, after having left the enclosed room, that the skill and capabilities of one and the other be out in the open for all to see.

> 3rd: Jerusalem insists that Rocca—not having earned the chapelmastery through established procedure—not be permitted to govern the Chapel except in the absence or sickness of the appointed chapelmaster.[40]

During the 1750s, Jerusalem set in motion a series of reforms that were to shape the course of musical activities in Mexico well into the next century. He complained of the use of antiquated notational practices, especially the lingering use of "white notation" from the Renaissance that still persisted in Mexican cathedral practice; he preferred instead the modern system with quarter notes, half notes, and so on, where the stems are affixed to the side of the note heads instead of being centered on a note head's top or bottom. He advocated the shaping of note heads as ovals instead of rectangles and diamonds. (If we put this in the context of our earlier discussions, we can see that Jerusalem was ridding the cathedral of *canto figurado* and *canto de órgano* notational practices and their attendant styles.) Old mensuration signs that were carryovers from Renaissance white notation were discarded in favor of time signatures that we would recognize today (such as 3/8 time, 3/4 time, etc.). His reforms branched out into the literary texts as well. He was irked by the overly obtuse and stretched metaphors of Baroque poetry that had become so convoluted that almost no one in the sanctuary could understand the "point" of a composition on only one hearing. In fact, for the Christmas *villancicos* of 1756, Jerusalem sought out a new poet, other than Francisco de Selma, who had normally supplied these texts, in clear displeasure with the contorted, labyrinthine imagery that Selma penned.[41] (This poet is the same artist who caused Jerusalem's ire for conducting the choir without Jerusalem's express permission.) One of the last and most enduring reforms during Jerusalem's tenure as chapelmaster was his expansion of the orchestral resources in 1759. He persuaded the cathedral to fund a trip by Antonio Palomino to Spain in order to purchase the instrumental resources for a more substantial and updated orchestra. They granted him two years' salary for the trip. He was to work with the chapter's agent in Cádiz, the widow of José Díaz de Guitlán, who was then to ship the instruments back to Mexico as soon as possible. The shopping list had everything one would want for a "Classical" orchestra:

> six violins by the Neapolitan Gallani or even better makers if there are
>   any available
> two short oboes and two long ones
> two transverse flutes with mechanisms for lifting and raising
> two recorders and two piccolos
> two long flutes pitched in B flat
> two portable organs from Naples or any other place where they make nice
>   ones—with eight or nine registers—but it should have only the pipes
>   and soundbox so that it can be assembled here
> two high clarion trumpets pitched in F
> a pair of timpani made with the greatest care possible so that it is possible
>   to tune them to D with the greatest perfection
> two horns—keeping in mind those that the cathedral already has—so
>   that the old ones and the newly requested ones might serve our needs
>   even better[42]

If the 1750s had been stressful and not particularly fruitful for Jerusalem, the opposite can be said of the last ten years of his life. In a complete turnaround, he did an about-face, cleaned up his personal life, and immersed himself in an outpouring of compositional creation that was both prodigious and profoundly sublime. Some of the most architecturally sound and monumentally conceived musical works of the eighteenth century (and I include Europe in this sweeping praise) issued from his writing desk in the 1760s, such as the *Matins for Saint Peter* (1762), *Matins for the Assumption of the Virgin* (1762), *Matins for Our Lady of*

Guadalupe (1764), *Matins for San José* (1766), and *Matins for the Conception of the Virgin* (1768), in addition to a handful of major concerted masses and more than a dozen spectacular Vespers Psalms.[43] In addition, there is a wealth of undated material by Jerusalem in the archives, the bulk of which probably was created during this richly productive decade.

During this time, Jerusalem's son Pedro entered the services of the cathedral as a violinist or cellist, but apparently he had been taught composition and performance skills on other instruments as well. Ignacio had obviously restored himself to good graces with the cathedral chapter and hierarchy, for in 1766 they gave him a raise, his salary increasing to 800 pesos annually, in gratitude for all his hard work and diligence—the opposite to conditions in the 1750s.[44] Near the end of his life we find him still chipping away at the "outside" artists who were cutting in on the cathedral chapel's lucrative side jobs. When Antonio Rafael del Portillo, a professor at the Royal University of Mexico, petitioned for a permanent, formally established music chapel at the university (with Portillo selected to lead the group), Jerusalem was quick to nip this proposal in the bud. He insisted that Portillo and his ensemble, plus other professional musicians and freelancers in the city, attend a royal hearing (*real audiencia*) on 26 May 1769. And he put his foot down with respect to those pesky musicians who were employed at convents and monasteries but accepted temporary jobs on the side; it was one of Jerusalem's pet peeves, and he sought to have it decreed that musicians were limited in their service to the actual church, convent, or institution that employed them (implicitly trying to put an end to the freelance work that was cutting into Jerusalem's expected moneys). He also wanted to beef up the quality of musician in his service at the Mexico City Chapel, so he instituted rigorous exams in the musical arts for any applicant in the cathedral's music establishment.[45]

Ignacio de Jerusalem died at 8:00 o'clock in the evening on 15 December 1769—the same year that Father Junípero Serra arrived in Alta California. The cathedral chapter contributed fifty pesos to help defray the costs of his burial. His passing was observed by Tollis de la Rocca at the chapter meeting.[46] The tender and respectful language expressed in the capitular acts at his death is of a completely different character than the exasperated tone expressed in the mid-1750s. The tentative and unenthusiastic way the chapter had granted him the chapelmastery in 1750 was at the opposite end of the spectrum from their attitude at his death. They respected and wholeheartedly embraced their master's craft. In fact, they initiated the business dealings to purchase from the Jerusalem family the composer's original scores, an action that up to that point had never taken place in the cathedral's history of almost three centuries of music making. This passion for their fallen chapelmaster's music was unprecedented.

It is well to remember that during the eighteenth century whenever a cathedral, church, or secular patron commissioned a work, it expected the composer to conceive and write out a new work and then supply the client with the individual performance parts for each player to read. The score, however, was not part of the package but was instead the composer's *personal* property.[47] It is rather like the ownership of a computer in our present era. Whenever someone asks me to compose a work, I use my computer to create it and to help me hammer out the nitty-gritty details of who will play what notes, and so on—so when all is said and done, I plop the necessary performance parts on the stands of the individual play- ers, but I would not dream of handing over my computer. It's mine! That is exactly the case with scores in the eighteenth century. The composer wrote out the sketch of all the parts in score format (called the *borrador*) so that he could coordinate and refine all the necessary compositional details. He then had the copyist write out the performance parts from the score and had them delivered to the paying institution. The score remained in the composer's hands because it really was not needed to realize the piece, at least until the invention of the "conductor."

In the eighteenth century the leader of the ensemble (most often the keyboard- ist playing the continuo line from the organ bench) would hold things together by means of the *guión*, or "guide"—but that was little more than the basso con- tinuo part with an infrequent cue to help the director-keyboardist keep his place and hold things together. In the case of Jerusalem, we can assume he probably directed from the first stand of the violin section. In either case, the score would have been a luxury and was not part of the package deal. That explains why there is almost a complete lack of scores in cathedral archives. There are no extant scores by the Mexican masters Hernando Franco, Juan Gutiérrez de Padilla, Francisco López de Capillas, Gaspar Fernandes, Antonio de Salazar, and so on. Out of all of Manuel de Sumaya's pieces that he wrote during his tenure as the chapelmaster of the Mexico City Cathedral and then privileged composer in Oaxaca, I know of only *one* score: "Ciclo y mundo."[48] All that we have for his remaining works is the individual performing parts. Not surprisingly, this is also the case with all of the California sources. There is not a single *score* for concerted works with voices and instruments in any California mission or archive; we have instead only the indi- vidualized performance sheets that then have to be put together, piece by piece like a jigsaw puzzle, in order for the musical "image" to be discernible.

And that brings us back to Jerusalem's scores. The fact that the chapel vigor- ously sought out the autograph scores for the compositions for which they already had the performance parts shows a deep reverence and respect that completely reverse the lukewarm, semi-insulting assessment he had received from that same body when he first took his post in 1750. The cathedral chapter negotiated with the Count of Berrio to pay 500 pesos (equivalent to a year's salary!) for the stack of 174 works by Jerusalem in his possession. During the negotiations, the cathedral scribe observes that Jerusalem "was admired even by the intelligencia, and that he was regarded as a miracle."[49] The story does not end there. The Count of Ber- rio apparently donated the entire sum of this sale to Pedro de Jerusalem's widow, Ignacio's daughter-in-law. According to Estrada, Pedro had died earlier of a gun- shot wound.[50]

Jerusalem's artistic influence cast a long shadow on the Viceroyalty of Mexico. His works are found in the cathedrals of Mexico City, Puebla, Morelia, Durango, and Guatemala City, as well as in the Sánchez Garza Collection in CENIDIM in Mexico City, the Basilica of Guadalupe in Mexico City, Cuenca (Spain), and even Washington, D.C. No composer (whose works can be identified with any reliability) is more represented in the California missions than he. Eight years after Jerusalem's death, his legacy was recalled with nostalgic affection by the writer Juan de Viera, who unreservedly heaps praise on the cathedral musicians and their beloved chapelmaster. De Viera explains:

> The choir consists of twenty-five individuals who are the Dean, Archdean, Chantre, Treasurer, Dignitaries, Canons, Salaried, and Half-Salaried. The Cathedral's Music Chapel is the most select, skilled, and knowledgeable of any that can be found in America. Indeed, its individuals (which are fifty in number) for the most part are disciples of Maestro Jerusalem, an Italian who is never very restrained. There are no instruments of this choir that are not heard on an almost daily basis, instruments such as organ, violins, violas, contrabasses, transverse flutes, oboes, recorders and piccolos, horns and clarion trumpets. Each of the musicians garners a salary corresponding [to his quality] of no less than 500 pesos and going as high as 1,000 pesos. The number of musicians (not counting the choir boys and chaplains) reaches fifty individuals, and the Cathedral Chapter does not fail to raise musicians' salaries based on their abilities. These abilities are so substantial that one night—it being Wednesday of Holy Week— I heard a group of Europeans huddled together and say that "even Toledo and Seville did not achieve such magnificence—they seemed more like a choir of angels than of humans."[51]

Francisco Javier García Fajer, "El Españoleto": His Biography

The three composers who are represented in the California mission archives with ambitious, elegant, concerted works for choir and orchestra each hailed from a different geographic region; Jerusalem was Italian, Sancho was Mallorcan, and García Fajer was Aragonese. Each of them was raised in a family of professional musicians. Francisco Javier García Fajer was born in Nalda, Logroño, to Juan Bautista García and Manuela Faxer on 2 December 1730.[52] As a youth he was a member of the choir school at the Zaragoza Cathedral (the Colegio de Infantes de las Catedrales de Zaragoza). He probably began his musical studies under the tutelage of Luis Serra.[53] As a young man he then ventured to Italy, where he spent several years as the chapelmaster at the Seo of Terni (1754–56) and probably some time in Rome as well, where Arnold Loewenberg suggests that García Fajer was the singing master at the church of Caterina Gabrielli.[54] During his residency to Italy, he received the appellation of his homeland, "El Españoleto" or "Lo Spagnoletto"—reminiscent of the famous Spanish painter "El Greco," who had moved to Iberia from his native Greece.[55] His years in Italy were fruitful ones, as testified by several large-scale operas in Rome in 1754 and 1756, as well as his oratorio *Tobias* (1752).[56] We know that he applied for the chapelmastery of Toledo Cathedral sometime in the mid-1700s, since Latassa cites an eight-voice mass by him that was the examination piece during the chapelmastery's *oposiciones*.[57] Upon his return to his native Spain, García Fajer triumphed in the contest for the vacant post of chapelmaster in the Seo de Zaragoza, where he was appointed on 20 May 1756.[58] He exerted considerable sway on compositional style in late eighteenth-century Spain and continued to write profusely until his death on 26 February 1809.

Like Christoph Willibald Gluck, who was largely responsible for reforming operatic "excesses" during the Enlightenment, so García Fajer instituted a series of reforms that reshaped expectations in Spanish cathedral music in the Classical era. He felt that the vernacular-texted *villancicos* that had served as a core to sacred Matins services for two and a half centuries were too rowdy, crass, and demeaning to provide a respectful and dignified atmosphere required of worship in the sanctuary. As a result, he advocated the replacement of the eight *villancicos* with eight Latin Responsories—the texts that had previously occupied the privileged position in Matins as far back as the early Middle Ages. For García Fajer, the rejection of the *villancico* was a rejection of "accessible" street music that pandered to shallow public taste; for him, a return of the Responsory to Matins was a return to the noble, the elevated, and the traditional. His case was taken up by many composers and was quite successful—a remarkable triumph given the public's insatiable appetite for the spunky, fun-loving *villancicos*.[59]

The sacred compositions of "El Españoleto" can be found spread across the Hispano-American world, in such locations as El Escorial, Santiago de Compostela, Zaragoza, Daroca, Jaca, Valencia, Málaga, Barcelona, Mexico City, Puebla, Santiago de Chile, and Lima.[60] Andrés Sas Orchassal identifies an "Ynvitatorio... de Difuntos" and "Parce michi [*sic*]... de Difuntos" by García Fajer in the Lima Cathedral.[61] The cathedrals of Mexico City and Puebla have important works by our composer.[62]

The Orchestra in California

Before addressing the specific musical features of Jerusalem's and García Fajer's masses in California, it is worth pondering whether or not the pieces could actually have been played in this region, the most remote of the Spanish Empire. As we saw in chapter 1, the San Antonio Mission had a full orchestra with the same instrumentation that was typical of the era. This is proven by Sancho and Cabot's assessment of music activities at the mission they submitted in 1814 that states the "neophytes have a lot of musical talent, and they play violins, cello, flutes, horn, drum, and other instruments that the Mission has given them [implying that there were even more kinds of instruments available and that they collectively comprised a full orchestra]." That full orchestral performance was a regular affair at the San Antonio Mission is further demonstrated through Bill Summers's research in which he uncovered the instrument inventories for a handful of missions, including San Antonio. He cites a pertinent document for that mission (now housed at the Santa Barbara Mission Archive-Library) that lists the instruments in its possession in the year 1842: "four new violins, another old one, another one called a bass, one drum, four flutes, another new one, a horn, a valveless trumpet, two triangles, an old choirbook with ten or eleven masses."[63] This is the perfect "top-dominated" orchestra that arose in the late 1700s and early 1800s and fits hand in glove with Sancho and Cabot's commentary of life at the San Antonio Mission. Summers continues with impressive instrument lists from the Santa Clara Mission (in 1851) and the Santa Barbara Mission (in 1834). The former owned "one large bass, three medium basses, thirteen violins, three more [new ones?], one side drum, one regular drum, one choirbook with velum pages, two triangles, and several unbound sheets of music."[64] The Santa Barbara Mission owned "four flutes, three valveless trumpets, two valveless horns, two cellos, one Turkish crescent, one bass drum, two drums, sixteen [older] violins, one organ with six registers and a four-octave keyboard, four of our own violins [that we made?], three triangles, and four brand-new violins."[65] In each of these missions, we have the instrumentation that would have been ideal for performing the concerted masses of Ignacio de Jerusalem and Juan Manuel García Fajer, both of whom are represented in the California mission repertoire. It is no coincidence that the musicians with whom I have dealt extensively in the previous chapters—Juan Bautista Sancho, Narciso Durán, and Florencio Ibáñez—were the very leaders of music activities at the three aforementioned missions with impressive instrument inventories, the San Antonio Mission, Santa Barbara Mission, and Santa Clara Mission, respectively.

Sancho and Ibáñez were trained chapelmasters from Spain and would have had the know-how to get an orchestra up and running in their new California outposts. In the case of Durán, we do not have the same early training that would automatically qualify him, but we *do* have the memoirs of Alfred Robinson and Sir George Simpson. Both writers mention Durán and his musical institutions in such convincing and glowing terms that we have to include Durán's two missions (initially San José Mission and later Santa Barbara Mission) as potential locations where Jerusalem's music could have been performed. John Koegel and Francis Price have examined two requests by Durán to beef up the instrumental resources of San José, asking for a "bass viol and four violins" in 1820 and for a "bass viol and strings" in 1826,[66] and Alfred Robinson, who attended services at San José, recalls the impressive music experience under the guiding hand of Narciso Durán:

> Mass was soon commenced, and Padre Viader at the usual period of the ceremony ascended the pulpit, and delivered an explanatory sermon relative to the celebration of the day. The music was well executed, for it had been practiced daily for more than two months under the particular supervision of Father Narciso Durán. The number of the musicians was about thirty; the instruments performed upon were violins, flutes, trumpets, and drums; and so acute was the ear of the priest that he would detect a wrong note on the part of either instantly, and chide the erring performer. I have often seen the old gentleman, bareheaded, in the large square of the Mission beating time against one of the pillars of the corridor, whilst his music was in rehearsal.[67]

Mariano Guadalupe Vallejo provides another intriguing account of father Durán's choir and orchestra at the San José Mission. It traces over some of the points also made by Robinson, such as his acute sense of pitch and performance expectations, but expands on the role of the choir in mission society as a place of honor and prestige. His estimate of around twelve orchestral players matches perfectly with the instrumentation of the "Classical" orchestras of New Spain and Iberia at the turn of the century.[68] Vallejo recalls:

Many young Indians had good voices, and they were selected with great care to be trained in singing for the church choir. It was thought such an honor to sing in church that the Indian families were all very anxious to be represented. Some were taught to play on the violin and other stringed instruments. When Father Narciso Durán, who was the President of the Franciscans in California, was at the Mission San José, he had a church choir of almost thirty well-trained boys to sing the mass. He was himself a cultivated musician, having studied under some of the best masters in Spain, and so sensitive was his ear that if one string was out of tune he could not continue his service, but would at once turn to his choir, call the name of the player, and the string that was out order, and wait until the matter was corrected. As there were often more than a dozen players on instruments, this showed high musical ability. Every prominent Mission had fathers who paid great attention to training the Indians in music.[69]

Later, in the early 1830s, all the Spanish friars in northern California were forced to relocate to the southern missions to make room for the newly arrived and politically favored Mexican friars. Father Durán made the trek from San José to his new life in Santa Barbara, and it was there in 1842 that Sir George Simpson passed through. His intriguing recollection of a music performance in the Santa Barbara Mission while Durán was the presiding padre bears repeating here:

To continue our survey of the church, the walls were covered with the usual assortment of pictures and images, while from the ceiling were suspended several beautiful chandeliers, by means of flags of silk, of various colors, spangled with silver and gold. In the music gallery there was a small but well-tuned organ, on which a native convert was executing several pieces of sacred music with considerable taste, and amongst them, to our great surprise, Martin Luther's hymn [Ein feste Burg (A mighty fortress)]. This man was almost entirely self-taught, possessing, like most of his race, a fine ear and great aptitude; and though his countenance was intelligent enough, yet his dress was rather a singular one for an organist on active service, consisting of a handkerchief that confined his black locks, and a shirt of rather scanty longitude around his waste [*sic*].

Besides the organ, the choir mustered several violins, violoncellos, triangles, drums, flutes, bells, etc., with a strong corps of vocalists; and had we been able to wait until the 2d of February we should have enjoyed a grand treat in the musical way, as the bishop was then to celebrate pontifical mass with the full force of voices and instruments. Immense preparations were made for this religious festival, some of them being, according to our notions, of a very peculiar kind. Fireworks, for instance, were, if possible, to be exhibited; and as gunpowder could not be obtained for love or money, either for this purpose or for the giving of signals, we won the hearts of the bishop, priests, graduates, servants, and all, by promising to present them with a barrel of the needful from the ship.[70]

In addition to anecdotal accounts of music making in the missions, one can get a sense of the instrumental demands and expectations across California in the early 1800s by perusing the requests for music instrument shipments to the missions. These requests were channeled through the *casa matriz,* or motherhouse, of the Apostolic College of San Fernando in Mexico City. Of course, a request for any given year does not actually tell us a particular mission's *inventory,* that is, what it already has on hand; instead, these petitions are "purchase orders" that itemize what the petitioner is hoping will be sent for the upcoming year. The large tome of shipment requests between 1806 and 1808, now preserved in the Archivo General de la Nación in Mexico City (AGN, Hacienda, N° 53860), shows a veritable demand for orchestral instruments and their necessary accessories such as strings and rosin.[71] (These itemized requests also show that the missions were assembling large plucked string ensembles of guitars and families of *bandolas* in assorted sizes; we might guess that these groups constituted the "orchestra" for the *canto figurado* passages.) In item C-4 in appendix C online, I include all the documents in AGN, Hacienda, N° 53860 that concern music instrument shipments, but I include here a few sample petitions:

San Francisco Mission, *Expediente 3,* 3 January 1806, requesting shipment of "2 violins, 2 cellos, 2 contrabasses, 2 large *bandolas,* 2 horns, 1 clarion trumpet, 2 guitars, 2 flutes, 2 oboes, 2 clarinets, 2 sets of cymbals, a drum and bass drum, 2 triangles, and 2 complete assortments of strings." They even ask for a barrel organ, if there is enough money left over. Signed "Fr. Martín de Landaeta."[72]

San Luis Rey Mission, *Expediente 19,* 7 January 1806, requesting a shipment of "1 cello, 2 violins, 2 transverse flutes, 2 Royal trumpets [fanfare trumpets?], 2 large *bandolas,* 2 bass *bandolas,* 2 guitars, 2 triangles, 1 clarinet, and 1 drum." Signed "Fr. Antonio Peyri" and "Fr. Jose Garcia."[73]

San José Mission, *Expediente 63,* 31 January 1807, requesting a shipment of "6 violins, 1 contrabass, 2 hunting horns and 1 triangle." Then there is an addendum on the next page asking for "1 spinet, and 4 volumes of explanatory lessons on harmony." Signed "Fr. Narciso Duran."[74]

Of course, it would be fallacious to assume on the basis of a few purchase orders that all the twenty-one missions had astounding musical establishments along the lines of Bach's Thomaskirche in Leipzig and could mount a production of complicated *música moderna*. Also, possession of a large instrument inventory does not mandate that all those instruments were used together all the time. Travelers' accounts imply that chamber ensembles might have been the common sonority at some missions (even at some with a hefty music instrument collection). Otto von Kotzebue's diary entry for the Dolores Mission in San Francisco for 4 October, 1816, comments that at mass, the kneeling congregation was moved by the music, for it "seemed to afford them much pleasure, and which was probably the only part they comprehended during the whole service. The orchestra consisted of violoncello, a violin, and two flutes; these instruments were played by little half-naked Indians and were very often out of tune."[75] On a day in 1827, however, this same mission used a more robust ensemble with richer orchestration: eight violins, two bass viols, and two drums—all under the direction of Padre Tomás Esténaga.[76] These two different views are not so much contradictory as complementary: instrumental ensembles at any given mission could vary.

Some institutions' musical groups were midsize, able to cover the bases but not as richly as the large orchestras in San Antonio, Santa Clara, San José, or Santa Barbara. They offered three-voiced texture composed of two treble instruments plus a basso continuo line (as opposed to a "string quartet" division). This three-voice texture was the basis for the string writing in almost every sacred work from Spain and the Hispano-American world, from the early 1700s through the early 1800s. Not surprisingly, then, we find several missions filling the bill in a minimal way by having one performer per part—that is, with two violins or flutes plus a continuo ensemble consisting of a cello or bass and whenever possible an additional chordal instrument to enrich the harmonies. When Harrison G. Rogers traveled to the San Gabriel Mission on 11 December 1826, he heard a "band of musick that played for two hours…consisting of two small violins, one bass viol, a trumpet, and a triangle."[77] On 24 May 1842, William Dane Phelps provides a similar portrait when he attended mass at the San Diego Mission. He recalls, "Mass was said, and anthems were sung. The orchestra consisted of about a dozen Indians who sang with good voices and performed on a hand organ & base [*sic*] & kettle drum, two fiddles and a tambourine."[78] Yet another mission with a healthy musical life must have been the San Luis Rey Mission. At the opening of the 1840s, Count Eugène Duflot de Mofras finds himself at this mission, and in describing its educational system he implies that a varied orchestral palette was available for music performance. He states, "Indian children are educated in the schools together with the children of the white colonists. A limited number, selected from pupils who display the most intelligence, study music—elementary singing, the violin, flute, horn, violoncello, and other instruments."[79] One startling aspect of nearly all these inventories and travelers' accounts is the appearance of percussion instruments such as the numerous drums, jingling Turkish crescent, and triangle. Even the smallest chamber groups often contained a drum or triangle. With those timbres, the California music ensembles must have had significantly different sonorities in their sacred music than their European or even Mexican counterparts. Granted, these "exotic" sounds did surface in European music of the time, but only in military music or opera, as in Mozart's *Die Entführung aus dem Serail* or *The Abduction from the Seraglio*.

Provenance of the Sources

Before trying to determine whether or not these pieces were actually performed in California, we must first address the issue of provenance. Where did the sheets come from, and what were they for? A critical part of the answer to those questions goes back to the investigative fieldwork of John Koegel. As I mentioned in chapter 5 when dealing with the music of Juan Bautista Sancho, it was Koegel who unearthed the invaluable stack of "anonymous" performance parts for three masses while at the Archival Center of the Archdiocese of Los Angeles at the San Fernando Mission. He is the undisputed authority on music in California and the American Southwest during the late 1800s and early 1900s, but these papers looked to him like music from an earlier time period than his main area of investigation. He was right on the mark, too. Deciding to pursue his hunch, he kindly gave me a call, since I am a specialist in eighteenth-century Mexican choral music, and asked if I wanted to come down, have a look, and try my hand at deciphering the clues. Thrilled, I raced down to the archive and with the generous assistance of Monsignor Francis Weber—who is a first-rate scholar in his own right—began to pore over the manuscript sheets. There were a few loose sheets with some mass movements, a sequence, a Spanish song or two, and so on, and there was an oblong book with twelve folios in score format; it contained an Italian aria that was retexted with Latin and Spanish lyrics. These fascinating sources became the central focus of William Summers's highly informative and groundbreaking article, "*Opera seria* in Spanish California: An Introduction to a Newly-Identified Manuscript Source."[80] In addition, though, there was an enormous stack of a few hundred sheets that contained the music for three masses (one in F major that was pastoral in character, one in D major with a military flair, and another thrilling polychoral mass in D major).

Not surprisingly, there were no scores for these three masses (for the reasons I discussed previously in this chapter), only folded gatherings of performance parts that could be set on the music stands of the various singers and instrumentalists. They had no ascriptions, no titles, and no dates—nothing to help clarify authorship or the era when they were written except for stylistic aspects. Nevertheless, my heart began to pound; when I began to sing through the lines, they sounded to me like the musical compositions of Ignacio Jerusalem. I had become familiar with his works while living in Mexico City in 1988–89 on a grant from the National Endowment for the Humanities to study the life and music of Santiago de Murcia, another composer similar to Jerusalem in that they both left Europe as young men to make their way in the New World. Monsignor Weber allowed me to come down to the mission two weeks later with my camera and copy stand, and I began clicking away. There were a *lot* of pages; in fact, the cost of developing the film ran to more than a thousand dollars. Then came the task of putting the pieces together, which was a thorny task, since many of the performance parts were missing. None of the continuo or organ lines was extant, so the entire bottom register of the pieces was up for grabs. I had to make something up that would support and reinforce the upper voices. Moreover, the first violin part for the *Mass in F* was nowhere to be found. Once I had the tunes in hand and had reconstructed provisional scores, I began my search for concordant versions, digging through microfilms and even returning to Mexico City on a few occasions with the hope of filling in the holes and maybe even identifying the author(s) and date(s) of composition. The work paid off: I eventually identified the *Mass in F major* as a composition by Ignacio de Jerusalem and the militaristic *Mass in D major* as the work of Francisco Javier García Fajer, more commonly known as "El Españoleto."[81] (For a facsimile of the Violin I part from García Fajer's *Mass in D major,* consult photo B-58 in appendix B online.) I have not yet found a concordant source for the third mass in the grouping, the *Polychoral Mass in D* at the San Fernando Mission, but for orthographic and stylistic reasons I argue that the probable composer is Jerusalem.[82] For all three masses in the San Fernando Mission, the paper stock is identical. Their physical dimensions are the same, with ten staves per page being the preferred format for the *Mass in F* and *Polychoral Mass in D,* but with twelve staves per page being the norm for the García Fajer *Mass in D.*[83] The three mass manuscripts share the same watermarks, and all the sheets have the same texture.[84] There are several scribal hands at work in these compositions, but the notational conventions resemble each other very closely.[85] Given the common paper stock, the overlap of scribal efforts between masses, and the tremendous similarities in notational procedures for all three works, it is clear that the three masses were prepared in the same location at roughly the same time. Furthermore, this reinforces my argument that the *Polychoral Mass in D* that bears no explicit ascription nevertheless could be a mass by Ignacio de Jerusalem. The other two masses in the San Fernando Mission have irrefutable ties to the repertoire of the Mexico City Cathedral during his tenure there, and it would not be shocking if this third one did as well (although that theory would have to be based on the unproven assumption that there was once a "model" for this mass in the cathedral that is now lost).

Fragments from a fourth large-scale mass in G major, for two choirs and orchestral accompaniment, is found at the Santa Barbara Mission.[86] Robert Stevenson was one of the first to mention this mass, accurately identifying it as a piece by Ignacio de Jerusalem, and it later became the topic of George Harshbarger's doctoral dissertation—particularly useful for its appendix that includes a complete score for the mass.[87] In order to complete the mass, Harshbarger used a microfilm of a concordant version found in the Puebla Cathedral, but curiously, he states that this source is missing the second horn part, the first soprano part, and portions of the soprano and alto from Choir II. In truth, the Puebla source *is* complete, but one has to look earlier on the same microfilm to gather the "missing" portions. In addition, there is another concordant version of this mass in the Mexico City Cathedral.[88] The *Polychoral Mass in G* might have been the mass that garnered attention back in 1898 when the Reverend Joachim Adam described the presence of Jerusalem's music in Bishop Montgomery's library at the end of the nineteenth century.[89] This mass has been praised by Bill Summers for its superb quality in many of his publications, declaring it to be one of most important creations in the California repertoire.[90]

Returning to our initial question, Were these masses actually *performed* in the California missions? The musical sheets, taken by themselves, fill in only a bit of the puzzle. For instance, if we encounter a sheet of music in a particular location today, it does *not* prove that it was performed by the friars and neophytes at that same institution back in 1770 or 1820! Manuscripts can migrate from place to place, from archive to archive, just like autumn leaves that grow on one tree but later get blown across the neighborhood and decay wherever the wind has taken them. So it might be with these masses. We need to try to retrace that path of the leaves of manuscript paper with Jerusalem's music and determine where the winds of time have blown them and how they arrived at their present destinations. Another aspect of these music sheets must be scrutinized as well—their *purpose*. Sometimes a musician collects reference copies of cherished pieces for "reading" enjoyment in the privacy of one's own home, with no intention of ever performing them in public. That might be the case here; they might be personal copies for an individual friar's reading pleasure. Alternatively, the opposite might be true; they might have been in the service of spectacular music performances in the mission sanctuaries. All possibilities must be considered if we are to piece together our puzzle with any accuracy.

Addressing first the issue of *how* the music sheets got to their present locations, we first have to find the "tree" on which the leaves grew. It is significant that the stack of music that Koegel discovered at the San Fernando Mission contains so much material in the hand of Juan Bautista Sancho, as well as the masses of Jerusalem and García Fajer. That connection is not casual. In conversations with Bill Summers, he has proposed to me that it was Juan Bautista Sancho who initially had the Jerusalem masses in his possession and that they later found their way to the San Fernando Mission. I am in complete agreement. In fact, it is quite possible that the avenue for this migration of materials was Sancho's close friend Pedro Cabot. After Sancho's death in 1830, a new domineering governor came to power, José Figueroa, who forcibly replaced the Spanish padres with Mexican ones from Zacatecas. With each passing day, the native-born Spaniards were made less and less welcome. Eventually Pedro Cabot, Sancho's lifelong friend, was forced to flee San Antonio in 1834, ceding the mission to his "replacement," Jesús María Vásquez del Mercado. When Cabot retreated, he sought out one of the few safe havens that welcomed these Spanish refugees—the San Fernando Mission in the Los Angeles basin. I argue, therefore, that Pedro Cabot carried with him the things that he valued most when he escaped to the San Fernando Mission, and that chief among those treasures were the musical gems of his friend Juan Sancho.[91]

With respect to the second aspect of our question (what was the *purpose* of these manuscripts?), we need to consider the actual physical construction of the papers themselves. As we have observed, all the California sources for these four masses consist exclusively of performance parts; there is not a single full score among them. That would argue against the possibility that they were brought to this northern frontier for the personal reading pleasure of a friar. Performance parts have a practical purpose, and the fact that so many of the parts are missing seems to indicate that the parts were *used*. The parts are not pristine and complete; instead, they are piecemeal, and the *Polychoral Mass in G* shows signs of heavy use.

So, when we survey all the terrain that we have covered, the picture becomes clear. These magnificent masses were part of the living, sounding, performed repertoire in California as evidenced by the following clues: the instruments necessary for performance were found in the mission inventories; a few friars (especially Juan Bautista Sancho) had impressive musical training and expertise that could have been applied in the music education of Native American neophytes on the shores of California; travelers and friars described the scale and sonorities that match up with the Jerusalem and García Fajer compositions; the friars spent their missionary training in Mexico, where these works were part of the central literature and where these same pieces are found grouped together by their physical bindings and other orthographic characteristics; and the condition of the manuscript sheets in California and the fact that there are many missing pieces point toward a performance tradition of living music in the missions as opposed to mere reference usage by friars in their libraries.

Musical Aspects of Jerusalem's and García Fajer's Masses

Ignacio de Jerusalem, more than any other artist of the eighteenth century, brought the new trend of the *galant* style to the Viceroyalty of Mexico.[92] Several of his traits reflect the birth of the new "Classical" period. Rhythmic variety abounds. Long notes are followed by short ones, dotted rhythms give way to smooth passages that in turn fall into lilting triplets. When there are dotted rhythms, they often are "reversed," with the short note of the pair falling on the *downbeat,* succeeded immediately by the longer value (in a Scotch snap or Lombardic rhythm of short-long, short-long, etc.) as opposed to the Baroque preference for rhythms that bump along long-short, long-short, and so forth. The almost frenetic harmonic rhythms of Bach and Sumaya, where a chord change can occur on every other pulse, are replaced by a much slower harmonic rhythm by Jerusalem and Haydn. Bach's bass lines and those of his Baroque contemporaries are almost hectic in their busy march from harmony to harmony; in the Classical works of a Haydn or Jerusalem, however, the basses frequently drum away on steady repeated bass notes, stubborn in their intransigent reluctance to move from persistent iterations of the same pitch. While Bach distributes the compositional interest throughout the spectrum of registers and voices, Jerusalem and his Classical peers rid themselves of the multiple musical conversations and incessant egalitarian banter of Baroque polyphony and instead focus the ear on a single melodic thread at any given moment. The resulting texture is homophonic and top-dominated, a treble melody wafting along and buoyed up by the subordinate accompaniment. That is not to say that contrapuntal passages are nonexistent; but in Jerusalem's music and that of his contemporaries (such as Leonardo Leo, Joseph Haydn, Michael Haydn, and José de Nebra), the tapestry of interweaving melodic lines is confined to specific locations in compositions such as the concluding fugues of Gloria movements or the central section of a Kyrie. And the fugues themselves have an entirely different character than the fugues of Bach. The "serious" sound of North German polyphony in Lutheran territory does not provide the model for Jerusalem's more translucent and airy counterpoint. In fact, Jerusalem's fugues—like Mozart's—do not sound "heavy." They provide a curious contradiction: intellectually, we understand that the counterpoint is complicated and difficult to write, but aurally these fugues *sound* almost as if they are a filigree of exuberant, lighthearted melody. Furthermore, Jerusalem generally launches his fugues with the counter-subject accompanying the subject from the very beginning as opposed to delaying the countersubject until the second fugal entrance. This structural feature is actually part of the Spanish norm of Classicism. We see it in the masses of José de Nebra (who serves as the explicit model for Jerusalem's compositions), as well as the foot-tapping and invigorating fugue that concludes Antonio de Sarrier's thrilling *Overtura* found in Mexico's Conservatorio de las Rosas.[93] Jerusalem's expertise on the violin reveals itself in his sacred writing. Whereas we can easily imagine Sumaya conducting the Mexico City Cathedral chapel choir from the organ bench in the early 1700s (and Sumaya was a spectacular keyboardist), with Jerusalem our mind's eye sees a different picture—we can see Jerusalem with violin in hand, leading the choir and orchestra from the first violin stand, throwing in the feverish splashes of violinist virtuosity that are seen adorning his compositions, including each of the masses found in California. As will be seen, it is also the violin, not the keyboard, that often provides the compositional gestures and motifs that glue together the larger structure. Jerusalem's violin often provides the energetic engine of a movement that pushes the line forward; it is the perfect force to counterbalance the rather static harmonic rhythm that tends more toward stasis than propulsion. In addition, Jerusalem uses an increase in surface rhythm to propel the listener through the phrase. Often, as in the Gloria to the *Polychoral Mass in D*, he etches out the melodic outline in even, bold quarter notes that gradually shift into faster and faster rhythms until—eventually—the instruments and voices are racing through a forest of sixteenth notes. The acceleration of this "surface rhythm" is one of the most exhilarating aspects of Jerusalem's compositional style.

Structurally, Jerusalem is a master architect. When presented with a long text (such as the Gloria, Credo, Magnificat, *Dixit Dominus*, and the like), he usually subdivides the verbiage into meaningful sections or "numbers," giving each its own mood, meter, tempo, and tonality—in much the same way that Bach divides the texts for his cantatas. Within this varied salad of moods and musical character afforded in "numbers" compositions, Jerusalem nevertheless generally bonds together the larger whole by all sorts of ingenious structural glues. In the *Polychoral Mass in G*, he links movements by utilizing similar endings or beginnings to various movements. This same mass and the *Mass in F* are further put together cohesively by Jerusalem's application of a unifying rhythm that is attached to recurring meters in a specific work. Jerusalem is a master chef; each mass has its own "flavor." The *Mass in F* is peppered with the gently energized Scotch snaps that are found throughout the piece. The *Polychoral Mass in G,* in contrast, has far fewer Scotch snaps but instead wafts along with a pastoral feeling, exploring the lilt of 6/8 compound meter that was associated with Elysian, peaceful tranquillity in staged works of the era. The divvying up of the text into subsections is counteracted by the larger structural gesture. Often, movements are "open-ended," with a sense of suspenseful tension demanding resolution—that is then satisfied by the opening strains of the ensuing movement. In that way, Jerusalem draws us through the work, movement by movement, with no sense of completion until we arrive at the ultimate finish line. He prepares the passage from movement to movement carefully, by selecting the proper key destinations that will fall into place as inevitabilities. In that respect, the choice of keys reminds one of Mozart's key schemes in the ensemble finales to his operas. He framed the house (i.e., he chose the key destinations of the movements themselves) before he began adorning the walls with pictures and framed photos (i.e., before he started filling in the more minuscule melodic details). The formal scheme of the *Mass in F* is as finely milled as the tonal scheme for *The Marriage of Figaro.*

Another recurring aspect of Jerusalem's craftsmanship involves the floor plan for his "numbers" compositions. (See figure 7-1.) His Kyrie movements are nearly always framed; a slow and chordal "Kyrie" usually gives way to a more excited and contrapuntal "Christe," only to return to a few measures of broad, rich chords in a concluding "Kyrie." His Gloria movements could be mistaken for the blueprint of a Bach cantata. Both composers often distribute the text sections into five large regions. The first, middle, and final movements are nearly always choral sections with rich, full sonorities. The second and fourth movements, which are interpolated in between these choral regions, feature solo voices or chamber ensembles. Within this general scheme, more refined details seem to resurface in work after work issued from the pen of Ignacio de Jerusalem. As with Bach canatatas, the first movement or section is often the most magnificent and meatiest; it exhibits the most substantial interplay of voices and richest sonorities. The middle section is often more "flavorful" than the opening movement but not as overpowering. The final movement is often a joyous fugue or a jaunty 3/8 dance to the finish—or both of these combined into one jocular fugue in a brisk triple meter. Jerusalem's "solo" movements have their recurring tendencies as well. Movement II usually begins as if it were a sedate solo aria, but the melody soon shifts to another singer, who then passes the melodic baton to yet another soloist. They then all combine in a mellifluous ensemble as the team blend in rich harmonies. The fourth movement similarly features smaller resources than movements I, III, and V, but more often Jerusalem drafts its measures so that the spotlight falls on a single vocalist. This is the perfect progression of architectural sound: the solo aria shows off the solo voice in all its agility and expressive clarity, and this serves as the perfect foil to prepare for the bold sounds of the choir that initiate movement V, followed by its exciting dash to the finish in triple meter, often with the banter of fugal entrances. This blueprint could be applied to the experience of listening to Bach's *Cantata*

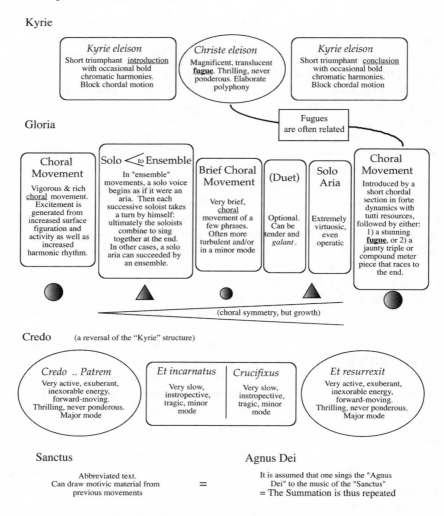

Figure 7-1 Symmetry and growth in Jerusalem's Masses

140, "Wachet auf," his Cantata 40, "Ein feste Burg," Jerusalem's Vespers Psalm Dixit Dominus, his fabulous Te Deum that tied up his Matins services, or any of the three Glorias in the masses of the California missions.

The shorter movements of the Sanctus and Agnus Dei are treated quite differently than the longer "numbers" selections and present a real puzzlement. If one examines the performance parts for Jerusalem's *Mass in F,* his *Polychoral Mass in G,* and the *Polychoral Mass in D,* one is immediately struck by the peculiar absence of one of the core movements of the Mass Ordinary—the Agnus Dei is nowhere to be found. It is obvious that no notated sheets are missing, because some of the performance parts in the San Fernando Mission have blank staves after the conclusion of the Sanctus that could have been utilized for this phantom movement, and some of the brass parts even snip off the sheet after the final bars of the Sanctus, presumably so that the musician could use the blank staves for another purpose. In the remote outback of the California frontier, a few staves of music paper were a valuable commodity and were not casually wasted. In short, the Agnus Dei was not misplaced or simply "lost" but was obviously not even written down. If we start digging through other archives, we discover that the omission of a notated Agnus Dei in New World mass settings was so common that it could be considered the norm—as natural and expected as French fries in a hamburger joint. For example, the Agnus Dei is missing from many masses by Jerusalem, Seijas (Seixas?), Lazo, Alba, Capitán, Mir, Ochando, Eladio, de la Rocca, and Zipoli.[94]

And that presents a quizzical problem, due to that fact that the Agnus Dei is as obligatory to the Mass as are the wheels to a car. We are left with an intriguing question, How do we fill in the gaping hole where the Agnus Dei should be sung? A perusal of other Baroque and Classical compositions in the Hispano-American world helps to answer this question. One of the most revelatory clues appears in the *Missa a 4 y 8* by Alba in the Conservatorio de las Rosas in Morelia. The *acompañamiento* or basso continuo line for Choir I has the instruction "Sanctus: y Agnus por esta," presumably indicating "Sanctus and Agnus with this same music." The first soprano for this same work has similar instructions: "Agnus por Sanctus," or "Agnus with [the same music as the] Sanctus"; it then has an added page with the identical music as the Sanctus but with the new words of the Agnus Dei as the text underlay. The same procedure occurs in the Mexico City Cathedral in the *Missa a 3 por Seijas* (probably the great Portuguese master Carlos Seixas who was a protégé of Scarlatti).[95] The accompaniment part indicates "Agnus por Sanctus," and the vocal parts have *both* Sanctus and Agnus Dei texts placed below the pitches. Joseph Lazo Valero's *Misa a 5* in Puebla is missing the Agnus Dei in all the instrumental parts but is copied out in the vocal parts; as might be expected, the music for the voices' Sanctus and Agnus Dei is identical.[96] Therefore, given this long tradition, it was not necessary for Jerusalem even to bother to sketch out his Agnus Dei—he had already done his composing when he had worked out the previous Sanctus.[97]

Jerusalem shows a proclivity, as do his fellow Classical composers in Mexico and much of Europe, to require the wind and brass players to double on other instruments. In the *Mass in F* at the San Fernando Mission, the oboists have to put down their reed instruments and take up their flutes, and later they switch to yet another instrument, the *octavino* (apparently some sort of flute playing in the piccolo register). In Jerusalem's *Dixit Dominus* found in the Puebla Cathedral, the brass players switch back and forth between natural horns and clarion trumpets, an impressive and excruciatingly demanding skill given the different embouchures required of both instruments. Apparently, brass players in Mexico were like switch-hitters on baseball teams; the skills were in high demand, and a performer who could develop this ambidextrous feat was imminently employable. The payment records for the Feast of San Pedro Arbués in the late 1600s and first half of the 1700s show that the cathedral's music chapel had two "indios" (meaning full-blooded Native Americans with no touch of mestizo or Spanish blood) as their clarion trumpet players, who could also switch on a moment's notice to valveless horns.[98]

The *Polychoral Mass in G* by Ignacio de Jerusalem

Jerusalem carves each movement from the same emotional core, shaping a lilting, pastoral feeling with the prevalent 3/8 and 6/8 meters. This gently elegiac feeling surfaces at the beginning of the Gloria ("Et in terra pax") and its ending ("Amen") as well as in the closing of the Credo ("Et vitam venturi"). If one plays the Nebra Gloria from his *Polychoral Mass in G* with his Gloria in this mass, one finds kindred idyllic spirits, not only in the choice of key but also in the pastoral compound meters. In Jerusalem's mass, both the Gloria and the Credo resemble each other in the lilt of their brisk triple meters, fughetta entrances, and clever use of space and silence in the breathless articulations of "a...men,...a...men" that pull phrases to a close. As each voice group enters with the fughetta's subject, no distracting material muddies the crystalline texture, so the melodic lines remain transparently clear. The full choral resources are mustered, however, before the melodic line's completion, so the rich choral exclamations punctuate each phrase's conclusion.

Just as the Gloria and Credo are conjoined, so are the Kyrie and Credo. For both movements, the orchestra and choirs proclaim the tune in unison textures during the opening bars. Their tunes highlight the same scale degrees: they start on the tonic, leap up a third, descend back to tonic, and then have a prominent octave leap downward on the dominant (1...3,2,1 / 5'-5). In yet another pairing, the Credo and Sanctus are coupled like a pair of train cars; the closing moments of the Credo's "Vitam venturis" are hooked like a clasp to the beginning of the Sanctus that is made of the same material. At its essence, this clasp is forged from a variant of the primal tune we had heard at the beginning of the Gloria and Credo: after starting on the tonic G, it rises up a fourth to C, falls down stepwise to a prominent arrival on B, after which it falls yet again and then takes a few "catchy" jogs before cadencing on its home tonic of G.

Internally, threads connect other sections of Jerusalem's mass as well. In those movements in duple meter, the fabric of melodic motives is the same: Jerusalem uses the recurring rhythmic gestures ♪♩♪♪ | ♪♪♩♪ in the "Domine Deus," the "Deum de Deo," the section "Et resurrexit," and "Et in spiritum." The filial relationship is even more striking given the similar tempos (andante or lento) of all four sections. In the "Domine Deus" and "Deum de Deo," Jerusalem prepares our ears for their thematic resemblance by yet another compositional detail saved for these two parallel moments: he delegates the initial presentation of the tune to the same vocal soloist—the alto.

As mentioned earlier, Jerusalem enjoys linking the various sections of a "numbers" movement by leaving the end section open-ended, poised in suspense on an unresolved harmony whose tension is then dispelled by the opening measures of the next movement. In that respect, this mass's Kyrie, Gloria, and Credo are rather like a row of dominoes all stacked upright but ready to fall forward at the appropriate moment, pushing from one to the next, until the last tile falls. For example the subsections of the Gloria do not come to closure but instead move ever forward, tumbling from neighbor to neighbor with V-to-I harmonic energy, as can be seen in figure 7-2.

Jerusalem also develops a vocal strategy for each major work that is unusual and specific for that one composition; in the *Polychoral Mass in G,* he often shines the spotlight on a solo bass voice from Choir II. Under normal circumstances, Choir I in the cathedral personnel consisted of four single voices: soprano 1, soprano 2, alto, and tenor. For Jerusalem to draw upon a different voice type—a bass—and one from the "other" more massive Choir II, was an unorthodox yet highly effective experiment. It is rather like the use of trombones in Beethoven's Symphony no. 9. For modern listeners who are looking back over their shoulders in time, past centuries of Stravinsky, Mahler, acid rock, and earsplitting heavy metal, the blasting away of a few trombones in Beethoven's orchestra hardly draws our attention; but during Beethoven's time, their reverberant, thunderous entrance in the triumphant finale to that symphony surely raised eyebrows. Similarly, Jerusalem's dressing up of the bass vocalist as a commanding general in this mass must have seemed

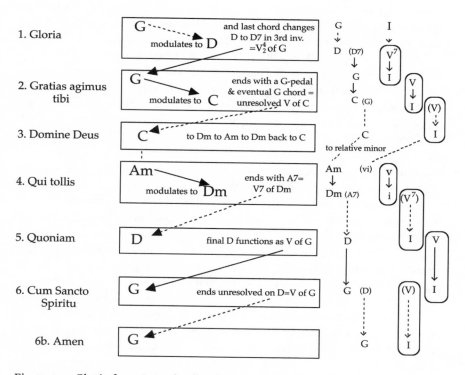

Figure 7-2 Gloria from Jerusalem's Polychoral Mass in G

a novel adventure in stentorian resonance. He doles out major solos in the Gloria's "Qui tollis" movement; the Credo's opening "Patrem omnipotentem," "Deum de Deo," "Et resurrexit," and closing "Et in Spiritum Sanctum"; and the final moments of the Sanctus, where the soloist proclaims the last rumbling "Hosanna in excelsis" from the bass register. Whereas the other four star vocalists from Choir I often combine with each other in ever-changing duets, trios, and quartets, the growling bass of Choir II is treated differently than these four. In most movements, he is not tied to the other vocal soloists in a chamber grouping but instead is either a trooper with the rest of Choir II or a single commander standing alone in the musical fray. One notable exception, however, is the winsome "Domine Deus" in the Gloria that features the alto and bass soloists in an endearing duet. It very well might be the most exquisite moment of the mass.[99] (See figure 7-3.)

This same movement also delves into yet another aspect of Jerusalem's avant-garde "Classicism"—the use of abridged sonata form, replete with clear differentiation of contrasting themes and an initial tonal conflict that is eventually resolved in a recapitulation of all thematic ideas in the same tonic key. Jerusalem builds this movement in true Haydnesque fashion. He begins with an introductory ritornello in C major based on the principal theme (*P*), the violins singing through the tune's variegated rhythms, wistful sigh figures, and sprightly Scotch snaps. The alto soloist then takes charge, singing the tune to the lyrics, "Domine Deus, Rex caelestis" (Lord God, Heavenly King). With the words "Deus Pater omnipotens" (God the *Father* Almighty), the bass voice elicits a new melody (*2P*) and dispels the higher octave of the alto, appropriately depicting God's "fatherliness" in the low register. A transition (*T*) ensues, fabricated from a new idea in the alto voice that wafts above the bass, who continues to plow forward with the same *2P* material, but now directed to the new tonal center of the dominant G major. Having arrived in new tonal terrain, the secondary theme (*S*) occurs right on cue, the alto and bass finally singing together in a tender duet of parallel sixths, full of poignant rapture at the text "Lord God, Lamb of God." The pair then ties off the exposition with a subdued closing theme (*K*), after which the strings banter through seven measures of retransition (i.e., a concise development section) whose path leads us inexorably back to the tonic. True to form, the recapitulation of materials begins with the reappearance on the scene of the principle themes *P* and *2P*—but at the rehoned transition we are in for a surprise. Jerusalem plunges us into the somber landscapes of D minor and then A minor, stretching, building, smelting, and reforging the ideas we have heard before and prolonging this journey until this section becomes a true development section unto itself. Whereas the "expected" development that is tucked between the exposition and recapitulation was a curt seven measures, this more ambitious *T* section distends to three times that size, all of it traversing the unsettling turf of minor tonalities. The secondary theme's luminous arrival on the scene—now in the consoling tonic key of C major—causes the previous suspenseful anxiety to evaporate. Buoyed by the tender contentment of the *S* theme, the alto and bass sing their dulcet duet of parallel thirds and sixths and, by movement's end, bring the listener back to a world of adoring empathy.

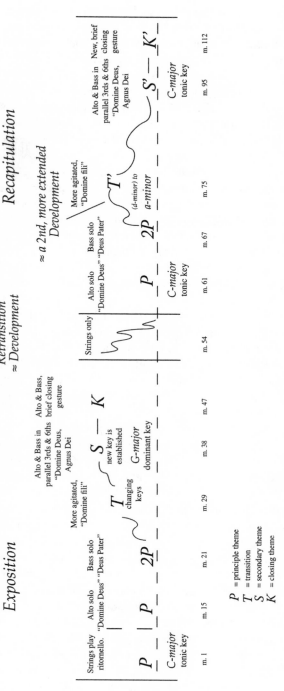

Figure 7-3 "Domine Deus" from Jerusalem's *Polychoral Mass in G*

Another movement in the Gloria, "Qui tollis peccata mundi," has thematic differentiation of a principle and secondary theme and a later recapitulation of the pair. This movement could be considered to be in sonata form were it not for the lack of any real modulation away from tonic in the exposition. In mid-eighteenth-century Mexico, the sonata form was more likely to appear in the solo or duet movements of a "numbers" mass or other large-scale creation than in the full-bodied choral movements. That is certainly the case with the "Domine Deus" and "Qui tollis" movements from Jerusalem's *Polychoral Mass in G,* and similar treatment of sonata-allegro form as found in Giacomo Rust's "Beatam me dicent omnes" that Jerusalem folds into his *Matins for Our Lady of Guadalupe* and *Matins for the Assumption of the Virgin.*[100]

The word painting we had seen as early as Jerusalem's examination piece, "A la milagrosa escuela," comes to the fore in this mass as well. In the Gloria, he colors the text's moods with changes in modality from major to minor, shifts in tempo, density of texture. In the "Qui tollis" movement, he sets the concept of sin in A minor and has the phrases fall with sigh figures, accompanying the text's plea for mercy. Texturally, he begins each prayerful idea by a solo singer, a lone voice before the Creator, but at the text's arrival on the words "miserere nobis" (have mercy upon us!) or "suscipe deprecationem nostram" (receive our prayer), he has everyone sing in plangent supplication, begging that their prayer will be heard. Their passionate appeals sound almost desperate as the choirs declaim the words "miserere" (have mercy) and "suscipe" (hear us), over and over, in anxious repetition. Moreover, the last phrase's tortured chromaticism further heightens their distress. The Credo, too, has its distinctive moments. After the opening incipit intoned by the cantor, the piece begins with amassed choral and instrumental resources declaring in unison, "I believe in one God, the father almighty." Here there is no strife, turmoil, or dissent; all the musicians perform *one* thing. (Jerusalem begins his *Dixit Dominus* in the Puebla Cathedral and the opening Kyrie of this mass in the same way, with all playing in a monophonic texture.) When the Credo's text arrives at the presentation of Jesus as part of the Trinity, the music transforms itself into tender duets; we have moved from the sonorities of imperial majesty for the Father and become more gentle and introspective for the less-imposing Son. The "Deum de Deo" section grows, first presenting a string of vocal solos and then layering them together with the chorus to generate a full, lush wash of sound for the concluding sentiment, "[God] came down from heaven, for us men and for our salvation." With the ensuing words, "and was made man by the Holy Spirit," the strings fall in weeping eighth notes over a sorrowful largo tempo and G-minor tonality as the choirs' block chords respond back and forth antiphonally. The combination of choices by Jerusalem probes the depth of man's frailty. As we have seen in so many other instances, Baroque and Classical composers chose to set the Credo's lines "et incarnatus est" in a minor key and unhurried tempo in order to meditate on the somber implications of man's mortality and weaknesses, and to prepare the way musically for the Credo's reflections on the Crucifixion. Keeping those same expectations in mind, it must have been shocking for eighteenth-century audiences to have heard Jerusalem's ensuing portrayal of the Passion in the "Crucifixus" movement. It blasts forward from the get-go in G major, an allegro tempo, and marching energy by all of the combined musical resources. He has jumped the gun, so to speak, already anticipating the joy of the Resurrection, but he has given us that optimistic vision as early as the Cross that made that transformation possible. The string writing becomes even more active, and the choirs exchange volleys of antiphonal sound all through the "Resurrexit," raising the listener's spirits ever higher. The ensuing movement has exquisitely subtle text painting as well. In depicting the Holy Spirit in "Et in Spiritum Sanctum," he provides an extended instrumental ritornello where the horns twice take the melodic spotlight; the music is "voiceless" as is the noncorporeal essence of the Holy Spirit. When the text finally does resound, it is through the soprano soloist, the most airy and ethereal voice available. When the text tells us that the Holy Spirit "proceeds from the *Father* and the Son," Jerusalem returns to a metaphor he had set up earlier by having the bass voice (the most "fatherly" of all) sing the important line "qui cum *Patre* et Filio." The Credo's closing moments embark on a fugue that reminds us of the Gloria's "Amen," once again tying together the mass as a whole.

The *Mass in F* by Ignacio de Jerusalem

Jerusalem's *Mass in F* (1768) is one of his last works before his death in 1769. Just as he gave a pastoral feeling to the *Polychoral Mass in G,* so he supplies the *Mass in F* with its own, more elegiac personality. He infuses its character with a lilting grace and unprecedented interest in orchestral color. Stylistically, it is his most "Classical" or *galant,* and the increased emphasis on independent woodwind color echoes the same transformation in Mozart's life. The ritornellos put on view luminescent solo passages for the horns and oboes. Jerusalem broadens his timbral palette by having the oboists switch to flutes in the "Laudamus te," "Domine Deus," and "Crucifixus" sections, and to *octavinos* (probably a type of sopranino recorder) in the Gloria's "Quoniam tu solus" and Credo's "Et in spiritum sanctum." Here again, his multihued orchestration is in the spotlight, the pair of obbligato flutes providing a glowing sheen to the "Laudamus te" and "Domine Deus." In addition, Jerusalem's Classical tendencies are on display in this mass's exquisite tunes: his melodies forever explore new rhythmic patterns and a nearly infinite variety of ornamental figuration.

He also forges a certain cogency to the *Mass in F* by utilizing extremely similar techniques in parallel passages. The two soloistic movements in the Gloria (the soprano aria "Laudamus te" and the duet for soprano and tenor "Domine Deus") share a common syntax and musical grammar. Both present a broad spectrum of rhythms, duplets fluidly transforming into triplets, Scotch snaps juxtaposed against steady bass lines. The violins open both movements with the jagged edges of Scotch snaps—and in both movements, those jagged edges are soon sanded over and smoothed out by evenly spaced triplets. The continuo line is almost static in its slow harmonic rhythm and its implacable quarter-note motion. Orchestral colors are similar; both have the woodwind players exchange their oboes for flutes. Both feature the solo soprano (although the "Domine Deus" is gradually transformed into a duet later when the tenor also joins in). The first vocal entrances have a perceived propinquity in the way the soprano ascends upward from the first scale degree over static tonic harmony, doubled by violins layered over static tonic harmonies. The two works are blood relations.

The *Mass in F* also is glued together through remarkably similar violin figuration in its 3/4 andante movements. A recurrent gesture, seen at the beginning of five movements, is based on the gradual ascent of the tonic harmony with its culminating arrival on the high *c"*. The gesture is seen most clearly at the "Cum sancto spiritu" section at the close of the Gloria, and the first section of the Credo, where their bowings are replicated in the manuscript scores. The choral voicing is nearly identical, and the chord progression maps out a I-IV-V⁷-I progression. Passages with some similar traits occur at the beginning of the Kyrie and in the Credo's "Et incarnatus est" section. An inverted variant of the motive in descending motion initiates the Gloria's "Qui tollis." Although arpeggiated triads are not all that rare in general, they *are* relatively uncommon as incipit gestures in Jerusalem's music, yet he uses that gesture five times in this mass. This clearly appears to be deliberate connateness, not casual accident, given the prominent placement of these triads as initiating gestures, the wide span of its two octaves, the shared arrival points most often of a high *c"* and its frequent recurrence throughout the mass.

In drafting the Kyrie, Jerusalem struck upon a novel structural design unique in the literature (or at least with regard to eighteenth-century mass settings from the New World). Instead of tying things off at the end of the Kyrie with a triumphant declaration of the tonal center *F* and a full stop—which is what we expect—he comes to the Kyrie's end, precariously poised on the unstable dominant chord. We are left, teetering on a tonal precipice, and the suspense is not resolved until we plunge into the beginning of the Gloria (tipping from the dominant to the tonic). It is the same sort of "falling dominoes" that we observed within the Gloria of the *Polychoral Mass in G*, but in that instance the connecting device was applied only *internally*, within the boundaries of the Gloria itself. Here, in the *Mass in F*, he bonds into one large, composite boulder, the Kyrie and Gloria together. It is rather like Beethoven's ingenious welding together of the scherzo and finale to his Symphony no. 5 and, likewise, his running together of the final three movements of his Symphony no. 6 into one, long extended gesture. In this latter work, Beethoven presents a peasant dance and then interrupts it by a torrential storm. Then—without pause—the sun's rays come out to dispel the thunderstorm's ferocity. For both Jerusalem and Beethoven, their genius was not merely the invention of musical glue to connect items but their decision to apply this musical glue to ever-larger and monumental architectural structures.

The mass's Kyrie prepares the path that the other movements will trod: the oboes and horns often blaze this trail, answering back and forth in antiphonal dialogue. Their conversation is taken up or alluded to in the following movements; by the time thirty seconds have passed, Jerusalem has told us that the wind instruments will be front and center for the evening's musical episodes. Jerusalem's fingerprints can be found in many of the Kyrie's details. Its opening vocal statement of the "Kyrie eleison" in bold unison is much like the Credo's "Patrem omnipotentem" from the *Polychoral Mass in G* or monolithic exclamations in Jerusalem's *Dixit Dominus* in G major. The Christe portion of the Kyrie shifts continents; we now find ourselves in a lilting minuet with immense rhythmic variety and ingenuity. Normally, Jerusalem ends the Kyrie movement with a few bold strokes in homorhythmic exclamations by the full choir(s) and orchestra. And in some respects, that is what we encounter here: but as we just observed, this ending is peculiar in its suspenseful lack of closure. We are shoved out of the Christe's minuet and into the ensuing Kyrie initially by the strings' Scotch snaps and are then pushed further along by the vigorous sprinting of the violins' sixteenth notes and tense dotted rhythms of choral statements. We arrive at the cliff's edge. When we then fall into the exuberantly joyous allegro of the Gloria, all of the Kyrie's unsettling problems have been cheerily resolved.

The Gloria pulls together all of the "personality" traits already revealed in the Kyrie. The oboes interject themselves as independent, autonomous voices—just as they did in the Kyrie—and realize the instrumental interpolations that separate the blocks of choral writing. Jerusalem casts the second movement of the Gloria, "Laudamus te," as a solo aria for soprano with a pair of flutes that act as obbligato companions. As always, the solo numbers (such as this "Laudamus te") provide the most palpable examples of Jerusalem's *galant* melodies that unravel in ever-changing surface rhythms. Jerusalem's compositional gifts come to the fore in the remaining movements, where he captures the tumultuous (in the A-minor turbulence of the "Gratias agimus tibi"), the sublime (in the gracious duet for soprano and tenor, "Domine Deus," permeated with its Scotch snaps and flute interjections), the impulsively tense (in the D-minor "Qui tollis" with its emotive and sometimes jagged orchestral writing), the serene and bucolic (in the blissful lilt of "Quoniam tu solus" in its pastoral 6/8 meter and countrified *octavinos*), and the jovial (in the triple-meter "Amen" that trips along joyously to the finish).

The Credo's opening bars make an audible reference back to the closing moments of the previous movement. The bonds they share are stamped from the same die. The Gloria's "Cum Sancto Spiritu" and the Credo's beginning both explore tutti sonorities in triple meter with astoundingly similar violin figuration. Moreover, the opening harmonies of the choir deliver the same chords in both movements. The oboes and horn are major actors in the musical drama, just as they were in the previous scenes.

The word painting of the *Mass in F* is on a par with that of the *Polychoral Mass in G* as evidenced in the Credo. Man's mortality and flawed character are expressed in the "Et incarnatus" movement by a descent into the mass's parallel minor (the key of F minor), accompanied by a reduction in scoring. Three solo vocalists trace out the heartfelt lines, leading us into the "Crucifixus." Here again, Jerusalem senses the joy of Easter sunrise that will come even while singing of the Cross; he sets the "Crucifixus" in a major key (B-flat major) just as he did in the *Polychoral Mass in G*, but this time his exuberance is tempered by the andante tempo as opposed to the almost frenetic allegro of the latter mass. In yet another suggestive detail, he adds fermatas on the last words of the "Et resurrexit" movement, so that as the choir sings "non erit finis" (world without end), he gives the note values a sort of psychological eternity—they are not summarily snipped off by a predetermined value but have, in a sense, a value "without end." The last movement of the *Mass* in F exhibits typical Jerusalem characteristics. The solo voices bring us the tune, alternating between the tonic and the dominant for their respective entrances. In between these melodic threads, the choir erupts with their culminating "amens," interrupting the soloistic textures with full-bodied explosions of choral writing. The effect is thrilling.

The *Polychoral Mass in D,* Perhaps by Ignacio de Jerusalem

A third mass in the mission repertoire can join the *Polychoral Mass in G* and the *Mass in F* as a likely member of the Jerusalem family. Although there are no ascriptions in the manuscript, nearly all of the *galant* features and Jerusalem's idiosyncratic tendencies are prevalent in this mass as well; his stylistic fingerprints are seen in the phrasing, homophonic texture, orchestration, fugal writing, use of recurring motives to create cohesive unity, architectural design, word painting, choral writing, violinistic virtuosity, shifts in rhythmic contours, slow harmonic rhythm, and so on. (See photo 7-1.)

Structurally, we have seen Jerusalem build his Kyrie like a sandwich in his other masses—and he does so here, as well. In fact, every movement of the *Polychoral*

Photo 7-1 "Tiple de 1° Coro," p. 5, from Jerusalem, [?] *Polychoral Mass in D,* San Fernando Mission, Archival Center of the Archdiocese of Los Angeles, manuscript J-1, p. 3. (Permission to include this image, courtesy of the ACALA; photo by the author.)

Mass in D is based on the pattern of outside movements enclosing a center of dissimilar elements. In the opening movement, the slower outer sections (with their "Kyrie eleison" text) often exhibit great harmonic daring and bold chromaticism, and they serve as the external bread that encompasses the quicker, meatier, and more ambitious counterpoint of the "Christe eleison" in the middle allegro. Nebra, too, frames the central, fugal writing of his "Christe eleison" with Kyrie sections on either side that are of a more chordal or homophonic nature. However, his outer units, the "bread" of his sandwich, are usually "thicker" than Jerusalem's. Whereas the Kyrie sections in Nebra's *Polychoral Mass in G* are large enough that they can almost stand alone as satisfying units unto themselves, Jerusalem's Kyrie sections are but a few measures in length and serve only as a preparation and a sort of coda for the central Christe, the calorie-laden center of the meal. The Kyrie portions make very little sense, left alone as musical orphans. García Fajer has an entirely different approach in his *Mass in D* than either Nebra or Jerusalem. After a long instrumental introduction of militaristic excitement and static harmonic rhythm, he sets up one long vocal movement that swells in energy and excitement. Their structure is end-weighted and has no vestiges of the "sandwich" model as realized by Jerusalem or Nebra.

Just as the Kyrie has two outside sections that embrace a central, contrasting section, so the Credo begins and ends with high-spirited movements in the jubilant key of D major, and folded within these boundaries are contrasting sections of a completely different character: they edge forward to a lugubrious adagio tempo and the lamenting strains of D minor. The Kyrie and Credo, then, are rather like mirror images of the other. The Kyrie maps out a *slow-fast-slow* pattern; flipping the image, the Credo is built on a *fast-slow-fast* pattern. Of course, the text itself motivates this design, for the confirmation of faith at the outset is aptly set with the dynamic vitality of cut time and an allegro tempo. The reflections on the suffering and Crucifixion of Christ are almost always in minor, and the Resurrection described in the Credo habitually presents the opportunity to return to faster tempos and major tonalities, in this case a brisk allegro and the beaming joy of D major.

We get yet another manifestation of the "sandwich" design with regard to the Sanctus and Agnus Dei. As we observed earlier, Jerusalem intended for the Sanctus's music to be repeated intact as the choir supplied the substituted Agnus Dei text. The Sanctus and Agnus Dei are separated from each other by three very brief recitations: the Canon (the blessing of the bread and wine for Communion); the Lord's Prayer; and the *Pax domini* (in which the celebrant makes the sign of the cross over the Communion chalice and says, "The peace of the Lord be with you always, and with Thy spirit"). We could liken the robust, orchestrally accompanied Sanctus and Agnus Dei to two external slices of bread, and in between are tucked the three thin slices of "recited" pastrami. If we examine the Gloria in this same structural context, it too could be viewed as a sort of symmetrical club sandwich, with thick, orchestral-and-choral slices of bread at the beginning, middle, and end, and with thinner solo, duet, and chamber ensemble movements (i.e., the slices of luncheon meats, lettuce, and cheese) tucked tidily in between.

Figure 7-4 Christe and Amen fugal subjects from Jerusalem's *Polychoral Mass in D*

The point of all this food imagery is to establish that Jerusalem and his Classical contemporaries in the eighteenth century were steeped in the Enlightenment and rational empiricism. The astounding simplicity and balance of Newtonian equations or Leibniz's calculations on potential and kinetic energy find their corollaries in the direct balance of sonata form in a Haydn string quartet, the symmetrical organizational patterns of Bach's cantatas, the crystalline logic of tonal structures in the ensemble finales for Mozart's operas, or—in the New World of Mexico and California—the underlying, formational constructions of the various movements in Jerusalem's mass settings. If one experiences the *Polychoral Mass in D,* one is struck with the recurring morphotic symmetry of these framed "sandwich" structures and their natural organic logic.

An even stronger bond that serves to glue together the various movements into one cohesive whole is the use of recurring motives that get recycled in different movements. The main theme of the Christe eleison fugue that appears early in the mass and that of the Amen fugue at the Gloria's conclusion grow from the

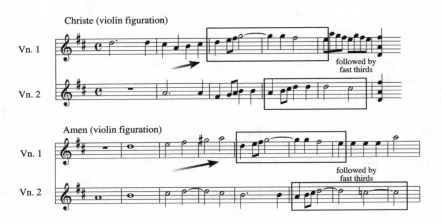

Figure 7-5 Christe and Amen violin figurations from Jerusalem's *Polychoral Mass in D*

same motivic cell, as can be seen in figure 7-4. Similarly, the violin figuration in those fugues is engendered from the same melodic plasma. (See figure 7–5.)

One could argue that the core elements of the fugal subject (i.e., the stepwise ascent from D to G and the downward slope back to D) are adopted as well at the beginning of the Sanctus in the violin parts. Visually, the relationship is somewhat concealed, since their top-sounding note in measure 1 is an F sharp, not the necessary D. But the page is elusive. If one *listens* to the passage (and not just *looks* at the page), the D is unmistakably present. In fact, it sounds humongous because the strings initiate the passage in full D-major chords as triple stops. The bow races across the strings: we do not hear the components of the individual pitches as much as we hear the conglomerate harmony—which is a weighty D major. If we allow that one "harmonic" substitution at the beginning of the Sanctus, then the melodic contour of the aforementioned fugues (D–E–F#–G–F#–E–D) is clearly audible. (See figure 7-6.)

Violin figuration from the end of the Credo also resurfaces in the Sanctus, linking them with a common genetic code. The infectious verve of the Credo's concluding section, "Et resurrexit," is powered largely by the energetic violins, which chatter away in bustling effervescence. Interspersed between the choral blocks, the strings launch into a highly distinctive theme that initially dips, then leaps up an octave, where it remains suspended for a moment, skating across the bar line, and then tumbles downward in a rush of sixteenths. It is quite catchy and serves as a closing gesture to punctuate the end of the B-minor and E-minor excursions within the movement. In the Sanctus, the violins once again take this motivic cell, using it to punctuate the first phrase of the piece (m.3), just as they had closed off

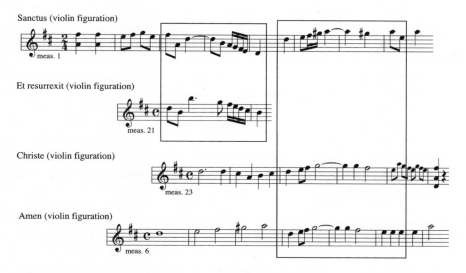

Figure 7-6 Thematic unity between the Sanctus and the other movements of Jerusalem's *Polychoral Mass in D*

phrases in the "Et resurrexit" movement. In short, not only does the motive resurface, but it serves the same grammatical function in both locations.

The Sanctus, then, serves as a sort of thematic reminiscence of what came before. In the first four measures of the violin part we hear the following unifying attributes: an allusion to the fugal subject that the voices sing in the Christe eleison and Amen movements; a replication of the strings' punctuating motive from "Et resurrexit"; and then the violin figuration from the fugues. Thus, in the span of four measures, Jerusalem has drawn together elements of all the preceding movements and woven them together into the unobtrusive accompaniment in the Sanctus.

Word painting is seen throughout the *Polychoral Mass in D*. For instance, the opening movement of the Gloria, "Et in terra pax," sets out in squarely hewn quarter notes, affirming with conviction the opening line, "Peace on earth, good will to men." As the movement progresses, there is more and more surface activity until the movement's end is rich in sixteenths and sextuplets that drive the piece forward with unflagging energy. Increased or decreased activity is not introduced arbitrarily, however, but instead is inserted to match the text. For example, the voices extend their melodic note values, holding their harmonies in ardent affection, at the words "We adore thee" (Adoramus te). Next, eruptions of sixteenth notes soon infect the texture, bursting forth on the line "We glorify thee" (Glorificamus te). The sense of tranquil adoration and that of excited exaltation are thus differentiated by the amount of rhythmic motion in the musical texture. In addition, the composer (probably Jerusalem) changes the length of time between vocal entrances to accelerate a sense of growing excitement. At first the two choirs wait at least a measure between their answering echoes; by movement's end, they follow on each other's heels, answering the other with choral volleys after only half a measure, well before the completion of the other group's phrase.

Just as the rhythmic values compress or expand in the opening of the Gloria in order to reflect the text, so Jerusalem draws out the note values in the "Qui tollis" when the choir asks, "Have mercy upon us, Oh Lord" (miserere nobis). In the *Polychoral Mass in G*, Jerusalem had used anxious repetition to reflect the man's supplication for mercy; in the *Polychoral Mass in D*, the same feeling is achieved, but through stretching and elongating the note values while simultaneously declaiming the prayer in tortuously chromatic harmonies, again infusing the text with suffering passion.

The solo movement "Quoniam tu solus" is highly operatic in its theatrical virtuosity. If this turns out to be by Jerusalem, we might have a glimpse here of the sort of thing he wrote when he was in charge of the Coliseo. Like the other movements, it too is chock-full of word painting. It is crafted primarily from two short phrases, the first that maps out a jagged descent over the tonic harmony, and the second that races upward, higher and higher in an unstoppable dotted rhythm. It is this latter idea that is developed by the violins in a kind of stretto counterpoint, the second violin following the first violin in canonic imitation so closely (only an eighth-note delay) that it is in danger of being ticketed for tailgating. It is this second motive, with its irrepressible upward motion, that is most developed through repetition in a sequence. In short, the heart and soul of this movement is this ascending idea—and what better way than this to express the text, "Lord, you alone are the most high."

The Credo starts and ends in a brisk allegro and major tonality (D major), but it has the expected excursions to minor tonality and slower tempo (in this case, a doleful adagio) that we have seen as standard rhetorical devices of this period to reflect man's failings and mortality. But there are new touches in these two middle movements that deal with Christ's coming to earth and Crucifixion ("Et incarnatus" and "Crucifixus") that further enhance the tragic solemnity. Only the four vocalists from Choir I sing, making the texture more solitary and introspective. Jerusalem provides a sense of foreboding by the octave leap in the strings that then trace out a cheerless D-minor tonality, and immediately after the choir's first announcement of God's coming to earth in corporeal form ("Et incarnatus est"), he has the violins follow with a phrase built of large, jagged leaps that stumble forward in ungainly dotted rhythms almost as if they are weary or clumsy. With each leap, the violins seem to strive to attain the height of the previous jump, but they never succeed; instead, they become more exhausted with each cumbersome attempt, losing altitude with each lunge forward, and eventually falling back down to be grounded on the lowest pitch of the phrase. In some ways, this "clumsy" gesture is built of the same disjointed, gawkish leaps utilized by Beethoven in the middle movement of his String Quartet in A minor, op. 132, in which he too explicitly describes a man's wounds and a halting recuperation. Beethoven places a heading before this movement, "Holy Song by a Convalescent to the Divinity, in the Lydian Mode." After a few minutes he introduces a new thematic idea that he labels "Feeling New Strength" that plods forward with the awkward determination of someone learning again how to walk in the heroic but painful rehabilitation process.[101] These same lumbering steps in Beethoven can be compared to Jerusalem's musical portrayal of Christ's ponderous steps as he carried the cross. In the "Crucifixus" section of the Credo, the violins leap upward and fall back—just as they had done in the previous "Et incarnatus" movement—but here the leaps are even more enormous, and the stumbling returns to the lower octaves are even more pained and ungainly. In fact, they sound breathless, valiant, and exhausted. The vocal writing between these two movements is also remarkably similar. The singers begin on the same pitches in both sections, initially moving in declamatory quarter notes, and tracing out a brief phrase that resolves momentarily with an unstressed V-to-i cadence by measure 2. The imitative passages in both movements are generally initiated by the same gesture: the alto and tenor set the phrase in motion, and then they are joined by the pair of soprano soloists. In short, the compositional devices between these two movements are so remarkably similar that they present us with a sort of balanced equation: the coming to earth of God in human form (the premonition of God's sacrifice) is on one side of the fulcrum, and the Crucifixion (the actual manifestation of that altruistic gift) is on the other.

The "Resurrexit" dispels the gloom with vivacious string writing in the movement's ritornello. The feverish sixteenth-note runs in the violins propel the movement forward with exuberant joy. There is a momentary detour from the beaming of optimism of D major upon the arrival of the text "the living and the dead" (vivos et mortuos), where we cadence in B minor. However, that shadow is obliterated immediately by the sunny disposition of the next phrase. The only other place that has a glimpse of anything other than unmitigated joy is the passage about the remission of sins. The harmonies become unstable and even contorted for two measures in depicting the temptations and perversity of sin, but as before, we race past this glimpse of the darker side of human nature and onward to the triumph of the final measures. The final words of the Credo radiate joy and elated optimism: "I look for the resurrection of the dead and *the life of the world to come, amen*" (Et expecto resurrectionem mortuorum, et vitam venturi saeculi, amen). The last words envision a heavenly afterlife, and that divine setting is painted musically by a shift in meter from common time to an irrepressibly ecstatic 3/8 meter. As is so often the case in the composer's craft, the Trinity is deliberately personified by the perfect "threeness" of triple meter. And theology aside, the movement's closing moments are euphoric simply because of the thrilling writing and the brisk speed with which each measure flies by. The effect leaves one breathless.

The Sanctus has a tough job to fill, following after the rapturous joy and theatrical magnificence of the Credo. It succeeds not through confronting the feverish activity or splendor head-on but through reflective summation. As I commented earlier, most of the essential motives of this mass are jam-packed into the first four measures of the Sanctus, tying everything up into one final bundle.

Notes

1. Robert Stevenson, "Ignacio de Jerusalem (1707–1769): Italian Parvenu in Eighteenth-Century Mexico," *Inter-American Music Review*, 16, no. 1 (Summer–Fall 1997), 57–61; he cites as his source for biographical information the research of Giuseppe A. Pastore and Luisa Cosi, *Pasquale Cefaro musicista salentino del XVIII secolo* (Lecce: Milella, 1980).

2. See María Gembero Ustárroz, "Documentación de interés en el Archivo General de Indias en Sevilla," *Revista de Musicología*, vol. 24, nos. 1–2 (2001), 22, drawing upon the document "Contratación, 5486, N.3, R.15, docs. 1 & 2" dated 19 April 1743 in the Archivo General de las Indias in Seville. Also consult María Gembero Ustárroz, "Relaciones musicales entre España e Hispanoamérica en los siglos XVII y XVIII," p. 33 of the handout for lecture on 3 July 2003 at the international conference "El Barroco Musical en Hispanoamérica (siglos XVII y XVIII)" as part of the Cursos Internacionales «Manuel de Falla»" in affiliation with the 34 Festival Internacional de Música y Danza, Granada, Spain. A revised and expanded version of this handout has appeared as Gembero Ustárroz's "Migraciones de músicos entre España y América (siglos XVI–XVIII): Estudio preliminar," in *La música y el Atlántico: Relaciónes musicales entre España y Latinoamérica,* ed. by María Gembero Ustárroz and Emilio Ros-Fábregas (Granada, Spain: Editorial Universidad de Granada, 2007), 17–58. See esp. 34–37, 40, 45, and 53.

3. María Gembero Ustárroz provides the following data, extracted from the license for embarkation to Mexico dated 8 April 1743, in the Archivo General de las Indias: "Testigos que declararon a su favor, edad de los mismos y duración de su relación con el músico sobre el que informan: *Ignacio Jerusalem Stella:* 1) *Antonio Saul,* 'vecino' de Cádiz (41 años), músico del Batallón de Marina. Conocía a Jerusalem desde antes de 1718 y lo había tratado en Nápoles y Cádiz; 2) *Paolino dell'Anno (Paulino de Lano),* (33 años), músico del Regimiento de Zamora, 'residente' de Cádiz. Conocía a Jerusalem desde *ca.* 1719, y lo había tratado en distintos reinos; 3) *Nicolás Pierro* (43 años), 'residente' en Cádiz. Conocía a Jerusalem desde *ca.* 1735, y lo había tratado 'en distintos parajes'." See Gembero Ustárroz, "Relaciones musicales entre España e Hispanoamérica," 33.

4. The history of Mexico City's Coliseo is meticulously detailed in the contemporary account of Luis González Obregón, *Época Colonial, México Viejo: Noticias históricas tradiciones, leyendas y costumbres por Luis González Obregón. Nueva edición aumentada y corregida, con profusión de ilustraciones: Dibujos originales, retratos, vistas, planos, sacados de antiguos cuadros al óleo, láminas y litografías; y fotografías, tomadas directamente de monumentos, monedas y medallas* (Mexico City: Editorial Patria, 1945). Chapter 35 on pp. 343–47 deals with the Antiguo Coliseo, and the ensuing chapter 36 on pp. 348–64 is directed toward the Nuevo Coliseo. The source is invaluable for its illustrations revealing the layout of the theaters, the location of seating, the price of admission, attendance, rent, salaries, number of employees and size of orchestra, and annual income.

5. There is considerable confusion regarding the date of Jerusalem's departure from Spain for Mexico. The eighteenth-century writer Juan de Viera tells us in his *Breve compendiossa naracion de la Ciudad de Mexico* (1777) that Josef de Cárdenas received permission to go to Cádiz to recruit new members for the musical theater in Mexico City, the Coliseo, in 1742. As has been noted, Jerusalem was one of the musicians that Cárdenas contracted to go to Mexico City, and most scholars have used these data to establish Jerusalem's presence in the New World in that same year. See Robert Stevenson, "La música en el México de los siglos XVI a XVIII," in *La Música de México. I. Historia, 2. Periodo Virreinal (1530 a 1810)*, ed. by Julio Estrada, Instituto de Investigaciones Estéticas (Mexico City: UNAM, 1986), 68; and my own articles "Hidden Structures and Sonorous Symmetries: Ignacio de Jerusalem's Concerted Masses in 18th-Century Mexico," in *Res musicae: Essays in Honor of James Pruett*, ed. by Paul R. Laird and Craig H. Russell (New York: Harmonie Park Press, 2001), 135–59; and "Jerusalem, Ignacio de," in *The New Grove Dictionary of Music and Musicians*, 2nd ed., ed. by Stanley Sadie (London: Macmillan, 2001), vol. 13, pp. 15–17.

The modern edition of Juan de Viera's *Breve compendiossa naracion de la Ciudad de Mexico*, with annotations and commentary by Gonzalo Obregón, states that Jerusalem's journey to the New World took place in 1744. In truth, the dates of 1742 and 1744 are both in error. The actual documentation for Jerusalem's departure from Cádiz—discovered in the Archivo General de las Indias by María Gembero Ustárroz—tells us that he received his license to travel (*expediente de viajeros*) from Spain to Mexico on 19 April 1743. See Br. Juan de Viera, *Breve compendiossa naracion de la Ciudad de Mexico (1777)*, prologue and notes by Gonzalo Obregón (México City and Buenos Aires: Editorial Guarania, 1952), 111n26; Gembero Ustárroz, "Documentación de interés en el Archivo General de Indias," 22n34; and Gembero Ustárroz, "Relaciones musicales entre España e Hispanoamérica," 33.

6. "Mas lo que elevó el coliseo a un grado sobresaliente fué la afición del Señor Don Josef Cárdenas, Administrador del Real Hospital de Naturales, y contador honorario del Real Tribunal de Cuentas. En 1742 consiguió permiso de S.M. para ajustar en Cádiz algunas habilidades para este coliseo, y en ese año y en el siguiente ajustó a Josef Ordóñez e Isabel Gamarra su mujer, con sus dos hijas Vicenta y Josefa, de las cuales esta última fué después dama del teatro con mucha reputación, y casó con el célebre Panseco. Ajustó a Juan Gregorio Panseco, natural de Milán, músico de los batallones de Marina y sobresaliente en los instrumentos de violín, violón y flauta travesera; a Josef Pisoni del Ducado de Milán, sobresaliente en violín, trompa de caccia y maestro de danza; a Juan Bautista Arestin, francés sobresaliente en violín y violón; a Gaspar y Andrés Espinosa, que tocaban flauta travesera, trompa de caccia, oboe y violín; a Benito Andrés Preibus, del Puerto de Santa María, que tenía la misma habilidad que los dos anteriores; a Francisco Rueda y Petronila Ordóñez su mujer, destinados en el teatro de Barcelona, el marido sobresaliente en violín y trompa caccia, y la mujer, famosa actriz y excelente cantarina, que se acompañaba grandemente a sí misma con violín y guitarra, y finalmente, el célebre músico compositor, Don Ignacio Jerusalén, natural de la ciudad de Leche en el reino de Nápoles, maestro de capilla, que fue después de esta Santa Iglesia Catedral, que en los maitines de su composición, tocados en la misma del Jueves Santo del año de 1753, a más del numerosísimo concurso, que para oirlos hubo, asistieron los Exmos. Señores Virreyes." Published initially in the *Prólogo a las constituciones y ordenanzas para el régimen y gobierno del Hospital Real y general de los indios de esta Nueva España, mandadas guardar por Su Magestad en real cédula de 27 octubre de 1776. Con licencia del Superior Gobierno, impresas en México en la nueva oficina madrileña de D. Felipe de Zúñiga y Ontiveros, calle de la Palma, año de 1778*, and quoted in full in Luis González Obregón, *Época Colonial, México Viejo:*

Noticias históricas tradiciones, leyendas y costumbres por Luis González Obregón. Nueva edición aumentada y corregida, con profusión de ilustraciones: Dibujos originales, retratos, vistas, planos, sacados de antiguos cuadros al óleo, láminas y litografías; y fotografías, tomadas directamente de monumentos, monedas y medallas (Mexico City: Editorial Patria, 1945), 343, 345–46.

María Gembero Ustárroz provides further information on these travelers in her article "Documentación de interéses en el Archivo General de las Indias," esp. 22 and 22n34. Drawing upon the document Contratación, 5486, no. 3, R. 15, docs. 1 and 2, dated 19 April 1743, in the Archivo General de las Indias, she tells us that the assembled group of artists consisted of Ignacio de Jerusalem; the Spanish musicians and actors Andrés de Espinosa, Francisco Muñoz, Juan Ordóñez [= "Josef Ordóñez" mentioned in the *Prólogo a las constituciones*], Gregorio Paneco [= "Panseco"], Francisco Rueda and his wife, Petronila Ordóñez; the Frenchman Juan Arestin, whose birthplace was Aix-en-Provence, and the Italian José Pissoni of Milan [= the "Josef Picado," mentioned in the *Prólogo a las constituciones*]. Gembero Ustárroz further lists the artists' family members on the journey, including Jerusalem's wife, Antonia Sixto, and their two children, Salvador and Isabel; Juan Ordóñez's wife, Isabel Gamarra, and their children, Josefa, Vicenta, Maribel, and Luis; Francisco Rueda's wife, Petronila Ordóñez (who was herself an actress and musician), along with their son, José.

7. Jesús Estrada has compiled and published the most extensive primary documentation concerning Jerusalem's life, particularly with respect to this critical period in the Mexico City Cathedral. Estrada quotes this document from the Actas del Cabildo in Mexico City (but without specifying the location of the volume or page number), stating: "se podía conseguir que entrase a cubrirla un hijo de don Ignacio de Jerusalén, llamado Salvador" and continuing that Ignacio is "maestro de Coliseo…es muy inteligente en toda música y composición y el sobrepunto, que es él que sólo lo sabe." The final passage words close "que por amor del hijo asistiría y podían aprovechar mucho los niños." See Jesús Estrada, *Música y músicos de la época virreinal,* prologue, revision, and notes by Andrés Lira (MexicoCity: Biblioteca Secretaría de Educación Pública, 1973), 124. For a study of Jerusalem's musical importance in other Mexican institutions such as girls' schools and music conservatories (especially the Colegio de San Miguel de Bethlen), consult Luis Lledías's "La didáctica musical dentro de un conservatorio femenino novohispano," in *Música Colonial Iberoamericana: Interpretaciones en torno a la práctica de ejecución y ejecución de la práctica. Actas del V Encuentro Simposio Internacional de Musicología* (Santa Cruz, Bolivia: Asociación Pro Arte y Cultura, 2004), 83–92.

8. "Y tratándose sobre su mucha destreza en el violón [violín] y grande inteligencia en la música, pues es el único compositor que había en esta ciudad y que aun en España…que tocaba como violón en la orquesta, esto no le perjudicaba…que el ingreso a ella [la catedral de México] no la embarazaría don Joseph de Cárdenas, no obstante lo escriturado." Estrada, *Música y músicos de la época virreinal,* 125.

9. "300 pesos por el violón, del que era insigne, y 200 pesos por maestro de los niños infantes." They also require "que componga los villancicos que se ofrecieren…llevando lo que en los aniversarios de San Pedro, Asunción, Guadalupe y demás tiene asignado por dicha composición…y que con esto y las obvenciones correspondientes a la renta de 500 pesos podía quedar contento." Ibid.

10. Ibid., 126–27.

11. Estrada provides the documentation and quotations for Jerusalem's work in the cathedral in the late 1740s, stating that Jerusalem's clothing allowance on 31 July 1746 provided him with attire "en sotana y sobrepelliz, traje muy clerical." Jerusalem's complaint against his absent musicians reads: "Varios músicos vacantes están ajustados [contratados] con otros líricos para en su compañía hacer una función en la iglesia de Jesús Nazareno." Jerusalem's description of his sorry state of dress on 31 July 1746 when he asks for more money reads: "por hallarse totalmente desnudo." See ibid., 128.

12. "don Domingo, por sus necesidades y especies, no cuida de nada; por lo que la capilla se halla sin gobierno." Ibid., 129.

13. Ibid., 129–30.

14. "*O Emanuele Rex*…con la melodía gregoriana propia, para que fuese empleada como *cantus firmus* en la composición en contrapunto a 4 voces, llevando el tiple el canto llano y con término de 24 horas." Ibid., 130–31.

15. Jesús Estrada identified "A la milagrosa escuela" as the *villancico* test piece that Jerusalem composed on the occasion of the *oposiciones* for the chapelmastery of the Mexico City Cathedral in 1750. See ibid., 132–33. Lincoln Spiess and Thomas Stanford transcribed the work and include a complete performance score for "A la milagrosa escuela" (but dated as 1765 instead of 1750) with an accompanying English translation in their useful guide, *An Introduction to Certain Mexican Musical Archives*, Detroit Studies in Music Bibliography, No. 15 (Detroit: Information Coordinators, 1969), in unnumbered pages appended to the back of the volume. There are at least two sound recordings available of this composition: *A la milagrosa escuela: Ignacio Jerusalem y Stella (1710c.–1769)*, Coro y Conjunto de Cámara de la Ciudad de México, dir. by Benjamín Juárez Echenique, Universidad Nacional Autónoma de México and Instituto de Investigaciones Bibliográficas and la Biblioteca Nacional de México (Mexico City: Urtext, 1997); and *300 [Tres Cientos] Años de Música Colonial Mexicana*, Capilla Virreinal de la Nueva España, directed by Aurelio Tello (Mexico City: Instituto Nacional de Bellas Artes-SACM, 1993), distributed by Fonarte Latino, S.A., under the number CDDP 1230. According to E. Thomas Stanford's recent catalogue of Mexican archives, the original score for "A la milagrosa escuela de Pedro" is found in the Archive of the Mexico City Cathedral under the assignation "Legajo XXII." It is located on the microfilm collection of the Mexico City Cathedral on Rollo V (that can be consulted at the microfilm readers in the branch of Subdirección de Documentación on the second floor of the Archivo Histórico Nacional de Antropología). Observe that there are a series of films with Arabic numerals and a series in Roman numerals, so the designation of "Rollo V" should not be casually interchanged with "Rollo 5," for they are different films. See Stanford, *Catálogo de los Acervos musicales de las Catedrales Metropolitanas de México y Puebla de la Biblioteca Nacional de Antropología e Historia y otras colecciones menores* (Mexico City: Instituto Nacional de Antropología e Historia, Gobierno del Estado de Puebla, Universidad Anahuac del Sur, Fideicomiso para la Cultura México/USA, 2002), 207.

16. For the full effect of the solfege syllables to be enjoyed, it is worth remembering that sight-singing of the time could start the six-note pattern (or hexachord) on either C or G. One hexachord then results with the syllables do–re–mi–fa–so–la applying to the pitches C–D–E–F–G–A and the other hexachord matched up with the notes G–A–B–C–D–E. As a result, when the text has the syllable do, it can apply equally to either the note C or G; the syllable re could apply to either D or A; the syllable mi corresponds to the pitches E or B, and so on.

17. In Jerusalem's setting of the *coplas* as printed in the text, he starts his hexachord on either C or G, as explained in the previous footnote and depending on the vocal tessitura of the particular singer. As a result, in this particular example the re's match up with either the notes D or A; the mi's match up with either E or B; the fa's match up with either F or C; the sol's match up with either G or D; and the la's match up with either A or E.

18. The definitive authority on Sumaya's life and music is Aurelio Tello. His volumes through CENIDIM in Mexico City not only are treasure troves for performing editions of Sumaya's works but also are rich in new biographical information. Consult Tello's introduction to *Manuel de Sumaya, Cantadas y Villancicos de Manuel de Sumaya*, rev. ed., trans. by Aurelio Tello, 3rd publ. of Archivo Musical de la Catedral de Oaxaca, vol. 7 of Tesoro de la Música Polifónica en México (Mexico City: CENIDIM, 1994); and his introduction to *Misas de Manuel de Sumaya*, rev., ed., trans. by Aurelio Tello, 4th publ. of Archivo Musical de la Catedral de Oaxaca, vol. 8 of Tesoro de la Música Polifónica en México (Mexico City: CENIDIM, 1996); plus Tello's *Archivo Musical de la Catedral de Oaxaca: Catálogo*, Serie Catálogos, vol. 1 (Mexico City: CENIDIM, 1990); and his *Archivo Musical de la Catedral de Oaxaca: Antología de Obras*, Tesoro de la Música Polifónica en México, vol. 4 (Mexico City: CENIDIM, 1990). I also address the contest for the chapelmastery of the Mexico City Cathedral in my article "Manuel de Sumaya: Reexamining the A Cappella Choral Music of a Mexican Master," in *Encomium Musicae: Essays in Memory of Robert J. Snow*, ed. by David Crawford and G. Grayson Wagstaff, Festschrift Series, No. 17 (Hillsdale, N.Y.: Pendragon Press, 2002), 91–106, esp. 93–94. Other major contributions explaining Sumaya's career and output include two giants in the field. See Estrada, *Música y músicos de la época virreinal*, esp. 102–21; and Stevenson's numerous essays in this area of research, including "Baroque Music in Oaxaca Cathedral: Mexico's Most Memorable Indian Maestro," *Inter-American Music Review*, vol. 1, no. 2 (Spring–Summer, 1972), esp. 196–202; "Manuel Sumaya en Oaxaca," *Heterofonía*, vol. 12, no. 64 (January–February, 1979),

3–9; "Mexico City Cathedral Music: 1600–1750," *The Americas,* vol. 21, no. 2 (October 1964), esp. 130–35; *Music in Mexico: A Historical Survey* (New York: Thomas Y. Crowell, 1952), pp. 149–53; "La música en la Catedral de México: 1600–1750," *Revista Musical Chilena,* vol. 19, no. 92 (April–June 1965), esp. 27–31. Stevenson located the original manuscript parts for Sumaya's test piece, "Solfa de Pedro," in the Guatemala City Cathedral, from which can be derived that he wrote the piece on 27 May 1715. The public "exam" or premiere of the work took place on 3 June, and he was voted in as chapelmaster by the cathedral chapter on 7 June. See Stevenson, *Renaissance and Baroque Musical Sources in the Americas* (Washington, D.C.: General Secretariat, Organization of American States, 1970), 105. I would like to thank Robert Snow for having sent me photographs of this same source, from which I made a performing edition of "Solfa de Pedro" (Los Osos, Calif.: Russell Editions, 1992). Using this score, the acclaimed choir Chanticleer made a stellar recording of the work: *Mexican Baroque: Music from New Spain,* Chanticleer and Chanticleer Sinfonia, dir. by Joseph Jennings, Series: Das Alte Werke (Hamburg: Teldec, 1994), CD, Teldec 4509-93333-2.

One of the most important publications concerning Sumaya's output is Javier Marín López's "Una desconocida colección de villancicos sacros novohispanos (1689–1812): El Fondo Estrada de la Catedral de México," in *La música y el Atlántico: Relaciónes musicales entre España y Latinoamérica,* ed. by María Gembero Ustárroz and Emilio Ros-Fábregas (Granada: Editorial Universidad de Granada, 2007), 311–57.

19. Estrada quotes the chapter's demands, stating that they asked for "contrapunto de carrera, fugas, cánones, pasos forzados, ligación y demás contrapuntos que se pueden hacer, para que se reconozca saberlos y poder componer en ellos." See Estrada, *Música y músicos de la época virreinal,* 133.

20. Estrada's account of this situation bears quoting in full. He states with regard to the committee's tribunal on 10 July 1750: "A la sesión se invitó a los examinadores, quienes dijeron que a Jerusalén 'se le hicieron preguntas y repreguntas... sobre las que hubo disputas y controversias acostumbradas en estos casos' y que tanto ellos como el examinado, tropezaron con la dificultad del idioma y no llegaron a saber bien 'si lo que le preguntaban no lo entendía o no lo sabía; o si lo que respondía, los examinadores a su vez tampoco lo entendían.'" See ibid.

21. "Es cierto que nos fue, y aun [no es], muy difícil formar concepto cabal de hasta dónde pueda extenderse su comprensión y suficiencia... [de Jerusalén, quien]... se defendía escaseando y tropezando en la explicación y en las voces; vimos también que, con notable agilidad y expedición, se desembarazaba y respondía a lo que se le preguntaba con la pluma en la mano, haciendo y formando de repente sobre papel rayado [pautado] lo que se le mandaba que hiciese." Quoted in ibid., 134.

22. "Como en dicho examen hiciese juramento, *tacto pectore,* de cumplir mi obligación e informar lo que fuese verdad, para no gravar mi conciencia, digo que: un maestro de capilla de una catedral debe ser un compendio de las habilidades de los músicos, de suerte que lo que otro ignora, el maestro lo sepa; y lo que otros saben, el maestro no lo ignore.... Esto en Jerusalén no se verifica." Ibid..

23. Ibid., 134–35.

24. Estrada provides an excerpt from the Actas del Cabildo in the cathedral, dated 16 January 1751, in which Antonia makes her request for funds, stating "pues está atrasado a causa de una grave enfermedad que tuvo de un tabardillo y que ahora convalece de él." Interestingly, the excerpt that Estrada includes from this document refers to Ignacio's wife as "Antonia de Estrada"—not as "Antonia Sixto," "Antonio Sixto de Jerusalem," or "Antonia de Jerusalem." See ibid., 135.

25. Ibid., 135–36.

26. González Obrégon, *Época Colonial, México Viejo,* 346.

27. Robert Stevenson provides a quotation from one of the Mexico City clerics who complains of Jerusalem's slow pace in completing his mass in the style of Nebra: "'dicha gratificación, para que fuese de más consideración, se podía guardar para quando el dicho Hyerusalem acauasse de hazer una missa nueva que estaba trabajando con mucha especiallidad, al modo de la de Nebra, y que su señoría asseguraba que la acauaria en todo este año,' por encargo del arzobispo, y que 'esperaba verla terminaba antes de diciembre 31.'" Stevenson, "La música en el México de los siglos XVI a XVIII," in *La Música de México. I. Historia, 2. Periodo*

Virreinal (1530 a 1810), ed. by Julio Estrada, Instituto de Investigaciones Estéticas (Mexico City: UNAM, 1986), 68.

Several new editions of Nebra's works have been a godsend for those interested in the jewels of eighteenth-century Spain, including *Cuatro villancicos y una cantada de José de Nebra (1702–1768),* study and transcription by María Salud Álvarez Martínez, Polifonía Aragonesa, vol. 10 (Zaragoza: Institución «Fernando el Católico», Sección de Música Antigua, Excma. Diputación Provincial, 1995); and *Misa "Laudate nomen Domini" a 8 voces, oboes, violines, viola y bajo continuo,* study and transcription by María Salud Álvarez Martínez, Obra selecta, Música litúrgica. I. Misas (Zaragoza: Institución «Fernando el Católico», Sección de Música Antigua, Excma. Diputación Provincial, 1998).

In addition, several superb recordings of Nebra's music have been released in the last ten years, including *José de Nebra (1702–1768): Miserere and excerpts from "Iphigenia en Tracia,"* Al Ayre Español, dir. by Eduardo López Banzo, BMG and Deutsche Harmonia Mundi, 2001, CD LC-00761, No. 05472–77532–2; *José de Nebra (1702–1768): Dos Lamentaciones y Oficios de Difuntos para Fernando VI y Bárbara de Braganza,* Estil Concertant and Victoria, Cor de Cambra de Valencia, dir. by Josep R. Gil-Tárrega, Sociedad Española de Musicología, El Patrimonio Musical Hispano, and Comunidad de Madrid (Consejería de Educación), 1999, Ref. DCD/106, Dep. Leg. GC/1437/1999; *José de Nebra (1702–1768): Viento es la dicha de amor,* Coro Capilla Peñaflorida, dir. by Jon Bagües and Ensemble Baroque de Limoges, dir. by Christopher Coin, Auvidis Ibérica, and Audvidis Valois, in conjunction with Fundación Caja de Madrid and the Comunidad de Madrid, 1996, Valois V4752; and *Madrid 1752: Sacred Music from the Royal Chapel of Spain,* Madrid Barroco, Baroque Orchestra of Madrid, dir. by Grover Wilkins, Dorian Recordings, 2001, DOR-93237. This last recording contains a sizable portion of José de Nebra's *Maitines para Navidad* from 1752.

28. For important recent research on José de Nebra, consult María Salud Álvarez Martínez, "José de Nebra a la luz de las últimas investigaciones," *Anuario Musical,* vol. 47 (1992), 153–73; María Salud Álvarez Martínez, "José y Manuel Blasco de Nebra: La otra cara de la familia de Nebra Blasco," *Revista de Musicología,* vol. 15, no. 2 (1992), 775–813; Rainer Leonhard Kleinertz, "*Iphigenia en Tracia:* Una zarzuela desconocida de José de Nebra en la Biblioteca del Real Monasterio de San Lorenzo del Escorial," *Anuario Musical,* vol. 48 (1993), 153–64; Antonio Martín Moreno, *Siglo XVIII,* vol. 4 of *Historia de la música española,* series directed by Pablo López de Osaba (Madrid: Alianza Editorial, 1985); Nicolás A. Solar-Quintes, "El compositor español José de Nebra (†11-VII-1768): Nuevas aportaciones para su biografía," *Anuario Musical,* vol. 9 (1954), 179–206; and María Salud Álvarez Martínez, "Nebra Blasco, José de," *Diccionario de la Música Española e Hispanoamericana,* dir. by Emilio Casares Rodicio, adjunct directors, José López-Calo and Ismael Fernández de la Cuesta, 10 vols., (Madrid: Sociedad General de Autores y Editores, 2000), vol. 7, pp. 1002–9.

29. Estrada quotes the demand of the Coliseo: Jerusalem was under the "obligación de hacer toda la música que se ofreciese." See Estrada, *Música y músicos de la época virreinal,* 136–37.

30. "Que han pasado sólo 3 meses y 19 días y que se le han entregado [ya a Jerusalén] 557 pesos y 4 reales en géneros y parte de pago en mayor cantidad que quedó debiendo en la casa que habitó." The request for restitution continues that "se le pague al mencionado señor Calvo 225 pesos y 6 reales." See ibid., 137.

31. Estrada gives a full account of the lawsuit as it transpired. It is fascinating that the excerpted quotations that address Jerusalem's concerns (we would assume by Jerusalem) are written in the third person instead of first person (perhaps an idiosyncratic aspect of formalized legal prose in the mid–eighteenth century?). Estrada states: "Jerusalem...aclara 'que el dinero que recibió del...Coliseo, 400 pesos, los ganó en sus mesadas; y los otros 400 pesos, su mujer los sacó en la tienda del señor Calvo en géneros...' Pide el cabildo que no le retenga el pago de sus obvenciones, 'que si bien es cierto que gana la renta de 800 pesos [en la catedral], sin embargo no le alcanza para mantenerse, por quitársele dinero para el pago de su adeudo.' Suplica además 'que se le quiten los puntos por sus faltas a la Escoleta [Pública] de los músicos' y aclara en tono de petición que 'no puede costearse en sus composiciones de copiante y poeta,' es decir, que no podía pagar al copiante de música ni al poeta que componía la letra para sus composiciones." Ibid., 137–38.

32. The chapelmaster should have a "vida ordenada y buenas costumbres." See ibid., 137.

33. There is a paucity of information on Matheo Tollis de la Rocca (or "de la Roca"), in spite of his importance in the history of Western music (especially in the New World) and the quality of his compositions. The most important scholarly work on de la Rocca is Dianne Lehmann's recently completed master's thesis, "A Diamond among Jewels: Matheo Tollis de la Rocca and His Place in Mexican Vice-Regal Music," University of California, Santa Cruz, 2005. Lehmann worked extensively with primary sources in the Mexico City Cathedral and in the Archivo General de la Nación in Mexico City, and her work supplants and replaces the previous principal source of information for Tollis de la Rocca's life, Estrada's *Música y músicos de la época virreinal,* esp. 138–45, 148–61. Her discoveries force us to revise the long-held view that de la Rocca was Italian. See, for example, Estrada, *Música y músicos de la época virreinal,* 138. Robert Stevenson, however, was correct in stating that Tollis de la Rocca was "presumably of Spanish birth." See Stevenson, "Tollis de la Roca," *New Grove Dictionary of Music and Musicians,* ed. by Stanley Sadie (London: Macmillan, 1980), vol. 19, p. 30; and Stevenson, "José Manuel Aldana y Matheo Tollis de la Roca," *Heterofonía,* vol. 5, no. 30 (May–June, 1973), 17. Dianne Lehmann can now confirm without doubt Stevenson's hunch; de la Rocca was a native-born Spaniard.

34. Estrada, *Música y músicos de la época virreinal,* 138–39.

35. "maestro de clave y órgano, y de profesión compositor para iglesias y catedrales...que desea servir a esta santa iglesia con plaza de organero u otra proporcionada a su mérito...pidiendo al cabildo se sirva admitirlo...haciendo las pruebas que parecieren más convenientes, así en componer misas, salmos u otros cantos..." Ibid., 140.

36. Ibid., 141–42. According to the Actas of the chapter, Jerusalem failed, "para componer, lo que es su obligación de hacer" (141). The Actas spell out Tollis de la Rocca's duties. They included "suplir las faltas de aquel incumplido en las escoletas, o como organista, o como tocador de clave en el canto de arias" (141). Later, they assess his personal qualities as including "la prontitud, la honra y la juicio con que responde a todo lo que se le encarga que haga" (141–42).

37. "Don Francisco de Selma echa el compás en el coro sin tener derecho...ye esto es en su desdoro, ya que sólo él es el que tiene privilegio de dirigir..." The Actas, as usual, in recording Jerusalem's arguments place them in the third person as opposed to first-person quotations. I have changed the quotation, providing Jerusalem's "original" testimony as opposed to the secondary description of it in third person. Quotation in Estrada, *Música y músicos de la época virreinal,* 140–41.

38. Ibid., 142–43. Although Estrada does not give the date or precise context, we can assume that he is referring to her death in 1758, for any Spanish chapelmaster would have been expected to compose works of mourning and lament to honor the fallen Spanish monarch. María Bárbara was born in Portugal in 1711 and was heir apparent until the birth of her younger brothers, Peter and Joseph. She later married Fernando VI, who became king of Spain. Her love of music is legendary, and it was for her that Domenico Scarlatti wrote the amazing complex and technically demanding keyboard sonatas that pushed the limits of keyboard virtuosity in the mid–eighteenth century.

39. Jerusalem's testimony as it appears in the Actas asserts: "no ser cierto [el] haberse negado a componer música para las honras de la reina María Bárbara de Portugal, a menos que fuesen pagadas...que todo esto era intriga de don Matheo." The *chantre*'s demands of Jerusalem to compose some music were notarized "según lo escriturado." His explanation of his desperate collaboration with Tollis de la Rocca reads as follows: "para que arreglarse unos papeles de una misa de Bassani a fin de contar con la música que había de ponerse en las honras." See ibid., 142.

40. "1°, que no usurpe Tollis las funciones de maestro de capilla por erección, y que sólo por enfermedad o ausencia del titular, gobierne la capilla; 2°, que se reconozca por un titular [facultado] si della Rocca o Jerusalén son peritos en el arte de la composición o cuál de los dos se halla más apto para el magisterio: que los encierren en una sala, sin instrumento alguno y sin más que tintero en donde *tirarse* sobre una antífona del canto llano, lo que más ha de practicar Rocca, y éste que me ponga las dificultades que quisiere que yo siga...que luego de salidos de la sala se reconozca la capacidad de uno y de otro; 3°, insiste Jerusalén que no siendo Rocca maestro por erección, no se le deje gobernar la capilla sino sólo en ausencia o enfermedad del titular." Ibid., 143.

41. Stevenson, "La música en el México de los siglos XVI a XVIII," 68.

42. "6 Violines de Gallani el Napolitano o de otro mejor fabricante si lo hubiere/ 2 Obues Cortos y 2 Largos/ 2 Flautas Trabisieras con sus piezas de Alzar y Vajar/ 2 Flautas Dulzes con 2 Octauinas/ 2 Flautas Largos por Be.Fa.Be.Mi/ 2 Órganos portátiles Napolitanos o de otra parte donde se fabriquen bien, de ocho o nuebe rexistros, traiendo no más que la cañutería y su secreto para que aquí se armen/ 2 clarines Octauinos de Fe.Fa.Vt / Vn Par de Timbales, en que pondrá todo el esmero posible para que se logren de la maior perfección por De.La.Sol.Re / 2 Trompas, teniendo presente las que la Iglesia tiene, para que estas y que de nuevo se piden, puedan servir de más." The details are provided in José Antonio Guzmán Bravo, "La música instrumental en el Virreinato de la Nueva España," in *La música de México,* 133, citing his original source as being the "Actas capitulares," vol. 43, f. 298. See also Stevenson, "La música en el México de los siglos XVI a XVIII," 53–54.

43. Two of Jerusalem's most important Matins services are his *Maitines para Nuestra Señora de Guadalupe* of 1764. He borrowed several of its Responsories from some of his previous compositions, in much the same way that Handel recycled much of his material in his oratorios. Excluding the duplicate copies of the Responsories that are found as "separate" compositions as well as essential members of the larger service, the manuscript for this composition are found in the Mexico City Cathedral as "Invitatori° i Himno â 4°. con VVs. Trompas i Baxo A N. S. d^e Guadalupe. S.M. Jerusalem. 21 p^s. Son 24 ff., 1764" under the call number E814, Ct., Leg. C.c.9, AM0605–0606; the second portion of this folder also contains the scores for "Ocho Responsorios para los Maytines de la Aparación de Nuestra Señora de Guadalupe." These manuscripts of the *Maitines para Nuestra Señora de Guadalupe* at the Mexico City Cathedral are also found on Rollos 16 and 17 of the microfilm collection "Archivo Musical de la Catedral Metropolitana de México," available at the Subdirección de Documentación, Museo Nacional de Antropología e Historia, Mexico City. The score for the *Te Deum* that almost certainly concluded this Matins service is found in the Mexico City Cathedral under the call number E8.6, C1, Leg. C.c.1, AM0554–0555. Another worthy composition is Jerusalem's *Matins for the Conception* from 1768, found in the Mexico City Cathedral as "Ynvitatorio e Himno y Sinco Responsorios a dos VVs. Trompas i Bajo. Para los Maitines de la Virgen de la Concep^n. Por el S. M° D. Ygnacio Jerusalem. Año 1768," under the call number E815, C1, Leg. C.c.10, AM0607–0609. The aforementioned *Matins for Guadalupe* and *Matins for the Conception* can be consulted on Rollo 5 of the Mexico City Cathedral microfilm series. The *Te Deum* is located on Rollo 43.

One can obtain much invaluable information on Jerusalem's manuscripts in Mexican cathedrals and research archives in E. Thomas Stanford, *Catálogo de los Acervos musicales.* In addition to citing the aforementioned services, he lists the important compositions: *Maitines para San Pedro* (1762), E.b.12, found on Rollo 12 of the Mexico City Cathedral microfilm series [Stanford, p. 78]; *Maitines para la Asumpción* (1762), E.b.11, Rollos 33 and 42 [Stanford p. 78]; *Maitines para San José* (1766), E.b.9, Rollo 33 [Stanford p. 77].

I have reconstructed and published a complete score of Jerusalem's *Matins for the Virgin of Guadalupe* of 1764 (Russell Editions, 1997). The inspiring choir Chanticleer from San Francisco and I collaborated on a recording of this same work (although we sadly did not have the funds to record the entire three hours of music). It was released as *Ignacio de Jerusalem. Matins for the Virgin of Guadalupe,* Chanticleer and Chanticleer Sinfonia, dir. by Joe Jennings, compact disc, Teldec 3984–21829–2 (Hamburg: Teldec, 1998). Jerusalem's *Matins for the Virgin of Guadalupe* was the main theme that I treated in "The Apparition of the Virgin of Guadalupe and her 'Reappearance' in the Choral Masterpieces of 18th-Century Mexico," paper presented at the annual meeting of the American Musicological Society (Phoenix, 30 October–2 November 1997) and at the annual convention of the College Music Society (Cleveland, 13–16 November 1997). My program notes for Chanticleer's tour of this same piece also delve into this topic.

The *Matins for the Virgin of Guadalupe* contains a prologue section of introductory material and then three full Nocturns that are roughly equivalent in size and scale to the acts of an opera or oratorio. Each of the Nocturns starts with thinner textures and less concerted material, but it then builds in texture and energy in much the same way an act in a Mozart opera builds from smaller arias to gradually bigger ensembles, eventually culminating in a flurry of activity. For further publications that touch upon this particular Matins composition, consult Ricardo Miranda, "El mito recuperado: Música para la Virgen de Guadalupe,"

Heterofonía, vols. 120–21 (January–December 1999), 157–59; Miranda's "Rosas decembrinas en el escenario barroco: Mito y representación en los maitines guadalupanos," *La música y el Atlántico: Relaciónes musicales entre España y Latinoamérica*, ed. by María Gembero Ustárroz and Emilio Ros-Fábregas (Granada: Editorial Universidad de Granada, 2007), 397–414; and Lydia Guerberhof Hahn, "Música del archivo de la Basílica Santa María de Guadalupe de México dedicada a la Virgen de Guadalupe," *Heterofonía*, vols. 120–21 (January–December 1999), 80–90.

Jerusalem wrote other pieces in veneration of the Virgin of Guadalupe as well; Ireri Elizabeth Chávez Bárcenas explores the historical, social, racial, iconographic, and musical elements of music dedicated to the Virgin of Guadalupe and emphasizes Jerusalem's *Non fecit taliter* as the core example in her thesis. See Chávez Bárcenas's "*Non fecit taliter omni nationi: Muestras de la felicidad mexicana en la música e iconografía guadalupana del siglo XVIII*," tesis profesional, Licenciatura en Música [master's thesis], Universidad de las Américas, Puebla (México), 2006.

44. Estrada, *Música y músicos de la época virreinal*, 143–44.

45. Isabel Pope, "Documentos relacionados con la historia de la música en México," *Nuestra Música* (Mexico), vol. 6, no. 21 (Spring 1951), 14–15, 22.

46. Estrada, *Música y músicos de la época virreinal*, 145–46.

47. Juan José Carreras explains that normally the composers kept their own scores, even against protests of the *cabildo*. For an accurate explanation concerning "ownership" of a composer's score, consult Juan José Carreras's "Repertorios catedralicias en el siglo XVIII: Tradición y cambio en Hispanoamérica y España," *Revista de Musicología*, vol. 16, no. 3 (1993), 1197–1204.

48. It should be noted that the "complete" microfilming of the Mexico City Cathedral music archive by E. Thomas Stanford and Oscar Huete in 1969 is not actually complete at all, because Jesús Estrada had taken home many of the most fabulous gems while he was writing his book on Mexican cathedral music. Thus, when Stanford and Huete clicked away, they had no way of knowing about the treasure trove that had been temporarily removed from the archive's shelves. Therefore, this work is not available in the microfilm collection of the cathedral's holdings that can be consulted at the Archivo Histórico Nacional de Antropología. Much to the credit and honesty of the Estrada family, they recently saw to it that the manuscripts were returned to their rightful owners in the cathedral, and this collection (that fits in two enormous cardboard boxes in acid-free folders) is now identified in the cathedral as the "Colección Jesús Estrada." The Sumaya score for "Ciclo y mundo" in this collection is of inestimable value, since it is the earliest work in score format in Mexico, and maybe in the Americas. It is a Christmas *villancico* for two violins, basso continuo, and four voices (SSAB). Its call number is "78)27, Colección Jesús Estrada" in the Mexico City Cathedral archive. Other holdings in this collection include fifty-one pieces by Antonio de Salazar (the chapelmaster who preceded Sumaya and was his teacher), thirty-eight works by Sumaya, and major works by such composers as Jerusalem, Tollis de la Rocca, Antonio de Juanas, Dallo y Lana, and López Capillas.

49. "Era admirado aun por los inteligentes y era considerada como milagro." Estrada, *Música y músicos de la época virreinal*, 146.

50. Ibid.

51. "Compónese su Choro de veinticinco individuos que son los Sres. Deán, Arcediano, Chantre, Tesorero, Dignidades, Canónigos, Racioneros y Medio-racioneros. Su capilla de música es la más selecta, diestra y sabia de quantas tiene la América, pues sus individuos (que son cincuenta) son la mayor parte discípulos del nunca bien ponderado italiano, el Maestro Jeruzalém. No hai instrumentos assí órgano, violines, violas, contrabajos, flautas, traveseras, oboes, flautas dulces y octavinos, trompas y clarinetes [*sic*] que no se oigan resonar en este Choro quasi diariamente. Cada uno de los músicos tiene una renta correspondiente que la que menos llega a quinientos pesos fuertes, subiendo otros hasta mil pesos, llegando el número de ellos, sin los seises y capellanes de Choro, a cincuenta individuos, y el Cabildo no repara en acrecer las rentas según las habilidades. Estas son tantas que estando una noche de Miércoles Santo una pandilla de Europeos de esfera, les oí decir que no llegaba Toledo ni Sevilla a tanta magnificencia más parecía Choro de ángeles que de hombres." Juan de Viera, *Compendiosa narración de la ciudad de México* [1777], 33–34. The modern edition of Viera's *Compendiosa*

narración edited by Gonzalo Obregón cites "clarinetes," but it is highly likely that the original edition had "clarines" instead of "clarinetes," thus indicating clarion trumpets. This sort of trumpet was in standard usage at this time, and clarinets did not appear in the cathedral until well into the nineteenth century.

52. Biographical information concerning Francisco Javier García Fajer can be gleaned primarily from the following investigative writings: Juan José Carreras, *La música en las catedrales durante el siglo XVIII: Francisco J. García «El Españoleto» (1730–1809)* (Zaragoza: Diputación Provincical Institución «Fernando el Católico» Zaragoza, 1981) esp. 65–78; Carreras, "García Fajer, Francisco Javier [El Españoleto, Lo Spagnoletto]," in the *Diccionario de la Música Española e Hispanoamericana*, dir. by Emilio Casares Rodicio (Madrid: Sociedad General de Autores y Editores, 2000), vol. 5, pp. 448–49; Juan José Carreras and Raúl Fraile, "García Fajer, Francisco Javier," in *The New Grove Dictionary of Music and Musicians*, 2nd ed., ed. by Stanley Sadie (London: Macmillan, 2001), vol. 9, pp. 528–29; and Antonio Martín Moreno, *Siglo XVIII*, vol. 4 of *Historia de la música española*, series directed by Pablo López de Osaba (Madrid: Alianza Editorial, 1985), esp. 139–40. García Fajer's birth and family tree have been explored by Lynn Kurzeknabe, who discovered the composer's baptismal certificate; she tells us that García Fajer's paternal grandparents were Pedro García and María Bergan, and his maternal grandparents were Joseph Faxer and Manuela Fandos. Cited in Carreras, *La música en las catedrales*, 65n111.

53. Carreras tells us that the connection between García Fajer and his putative teacher, Luis Serra, was first stated by Rafael Mitjana, "Espagne," in the *Encylopédie de la musique et Dictionnaire du Conservatoire* (Paris, 1920), but observes that no documents have been found to confirm this relationship. See Carreras, *La música en las catedrales*, 70; also see Martín Moreno, *Siglo XVIII*, 133.

54. Loewenberg's claims are provided in Carreras's biography of García Fajer. See Carreras, *La música en las catedrales*, 67.

55. Ibid., 65–67; Martín Moreno, *Siglo XVIII*, 133.

56. Carreras explores the stage works of García Fajer in his tome on the composer; utilizing the findings listed by V. Manferrari and the *Dizzionario universale delle opere melodramatiche* (Florence, 1954–55), Contributi alla Biblioteca bibliografica italiana, IV, VIII, and X. Carreras cites the following works composed by García Fajer during his sojourn to Rome: *La Finta Schiava*, intermezzo due atti in Roma teatro della pace, Carnevale 1754; *Pompeo Magno*, Tragedia, 3 atti, Teatro Alibert o delle Dame, Carnevale 1755; *Pupilla*, Farsa, Due atti, 7 December 1755, Ducato di Baden, Mannheim, teatro di Corte, 21 November 1758; and *Lo sculptore*, Intermezzo 1 atto, Roma Teatro Valle, Carnevale 1756. Many of the scores and librettos are extant, presently housed at the British Library and the Liceo Musicale di Bologna. Carreras also observes that the score for the oratorio *Tobias* is preserved in the Gesellschaft der Musikfreunde in Vienna. See Carreras, *La música en las catedrales*, 74, 75, 95.

57. "Misa a ocho voces de gran propiedad y armonia para la oposición de Magisterio de capilla de la Santa Iglesia de Toledo" (Mass for eight voices of great tastefulness and harmony for the job contest for the Chapelmaster of the Holy Cathedral of Toledo). The citation is found in F. Latassa, *Bibliotecas Antigua y Nueva de Escritores Aragoneses de Latassa aumentadas en forma de Dicc. Bibliográfico-Biográfico por Don Miguel Gómez Uriel* (Zaragoza, 1884), cited in Carreras, *La música en las catedrales*, 66.

58. Information gleaned from Antonio Lozano González, A., *La música Popular, Religiosa y Dramática en Zaragoza. Desde el siglo XVI a nuestros días. Con prólogo de Felipe Pedrell* (Zaragoza: Tip. de Julián Sanz y Navarro, 1895), cited in Carreras, *La música en las catedrales*, 67.

59. For an exploration of García Fajer's reforms and their adoption in Spanish institutions, consult Martín Moreno, *El Siglo XVIII*, 133–40; and Craig H. Russell, "Spain in the Enlightenment," in *The Classical Era: From the 1740s to the End of the 18th century*," ed. by Neal Zaslaw, vol. 5 of *Man and Music*, gen. ed. Stanley Sadie (London: Macmillan, 1989), esp. 352.

60. See Carreras. *La música en las catedrales*, 79; Martín Moreno, *Siglo XVIII*, 139–40.

61. Andrés Sas Orchassal, *La música en la Catedral de Lima durante el Virreinato*, 3 vols., *Primera Parte: Historia General*, Colección de Documentos para la Historia de la Música en el Perú (Lima: Universidad Nacional Mayor de San Marcos and Casa de Cultura del Perú, 1971), 193.

62. The Mexico City Cathedral possesses copies of "Missa del Españoleto. Baxo general de la Sta Igl^a de Mex^{co} N.S.," E.9.16 C2 Leg. D.c.9 AM0671; "Dixit Dominus," Leg. D.c.15; and "Laudate

Dominum a 8," Leg. D.c.15, no. 3. The first work mentioned above is available on Rollo 50 of the microfilm collection "Archivo Musical de la Catedral Metropolitana de México," available at the Subdirección de Documentación, Museo de Antropología e Historia, Mexico City. There is a concordant version of this mass in the Mission San Fernando. García Fajer is even more richly represented in the Puebla Cathedral: "Misa a 4," Leg. 10, no. 3; "Ofizio de Difuntos," Leg. 10, no. 4; "Misa," Leg. 17; "Misa a 4 y a 8" in D major, Leg. 62, No. 2; and "Magnificat a 4 y a 8" in G major, Leg. 62, no. 3. The citations are drawn from personal observation and from Tom Stanford's two exceedingly useful catalogues of Mexican cathedral resources: *Catálogo de los Acervos musicales de las Catedrales Metropolitanas de México y Puebla de la Biblioteca Nacional de Antropología e Historia y otras colecciones menores* (Mexico City: Instituto Nacional de Antropología e Historia, Gobierno del Estado de Puebla, Universidad Anahuac del Sur, Fideicomiso para la Cultura México/USA, 2002); and "Catalogue for the Archivo de Música Sacra Iglesia Metropolitana México, D.F.," microfilm collection done by Thomas Stanford with technical operator Oscar Arzate Huete, available for consultation in the Museo Histórico Nacional de Antropología.

63. "4 violines nuevos, 1 idem viejo, 1 idem grande llamad bajo, 1 tambor, 4 flautas, 1 idem nueva, 1 trompa, 1 clarin, 2 triangulos, 1 libro de coro ya viejo con 10 u 11 misas." See Summers, "The Spanish Origins of California Mission Music," in *Transplanted European Music Cultures: Miscellanea Musicologica,* Adelaide, Australia: Studies in Musicology, vol. 12, Papers from the Third International Symposium of the International Musicological Society, Adelaide, 23–30 September 1979, 123n7.

64. "1 bajo grande, 3 bajos medianos, 13 violines, 3 idem, 1 redublante, 1 tambor, 1 libro coral de pergamino, 2 triangulos y varios papeles de musica." Summers, "The Spanish Origins of California Mission Music," 116–17 and 125n29. John Koegel also deals with his inventory (but dates the source as 1851, whereas Summers dates it in 1852), placing it in the larger context of concerted vocal and instrumental performance in the missions in his excellent paper that he delivered for the Sonneck Society in 1993 and the accompanying handout that he distributed, "*Órganos, Violines, Cornetos, y Tambores:* Musical Instruments in *Mission, Presidio, Pueblo* and *Rancho* in Spanish and Mexican California, Arizona, New Mexico, and Texas," paper presented at the annual meeting of the Sonneck Society for American Music, Pacific Grove, California, February 1993.

A few words on terminology are in order here. It is unclear what the scribe intended by distinguishing between a *bajo grande* and the *bajo mediano*. It is quite possible that the "medium-sized" bass was the Mexican *tololoche,* a bass string instrument larger than a cello but a bit smaller than a typical contrabass that one finds in the symphony orchestra today. I have seen folkloric "pop" bands in Mexico with *tololoches* with only three strings. If that is the case, perhaps the mission had three basses of the *tololoche* variety and one "normal" double bass.

The *redublante* is probably just an alternate spelling of *redoblante,* defined in the *Diccionario moderno español-inglés* as a "side drum." See *Diccionario moderno español-inglés, English-Spanish Larousse,* ed. by Ramón García-Pelayo y Gross and Micheline Durand (Paris: Ediciones Larousse, 1979), 772. Next, the inventory lists a *tambor* and clearly regards it as a separate classification from the *redoblante.* Perhaps this *tambor* is a tenor drum, larger and deeper than the *redoblante.* For a discussion of side drums (*redoblantes*) and tenor drums (*tambores?*), consult James Blades, "Drum," in *The New Grove Dictionary of Music and Musicians* (London: Macmillan, 1980), vol. 5, pp. 639–49, esp. 647–48.

65. "4 flautas, 3 clarinets, 2 trompas, 2 violones, 1 chinesco, 1 bombo, 2 tambores, 16 violines, 1 organo con 6 registros y un teclado y quatro diapasones, 4 violines nuestros, 3 triangulos, 4 violines nuevos." Summers, "The Spanish Origins of California Mission Music," 123n7. Summers provides this information as well in his article "Orígenes hispanos de la música misional de California," *Revista Musical Chilena,* nos. 149–150 (1980), 36n7. In the former article he spells the second item on the list as *clarinets,* and in the latter article he spells the same item as *clarinetes.* The *chinesco* is a Turkish crescent (sometimes called a Jingling Johnny or a Chinese pavilion). It was of Turkish origin in the Janissary bands and is constructed of a pole with metal cross beams in the shape of crescents from which are suspended many small bells. At the top of the pole is a Chinese pavilion—hence its name—or some symbol of a military standard. As with cymbals, bass drums, and triangles—that were also of Turkish origin—they migrated

from the Janissary bands to other European bands and orchestras in the eighteenth century. See *Diccionario moderno español-inglés*, 271; and James Blades, "Turkish Crescent," in *The New Grove Dictionary of Music and Musicians*, vol. 19, p. 279. The *bombo* is a bass drum.

   With regard to the *clarinets* in the inventory, I strongly suspect that the spelling in the original document was *clarines* (with no *t*), the name for the valveless trumpet. Clarion trumpets were standard instruments in the cathedrals and churches of Spain and its colonies in the New World, unlike clarinets, which are not mentioned in the Mexico Cathedral until well into the nineteenth century. The *Polychoral Mass in D* (perhaps by Jerusalem) whose performance parts are now in the San Fernando Mission requires *clarines,* as does the *Mass in D* by García Fajer, also preserved in the San Fernando Mission. It would make perfect sense to have these instruments in a mission inventory, since they were needed for these two mission masses (and probably for other works as well). Additionally, many travelers such as Alfred Robinson and Harrison G. Rogers mention "trumpets" in their prose descriptions of mission life, yet the word *trompeta* never shows up (to my knowledge) in the Spanish writings of the friars. And it is necessary to recall that their use of the term *trompa* referred to the valveless French horn, *not* the trumpet. The *clarines* in the inventories, however, would match up with the *trumpets* described by the British and Yankee travelers. Lastly, *clarines* would have been present at any of the presidios in California: they were a mandatory part of any military music ensemble as part of their "drum and bugle corps."

   Joseph Halpin also discusses this inventory in his study "Musical Activities and Ceremonies of Mission Santa Clara de Asis," *California Historical Society Quarterly,* vol. 50, no. 1 (March 1971), 41.

   66. Koegel, "*Órganos, Violines, Cornetos, y Tambores*"; Francis Price, "Letters of Narciso Durán from the Manuscript Collections in the California Historical Society Library," *California Historical Society Quarterly,* pt. 2 in vol. 37, no. 3 (September 1958), 250.

   67. Alfred Robinson, *Life in California: A Historical Account of the Origin, Customs, and Traditions of the Indians of Alta-California,* foreword by Joseph A. Sullivan (Oakland, Calif.: Biobooks, 1947), 72.

   68. A common grouping would consist of three first violins, three second violins, a cello, a bass, a harp and/or guitar, a pair of horns, and a pair of oboes or flutes. See notes 117–120 in chapter 1 regarding Spanish orchestras of the late eighteenth and early nineteenth centuries.

   69. Mariano Guadalupe Vallejo, "Ranch and Mission Days in Alta California," *The Century Magazine,* vol. 41, no. 2, series 19 (December 1890), 186.

   70. Sir George Simpson, *Narrative of a Voyage to California Ports in 1841–42. Together with Voyages to Sitka, the Sandwich Islands and Okhotsk. To which are added: Sketches of Journies across America, Asia, and Europe. From the Narrative of a Voyage around the World,* edited, corrected, and with a foreword by Thomas C. Russell (San Francisco: Private Press of Thomas C. Russell, 1930), 129–30.

   71. AGN: Número de Registro 53860, Grupo Documental 8, Archivo de Hacienda, Número de Soporte, 283, "TEMPORALIDADES Misiones en California" (hereafter abbreviated to "AGN, Hacienda, N° 53860").

   72. "1 Organo de cilindro, si hai proporcion ... 2 biolones / 2 biolines / 2 bandolones / 2 bajos [de ?] / 2 trompas / 1 clarin / 2 guitarras / 2 flautas 16 p[eso]s. / 2 oboes / 2 clarinetes / 2 juegos de platillos / 2 triangulos/ 1 tambor, y tambora / 2 surtidos de cuerdas." Part of Expediente 3, "Memoria que la Misión de N. S. P. Sn. Francisco pide por el año de 1807, fecha en 31 Enero de 1806," in AGN, Hacienda, N° 53860.

   73. "1 Violon / 2 Violines / 2 Flautas traveseras / 2 Trompas reales / 2 Bandolones / 2 Basos e Bandolon / 2 Guitarras / 2 Triangulos / 1 Clarinete / 1 Tambora." Part of Expediente 19, "Memoria perteniciente â esta Mision de Sⁿ Luis Rey en el año 1807," in AGN, Hacienda, N° 53860.

   74. "6 violines, 1 violon baxo, 2 trompas de caza y 1 triangulo" and later "Anadido en corta ... 1. Espineta / 4. Tomos de serm⁻s [sermones?] de armonia." Part of Expediente 63, "Memoria qᵉ piden los PP. M⁻itros. de la Mision del Sr. S. Jose para el año de 1808," in AGN, Hacienda, N° 53860.

   75. See Kotzebue's accounts as covered in Robert Kirsch and William S. Murphy, "The Russians in California," in *West of the West: Witnesses to the California Experience,*

1542–1906. The Story of California from the Conquistadores to the Great Earthquake, as Described by the Men and Women Who Were There (New York: Dutton, 1967), 147–55, esp. 151; Fr. Owen da Silva, O.F.M., *Mission Music of California: A Collection of Old California Mission Hymns and Masses* (Los Angeles: Warren F. Lewis, 1941), 9; Larry Warkentin, "The Rise and Fall of Indian Music in the California Missions," *Latin American Music Review*, vol. 2, no. 1 (1981), 54; Koegel, "*Órganos, Violines, Cornetos, y Tambores*"; and August C. Mahr, *The Visit of the "Rurick" to San Francisco in 1816* (Palo Alto, Calif.: Stanford University Press, 1932).

76. Da Silva, *Mission Music of California*, 8.

77. Robert Stevenson, "Music in Southern California: A Tale of Two Cities," *Inter-American Music Review*, vol. 10, no. 1 (Fall–Winter 1988), 56. Other descriptions of music at the San Gabriel Mission tell of other instrumental usage there as well, although there is no hint as to how many of each instrument played and to whether or not they doubled each other or the voices or—on the other hand—whether they played independent lines. José de Lugo (who must have been the source for Bancroft when he provides this same information in his *California Pastoral*) states that San Gabriel had an Indian orchestra with flutes, guitars, violins, drums, triangles, and cymbals. See Koegel, "*Órganos, Violines, Cornetos, y Tambores*"; and Hubert Howe Bancroft, *California Pastoral, 1769–1848*, vol. 34 of *The Works of Hubert Howe Bancroft* (San Francisco: San Francisco History Company, 1888), 427.

78. William Dane Phelps, *Alta California, 1840–1842: The Journal and Observations of William Dane Phelps, Master of the Ship "Alert*," introduce and edited by Briton Cooper Busch (Glendale, Calif.: Arthur H. Clark, 1983), 297.

79. M[onsieur Count Eugène] Duflot de Mofras, *Duflot de Mofras' Travels on the Pacific Coast*, 2 vols., translated, edited, and annotated by Marguerite Eyer Wilbur, foreword by Frederick Webb Hodge (Santa Ana, Calif.: Fine Arts Press, 1937), vol. 1, p. 134.

80. William John Summers, "*Opera seria* in Spanish California: An Introduction to a Newly-Identified Manuscript Source," in *Music in Performance and Society: Essays in Honor of Roland Jackson*, ed. by Malcolm Cole and John Koegel (Warren, Mich.: Harmonie Park Press, 1997).

81. The "anonymous" *Mass in F* is found in a concordant source in the Mexico City Cathedral as "E7.5, C1, Leg. D.b.14, AM0471," sometimes abbreviated simply to "Leg. D.b.14." The material can be consulted on Rollos 28 and 29 of the microfilm collection Archivo Musical de la Catedral Metropolitana de México, available at the Subdirección de Documentación, Museo de Antropología e Historia, Mexico City. This *legajo*, or folder, contains a full set of performance parts for use in the Cathedral as well as Jerusalem's *borrador*, his signed autograph score. It is in his hand, signed by him, and dated 1768. It should be noted that until recently the penciled identification at the top of the title page did not match the catalogue in the cathedral used for locating documents. Therefore, when I photographed the score it still read "D.b.13," but after I pointed out the discrepancy to the chief archivist, Lic. Salvador Valdés, the "D.b.13" has been erased and been replaced with the correct number, "D.b.14." The title page of this *legajo* reads: "No. 5. / MISA A 4 / CON VVIOLINES OBOES FLA/VTAS TROMPAS Y VAXO / CON RIFORSOS DE SEGVNDO CORO Y ORGANOS / Compuesta Por Don Ygnacio Jerusalem / Mtr̄o De Capilla / De la Santa Yglesia Metropolitana De Mexico / Año de 1768 / Son veinte y quatro Papeles." Although this is technically not a "polychoral" mass with two opposing choirs, it is clear from both the title and the way the parts are written that there is a contrast between the "weight" of the choral writing. At times, the fabric is simply four singers, with each singing his own line. At other times, the full choral resources are employed (probably twelve singers if we are to judge by the number of copied choral parts). Another point of interest is this mass has the *identical* colorful marbled paper used to bind it as the performance parts for the *Mass in D* by El Españoleto. This shared physical aspect binds these two sources together, proving that they were created in the same scriptorium; interestingly, it is these *same two masses* that are copied out into manuscript parts and surface in the San Fernando Mission. Apparently, the conjunction of these two masses—Jerusalem's *Mass in F* and García Fajer's *Mass in D*—is not entirely random or coincidental.

The "anonymous" *Mass in D* at the San Fernando Mission is found in a concordant source in the Mexico City Cathedral as "E.9.16, C2, Leg. D.c.9, AM0671," sometimes abbreviated as "Leg. D.c.9." The cover of each performance provides a cursory title for the larger work: the continuo line has "Missa del Españoleto / Baxo general / de la Sta Ygl^a de Mex^{co} / N.S. [or perhaps "N.1."]." Inside the cover of the first violin part is the ascription "La Dio a la Iglesia D^n Juan Bau^{ta} del Aguila siendo Chantre el Sr D^n J^n Manuel Barrienlos" (I, Don Juan Bautista del Aguila, donated this [mass] to the Church, the Chantre of the Chapel being Don Juan Manuel Barrienlos). The material can be consulted on Rollo 50 of the microfilm collection Archivo Musical de la Catedral Metropolitana de México in the Museo de Antropología e Historia. Although the California source makes no clear distinction between the vocal lines, the Mexican parts do, dividing the vocalists into Choir I (SSAB) with one performance part per line, and Choir II (SATB) with two performance parts per line. Thus, for the both the *Mass in F* and the *Mass in D* we have a choir consisting of twelve voices—the standard for the cathedral music of the middle and late eighteenth century. The instrumental lines include vn1 (2), vn2 (2), va, ob1, ob2, clarín 1, clarín 2, (i.e., valveless trumpets), hn1, hn2, baxo general, bc, org (2). The fascinating feature here is the existence of a *separate* viola part, a rarity even in Mexico, and even rarer in California. Mexican cathedrals had been using violas for a long time (and they probably were used in California as well), but they were relegated to the *acompañamiento* line and thus doubled the cello and bass but in a different octave. There was no reason, then, to write out a separate line for this instrument.

At this point it is necessary to correct an error that I made in 1992 and that has been repeated by scholars who have relied on my earlier work. When I first started work with these sources, in confusion I incorrectly observed that the *Mass in D* at the San Fernando Mission was composed by Ignacio de Jerusalem when, in fact, the mass is the work of García Fajer. The faulty citations appear in two of my articles. See Russell, "The Mexican Cathedral Music of Sumaya and Jerusalem: Lost Treasures, Royal Roads, and New Worlds," *Actas del XV Congreso de la Sociedad Internacional de Musicología* (Madrid, April 1992) published in the *Revista de Musicología*, vol. 16, no. 1 (1993), esp. 100, 108; and "Newly Discovered Treasures from Colonial California: The Masses at the San Fernando Mission," *Inter-American Music Review*, vol. 13, no. 1 (Fall–Winter, 1992), 5–9.

In addition to my faulty information, a recent error by James Sandos needs to be repaired. In his chapter on music in the missions, he observes, "De Jerusalem's masses were in the handwriting of Sancho, himself a choir director, who had heard them in Mexico City. Sancho transcribed them and brought them with him when he came to Alta California in 1804." See James A. Sandos, *Converting California: Indians and Franciscans in the Missions* (New Haven, Conn.: Yale University Press, 2004), 141. This is incorrect; none of the manuscripts in California with Jerusalem's music are in Juan Bautista Sancho's handwriting. The source of the confusion probably derives from the fact that the San Fernando Mission manuscript parts that contain the masses of Jerusalem and García Fajer are interspersed in the same large stack of music that also contains numerous loose sheets in Sancho's hand, as well as the fascinating booklet (identified by the sigla "As-3") with an aria based on a Metastasio libretto, *Artaserse*. Bill Summers's ingenious digging tracked down the source of the operatic text in this book and most of the other musical items tucked into its pages—and it was also Summers who first brought to our attention the fact that Sancho had scribbled the music for several independent pieces into the "blank measures" of this *Artaserse* booklet. (See Summers, "*Opera seria* in Spanish California.") Therefore, there is a peripheral link between Sancho and the Jerusalem manuscript part in that they are from the same collection of materials—but the Jerusalem masses are not in Sancho's hand. Bill Summers proposed to me (and I am in complete agreement) that the whole stack of materials was probably part of Sancho's personal collection during his lifetime.

82. There is an excellent recording of *The Polychoral Mass in D* (that I ascribe to Jerusalem) by the San Francisco choir Chanticleer. See *Mexican Baroque: Music from New Spain*. Their recording is based on my reconstruction of this mass.

83. The sheets measure 23 cm height by 31 cm width. García Fajer's *Mass in D* uses twelve staves per page with the sole exception of the alto part, which is on ten-staff paper. The *Polychoral Mass in D* uses ten staves per page for all the parts except for the two violin parts, which utilize twelve staves per page. Jerusalem's *Mass in F* uses ten staves per page for the vocal, violin 2, and organ parts: its two oboe and two horn parts are on twelve-staff paper.

84. One watermark that recurs in the paper for each of the three masses is that of a large "CS." The same is true for a large crescent with some irregular "dimples" on the inside arch.

The organ part for the *Mass in F* has one sheet with three crescent moons in a row. The *Mass in D* and the *Mass in F* have the following watermarks: a large "VB"; a flowered shield; half of a dimpled crescent with the large letters "LZ" placed below; and a florid seven-point crown. The *Polychoral Mass in D* does not have these latter watermarks, but their absence does not necessarily indicate that it is copied onto different paper stock. On the contrary, the two watermarks that do recur (the large "CS" and the dimpled crescent) are also found in the F-major and D-major masses. Furthermore, it has no watermark that is unique to this source. Regardless of watermark, the general texture, size, and feel of the paper are identical for all sheets. It is my opinion that the paper stock is basically the same for all three masses.

85. The fact that the hands differ is not surprising, since it was a standard feature in a scriptorium to divide the labor. In the Mexico City Cathedral, most often there was a separate copyist for Choir I and a different copyist for Choir II. I have found that often the brass parts are in a separate hand as well.

All the parts for the *Polychoral Mass in D* are in the same hand, except for the clarion trumpet parts, which are done by a different scribe. These trumpet parts have the word "Fin" written at the end of the piece, and the page has been cut below that word, apparently so the remaining music paper could be used elsewhere. Like that trumpet part in the *Polychoral Mass,* the last sheet of instrumental parts from the *Mass in F* are physically cut off, leaving only a partial sheet when there would have been a significant number of blank staves after the piece's conclusion. This is the case for the "Trompa 1ª," "Trompa 2ª," "Violin 2°," and "Organo" parts. The organ part for the *Mass in F* additionally has the word "Fin" at the conclusion of the "Sanctus"—as do the clarion trumpet parts from the *Polychoral Mass*. In addition, the organ part of the *Mass in D* and the bass vocal part of the *Mass in F* are so similar in their notational idiosyncrasies that they appear to be written by the same scribal hand. The same holds true for the "Violin 2°" parts of the F-major and D-major masses.

86. The *Polychoral Mass in G* is found in the Santa Barbara Mission Archive-Library as Docs. 11, 13, 14, and 25—although now the contents have been consolidated into the folder for Doc. 11. The other folders have a slip that refers the investigator to Doc. 11. Only a handful of the parts are still extant: "Tiple 2° De Primero Choro"; "Alto De Primero Choro"; "Tenor De 2° Choro"; and "Bajo de 2° Choro." Each of the parts is folded with the name of the vocal part written as an identifying title, along with the ascription "Jerusalen." This clearly contradicts Joseph Halpin's statement: "This mass is most likely one composed by Father Durán though the manuscript is untitled and unsigned." See Joseph Halpin, "A Study of Mission Music Located at Mission Santa Clara de Asís," M.A. thesis, San Jose State College, 1968, p. 30. According to George Harshbarger, this mass is "Manuscript 10" in the Santa Barbara Mission Archive-Library, but "Document 10" will actually lead the scholar to a polyphonic intoning formula for the *Te Deum*. See George A. Harshbarger, "The Mass in G by Ignacio de Jerusalem and Its Place in the California Mission Music Repertory," D.M.A. diss., University of Washington, 1985, 27.

87. Harshbarger mentions Stevenson's reference to Jerusalem and the presence of manuscripts parts for his *Polychoral Mass in G* at the Santa Barbara Mission. See Robert Stevenson, "Sixteenth- through Eighteenth-Century Resources in Mexico: Part III," *Fontes artis musicae* 25 (March–April 1978) 174; citation in Harshbarger, "The Mass in G," 48n1.

88. "In the present effort to reconstruct this mass, a concordance was sought in Mexico City. Another incomplete version of this mass, along with other pieces by the same composer, was found in the microfilm archive of the *Instituto Nacional de Antropología y Historia.* . . . The score in the Appendices of this study is a corrected, edited, and annotated compilation of both sources [i.e., the Santa Barbara parts and the Puebla parts] of the Mass in G by Ignacio [de] Jerusalem for two choirs, violins, *trompas*, and *acompañamiento*. Missing parts (second *trompa*, first soprano of the first choir, and portions of the soprano and alto of the second choir) were filled in, based on examination of the harmonic needs of this score and a close scrutiny of Jerusalem's compositional practices." See Harshbarger, "The Mass in G," 1–2. See also pp. 37–39. Harshbarger states that he used Rollo 17 of the Puebla Cathedral, relying on Legajo 70 (Harshbarger, "The Mass in G," 38). The material is elusive, however, because several folders must be combined and utilized in consort with each other in order to reconstruct the whole mass. The call number for the source and its exact instrumentation are as follows:

Puebla, Leg. 70, No. 1. "Missa â 4 y â 8, con Violines y Trompas. Compuesta por D^n Ygnacio Jerusalem. Maestro de Capilla de la Santa Yglesia Catedral de Mexico." The folder contains only the "Accompañamiento" part for the mass in G major, and remarkably, it includes an "Agnus Dei" movement that is absent in most of the other performance parts.

Puebla, Leg. 70, No. 2. "Misa a ocho con Violines y Trompas Por el Sõr Mtᵒo Jerusalem." The "Accompañamiento" part for the mass in G major. This does *not* include the "Agnus Dei."

Puebla, Leg. 69, No. 3. The same G-major mass as listed above. It includes hn1, hn2, vn1, vn2, bc, and also contains the choral parts for two choirs: SSAT/SATB.

Puebla, Leg. 69, No. 6. The same G-major mass as listed above. It contains vn1, vn2, hn1, and *some* of the vocal parts: It is missing the first soprano from Choir I, the "bajo" for Choir II, and the second horn. In addition, the folder contains a "bajete" for Choir I not found in the other *legajos*.

Given Harshbarger's statement that the second horn part and the first soprano for Choir II are missing, we can safely assume that he was relying on Legajo 69, No. 6, in the Puebla Archive for his reconstruction, not Legajo 70 as he states. Ironically, the "missing" material appeared on the same film but located earlier on the film and with different call numbers. Therefore, the inevitable errors that arise from Harshbarger's valiant attempt to think up the "missing parts" can now be corrected definitively with the composer's intentions now retrievable from these performance parts.

In addition to the Puebla concordant sources, there is also a folder in the Mexico City Cathedral Archive containing this mass as well:

Call number: E7.5, C1, Leg. D.b.15, AM0472. The title on the folder's cover states, "N. 1° / MISA A 8 / CON VIOLINES TROMPAS Y / BAXO/ Compuesta Por Don Ygnacio Jerusalem Mtᵒo / De Capilla de la Sta Yglesia Cathedral de Mexico / Son 23 Papeles."

This folder contains no score but many performance parts, including vn1 (2), vn2 (2), hn1, hn2, ob1, ob2, bc (2), org (2), and the vocal parts SSATB/SATB. There are two parts each for Choir II, yet only one part each for Choir I. Significantly, this is the only source with oboes included in the instrumentation.

There is an excellent recording of Jerusalem's *Polychoral Mass in G* based on the sources in the Mexican archives, transcribed by Thomas Stanford. See *México Barroco,* Schola Cantorum and Conjunto de Cámara de la Ciudad de México, dir. by Benjamín Juárez Echenique (Mexico City: Urtext, 1994), CD UMA2001.

89. "Among these music papers I find one called a mass for four voices with violin, tromb [*sic*], organ and bajo (bass viol), written by Ygnacio Jerusalem. Some of you, perhaps, are not aware that in the old times every mission had a set choir of musicians selected from among Indian neophytes. These sang mass and vespers and hymns accompanied by string and wind instruments....In some missions they had as many as one hundred players and singers, but they have nearly all disappeared. Once a year at least each one of them was given a new suit, and other privileges were granted to them to encourage them to serve in the choir." Rev. J[oachim], Adam, V.G., "Rare Old Books in the Bishop's Library," in *Publications of the Historical Society of Southern California,* vol. 5, no. 1 (1897), 154–56. I would like to thank both John Koegel and Bill Summers for independently bringing this information to my attention and for sending me a copy of the pertinent pages from this rather inaccessible journal.

Although Adam does not give a specific title to the composition that he saw, a possible candidate for this "mystery" piece would be the *Mass in G* for the following reasons. There are now *four* extant voice parts, and I suspect that Rev. Adam simply counted the folders when he described this as a four-voice mass. In addition to the expected string contingency, this mass emphasizes *trompas,* or horns, and that would account for the *tromb* [*sic*] that Rev. Adam mentions. Another worthy clue that indicates Adam was referring to Jerusalem's *Polychoral Mass in G* at the Santa Barbara Mission is his explicit mention of the composer, Jerusalem; it is worth noting again that this particular mass is the *only* one of the extant California manuscript sources that identifies the composer by name. An argument against my stated theory, however, is the absence—at least in modern times—of any extant instrumental parts in the California archives. If Adam had access *only* to the four vocal parts that we find today in Santa Barbara, there is no way for him to have known about the other instruments that he mentions with great specificity.

If Rev. Adam had seen the performance parts for the *Mass in F* now preserved at the Mission San Fernando, he probably would have mentioned the woodwind parts that predominate—the flutes or oboes. The *Polychoral Mass in D* in that same archive makes use of *clarines* (trumpets), *not trompas* (horns), arguing against this mass's candidacy as the one that Adam had seen. The *Mass in D* by García Fajer at Mission San Fernando is even more resplendent in its music resources than the aforementioned masses, using trumpets and oboes, in addition to the strings and horns. Again, if Adam had seen the extant sheets for this mass, he certainly would have included the broader instrumentation in his citation.

When all is said and done, the most likely case is that Rev. Adam was familiar with the manuscript parts for the *Polychoral Mass in G* by Ignacio de Jerusalem, but this theory does have its problems that need to be reconciled, and until more information is gleaned, there is no way of knowing exactly how Rev. Adam's statement relates *specifically* to the sources that we still have in our possession in the year 2009.

90. See Summers, "New and Little Known Sources of California Mission Music," *Inter-American Music Review*, vol. 11 (1991), 13–24; and Summers, "The Spanish Origins of California Mission Music," 126n31.

91. For a summary of this episode concerning the secularization of the missions and Cabot's transfer from San Antonio to San Fernando (with a brief stay at Mission San Miguel interpolated in between the other two missions), consult George Wharton James, *The Old Franciscan Missions of California,* new ed. (Boston: Little, Brown, 1925), 106–7.

92. Some of the material in this section appeared previously in my article "Hidden Structures and Sonorous Symmetries: Ignacio de Jerusalem's Concerted Masses in 18th-Century Mexico," in *Res musicae: Essays in Honor of James Pruett,* ed. by Paul R. Laird and Craig H. Russell (New York: Harmonie Park Press, 2001), 135–59.

93. For instance, the *Polychoral Mass in G* by José de Nebra found in Mexico City and in the Conservatorio de las Rosas in Morelia has a fabulous fugue in the midsection of the Kyrie and another even more thrilling one to draw the Gloria to a close. They resemble in character the fugues found in the same locations of the Kyrie and Gloria of the masses by Jerusalem. The Nebra mass is found in the Mexico City Cathedral as E9.2, C2, Leg. C.c.32, AM0652; in Morelia's Conservatorio de las Rosas the work is found on the microfilm of its collection (although the actual manuscript appears to be misplaced). Its title page reads, "Missa a 8 con Vns y Trompas. Nebra. Se copió en 1778." A similar ethereal yet exciting fugue is found as the concluding movement to Antonio Sarrier's three-movement *Overtura,* one of the most astoundingly crafted instrumental compositions to be found in the Western Hemisphere. Ricardo Miranda's research on this piece has revealed Sarrier to have been the second trumpeter (playing the *clarín*) in the Spanish court in the mid-1700s. His paper "Journies of Musical Pleasure: Antonio Sarrier's *Obertura* (Morelia, Eighteenth Century)" at the Dartmouth Conference "A Celebration of Latin American Music" in early February 1996 is now published as an expanded monograph, *Antonio Sarrier: Sinfonista y clarín* (Morelia, Mexico: Conservatorio de las Rosas, 1997). That monograph, in turn, has been reprinted in *Ecos, alientos y sonidos: Ensayos sobre música mexicana* (Xalapa, Veracruz, Mexico: Universidad Veracruzana and Fondo de Cultura Económica de México, 2001). The original manuscript is in the possession of the Conservatorio de las Rosas in Morelia. A modern edition is available through the Universidad Nacional Autónoma de México: Antonio Sarrier, *Sinfonia* (Mexico City: UNAM, 1983). Jorge Velazco conducted the RIAS-Sinfonietta of Berlin in a recording of this Sarrier symphony on the Koch-Schwann label (CD 311–035-G1) in Austria in 1982.

94. In all known masses by Jerusalem, he has chosen not to compose an Agnus Dei, except in a single instance: the only extant Jerusalem mass with a separate, autonomous movement labeled "Agnus Dei" is the *Missa a 4 "de los Niños"* (1767), in G major, for choir, violins 1 and 2, two oboes, two horns, organ, and continuo, in the Mexico City Cathedral, Legajos B.a.11 and B.a.13. It should be observed as well that the *Mass in D* by García Fajer in Mission San

Fernando *does* have an Agnus Dei. However, for sample examples of masses with a "missing" Agnus Dei, consult: "Misa a 3 de Seijas," Leg. 57, no. 3, in the Mexico City Cathedral; "Misa a 5," by Joseph Joachim Lazo Valero in Puebla Cathedral, Leg. 16, no. 11; "Missa a 4 con VVs. y Trompas y a 8 con Ripienos. Mro. Alba. Para el Colegio de Niñas de Sta. Roza María de esta Ciudad de Vallad[oli]d año de 1770," in the Conservatorio de las Rosas in Morelia; Polychoral Mass in F major by Alba, Mexico City Cathedral, Leg. D.c.3; "Misa a 4 con Violines, Trompas, y Vaxo, compuesta por el Sr. Mto. Myr [= Juan Mir]," in F major, Mexico City Cathedral, Leg. D.c.6., no. 1; "Misa a 4 con Violines, Trompas, y Vaxo, Compuesta por el Sr. Mir Yllus. [in A minor]," Mexico City Cathedral, Leg. D.c.6, no. 2; "Misa a 4 y 8 con Violines y clarines de el Mro. Thomas Ochando," Conservatorio de las Rosas; "Missa a 8 con Violines. Eladio," Conservatorio de las Rosas; "Missa a 5 con Ripieni, VVs, Obues [*sic*], Flautas, y Trompas (1771)" in F major, by Matheo Tollis de la Rocca, Mexico City Cathedral, Leg. C.b.9 (note: normally de la Rocca *does* include an "Agnus Dei" and even a separate "Benedictus" movement). The Zipoli Mass found on the compact disc *Lima–La Plata, Misions Jésuites,* Coro de Niños Cantores de Córdoba, Argentina and Ensemble Elyma, directed by Gabriel Garrido, vol. 1 of Les Chemins du Baroque (Paris: Association Française d'Action Artistique, K.617, 1992), omits the Agnus Dei, as does the Zipoli Mass in F major in *Inter-American Music Review,* 9, no. 2 (Spring–Summer 1988), 35–89. Yet another relevant source is T. Frank Kennedy, S.J., "Colonial Music from the Episcopal Archive of Concepción, Bolivia," *Latin American Music Review,* vol. 9, no. 1 (1988), 1–17. Kennedy delves into the masses by Zipoli with a "missing" Agnus Dei, including those at the Chiquitos Missions and Sucre, and his Mass for San Ignacio.

   95. Mexico City Cathedral, Leg. 57, no. 3.
   96. Puebla Cathedral, Leg. 16, no. 11.
   97. T. Frank Kennedy suggests that the "missing" Agnus Dei movements of Zipoli's masses could be performed instrumentally and not sung; due to the reasons stated above (with regard to instructions that are printed in the actual vocalists' parts), I think the procedure instead was to have the choir retext the Sanctus. See Kennedy, "Colonial Music from the Episcopal Archive of Concepción, Bolivia," 6–7.
   98. I discuss the payment records for the Festival of San Pedro Arbúes preserved in the Archivo General de la Nación in Mexico City in the two published versions of my paper that I delivered at the Fifteenth International Congress of Musicology in Madrid in 1992: "Musical Life in Baroque Mexico: Rowdy Musicians, Confraternities and the Holy Office," *Inter-American Music Review,* vol. 13, no. 1 (Fall–Winter 1992), 11–14; and "Rowdy Musicians, Confraternities and the Inquisition: Newly Discovered Documents Concerning Musical Life in Baroque Mexico," *Revista de Musicología,* vol. 16, no. 5 (1993), *Actas del XV Congreso Internacional de Musicología,* 2801–13. The second of these two versions is more complete, containing the charts that were distributed in the handout and that refer to the clarion trumpet players who were *indios.*
   99. The "Domine Deus" duet in Jerusalem's *Polychoral Mass in G* resembles in certain aspects the duet "¡Quo prodigio!" in his theatrical-*villancico Ay paysanos* found in the Mexico City Cathedral. The tunes' rhythms share a short-long-short emphasis in the opening bars, and the interaction and development of the voices is also vintage Jerusalem. The two singers have more independence initially, engaged in conversations where they alternate phrases or have one vocalist complete the melodic ideas of the other; later, they are layered more often in parallel thirds and sixths. "Que prodigio" is for two solo sopranos accompanied by strings; "Domine Deus," on the other hand, has the less common combination of alto and bass soloists. Jerusalem's autograph score for *Ay paysanos* is found in the Archive of the Mexico City Cathedral, E.8.10 C.1 Leg. C.c.5 AM0584.
   100. Jacob Rust's "Beatam me dicent omnes" is the last Responsory (number 8 of eight) for the *Maitines a Nuestra Señora de Guadalupe* (1764). The other seven are by Ignacio de Jerusalem. The score (in Jerusalem's handwriting) and parts for this work are in the Archivo de la Catedral Metropolitana in Mexico City under the call numbers Leg. C.c.9, no. 2 and Leg. C.c.10, no. 2. This same piece appears as Responsory no. 5 in Jerusalem's *Maytines de la Asunción de Nuestra Señora* under the call number Leg. C.c.6. In both cases, Rust is actually credited as the composer (and acknowledging authorship is not to be taken for granted in eighteenth-century sources). His name, however, appears as "Giacome" instead of the more conventional spelling,

"Giacom*o*." Giacomo Rust (also known as Jacob Rust) was born in Italy and attended the Torchini Conservatory in Naples. He later briefly served as the chapelmaster in Salzburg during Mozart's lifetime. All the dictionary entries claim he moved to Barcelona near the end of his life and became the chapelmaster there, but I have found no mention of him in any capacity in Barcelona. The Arxiu Capitular de la Santa Església Catedral Basílica de Barcelona (Archive of Barcelona Cathedral) has detailed records there of the chapel and musical activities—including who was serving as chapelmaster—and Rust appears nowhere in the lists. In short, the Barcelona connection is in error.

This particular Responsory is quite a remarkable creation in that it is simultaneously a complete sonata-allegro form and a rigorous march through the complex structure of repetitions as required in a medieval Responsory form. The work has been recorded by Chanticleer with David Munderloh as the soloist. See *Ignacio de Jerusalem: Matins for the Virgin of Guadalupe*. The score of the *Matins for the Virgin of Guadalupe* is available through Russell Editions, 541 Lilac Drive, Los Osos, CA 93402.

For those who wish to experience the "sonata form" in this piece, the orchestra presents the main theme in its ritornello, followed by the vocal entry where the exposition proper begins. There is a full development, and the recapitulation begins with the Doxology, "Gloria Patri et Filio." For information concerning Rust's life, consult "Rust, Giacomo," in the *Dizionario Enciclopedico Universale della Musica e dei Musicisti*, dir. by Alberto Basso (Torino: Unione Tipografico-Editrice Torinese, 1988), vol. 6, p. 507; "Rust, Giacomo," in the *Enciclopedia della Musica*, ed. and dir. by Claudio Sartori (Milano: Ricordi, 1964), vol. 4, p. 82; and "Rust [Rusti], Giacomo," in *The New Grove Dictionary of Music and Musicians*, 2nd ed., entry by Thomas Bauman and Ernst Hintermaier, ed. by Stanley Sadie, executive editor, John Tyrrell (Oxford: Oxford University Press, 2001), vol. 22, pp. 36–37.

101. Beethoven's markings in the middle, slow movement of String Quartet no. 15 in A minor, op. 132, are "Heiliger Dankgesang eines Genesenen an die Gottheit, in der lydischen Tonart" and then "Neue kraft fühlend."

Epilogue

IN SOME WAYS, I am left with the same task now—that of reflective summation—as I come to the closing moments of our journey through the music and culture of Alta California during the mission period. A few general "motives" are worth restating, as we look back on all that has been covered. The friars in California and their neophyte converts unquestionably produced and performed some of the most worthy artistic creations of the New World, and they did it by combining elements of antiquity with elements that were ultramodern at the time. Moreover, they molded together indigenous practices or religious worship in the Native American communities with those of the newly introduced Christian orthodoxy. One did not completely conquer or vanquish the other; instead, there was a negotiated creation of a new "recipe" that had not really been seen before the meeting of these peoples and ideas. Looking back at the terrain we covered, we can see now that the small snippets of paper on which much of this music is written do not intuitively portray the grandeur and splendor of much of the California tradition. The West Coast of North America—as with most places on this planet—developed pageantry and spectacle that were a meaningful part of the daily life of the participants and those in attendance. And the East Coast and Europe did not corner the market with respect to creative composers worthy of attention and inclusion in the history of the Americas. To the list of honored American composers from the Atlantic seaboard such as William Billings, Andrew Lawe, Lowell Mason, and Stephen Foster can be added names from another culture, another group of peoples, and the "other" American coast. Ignacio de Jerusalem in Mexico, and the Californians Juan Bautista Sancho, Narciso Durán, Florencio Ibáñez, and Esteban Tapís also are part of our American history. But the listing of their names in a few texts is not the real goal of my book. It is deeper than that.

My father used to emphasize the inherent value of each person. I remember well one day when he pulled me over, looked me in the eye to make sure I was attentive, and said to me in his most heartfelt voice, "Craig, don't ever underestimate *anybody*. Everybody (including the janitor who pushes the broom down the office building hallway where you might work) knows something important, something that you need to learn and to know! Everybody has a lifetime of learned wisdom that he or she can teach you, if you're only willing to listen." The same can be said for Californians long ago during the mission period. As a culture, we have underestimated for too long the successes, insights, and offerings of our American brethren of Spanish, Mexican, or Native American heritage.

In truth, the fundamental lesson we can learn from the music of the California padres and their choirs and orchestras, populated by highly trained and impressive Native American artists, is that humble people are capable of astoundingly sophisticated artistry. Sometimes, awe-inspiring beauty, magnificent splendor, heroic achievement, and profound insight are close at hand—all made by humble individuals who are living next door or in our own backyard. There is much we can learn about artistic beauty and the human condition from California mission music. It can enrich our lives—if we are only willing to listen.

Contents of the Online Appendices

Appendix A: Catalogue of California Mission Sources

San Fernando Mission, Archival Center of the Archdiocese of Los Angeles (ACALA)

San Juan Bautista Mission (SJB)

Santa Barbara Mission, Santa Barbara Mission Archive-Library (SBMAL)

Manuscript 3	Hymns, Canticles, Music for Holy Week Mass in Mode 6,	A: 282
Manuscript 4	Lamentations and *Misa de Mallorca*	A: 283
Manuscript 5	Gradual for the Liturgical Year	A: 285
Manuscript 6	Christmas Gradual and Mass	A: 288
Santa Inés Prayer Board		A: 289

Stanford University, Green Research Library

| M.0573 | Juan Bautista Sancho, *Misa en sol* | A: 290 |
| M.0612 | "Serra Choirbook" | A: 296 |

University of California at Berkeley, Department of Music

| WPA Folk Music Project. Items 45–87, Box 2 of 12 | A: 302 |

Appendix B: Photos of Missions and Mission Music Sources

Some of the color photos found here on the Oxford University Press Web site also appear as black-and-white images printed in the paper volume of this book. The indicators in the left column help locate the photos on the Web site (usually in color); the indicators in the far right column direct the reader to images as found in the printed text (in black-and-white). For more complete citations of the specific music sources, consult appendix A: Catalogue of California Mission Sources.

1. *The Bancroft Library*

All images in this section, courtesy of The Bancroft Library, University of California, Berkeley.

C-C-59. Choirbook in the hand of Narciso Durán

		Page or Folio in the document	Photo number in this book
B-1	Narciso Durán's preface to choirbook C-C-59	fol. i	
B-2	Durán's preface, continuation	fol. i^v	
B-3	Durán's preface, continuation (For a complete translation of this *Prólogo*, see entry C-1 in appendix C online)	fol. ii	
B-4	*Veni sancte spiritus*	p. 27	
B-5	*Dies irae* (flaps up)	p. 69a	2-1

Ms. C-C-73:16. Diary of Juan Bautista Sancho

Ms. C-C-73:17. Sancho's translation of the last rites

Pictorial images of the California Missions

B-23   San Diego Mission
        Creator and date unknown. From the Robert B. Honeyman Jr.
        Collection of Early California and Western American Pictorial
        Material. Colored lithograph. Original size, 23.3. × 30 cm. Call
        number: BANC PIC 1963.002:0478:12-A.

B-24   San José Mission ("View of San Jose Mission")
        Henry Chapman Ford, 1883. From the Robert B. Honeyman
        Jr. Collection of Early California and Western American
        Pictorial Material. Etching. Original image size, 17.1
        × 32.8 cm (but the entire sheet is 36.2 × 45.3 cm). Call
        number: BANC PIC 1963.002:0918:21-ffALB.

B-25   San Juan Bautista Mission ("Mission of San
        Juan Bautista")   4-1
        Edward Vischer, 1862. Colored drawing from the Collection:
        "The Mission Era: California Under Spain and Mexico and
        Reminiscences." Original size, 14.7 × 23 cm. Call number:
        BANC PIC 19xx.039:29-ALB.

B-26   Santa Inés Mission ("View of Santa Ines Mission")
        Henry Chapman Ford, 1883. From the Robert B. Honeyman
        Jr. Collection of Early California and Western American
        Pictorial Material. Etching. Original image size, 17.6 ×
        32.7 cm (but the entire sheet is 37 × 46.1 cm). Call number:
        BANC PIC 1963.002:0918:09-ffALB.

B-27   Soledad Mission ("Mission of La Soledad")
        Henry Miller, "California Mission Sketches," 1856. Pencil
        drawing. Original size, 28 × 45 cm. Call number: BANC PIC
        1905.00006-B (no. 21 of 38).

2. California Historical Society

Photos courtesy of the California Historical Society.

Durán, Father Narciso, Letter (No. 30). January 7, 1821 from Father Narciso
Durán Letters, 1806-1827, Vault MS 17. A request for an organ to be sent to the
San José Mission. (See a complete translation in appendix C.)

B-28   Durán's letter requesting an organ (recto side)
B-29   Durán's letter requesting an organ (verso side)

3. California Polytechnic State University

All images in this section, courtesy of Special Collections and University
Archives, California Polytechnic State University.

California Travel and Promotional Ephemera Coll. F970 .M6 C24

B-30   San Buenaventura Mission
B-31   San Carlos Borromeo Mission
B-32   San Fernando Rey de España Mission
B-33   San Francisco de Asís Mission
B-34   San Francisco Solano Mission
B-35   San José Mission
B-36   San Juan Bautista Mission
B-37   Santa Barbara Mission
B-38   Santa Clara Mission
B-39   Santa Cruz Mission
B-40   Santa Inés Mission

Julia Morgan Papers

B-41   San Antonio Mission interior, 6-B-78-04-01
B-42   San Antonio Mission exterior, 6-B-78-04-02

4. Carmel Mission

Permission to include these images, courtesy of the Carmel Mission. Photographs by the author.

Carmel Mission Ms. 2, "Antiphonary," *Ms. 308.1955.46.139*

B-43   *Veni Creator Spiritus*   fol. 4   3-2
B-44   *Veni Creator,* continuation
           ("charitas…")   fol. 4v

Carmel Mission Ms. 3, "Folio of Chant Music"

B-45   *Ecce justus ecce palma*   fol. 1

5. San Fernando Mission, Archival Center of the Archdiocese of Los Angeles (ACALA)

Permission to include these images, courtesy of the Archival Center of the Archdiocese of Los Angeles. Photographs by the author.

Artaserse Ms., As-3

B-46   "Quando Fernando se ausenta"   fol. 5v   5-12

B-47	*Regina caeli lætare* and "Laudamus te" from the *Gloria del 5° tono*	fol. 9v	
B-48	"España de la guerra"	fol. 11v	

Manuscript A320

B-49	Kyrie and first part of Gloria from the "Misa Catalana, Tono 5" *(Misa de Cataluña)*	pp. 1-2	6-2
B-50	*Jesu Ex mitis Jerusalem ingressus*	pp. 13-14	
B-51	"Para la distribución de los Ramos"	p. 26	

Manuscript S-1

B-52	"Kyris [*sic*] Clasichs" and "Credo de Jesús"	p. S-1	

Manuscript S-2

B-53	"Kyris [*sic*] Clasichs" and *Lauda Sion Salvatorem*	p. S-2	1-8

Manuscript S-5

B-54	*Salve Regina* and Compline service	p. S-5	3-3
B-55	Compline service, continuation	p. S-5v	

Manuscript J-1, Jerusalem[?], *Polychoral Mass in D*

B-56	Jerusalem [?], "Tiple de 1° Coro," p. 3	J-1	7-1
B-57	Jerusalem [?], "Violin 1°," p. 5	J-1	

Manuscript E-1, García Fajer "El Españoleto," *Mass in D*

B-58	García Fajer, "Violin Primero," p. 5	E-1, p. 5

6. San Juan Bautista Mission

Permission to include these images, courtesy of the San Juan Bautista Mission. Photographs by the author.

Manuscript 1

B-59	*Veni Sancte Spiritus* (and more chant for Pentecost)	p. 41

Manuscript 2

7. Santa Inés Mission

Photos B-61, B-67, and B-70 courtesy of Old Mission Santa Inés. The remaining photographs by the author.

Manuscript 1

Manuscript 2

Manuscript 5

Manuscript 6

8. Santa Barbara: Santa Barbara Mission Archive-Library (SBMAL)

Permission to include these images, courtesy of the Santa Barbara Mission Archive-Library. Photographs by the author.

Document 1, Durán Choirbook

Document 2, Choirbook from the San Rafael Mission

B-75	*Sacris solemniis*	p. 65	
B-76	"Misa chiquita de La, y Tocata de La"	p. 75	
B-77	*Te Deum* [intoned in polyphony]	p. 84 & 85	3-4
B-78	Kyrie from the *Misa del quinto tono*	p. 127	
B-79	*¡O qué suave!*	p. 140	
B-80	*¡O pan de vida!*	p. 141	
B-81	*¡O Rey de corazones!*	pp. 142-43	
B-82	"Tocata"	p. 152	

Document 3, "Misa a trez de Cataluña" (signed "Pacífico Capéñaz")

B-83	Kyrie from the *Misa de Cataluña*	p. 1

Marcos y Navas, Francisco. *Arte, o compendio general del canto-llano, figurado y órgano,* Copy MT860 M37 1776.

B-84	Title page	Title	1-2
B-85	Bastard title page, with Juan Bautista Sancho's signature	Bt.Title	

Pérez Martínez, Vicente. *Prontuario del cantollano gregoriano.* Copy M2907 L99 P47 vols. 1 and 2.

B-86	Title page		1-4
B-87	*Cibavit eos*	II, p. 671	
B-88	*Dies irae*	II, p. 690	
B-89	*Benedictus qui venit*	II, p. 1071	

9. Santa Clara University, Archive of the Orradre Library (Santa Clara Mission)

Permission to include these images, courtesy of the Santa Clara University Archive. Photographs by the author.

Santa Clara Ms. 1, Mass of Saint Dominic

B-90	*In medio Ecclesiæ,* Introit	p. 1

Santa Clara Ms. 3, choirbook in the hand of Florencio Ibáñez (and Pedro Cabot).

B-91	Requiem	p. 1

Santa Clara Ms. 4, choirbook in hand of Narciso Durán

10. *The Smithsonian Institution*

Photos courtesy of the Smithsonian Institution National Anthropological Archives

"Prayerboard with Liturgy Written in Spanish 1817," Ms. 1082

B-115   Smithsonian prayerboard, recto side   5-14
B-116   Smithsonian prayerboard, verso side

11. Stanford University

Photos courtesy of Stanford University

Juan Bautista Sancho, *Misa en sol*, M.0573

B-117   *Bajo* part, 1st page of the Credo   5-15
B-118   *Tiple 1* part, 2nd page (fol. 1v) of the Gloria

Serra choirbook, M.0612

B-119   Kyrie from the *Missa Toledana. Quarto Tono*   fol. 15   1-3
B-120   Gloria from the *Missa Toledana*   fol. 15v

12. University of California at Berkeley, Department of Music

Photos courtesy of the Department of Music and Music Library at the University of
California at Berkeley. The photo identification numbers to the right are those that
are written in pencil on the actual photos preserved in the WPA collection in the
Music Library of the Department of Music at the University of California at Berkeley.

WPA Folk Music Project. Items 45-87, Box 2

B-121	"Ecos a duo," title page, WPA folder 50	Photo z-1	
B-122	"Baix, Credo a duo," WPA folder 51	Photo c-2	5-13
B-123	"Credo Artanense," WPA folder 52	Photo Aa-1	5-6
B-124	"Día 21 de Maio cerca las once de la noche," (last page), WPA 52	Photo Aa-2	5-7
B-125	"Credo de Jesús," WPA folder 63	Photo I-1	
B-126	*Tiple 1°* (Soprano) from Gloria, 5° tono, WPA folder 64	Photo L-4	
B-127	*Baxo* part for "Credo Italiano," WPA folder 66	Photo J-5	
B-128	"Missa de los Angeles â 4 voces" (cover page), WPA folder 69	photo G-1 Photo G-1	5-8
B-129	*Tiple 1°* part of "Missa de los Angeles â 4 voces," WPA folder 69	Photo G-2	
B-130	*Acompañamiento* (Continuo line) for the Gloria and Credo, 5° tono, WPA folder 70	Photo Ab-2	

B-156   Lynn Bremer (Director), Jeremy "Spud" Schroeder,
      Brother Tim at the SBMAL

Santa Clara Mission

B-157   Santa Clara Mission, front with flowers

Appendix C: Translations of Primary Texts

C-4. Music inventory requests for the missions, 1805–1809   C: 38

Archivo General de la Nación, Número de Registro 53860,
   Número de Soporte, 283

C-5. Preface to the Ramón Yorba Manuscript   C: 57

Ms. C-C-73/108c (vol. 1) at The Bancroft Library

Appendix D: Music Editions

D-1. Juan Bautista Sancho, *Misa de los Angeles*

Based on WPA folder 69 at the Department of Music, University of California
at Berkeley. The chant is drawn from San Juan Bautista Ms. 1, p. 92.

Kyrie	1
Gloria	4
Credo Dominical. Tono 6	10
Sanctus	19
Agnus Dei	20

D-2. Juan Bautista Sancho, Gloria from the *Misa del quinto tono*

Based on WPA folder 64 and WPA folder 70 at the Department of Music,
University of California at Berkeley.

D-3. Juan Bautista Sancho, *Misa en sol*

Based on M.0573 at Stanford and WPA folders 52, 65, and 70 at the
Department of Music, University of California at Berkeley.

Kyrie	1
Gloria	
Et in terra pax (*Andante*)	9
Laudamus te (*Adagio*)	11
Gratias agimus tibi (*Allegro*)	18
Quoniam tu solus (*Presto*)	30
Credo, 5to tono, alternando con el Credo Artanense.	39
Sanctus	53
Agnus Dei	56

D-4. Ignacio de Jerusalem, Kyrie and Gloria from the *Mass in F*

Based on manuscripts in folder J-2 at the Archival Center of the
Archdiocese of Los Angeles at the San Fernando Mission.
Kyrie

Gloria

D-5. Ignacio de Jerusalem [?], excerpts from the *Polychoral Mass in D*

"Quoniam tu solus," "Cum Spiritu Sancto," and "Amen" from the Gloria. Based on manuscripts in folder J-1 at the Archival Center of the Archdiocese of Los Angeles at the San Fernando Mission.

D-6. *Lauda Sion Salvatorem,* using *alternatim* technique

Based on manuscript S-2 in the Archival Center of the Archdiocese of Los Angeles at the San Fernando Mission; choirbook C-C-59 at the Bancroft Library, p. 70; Santa Barbara Doc. 1, p. 122; and Santa Clara Ms. 4, p. 17.

D-7. *Lauda Sion Salvatorem,* using *canto figurado* technique

Based on manuscript S-2 in the Archival Center of the Archdiocese of Los Angeles at the San Fernando Mission (in the hand of Juan Bautista Sancho).

D-8. Gozos al Señor San José, "Para dar luz inmortal"

Based on Santa Clara Ms. 4, p. 63; and choirbook C-C-59 at the Bancroft Library, p. 98.

D-9. *Gozos de la Purísima,* "Para dar luz inmortal"

Based on Santa Clara Ms. 4, p. 64; and choirbook C-C-59 at the Bancroft Library, p. 121.

D-10. *Dulce Esposo de María*

Based on Santa Clara Ms. 4, p. 62; choirbook C-C-59 at the Bancroft Library, p. 56; and San Juan Bautista Ms. 1, p. 110.

D-11. *Misa del quarto tono*

Based on choirbook C-C-59 at the Bancroft Library, pp. 122-27; Santa Clara Ms. 4, pp. 123-27; Santa Barbara Doc. 1, pp. 30-42; Santa Barbara Doc. 2, pp. 118-26; and Santa Barbara Doc. 21B, fols. 1-1v. Chant from the *Missale Romanum,* in the Santa Clara Mission, Hoskin 77, p. 239.

Kyrie	1
Gloria	6
Credo	12
Sanctus	22
Agnus Dei	26

D-12. *Credo Artanense.*

Based on WPA folder 52, with some ambiguities clarified in WPA folders 51 and 65.

Appendix E: Bibliography

Index